Law
and
Society

Seventh Edition

Steven Vago

Saint Louis University

Upper Saddle River, New Jersey 07458

Library of Congress Cataloging-in-Publication Data

VAGO, STEVEN.
  Law and society / Steven Vago.—7th ed.

    p. cm.
  Includes bibliographical references and index.
  ISBN 0–13–097958-9 (alk. paper)
  1. Sociological jurisprudence. I Title.
  K370.V33 2003
  340'.115—dc21   2002022480

AVP, Publisher: *Nancy Roberts*
Acquisition Editor: *Christopher DeJohn*
Managing Editor (Editoral): *Sharon Chambliss*
Editorial Assistant: *Christina Scalia*
AVP Director of Manufacturing and Production: *Barbara Kittle*
Executive Managing Editor (Production): *Ann Marie McCarthy*
Production Liaison: *Fran Russello*
Editorial/Production Supervision: *Kim Gueterman*
Prepress and Manufacturing Buyer: *Mary Ann Gloriande*
Cover Director: *Jayne Conte*
Cover Designer: *Bruce Kenselaar*
Copyeditor: *Ann Sieger*
Marketing Manager: *Amy Speckman*

This book was set in 10/12 Palatino by DM Cradle Associates.
and was printed and bound by R.R. Donnelley & Sons Company.
The cover was printed by Phoenix Color Corp.

© 2003, 2000, 1997, 1994, 1991, 1988, and 1981
by Pearson Education, Inc.
Upper Saddle River, New Jersey 07458

Printed in the United States of America
10 9 8 7 6 5 4 3 2 1

ISBN 0-13-097958-9

Pearson Education LTD., *London*
Pearson Education Australia PTY, Limited, *Sydney*
Pearson Education Singapore, Pte. Ltd.
Pearson Education North Asia Ltd., *Hong Kong*
Pearson Education Canada, Ltd., *Toronto*
Pearson Educación de Mexico, S.A. de C.V.
Pearson Education—Japan, *Tokyo*
Pearson Education Malaysia, Pte. Ltd.
Pearson Education, *Upper Saddle River, New Jersey*

To Kathe, as always

Contents

4   LAWMAKING   152

5 LAW AND SOCIAL CONTROL   191

6 LAW AND DISPUTE RESOLUTION   247

7   LAW AND SOCIAL CHANGE   302

8   THE LEGAL PROFESSION   340

Preface

Over the past twenty years, the previous and progressively more comprehensive editions of this book not only became popular with law and society scholars, but were adopted as textbooks in more than 350 colleges and universities in the United States and abroad. Extra printings for each edition along the way confirmed the usefulness of the text and the growing interest in the subject matter. This seventh edition is a result of the wide acceptance and demonstrated utility of the earlier versions. While reflecting the intent, perspectives, and basic plan of preceding versions, this edition continues to enhance the message with extensive new input. The material is more focused, reorganized and presented in a more integrated and relevant way for the benefit of students. The book remains in tune with ongoing global changes in legal systems and extensively incorporates the most recent theoretical developments and the latest research results. Much of the book has been rewritten to further increase clarity and readability and to include new trends, concerns, and controversies. The temptation to engage in merely cosmetic changes and verbiage alterations that are common in revisions has been successfully resisted. If a particular section was up-to-date, clear and useful, I did not change it just for the sake of change. Throughout the various revisions, my purpose remained the same: to prepare a book that is pedagogically sound, full with ideas and insights, informative and provocative to read, and distinctive in its coverage of the subject.

A substantial amount of new material has been included in this edition. The coverage now includes detailed and up-to-date discussions on the transformation of legal systems in Central and Eastern Europe and the former Soviet Union and some of the unintended consequences that promoted organized crime; critical race theory; community policing in Japan; trends in sentencing guidelines; and a variety of new developments in alternative dispute resolution and in the death penalty controversy. The many changes that have been suggested by students and reviewers have been considered and incorporated. All the chapters have been fully updated and expanded to reflect ongoing trends and current developments. There are close to 375 new resources and references, a significantly expanded list of further readings at the end of each chapter, and I have greatly increased the number of cross-cultural illustrations. I made a point once again of further emphasizing clarity of language at the expense of professional jargon.

The objective of this book is to serve as an undergraduate text in one-term courses. Although the book was written primarily for college students, anyone with an interest in law and society will find it useful, informative and provocative. The classroom tested and refined material has been organized and presented in a logical fashion, and each chapter builds on the previous one. Should one prefer a different organization of the contents, it would not detract from the value of the book. For example, if one desires, Chapter 9, Researching Law in Society, can be read after Chapter 2, Theoretical Perspectives, rather than at the end of the book. For a quick chapter overview, some readers may want to look at the detailed summaries. The suggested further readings are designed to provide a starting point for interested readers to pursue further a particular topic and to reflect alternative perspectives.

As I noted in previous editions, the study of the interplay between law and society is fundamentally eclectic. Knowledge about it has accumulated haphazardly. Intellectual developments in the field are influenced by a number of theoretical perspectives, resulting in a variety of strains of thought and research. In a sense, once again, more questions will be raised than answered. The abundance of unanswered questions and unexpected developments keeps the study of law and society challenging and appealing.

Writing a book always requires the cooperation, support and encouragement of many people. Prentice Hall reviewers Carol Bohmer, Ohio State University, Margaret Platt Jendrek, Miami University–Ohio; Suzanne Samuels, Seton Hall University; and Jeffery T. Ulmer, Pennsylvania State University made insightful and valuable suggestions. I also thank the many students (who over the years read and commented on and constructively criticized the multiple versions of the manuscript) for their no-nonsense feedback, demand for clarity, aversion to redundancy, reluctance to take things for granted, and willingness to talk back to their professor. Once again, without sounding redundant, it was most gratifying to work with production editor Kim Gueterman who superbly orchestrated the completion of this book. I am especially appreciative of the work of Ann Sieger who did an excellent job of editing this manuscript. The index was expertly prepared by Aristide Sechandice. As with the preceding editions and other scholarly endeavors, this work could not have been realized without the continuous generous pecuniary, moral, and spiritual support of the Vago Foundation, which **alone** provided the necessary infrastructure, secretarial services, library assistance, and magnanimously covered all expenses incurred in the preparation of this book.

Steven Vago
Bellingham, Washington
and Harrison Hot Springs, British Columbia

1
Introduction

With the advent of the twenty-first century, law increasingly permeates all forms of social behavior. Its significance and pervasiveness resonate on all walks of life. In subtle and, at times, not so subtle ways, a complex and voluminous set of laws governs our entire existence and our every action. It determines registration at birth and the distribution of possessions at death. Laws regulate prenuptial agreements, marriage, divorce, and the conduct of professors in the classroom. Laws set the speed limit and the length of school attendance. Laws control what we eat and where and what we buy and when, and how we use our computers. Laws protect ownership and define the boundaries of private and public property. Laws regulate business, raise revenue, provide for redress when agreements are broken, and uphold social institutions, such as the family. Laws protect the prevailing legal and political systems by defining power relationships, thus establishing who is superordinate and who is subordinate in any given situation. Laws maintain the status quo and provide the impetus for change. Finally, laws, in particular criminal laws, not only protect private and public interests but also preserve order. There is no end to the ways in which the law has a momentous effect upon our lives.

The principal mission of this book is to serve as a text in undergraduate courses on law and society. The large number of predominantly recent references cited also makes the text a valuable source for both graduate students engaging in research on the sociology of law; instructors who may be teaching this subject for the first time; and anyone else wanting to gain greater insight and understanding of the intricacies of law and society. Because the book has been written originally for the undergraduate student, I opted for an eclectic approach to the often controversial subject matter without embracing or advocating a particular position, ideology or theoretical stance. To have done so would have been too limiting for a text, since important contributions would have been excluded or would have been considered out of context. Thus, the book does not propound a single thesis or position; instead, it exposes the reader to the dominant theoretical perspectives and sociological methods used to explain the interplay between law and society in the social science literature. Should any reader care to follow up on a theoretical perspective or practical concern, or advocate or defend a certain position, the chapter topics, references and suggested further readings will provide the necessary first step toward the further exploration of most law and society related issues.

OVERVIEW

Since the earliest time, in every human society there have been mechanisms for the declaration, alteration, administration, and enforcement of the rules by which people live. Not all societies, however, utilize a formal legal system (courts, judges, lawyers, and law enforcement agencies) to the same degree. For example, throughout the third world, the formal systems of property rights taken for granted in advanced nations simply do not exist. As the renowned economist Hernando de Soto (2001) points out in his influential book, *The Mystery of Capital,* 80 percent of the poor people in the developing world cannot identify who owns what, addresses cannot be verified, and the rules that govern property vary from neighborhood to neighborhood or even from street to street. The notion of holding title to property is limited primarily to a handful of elites whose assets are "paperized" in the formal documents and legal structures common in the West.

Further, traditional societies rely almost exclusively on custom as the source of legal rules and resolve disputes through conciliation or mediation by village elders, or by some other moral or divine authority. As for law, such societies need little of it. Traditional societies are more homogeneous than modern industrial ones. Social relations are more direct and intimate, interests are shared by virtually everyone, and there are fewer things to quarrel about. Since relations are more direct and intimate, nonlegal and often informal mechanisms of social control are generally more effective.

As societies become larger, more complex, and modern, homogeneity gives way to heterogeneity. Common interests decrease in relation to special interests. Face-to-face relations become progressively less important, as do kinship ties. Access to material goods becomes more indirect, with a greater likelihood of unequal allocation, and the struggle for available goods becomes intensified. As a result, the prospects for conflict and dispute within the society increase. The need for explicit regulatory and enforcement mechanisms becomes increasingly apparent. The development of trade and industry requires a system of formal and universal legal rules dealing with business organizations and commercial transactions, subjects that are not normally part of customary or religious law. Such commercial activity also requires guarantees, predictability, continuity, and a more effective method for settling disputes than that of trial by ordeal, trial by combat, or decision by a council of elders. As one commentator has noted: "The paradox . . . is that the more civilized man becomes, the greater is man's need for law, and the more law he creates. Law is but a response to social needs" (Hoebel, 1954:292).

In the eloquent words of Oliver Wendell Holmes, Jr. (1881:5), "The law embodies the story of a nation's development through many centuries" and every legal system stands in close relationship to the ideas, aims, and purposes of society. Law reflects the intellectual, social, economic, and political climate of its time. Law is inseparable from the interests, goals, and understandings that deeply shape or compromise social and economic life (Posner, 2001; Sarat and Kearns, 2000). It also reflects the particular ideas, ideals, and ideologies that are part of a distinct "legal culture"—those attributes of behavior and attitudes that make the law of one society different from that of another, that make, for example, the law of the Eskimos different from the law of the French (Friedman, 1998, 2002).

In sociology, the study of law embraces a number of well-established areas of inquiry (Cotterrell, 1994; Friedrichs, 2001). The discipline is concerned with values, interaction patterns, and ideologies that underlie the basic structural arrangements in a society, many of which are embodied in law as substantive rules. Both sociology and law are concerned with norms—rules that prescribe the appropriate behavior for people in a given situation. The study of conflict and conflict resolution are central in both disciplines. Both sociology and law are concerned with the nature of legitimate authority, the mechanisms of social control, issues of human rights, power arrangements, the relationship between public and private spheres and formal contractual commitments (Baumgartner, 1999; McIntyre, 1994; Selznick, 1968:50). Both sociologists and lawyers are aware that the behavior of judges, jurors, criminals, litigants and other consumers of legal products is charged with emotion, distorted by cognitive glitches and failures of will, and constrained by altruism, etiquette or a sense of duty.

Historically, the rapprochement of sociology (along with economics, psychology and other social sciences) (Roesch, et al., 1999; Posner, 2001) and law is not novel. Early American sociologists, after the turn of the century, emphasized the various facets of the relationship between law and society. E. Adamson Ross (1922:106) considered law as "the most specialized and highly furnished engine of control employed by society." Lester F. Ward (1906:339), who believed in governmental control and social planning, predicted a day when legislation would endeavor to solve "questions of social improvement, the amelioration of the conditions of all the people, the removal of whatever privations may still remain, and the adoption of means to the positive increase of the social welfare, in short, the organization of human happiness."

study of law
use of law
to regulate conduct

The writings of these early sociologists have greatly influenced the development of the school of legal philosophy that became a principal force in American sociological jurisprudence. [Sociological jurisprudence is the study of law and legal philosophy, and the use of its ideas in law to regulate conduct (Lauderdale, 1997:132). It is based on a comparative study of legal systems, legal doctrines, and legal institutions as social phenomena and considers law as it actually is—the "law in action" as distinguished from the law as it appears in books.] Roscoe Pound, the principal figure in sociological jurisprudence, relied heavily on the findings of early sociologists in asserting that law should be studied as a social institution. For Pound (1941:18), law was a specialized form of social control that exerts pressure on a person "in order to constrain him to do his part in upholding civilized society and to deter him from anti-social conduct, that is, conduct at variance with the postulates of social order."

Interest in law among sociologists grew rapidly after the Second World War, which ended in 1945. In the United States, some sociologists became interested in law almost by accident. As they investigated certain problems, such as race relations, they found law to be relevant. Others became radicalized in the mid- and late 1960s, during the period of the Vietnam War, and their work began to emphasize social conflict and the functions of stratification in society. It became imperative for sociologists of the left to dwell on the gap between promise and performance in the legal system. By the same token, those sociologists defending the establishment were anxious to show that the law dealt with social conflict in a legitimate fashion. At the same time, sociological interest in law was further enhanced by the infusion of public funds into research evaluating a variety of law-based programs designed to address social problems in the United States (Ross, 1989:37). These developments provided the necessary impetus for the field of law and society which got its start in the mid-1960s with the formation of the Law and Society Association and the inauguration of its official journal, the *Law & Society Review* (Abel, 1995:9; *Law & Society Review*, 1995:5). These efforts will undoubtedly be sustained by the aftermath of the tragic events following the World Trade Center and Pentagon terrorist attacks on September 11, 2001.

Currently, a number of universities offer undergraduate, graduate or joint degree programs in law and society, such as the School of Justice Studies at Arizona State University, the Jurisprudence and Social Policy at University of California—Berkeley, the Department of Law, Jurisprudence and Social Thought at Amherst College, University of Wisconsin, and University of Massachusetts—Amherst. There are also a number of major research institutes such as the Center for Law and Society at Berkeley, the Institute for Law and Society at New York University and the Institute for Legal Studies at the University of Wisconsin (Abel, 1995:10).

But interest in law and society is not confined to the United States. Adam Podgorecki, a Polish sociologist, has analyzed a number of distinct national styles in social-science work related to law. Scandinavian scholars have emphasized the social meaning of justice. In particular, they have investigated knowledge of the law and attitudes toward it. Italian social scientists have been concerned with empirical investigations of judges and the process of judging. With the end of the Soviet Union, the legitimacy of its law also died. Russian social scientists are now looking into the processes involved in the transformation of socialist legal systems into more Western, market-oriented ones with studies on privatization, joint-ventures, leadership successions and the reintroduction of juries in criminal cases. German sociologists are studying the socio-legal implications of reunification, changing demographic composition of the population due to immigration and the ways of coping with economic contrast and rising nationalism. Additionally, there is a flourishing interest in law and society in Japan, initiated by the many problems Japan experienced with the reception of European law and more recently by the growing anti-Japan sentiments brought about by perceptions of "unfair" trade practices. Both nationally and internationally, a number of organizations have been formed and centers established to study the multifaceted interaction between law and society (Rehbinder, 1975:13–48). More recently, the International Institute for the Sociology of Law was founded in 1988 by the International Sociological Association (Research Committee on Sociology of Law) and the Basque government. The Institute is located in the Old University of Onati (Spain), and by the mid-1990s it had a full-fledged masters program and an International Doctorate in Sociology of Law program. By early 2002, the success and reputation of the Institute created a long list of applicants anxious to gain admission.

Few sociologists concerned with the study of law and society would question Eugen Ehrlich's oft-quoted dictum that the "center of gravity of legal development lies not in legislation, nor in juristic science, nor in judicial decision, but in society itself" (Ehrlich, 1975: Foreword). I share I. D. Willock's (1974:7) position that "in so far as jurisprudence seeks to give law a location in the whole span of human affairs it is from sociology that it stands to gain most." Sociological knowledge, perspectives, theories, and methods are not only useful but also axiomatic for the understanding and possible improvement of law and the legal system in society.

But the study of law by sociologists is somewhat hampered by difficulties of interaction between sociologists and lawyers. Language-based approaches to issues are different in the two professions (Conley and O'Barr, 1998) and as Edwin M. Schur correctly notes, "In a sense . . . lawyers and sociologists `don't talk the same language,' and this lack of communication undoubtedly breeds uncertainty in both professions concerning any involvement in the other's domain, much less any cooperative interdisciplinary endeavors." He goes on to say: "Sociologists and lawyers are engaged in quite different sorts of enterprises," and notes that "the lawyer's characteristic need to make decisions, here and now, may render him impatient with the sociologist's apparently unlimited willingness to suspend final judgment on the issue . . ." (Schur, 1968:8). The complexity of legal terminology further impedes interaction. There is a special rhetoric of law (Garner, 2001; Sarat and Kearns, 1994) and it has its own vocabulary; terms like *subrogation* and *replivin* and *respondeat superior* and *chattel lien* abound. Lawyers use a special arcane writing style, at times replete with multiple redundancies such as *made and entered into, cease and desist, null and void, in full force and effect,* and *give, devise and bequeath*. Not surprisingly, "Between specialized vocabulary and arcane style, the very language of the law defies lay understanding" (Chambliss and Seidman, 1982:119). There is a move underway to combat such legalese, and lawyers and law schools are beginning to learn that good English makes sense (Gest, 1995). The "linguistically challenged profession" (Glaberson, 2001) is further beset by difficulties involving the complexities of legal writing (and the need to translate it into plain English (Garner, 2001)) and the forms of irritating documentation called sentence citations, (see e.g., *Bush v. Gore*, 531 U.S. 98, 121 S. Ct. 525, 148 L. Ed. 2d 388 (2000)), which tend to appear in mid-sentence. Not surprisingly, there is no a move underway to clean up legal documents by putting citations at the bottom of the page. Legal citations can include references to the date, volume and page number of legal publications where precedents can be found.

Problems of interaction are also brought about and reinforced by the differences in professional cultures (Davis, 1962). Lawyers are advocates; they are concerned with the identification and resolution of the problems of their clients. Sociologists consider all evidence on a proposition and approach a problem with an open mind. Lawyers to a great extent are guided by precedents, and past decisions control current cases. In contrast, sociologists emphasize creativity, theoretical imagination, and research ingenuity. Law represents specific individuals and organizations within the legal system (Walker and Wrightsman, 1991:179). The pronouncements of law are predominantly prescriptive: They tell people how they should behave and what will happen to them if they do not. In sociology, the emphasis is on description, on understanding the reasons why certain groups of people act certain ways in specific situations. The law *reacts* to problems most of the time; the issues and conflicts are brought to its attention by clients outside the legal system. In sociology, issues, concerns, and problems are generated within the discipline on the basis of what is considered intellectually challenging, timely, or of interest to funding agencies.

These differences in professional cultures are, to a great extent, due to the different methods and concepts lawyers and sociologists and other social scientists (see, for example, Mattei, 1997) use in searching for "truth." Legal

WHAT IS TRUTH?

thinking, as Vilhelm Aubert (1973:50–53) explains, is different from scientific thinking for the following reasons:

1. Law seems to be more inclined toward the particular than toward the general (e.g., what happened in a specific case).
2. Law, unlike the physical and social sciences, does not endeavor to establish dramatic connections between means and ends (e.g., the impact the verdict has on the defendant's future conduct).
3. Truth for the law is normative and nonprobabilistic; either something has happened or it has not. A law is either valid or invalid (e.g., did a person break a law or not).
4. Law is primarily past and present-oriented and is rarely concerned with future events (e.g., what happens to the criminal in prison).
5. Legal consequences may be valid even if they do not occur; that is, their formal validity does not inevitably depend on compliance (e.g., the duty to fulfill a contract; if it is not fulfilled, it does not falsify the law in question).
6. A legal decision is an either-or, all-or-nothing process with little room for a compromise solution (e.g., litigant either wins or loses a case).

Of course, these generalizations have their limitations. They simply highlight the fact that law is an authoritative and reactive problem-solving system that is geared to specific social needs. Since the emphasis in law is on certainty (or predictability or finality), its instrumentation often requires the adoption of simplified assumptions about the world. The lawyer generally sees the law as an instrument to be wielded, and he or she is more often preoccupied with the practice and pontification of the law than with its consideration as an object of scholarly inquiry.

Perhaps the question most frequently asked of any sociologist interested in law is, "What are you doing studying law?" Unlike the lawyer, the sociologist needs to "justify" any research in the legal arena and often envies colleagues in law schools who can carry out such work without having to reiterate its relevance or their own competence. Yet, this need for justification is not an unmixed evil, since it serves to remind the sociologist that he or she is not a lawyer but a professional with special interests. Like the lawyer, the sociologist may be concerned with the understanding, the prediction, and perhaps even the development of law. Obviously, the sociologist and the lawyer lack a shared experience, a common quest. At the same time, increasingly, sociologists and lawyers work together on problems of mutual interests (such as research on jury selection, conflict resolution, delinquency, crime, demographic concerns and consumer problems) and are beginning to see the reciprocal benefits of such endeavors. Sociologists also recognize that their research has to be adopted to the practical and pecuniary concerns of lawyers if it is to capture their interest. In view of the vocational orientation of law schools and the preoccupation of lawyers with legal doctrine, it is unlikely that research aimed at theory building will attract or retain the attention of most law students and professors (Posner, 1996:327–330).

CONCEPTUALIZATIONS OF LAW

In ordinary parlance, the term "law" conjures up a variety of images. For some, law may mean getting a parking ticket, not being able to get a beer legally if under age, or complaining about the local "pooper-scooper" ordinance. For others, law is paying income tax, signing a prenuptial agreement, being evicted, or going to prison for growing marijuana. For still others, law is concerned with what legislators enact or judges declare. Law means all the above and more. Even among scholars, there is no agreement on the term. The purpose here is to introduce some of the classic and contemporary conceptualizations of law to illustrate the diverse ways of defining it.

The question "What is law?" haunts legal thought, and probably more scholarship has gone into defining and explaining the concept of law than into any other concept still in use in sociology and jurisprudence. Comprehensive reviews of the literature by Ronald L. Akers and Richard Hawkins (1975:5–15), Lisa J. McIntyre (1994:10–29) and Robert M. Rich (1977) indicate that there are almost as many definitions of law as there are theorists. E. Adamson Hoebel (1954:18) comments that "to seek a definition of the legal is like the quest for the Holy Grail." He cites Max Radin's warning: "Those of us who have learned humility have given over the attempt to define law." In spite of these warnings, law *can* be defined. In any definition of law, however, we must keep Julius Stone's (1964:177) admonition in mind that " 'law' is necessarily an abstract term, and the definer is free to choose a level of abstraction; but by the same token, in these as in other choices, the choice must be such as to make sense and be significant in terms of the experience and present interest of those who are addressed."

In our illustrative review of the diverse conceptualizations of law, let us first turn to two great American jurists, Benjamin Nathan Cardozo and Oliver Wendell Holmes, Jr. Cardozo (1924:52) defines law as "a principle or rule of conduct so established as to justify a prediction with reasonable certainty that it will be enforced by the courts if its authority is challenged." Holmes (1897:461) declares that "the prophecies of what the courts will do in fact, and nothing more pretentious, are what I mean by the law." For Holmes, judges make the law on the basis of past experience. In both of these definitions, the courts play an important role. These are pragmatic approaches to law as revealed by court-rendered decisions. Although implicit in these definitions is the notion of courts being backed by the authoritative force of a political state, these definitions of law seem to have a temporal character: What is the law at this time?

From a sociological perspective, one of the most influential conceptualizations of law is that of Max Weber. Starting with the idea of an *order* char-

Weber:
Law is a legitimate that order carries a probability that it will be applied thru coercion

acterized by legitimacy, he suggests: "An order will be called *law* if it is externally guaranteed by the probability that coercion (physical or psychological), to bring about conformity or avenge violation, will be applied by a *staff* of people holding themselves specially ready for that purpose" (Weber, 1954:5). Weber argues that law has three basic features that, taken together, distinguish it from other normative orders, such as custom or convention. First, pressures to comply with the law must come externally in the form of actions or threats of action by others regardless of whether a person wants to obey the law or does so out of habit. Second, these external actions or threats always involve coercion or force. Third, those who instrument the coercive threats are individuals whose official role is to enforce the law. Weber refers to "state" law when the persons who are charged to enforce the law are part of an agency of political authority.

Weber contends that customs and convention can be distinguished from law because they do not entail one or more of these features. Customs are rules of conduct in defined situations that are of relatively long duration and are generally observed without deliberation and "without thinking." Customary rules of conduct are called usages, and there is no sense of duty or obligation to follow them. Conventions, by contrast, are rules for conduct and they involve a sense of duty and obligation. Pressures, which usually include expressions of disapproval, are exerted on individuals who do not conform to conventions. Weber (1954:27) points out that unlike law, a conventional order "lacks specialized personnel for the instrumentation of coercive power."

Although a number of scholars accept the essentials of Weber's definition of law, they question two important points. First, some contend that Weber places too much emphasis on coercion and ignores other considerations that may induce individuals to obey the law. For example, Philip Selznick (1968; 1969:4–8) argues that the authoritative nature of legal rules brings about a special kind of obligation that is not dependent on the use or threat of coercion or force. Many laws are obeyed because people feel it is their duty to obey. The second point concerns Weber's use of a special staff. Some scholars claim that Weber's definition limits the use of the term "law" in cross-cultural and historical contexts. They argue that the word "staff" implies an organized administrative apparatus that may not exist in certain illiterate societies. E. Adamson Hoebel (1954:28), for instance, proposes a less restrictive term by referring to individuals possessing "a socially recognized privilege," and Ronald L. Akers (1965:306) suggests a "socially authorized third party." Of course, in modern societies, law provides for a specific administrative apparatus. Still, these suggestions should be kept in mind while studying the historical developments of law or primitive societies (see, for example, Pospisil, 1971; 1978).

From a different perspective, Donald Black (1976:2; 1989:121; 1998:1–26, 2001:18), a leading figure in law and society studies, contends that

Def. of law & custom
Law:
① External pressure to comply
② Pressure involves force or coercion
③ Coercion used by official designated to enforce law

law is essentially governmental social control. In this sense, law is "the normative life of a state and its citizens, such as legislation, litigation, and adjudication" (Black, 1976:2). He maintains that several styles of law may be observed in a society, each corresponding to a style of social control. Four styles of social control are represented in law: penal, compensatory, therapeutic, and conciliatory. In the penal style, the deviant is viewed as a violator of a prohibition and an offender to be subjected to condemnation and punishment (for example, a drug pusher). In the compensatory style, a person is considered to have a contractual obligation and, therefore, owes the victim restitution (for example, a debtor failing to pay the creditor). Both of these styles are accusatory where there is a complainant and a defendant, a winner and a loser. According to the therapeutic style, the deviant's conduct is defined as abnormal; the person needs help, such as treatment by a psychiatrist. In the conciliatory style, deviant behavior represents one side of a social conflict in need of resolution without consideration as to who is right or who is wrong (for example, marital disputes). These last two styles are remedial, designed to help people in trouble and ameliorate a bad social situation. Elements of two or more of these styles may appear in a particular instance, for example, when a drug addict is convicted of possession and is granted probation contingent upon his or her participation in some kind of therapy program.

The foregoing definitions illustrate some of the alternative ways of looking at law. It is the law's specificity in substance, its universality of applicability, and the formality of its enactment and enforcement that set it apart from other devices for social control. Implicit in these definitions of law is the notion that law can be analytically separated from other normative systems in societies with developed political institutions and specialized lawmaking and law-enforcement agencies. The paramount function of law is to regulate and constrain the behavior of individuals in their relationships with one another. Ideally, law is to be employed only when other formal and informal methods of social control fail to operate or are inadequate for the job. Finally, law can be distinguished from other forms of social control primarily in that it is a formal system embodying explicit rules of conduct, the planned use of sanctions to ensure compliance with the rules, and a group of authorized officials designated to interpret the rules and apply sanctions to violators (Davis, 1962:39–63). From a sociological perspective, the rules of law are simply a guide for action. Without interpretation and enforcement, law would remain meaningless. As Henry M. Hart (1958:403) points out, law can be analyzed sociologically as a "method" of doing something. In this context, law can be studied as a social process, instrumented by individuals during social interaction. Sociologically, law consists of the behaviors, situations, and conditions for making, interpreting, and applying legal rules that are backed by the state's legitimate coercive apparatus for enforcement.

TYPES OF LAW

The content of law may be categorized as *substantive* or *procedural*. *Substantive* laws consist of rights, duties, and prohibitions administered by courts—which behaviors are to be allowed and which are prohibited (such as prohibition against murder or the sale of narcotics). *Procedural* laws are rules concerning just how substantive laws are to be administered, enforced, changed, and used by players in the legal system (such as filing charges, selecting a jury, presenting evidence in court or drawing up a will).

At times a distinction is made between *public* law and *private* law (Johnson, 1977:59–60). *Public* law is concerned with the structure of government, the duties and powers of officials, and the relationship between the individual and the state. "It includes such subjects as constitutional law, administrative law, regulation of public utilities, criminal law and procedure, and law relating to the proprietary powers of the state and its political subdivisions" (Davis, 1962:51). *Private* law is concerned with both substantive and procedural rules governing relationships between individuals (the law of torts or private injuries, contracts, property, wills, inheritance, marriage, divorce, adoption, and the like).

A more familiar distinction is between *civil* law and *criminal* law. As noted, *civil* law, as private law, consists of a body of rules and procedures intended to govern the conduct of individuals in their relationships with others. Violations of civil statutes, called *torts*, are private wrongs for which the injured individual may seek redress in the courts for the harm he or she experienced. In most cases, some form of payment is required from the offender to compensate for the injury he or she has caused. Similarly, one company may be required to pay another a sum of money for failing to fulfill the terms of a business contract. The complainant firm is thus "compensated" for the loss it may have suffered as a result of the other company's neglect or incompetence. *Criminal* law is concerned with the definition of crime and the prosecution and penal treatment of offenders. Although a criminal act may cause harm to some individual, crimes are regarded as offenses against the state or "the people." A crime is a "public," as opposed to an "individual" or "private," wrong. It is the state, not the harmed individual, that takes action against the offender. Furthermore, the action taken by the state differs from that taken by the plaintiff in a civil case. For example, if the case involves a tort, or civil injury, compensation equivalent to the harm caused is levied. In the case of crime, some form of punishment is administered. Henry M. Hart suggests that a crime ". . . is not simply antisocial conduct which public officers are given a responsibility to suppress. It is not simply any conduct to which a legislature chooses to attach a 'criminal' penalty. It is a conduct which, if duly shown to have taken place, will incur a formal and solemn pronouncement of the moral condemnation of the community" (1958:404). In Hart's view, both the condemnation and the consequences that follow may be regarded as constituting the punishment. Occasionally, a criminal action may be followed up by a civil suit such as in a rape case where the victim may seek financial compensation in addition to criminal sanctions.

A distinction can also be made between civil law and common law. In this context, civil law refers to legal systems whose development was greatly influenced by Roman law, a collection of codes compiled in the Corpus Juris Civilis (Code Civil). Civil-law systems are codified systems, and the basic law is found in codes. These are statutes that are enacted by national parliaments. France is an example of a civil-law system. The civil code of France, which first appeared in 1804, is called the Code Napoleon and embodies the civil law of the country. By contrast, common law resisted codification. Law is not based on acts of parliament but on case law, which relies on precedents set by judges to decide a case (Friedman, 1998, 2002). Thus, it is "judge-made" law as distinguished from legislation or "enacted" law. Law in the United States may be further divided into the following branches: constitutional law, case law, statutory law, executive orders, and administrative law. Constitutional law is a branch of public law. It determines the political organization of the state and its powers while also setting certain substantive and procedural limitations on the exercise of governing power. Constitutional law consists of the application of fundamental principles of law based on that document, as interpreted by the Supreme Court. Case law is enacted by judges in cases that are decided in the appellate courts. Statutory law is legislated law—law made by legislatures. Executive orders are regulations issued by the executive branch of the government at the federal and state levels. Finally, administrative law is a body of law created by administrative agencies in the form of regulations, orders, and decisions. These various categories of laws will be discussed and illustrated later in the text.

MAJOR LEGAL SYSTEMS

In addition to the types of law, there is a large variety of legal systems (see, for example, Johansen, 1998). The dominant legal systems that exist in various forms throughout the world are the Romano-Germanic (civil law), common law, socialist law, and Islamic law (David and Brierley, 1985). The Romano-Germanic systems predominate in Europe, in most of the former colonies of France, Germany, Italy, Spain, Portugal, and Belgium, and in countries that have westernized their legal systems in the nineteenth and twentieth centuries. Common-law systems are predominant in English-speaking countries. Islamic systems are found in the Middle East and some other parts of the world to which Islamic religion has spread. Socialist legal systems prevail in the People's Republic of China, Vietnam, Cuba, and North Korea. Remnants of socialist systems are still found in the former Soviet Union and Eastern European countries.

Romano-Germanic System

The Romano-Germanic, or civil, law refers to legal science that has developed on the basis of Roman *ius civile* or civil law (Abel and Lewis, 1988, Vol. 2). The foundation of this system is the compilation of rules made in the sixth century A.D. under the Roman emperor Justinian. They are contained in the Code of Justinian and have evolved essentially as private law, as means of regulating private relationships between individuals. After the fall of the Roman Empire, the Code of Justinian competed with the customary law of the Germanic tribes that had invaded Europe. The code was reintroduced in law school curricula between A.D. 1100 and 1200 in northern Europe, then spread to other parts of the continent. Roman law thus coexisted with the local systems throughout Europe up to the seventeenth century. In the nineteenth century, the Napoleonic codes, and subsequently the code of the new German Empire of 1900 and the Swiss code of 1907, are examples of the institutionalization of this legal system.

Codified systems are basic laws that are set out in *codes*. A *code* is simply a body of laws (see, for example, Kevelson, 1994). These are statutes enacted by national parliaments that arrange whole fields of law in an orderly, comprehensive, and logical way. Today, most European countries have national codes based on a blend of customary and Roman law that makes the resulting systems members of the Romano-Germanic legal tradition.

Common-Law System

Common law is characteristic of the English system, which developed after the Norman Conquest in 1066. The law of England as well as those laws modeled on English law (such as the laws of the United States, Canada, Ireland, and India) resisted codification. Law is not based on acts of parliament but on case law, which relies on precedents set by judges in deciding a case (Friedman, 1998, 2002). Thus, it is "judge-made" law as distinguished from legislation or "enacted" (statutory) law. The doctrine of "precedent" is strictly a common-law practice. The divisions of the common law, its concepts, substance, structure, legal culture, vocabulary, and the methods of the common-law lawyers and judges are very different, as will be demonstrated throughout the book, from those of the Romano-Germanic, or civil, law systems (see, for example, Abel and Lewis, 1988, Vol. 1).

Socialist Legal System

Although there are multiple versions of it, the origins of the socialist legal system can be traced back to the 1917 Bolshevik Revolution, which gave birth to the Union of Soviet Socialist Republics. The objectives of clas-

Socialist
law — all statutes
expressed by people
cts apply law — don't
create it

14   Chap. 1   Introduction

sical socialist law are threefold. First, law must provide for national security. Ideally, the power of the state must be consolidated and increased to prevent attacks on the socialist state and to assure peaceful coexistence among nations. Second, law has the economic task of developing production and distribution of goods on the basis of socialist principles so that everyone will be provided for "according to his needs." The third goal is that of education: to overcome selfish and antisocial tendencies that were brought about by a heritage of centuries of poor economic organization.

The source of socialist law is legislation, which is an expression of popular will as perceived by the Communist Party. The role of the court is simply to apply the law, not to create or interpret it. Even today, for example, judges in China are not required to have any legal training, and few do. Most hold their positions because they have close connections with local governments, who are eager for quick convictions (Smith, 2001).

Socialist law rejects the idea of separation of powers. The central notion of socialist law is the notion of ownership. Private ownership of goods has been renamed "personal ownership," which cannot be used as a means of producing income. It must be used only for the satisfaction of personal needs. Socialist law is unique with respect to "socialist" ownership, of which there are two versions: collective and state. A typical example of collective ownership is the *kolkhozi*, or collective farm, which is based on nationalized land. State ownership prevails in the industrial sector in the form of installations, equipment, buildings, raw materials, and products. In a socialist legal system, the real question of property is not who owns it, but by whom and how such property is exploited (David and Brierley, 1985). Versions of this type of legal system still exist in China, Cuba, North Korea, and Vietnam (see, for example, Zatz, 1994).

The collapse of communism in the Soviet Union and the former Eastern-bloc countries, the dissolution of the political and economic institutions that guaranteed the conservation of communist structures, the reintroduction of a multiparty system, and general democratization of political life had immediate implications for the socialist legal system (Tismaneanu, 1992). These developments brought about by transitions require a reconceptualization of the basic notions of property, authority, legitimacy, and power, and even of the very idea of law (see, for example, Elster, 1995).

As part of the unexpected and unforeseen dramatic transformations now taking place in Eastern Europe and the former Soviet Union (Collins, 1995), the newly established independent states are experimenting with workable alternatives to the socialist rule of law in their attempts to create a climate for a system of laws receptive to and facilitative of democratic forms of market economies and civil liberties (Alexander and Skapska, 1994; Bryant and Mokrzycki, 1994; Milor, 1994). Although the problems involved in the transition vary from country to country according to unique historical and political circumstances, all the states face common concerns, such as establishment of a new political ideology, creation of new legal rights, the imposition of sanctions on former elites, and new forms of legitimization. Among the practical problems are the creation of new property rights; the attainment of consensus in lawmaking; the formulation and instrumentation of new laws on such matters as privatization; joint ventures; restitution for and rehabilitation of victims of the overturned regime; revision of criminal law; the rise of nationalistic, antiforeign, and anti-Semitic sentiments; and multiparty electoral behavior. There is also a whole slate of legal issues previously denied public attention by socialist law, such as prostitution, drug abuse, unemployment, and economic shortages. There are also significant structural changes taking place that are composed of newly democratic parliamentary lawmaking, conversion of the judicial system, and the awakening of alternative political parties. There are, finally, concerns with the development of new law school curricula, selection of personnel, and replacement or resocialization of former members of the Communist Party still occupying positions of power.

So far, the transition has been slow, uneven and its scope limited. There has been no effort to remove judges who grew up under the old regime. The constitutions have yet to be revised, although there is much talk about them (Klingsberg, 1992). There is a shortage of defense attorneys (Erlanger, 1992). As of November 1993, Russian law permits accused criminals to request a trial by jury (Stead, 1994). But the powers of prosecutors have remained largely unreformed since Stalin's day. They remain hugely influential, heavy-handed, unaccountable and corrupt, and prosecutors can get almost anyone arrested under Russia's vague and contradictory laws, and usually convicted too (*Economist*, 2001).

Perhaps the biggest task facing the new lawmakers is the creation of a legal climate aimed at stimulating foreign investments. Westerners need to be assured about the safety of their investments, which requires the creation of a legal infrastructure based on democratic principles. New laws are needed on repatriation of profits, property rights, privatization, and the movement of goods.

But the greatest challenge confronting the post-Communist regimes is crime management (see, for example, Friedman, 2000; Perlez, 1995). In Russia and in its former satellites, the Soviet criminal code has not been significantly altered and it resulted in some unexpected developments. It is better suited to catch political dissidents than to inspire respect for law and order. The laws are aimed at defending the totalitarian state, not the individual. Presidential decrees and legislative acts have expanded the boundaries of life—from the right to buy and sell property to the freedom to set up banks and private corporations—but the notoriously inefficient courts have no legal basis for interpreting these decrees, much less enforcing them. Consequently, the police cannot formally tackle organized criminal activity because under present law only individuals can be held criminally culpable.

Not surprisingly, the number of organized criminal groups in Russia more than quadrupled during the last decade of the twentieth century (Gaddy et al., 1995; Friedman, 2000; Ryan and Rush, 1997).

Criminal groups now operate in every region and the *Mafiya* is ubiquitous internationally and nationally (Friedman, 2000; Handelman, 1995). For example, prostitution networks in Western Europe, involving several hundreds of thousands of women each year from former Soviet-bloc countries, are run mostly by Russians and Ukrainians and generate huge profits. They collect several thousand dollars per woman at each stage of her odyssey (passport, journey, placement, etc.) and "middlemen" average about $20,000 per person (Paringaux, 1998:18).

In cities all across the nation, gangs operate with near impunity, practicing fraud and extortion, conducting illegal trade, bribing and corrupting officials and viciously murdering anyone who gets in their way. One base of support for the Russian Army's invasion of Chechyna in late 1994 was competing crime syndicates elsewhere in Russia (Meier, 1995). In 1993, Russia saw 335,000 crimes officially designated as racketeering and nearly 30,000 premeditated murders. In Moscow, the slaughter included over 1,400 gangland assassinations, with probably thousands more that went unrecorded. By the end of the first quarter of 1994, the toll was running at 84 murders a day, giving Russia the dubious distinction of surpassing the United States' homicide rate—in fact more than doubling it. The bulk were contract killings due to conflicts in commercial and financial activities (Viviano, 1995).

Almost every small business across Russia pays protection money to some gang. Some authors even raise questions such as "Is Sicily the future of Russia?" (Varese, 2001). Vast fortunes in raw materials—from gold to petroleum—are smuggled out through the porous borders in the Baltics by organized groups who have bribed their way past government officials, and ministries and municipal governments peddle property and favors. Official corruption is rampant and along with tax instability, licensing confusion and disregard for intellectual property rights they serve as disincentives to the kind of private Western investment Russia needs to create jobs and a functioning market economy (Erlanger, 1995).

Despite attempts to establish a "dictatorship of law" in the new Russia (Wines, 2001) the conditions remain chaotic, and the authors of an influential paper in the *Brookings Review* contend that many Russians still believe that organized crime is beneficial for the economy (Gaddy et al., 1995). Businesspeople perceive organized crime as a necessary evil. Although it is hard to acknowledge, the Mafia confers certain benefits. The protection rackets offer security against other types of "disorganized" crime that might affect their clients. Dispute resolution is another Mafia service. But perhaps the biggest contribution of the Mafia to orderly market transactions is contract enforcement. In today's Russia, contracts have little force. Failure to adhere to a contract—to pay for goods or services ordered or delivered—

exacts virtually no official sanctions. Close to half of the aggregate volume of accounts receivable in all Russian industry are delinquent. Since the Russian state is unwilling or unable to provide public enforcement of private contracts, the interim alternative is to privatize enforcement. It is one of the private solutions businesspeople use when they need protection for their transaction. It also makes a nice argument in support of functionalist theorizing in sociology.

Islamic Legal System

Islamic law, unlike the previously discussed systems, is not an independent branch of knowledge. Law is integral to Islamic religion, which defines the character of the social order of the faithful who create laws in the name of God (Ahmad, 2001; Al-Azmeh, 1988; Cooper, et al., 2000; Lippman et al., 1988; Neusner and Sonn, 1999). "Islam" means "submission" or "surrender" and implies that individuals should submit to the will of God. Islamic religion states what Muslims must believe, and includes the *Shari'a* ("the way to follow"), which specifies the rules for believers based on divine command and revelation. Unlike other systems of law based on judicial decisions, precedents, and legislation, Islamic law is derived from four principal sources. They include the *Koran*, the word of God as given to the Prophet. This is the principal source of Islamic law. The second source is the *Sunna*, which are the sayings, acts, and allowances of the Prophet as recorded by reliable sources in the Tradition (*Hadith*). The third is *judicial consensus*; like precedent in common law, it is based on historical consensus of qualified legal scholars, and it limits the discretion of the individual judge. *Analogical reasoning* is the fourth primary source of Islamic law. It is used in circumstances not provided for in the Koran or other sources. For example, some judges inflict the penalty of stoning for the crime of sodomy, contending that sodomy is similar to the crime of adultery and thus should be punished by the same penalty the Koran indicates for adultery. In the same vein, a female would get half the compensation a male would receive for being the victim of the same crime, since a male is entitled to an inheritance twice that of a female. In addition to these principal sources, various supplementary sources, such as custom, judge's preference, and the requirements of public interest, are generally followed.

Shari'a legal precepts can be categorized into five areas: acts commanded, recommended, reprobated, forbidden, and left legally indifferent. Islamic law mandates rules of behavior in the areas of social conduct, family relations, inheritance, and religious ritual, and defines punishments for heinous crimes including adultery, false accusation of adultery, intoxication, theft, and robbery. For example, in the case of adultery, the proof of the offense requires four witnesses or confession. If a married person is found guilty, he or she is stoned to death. Stones are first thrown by witnesses, then by the judge, followed by the rest of the community. For a woman, a grave is dug to receive the body. The punishment for an unmarried person is 100 lashes (Lippman et al., 1988:42). For theft, the penalty of hand amputation is often used. Even grooming can be a man's undoing. In Afghanistan, as the formerly-ruling Taliban interpret the Koran, an adult male is obliged not only to grow a beard but also to leave the hairy underbrush unmolested by scissors. Patrols from the General Department for the Preservation of Virtue and Prevention of Vice are getting tough on trimmed beards in Kabul and now snatch violators from the bazaars and take them to a former maximum security prison for 10 days of religious instructions (Bearak, 1998).

Although such practices are susceptible to interpretations that can and do create conflicts between religious doctrine and human rights (see, for example, Mayer, 1999), they must be examined within the philosophy of Islam and in the spirit of true theoretical inquiry for justification—or even understanding, for Islamic justice is based on religious and philosophical principles that are quite alien to most western readers (Souryal and Potts, 1994). Punishments and rules not defined by historical sources of Shari'a are left to decision by contemporary government regulations and Islamic judges. This practice permitted an evolution of Shari'a law to reflect changing social, political, and economic conditions.

It is important to remember that the sanctions attached to the violation of Islamic law are religious rather than civil. Commercial dealings, for example, between Muslims and Westerners are covered by governmental rules comparable to administrative law in the United States. The fundamental principle of Islam is that of an essentially theocratic society, and Islamic law can be understood only in the context of some minimum knowledge of Islamic religion and civilization. Thus, care should be exercised in discussing or analyzing components of Islamic law out of context and in isolation.

FUNCTIONS OF LAW

Why do we need law, and what does it do for society? More specifically, what functions does law perform? As with the definition of law, there is no agreement among scholars of law and society on the precise functions, nor is there consensus on their relative weight and importance. A variety of functions are highlighted in the literature (see, for example, Aubert, 1969:11; Bredemeier, 1962:74; Mermin, 1982:5–10; Nader and Todd, 1978:1; Pollack, 1979:669; Rawls, 2001; and Sampford, 1989:116–120) depending on the conditions under which law operates at a particular time and place. The recurrent major themes include social control, dispute settlement, and social change. I shall now consider them briefly. These functions of the law will be examined in detail in the chapters dealing with social control, conflict resolution, and social change.

Handwritten margin notes (top): Need formalized systems of social control when: ① great diversity in pop ② lack of direct communic. ③ absence of sim. values/attitudes/standards ④ economic inequities ⑤ rising expectations ⑥ competitive struggle btwn group w/ diff interest

Social Control

In a small, traditional, and homogeneous society, behavioral conformity is ensured by the fact that socializing experiences are very much the same for all members. Social norms tend to be consistent with each other, there is consensus about them, and they are strongly supported by tradition. Social control in such a society is primarily dependent upon self-sanctioning. Even on those occasions when external sanctions are required, they seldom involve formal punishment. Deviants are mostly subjected to informal mechanisms of social control, such as gossip, ridicule, or humiliation. Although they exist, banishment or forms of corporal punishment are rare.

Even in a complex, heterogeneous society, such as the United States, social control rests largely on the internalization of shared norms. Most individuals behave in socially acceptable ways, and, as in simpler societies, fear of disapproval from family, friends, and neighbors is usually adequate to keep potential deviants in check. Nevertheless, the great diversity of the population; the lack of direct communication between various segments; the absence of similar values, attitudes, and standards of conduct; economic inequities, rising expectations and the competitive struggles between groups with different interests have all led to an increasing need for formal mechanisms of social control. Formal social control is characterized by "(1) explicit rules of conduct, (2) planned use of sanctions to support the rules, and (3) designated officials to interpret and enforce the rules, and often to make them" (Davis, 1962:43).

In modern societies, there are many methods of social control, both formal and informal. Law is considered one of the forms of formal social control. In the inimitable words of Roscoe Pound (1941:249): "I think of law as in one sense a highly specialized form of social control in developed politically organized society—a social control through the systematic and orderly application of the force of such a society."

Handwritten margin notes (right): Methods of S.C.: Formal ① Law ② ③ firing ④ promotion ⑤ relocation Compensation manipulation

Lawrence M. Friedman calls attention to two ways in which law plays an important role in social control:

> In the first place, legal institutions are responsible for the making, care and preservation of those rules and norms which define deviant behavior; they announce (in a penal code, for example) which acts may be officially punished and how and which ones may not be punished at all. In the second place, the legal system carries out many rules of social control. Police arrest burglars, prosecutors prosecute them, juries convict them, judges sentence them, prison guards watch them, and parole boards release them. (1977:11)

Of course, as we shall see, law does not have a monopoly on formal mechanisms of social control. Other types of formal mechanisms (such as firing, promotion, demotion, relocation, compensation manipulation and so forth) are found in industry, academe, government, business, and various private groups (Selznick, 1969).

Dispute Settlement

As Karl N. Llewellyn so aptly put it:

> What, then, is this law business about? It is about the fact that our society is honeycombed with disputes. Disputes actual and potential, disputes to be settled and disputes to be prevented; both appealing to law, both making up the business of law. . . . This doing of something about disputes, this doing of it reasonably, is the business of law. (1960:2)

By settling disputes through an authoritative allocation of legal rights and obligations, the law provides an alternative to other methods of dispute resolution. Increasingly, people in all walks of life let the courts settle matters that were once resolved by informal and nonlegal mechanisms, such as negotiation, mediation, or forcible self-help measures. It should be noted, however, that law deals only with disagreements that have been translated into legal disputes. A legal resolution of conflict does not necessarily result in a reduction of tension or antagonism between the aggrieved parties. For example, in a case of employment discrimination on the basis of race, the court may focus on one incident in what is a complex and often not very clear-cut series of problems. It results in a resolution of a specific legal dispute, but not in the amelioration of the broader issues that have produced that conflict.

Social Change

Many scholars contend that a principal function of law in modern society is social engineering. It refers to purposive, planned, and directed social change initiated, guided, and supported by the law. Roscoe Pound captures the essence of this function of law in stating:

> For the purpose of understanding the law of today, I am content to think of law as a social institution to satisfy social wants—the claims and demands involved in the existence of civilized society—by giving effect to as much as we need with the least sacrifice, so far as such wants may be satisfied or such claims given effect by an ordering of human conduct through politically organized society. For present purposes I am content to see in legal history the record of a continually wider recognizing and satisfying of human wants or claims or desires through social control; a more embracing and more effective securing of social interests; a continually more complete and effective elimination of waste and precluding of friction in human enjoyment of the goods of existence—in short, a continually more efficacious social engineering. (1959:98–99)

In many instances law is considered a "desirable and necessary, if not a highly efficient means of inducing change, and that, wherever possible, its institutions and procedures are preferable to others of which we are aware" (Grossman and Grossman, 1971:2). Although some sociologists disagree with this contention (for example, Quinney, 1974), law is often used as a method of social change, a way of bringing about planned social change by the government. Social change is a prominent feature of modern welfare states. For example, part of the taxes a government collects goes to the poor in the form of cash, food stamps, medical and legal benefits, and housing (Friedman, 1998, 2002). I shall return to this social change function of the law in the discussion of law and social change in Chapter 7.

DYSFUNCTIONS OF LAW

Although law is an indispensable and ubiquitous institution of social life, it possesses—like most institutions—certain dysfunctions that may evolve into serious operational difficulties if they are not seriously considered. These dysfunctions stem in part from the law's conservative tendencies, the rigidity inherent in its formal structure, the restrictive aspects connected with its control functions, and the fact that certain kinds of discriminations are inherent in the law itself.

The eminent social scientist Hans Morgenthau (1993:418) suggests that "a given status quo is stabilized and perpetuated in a legal system" and that the courts, being the chief instruments of a legal system, "must act as agents of the status quo." Although this observation does not consider fully the complex interplay between stability and change in the context of law, it still contains an important ingredient of truth. By establishing a social policy of a particular time and place in constitutional and statutory precepts, or by making the precedents of the past binding, the law exhibits a tendency toward conservatism. Once a scheme of rights and duties has been created by a legal system, continuous revisions and disruptions of the system are generally avoided in the interests of predictability and continuity. Social changes often precede changes in the law. In times of crisis, the law can break down, providing an opportunity for discontinuous and sometimes cataclysmic adjustments. Illustrations of this include the various first-aid legal measures used during an energy crisis, such as the rationing of gasoline purchases.

Related to these conservative tendencies of the law is a type of rigidity inherent in its normative framework. Since legal rules are couched in general, abstract, and universal terms, they sometimes operate as straitjackets in particular situations. An illustration of this is the failure of law to consider certain extenuating circumstances for a particular illegal act; for example, stealing because one is hungry or stealing for profit.

A third dysfunction of the law stems from the restrictive aspects of normative control. Norms are shared convictions about the patterns of behavior that are appropriate or inappropriate for the members of a group. Norms serve to combat and forestall anomie (a state of normlessness) and social disorganization. Law can overstep its bounds, and regulation can turn into overregulation, in which situation control may become transformed into repression. For example, in nineteenth-century America, public administration was sometimes hampered by an overrestrictive use of the law, which tended to paralyze needed discretionary exercises in governmental power (Pound, 1914:12–13).

Donald Black's (1989) contention that certain kinds of discrimination are inherent in law itself can also be construed as a fourth dysfunction. Rules, in principle, may apply to everyone, but legal authority falls unevenly across social place. A quote from his oft-cited book, *Sociological Justice*, aptly illustrates this point: "The law in its majestic equality . . . forbids the rich as well as the poor from sleeping under bridges, begging in the streets, and stealing bread" (1989:72). He argues that social status (regardless of race), the degree of intimacy (for example, family members versus friends versus strangers), speech, organization, and a number of other factors all greatly influence the use and application of law. For example, when a black person is convicted of killing a white person in America, the risk of capital punishment far exceeds every other racial combination. In Ohio, the risk of capital punishment is approximately 15 times higher than when a black is convicted of killing another black; in Georgia, over 30 times higher; in Florida, nearly 40; and in Texas, nearly 90 times higher. Similarly, sentencing for negligent homicide with a car is by far the most severe when the victim's status is higher than that of the offender's (1989:10).

Undoubtedly, the list of dysfunctions of law is incomplete. One may also include a variety of procedural inefficiencies, administrative delays, and archaic legal terminologies. At times, justice is denied and innocent people are convicted (Yant, 1991). There is the cost of justice to the middle class and its unavailability to the poor, to the consumer, and to minority-group members. Questions also can be raised regarding the narrowness of legal education and the failure of ethical indoctrination, laws being out-of-date, inequitable criminal sentencing, lack of clarity of some laws resulting in loopholes and diverse interpretations, and the dominating use of law by one class against another (Rostow, 1971; Strick, 1977). Finally, critics of the law point to the current rage for procedure and to "government by judges" as being particularly dysfunctional in a world as complex as ours (Crozier, 1984:116–117).

PARADIGMS OF SOCIETY

Sociological discussions of law in society often take place in the context of one of two ideal conceptions of society: the *consensus* and the *conflict* perspectives. The former describes society as a functionally integrated, relatively stable system held together by a basic consensus of values. Social order is considered as more or less permanent, and individuals can best achieve their interests through cooperation. Social conflict is viewed as the needless struggle among individuals and groups who have not yet attained sufficient understanding of their common interests and basic interdependence. This perspective stresses the cohesion, solidarity, integration, cooperation, and stability of society, which is seen as united by a shared culture and by agreement on its fundamental norms and values.

The conflict perspective, in direct opposition, considers society as consisting of individuals and groups characterized by conflict and dissension and held together by coercion. Order is temporary and unstable because every individual and group strives to maximize its own interests in a world of limited resources and goods. Social conflict is considered as intrinsic to the interaction between individuals and groups. In this perspective, the maintenance of power requires inducement and coercion, and law is an instrument of repression perpetuating the interests of the powerful at the cost of alternative interests, norms, and values.

But, as Ralf Dahrendorf aptly points out, it is impossible to choose empirically between these two sets of assumptions: "Stability and change, integration and conflict, function and 'dysfunction,' consensus and constraint are, it would seem, two equally valid aspects of every imaginable society" (1958:174–175) When law in society is viewed in one of these two perspectives, not surprisingly, quite disparate conceptions of its basic role emerge. Let us examine in some detail the role of law in these two perspectives.

The Consensus Perspective

The consensus perspective considers law as a neutral framework for maintaining societal integration. One of the best-known and most influential legal scholars, Roscoe Pound (1943, 1959), views society as composed of diverse groups whose interests often conflict with one another but are in basic harmony. He considers certain interests as essential for the well-being of society and maintains that the reconciliation between the conflicting interests of the diverse groups in society is essential to secure and maintain social order. In his words, law

> is an attempt to satisfy, to reconcile, to harmonize, to adjust these overlapping and often conflicting claims and demands, either through securing them directly and immediately, or through securing certain individual interests, or through delimitations or compromises of individual interests, so as to give effect to the greatest total of interests or to the interests that weigh most in our civilization, with the least sacrifice of the scheme of the interests as a whole. (Pound, 1943:39)

In Pound's view, law in a heterogeneous and pluralistic society, such as the United States, is best understood as an effort at social compromise with an emphasis on social order and harmony. Pound argues that the historical

[handwritten: purpose of law is to maintain harmony by controlling interests & social integration]

development of law demonstrates a growing recognition and satisfaction of human wants, claims, and desires through law. Over time, law has concerned itself with an ever wider spectrum of human interests. Law has more and more come to provide for the common good and the satisfaction of social wants (Pound, 1959:47). He considers law a form of "social change" directed toward achieving social harmony. Pound argues that the purpose of law is to maintain and to ensure those values and needs essential to social order, not by imposing one group's will on others, but by controlling, reconciling, and mediating the diverse and conflicting interests of individuals and groups within society. In brief, the purpose of law is to control interests and to maintain harmony and social integration.

Talcott Parsons (1962:58) concurs with this view by suggesting that "the primary function of a legal system is integrity. It serves to mitigate potential elements of conflict and to oil the machinery of social intercourse." Other sociologists, such as Harry C. Bredemeier (1962), accept this perspective and believe that it is necessary for society to supplement informal with formal mechanisms for generating and sustaining interpersonal cooperation. Proponents of the consensus perspective further maintain that law exists to maintain order and stability. Law is a body of rules enacted by representatives of the people in the interests of the people. Law is essentially a neutral agent, dispensing rewards and punishments without bias. A fundamental assumption of this perspective is that the political system is pluralistic, that society is composed of a number of interest groups of more or less equal power. The laws reflect compromise and consensus among these various interest groups and the values that are fundamental to the social order (Chambliss, 1976:4).

The Conflict Perspective

[handwritten: → law used to control & oppress ruling by class]

In marked contrast to the consensus perspective, the conflict view considers law as a "weapon in social conflict" (Turk, 1978) and an instrument of oppression "employed by the ruling classes for their own benefit" (Chambliss and Seidman, 1982:36). From this perspective, the transformation of society from a small, relatively homogeneous social group to a network of specialized groups is brought about by the evolution of both distinct sets of interests and differences in real power between groups. When diverse groups come into conflict, they compete to have their interests protected and perpetuated through the formalization of their interests into law. On the basis of this idea, Richard Quinney argues that rather than being a device to control interests, law is an expression of interests, an outgrowth of the inherent conflict of interests characteristic of society. According to Quinney:

> Society is characterized by diversity, conflict, coercion, and change, rather than by consensus and stability. Second, law is a *result* of the operation of interests, rather than an instrument that functions outside of particular interests. Though

law may control interests, it is in the first place *created by* interests of specific persons and groups; it is seldom the product of the whole society. Law is made by men, representing special interests, who have the power to translate their interests into public policy. Unlike the pluralistic conception of politics, law does not represent a compromise of the diverse interests in society, but supports some interests at the expense of others. (1970:35)

Proponents of the conflict perspective believe that law is a tool by which the ruling class exercises its control. Law both protects the property of those in power and serves to repress political threats to the position of the elite. Quinney (1975:285) writes that whereas the state, contrary to conventional wisdom, is the instrument of the ruling class, "law is the state's coercive weapon, which maintains the social and economic order," and supports some interests at the expense of others, even when those interests are that of the majority.

But advocates of this position overstate their case. Not all laws are created and operated for the benefit of the powerful ruling groups in society. Laws prohibiting murder, robbery, arson, incest, and assault benefit all members of society, regardless of their economic position. It is too broad an assumption that powerful groups dictate the content of law and its enforcement for the protection of their own interests. As we shall see in Chapter 4, all kinds of groups are involved in lawmaking, although the powerful groups do have a substantial voice in the lawmaking process.

These two perspectives of society—consensus and conflict—are ideal types (that is, abstract concepts used to describe essential features of a phenomenon). Considering the operation of legal systems in society, there may be an element of truth in both. Sociologists who are influenced by Karl Marx, Georg Simmel, Lewis Coser, and Ralf Dahrendorf generally tend to embrace the conflict perspective of law in society. One of their justifications for taking this theoretical stance is that this approach emphasizes the role of special-interest groups in society. For example, the power of economic and commercial interests to influence legislation is illustrated by William J. Chambliss in his study of vagrancy statutes. He notes that the development of vagrancy laws paralleled the need of landowners for cheap labor during the period in England when the system of serfdom was collapsing. The first of these statutes, which came into existence in 1349, threatened criminal punishment for those who were able-bodied and yet unemployed—a condition that existed when peasants were in the process of moving from the land into the cities. The vagrancy law served "to force laborers (whether personally free or unfree) to accept employment at a low wage in order to insure the landowner an adequate supply of labor at a price he could afford to pay" (Chambliss, 1964:69). Subsequently, vagrancy statutes were modified to protect the commercial and industrial interests and to ensure safe commercial transportation. In the late nineteenth and early twentieth centuries in the

United States, vagrancy laws were used again to serve the interests of the wealthy. Agricultural states during harvest time enforced vagrancy laws to push the poor into farm work. In periods of economic depression, similar laws were used to keep the unemployed from entering the state (Chambliss and Seidman, 1982:182). This is just one illustration to show how law came to reflect the particular interests of those who have power and influence in society. I shall return to the role of interest groups dealing with decision-making processes in the context of lawmaking in Chapter 4.

OPTIONS FOR SOCIOLOGISTS

As with the approaches to the study of law and society, divergences of opinion also characterize the question of what role sociologists should play in such endeavors. This question, to a substantial degree, polarized the discipline. Some sociologists consider their role primarily to synthesize material and to provide instructional packages for students and interested laymen (see, for example, Friedrichs, 2001; Sutton, 2001); Others consider their role as describing and explaining social phenomena objectively. They are concerned with the understanding of social life and social processes, and they go about their research in an alleged value-neutral and empirical fashion. They accept as scientific only those theoretical statements whose truth can be proven empirically. They are guided by Max Weber's notion of sociology as "a science which seeks to understand social action interpretively, and thereby to explain it causally in its course and its effects" (Weber, 1968:3). They believe that the discovery of causal laws is the ultimate goal of sociology, but the understanding of peoples' motives is central.

Others, however, go beyond the notion of *verstehen* (to understand). Sociologists who claim to be dialectical and critical in their orientation do not seek merely to describe and explain social events. They, as scientists, assert their right to criticize. The standards of evaluation upon which their criticism is based, and which these sociologists deduce from the nature of human beings and from considerations about social development, cannot always be empirically tested. To them, empirical research is necessary insofar as it provides and explains the data, but it is, so to speak, only a first step toward the essential criticism. They believe that the task of sociology is to account for human suffering. They aim at demystifying the world; to show people what constrains them and what are their routes to freedom. Their criticisms are prompted by their belief that the human condition and the social order have become unbearable. These critics believe that they have a responsibility not only to identify the factors that have precipitated a deleterious condition but also to provide, through theoretical and empirical efforts, ways to rectifying or redressing it. In the context of law and society studies, illustrations of such attempts over the past three decades include Jerold S. Auerbach's *Unequal Justice* (1976), Maureen Cain and Christine B.

Harrington's *Lawyers in a Postmodern World; Translation and Transgression* (1994), Paul Campos' *Jurismania: The Madness of American Law* (1998), Alan M. Dershowitz's *The Abuse Excuse, And Other Cop-outs, Sob Stories, and Evasions of Responsibility* (1994), Leonard Downie's *Justice Denied* (1972), Daniel A. Farber and Suzanna Sherry's *Beyond All Reason: The Radical Assault on Truth in American Law* (1997), Macklin Fleming's *Lawyers, Money, and Success: The Consequences of Dollar Obsessions* (1997), Mary Ann Glendon's *A Nation Under Lawyers: How the Crisis in the Legal Profession Is Transforming American Society* (1994), Paul G. Haskell's *Why Lawyers Behave As They Do* (1998), Philip K. Howard's two critical volumes, *The Death of Common Sense, How Law Is Suffocating America* (1994) and *The Lost Art of Drawing the Line: How Fairness Went Too Far* (2001), Richard Quinney's *Critique of Legal Order* (1974), Gerry Spence's *With Justice for None* (1989), Ann Strick's *Injustice for All* (1977), and Martin Yant's *Presumed Guilty: When Innocent People Are Wrongly Convicted* (1991).

Finally, for some sociologists, criticism is interconnected with practice. They endorse the role of being simultaneously a student and an agent of social action. They are guided by *praxis*, or the wedding of theory and action. Because of their knowledge of social conditions, they are obligated to take action. This position is associated with a Marxist tradition. It is based on the notion that knowledge generated from an analysis of a specific historical situation may be used as an argument for intervention. Sociologists in such situations try to demystify, clarify, and show individuals the source of their misery and the means of overcoming it. In a Marxian context, praxis means what people do, as contrasted with what they think. "Praxis is a revolutionary form of social practice (i.e., it contributes to the humanization of people by transforming reality from alienation to hopefully better future). The concept is both a means of consciously shaping historical conditions and a standard for evaluating what occurs in any historical order. Marx maintains that a dialectical relationship exists between theory and praxis" (Reasons and Rich, 1978:431). Thus, sociologists of this perspective actively advocate changes in law and legal institutions wherever needed and work for the reformation of both the criminal system and the criminal law when warranted (Krisberg, 1978).

These controversies beset the "proper" role of sociologists in the discipline. Based on one's values, ideologies, and conception of sociology, and a plethora of other considerations, one may prefer to be a detached observer of social life, a critic of the social order, or an active agent of change. These roles, fortunately, are not mutually exclusive. Depending on the nature of the issue under consideration, the degree of commitment to and involvement in that issue, one may freely select among these alternatives. As an intellectual enterprise, sociology is flexible enough to accommodate these diverse positions. In a sense, they contribute to a greater understanding of the complicated interplay between law and society.

SUMMARY

In sociology, the study of law touches a variety of well-established areas of inquiry. It incorporates values, ideologies, social institutions, norms, power relations, and social processes. Since World War II, there has been a growing interest in law among sociologists both in the United States and abroad. Some of the examples of the study of law and society include the effectiveness of law, the impact of law on society, methods of dispute resolution, and research on judicial, legislative, and administrative processes. There are still some obstacles to interaction between sociologists and lawyers, however, as a consequence of differences in terminology, perception of the role of law in society, methodology, and professional culture. Yet, in spite of these difficulties, collaboration is on the increase between members of the two professions.

Scholarly debate over a proper definition of law has long preoccupied scholars in jurisprudence and in the social sciences. In our illustrative definitions, it was noted that law is a form of social control with explicit sanctions for noncompliance, and it consists of the behaviors, situations, and conditions for creating, interpreting, and applying legal rules.

The content of law may be considered as substantive or procedural. A distinction is made also between public law and private law, as well as between civil law and criminal law. Common law generally refers to "judge-made" law or "case" law, as differentiated from statutory or enacted law. The principal legal systems in the world today include the Romano-Germanic (civil law), common law, socialist law with its current ramifications and problems of transition, and Muslim law.

Law performs a multitude of functions in society. It is difficult to arrive at a satisfactory and meaningful list of functions. Still, there seems to be a great deal of emphasis in the literature on the recurrent social control, dispute settlement, and social change functions of law. But law, like other social institutions, possesses certain dysfunctions as a result of law's conservative tendencies, the rigidity inherent in its formal structure, the restrictive aspects connected with its social control functions and the fact that certain kinds of discriminations are inherent in the law itself.

Sociological analyses of law and society are generally based on two ideal views of society—consensus and conflict perspectives. The former considers society as a functionally integrated, relatively stable system held together by basic consensus of values. The latter conceives of society as consisting of groups characterized by conflict and dissension on values and held together by some members who coerce others. These dialectic models of society are ideal types. Taken toward the operation of the lawmaking organizations, there may be an element of truth in both. In this context, perhaps an eclectic approach is best.

In addition to divergences in the way of studying law in society, controversies also beset the "proper" role sociologists should play in the study of law and society. Some sociologists maintain that their role is to try to understand, describe, and empirically analyze social phenomena in a more or less value-free context. Others argue that it is the responsibility of social scientists to criticize malfunctioning components of, and processes in, a social system. Still others are guided by the notion of praxis; they seek to combine theory with practice, and their objective is to try to redress deleterious social conditions by means of legal action. Of course, these divergent positions are not mutually exclusive, and an awareness of these perspectives on the role of sociologists can contribute to a greater understanding of the intricate interplay between law and society.

SUGGESTED FURTHER READINGS

RICHARD L. ABEL (ED.), *The Law & Society Reader*. New York: New York University Press, 1995. A series of groundbreaking articles that have all appeared in the *Law & Society Review*.

MARY P. BAUMGARTNER (ED.), *The Social Organization of Law*. 2nd ed. San Diego, CA: Academic Press, 1999. A set of empirical studies on how social factors affect legal behavior.

JOHN M. CONLEY, and WILLIAM M. O'BARR, *Just Words: Law, Language, and Power*. Chicago: University of Chicago Press, 1998. A good attempt to show how the microdynamics of the legal process and the major questions of justice can be explored through the field of socio-linguistics.

JOHN COOPER, RONALD L. NETTLER and MOHAMED MAHMOUD (EDS.), *Islam and Modernity*. New York: I. B. Tauris Publishers, 2000. A compendium of articles that provides a background for the interplay between law and Islamic religion.

ROGER COTTERRELL (ED.), *Law and Society*. New York: New York University Press, 1994. A diverse collection of "big-name" articles on the various facets of the field. An excellent supplement to Abel's compendium.

JAMES E. DUKE, *Conflict and Power in Social Life*. Provo, UT: Brigham Young University Press, 1976. An easy to read review of the influential and important conflict theories in sociology. It provides several ramifications of the conflict model of society.

LAWRENCE M. FRIEDMAN, *Total Justice*. New York: Russell Sage Foundation, 1985. A short and highly readable book on law and the legal system in the United States.

ROBERT L. FRIEDMAN, *Red Mafiya: How the Russian Mob Has Invaded America*. Boston: Little, Brown and Company, 2000. An interesting account of Russian organized crime. It is bloodier than Corliano's *Godfather*, and reads almost as well.

BRYAN A. GARNER, *Legal Writing in Plain English: A Text with Exercises*. Chicago: University of Chicago Press, 2001. Just to show that it can be done.

E. ADAMSON HOEBEL, *The Law of Primitive Man: A Study in Comparative Legal Dynamics*. Cambridge: Harvard University Press, 1954. A highly influential treatise on the cross-cultural study of the dynamics of law. A must for students interested in law from an anthropological perspective.

HERBERT JACOB, *Law and Politics in the United States*. 2nd. ed. Ft. Washington, PA: HarperCollins College Publishers, 1995. An informative and clear overview of the components and processes of the American legal system.

MITCHELL S. G. KLEIN, *Law, Courts, and Policy*. Englewood Cliffs, NJ: Prentice Hall, 1984. See in particular Chapter 1, which is a good overview of law and society from the perspective of political science.

RICHARD LEMPERT and JOSEPH SANDERS, *An Invitation to Law and Social Science*. New York: Longman, 1986. An interdisciplinary analysis of law and the legal system written by two law professors for students in both law and the social sciences.

LISA J. MCINTYRE, *Law in the Sociological Enterprise: A Reconstruction*. Boulder, CO: Westview Press, 1994. A sophisticated discussion of how law permeates the relationships of modern society.

JOHN MONAHAN and LAURENS WALKER, *Social Science in Law: Cases and Materials*. 4th ed. Westbury, NY: The Foundation Press, Inc., 1998. See especially the first chapter on the jurisprudential origins of social science in law.

RONALD ROESCH, STEVEN D. DART, and JAMES R. P. OGLOFF (EDS.), *Psychology and the Law: The State of the Discipline*. New York: Plenum Publishing Corporation, 1999. An overview of current key issues and contributions of psychology to the understanding of law, legal systems and processes. A useful supplement to the law and society literature.

NORBERT ROULAND, *Legal Anthropology*. Trans. Philippe G. Planel. Stanford, CA: Stanford University Press, 1994. An excellent discussion of law and legal systems from an anthropological perspective.

PATRICK J. RYAN and GEORGE E. RUSH (EDS.), *Understanding Organized Crime in a Global Perspective*. Thousand Oaks, CA: Sage Publications, Inc., 1997. See in particular the articles on organized crime in Russia and Eastern Europe and the predictions for the next century.

AUSTIN SARAT and THOMAS R. KEARNS (EDS.), *Law in the Domains of Culture*. Ann Arbor: The University of Michigan Press, 2000. A collection of essays on law's relations to culture and on the role of cultural analysis of law.

A. W. B. Simpson, *Invitation to Law*. Oxford, England: Basil Blackwell, 1988. A provocative and mordant examination of law and the emergence of the British legal system.

JUNE STARR and JANE F. COLLIER (EDS.), *History and Power in the Study of Law: New Directions in Legal Anthropology*. Ithaca, NY: Cornell University Press, 1989. A compendium of 14 articles by anthropologists, sociologists, and law professors from North America and Europe on the various facets of the interplay between law and society.

MARJORIE S. ZATZ, *Producing Legality: Law and Socialism in Cuba*. New York: Rutledge, 1994. A readable exploration of Cuba's legal system and a good resource for anyone interested in the comparative study of legal systems.

REFERENCES

ABEL, RICHARD L. 1995. "What We Talk About When We Talk About Law." Pp. 1–10 in Richard L. Abel (ed.), *The Law & Society Reader*. New York: New York University Press.

ABEL, RICHARD L., and PHILIP S. C. LEWIS (EDS.). 1988. *Lawyers in Society: The Common Law World*. Vol. 1. Berkeley and Los Angeles: University of California Press. 1988. *Lawyers in Society: The Civil Law World*. Vol. 2. Berkeley and Los Angeles: University of California Press.

AHMED, ALI. 2001. *Cosmopolitan Orientation of the Process of International Environmental Lawmaking: An Islamic Law Genre*. Lanham, MD: University Press of America.

AKERS, RONALD L. 1965. "Toward a Comparative Definition of Law," *Journal of Criminal Law, Criminology, and Police Science* 56 (September): 301–306.

AKERS, RONALD L., and RICHARD HAWKINS (EDS.). 1975. *Law and Control in Society*. Englewood Cliffs, NJ: Prentice Hall.

ALEXANDER, GREGORY S. and GRAZYNA SKAPSKA (EDS.). 1994. *A Fourth Way? Privatization, Property, and the Emergence of New Market Economies*. New York: Routledge.

AL-AZMEH, AZIZ (ED.). 1988. *Islamic Law: Social and Historical Contexts*. London: Routledge.

AUBERT, VILHELM (ED.). 1969. *Sociology of Law*. "Introduction." Pp. 9–14. Harmondsworth, England: Penguin. 1973. "Researches in the Sociology of Law." Pp. 48–62 in Michael Barkun (ed.), *Law and the Social System*. New York: Lieber-Atherton.

AUERBACH, JEROLD S. 1976. *Unequal Justice*. New York: Oxford University Press.

BAUMGARTNER, MARY P. (ED.). 1999. *The Social Organization of Law*. 2nd ed. San Diego, CA: Academic Press.

BEARAK, BARRY. 1998. "Afghan Beard Code: Like Castro Si, Pavarotti No," *New York Times* (October 13): A4.

BLACK, DONALD. 1976. *The Behavior of Law*. New York: Academic Press. 1989. *Sociological Justice*. New York: Oxford University Press. 1998. *The Social Structure of Right and Wrong*. Revised ed. San Diego, CA: Academic Press. 2001. "The Geometry of Law: An Interview with Donald Black," Draft: April 15, 2001. Forthcoming in the Brazilian *Review of Criminal Sciences*.

BREDEMEIER, HARRY C. 1962. "Law as an Integrative Mechanism." Pp. 73–90 in William J. Evan (ed.), *Law and Sociology: Exploratory Essays*. New York: Free Press.

BRYANT, CHRISTOPHER and EDMUND MOKRZYCKI (EDS.). 1994. *The Great Transformation? Change and Continuity in East Central Europe*. New York: Routledge.

CAIN, MAUREEN and CHRISTINE B. HARRINGTON (EDS.). 1994. *Lawyers in a Postmodern World: Translation and Transgression*. New York: New York University Press.

CAMPOS, PAUL F. 1998. *Jurismania: The Madness of American Law*. New York: Oxford University Press.

CARDOZO, BENJAMIN NATHAN. 1924. *The Growth of the Law*. New Haven: Yale University Press.

CHAMBLISS, WILLIAM J. 1964. "A Sociological Analysis of the Law of Vagrancy," *Social Problems* 12 (1) (Summer):67–77. 1976. "Functional and Conflict Theories of Crime: The Heritage of Emile Durkheim and Karl Marx." Pp. 1–28 in William J. Chambliss and Milton Mankoff (eds.), *Whose Law? What Order? A Conflict Approach to Criminology*. New York: John Wiley.

CHAMBLISS, WILLIAM, and ROBERT SEIDMAN. 1982. *Law, Order, and Power*. 2nd ed. Reading, MA: Addison-Wesley.

COLLINS, RANDALL. 1995. "Prediction in Macrosociology: The Case of the Soviet Collapse," *American Journal of Sociology*. 100, (6) (May): 1552–1593.

CONLEY, JOHN M. and WILLIAM M. O'BARR. 1998. *Just Words: Law, Language, and Power*. Chicago: University of Chicago Press.

COOPER, JOHN, RONALD L. NETTLER and MOHAMED MAHMOUD (EDS.). 2000. *Islam and Modernity*. New York: I. B. Tauris Publishers.

COTTERRELL, ROGER (ED.). 1994. *Law and Society*. New York: New York University Press.

CROZIER, MICHEL. 1984. *The Trouble with America*. Trans. Peter Heinegg. Berkeley and Los Angeles: University of California Press.

DAHRENDORF, RALF. 1958. "Toward a Theory of Social Conflict," *Journal of Conflict Resolution*, no. 2 (June): 170–183.

DAVID, RENE, and JOHN E. BRIERLEY. 1985. *Major Legal Systems in the World Today*. 3rd ed. London: Stevens & Sons.

DAVIS, F. JAMES. 1962. "Law as a Type of Social Control." Pp. 39–63 in F. James Davis et al. (eds.), *Society and the Law: New Meanings for an Old Profession*. New York: Free Press.

DE SOTO, HERNANDO. 2001. *The Mystery of Capital, Why Capitalism Triumphs in the West and Fails Everywhere Else*. New York: Basic Books.

DERSHOWITZ, ALAN M. 1994. *The Abuse Excuse, And Other Cop-outs, Sob Stories, And Evasions of Responsibility*. Boston: Little, Brown and Company.

DOWNIE, LEONARD. 1972. *Justice Denied*. Baltimore: Penguin.

ECONOMIST. 2001. "A Survey of Russia—Putin's Choice," (July 21): 1–16.

EHRLICH, EUGEN. 1975. *Fundamental Principles of the Sociology of Law*, Foreword. New York: Arno Press. Trans. Walter L. Mall. Originally published by Harvard University Press, 1936.

ELSTER, JON. 1995. *Archives Europeenes de Sociologie*. 36 (1), (Sommaire): 105–134.

ERLANGER, STEVEN. 1992. "Two Novelties in Russian Courts: Defense Lawyers and Jury Trial," *New York Times* (May 11): A1, A4. 1995. "A Corrupt Tide in Russia From State-Business" (July 3): A1, A5.

FARBER, DANIEL A., and SUZANNA SHERRY. 1997. *Beyond All Reason: The Radical Assault on Truth in American Law*. New York: Oxford University Press.

FLEMING, MACKLIN. 1997. *Lawyers, Money, and Success: The Consequences of Dollar Obsessions*. Westport, CT: Quorum.

FRIEDMAN, LAWRENCE M. 1975. *The Legal System: A Social Science Perspective*. New York: Russell Sage Foundation. 1977. *Law and Society: An Introduction*. Englewood Cliffs, NJ: Prentice Hall. 1998. *American Law: An Introduction*. 2nd ed. New York: W.W. Norton & Co., Inc. 2002. *American Law in the Twentieth Century*. New Haven: Yale University Press.

FRIEDMAN, ROBERT L. 2000. *Red Mafiya: How the Russian Mob Has Invaded America*. Boston, MA: Little, Brown and Company.

FRIEDRICHS, DAVID O. 2001. *Law in Our Lives, An Introduction*. Los Angeles, CA: Roxbury Publishing Co.

GADDY, CLIFFORD, JIM LEITZEL and MICHAEL ALEXEEV. 1995. "Mafiosi and Matrioshki: Organized Crime and Russian Reform," *Brookings Review* 13 (1) (Winter): 26–30.

GARNER, BRYAN A. 2001. *Legal Writing in Plain English: A Text with Exercises*. Chicago: University of Chicago Press.

GEST, TED. 1995. "Combating Legalese: Law Schools Are Finally Learning That Good English Makes Sense," *U.S. News & World Report* (March 20): 78–81.

GLABERSON, WILLIAM. 2001. "Legal Citations Are on Trial in Innovation v. Tradition," *New York Times* (July 8): A1.

GLENDON, MARY ANN. 1994. *A Nation Under Lawyers: How the Crisis in the Legal Profession Is Transforming American Society*. New York: Farrar, Straus, and Giroux.

GROSSMAN, JOEL B., AND MARY H. GROSSMAN (eds.). 1971. "Introduction." Pp. 1–10 in *Law and Change in Modern America*. Pacific Palisades, CA: Goodyear.

HANDELMAN, STEPHEN. 1995. *Comrade Criminal, Russia's New Mafiya*. New Haven, CT: Yale University Press.

HART, HENRY M., JR. 1958. "The Aims of the Criminal Law," *Law and Contemporary Problems*, no. 23 (Summer): 401–441.

HASKELL, PAUL G. 1998. *Why Lawyers Behave As They Do*. Boulder, CO: Westview Press.

HOEBEL, E. ADAMSON. 1954. *The Law of Primitive Man: A Study of Comparative Legal Dynamics*. Cambridge: Harvard University Press.

HOLMES, OLIVER WENDELL, JR. 1897. "The Path of the Law," *Harvard Law Review*, no. 10 (March): 457–461. 1963. *The Common Law*. Cambridge: Harvard University Press. Mark D. Howe (ed.). Originally published in 1881.

HOWARD, PHILIP K. 1994. *The Death of Common Sense, How Law Is Suffocating America*. New York: Random House. 2001. *The Lost Art of Drawing the Line: How Fairness Went Too Far*. New York: Random House.

JOHANSEN, BRUCE ELLIOTT (ED.). 1998. *The Encyclopedia of Native American Legal Tradition*. Westport, CT: Greenwood Publishing Group.

JOHNSON, ALAN V. 1977. "A Definition of the Concept of Law," *Mid-American Review of Sociology* 2 (1) (Spring): 47–71.

KEVELSON, ROBERTA (ED.). 1994. *Codes and Customs; Millennial Perspectives*. New York: Peter Lang.

KLINGSBERG, ETHAN. 1992. "Judicial Review and Hungary's Transition from Communism to Democracy. The Constitutional Court, the Continuity of Law, and the Redefinition of Property Rights," *Brigham Young University Law Review 1992*, no. 1: 41–144.

KRISBERG, BARRY. 1978. "The Sociological Imagination Revisited." Pp. 455–470 in Charles E. Reasons and Robert M. Rich (eds.), *The Sociology of Law: A Conflict Perspective*. Toronto: Butterworths.

LAW & SOCIETY REVIEW. 1995. "From the Editor," 29 (1): 5–9.

LAUDERDALE, PAT. 1997. "Indigenous North American Jurisprudence," *International Journal of Comparative Sociology* 38 (1–2) (June): 131–149.

LIPPMAN, MATTHEW, SEAN MCCONVILLE, and MORDECHAI YERUSHALMI. 1988. *Islamic Criminal Law and Procedure*. New York: Praeger.

LLEWEWLLYN, KARL N. 1960. *The Bramble Bush*. Dobbs Ferry, NY: Oceana Publications, Inc. Originally published in 1930.

MATTEI, UGO. 1997. *Comparative Law and Economics*. Ann Arbor, MI: The University of Michigan Press.

MAYER, ANN ELIZABETH. 1999. *Islam and Human Rights: Tradition and Politics*. Boulder, CO: Westview Press.

MCINTYRE, LISA J. 1994. *Law in the Sociological Enterprise: A Reconstruction*. Boulder, CO: Westview Press.

MEIER, ANDREW. 1995. "The Chechen Mafia: The Real Reason Yeltsin Invaded," *New Republic* 212 (17) (April 24): 16–18.

MERMIN, SAMUEL. 1982. *Law and the Legal System: An Introduction*. 2nd ed. Boston: Little, Brown.

MILOR, VEDAT (ED.). 1994. *Changing Political Economies: Privatization in Post-Communist and Reforming Communist States*. Boulder, CO: Lynne Rienner Publishers.

MORGENTHAU, HANS. 1993. *Politics Among Nations*. New York: McGraw-Hill. Revised by Kenneth W. Thompson.

NADER, LAURA, and HARRY F. TODD, JR. (EDS.). 1978. "Introduction." Pp. 1–40 in *The Disputing Process—Law in Ten Societies*. New York: Columbia University Press.

NEUSNER, JACOB and TAMARA SONN. 1999. *Comparing Religions Through Law: Judaism and Islam*. New York: Routledge.

PARINGAUX, ROLAND-PIERRE. 1998. "Prostitution Takes a Turn for the West," *Guardian Weekly* 158 (21) (May 24): 18.

PARSONS, TALCOTT. 1962. "The Law and Social Control." Pp. 56–72 in William M. Evan (ed.), *Law and Sociology: Exploratory Essays*. New York: Free Press.

POLLACK, ERVIN H. 1979. *Jurisprudence: Principles and Applications*. Columbus: Ohio State University Press.

PERLEZ, JANE. 1995. "Poles Dismayed at Unchecked Crime,"*New York Times* (June 19): A5.

POSNER, RICHARD A. 1996. *The Federal Courts: Challenge and Reform*. Cambridge: Harvard University Press. 2001. *Frontiers of Legal Theory*. Cambridge: Harvard University Press.

POSPISIL, LEOPOLD J. 1971. *Anthropology of Law: A Comparative Theory*. New York: Harper & Row, Pub. 1978. *The Ethnology of Law*. 2nd ed. Menlo Park, CA: Cummings Publishing Company.

POUND, ROSCOE. 1914. "Justice According to Law," *Columbia Law Review* 14 (1): 1–26. 1941. *In My Philosophy of Law*. St. Paul, MN: West Publishing Company. 1943. "A Survey of Social Interests," *Harvard Law Review*, no. 57 (October): 1–39. 1959. *An Introduction to the Philosophy of Law*. New Haven: Yale University Press.

QUINNEY, RICHARD. 1970. *The Social Reality of Crime*. Boston: Little, Brown. 1974. *Critique of Legal Order: Crime Control in Capitalist Society*. Boston: Little, Brown. 1975. *Criminology: Analysis and Critique of Crime in America*. Boston: Little, Brown.

RAWLS, JOHN. 2001. *Justice as Fairness. A Restatement*. (ed. Erin Kelly). Cambridge: The Belknap Press/Harvard University Press.

REASONS, CHARLES E., and ROBERT M. RICH (EDS.). 1978. *The Sociology of Law: A Conflict Perspective*. Toronto: Butterworths.

REHBINDER, MANFREID. 1975. *Sociology of Law: A Trend Report and Bibliography*. The Hague: Mouton.

RICH, ROBERT M. 1977. *The Sociology of Law: An Introduction to Its Theorists and Theories*. Washington, DC: University Press of America.

ROESCH, RONALD, STEVEN D. DART, and JAMES R. P. OGLOFF (EDS.). 1999. *Psychology and the Law: The State of the Discipline*. New York: Plenum Publishing Corporation.

ROSS, E. ADAMSON. 1922. *Social Control*. New York: MacMillan. Originally published in 1901.

ROSS, LAURENCE H. 1989. "Sociology and Legal Sanctions," Pp. 36–49 in Martin Lawrence Friedland (ed.), *Sanctions and Rewards in the Legal System: A Multidisciplinary Approach*. Toronto: University of Toronto Press.

ROSTOW, EUGENE V. (ED.). 1971. *Is Law Dead?* New York: Simon & Schuster.

RYAN, PATRICK J. and GEORGE E. RUSH (EDS.). 1997. *Understanding Organized Crime in a Global Perspective*. Thousand Oaks, CA: Sage Publications, Inc.

SAMPFORD, CHARLES. 1989. *The Disorder of Law: A Critique of Legal Theory*. Oxford, England: Basil Blackwell.

SARAT, AUSTIN, and THOMAS R. KEARNS (EDS.). 1994. *The Rhetoric of Law*. Ann Arbor: The University of Michigan Press. 2000. *Law in the Domains of Culture*. Ann Arbor: The University of Michigan Press.

SCHUR, EDWIN M. 1968. *Law and Society: A Sociological View*. New York: Random House.

SELZNICK, PHILIP. 1968. "Law: The Sociology of Law," *International Encyclopedia of the Social Sciences*, no. 9: 50–59. New York: Free Press. 1969. *Law, Society and Industrial Justice*. New York: Russell Sage Foundation.

SOURYAL, SAM S. and DENNIS W. POTTS. 1994. "The Penalty of Hand Amputation for Theft in Islamic Justice, " *Journal of Criminal Justice* 22 (3) (May–June): 249–265.

SMITH, CRAIG S. 2001. "Torture Hurries New Wave of Executions in China," *New York Times* (September 9): A1, A8.

SPENCE, GERRY. 1989. *With Justice for None*. New York: Times Books.

STONE, JULIUS. 1964. *Legal System and Lawyer's Reasonings*. Stanford: Stanford University Press.

STRICK, ANNE. 1977. *Injustice for All*. New York: Penguin.

STEAD, DEBORAH. 1994. "Crime and Punishment—And Now Trial By Jury," *Business Week* (January 17): 20–22.

SUTTON, JOHN R. 2001. *Law/Society: Origins, Interactions, and Change*. Thousand Oaks: CA: Pine Forge Press.

TISMANEANU, VLADIMIR. 1992. *Reinventing Politics: Eastern Europe from Stalin to Havel*. New York: Free Press.

TURK, AUSTIN T. 1978. "Law as a Weapon in Social Conflict." Pp. 213–232 in Charles E. Reasons and Robert M. Rich (eds.), *The Sociology of Law: A Conflict Perspective*. Toronto: Butterworths.

VARESE, FEDERICO. 2001. "Is Sicily the Future of Russia? Private Protection and the Rise of the Russian Mafia," *Archives Europeennes de Sociologie* 42 (1): 186–221.

VIVIANO, FRANK. 1995. "The New Mafia Order, Organized Crime in Russia, Mexico, and Elsewhere," *Mother Jones* 20 (3) (May–June): 44–55.

WALKER, NANCY PERRY, and LAWRENCE S. WRIGHTSMAN. 1991. *The Child Witness: Legal Issues and Dilemmas*. Newbury Park, CA: Sage Publications.

WARD, LESTER F. 1906. *Applied Sociology*. Boston: Ginn.

WEBER, MAX. 1954. *Law in Economy and Society*. Ed. Max Rheinstein and trans. Edward Shils and Max Rheinstein. Cambridge: Harvard University Press. 1968. *Economy and Society*. Trans. Guenther Roth and Claus Wittich. New York: Bedminster Press.

WILLOCK, I. D. 1974. "Getting on with Sociologists," *British Journal of Law and Society* 1(1): 3–12.

WINES, MICHAEL. 2001. "Russian's Latest Dictator Goes By the Name of Law," *New York Times* (January 21): WK3.

YANT, MARTIN. 1991. *Presumed Guilty: When Innocent People Are Wrongly Convicted*. Buffalo: Prometheus Books.

ZATZ, MARJORIE S. 1994. *Producing Legality: Law and Socialism in Cuba*. New York: Rutledge.

2
Theoretical
Perspectives

This chapter examines the evolution of legal systems and reviews some of the principal classical and contemporary theories of law and society. At the outset, it should be acknowledged that there is no single, widely accepted, comprehensive theory of law and society (or of anything else in the social sciences). The field is enormously complex and polemical, and individual explanations have thus far failed to capture fully this complexity and diversity. This is, of course, not due to lack of effort. On the contrary, sociological theories of law abound (Arrigo, 1999; Rich, 1978; Rokumoto, 1994; Trevino, 1996). Of the vast amount of literature, this chapter deals briefly with only a few of the important classical and contemporary theories of law and society. This approach serves certain purposes. It provides the reader with some conception of the development and content of these different theories and how they relate to one another. Although the discussion of these theories clearly shows the complex and multifaceted nature of the relationship between law and society, it also serves as a means of differentiating, organizing, and understanding a great mass of material. Thus, although the concern is to suggest the magnitude and diversity of the field, an attempt is also made to lend order to that magnitude and diversity.

A cautionary note is in order with regard to the procedures followed in this chapter for grouping various theories. It will become clear that many theories of law and society tend to overlap. For example, the reader may find that a theory which has been placed under the heading of "The European Pioneers" will contain similar elements to those embodied in "Classical Sociological Theorists." Any such effort at classification of theories should be viewed as essentially a heuristic device to facilitate discussion rather than to reflect the final status of the theories considered.

Just like with general sociological theories (see, for example, Adams and Sydie, 2001) there are many ways of categorizing the more specific law and society theories. They may be considered from the disciplinary perspectives of jurisprudence, philosophy of law, sociology of law, and anthropology of law. They can also be listed under the headings of sociology of civil law, sociology of criminal law, sociological jurisprudence, and anthropology of law (Rich, 1978), grouped by various theoretical trends, such as natural law, historical and analytical jurisprudence, utilitarianism, positivism, and legal realism (Bodenheimer, 1974; Pollack, 1979) or under various perspectives such as Marxian, Weberian, and Durkheimian (Trevino, 1996). Any attempt to categorize theories under particular labels is open to question. The present effort should not be an exception. The categories used are in some ways arbitrary, since they can be increased or decreased depending on one's objectives. These categorizations simply provide some semblance of order for the principal theoretical approaches to law and society. In the schema employed, the diverse theories are presented in a chronological order, with an emphasis on influential classical and contemporary theories. Finally, due to the tyranny of space, there are more theorists and theories omitted than included. Those who wish to gain further knowledge about classical or modern theoretical concerns, the Suggested Further Readings will provide a useful point of departure.

EVOLUTION OF LEGAL SYSTEMS

Formal codified law emerges when the social structure of a given society becomes so complex that regulatory mechanisms and methods of dispute settlement no longer can be dependent on informal customs and social, religious, or moral sanctions. Formal and institutionalized regulatory mechanisms come into being when other control devices are no longer effective. Changes in the organization of a society from kinship and tribe to a territorially based political organization inevitably result in changes in the legal system. The basic content of the law and legal system concomitantly will become more complex, specialized, and statutory as the economy grows more complex and diversified, industrialization increases, and social institutions become more stratified and specialized.

Historically, legal development and industrialization, urbanization, and modernization are closely intertwined. In a small, homogeneous society with little division of labor and a high degree of solidarity, informal sanctions are sufficient to keep most behavior in line with the norms. An ideal example is the community on Tristan da Cunha, an isolated island in the middle of the South Atlantic Ocean. A few hundred people live there, growing potatoes and catching fish. When social scientists visited the island in the 1930s, they were amazed to see how "law-abiding" these people were, even though they had nothing resembling law as we know it. There was no serious crime on the island that anyone could recall, no police, courts, jails, or judges. There was no need for them. People in the community relied on informal mechanisms of social control such as shaming and open disapproval, which can be effective and severe in their own way. Such forms of control work in small, homogeneous, face-to-face communities (Friedman, 1998, 2002).

But in a modern, heterogeneous, and complex society, formal norms and sanctions are necessary to control behavior so that society can continue to function in an orderly and predictable fashion. The presence of law and a legal system is essential to the maintenance of social order.

The reciprocal relationships between society and the legal system during their parallel development are perplexing issues that have been conceptualized vaguely in the sociological literature. Jonathan H. Turner points out that

> linkages between law and society are often left implicit; change in the relative importance of these linkages is frequently not discussed; and there is a tendency to place too heavy an emphasis on single variables and thereby ignore the multiplicity of institutional influences on legal development. (1974:3)

Turner (1972:242) views legal development as a form of institutional adjustment to the ubiquitous problems of control and coordination facing modernizing society. He reasons that modernization inevitably generates conflict, tension, strains, and disjunctures that can force the modernization of law in society. It should be noted, however, that although there is some overall pattern of legal development, the specifics vary from society to society as a result of unique conditions, such as geographical location, historical events, conquest, and prevailing political and social forces. As a result, it is impossible to trace legal development from a primitive to a modern profile for one society because changes in geographical boundaries, wars, and other events would obscure unilineal development. For instance, a highly developed system of Roman law was imposed upon primitive legal systems during the expansion of the Empire, "with the result that a developmental jump occurred in these primitive legal systems" (Turner, 1972:242).

Developmental models, although controversial, have been used in almost every field of social science. Their use is justified by the attempt to make sense of history, which requires an appreciation of directionality, growth, and decay (Nonet and Selznick, 1978:19). The early sociologists all believed in the progressive development of social patterns over long periods of time (Vago, 1999:44–53). Similar beliefs are also present in psychology. Consider, for example, the stages of growth to psychological maturity in Freudian theory, or the development of personality in the theories of Piaget (1932). Similarly, in economics, Walt W. Rostow (1961) talks about the stages of economic growth from preconditions for takeoff to the age of high mass consumption. In the same vein, students of modern organization talk rather freely of three stages: prebureaucratic, bureaucratic, and postbureaucratic (Bennis, 1966:3–15). Developmental models can deal with transformations at various levels in society, such as individual, group, community, organization, and social institutions, or they may deal with the transformation of entire societies. The underlying theme in developmental models is the identification of forces that, having been set in motion at one stage, produce a characteristic outcome in another stage.

Thus, it is not surprising that Pound (1959:366), among others, finds it "convenient to think of . . . stages of legal development in systems which have come to maturity." The law and society literature suggests that the more complex the society, the more differentiated the legal system (Schwartz and Miller, 1975). Underlying this proposition is the notion that legal development is conditioned by a series of integrative demands stemming from society's economic, political, educational, and religious institutions. Based on the complexity and magnitude of the interplay among these institutions and between these institutions and the law, several types of legal systems may be identified in the course of societal development. There is practically no limit to the variability of legal systems, and many scholars have developed typologies to capture this diversity (such as Diamond, 1971; Pospisil, 1971:97–126; Wormser, 1962). These typologies seldom correspond fully to the real world, but they are essential in an analytical discussion dealing with the types of legal systems. From a developmental perspective, some general types can be isolated, and following Turner's illustrative and timeless categories (1972:216–230), the primitive, transitional, and modern legal systems will be examined. Before proceeding, it should be noted that the terms "primitive" and "traditional" law and legal systems are often used interchangeably in the literature (see, for example, Rouland, 1994).

Primitive Legal Systems

Primitive legal systems are typically found in hunting and gathering, and simple agrarian societies. The laws are not written or codified; they are permeated by customs, tradition, religious dogmas, and values. Primitive laws often coexist with ancient norms, and are also comparatively undifferentiated. There is, however, some distinction between *substantive* and *procedural* laws. *Substantive laws* consist of rights, duties, and prohibitions concerning what is right, wrong, permissible, and unpermissible. *Procedural laws* are rules regarding just how substantive law is to be administered, enforced, changed, and used in the mediation of disputes. Subsequent differentiation of types at later stages of legal evolution can be encompassed under these two general types of law.

The functions of law in primitive societies are essentially the same as those in more advanced societies (Rouland, 1994: 153–299). Laws preserve important cultural elements, they coordinate interaction, settle disputes, check deviance, and regularize exchanges. Laws also legitimize existing inequalities. In addition: "By codifying, preserving, and enforcing certain key kinship rules (usually descent and authority), religious rituals and dogmas, and the chief's right to enact laws, differences in power and privilege are preserved and made to seem appropriate" (Turner, 1972:220).

In primitive societies, there are no well-developed political subsystems, and the polity is composed of kin leaders, councils of elders or chiefs, and various religious leaders. Legislators are political bodies and, as such, do not formally exist in primitive societies. In such societies, judges and political leaders (elders, and the like) are one and the same. The emphasis is on court-enacted law (common law) rather than legislative law enacted by political bodies (statutory law). Although the distinction between the two in primitive societies does not exist (because courts are political and their decisions constitute legislation), chiefs or elders can enact both substantive and procedural laws. Because there are no written laws, the chief-legislator can strike, rescind, or change old laws more easily than the modern legislator; and if such action appears reasonable, little resistance is offered. Obviously, getting old laws off the books in modern societies is rarely that easy.

Courts, like the police force, are temporarily assembled and then dispersed as disputes arise and are settled. Although they are provisional, the courts comprise at least two clearly differentiated roles: that of the judges, who hear evidence and make decisions in accordance with laws, and that of litigants, who have to abide by the judges' decision. Occasionally, a third role can be identified in such courts, that of a representative "lawyer" who pleads the case for a litigant. As the legal system develops, these roles become more clearly differentiated. In primitive societies, however, these three procedures are sufficient to maintain a high degree of societal integration and coordination.

Transitional Legal Systems

Transitional legal systems are characteristic of advanced agrarian and early industrial societies where the economic, educational, and political subsystems are increasingly differentiated from kinship relationships. As a result of increases in integrative problems, the legal subsystem becomes more complex and extensive, as evidenced by a clear-cut differentiation in basic legal elements—laws, courts, enforcement agencies, and legislative structures. In the transitional stage, most of the features of the modern legal system are present, but not to the same degree. Law becomes more differentiated from tradition, customs, and religious dogma. There is a distinction between *public* and *private* law. The former is concerned with the structure of government, the duties and powers of officials, and the relationships between the individual and the state, and the latter regulates relations among nonpolitical units. *Criminal* law also becomes distinguishable from *torts*. *Criminal* law denotes wrongs against the state, the community, and the public. *Torts* are laws pertaining to private wrongs of parties against each other rather than against the state or the public. There is, similarly, a clearer differentiation between procedural and substantive laws, and as the types of laws increase, laws become systems of rules (Friedman, 1975:291–309).

The increased differentiation of laws is reflected in the increased complexity of the courts. Accompanying this differentiation is the emergence of at least five distinct types of statuses: judge; representative or lawyer; litigant; court officials and administrators; and jurors. The roles of judges and lawyers become institutionalized, requiring specialized training. In transitional legal systems, written records of court proceedings become more common, contributing to the emergence of a variety of administrative roles, which, in turn, leads to the initial bureaucratization of the court.

With the development of clearly differentiated, stable, and autonomous courts, legal development accelerates for the following reasons:

> (1) Laws enacted by the growing legislative body of the polity can be applied systematically to specific circumstances by professionals and experts. This means that laws enacted by the centralizing polity have institutional channels of application. (2) Where political legislation of laws is absent, an established court can enact laws by handing down Common-Law precedents. Such common laws tend to fit nicely the structural conditions in a society, since they emerge out of attempts to reconcile actual and concrete conflicts. (Turner, 1972:222)

Initially, courts are localized and characterized by common-law decisions. In time, their conflicting and overlapping rules provide an impetus for the unification of a legal system, eventually leading to a more codified system of laws.

There is also the emergence of explicit, relatively stable, and somewhat autonomous police roles in transitional legal systems. Concomitant with the development of police roles is the emergence of legislative structures. This results in a clear differentiation of legislative statuses from judicial (courts) and enforcement (police) statuses. Legislating new laws or abolishing old ones is no longer a matter of a simple decree. In transitional legal systems, a small cluster of statuses, whether organized in a forum, a senate, or a royal council, can enact laws. Initially, these laws are dominated by a political elite and are responsive to its demands. Later on, legislative changes become more comprehensive, involving a group of laws pertaining to general problem areas. With the enactment of more comprehensive statutes and codes, a system of civil law begins to emerge to supplement common law. The development of civil codes is stimulated by an established court system and police force, a pool of educated lawyers and judges, a background of common law, and a degree of political and national unity. The functions of law in transitional legal institutions are essentially similar to those in primitive systems—perhaps a bit more complex, and at the same time, less successful in resolving integrative problems. Structural differentiation becomes more complex. Political development increases, bringing with it inequities in power and wealth. In such situations, civil law tends to legitimize these inequalities.

Modern Legal Systems

In modern legal systems, we find all the structural features of transitional systems present, but in greater and more elaborate arrangements. Turner notes: "Laws in modern legal systems are extensive networks of local and national statutes, private and public codes, crimes and torts, common and civil laws, and procedural and substantive rules" (1972:225). A distinctive feature of modern legal systems is the proliferation of public and procedural laws, referred to as *administrative* law. Another aspect is the increasing proportion of statutory law over common law. Legislation, as a result of political development, becomes a more acceptable method of adjusting law to social conditions. There are also clear hierarchies of laws, ranging from constitutional codes to regional and local codes.

Courts, in modern legal systems, have an important role in mediating and mitigating conflict, disputes, deviance, and other sources of malintegration. The roles of lawyers and judges become highly professionalized, with licensing requirements and formal sanctions. The various administrative statuses—clerks, bailiffs, and public prosecutors—specialize, proliferate, and become heavily bureaucratized. The jurisdictions of courts are specified with clearly delineated appeal procedures. Cases unresolved in lower courts can be argued in higher courts that have the power to reverse lower court decisions.

In modern legal systems, laws are enforced and court decisions are carried out by clearly differentiated and organized police forces, which are organized at the local, state, and federal levels. Each force possesses its own internal organization, which becomes increasingly bureaucratized at the higher levels. In addition to police forces, regulatory agencies (such as the Food and Drug Administration, the Federal Trade Commission or the Federal Aviation Administration) regularly enforce and oversee compliance with laws. Administrative agencies, as will be discussed in Chapters 4 and 5, also make and interpret laws in the context of their own mandates.

Legislative bodies at various levels proliferate. There is a greater emphasis on integrative problems and on enacting comprehensive laws. Accompanying the emergence of a stable legislature, well-planned and comprehensive law enactment can become an effective mechanism of social change.

Inherent in modern legal systems is the notion of "modern" law. Marc Galanter (1977) in a classic and influential article, "The Modernization of Law," sets forth a comprehensive conceptualization of contemporary law that remains among the most widely cited even today. His model, not a description, includes 11 salient features that characterize the legal systems of the industrial societies of the last century, and many of them can be found in modern societies as well. He argues that "modern law consists of rules that are uniform and unvarying in their application" (1977:1047). The same rules and regulations are applicable to everyone. Modern law is also "transactional." Rights and duties stem from "transactions." They are not "aggregated in unchanging clusters" prescribed to an individual by ascribed status. Galanter insists that modern legal norms are "universalistic"; that is, their application is predictable, uniform, and impersonal. Further, the system, to be uniform and predictable, operates on the basis of written rules and has a regular chain of command. The system is "rational" in the Weberian sense, and "rules are valued for their instrumental utility in producing consciously chosen ends, rather than for their formal qualities" (1977:1048). Such a system is run by full-time professionals whose "qualifications come from mastery of the techniques of the legal system itself, not from possession of special gifts or talents or from eminence in some other area of life" (1977:1048). Professionals run the law; lawyers replace "mere general agents" as the legal system grows more complex. The system is "amenable." It can be changed and it does not have "sacred fixity." Says Galanter: "Legislation replaces the slow reworking of customary law" (1977:1048). It is also "political"—that is, tied to the state, which has a monopoly on law. Finally, legislative, judicial, and executive functions are "separate and distinct" in modern law.

Thus far, we have identified some of the preconditions necessary for the development of modern legal systems. Let us now consider some of the theories accounting for those developments.

THEORIES OF LAW AND SOCIETY

The preceding section dealt with some general types of legal systems as they correspond to various stages of modernization and social development. The present section addresses two questions emerging from the previous discussion: Why did changes in the legal system take place? And what factors contributed to legal development from a historical perspective? In attempting to answer these questions, we can distinguish two general issues. The first is the issue of legal development in any society. The second concerns forces that produce or prevent change in the legal system.

Theorists of law and society have long been preoccupied with efforts to describe the broad historical course of legal development and to analyze the factors that influence legal systems. The literature is extensive, going back several centuries. The investigation of legal development has traditionally been the concern of scholars in a variety of fields. In view of the limits set for this study, no attempt is made here to provide a comprehensive and systematic review of principal theories and schools. Certain prominent theorists will, however, be considered.

Among the theorists to be presented, there is more or less general agreement that societal and legal complexities are interrelated. Beyond that, there is little consensus. The particular theorists differ as to detail and interpretation of the general relationship between legal change and social change. It is hoped that the following sample of theorists from various disciplines, historical periods, and countries will provide a better understanding of the diverse issues involved in the investigation of the multifaceted relations between law and other major institutions of society.

The European Pioneers

In Europe, for centuries law has been considered as an absolute and autonomous entity, unrelated to the structure and function of the society in which it existed (see, for example, Feinberg and Gross, 1995). The idea of natural law constitutes the basis for this exposition of law. The origins of natural law can be traced back to ancient Greece. Aristotle maintains that natural law has a universal validity and is based on reason that is free from all passion. St. Thomas Aquinas argues that natural law is part of human nature, and through natural law, human beings participate as rational beings in the eternal laws of God.

The idea of natural law is based on the assumption that through reason, the nature of human beings can be known, and that this knowledge can provide the basis for the social and legal ordering of human existence (see, for example, Belliotti, 1992:17–44). Natural law is considered superior to enacted law. It is "the chief tenet of natural law that arbitrary will is not legally final" (Selznick, 1961:100). An appeal to higher principles of justice is always permissible from the decrees of a lawmaker. When enacted law does not coincide with the principles of natural law, it is considered unjust. For example, pro-life proponents argue that laws providing for abortion on demand are contrary to the tenets of natural law.

Under the influence of natural law, many European scholars believed that law in any given society was a reflection of a universally valid set of legal principles based on the idea that through reason, the nature of man can be ascertained. This knowledge could then become the basis for the social and legal order of human existence. From the middle of the nineteenth century, however, the idea of natural law was largely displaced by historical and evolutionary interpretations of law, and by legal positivism, which considered the legal and the moral to constitute two quite separate realms. These two views of the law sought to explain the law causally in terms of ethnological factors, or by reference to certain evolutionary forces that pushed the law forward along a predetermined path. Many theorists sought to discourage philosophical speculation about the nature and purposes of law and concentrated on the development and analysis of positive law laid down and enforced by the state. The most notable among these scholars include Baron de Montesquieu in France, Herbert Spencer, and Sir Henry Sumner Maine in England. I shall now consider their theories in some detail.

Baron de Montesquieu (1689–1755) Charles-Louis de Secondat, Baron de Montesquieu, was born near Bordeaux, France, to a wealthy family. He inherited a seat in the Parliament of Bordeaux and was active in politics most of his life. Well educated by his family, he was a most influential writer against the absolutism of the French monarchy.

Montesquieu challenges the underlying assumptions of natural law by presenting a radically different conceptualization of law and society. He considers law integral to a particular people's culture. The central thesis of his *Spirit of Laws* (1886) is that laws are the result of a number of factors in society such as customs, physical environment, and antecedents, and that laws can be understood only in the context of particular societies. He further posits that laws are relative and that there are no "good" or "bad" laws in the abstract. This proposition ran contrary to the opinions of the day. Each law, Montesquieu maintains, must be considered in relation to its background, its antecedents, and its surroundings. If a law fits well into this framework, it is a good law; if it does not, it is bad.

But Montesquieu's fame rests above all on his political theory of the separation of powers. According to this theory, a constitution is composed of three different types of legal powers: legislative, executive, and judicial, each vested in a different body or person. The role of the legislature is to enact new laws; of the executive, to enforce and administer the laws as well as to determine policy within the framework of those laws; and of the judiciary, simply to interpret the laws established by the legislative power. This neat classification had considerable influence on the form of constitution subsequently adopted by the newly created United States of America after the Declaration of Independence (Bodenheimer, 1974:49) and would greatly affect constitutional thinkers in other countries as well throughout the late 18th and 19th centuries.

Leopold Pospisil (1971:138), in his analysis of Montesquieu's contributions, aptly remarks: "With his ideas of the relativity of law in space as well as in time, and with his emphasis on specificity and empiricism, he can be regarded as the founder of the modern sociology of law in general and of the field of legal dynamics in particular."

Herbert Spencer (1820–1903) Spencer was born in Derby, England. His education was largely informal and undisciplined, strongly influenced by the family's anti-establishment and anti-clerical views. His writings reflect those influences. Spencer, the British philosopher and sociologist, was a major figure in the intellectual life of the Victorian era.

Contrary to the doctrines of natural law, in nineteenth-century England, Herbert Spencer provides the philosophical underpinnings for the theory of unregulated competition in the economic sphere. Strongly influ-

[handwritten margin notes: "believed law developed under natural selection —" "survival of the fittest didn't want to help poor/weak"]

enced by Charles Darwin, Spencer draws a picture of the evolution of civilization and law in which natural selection and the survival of the fittest are the primary determining factors. Evolution for Spencer consists of growing differentiation, individuation, and increasing division of labor. Civilization is the progress of social life from primitive homogeneity to ultimate heterogeneity. He identifies two main stages in the development of civilizations: a primitive or military form of society, with war, compulsion, and status as regulatory mechanisms, and a higher or industrial form of society, with peace, freedom, and a contract as the controlling devices.

Spencer is convinced that in his second stage, human progress is marked by a continual increase in individual liberty and a corresponding decrease in governmental activities. Government, he believes, would gradually confine its field of action to the enforcement of contracts and the protection of personal safety. He strongly opposes public education, public hospitals, public communications, and any governmental programs designed to alleviate the plight of the economically weaker groups in society. He is convinced that social legislation of this type is an unwarranted interference with the laws of natural selection (Spencer, 1899).

Spencer's ideas on law influenced a number of early sociologists in the United States. For example, William Graham Sumner advocates a position essentially similar to that of Spencer. He, too, sees the function of the state limited to that of an overseer who guards the safety of private property and sees to it that the peace is not breached. He favors a regime of contract in which social relations are regulated primarily by mutual agreements, not by government-imposed legal norms. He argues that society does not need any supervision. Maximum freedom of individual action should be promoted by law. He considers attempts to achieve a greater social and economic equality among men ill-advised and unnatural.

> Let it be understood that we cannot go outside of this alternative: liberty, inequality, survival of the fittest; not liberty, equality, survival of the unfittest. The former carries society forward and favors all its best members; the latter carries society downward and favors all its worst members. (Sumner, 1940:25)

[handwritten margin note: "laissez-faire"]

To a great extent, the *laissez-faire* doctrines of courts and legislatures in the United States, perhaps consciously or unconsciously, reflected the economic and social philosophy of Spencer and Sumner. Up until fairly recently, for example, legislative policies designed to equalize the bargaining power of management and labor, to protect the health and subsistence of marginal groups, or to interfere with that freedom of contract which was considered the true birthmark of an advancing civilization, did not appear to be widespread. In part, these are still discernible in the current conservative attitudes that place the rights of wealthier groups above those of the disfavored members of society.

Sir Henry Sumner Maine (1822–1888)   Maine was born in Scotland and died in Cannes, France. He was educated at Cambridge and, after holding various teaching positions in England, as well as various administrative appointments in India, he returned to Cambridge. There he was elected master of Trinity Hall and finished his career as professor of international law. He was among the first theorists to argue that law and legal institutions must be studied historically if they are to be understood.

Maine contends that the legal history of people shows patterns of evolution that recur in different societies and in similar historical circumstances. He argues that there do not exist infinite possibilities for building and managing human societies; certain political, social, and legal forms reappear in seemingly different garb, and if they reappear, they manifest themselves in certain typical ways. For example, Roman feudalism produced legal rules and legal institutions strikingly similar to English feudalism, although differences can also be demonstrated.

One of his general laws of legal evolution is set forth in his classical treatise, *Ancient Law*:

> The movement of the progressive societies has been uniform in one respect. Through all its course it has been distinguished by the gradual dissolution of family dependency and the growth of individual obligation in its place. The Individual is steadily substituted for the Family, as the unit of which civil laws take account. The advance has been accomplished at varying rates of celerity, and there are societies not absolutely stationary in which the collapse of the ancient organization can only be perceived by careful study of the phenomena they present. But, whatever its pace, the change has not been subject to reaction or recoil, and apparent retardations will be found to have been occasioned through the absorption of archaic ideas and customs from some entirely foreign source. Nor is it difficult to see what is the tie between man and man which replaces by degrees those forms of reciprocity in rights and duties which have their origin in the Family. It is Contract. Starting, as from one terminus of history, from a condition of society in which all the relations of Persons are summed up in the relations of Family, we seem to have steadily moved towards a phase of social order in which all these relations arise from the free agreement of Individuals. (1861:170)

Thus, Maine arrives at his often-quoted dictum that "the movement of the progressive societies has hitherto been a movement from Status to Contract" (1861:170). Status is a fixed condition in which an individual is without will and without opportunity. Ascribed status prevails, legal relations depend on birth or caste. It is indicative of a social order in which the group, not the individual, is the primary unit of social life. Every individual is enmeshed in a network of family and group ties. With the progress of civilization, this condition gradually gives way to a social system based on contract. Maine argues that a progressive civilization is manifested by the emergence of the independent, free, and self-determining individual, based on achieved status, as the primary unit of social life. He suggests that the emphasis on individual achievement and voluntary contractual relations set the conditions for a more mature legal system that uses legislation to bring society and law into harmony. In essence, his argument is that in modern societies legal relations are not conditioned by one's birth but depend on voluntary agreements.

Classical Sociological Theorists

Early sociologists have recognized the essential interrelation between legal institutions and the social order. In this section, the influential theoretical explanations of law and society of Karl Marx, Max Weber, and Emile Durkheim are explored.

Karl Marx (1818–1883)   Karl Heinrich Marx was born into a comfortable middle-class family in Trier, Germany. He studied law and literature at the universities of Bonn and Berlin before moving to Paris and subsequently to England where he did most of his writing, much of it in collaboration with his financial mentor, Friedrich Engels. He died on March 14, 1883, in London.

Of all the social theorists, few are as important, brilliant, or original as Karl Marx. Part philosopher, part economist, part sociologist, and part historian, Marx combines political partisanship with deep scholarship. Marx, and the subsequent ideology of Marxism, may have caused more social change than any other force in the modern world, in both developed and developing societies (Barber, 1971:260).

Marx postulates that every society, whatever its stage of historical development, rests on an economic foundation. He calls this "mode of production" of commodities, which has two elements. The first is the physical or technological arrangement of economic activity. The second is "the social relations of production," or the indispensable human attachments that people must form with one another when engaged in economic activity. In his words:

The sum total of these relations of production constitutes the economic structure of society—the real foundation, on which rise legal and political superstructures and to which correspond definite forms of social consciousness. (Marx, 1959:43)

For Marx the determinant variable is the mode of production. Changes in this produce changes in the way in which groups are attached to production technology. This economic determinism is reflected in Marx's theory of law.

Marx's theory of law, which has greatly influenced social and jurisprudential thinking throughout the world, may be summarized in three principal assumptions: (1) Law is a product of evolving economic forces; (2) law is a tool used by a ruling class to maintain its power over the lower classes; and (3) in the communist society of the future, law as an instrument of social control will "wither away" and finally disappear.

The idea that law is a reflection of economic conditions is integral to the doctrine of "dialectical materialism." According to this doctrine, the political, social, religious, and cultural order of any given epoch is determined by the existing system of production and forms a "superstructure" on top of this economic basis. Law, for Marx, is part of this superstructure whose forms, content, and conceptual apparatus constitute responses to economic developments. This view maintains that law is nothing more than a function of the economy but without any independent existence.

In societies with pronounced class distinctions, the means of production are owned and controlled by the ruling class. Marx's theory of law is the characterization of law as a form of class rule and dominance (Collins, 1996). While addressing the bourgeoisie of his day in his *Communist Manifesto*, Marx (1955:47) writes: "Your jurisprudence is but the will of your class made into a law for all, a will whose essential character and direction are determined by the economic conditions of existence of your class." Marx further argues that law, as a form of class rule, is sanctioned by public authority, which has the power of enforcement through the use of armed bodies.

Finally, Marx suggests that after the revolution, when class conflict is resolved and the institution of private property is replaced by a communist regime, law and the state, hitherto the main engines of despotism and oppression, will "wither away." There will be no need for coercion, since everyone's needs will be fulfilled and universal harmony will prevail. According to this view, there will be no need for law in the future—a future that will be the final stage of humanity's evolution because stateless and lawless communism shall exist forever.

Max Weber (1864–1920)   Weber was born near Erfurt, Germany into a middle-class professional family. He studied at the universities in Heidelberg and Berlin (where he earned a Ph.D.) and became a professor of economics. He traveled to the United States, where, among other cities, he visited St. Louis during the 1904 World's Fair. Upon returning to Germany, he devoted his life to writing and teaching. Max Weber played a crucial role in the development of sociology. His significance is not merely historical; he remains an ever-present force in comtemporary sociology. He occupies a central position among the law and society theorists.

Weber's typology of legal systems is based on two fundamental distinctions (1954:63). First, legal procedures are rational or irrational. *Rational* procedures involve the use of logic and scientific methods to attain specific objectives. *Irrational* procedures rely on ethical or mystical considerations such as magic or faith in the supernatural. Second, legal procedures can proceed, rationally or irrationally, with respect to formal or substantive law. *Formal* law refers to making decisions on the basis of established rules, regardless of the notion of fairness. *Substantive* law takes the circumstances of individual cases into consideration along with the prevailing notion of justice. These two distinctions create four ideal types, which are seldom, if ever, attained in their pure form in specific societies.

1. *Substantive irrationality.* This exists when a case is decided on some unique religious, ethical, emotional, or political basis instead of by general rules. An example of this would be when a religious judge makes a decision without any recourse to explicit rules or legal principles.
2. *Formal irrationality.* This involves rules based on supernatural forces. It is irrational because no one tries to understand or clarify why it works and formal because strict adherence is required to the procedures. The Ten Commandments, for example, were enacted in a formally irrational way: Moses, claiming direct revelation, presented the tablets and announced, "This is the Law." Other examples would include the use of ordeals and oaths.
3. *Substantive rationality.* This is based on the application of rules from nonlegal sources such as religion, ideology, and science. It is rational because rules are derived from specific and accepted sources and substantive because there is a concern for justness of outcomes in individual cases. The efforts of Ayatollah Khomeini in Iran to make decisions on the basis of the Koran would be an example of substantive rationality.
4. *Formal rationality.* This involves the use of consistent, logical rules independent of moral, religious, or other normative criteria that are applied equally to all cases. An example of this is modern American or Western law.

While referring to both formal and substantive rationality, Weber identifies three types of administration of justice: (1) *Kahdi* justice, (2) empirical justice, and (3) rational justice. *Kahdi* justice is dispensed by the judge of the Islamic *Shari'a* Court. (See Chapter 1 for a detailed discussion of Islamic law and Huff and Schlucter, 1999.) It is based on religious precepts and is so lacking in procedural rules as to seem almost completely arbitrary. The *Koran* contains the revealed word of God, and this bible forms the heart of the Islamic legal system in such countries as Iran and Pakistan. Empirical justice, the deciding of cases by referring to analogies and by relying on and interpreting precedents, is more rational than *Kahdi* justice, but notably short of complete rationality. Weber argues that modern law is rational, whereas traditional and primitive laws were irrational, or at least, less rational. Rational justice is based on bureaucratic principles. The rational legal system is basically universalistic; the irrational is particularistic. The rational legal system looks toward contract, not toward status (Parsons, 1964:339). Rationality can be further based on adherence to "eternal characteristics" (observable concrete features) of the facts of the case. However, Weber perceives that Western law, with its specialized professional roles of judges and lawyers, is unique in that it is also reliant on the "logical analysis of meaning" of abstract legal concepts and rules.

Modern society differs from its past in many ways, which Max Weber sums up in a single concept: the *rational*. Modern society is in pursuit of the rational. Weber contends that the modern law of the West has become increasingly institutionalized through the bureaucratization of the state. He points out that the acceptance of the law as a rational science is based on certain fundamental and semilogical postulates, such as, that the law is a "gapless" system of legal principles, and that every concrete judicial decision involves the application of an abstract legal proposition to a concrete situation. There is little doubt that Weber captures, in his idea of rationality, a crucial feature of modern legal systems. It is rather ironic that soon after Max Weber's death in 1920, rational law in Germany was in part replaced by a faith in the intuition of a charismatic leader—Adolph Hitler.

Emile Durkheim (1858–1917)   Durkheim was born in Epinal, France. In keeping with family tradition, he was destined for the rabbinate. Although part of his early education was spent in a rabbinical school, he broke with Judaism soon after his arrival in Paris. After attending the *Ecole Normal Superieure,* he taught at the Faculty of Letters at Bordeaux and was subsequently appointed professor and chair of sociology and education at the Sorbonne. Durkheim founded *Anne sociologique,* the first social science journal in France, and wrote several important treatises in sociology.

Emile Durkheim outlines his thesis on law in society in his influential work, *The Division of Labor in Society* (1964). While tracing the development of social order through social and economic institutions, Durkheim sets forth a theory of legal development by elucidating the idea that law is a measure of the type of solidarity in a society. Durkheim maintains that there are two types of solidarity: mechanical and organic. *Mechanical* solidarity prevails in relatively simple and homogeneous societies where unity is ensured by close interpersonal ties, similarity of habits, ideas, and attitudes. *Organic* solidarity is characteristic of modern societies that are heterogeneous and differentiated by a complex division of labor. The grounds for solidarity are the interdependence of widely different persons and groups performing a variety of functions.

Corresponding to these two forms of solidarity are two types of law: repressive and restitutive. Mechanical solidarity is associated with repressive and penal law. In a homogeneous, undifferentiated society, a criminal act offends the collective conscience, and punishment is meant to protect and preserve social solidarity. Punishment is a mechanical reaction. The wrongdoer is punished as an example to the community that deviance will not be tolerated. There is no concern with the rehabilitation of the offender.

In modern heterogeneous societies, repressive law tends to give way to restitutive law with an emphasis on compensation. Punishment deals with restitution and reparations for harm done to the victim. Crimes are considered acts that offend others and not the collective conscience of the community. Punishment is evaluated in terms of what is beneficial for the offender and is used for rehabilitation.

Stated concisely, Durkheim's position is that penal law reflects mechanical solidarity. Modern society is bound together by organic solidarity—interdependence and division of labor flowing out of voluntary acts. Society is complex—its parts are highly specialized. Through contracts, which are the main concern of modern law, people arrange their innumerable, complex relationships. Contracts and contract laws are central to modern society and influence the course of societal development through the regulation of relationships.

Although Durkheim's concern is not with the elaboration of a general framework or methodology for the sociological analysis of law, his interest in law "resulted in the school that formed around him developing a considerable interest in the study of law as a social process" (Hunt, 1978:65). His ideas on law also provided an important background to subsequent discussions concerning the nature of primitive law and the nature of crime. Although it may be questionable that "he made a serious contribution to the development of systematic legal sociology" (Gurvitch, 1942:106), he certainly made an important contribution to our understanding of the relationship between law and social solidarity and legal evolution (McIntyre, 1994:77–78).

Sociolegal Theorists

The theorists that will be considered in this section argue that law cannot be understood without regard for the realities of social life. Since the beginning of the twentieth century, scholars of jurisprudence and of related disciplines on both sides of the Atlantic have reflected the influence of the social sciences in their analysis of legal development. The more prominent ones that shall be included in our analysis are Albert Venn Dicey, Justice Oliver Wendell Holmes, Jr., and E. Adamson Hoebel.

Albert Venn Dicey (1835–1922)   Dicey (1905), an English legal scholar, was born in Lutterworth, Northhamptonshire. For several generations, his family owned and edited a newspaper, and over time they became prosperous. Dicey was educated at Oxford. He assisted in the founding of law schools in Manchester where he was elected the prestigious Vinerian Chair. Later he accepted a professorship and returned to Oxford where he spent the rest of his life.

Dicey offers what has become a classic theory on the influence of public opinion on social change in his lectures given at Harvard Law School in 1898. He traces the growth of statutory lawmaking and the legal system in the context of the increasing articulateness and power of public opinion. He notes that the process begins with a new idea that "presents itself to some one man of originality or genius." He has in mind such individuals as Adam Smith and Charles Darwin. Next, the idea is adopted by supporters who "preach" it to others. As time passes, "the preachers of truth make an impression, either directly upon the general public or upon some person of eminence, say a leading statesman, who stands in a position to impress ordinary people and thus to win the support of the nation" (Dicey, 1905:23). As Dicey points out, however, something must happen so that people will listen to a truly new idea and change their values. He talks of "accidental conditions" that enable popular leaders to seize the opportunity. As an example he gives the Irish famine, which enabled Cobden and Bright to gain acceptance of Adam Smith's doctrine of free trade.

Public opinion for Dicey is "the majority of those citizens who have at a given moment taken an effective part in public life" (1905:10). Dicey talks of the "gradual, or slow, and continuous" (1905:27) developments of tides of public opinion in England. Generally, he maintains, there are few abrupt changes. Ideally, legislators should reflect and act upon public opinion, but judges (even more than legislators) lag behind public opinion. Dicey concedes that although judges are "guided to a considerable extent by the dominant current of public opinion" (1905:363), "they are also guided by professional opinions and ways of thinking which are, to a certain extent, independent of and possibly opposed to the general tone of public opinion" (1905:364). He then concludes, "they are men advanced in life. They are for the most part persons of a conservative disposition" (1904:364).

Dicey is also known for his famous doctrine of "the rule of law." The doctrine has three aspects: First, no one is punishable except for a distinct breach of law and, therefore, the rule of law is not consistent with arbitrary or even wide discretionary authority on the part of the government. Second, the rule of law means total subjection of all classes to the law of the land, as administered by the law courts. Third, individual rights derive from court precedents rather than from constitutional codes.

From a sociological perspective, Dicey's most crucial contribution to law and society is the recognition of the importance of public opinion in legal development. As Lord Tangley (1965:48) observes: "We are indebted to Professor Dicey for many things—he established for all time the relationship between public opinion and law reform and traced its course through the nineteenth century."

Oliver Wendell Holmes, Jr. (1841–1935)   Holmes was born in Boston, Massachusetts, and was named after his famous father, the writer and physician. After his service in the American Civil War, he entered Harvard Law School and subsequently became a professor there. He was appointed to the United States Supreme Court in 1902 where he remained for three decades.

The distinguished American judge and legal philosopher Oliver Wendell Holmes, Jr. is considered one of the founders of the "legal realism" school (Novick, 1989; White, 2000). This is based on the conception of the judicial process whereby judges are responsible for formulating law, rather than merely finding it in law books. The judge always has to exercise choice when making a decision. He decides which principle will prevail and which party will win. According to the legal realists' position, judges make decisions on the basis of their conceptions of justness before resorting to formal legal precedents. Such precedents can be found or developed to support almost any outcome. The real decisions are based on the judge's notion of justness, conditioned, in part, by values, personal background, predilections, and so forth. They are then rationalized in the written opinion.

Holmes stresses the limits that are set to the use of deductive logic in the solution of legal problems. He postulates that the life of law has been experience and not logic and maintains that only a judge or a lawyer who is acquainted with the historical, social, and economic aspects of the law will be in a position to fulfill his or her functions properly.

Holmes assigns a large role to historical and social forces in the life of law, while de-emphasizing the ethical and ideal elements. He considers law largely as a body of edicts representing the will of dominant interests in society, backed by force. Although he admits that moral principles are influential in the initial formulation of the rules of law, he is inclined to identify morality with the taste and value preferences of shifting power groups in society. Schwartz notes: "Holmes was part of the generation that had sat at the feet of Darwin and Spencer and he could never shed his Darwinist outlook" (1974:151). His basic philosophy is that life is essentially a Darwinian struggle for existence and that the goal of social effort was to "build a race" rather than to strive for the attainment of humanitarian ethical objectives.

In his often-quoted essay "The Path of the Law," Holmes (1897:458) outlines some of his basic propositions and states that "a legal duty so called is nothing but a prediction that if a man does or omits certain things he will be made to suffer in this or that way by judgment of a court." A pragmatic approach to law, he declares, must view the law from the point of view of the "bad man." Such a person does not care about the general moral pronouncements and abstract legal doctrines. What is important is simply what the courts are in fact likely to do.

He argues that any sense of absolute certainty about the law was bound to be illusory.

> Behind the logical forms lies a judgment as to the relative worth and importance of competing legislative grounds, often an inarticulate and unconscious judgment, it is true, and yet the very root and nerve of the whole proceeding. You can give any conclusion a logical form. (Holmes, Jr., 1897:465-466)

Lawyers and judges should be aware of this and should "consider the ends which the several rules seek to accomplish, the reasons why those ends are desired, what is given up to gain them, and whether they are worth the price" (Holmes, Jr., 1897:476).

   E. Adamson Hoebel (1906–1993)   Edward Adamson Hoebel was born in Madison, Wisconsin. He received his A.B. from the University of Wisconsin, M.A. from New York University, and a Ph.D. in anthropology from Columbia University. He was president of the American Ethnological Society and the American Anthropological Association and Regent's Professor of Anthropology at University of Minnesota for 18 years until his retirement in 1972.

   A leading and highly respected and influential American scholar in the field of anthropology of law, Hoebel was much influenced by Karl N. Llewellyn, a brilliant lawyer with social science skills and interests. The two men collaborated on an analysis of the "law ways" in traditional Cheyenne society. The emphasis on the "law-jobs" having both a "pure survival" or "bare bones" aspect for the society and a "questing" or "betterment" value (Llewellyn and Hoebel, 1941: Ch. 3) contributed significantly to the development of a modern functional approach to the legal system. I shall return to this point in the discussion on the functionalist approach later in this chapter.

   Hoebel's (1954:288–333) views on the development of legal systems are presented in the concluding chapter, entitled "The Trend of the Law," in his book *The Law of Primitive Man*. Hoebel (1954:288) notes that "there has been no straight line of development in the growth of law." His description of trends in legal development is based on the assumption that cultures of contemporary primitive societies exhibit characteristics that are similar "to those that presumably prevailed in the early cultures of the infancy of mankind" (1954:290). He considers law and the legal system as a property of a specific community or subgroup of a society, and states: "Without the sense of community there can be no law. Without law there cannot be for long a community" (1954:332). Consequently, law exists to some extent even in the simplest societies.

   Hoebel begins his description of the trend of law with a discussion of the "lower primitive societies"—the hunters and gatherers, such as the Shoshone Indians and the Andaman Islanders. Almost all relations in such a society are face-to-face and intimate. The demands imposed by culture are relatively few. Ridicule is a potent mechanism of social control. Taboo and the fear of supernatural sanctions control a large area of behavior. Special interests are few, for there is little accumulated wealth. Conflict arises mostly in interpersonal relations. Repetitive abuse of the customs and codes of social relations constitutes a crime, and the offender may be beaten or even killed by the members of the community. Hoebel writes: "Here we have law in the full connotation of the word—the application, in threat or in fact, of physical coercion by a party having the socially recognized privilege-right of so acting. First the threat—and then, if need be, the act" (1954:300).

Among the more organized hunters, the pastoralists and the rooter-gardening peoples, such as the Cheyenne, Comanche, Kiowa, and Indians of the northwest coast of North America, the size of the group and the increased complexity of the culture make possible a greater divergence of interests between the members of society. Conflicts of interest grow, and the need arises for legal mechanisms for settlement and control of the internal clash of interests. Private law emerges and spreads, although much of the internal social control problems are handled on other than a legal basis.

In the tribes, a more formalized chieftanship develops, with a tendency toward hereditary succession (Hoebel, 1954:309–310). Although homicide and adultery still represent major difficulties, the development of criminal law remains weak.

"The real elaboration of law begins with the expansion of the gardening-based tribes," such as the Samoans and the Ashanti (Hoebel, 1954:316). The gardening activity provides an economic foundation for the support of larger populations that can no longer maintain face-to-face relationships. With the formation of more communities: "The pressures to maintain peaceful equilibrium between the numerous closely interacting communities become intensified. The further growth of law and a more effective law is demanded" (1954:316). The attempt to establish the interest of the society as superior to the interests of kinship groups is the prime mover of law in this type of society. Allocation of rights, duties, privileges, powers, and immunities with regard to land becomes important, and "the law of things begins to rival the law of persons" (1954:316). "Clear-cut crimes" (1954:319) are established in the legal systems of these societies, and action for damages becomes even more frequent than on the preceding level.

For Hoebel, the "trend of law" is one of increasing growth and complexity in which the tendency is to shift the privilege-right of prosecution and imposition of legal sanctions from the individual and the kinship group to clearly defined public officials representing the society as such. Hoebel notes: "Damages have generally replaced death as penalties in civil suits" (1954:329). Hoebel maintains that this is how law developed in human societies through the ages, but the laws of particular societies have not followed a single line of development through fixed, predetermined, and universal stages. The development of legal systems in particular societies is characterized by a trend that only in general exhibits the features described here.

Contemporary Law and Society Theorists

A brief explanation is necessary for the inclusion of the particular contemporary theorists. Comprehensive macrolevel theoretical works on law and society are few. My intention in this section is to describe influential (and possibly controversial) theoretical developments that have taken place since the 1970s. The rationale for this preference is to illustrate some of the relatively recent advances in sociolegal theorizing on law and society. There are, of course, a number of other theorists (who will be alluded to in specific contexts) who could have been discussed. They include Raymond A. Belliotti (1992), *Justifying Law*; William Chambliss and Robert Seidman (1982), *Law, Order, and Power*; William M. Evan (1990), *Social Structure and Law: Theoretical and Empirical Perspectives*; Hyman Gross (1979), *A Theory of Criminal Justice*; Alan Hunt (1993), *Explorations in Law and Society; Toward a Constitutive Theory of Law*; Philippe Nonet and Philip Selznick (1978), *Law and Society in Transition: Toward Responsive Law*; Harold E. Pepinsky (1976), *Crime and Conflict: A Study of Law and Society*; and Charles E. Reasons (1974) and Charles Sampford (1989), *The Disorder of Law: A Critique of Legal Theory*. As illustrations of contemporary theorists, these and similar works tend to be limited in scope. By contrast, the ones chosen for examination attempt to account for law and society in their treatises from different but, at the same time, complementary perspectives. Their alternative viewpoints are also broad enough to include both the older theoretical perspectives and the more contemporary, specialized advancements.

Donald Black   Black received his doctorate in sociology in 1968 at the University Michigan. He held dual appointments in the Department of Sociology and the Law School at Yale and Harvard Universities. He joined University of Virginia in 1985 where he is University Professor of the Social Sciences.

In three influential volumes, *The Behavior of Law; Sociological Justice;* and *The Social Structure of Right and Wrong*, Donald Black (1976, 1989, 1998) sets forth a theory of law that he contends explains variations in law from a cross-national perspective, as well as among individuals within societies. As noted in Chapter 1, he considers law as governmental social control, which makes use of legislation, litigation, and adjudication. He distinguishes between behavior that is controlled by these means from behavior that is subject to other forms of social control, such as etiquette, custom, and bureaucracy.

Black contends that law is a quantitative variable that can be measured by the frequency by which, in a given social setting, statutes are enacted, regulations are issued, complaints are made, offenses are prosecuted, damages are awarded, and punishment is meted out. Consequently, the quantity of law varies from society to society and from one historical period to another in a given society. Different organizations in a society may have more or less law both for themselves and in regard to other groups and organizations.

The direction of law (that is, the differential frequency and success of its application by persons in different social settings) also varies. So is the style of law that, as I mentioned earlier, may be accusatory (with penal or compensatory consequences) or remedial (with therapeutic or conciliatory consequences).

Next, Black develops a number of propositions that explain the quantity, direction, and style of law in regard to five measurable variables of social life: stratification, morphology, culture, organization, and social control. *Stratification* (inequality of wealth) can be measured in such ways as differences in wealth and rates of social mobility. *Morphology* refers to those aspects of social life that can be measured by social differentiation or the degree of interdependence (for example, the extent of division of labor). *Culture* can be measured by the volume, complexity, and diversity of ideas, and by the degree of conformity to the mainstream of culture. *Organization* can be measured by the degree to which the administration of collective action in political and economic spheres is centralized. Finally, the amount of nonlegal *social control* to which people are subjected is a measure of their respectability, and differences between people indicate normative distance from each other.

On the basis of sociological, historical, and ethnographic data, Black arrives at a number of conclusions. He points out that the quantity of law varies directly with stratification rank, integration, culture, organization, and respectability, and inversely with other forms of social control. Thus, stratified societies have more law than simple ones, wealthy people have more law among themselves than poor people, and the amount of law increases with the growth of governmental centralization.

The relationships between the quantity of law and the variables of differentiation, relational distance, and cultural distance are curvilinear. Law is minimal at either extreme of these variables and accumulates in their middle ranges. For example, law relating to contractual economic transaction is limited in simple societies where everyone engages in the same productive activity, and in the business world where manufacturers operate in a symbiotic exchange network.

The style of law varies with its direction: In relation to stratification, law has a penal style in its downward direction, a compensatory or a therapeutic style in its upward direction, and a conciliatory style among people of equal rank. In regard to morphology, law tends to be accusatory among strangers and therapeutic or conciliatory among intimates. Less organized people are more vulnerable to penal law and more organized people can count on compensatory law.

These patterns of stylistic variation explain, for example, why an offense is more likely to be punished if the rank of the victim is higher than that of the offender, but is more likely to be dealt with by compensation if their ranks are reversed, why accusatory law replaces remedial law in societies undergoing modernization, why members of subcultures are more vulnerable to law enforcement than conventional citizens, and why organizations usually escape punishment for illegal practices against individuals.

Over the years, Black's theory of law has generated considerable critical debate and analysis (see, for example, Wong, 1998). It has been referred to as a "crashing classic" (Nader, cited by Gottfredson and Hindelang, 1979:3) and as "the most important contribution ever made to the sociology of law. It is that and more" (Sherman, 1978:11). It should be noted, however, that Black's thesis has been subjected only to limited empirical investigation, mostly at the microsociological level. Consequently, it is criticized for being "circular" (Michaels, 1978:11) and because some of the propositions derived from the theory do not stand up well to the rigors of empirical testing at the macrosociological level (Doyle and Luckenbill, 1991; Gottfredson and Hindelang, 1979:3–18; and Lessan and Sheley, 1992). Regardless of these and other criticisms, Black's theory of law will continue to provide the impetus for a great deal of empirical work in coming years (see, for example, Cooney, 1997, on the decline of lethal conflict among social elites). His propositions are likely to be subjected to further testing, criticism, revision, reformulation, and possible rejection, especially his recently compiled ideas on the "geometry of law" (Black, 2001). But, as Sherman presciently noted shortly after the publication of *The Behavior of Law*, "whatever the substance or method, social research on law cannot ignore Black" (1978:15).

Roberto Mangabeira Unger   Unger was born in Brazil and is currently a professor of law at Harvard University. In *Law in Modern Society* (1976), he revives the sweeping scope of Max Weber's theorizing on law and places the development of rational legal systems within a broad historical and comparative framework. Unger locates the study of law within the major questions of social theory in general: the conflicts between individual and social interests, between legitimacy and coercion, and between the state and society. His main thesis is that the development of the rule of law, law that is committed to general and autonomous legal norms, could take place only when competing groups struggle for control of the legal system and when there are universal standards that can justify the law of the state.

Unger's analysis emphasizes the historical perspective. His goal is an understanding of modern law and society. He examines the nature of society, and compares rival systems (for example, the Chinese) with the Western tradition with the range of special types of law—customary or interactional law, regulatory law, and autonomous legal order. Customary or interactional law is "simply any recurring mode of interaction among individuals and groups, together with the more or less explicit acknowledgment by these groups and individuals that such patterns of interaction produce reciprocal expectations of conduct that ought to be satisfied" (1976:49). Bureaucratic or regulatory law for Unger "consists of explicit rules established and enforced by an identifiable government" (1976:50). This type of law is not a universal characteristic of social life: "It is limited to situations in which the division between state and society has been established and some standards of conduct have assumed the form of explicit prescriptions, prohibitions, or permissions, addressed to more or less general categories of persons and acts"

(1976:51). Unger calls the third type of law the legal order or legal system, which is both general and autonomous, as well as public and positive (1976:52). From an evolutionary perspective, these different types of law turn out to be stages, for they build upon one another, regulatory law upon customary law, the autonomous legal order upon regulatory law.

For Unger, law is indicative of the normative structure of social life. He contends that there are two competing forms of normative integration: consensual and instrumental. "Consensual law expresses the shared values of a group or community and manifests the stable structure in recurring interactions. Regulatory law is instrumental social control by political institutions through positive and public rules" (Eder, 1977:142). Unger considers autonomous law as both instrumental and consensual.

Unger accounts for these different types of law in an evolutionary context. The change of customary law into bureaucratic law is characterized by an extension of instrumental rules that have normative quality (state law, governmental sanctions). This extension of the instrumental rule is dependent upon the recognition of the consensual basis of law. Unger argues that sacred and natural law can provide the cultural context within which instrumental norms can be legitimized. The development of an autonomous legal order brings about a further extension of instrumental rules to everybody. Everyone can pursue his or her personal objectives as long as they do not infringe upon those of others. Laws set these limits. He notes, however, that this situation requires a further legitimization of the principles of law, and consensus must be generated by social contract and by agreement upon the criteria of substantive justice.

Unger (1998; Unger & West, 1998) is a prolific writer, and provides a fresh and unified, albeit somewhat controversial, solution to a number of problems in social theory—the problem of social scientific method, the problem of social order, and the problem of modernity (Sampford, 1989:145). His theory of law is useful for the analysis of changes in law, and he has generated a number of testable propositions that enable sociologists to study law at the synchronic and diachronic levels (Eder, 1977:143). His works are becoming increasingly recognized and appreciated in sociological circles.

CURRENT INTELLECTUAL MOVEMENTS IN LAW

As I have shown in Chapter 1, sociological discussions of the role of law in society generally take place in the context of two ideal conceptions of society: the consensus and conflict perspectives. The consensus perspective is grounded in the functionalist approach, and the conflict perspective in the conflict and Marxist approaches to the study of law in society. These are the two prevailing approaches in the sociological literature. Most sociologists opt for either a version of the functionalist or the conflict and Marxist approach to law and the legal system.

Functional analysis examines social phenomena with respect to their consequences for the broader society. Proponents of this approach ask specific questions such as: What does a kinship system do for society? What does law do for society? What are the "functions" of government, of social classes, or of any social phenomenon? (Turner, 1998: 7–76). In the context of the analysis of law, functionalists are concerned with the identification of the characteristics of legal phenomena, as well as indicating how legal institutions fit into the workings of the overall structure. Theorists embracing conflict and Marxist approaches emphasize the structuring of economic relations that provide, for them, the foundation for various specific studies of legal trends. I shall now consider these two approaches in some detail.

The Functionalist Approach

"Functionalism is," writes Robert A. Nisbet (1969:228), "without any doubt, the single most significant body of theory in the social sciences in the present century. It is often thought to be essentially a theory of order, of stability, of how society is possible." Historically, functionalism was brought into sociology by borrowing directly, and developing analogies for, concepts in the biological sciences. Biology, since the middle of the nineteenth century, frequently referred to the "structure" of an organism, meaning a relatively stable arrangement of relationships between the different cells, and to the "function" of the organism that considered the consequences of the activity of the various organs in the life process. The principal consideration of this organic analogy was how each part of the organism contributed to the survival and maintenance of the whole.

Sociologists distinguish between the manifest and the latent functions (Merton, 1957:19–84). Manifest functions are those that are built into a social system by design. They are well understood by group members. Latent functions are, by contrast, unintentional and often unrecognized. They are unanticipated consequences of a system that has been set up to achieve other ends. For example, the minimum wage law was enacted to provide unskilled laborers with an income slightly above poverty level. Unintentionally, however, this law contributed to the increase in teenage unemployment, particularly among black youths (Herbers, 1979), and reduced job prospects of low-wage earners. When the minimum wage increased, employers tended to hire more part-time than full-time workers, and the overall level of hiring was lower.

The basic tenets of functionalism are summarized in the following key assumptions (Van den Berghe, 1967:294–295):

1. Societies must be analyzed "holistically as systems of interrelated parts."
2. Cause and effect relations are "multiple and reciprocal."

3. Social systems are in a state of "dynamic equilibrium," such that adjustment to forces affecting the system is made with minimal change within the system.

4. Perfect integration is never attained, so that every social system has strains and deviations, but the latter tend to be neutralized through institutionalization.

5. Change is fundamentally a slow adaptive process, rather than a revolutionary shift.

6. Change is the consequence of the adjustment of changes outside the system, growth by differentiation, and internal innovations.

7. The system is integrated through shared values.

In sociology, functional analysis is as old as the discipline. Comte, Spencer, Durkheim, Malinowski, Radcliffe-Browne, Merton, and Parsons, to name a few, have engaged in the functional analysis of the social world (Turner and Maryanski, 1979:XI). The early theorists viewed the world in systematic terms (Turner and Maryanski, 1995:49–55). For them such systems were considered to have needs and prerequisites that had to be met to ensure survival. They viewed such systems as having normal and pathological states, thus suggesting a system of equilibrium and homeostasis. The social world was seen as composed of mutually interrelated parts, and the analysis of these connected and interdependent parts focused on how they fulfilled the requisites of the systems as a whole and how, thus, system equilibrium was maintained.

Ever since the classical sociological theorist Emile Durkheim postulated the notion that deviance could serve certain social functions in a society, sociologists have looked for evidence to support this contention. Durkheim had in mind the idea that a society needed deviance to continually reaffirm its boundaries of propriety. Functional arguments for the importance of deviance are intriguing. They provide a novel way of showing how certain institutions in a society, if not the society itself, continue to operate. Durkheim points out, for example, that without the existence of sinners, a church could not exist. Their very existence provides the opportunity for believers to reaffirm the faith that has been offended by the sinner. Thus, the worst thing that could happen to a church is to completely eliminate sin from the world and completely propagate the faith to society.

Functionalism is also present in legal anthropology. For example, in *The Cheyenne Way*, Karl N. Llewellyn and E. Adamson Hoebel (1941) outline their law-job theory about society as a whole. For societies to survive, there are certain basic needs that must be met. It is within this context that the wants and desires of individuals, their "divisive urges," assert themselves. The conflicts produced are unavoidable, but at the same time, essential to group survival. "The law-jobs entail such arrangement and adjustment of people's behaviour that the society (or the group) remains a society (or a group) and gets enough energy unleashed and coordinated to keep on functioning as a society (or as a group)" (1941:291). They consider the law-jobs as universal, applicable, and necessary to all groups and to all societies.

Functionalism is also evident in other writers. For example, in Jerome Frank's (1930) *Law and the Modern Mind,* the entire discussion of the "basic legal myth" and the associated "legal magic" is grounded in an examination of their functional consequences for the legal system. Similarly, Thurman Arnold's (1935) concern with the role of symbolism within legal institutions is consciously functionalist. Felix Cohen (1959) resorts also to functional analysis in his elaboration of "functional jurisprudence." More recently, the writing of Lon Fuller (1969) on law morality, Julius Stone's *Law and the Social Sciences* (1966), and Philippe Nonet's (1976) ideas on jurisprudential sociology are illustrative of the functionalist approach to the study of law and society.

Almost from the beginning, however, the functionalist approach was attacked both for alleged theoretical shortcomings and on ideological grounds. Criticisms included complaints that the whole notion of function is oversimplified. Questions such as "Functional for whom?" were raised, and not without grounds, for the interests and needs of different groups in a society are often in conflict. What may be functional for one group may be dysfunctional for another. Others argue that functional analysis is a static, antihistorical mode of analysis with a bias toward conservatism. Some sociologists even suggest that there is an implicit teleology in functional analysis, in that this mode of analysis inappropriately attributes purposes to social institutions as if they were conscious beings. As expected, a sizable amount of literature in the field has been devoted to both formulating and refuting these charges (see, for example, Turner and Maryanski, 1979; 1995). In spite of these criticisms, as Rich correctly points out: "It can be concluded that most sociology of law theorists are adherents to structural-functionalist theory" (1978:153).

Conflict and Marxist Approaches

Conflict and Marxist approaches are based on the assumption that social behavior can best be understood in terms of tension and conflict between groups and individuals. Proponents of these approaches suggest that society is an arena in which struggles over scarce commodities take place. Closely intertwined with the idea of conflict in society is the Marxian notion of *economic determinism.* Economic organization, especially the ownership of property, determines the organization of the rest of society. The class structure and institutional arrangements, as well as cultural values, beliefs, and religious dogmas, are, ultimately, a reflection of the economic organization of a society.

According to Marx, law and the legal system are designed to regulate and preserve capitalist relations. For the Marxists, law is a method of domination and social control used by the ruling classes. Law protects the interests of those in power and serves to maintain distinctions between the dominated and domineering classes. Consequently, law is seen as a set of rules that arise as a result of the struggle between the ruling class and those who are ruled. The state, which is the organized reflection of the interests of the ruling class, passes laws that serve the interests of this domineering class.

This breakdown of society into two classes—a ruling class that owns the means of production and a subservient class that works for wages—*inevitably* leads to conflict. Once conflict becomes manifest in the form of riots or rebellions, the state, acting in the interest of the ruling class, will develop laws aimed at controlling acts that threaten the interests of the status quo. As capitalism develops and conflict between social classes becomes more frequent, more acts will be defined as criminal.

It is not surprising, therefore, that many sociologists interested in law, and in particular, criminal law, have espoused this perspective. The conflict view of criminal law is most noticeable in the now controversial writings of Marxist criminologists. Quinney (1974a), for example, argues that law in capitalist society gives political recognition to powerful social and economic interests. The legal system provides the mechanism for the forceful control of the majority in society. The state and the legal system reflect and serve the needs of the ruling class. In *The Critique of Legal Order*, Quinney (1974b:16) argues that as capitalist society is further threatened, criminal law is increasingly used in the attempt to maintain domestic order. The underclass will continue to be the object of criminal law as the dominant class seeks to perpetuate itself. To remove the oppression, to eliminate the need for further reward, would necessarily mean the end of that class and its capitalist economy.

Similarly, William Chambliss and Robert Seidman take a conflict approach in their analysis of law. While emphasizing conflicting interests in society, they argue that "the state becomes a weapon of a particular class. Law emanates from the state. Law in a society of classes must therefore represent and advance the interests of one class or the other" (1982:72–73). For them, law is an instrument sought after and employed by powerful interest groups in society. Chambliss (1978:149) further reinforces the notion of law as an instrument of the powerful in society by specifically pointing out that "acts are defined as criminal because it is in the interests of the ruling class to so define them." Austin Turk (1978) also sees law as "a weapon in social conflict," an instrument of social order that serves those who are in power. The control of legal order represents the ability to use the state's coercive authority to protect one's interests. The control of the legal process further means the control of the organization of governmental decisions and the workings of the law, which diverts attention from more deeply rooted problems of power distribution and interest maintenance. Reasons (1974:103–104) considers crime as a phenomenon created by special interests who, with their definition of rectitude, create the laws of society.

Conflict theorists point out that most of the American criminal law comes directly from English common law. C. Ray Jeffery (1957) contends that acts such as murder, theft, trespassing, and robbery, problems that were once resolved in the kinship group, became crimes against the state when Henry II, King of England, centralized political power and declared them wrongs against the crown. Jerome Hall (1952) traces the growth of property and theft laws to the emergence of commerce and industrialization. With the advent of commerce and trade, a new economic class of traders and industrialists emerged, and the need to protect their business interests grew. As a result, new laws were established to protect the interests and economic well-being of the emergent class. These laws included the creation of embezzlement laws and laws governing stolen property and obtaining goods under false pretense. According to conflict theorists, notions of crime have their origins less in general ideas about right or wrong than in perceived threats to groups with the power to protect their interests through law.

Critics have not been kind to this type of argumentation, holding that it involves enormous simplification, reification, and absence of sensitivity to the complexity of social interaction (Manning, 1975:12). There are many who concede the validity of conflict and interest-group arguments but who, at the same time, contend that bold assertions about the "ruling class" conceal more than they reveal. Surely, lawmaking phenomena are more complex than implied in these statements that hint at a monolithic ruling class that determines legislative behavior and the creation of rules. In spite of these and other criticisms, Marxism exists in contemporary sociological theorizing and "must exist—because alienation exists. Alienation refers to the way in which human beings under capitalism do not control their work, but instead are dominated by their work and by the requirements of the profit-system" (Agger, 1979:1). Elements of the Marxist approach enter into a number of sociological studies on law and society and are influential on epistemological, methodological, and theoretical approaches, as evidenced, for example, in the works of Charles E. Reasons and Robert M. Rich (1978), who present the major paradigms in the sociology of law, with a particular emphasis on conflict and Marxist approaches.

Critical Legal Studies Movement

Critical legal studies (CLS but also referred to as CRITS) is a vibrant, refreshing, controversial and enduring addition to the ongoing jurisprudential debate on law, legal education and the role of lawyers in society (Belliotti, 1992:162–189; Kramer, 1995; Neacsu, 2000; Sampford, 1989: 143–146; Unger, 1983, 1986). It is widely considered, by critics and followers alike, to comprise some of the most exciting sociolegal scholarship around, and one sociologist of law described it as being "where the action is" (Trubek, 1984). The movement began with a group of junior faculty members and law students at Yale in the late 1960s who have since moved to other places. In 1977, the group organized itself into the Conference of Critical Legal Studies, which has over 400 members and holds an annual conference that draws more than 1,000 participants.

The movement has been greatly influenced by Marxist-inspired European theorists and its roots can be traced back to American legal realism (Tomasic, 1985:18). Legal realists in the 1920s and 1930s argued against the nineteenth-century belief that the rule of law was supreme. They contended, because a good lawyer could argue convincingly either side of a given case, there was actually nothing about the law that made any judicial decision inevitable. Rather, they pointed out, the outcome of a case depended largely, if not entirely, on the predilections of the judge who happened to be deciding it. Thus, far from being a science, the realists argued, law was virtually inseparable from politics, economics, and culture. They rejected the idea that law is above politics and economics.

Proponents of the movement reject the idea that there is anything distinctly legal about legal reasoning. As with any other kind of analysis, legal reasoning, they maintain, cannot operate independently of the personal biases of lawyers or judges, or of the social context in which they are acting. Furthermore, law is so contradictory that it allows the context of a case to determine the outcome. That attribute of law—its inability to cover all situations—is called *indeterminacy* (Trubek, 1984:578). Because law consists of a variety of contradictions and inconsistencies, judicial decisions cannot be the self-contained models of reasoning as they claim to be. Decisions rest on grounds outside of formal legal doctrine which are inevitably political.

Critical scholars also reject law as being value-free and above political, economic, and social considerations. Laws only *seem* neutral and independent, even those that reflect the dominant values in society. Moreover, laws legitimize those values that predominate in society. Therefore, laws legitimate the status quo. They maintain that law is actually part of the system of power in society rather than a protection against it.

Although proponents of the movement insist that their ideas are still tentative and evolving, their attacks on law and legal training have created a good deal of criticism. The movement has been called Marxist, utopian, hostile to rules, and incoherent. Critical legal scholars have been accused of favoring violence over bargaining, of advocating the inculcation of leftist values in legal education, and of being preoccupied with "illegitimate hierarchies" such as the bar (Schwartz, 1984); their approach to law is "nihilistic," and they teach cynicism to their students, which may result in "the learning of the skills of corruption." Nihilist law teachers with a proclivity for revolution are likely to train criminals, and they have, therefore "an ethical duty to depart from law school" (Carrington, 1984:227). It is unlikely that the controversy between proponents and opponents of the movement will be settled in the foreseeable future (Trubek and Esser, 1989). Further, although the movement has been fairly successful in questioning the validity of the Western legal system, it has failed, as the following sections will demonstrate, its major objective of developing and gaining broader support for new legal doctrines that are more representative of class, gender and race differences. So far, the most useful function of the movement is indicating the extent to which politics influences the legal system (Goodrich, 1993).

Feminist Legal Theory

Feminist legal theory is another intellectual movement of substantial influence, importance and impact. It is concerned with issues that are central to a broader intellectual and political feminist movement: sex based equality at the work place, reproductive rights, domestic violence, sexual harassment, rape, just to mention a few. It draws from the experiences of women and from critical perspectives developed in other disciplines in analyzing the relationship between law and gender (Frug, 1992a; Frazier and Hunt, 1998; Greenberg, Minow and Roberts, 1998). Unlike critical legal studies, which started in elite law schools and were inspired predominantly by notions of contemporary Marxism, feminist legal theories emerged against the backdrop of mass political movements (Rhode, 1991:334). These political backlashes for feminists included the defeat of the Equal Rights Amendment, setbacks in abortion rights, continued sexual subordination and exploitation in the profession of law, and the general prevalence of sexism in most walks of life. The recent "tough on crime" policies are also thought to have had a series of negative consequences on women: cuts from social services to pay for crime control can disproportionately affect women, women incur increased responsibility for family while men serve longer sentences, and women are often victimized as third parties by government when women are associated with criminals (Miller, 1998).

A dominant tendency in feminist legal theories is to regard men as the source of women's problems (Naffine, 1990:20). There is a strong conviction that male dominated jurisprudence perpetuates women as objects (Abrams, 1995; Eskridge and Hunter, 1997). Society is viewed as basically patriarchal, organized and dominated by men, and, as a result, not very hospitable to women. Not surprisingly, proponents of the theory consider it one of the most crucial challenges to contemporary law and legal institutions (Bartlett and Kennedy, 1991:1).

There are at least three predominant, although by no means mutually exclusive, themes in feminist legal literature. The first deals with women's struggle for equality in a male-dominated legal profession and in the broader society. Feminists challenge legal claims of fairness and the impartiality of law in dealing with women. The argument is that men directly or indirectly have endeavored to maintain their own power and to keep women in their place. There are many structural constraints to perpetuate inequality. One is law's respect for precedent. But for feminists, the emphasis on precedents raises two concerns. First, existing precedents tend to support and reinforce a status quo that may be more favorable to male than to female interests. Second, reasoning not based on precedent or accepted doctrine is often viewed as extreme and is less likely to be successful than arguments based on precedents. Examples of these two concerns include male-only combat rules, job security for pregnant women, and maternal child-custody preferences.

In the second broad theme of feminist legal scholarship, the argument of male bias is extended to include practically every feature of law. The law, according to this theme, is a reflection of a typical male culture, a masculine way of doing things. Law, therefore, is corrupted for women by its inherent masculinity. The task feminists face is to come up with a completely new law for women. Such law should be devoid of norms and characteristics that reinforce male prerogatives and female powerlessness about gender roles and private intentions. For example, the male legal culture dismisses or trivializes many problems that women face, such as sexual harassment and date-rape (Stein, 1999). They capture different subjective experiences of shared social realities: For the man, an office pass is sex (and pleasurable); for the woman, it is harassment (and painful). For the man, the dinner and its aftermath is a date (with certain expectations); for the woman, it is rape and frightening. Many gender-specific injuries are still dismissed as trivial (sexual harassment on the street); consensual (sexual harassment on the job); humorous (nonviolent marital rape); deserved or private (domestic violence); nonexistent (pornography); legally predetermined (marital rape, in states where legislatures have yet to outlaw it) (Frug, 1992b:808); or the use of battered women syndrome defense as an excuse to a variety of crimes, ranging from homicide to fraud (Coughlin, 1994).

The third dominant theme challenges the very concepts law invokes to support its contention that it is a just and fair institution. Contrary to professed notions, law is not value-neutral, objective, rational, dispassionate, and consistent. This is because law defines those concepts in a typically masculine way, ignoring or devaluing the qualities associated with the experience of women. Essentially, the problem is that law claims to be neutral in relation to the sexes (and other social categories); yet, the very way it argues for its neutrality is gender-biased. The particular style of maleness can best be illustrated by the concept of "rational person," a mythical legal subject who is coherent, rational, acts on *his* free will, and in ordinary circumstances can be held fully accountable for *his* actions (Naffine, 1990:1–23).

Feminists are pragmatists (Chafetz, 1997; Radin, 1991) and rely on feminist legal methods (Bartlett, 1991) to advance their cause. Feminists contend that without understanding feminist methods, law will not be perceived as legitimate or "correct." These methods, although not unique to feminists, seek to reveal features of a legal concern that more traditional approaches tend to ignore or suppress. There are three such basic methods (Bartlett, 1991:370–403).

One method asks the *woman question*, which is designed to probe into the gender implications of a social practice or rule. Asking the woman question compensates for law's failure to take into account experiences and values that are more typical of women than of men. Nowadays, feminists ask the woman question in many areas of the law. In the case of rape, they ask why the defense of consent deals with the perspective of the defendant and what he "reasonably" thought the woman wanted rather than the point of view of the woman and what she "reasonably" thought she conveyed to the defendant. The woman question asks why pregnancy is virtually the only medical condition excluded from state employee disability plans; why women cannot be prison guards on the same terms as men; and why conflict between family and work responsibilities is considered a private matter for women to resolve rather than a public concern involving the restructuring of the workplace. Essentially, the woman question shows how the predicament of women reflects the organization of society rather than the inherent characteristics of women.

Another method, *feminist practical reasoning*, deals with features not usually reflected in legal doctrine. The underlying assumption is that women approach the reasoning process differently from men, that women are more sensitive to situation and context, and that they tend to resist universal generalizations and principles. An example is minors' access to abortion. The notion of family autonomy seems to justify the legal requirement that a minor obtain parental consent before abortion. The young woman is immature, and parents are best suited to help her to decide whether or not to terminate her pregnancy. However, the often tragic and wrenching circumstances under which a minor may want to avoid notifying a parent about an abortion demonstrate the practical difficulties of the matter. Often, minors are traumatized by their parents' knowledge of their pregnancy. Women may be compelled to continue their pregnancy and subsequently give up the child for adoption, which is contrary to their intentions. Or they may be subjected to various forms of parental rejection or manipulation. Feminist practical reasoning challenges the legitimacy of the norms of those who claim to speak on behalf of the community, and they seek to identify perspectives not represented in the dominant monolithic male culture.

A third method, *consciousness-raising*, provides an opportunity to test the validity of legal principles through personal experiences of those who have been affected by those principles. The idea is to explore common experiences and patterns that come about from shared recollection of life events. It enables feminists to draw insights from their own experiences and those of other women and to use these newly formed insights to challenge dominant versions of social reality. In consciousness-raising sessions, women share their experiences publicly as victims of marital rape, pornography, sexual harassment on the job, or other forms of oppression or exclusion based on sexual orientation (Robson, 1994), in an attempt to alter public perception of the meaning to women of practices that the dominant male culture considers harmless or flattering.

Of course, feminist legal theory and its methods are not without their detractors. In part as a reaction to feminist legal scholarship, there is a nascent intellectual movement of critical studies of masculinity (see, for example, Collier, 1995; Hearn, 1992). The contention is that men are oppressed within patriarchy in a fashion comparable to women's oppression. It is not yet an institutionalized attempt at "men's liberation," albeit there are already efforts to legitimize the endeavors of politically powerful individuals and organizations to "improve" the legal rights of men (Collier, 1995:26). There is also a call for the development of a lesbian legal theory, "a theory about law that is relentlessly and intelligently lesbian," as a component of contemporary legal scholarship (Robson, 1992:37).

The assumption of a dominant androcentric homogenous legal culture is an exaggeration. It is more of a rhetorical than a factual contention. The classical Marxist polarization of the sexes into a dominant and a subordinate class, with the concomitant proletarianization of gender, represents a forceful argument but one of limited intellectual substance and appeal. In an attempt to depict the benefits that accrue to men in what is considered an essentially sexist institution, many feminists have overlooked the fact that not all men benefit equally from legal sexism. Indirectly and perhaps unintentionally, allusions are made only to successful white middle-class males, with their unique form of white middle-class masculinity while minority and gay males are excluded (Keen and Goldberg, 1998). A close examination of the principles and methods of law also reveals that there are many people who are omitted or maltreated on the basis of class, race, and ethnic background, in addition to gender. Thus, to assume that we are dealing with a clear-cut issue of "us versus them" gender-based exploitation is an oversimplification.

There are also some perplexing dilemmas confronting feminists. For example, there is no consensus in the literature about various options. In the context of male-only draft, statutory rape laws, and pregnancy, feminists have two choices: Either they claim equality for women on the basis of similarities between the sexes or they demand special treatment for women on the grounds of basic sexual differences. This difference-versus-similarity argument carries over into a variety of other areas. It is an either-or proposition, and critics maintain that feminists cannot have it both ways (Williams, 1991). Feminist legal theory also fails to address issues of democracy and citizenship (Higgins, 1997) and neglects the formulation of a positive theory of female sexuality (Franke, 2001). Still, in spite of these criticisms, feminist legal theory and its methods represent an important intellectual movement challenging traditional legal doctrine both in the United States (Bartlett and Harris, 1998; Bartlett and Kennedy, 1991; Frug, 1992; Greer, 2000; Naffine, 1990) and in Europe (Bernstein, 1994).

Critical Race Theory

Critical race theory is an eclectic, dynamic and growing movement in law with some 400 leading law review articles and a dozen books devoted to it (see, for example, Delgado and Stefancic, 2000).

Like feminist legal theory, critical race theory is concerned with questions of discrimination, oppression, difference, equality and the lack of diversity in the legal profession (Johnson, 1997). Although its intellectual origins go back much farther, the inception and formal organization of the movement can be traced back to a 1989 workshop on critical race theory in Madison, Wisconsin (Delgado and Stefancic, 2000; Delgado, 1994; Harris, 1994; Hayman, 1995; Scheppele, 1994). Many of the proponents have been previously involved with critical legal studies or feminist jurisprudence, and the 1989 conference effectively ratified critical race theory as an important component of legal theory. The critical race theory movement, along with the Latino focused critical legal scholarship or LatCrit (Valdes, 1997), attempts to rectify the wrongs of racism while acknowledging that racism is an inherent part of modern society. Racism is embedded in the system and proponents recognize that its elimination is impossible but at the same time they insist that an ongoing struggle to countervail racism must be carried out.

In a way, the word "critical" reflects a continuity between critical legal studies and critical race studies. Both seek to explore the ways in which law and legal education and the practices of legal institutions work to support and maintain a system of oppressive and inegalitarian relations. But CRITS do not generally look outside of the law to identify the forces that actually determine the content of legal rules while critical race theory prompts a recognition of the urgency of racial problems and an uncompromising search for real solutions rather than temporary and comforting stop-gap measures (Chang, 1993; Culp, 1994; Farber, 1994). The basic premise is that persons of color in the United States are oppressed and being oppressed creates fundamental disadvantages for those who are so treated. Critical race theory focuses on the experiences and situations of oppressed people of color, and provides an outlet for the concrete experiences of subordinates. Because of oppression, people of color perceive the world differently than those who have not had such experience. Critical race theory scholars can thus bring to legal analyses perspectives that were previously excluded. Through narratives and "story telling," some scholars share their experiences or the experiences of other people of color to make their presence felt in legal scholarship.

Critical race theorists extend traditional civil rights scholarship to locate problems beyond the surface of doctrine to the deep structure of American law and culture. Racism is viewed not only as a matter of individual prejudice and everyday practice, but also as a phenomenon that is deeply embedded in language and perception. Racism is a ubiquitous and inescapable feature of modern society, and despite official rhetoric to the contrary, race is always present even in the most neutral and innocent terms. Concepts such as "justice," "truth" and "reason" are open to questions that reveal their complicity with power. This extraordinary pervasiveness of unconscious racism is often ignored by the legal system.

Proponents of critical race theory have a commitment to a vision of liberation from racism through reason and efforts to separate legal reasoning and institutions from their alleged racist roots. Justice is still possible, and it is the property of both whites and nonwhites. Critical race theory seems confident that coming up with the correct theory of race and racism will lead to enlightenment, empowerment and, eventually, to emancipation.

As all other intellectual developments, critical race theory has also come in for criticism. There seems to be a contradiction between its commitment to radical criticism and its emphasis on racial emancipation. If the very language used to describe justice is infected by racism and gradations of power, what is the objective of critique? Another criticism is that it lacks a standard methodology and a set of common tenets. Further, it is also seen as a reformist project, not really new and distinguishable from traditional civil rights scholarship which set to eliminate discrimination but failed to achieve fully its stated objective. In the final analysis, critical race theory is a young intellectual movement which has the potential to have a profound effect on legal scholarship in the coming years.

SUMMARY

This chapter has traced the development of legal systems and has examined the principal theories of law and society. In a historical context, legal development, industrialization, urbanization, and modernization are closely intertwined. Legal development is conditioned by a series of integrative demands, stemming from society's economic, political, educational, and religious institutions. From a developmental perspective, the primitive, transitional, and modern legal systems were discussed. These three types are still present in the world's societies. Although one should be careful not to emphasize unilinear evolution, it can be inferred from the discussion that, to the extent legal change takes place in a society, it will follow more or less the pattern outlined. What distinguishes these legal systems from each other is the comparative degree of differentiation between basic legal elements. In the process of development, the once blurred elements of law, courts, legislation, and enforcement become increasingly separated from one another. Accompanying the emergence of laws, court systems, police force, and legislation is a trend toward increasing size, complexity, differentiation, and bureaucratization.

Among the theorists discussed, there seems to be more or less a general consensus that societal and legal complexities have gone hand in hand. Beyond that, there is little agreement. Many of the European pioneers discussed reacted in various ways to the influence of natural law and attempted to account for it from an evolutionary perspective. The classical sociological theorists covered have recognized the essential role of legal institutions in the social order and have made important explorations of the interplay between law and society. The sociolegal theorists were guided by social science principles in the development of their diverse perspectives on law and society. Making sense of the idea of law remains an ongoing enterprise, as evidenced by the efforts of the contemporary theorists discussed.

These efforts at explaining the interplay between law and society should be seen in the context of intellectual, political, and social climates of the particular theorists. In each historical epoch, every interpretation of social reality posits certain questions and provides certain answers. According to S. N. Eisenstadt (1972), tension is inherent in intellectual life because of the tendency to challenge the intellectual construction of social reality. If a theory of law and society is developed by one group of intellectuals, this will provide an incentive for others to view the matter in another way. Eisenstadt's insights account, in part, for the diverse explanations of the relationship between law and society and the nature, province, and function of law in society.

There are two currently widely accepted approaches to the study of law and society. Sociologists embracing the functionalist approach attempt, in various ways, to account for law in society within the overall framework of the theory that society consists of interrelated parts that work together for the purpose of maintaining internal balance. Sociologists advocating conflict and Marxist approaches to the study of law in society consider conflict inevitable and ubiquitous in societies, as a result of inescapable competition for scarce resources. They are preoccupied with debunking myths about society and advocating changes in what they regard as harmful social relations, structures, and processes that exist in today's social order. Proponents of the critical legal studies movement argue that there is nothing inherently rational, scientific, or neutral about the law—nothing that would dictate the outcome of a particular case. They maintain that law is riddled with contradiction and prejudice and that it is heavily in favor of the wealthy and powerful. Another movement of considerable influence is that of the feminist legal theory. Proponents challenge the impartiality of law in dealing with women and argue that law is a reflection of a typical male culture. Feminists rely on feminist methods that seek to reveal aspects of law that more traditional methods tend to ignore or suppress. Finally, proponents of critical race theory argue that the root causes of racial inequality still persist in American society, embedded in law, language, perception and structural conditions, and there must be an uncompromising search for real solutions rather than convenient stop-gaps.

SUGGESTED FURTHER READINGS

BRUCE A. ARRIGO, (ED.), *Social Justice/Criminal Justice: The Maturation of Critical Theory in Law, Crime, and Deviance*. Belmont, CA: West/Wadsworth, 1999. A collection of critical approaches by well-known contemporary theorists to law, crime and the criminal justice system.

KATHARINE T. BARTLETT and ROSANNE KENNEDY (EDS.), *Feminist Legal Theory: Readings in Law and Gender*. Boulder, CO: Westview Press, 1991. A balanced and provocative collection of articles on feminist legal theory and methods.

KATHARINE T. BARTLETT and ANGELA P. HARRIS, *Gender and Law: Theory, Doctrine, Commentary*. 2nd ed. New York: Aspen Law and Business, 1998. A comprehensive resource on feminist jurisprudence.

RAYMOND A. BELLIOTTI, *Justifying Law: The Debate over Foundations, Goals, and Methods*. Philadelphia: Temple University Press, 1992. A clear and concise review of historical and contemporary trends in jurisprudential thought.

EDGAR BODENHEIMER, *Jurisprudence: The Philosophy and Method of the Law* (rev. ed.). Cambridge: Harvard University Press, 1974. A review of the historical materials dealing with the development of jurisprudential thought with an emphasis on philosophical, sociological, historical, and analytical components of legal theory.

WILLIAM J. CHAMBLISS and MILTON MANKOFF, (EDS.), *Whose Law, What Order? A Conflict Approach to Criminology*. New York: John Wiley, 1976. A good illustration of the perspectives of conflict criminologists.

RICHARD COLLIER, *Masculinity, Law and the Family*. New York: Routledge, 1995. A controversial and thought-provoking book on the legal ramifications of critical studies of masculinity as a reaction in part to race and feminist legal scholarship.

HUGH COLLINS, *Marxism and Law*. New York: Oxford University Press, 1996. A clear and thorough treatment of the relationship between Marxian theory and law.

RICHARD DELGADO and JEAN STEFANCIC (EDS.), *Critical Race Theory, The Cutting Edge*. Philadelphia: Temple University Press, 2000. A collection of the best writings of a new generation of civil rights scholars in the fast growing legal genre of critical race theory.

WILLIAM M. EVAN (ED.), *The Sociology of Law: A Social-Structural Perspective*. New York: Free Press, 1980. *Social Structure and Law: Theoretical and Empirical Perspectives*. New York: Macmillan, 1990. Handy references for alternative theoretical approaches to the study of law in society.

LAWRENCE M. FRIEDMAN, *American Law; An Introduction*. 2nd ed. New York: W. W. Norton, 1998. A seminal work on the history and development of American law and legal system. *American Law in the Twentieth Century*, New Haven: Yale University Press, 2002. An excellent overview of law in the United States during the last century.

JUDITH G. GREENBERG, MARTHA L. MINOW and DOROTHY E. ROBERTS, *Women and the Law*. 2nd ed. New York: Foundation Press, 1998. A detailed overview of concrete legal problems of particular and current concern to women. The problems are grouped into three categories: women and work, women and the family, and women and their bodies.

ALAN HUNT, *The Sociological Movement in Law*. Philadelphia: Temple University Press, 1978. A comprehensive examination of the intellectual precursors of modern sociology of law, with an emphasis on Roscoe Pound, American legal realism, Emile Durkheim, and Max Weber.

LAW AND HUMAN BEHAVIOR, "Special Issue: Gender and the Law," 22 (1) (February), 1998. The entire issue is devoted to the examination of gender and law concerns. A good source for current research and applications.

SUSAN L. MILLER (ED.), *Crime Control and Women: Feminist Implications of Criminal Justice Policy*, Thousand Oaks, CA: Sage Publications, Inc., 1998. Using a feminist perspective, the collection of articles explores the adverse affects and unintended consequences of the U.S. crackdown on crime.

ERVIN H. POLLACK, *Jurisprudence: Principles and Applications*. Columbus: Ohio State University Press, 1979. A lengthy examination of diverse legal theories and their applications. A very useful book for prelaw students and essential for law students.

CHARLES E. REASONS and ROBERT M. RICH (EDS.), *The Sociology of Law: A Conflict Perspective*. Toronto: Butterworths, 1978. A compendium designed to present the major paradigms in the sociology of law, with particular emphasis on conflict and Marxist approaches.

ROBERT M. RICH, *The Sociology of Law: An Introduction to Its Theorists and Theories*. Washington: University Press of America, 1978. A handy review of principal theorists under the headings of sociology of law, sociology of criminal law, sociological jurisprudence, and anthropology of law.

KAHEI ROKUMOTO (ED.), *Sociological Theories of Law*. New York: New York University Press, 1994. A handy collection of classic, contemporary and cross-cultural articles on theoretical perspectives.

CHARLES SAMPFORD, *The Disorder of Law: A Critique of Legal Theory*. Oxford, England: Basil Blackwell, 1989. A useful source for additional discussion of a large number of important contemporary theorists from a critical perspective.

KIM LANE SCHEPPELE, "Legal Theory and Social Theory," *Annual Review of Sociology*, Annual 1994. Vol. 20, pp. 383–407, 1994. A concise and comprehensive review of recent developments in legal theory.

ROMAN TOMASIC, *The Sociology of Law*. London: Sage Publications, 1985. A compact overview of the various theoretical approaches to law and society, with a bibliography of close to a thousand references.

A. JAVIER TREVINO, *The Sociology of Law, A Biography of Theoretical Literature*. 2nd ed. Lewiston, NY: Mellen Press, 1998. A useful list of over 1,000 different references, culled from journal articles and books, which deal directly with the field of legal sociology.

A. JAVIER TREVINO, *The Sociology of Law, Classical and Contemporary Perspectives*. New York: St. Martin's Press, 1996. A recent review of classical and contemporary perspectives incorporating some original writings by theorists.

MAX WEBER, *Law in Economy and Society*. Ed. Max Rheinstein, and trans. Edward Shils and Max Rheinstein. Cambridge: Harvard University Press, 1954. Weber's most important writings on law, rich in historical material and major theoretical formulations.

G. EDWARD White, *Oliver Wendell Holmes, Sage of the Supreme Court*. New York: Oxford University Press, 2000. An insightful and informative biography of Holmes along with a review of some of his most important ideas and contributions.

REFERENCES

ABRAMS, KATHRYN. 1995. "Sex War Redux: Agency and Coercion in Feminist Legal Theory," *Columbia Law Review* 95 (2) (March): 304–376.

ADAMS, BERT N., and R. A. SYDIE. 2001. *Sociological Theory*. Thousand Oaks, CA: Pine Forge Press.

AGGER, BEN. 1979. *Western Marxism: An Introduction*. Santa Monica, CA: Goodyear.

ARRIGO, BRUCE A. (ED.). 1999. *Social Justice/Criminal Justice: The Maturation of Critical Theory in Law, Crime, and Deviance*. Belmont, CA: West/Wadsworth.

ARNOLD, THURMAN. 1935. *The Symbols of Government*. New Haven: Yale University Press.

BARBER, BERNARD. 1971. "Function, Variability, and Change in Ideological Systems." Pp. 244–262 in Bernard Barber and Alex Inkeles (eds.), *Stability and Social Change*. Boston: Little, Brown.

BARTLETT, KATHARINE T. 1991. "Feminist Legal Methods." Pp. 370–403 in Katharine T. Bartlett and Rosanne Kennedy (eds.), *Feminist Legal Theory: Readings in Law and Gender*. Boulder, CO: Westview Press.

BARTLETT, KATHARINE T., and ROSANNE KENNEDY (EDS.). 1991. *Feminist Legal Theory: Readings in Law and Gender*. Boulder, CO: Westview Press.

BARTLETT, KATHARINE T., and ANGELA P. HARRIS. 1998. *Gender and Law: Theory, Doctrine, Commentary*. 2nd ed. New York: Aspen Law and Business.

BELLIOTTI, RAYMOND A. 1992. *Justifying Law: The Debate over Foundations, Goals, and Methods*. Philadelphia: Temple University Press.

BENNIS, WARREN G. 1966. *Changing Organizations*. New York: McGraw-Hill.

BERNSTEIN, ANITA. 1994. "Law, Culture, and Harassment: Law and Workplace Harassment in the U.S. and Europe," *University of Pennsylvania Law Review*, 142 (4) (April): 1227–1311.

BLACK, DONALD. 1976. *The Behavior of Law*. New York: Academic Press. 1989. *Sociological Justice*. New York: Oxford University Press. 1998. *The Social Structure of Right and Wrong*. Revised ed. San Diego, CA: Academic Press. 2001. "The Geometry of Law: An Interview with Donald Black," Draft: April 15, 2001. Forthcoming in the *Brazilian Review of Criminal Sciences*.

BODENHEIMER, EDGAR. 1974. *Jurisprudence: The Philosophy and Method of the Law*. Rev. ed. Cambridge: Harvard University Press.

CARRINGTON, PAUL D. 1984. "Of Law and the River," *Journal of Legal Education* 34 (2) (June): 222–236.

CHAFETZ, JANET SALTZMAN. 1997. "Feminist Theory and Sociology: Underutilized Contributions for Mainstream Theory," *Annual Review of Sociology* 23: 97–121.

CHAMBLISS, WILLIAM J. 1978. "Toward a Political Economy of Crime." Pp. 191–211 in Charles E. Reasons and Robert M. Rich (eds.), *The Sociology of Law: A Conflict Perspective*. Toronto: Butterworths.

CHAMBLISS, WILLIAM, and ROBERT SEIDMAN. 1982. *Law, Order, and Power*. 2nd ed. Reading, MA: Addison-Wesley.

CHANG, ROBERT S. 1993. "Toward an Asian American Legal Scholarship: Critical Race Theory, Post-Structuralism, and Narrative Space." *California Law Review* 81 (5) (October): 1241–1323.

COHEN, FELIX. 1959. *Ethical Systems and Legal Ideals.* New York: Cornell University Press.

COLLIER, RICHARD. 1995. *Masculinity, Law and the Family.* New York: Routledge.

COLLINS, HUGH. 1996. *Marxism and Law.* New York: Oxford University Press.

COONEY, MARK. 1997. "The Decline of Elite Homicide," *Criminology* 35 (3) (August): 381–401.

COUGHLIN, ANNE M. 1994. "Excusing Women," *California Law Review,* 82 (1) (January): 1–93.

CULP, JEROME McCRISTAL, JR. 1994. "Colorblind Remedies and the Intersectionality of Oppression: Policy Arguments Masquerading as Moral Claims," *New York Law Review* 69 (1) (April): 162–196.

DIAMOND, ARTHUR S. 1971. *Primitive Law, Past and Present.* London: Methuen and Company, Ltd.

DELGADO, RICHARD. 1994. "Rodrigo's Ninth Chronicle: Race, Legal Instrumentalism, and the Rule of Law," *University of Pennsylvania Law Review* 143 (2) (December): 379–416.

DELGADO, RICHARD and JEAN STEFANCIC (EDS.). 2000. *Critical Race Theory, The Cutting Edge.* Philadelphia: Temple University Press.

DICEY, ALBERT VENN. 1905. *Lectures on the Relation Between the Law and Public Opinion in England During the Nineteenth Century.* London: MacMillan.

DOYLE, DANIEL P., and DAVID F. LUCKENBILL. 1991. "Mobilizing Law in Response to Collective Problems: A Test of Black's Theory of Law," *Law & Society Review* 25 (1): 103–116.

DURKHEIM, EMILE. 1964. *The Division of Labor in Society.* Trans. George Simpson. New York: Free Press. Originally published in 1893.

EDER, KLAUS. 1977. "Rationalist and Normative Approaches to the Sociological Study of Law," *Law & Society Review* 12 (1) (Fall): 133–144.

EISENSTADT, S. N. 1972. "Intellectuals and Tradition," *Daedelus:* 101 (2): 1–19.

ESKRIDGE, WILLIAM N. JR., and NAN D. HUNTER. 1997. *Sexuality, Gender, and the Law.* Westbury, NY: The Foundation Press, Inc.

EVAN, WILLIAM M. 1990. *Social Structure and Law: Theoretical and Empirical Perspectives.* Newbury Park, CA: Sage Publications.

FARBER, DANIEL A. 1994. "The Outmoded Debate Over Affirmative Action," *California Law Review,* 82 (4) (July): 893–934.

FEINBERG, JOEL and HYMAN GROSS (EDS.). 1995. *Philosophy of Law.* 5th ed. Belmont, CA: Wadsworth Publishing Company.

FRANK, JEROME. 1930. *Law and the Modern Mind.* New York: Coward-McCann.

FRANKE, KATHERINE M. 2001. "Theorizing Yes: An Essay on Feminism, Law, and Desire," *Columbia Law Review* (January): 101–181.

FRAZIER, PATRICIA A. and JENNIFER S. HUNT. 1998. "Research on Gender and the Law: Where Are We Going, Where Have We Been," *Law and Human Behavior* 22 (1) (February): 1–16.

FRIEDMAN, LAWRENCE M. 1975. *The Legal System: A Social Science Perspective.* New York: Russell Sage Foundation. 1998. *American Law: An Introduction.* 2nd ed. New

York: W. W. Norton & Co., Inc. 2002. *American Law in the Twentieth Century,* New Haven: Yale University Press.

FRUG, MARY JOE. 1992a. *Postmodern Legal Feminism.* New York: Routledge. 1992b. *Women and the Law.* Westbury, NY: The Foundation Press, Inc.

FULLER, LON. 1969. *The Morality of Law.* Rev. ed. New Haven: Yale University Press.

GALANTER, MARC. 1977. "The Modernization of Law." Pp. 1046–1060 in Lawrence M. Friedman and Stewart Macaulay (eds.), *Law and the Behavioral Sciences.* 2nd ed. Indianapolis: Bobbs-Merrill.

GOODRICH, PETER. 1993. "Sleeping with the Enemy: An Essay on the Politics of Critical Legal Studies in America," *New York University Law Review,* 68 (2) (May): 389–425.

GOTTFREDSON, MICHAEL R., and MICHAEL J. HINDELANG. 1979. "A Study of *The Behavior of Law,*" *American Sociological Review* 44 (1) (February): 3–18.

GREENBERG, JUDITH G., MARTHA L. MINOW and DOROTHY E. ROBERTS. 1998. *Women and the Law.* 2nd ed. New York: Foundation Press.

GREER, EDWARD. 2000. "Awaiting Cassandra: The Trojan Mare of Legal Dominance Feminism (Part I)," *Women's Rights Law Reporter* 21 (2) (Spring) 95–116.

GROSS, HYMAN. 1979. *A Theory of Criminal Justice.* New York: Oxford University Press.

GURVITCH, GEORGES. 1942. *Sociology of Law.* New York: Philo. Liby.

HALL, JEROME. 1952. *Theft, Law and Society.* 2nd ed. Indianapolis: Bobbs-Merrill.

HARRIS, ANGEL P. 1994. "Forward: The Jurisprudence of Reconstruction. Symposium: Critical Race Theory," *California Law Review* 82 (4) (July): 741–785.

HAYMAN, ROBERT L., JR. 1995. "The Color of Tradition: Critical Race Theory and Postmodern Constitutional Traditionalism," *Harvard Civil Rights-Civil Liberties Law Review* 30 (1) (Winter): 57–108.

HEARNS, JEFF. 1992. *Men in the Public Eye.* London: Routledge.

HERBERS, JOHN. 1979. "Changes in Society Holding Back Youth in Jobless Web," *New York Times* (March 11): A1, A44.

HIGGINS, TRACY E. 1997. "Democracy and Feminism," *Harvard Law Review* 110 (8) (June): 1657-1703.

HOEBEL, E. ADAMSON. 1954. *The Law of Primitive Man: A Study in Comparative Legal Dynamics.* Cambridge: Harvard University Press.

HOLMES, OLIVER WENDELL, JR. 1897. "The Path of Law," *Harvard Law Review,* no. 10 (March): 457–478.

HUFF, TOBY E. and WOLFGANG SCHLUCTER (EDS.). 1999. *Max Weber & Islam.* New Brunswick, NJ: Transaction Publishers.

HUNT, ALAN. 1978. *The Sociological Movement in Law.* Philadelphia: Temple University Press. 1993. *Explorations in Law and Society; Toward a Constitutive Theory of Law.* New York: Routledge.

JEFFERY, C. RAY. 1957. "The Development of Crime in Early English Society," *Journal of Criminal Law, Criminology and Police Science* 47:647–666.

JOHNSON, ALEX M., JR. 1997. "The Underrepresentation of Minorities in the Legal Profession: A Critical Race Theorist's Perspective," *Michigan Law Review* 95 (4) (February): 1005–1062.

KEEN, LISA and SUZANNE B. GOLDBERG. 1998. *Strangers to the Law: Gay People on Trial.* Ann Arbor, MI: The University of Michigan Press.

KRAMER, MATTHEW H. 1995. *Critical Legal Theory and the Challenge of Feminism: A Philosophical Reconception.* Lanham, Maryland: Rowman & Littlefield Publishers, Inc.

LESSAN, GLORIA T., and JOSEPH F. SHELEY. 1992. "Does Law Behave? A Macrolevel Test of Black's Propositions on Change in Law," *Social Forces* 70 (3) (March): 655–678.

LLEWELLYN, KARL N., and E. ADAMSON HOEBEL. 1941. *The Cheyenne Way: Conflict and Case Law in Primitive Jurisprudence.* Norman: University of Oklahoma Press.

MAINE, SIR HENRY SUMNER. 1861. *Ancient Law.* London: J. Murray.

MANNING, PETER K. 1975. "Deviance and Dogma," *British Journal of Criminology* 15 (1) (January): 1–20.

MARX, KARL. 1959. "A Contribution to the Critique of Political Economy." Pp. 42–46 in L. S. Feuer (ed.), *Marx and Engles: Basic Writing on Politics and Philosophy.* Garden City, NY: Doubleday.

MARX, KARL, and FRIEDRICH ENGELS. 1955. *The Communist Manifesto.* New York: Appleton-Century-Crofts. Originally published in 1848.

MCINTYRE, LISA JR. 1994. *Law in the Sociological Enterprise: A Reconstruction.* Boulder, CO: Westview Press.

MERTON, ROBERT K. 1957. *Social Theory and Social Structure.* New York: Free Press.

MICHAELS, PRISCILLA. 1978. "Review of Black's *The Behavior of Law*," *Contemporary Sociology* 7 (1) (January): 10–11.

MILLER, SUSAN L. (ED). 1998. *Crime Control and Women: Feminist Implications of Criminal Justice Policy.* Thousand Oaks, CA: Sage Publications, Inc.

MONTESQUIEU, BARON DE. 1886. *The Spirit of Laws.* Trans. Thomas Nugent. Cincinnati: Robert Clarke and Co. Originally published 1748.

NAFFINE, NGAIRE. 1990. *Law and the Sexes: Explorations in Feminist Jurisprudence.* Sydney, Australia: Allen & Unwin.

NEACSU, E. DANA. 2000. "CLS Stands for Critical Legal Studies, If Anyone Remembers," *Journal of Law and Policy* 8:415.

NISBET, ROBERT A. 1969. *Social Change and History.* New York: Oxford University Press.

NONET, PHILIPPE. 1976. "For Jurisprudential Sociology," *Law & Society Review* 10 (4) (Summer): 525–545.

NONET, PHILIPPE, and PHILIP SELZNICK. 1978. *Law and Society in Transition: Toward Responsive Law.* New York: Octagon Books.

NOVICK, SHELDON M. 1989. *Honorable Justice: The Life of Oliver Wendell Holmes, Jr.* Boston: Little, Brown.

PARSONS, TALCOTT. 1964. "Evolutionary Universals in Society," *American Sociological Review* 29 (3) (June): 339–357.

PEPINSKY, HAROLD E. 1976. *Crime and Conflict: A Study of Law and Society.* New York: Academic Press.

PIAGET, JEAN. 1965. *The Moral Judgment of the Child.* New York: Free Press. Originally published in 1932.

POLLACK, ERVIN H. 1979. *Jurisprudence: Principles and Applications.* Columbus: Ohio State University Press.

POSPISIL, LEOPOLD. 1971. *Anthropology of Law: A Comparative Theory.* New York: Harper & Row, Pub.

Pound, Roscoe. 1959. *Jurisprudence.* St. Paul, MN: West Publishing Company, Vols. 1 and 2.

QUINNEY, RICHARD. 1974a. *Criminal Justice in America.* Boston: Little, Brown. 1974b. *The Critique of Legal Order.* Boston: Little, Brown.

RADIN, MARGARET JANE. 1991. "The Pragmatist and the Feminist." Pp. 127–153 in Michael Brint and William Weaver (eds.), *Pragmatism in Law and Society.* Boulder, CO: Westview Press.

REASONS, CHARLES E. 1974. *The Criminologist: Crime and the Criminal.* Pacific Palisades, CA: Goodyear.

REASONS, CHARLES E., and ROBERT M. RICH (EDS.). 1978. *The Sociology of Law: A Conflict Perspective.* Toronto: Butterworths.

RHODE, DEBORAH L. 1991. "Feminist Critical Theories." Pp. 333–350 in Katharine T. Bartlett and Rosanne Kennedy (eds.), *Feminist Legal Theory: Readings in Law and Gender.* Boulder, CO: Westview Press.

RICH, ROBERT M. 1978. *The Sociology of Law: An Introduction to Theorists and Theories.* Washington, DC: University Press of America.

ROBSON, RUTHANN. 1992. "Embodiment(s): The Possibilities of Lesbian Legal Theory in Bodies Problematized by Postmodernisms and Feminisms," *Law & Sexuality, A Review of Lesbian and Gay Legal Issues,* 2 (Summer): 37–80. 1994. "Resisting the Family: Repositioning Lesbians in Legal Theory," *Signs,* 19 (4) (Summer): 975–997.

ROKUMOTO, KAHEI (ED.). 1994. *Sociological Theories of Law.* New York: New York University Press.

ROSTOW, WALT W. 1961. *The Stages of Economic Growth: A Non-Communist Manifesto.* New York: Cambridge.

ROULAND, NORBERT. 1994. *Legal Anthropology.* Translated by Philippe G. Planel. Stanford, CA: Stanford University Press.

SAMPFORD, CHARLES. 1989. *The Disorder of Law: A Critique of Legal Theory.* Oxford, England: Basil Blackwell.

SCHEPPELE, KIM LANE. 1994. "Legal Theory and Social Theory," *Annual Review of Sociology, Annual 1994.* Vol. 20, pp. 383–407.

SCHWARTZ, BERNARD. 1974. *The Law in America: A History.* New York: McGraw-Hill.

SCHWARTZ, LOUIS B. 1984. "With Gun and Camera through Darkest CRITS-Land," *Stanford Law Review* 36 (1 & 2) (January): 413–464.

SCHWARTZ, RICHARD D., and JAMES C. MILLER. 1975. "Legal Evolution and Societal Complexity." Pp. 52–62 in Ronald L. Akers and Richard Hawkins (eds.), *Law and Control in Society.* Englewood Cliffs, NJ: Prentice Hall.

SELZNICK, PHILIP. 1961. "Sociology and Natural Law," *Natural Law Forum* 6:84-108.

SHERMAN, LAWRENCE W. 1978. "Review of *The Behavior of Law*," *Contemporary Sociology* 7 (1) (January): 10–15.

SPENCER, HERBERT. 1899. *The Principles of Sociology* (II). New York: D. Appleton and Company.

STEIN, LAURA. 1999. *Sexual Harassment in America. A Documentary History.* Westport, CT: Greenwood Publishing Group, Inc.

SUMNER, WILLIAM GRAHAM. 1940. "The Challenge of Facts." Pp. 67–93 in Maurice R. Davie (ed.), *Sumner Today.* New Haven: Yale University Press. Originally published in 1886.

TANGLEY, LORD. 1965. *New Law for a New World.* London: Stephens and Sons.

TOMASIC, ROMAN. 1985. *The Sociology of Law.* London: Sage Publications.

TREVINO, A. JAVIER. 1996. *The Sociology of Law, Classical and Contemporary Perspectives.* New York: St. Martin's Press,

TRUBEK, DAVID M. 1984. "Where the Action Is: CRITS and Empiricism," *Stanford Law Review* 36 (1 & 2) (January): 575–622.

TRUBEK, DAVID M., and JOHN ESSER. 1989. " 'Critical Empiricism' in American Legal Studies: Paradox, Program, or Pandora's Box?," *Law & Social Inquiry* 14 (1): 3–52.

TURK, AUSTIN T. 1978. "Law as a Weapon in Social Conflict." Pp. 213–232 in Charles E. Reasons and Robert M. Rich (eds.), *The Sociology of Law: A Conflict Perspective.* Toronto: Butterworths.

TURNER, JONATHAN H. 1972. *Patterns of Social Organization: A Survey of Social Institutions.* New York: McGraw-Hill, 1974. "A Cybernetic Model of Legal Development," *Western Sociological Review* no. 5: 3–16. 1998. *The Structure of Sociological Theory.* 6th ed. Belmont, CA: Wadsworth Publishing Company.

TURNER, JONATHAN H., and ALEXANDRA R. MARYANSKI. 1979. *Functionalism.* Menlo Park, CA: Benjamin/Cummings.

TURNER, JONATHAN H., and ALEXANDRA R. MARYANSKI. 1995. "Is 'Neofunctionalism' Really Functional?" Pp. 49–62 in Donald McQuarie (ed.), *Readings in Contemporary Sociological Theory: From Modernity to Post-Modernity.* Upper Sadde River, NJ: Prentice Hall.

UNGER, ROBERTO MANGABEIRA. 1976. *Law in Modern Society: Toward a Criticism of Social Theory.* New York: Free Press. 1983. "The Critical Legal Studies Movement," *Harvard Law Review* 96 (3) (January): 561–675. 1986. *The Critical Legal Studies Movement.* Cambridge: Harvard University Press. 1998. *Democracy Realized: The Progressive Alternative.* New York: Verso.

Unger, RODERTO MANGADEIRA and CORNEL WEST. 1998. *The Future of American Progressivism: An Initiative for Political and Economic Reform.* Boston: Beacon Press.

VAGO, STEVEN. 1999. *Social Change.* 4th ed. Upper Saddle River, NJ: Prentice Hall.

VALDES, FRANCISCO. 1997. "Under Construction: LatCrit Consciousness, Community and Theory," *California Law Review* 85 (5) (October): 1087–1142.

VAN DEN BERGHE, PIERRE L. 1967. "Dialectic and Functionalism: Toward a Synthesis." Pp. 294–310 in N. Demerath and R. A. Peterson (eds.), *System Change and Conflict: A Reader on Contemporary Sociological Theory and the Debate Over Functionalism.* New York: Free Press.

WEBER, MAX. 1954. *Law in Economy and Society.* Ed. Max Rheinstein and trans. Edward Shils and Max Rheinstein. Cambridge: Harvard University Press. 1968. *Economy and Society.* Trans. Guenther Roth, and Claus Wittich. New York: Bedminster Press.

WHITE, G. EDWARD. 2000. *Oliver Wendell Holmes, Sage of the Supreme Court.* New York: Oxford University Press,

WILLIAMS, WENDY W. 1991. "The Equality Crisis: Some Reflections on Culture, Courts, and Feminism." Pp. 15–34 in Katharine T. Bartlett and Rosanne Kennedy (eds.), *Feminist Legal Theory: Readings in Law and Gender.* Boulder, CO: Westview Press.

WONG, K. C. 1998. "Black's Theory on the Behavior of Law Revisited II: A Restatement of Black's Concept of Law," *International Journal of Sociology* 26 (1) (March): 75–120.

WORMSER, RENE. 1962. *The Story of Law.* Rev. ed. New York: Simon & Schuster.

3
The Organization of Law

Nowadays, one way or another, law touches all of us. The contact may be pleasant or unpleasant, tangible or intangible, direct or indirect, but it is nonetheless a constant force in our lives. For a sociological understanding of law in society, we need to know about the social organization of law, the types of social arrangements and relations involved in the legal process, and the social characteristics of people who interpret and administer the law. The purpose of this chapter is to examine the social organization of legal systems in the context of the judicial, legislative, administrative, and enforcement agencies that carry out the official (and at times the unofficial) business of law.

COURTS

One of the most important functions of courts is to process disputes (see, for example, Mays and Gregware, 2001). By definition, a dispute is a conflict of claims or rights—an assertion of right, claim, or demand on one side, met by contrary claims on the other. When courts hear disputes, they attempt to decide (adjudicate) between or among those who have some disagreement, misunderstanding, or competing claims. Such disputes may arise between individuals, between organizations (private or governmental), or between an individual and an organization. Jones may sue Smith to recover damages caused by a traffic accident; acting under the provisions of a civil rights statute, the federal government may sue the state of Mississippi to force its officials to stop discriminating against blacks in the electoral process; the state of Missouri may charge Doe with burglary and bring him to court to answer the charge. When a judge renders the official judgment of the trial court in a civil or a criminal case as to the defendant's guilt or innocence, the process is called *adjudication*.

Unlike legislative and administrative bodies, courts do not place issues on their own agendas (see, for example, Abraham, 1998). Judges generally do not decide to make rulings about voting rights, racial discrimination, or abortion, and then announce their "decisions." Rather, courts are passive; they must wait until matters are brought to them for resolution. The passivity of courts places the burden on citizens or organizations to recognize and define their own needs and problems and to determine which require legal judgments. As Donald Black (1973:138) notes, this method of acquiring cases "assumes that each individual will voluntarily and rationally pursue his own interests." The courts are indifferent to those issues or disputes that individuals or organizations fail to notice or wish to ignore. This reactive nature of courts ensures that they consider disputes only after the injuries have taken place or the problems have developed.

In theory, courts differ from other kinds of dispute-regulation methods in that they are available to all members of society. In principle, everyone who has a dispute for which there is legal redress ought to be able to use the courts. Unlike dispute-settlement methods that are available only to specific groups in society (for example, college grievance committees or religious tribunals), courts are truly public. Judicial resolution of disputes entails both the application of legal knowledge and the interpretation of events. The role of courts is to interpret and to apply law. Such judicial interpretation of law is expected to be impartial. Judges are expected to be governed by legal principles, not by personal preferences or by political pragmatism.

Dispute Categories

The dispute-processing function of American courts, which will be discussed in detail in Chapter 6, is on the increase (see, for example, Palmer and Roberts, 1998). To understand what courts do, it is necessary to examine the kinds of disputes they process. Sheldon Goldman and Austin Sarat (1989:4–6) suggest that there are three important categories of disputes that provide the bulk of work of American courts. The first is called the *private* dispute. This kind of dispute is characterized by the absence of any initial participation by public authorities. For example, when a husband and wife quarrel, when two businesspersons debate the terms of a contract, when two automobiles collide, these events are likely to give rise to private disputes. Although they may occur in public places and may involve competing interpretations of law, they remain private as long as the government is not a party. Because these disputes arise more or less spontaneously in the course of normal social life, they are usually processed and managed without the intervention of government. Many of these private disputes can be dealt with in the general context of ongoing relationships or through some kind of bargaining and negotiation. For example, the husband and wife may seek marriage counseling, the businessperson may arrive at a compromise through negotiation, and a settlement may be reached for the car accident through an insurance company. At times, however, nonlegal intervention is insufficient for the disputing parties. The courts may be asked to settle disputes in a large variety of civil cases where a party seeks legal redress in a private interest, such as for a breach of contract or the use of a copyrighted story without permission.

The second category of disputes is called the *public-initiated* dispute. It occurs when the government seeks to enforce norms of conduct or to punish individuals who breach such norms. These kinds of public disputes emerge when society attempts to control and channel social behavior through the promulgation of binding legal norms. An illustration of the public-initiated dispute is the ordinary criminal case in which the state, or some official acting on its behalf, seeks to use the courts to determine whether a particular breach of law has occurred and whether sanctions should be applied. It is unique because it always involves and is governed by the law of the entire community. In the case of criminal law violation, dispute processing must occur in a public forum, for no society could allow the development of private mechanisms for the enforcement of breaches of public norms, since that could easily lead to anarchy. It should be noted, however, that not all public-initiated disputes are resolved or processed by means of judicial action. A variety of informal mechanisms, ranging from the warnings that a police officer may give to a traffic violator, to the prosecutor's choice not to go ahead with a criminal case, to the practice of plea bargaining, may be used to deal with breaches of public norms (Eisenstein and Jacob, 1977). Furthermore, disputes involving the breach of public norms are, at times, not called to the attention of public authorities. For instance, the husband who beats his wife may have committed a violation of public norms, but until a complaint is lodged with law enforcement agencies, their dispute remains private.

The third kind of dispute is the *public defendant* dispute. In this type, the government participates as a defendant. Such disputes involve challenges to the authority of some government agency or questions about the propriety of some government action that may be initiated by an individual or by an organization. In such cases, the courts are called upon to review the action of other branches of government. These disputes involve claims that the government has not abided by its own rules or followed procedures that it has prescribed. For instance, parents of children in racially segregated public schools might claim that school officials violated the Constitution's guarantee of equal protection of the laws. In general, such disputes come to court only after the aggrieved party has failed to remedy his or her grievance either through the political process or through procedures provided by the offending government agency.

These three types of disputes—private, public-initiated, and public defendant—represent, for the most part, the workload of American courts. It should be noted that, contrary to widespread beliefs, courts, in general, process rather than solve disputes. A court decision is seldom the last word in a dispute. For example, after a divorce decree, the aggrieving parties may continue to argue, not about settlements, but about visiting rights or proper supervision of children (see, for example, Sarat and Felstiner, 1995). Similarly, in many cities, court-ordered desegregation and busing did not resolve the issue of where children should go to school, not to mention the more enduring and underlying racial issues. Thus, it should be remembered that whether the disputes involve only two individuals who bring the case to court or whether cases have broader ramifications, court decisions are seldom the final word in a dispute. Let us now consider the structure of courts where decisions are rendered.

The Organization of Courts

The American court system is characterized by dual hierarchies. There are both state and federal courts operating side by side (see Figure 3–1). The structure is decentralized. Throughout American history, courts have been considered the third branch of government. Since they do not have an independent constitutional or political base, courts depend on the same political processes that sustain legislative and executive institutions. Each of the 50 states of the United States has its own court system, and, in addition, there is the federal court system. No two state court systems are alike; indeed, the differences both in the functions and in the labels given to American courts are many and bewildering, and no generalization is absolutely reliable for all states. Court systems have rarely been the product of long-range planning. Nearly all represent a series of patchwork accommodations to changing needs.

Although the organization and the structure of state court systems vary widely, in most states there are (1) trial courts (commonly called district courts), where most civil and criminal cases are originally heard, often before a jury; (2) intermediate courts of appeals, which primarily review cases decided at the trial court level; and (3) a court of last resort (commonly called a state supreme court), whose primary function is reviewing cases decided by the lower appeals courts.

Federal and state court systems are separate from each other. Most of the nation's legal business is settled in state courts under the provision of state law. However, state court decisions that involve a "federal question"—that is, decisions that present a question involving the Constitution (such as free speech) or federal laws (such as racial or sexual discrimination)—may be appealed to the U.S. Supreme Court.

The federal district courts carry most of the workload of the federal courts. At least one court of this type exists in every state, although some of the larger states are subdivided into several districts. There are 94 district courts and 649 district court judges. The number of judges and case filings range from 2 judges and a caseload of 589 in Vermont to 28 judges and 11,169

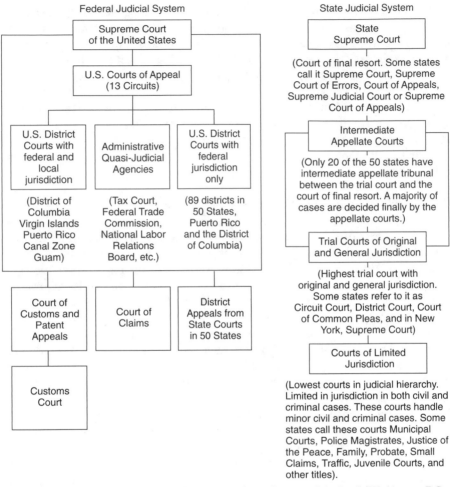

FIGURE 3-1   Court systems. *Source:* "The Supreme Court: Justice and the Law" (Washington, DC: *Congressional Quarterly*, 9th ed., 2001) p. 39.

filings in Manhattan, New York (Hughes, 1995:30–31). A single judge usually presides over trials in the district courts. Juries are used in about half of the more than 1 million criminal and civil cases decided each year by these courts.

In the hierarchy of the federal judiciary, the several courts of appeals are immediately above the district courts. The nation was divided in 2002 into 13 geographically defined jurisdictions, called "circuits." There is a court of appeals with a panel of three judges in each circuit. The chief function of these courts is to review decisions made by the district courts within their jurisdictions. They are also empowered to review the decisions of federal regulatory agencies, such as the Federal Trade Commission.

Thus, the typical court case begins in a trial court in the state or federal court system. Most cases go no further than the trial court. For example, the criminal defendant is convicted (by a trial or by a guilty plea) and sentenced by the court, and his or her case ends. The personal injury suit ends in a judgment by a trial court (or an out-of-court settlement by the parties while the court suit is pending), and the disputants leave the court system. Some litigants, however, who are not fully satisfied with the decision of a trial court may, by right, file an appeal. An appeal may take one of two forms: a trial *de novo* (a new trial) or a more limited review of specific aspects of a trial proceeding. For example, a criminal defendant believes that his or her con-viction was based on errors by the trial judge (such as the admission of evi-dence that should have been excluded) and seeks a new trial. In other instances, a litigant may seek a review of certain aspects of the trial based on procedural grounds. Most states have only one appellate court, usually known as the supreme court. This court hears appeals from all trial court decisions, criminal and civil, except those of minor courts. State supreme courts render the final decision for all cases involving state law. The U.S. Supreme Court renders the final verdict on all matters involving federal law or the federal Constitution (see, for example, Baum, 1998).

In the lower court, the burden of appealing falls on the losing party. In a criminal case, the prosecutor is prohibited from appealing an acquittal. The sole function of appellate courts is to correct errors committed in law by the trial courts. As disputes move from the trial to the appellate level, they are typ-ically transformed. They become almost exclusively disputes about law or about procedures; issues of law or questions concerning the way the trial was conducted are argued in appellate courts. Usually, the facts produced by the trial proceedings are not disputed at the appellate level. Time allotted for oral arguments before appellate courts is limited. Disputes are conducted prima-rily through briefs, motions, and memoranda. In a sense, disputes in appellate courts are a "lawyers' game." In trial courts, decisions are rendered by a sin-gle judge or shared by a judge and jury. In appellate courts, the decision-mak-ing process involves only judges. Some appellate courts have only a single judge, although most have several judges. Disputing in appellate courts is far removed in time and substance from the events that gave rise to the original disagreement. The original parties, their dispute, and its specific resolution become less important than the legal context into which they are placed.

Participants in Court Processes

Courts, as dispute-processing institutions, are composed of four dis-tinct groups of participants—litigants, lawyers, judges, and juries. These participants, in turn, bring to the judicial process diverse interests, values, and perspectives that influence the ways in which disputes are processed. I shall discuss these different types of participants separately.

Litigants   Since the principal function of courts is to process disputes, the most obvious participants must be the disputants. This group includes individuals, organizations, and government officials who are trying to settle disagreements and to regulate their own behavior and the behavior of others. Clearly, not all individuals, groups, or organizations can resort or are willing to resort to courts in their attempts to settle disputes. Questions of cost, efficiency, availability, the fulfillment of the legal requirements of a suit, and the nature of the dispute affect differently the potential users of courts. Consequently, two distinct types of litigants emerge.

In a classic study, Marc Galanter (1974) designates the two types of litigants as "one-shotters" and "repeat players" who have not changed over the years. They are distinguished by the relative frequency with which they resort to court services. As will be shown in Chapter 6, those who use the courts only occasionally are called one-shotters. Illustrations of one-shotters include an author suing his publisher for breach of contract, and a female professor filing charges against her university for alleged sexual discrimination in promotion. Repeat players are those who engage in many similar litigations over a period of time. Whereas one-shotters are usually individuals, repeat players are organizations, such as finance companies, moving companies, the Internal Revenue Service, or insurance companies. Their investment and interest in a particular case is moderately small. Because of their high frequency of participation in litigation, repeat players are more concerned with the ways a decision may affect the disposition of similar cases in the future than with the outcome of a single case (Ross, 1980). Repeat players can also invest greater resources in litigation than one-shotters, and their frequent appearances in court enable them to develop expertise. Such expertise is reflected in the way in which they select cases for litigation and in the manner in which they carry on disputes that have been transformed into lawsuits.

By contrast, participants who have only a one-time interest in litigation are generally more concerned with the substantive result of their case than the way in which the outcome may in the future affect the disposition of other cases. For example, the author in the preceding illustration is more concerned with winning his case against the publisher than with setting a precedent for similar cases. The IRS, on the other hand, is more interested in maintaining specific rules (such as those governing charitable deductions or computers) than with winning one particular case. Organizations, in general, participate in litigation as plaintiffs, and individuals participate as defendants. Both governmental and nongovernmental organizations have greater access to resources, and they are the most frequent initiators of court cases to process disputes between themselves and private individuals with whom they are dealing.

Lawyers   Law is a technical game and the players are highly trained in its complex rules and elusive categories. Without the assistance of attorneys, most individuals would be unable to activate the courts on their own behalf. The operation of courts is based on special standards and rules established by law. The process of identifying and applying rules requires special training and expertise, which is provided by members of the legal profession. Lawyers occupy an intermediary position between disputants and courts and transform litigants' complaints into legal disputes. Disputants generally need to retain the services of lawyers to receive advice about legal rules and how they apply to specific issues in dispute. By being familiar with both court operations and legal rules, lawyers are instrumental in determining whether a particular dispute warrants judicial intervention. Lawyers in effect play the role of gatekeepers for the judiciary (Hughes, 1995:109).

Lawyers are repeat players in the adjudication process. Only a small proportion of lawyers are involved in actual litigation. Most are concerned with specific nontrial activities, such as writing wills or carrying out routine transactions. As will be discussed in Chapter 8, some of the trial attorneys specialize in particular areas of the law (such as divorce or criminal law), and others represent only particular kinds of clients (such as corporations or universities) or limit themselves to particular clients within specified areas of law (such as taxes). Jonathan Casper (1972) distinguishes among types of trial lawyers by the manner in which they perceive their clientele. He argues that a small number of attorneys view themselves principally as representatives of public interests. These attorneys are concerned, for example, with consumer interests or with the protection of the environment. For them, individual cases are simply vehicles for achieving broad public objectives that generally necessitate major changes in the law. They prefer to take only cases they believe involve significant issues. The second type of lawyer represents particular interests or organizations. For example, some companies have their in-house lawyers whose principal role is to represent members of the organization.

The third type of lawyer, typically criminal defense lawyers, is most often involved in actual court work and, therefore, will be considered in greater detail. These lawyers are legal specialists who most closely approximate the public's preconception of lawyers. They handle a broad range of felonies and misdemeanors, with only a rare petty offense, traffic, or personal injury case (Wice, 1978:29–30). Although the role of defense lawyers is most often couched in the general term of "defending a client," they perform a number of specific roles. These include the roles of advocate, intermediary, and counselor (Cohn, 1976:261). In the primary role of *advocate*, defense lawyers take all possible steps within legal and ethical bounds to achieve a victory for the client, while protecting the rights of the client at each step of the criminal justice process. Often, this can best be accomplished by acting as an *intermediary* between the client and the law, working through negotiation and compromise to secure the best possible benefits from the system. The third role is that of *counselor*. It is the responsibility of defense to give advice to the client as to what to expect and what appears to be in the client's best interest. Although most people would agree that defense attorneys should perform the foregoing functions, it is often suggested that they fail to do so. For example, Abraham S. Blumberg echoes some of the still prevailing criticisms of defense lawyers. He argues:

> The real key to understanding the role of defense counsel in a criminal case is the fixing and collection of his fee. It is a problem which influences to a significant degree the criminal court process itself, not just the relationship of the lawyer and his client. In essence, a lawyer-client "confidence game" is played. (Blumberg, 1979:242)

Blumberg charges that defense lawyers make sure that the clients know that there is an important connection between fee payment and the zealous exercise of professional expertise, secret knowledge, and organizational "connections" in their behalf. He contends that defense lawyers manipulate their clients and stage-manage cases to offer at least the appearance of services. He calls the criminal lawyer a "double agent" because the main concern is to maintain good relations with members of the court organization. The defense lawyer may give the impression of being an impartial professional who will do everything possible for the client; however, he or she is, in reality, dependent on the goodwill of the prosecutor and the court.

The fourth type of trial lawyer perceives a lawyer's role primarily as serving individuals who retain him or her. These lawyers are often referred to as "hired guns" (Blumberg, 1979:238). They are interested only in the case in which they are involved, and they will do everything within legal and ethical limits to ensure favorable outcomes for their clients. In their view, they serve a case, not a cause. These different types of lawyers behave differently in advising clients whether to litigate and in preparing strategies of litigation.

Judges   Although a variety of officials work around courtrooms, none has the prestige of the judge, who is responsible for the administration of the court and its reputation for honesty and impartiality. The courtroom is designed so that attention is focused on the judge, who sits on a pedestal above the other participants. Any visitor to a courtroom will notice that the visitor's gallery never rises above the judge and that those who work in the courtroom are not allowed to sit or stand at the judge's level. The judge is the only official in the courtroom who wears special attire—a robe. When the judge enters the courtroom, everyone rises, and all attention is directed at him or her. The judge is addressed as "Your Honor," regardless of individual predilections (Jacob, 1984:10). The judge alone interprets the rules that govern the proceeding, although this power may be shared with a jury of laypersons and the judges see themselves as autonomous decision makers whom nobody bosses around (Jacob, 1997:3).

In addition to the basic adjudication functions and the control of the flow of litigation in the courtroom, the judge is also responsible for administering his or her own court. This entails a variety of "housekeeping" tasks, such as appointing clerical assistants, drawing up a budget, and making certain that the physical facilities are adequate for the court's operation. The judge is also instrumental in pretrial conferences and, by law, has a great deal of discretionary power (such as jury instruction on admission of evidence), which has important implications on the consideration and outcome of cases (Philips, 1998; Pinkele and Louthan, 1985). Because of this prestigious role, the judge also performs a variety of nonjudicial functions, such as appointing officials to public agencies (for example, the board of education, district attorneys in some states, and, at times, lucrative patronage positions).

Judges come from the middle or upper classes and have a history of party identification, if not activism (Carp and Stidham, 2001:210–214; Schmidhauser, 1979:49–55). Federal court judges are nominated by the president and confirmed by a majority vote in the U.S. Senate. These federal judges hold office for life, subject to removal only by impeachment or by conviction of a major crime. State and local judges are chosen by a variety of methods: Some are elected, some are appointed, and some are chosen by a method that combines election and appointment. In the combined election and appointment system, judges are appointed by an executive (such as a governor), and after completing a term in office, they must secure voter support to serve further terms. This type of system also has a selection procedure in which the executive's choice for a judgeship is screened through a commission or limited to nominees made by a commission. When elected, the majority of judges at the state level serve for a limited period, such as a six-year term (Volcansek and Lafon, 1988). Nowadays, running for judgeship can be an expensive proposition—judicial campaigns in many states now include large war chests, consultants and attack advertising. Some candidates for state supreme courts spend more than $1 million for campaigns. To combat interest group pressures, increased campaign fund-raising for judicial races and the resulting cynicism about the courts, public financing of judicial campaigns is an idea whose time has come (Glaberson, 2001). Table 3–1 reviews the selection processes and retention terms for judges by states as of June 1, 2001.

Almost all judges are lawyers in the United States, but only a small fraction of lawyers are, or ever become, judges (Friedman, 1998, 2002). By contrast, in civil-law countries, such as France and Italy, judges are civil servants and have different training and experience from practicing lawyers. Those who aspire to become judges take a competitive examination after law school. The ones who pass will become judges with a career of their own. Previous practice of law is not required. It is also unlikely that they will ever practice law. Their roles and functions are also different from their American counterparts of the adversarial system. Unlike in common-law countries,

TABLE 3–1 Method of Selection and Length of Initial and Retention Terms of General Jurisdiction Court Judges

By State and name of court, as of June 1, 2001

State/name of court(s)	Initial Selection Method[a]	Term	Retention Method	Term (in years)
Alabama				
Circuit court	Partisan election	6 years	Partisan election	6
Alaska				
Superior court	Nominating commission	Until next general election but not less than 3 years	Retention election	6
Arizona				
Superior court[b]	Nominating commission	Until next general election but not less than 2 years	Retention election	4
Arkansas				
Circuit court	Partisan election	4 years	Partisan election	4
California				
Superior court	Nonpartisan election or gubernatorial appointment[c]	6 years	Nonpartisan election[d]	6
Colorado				
District court	Nominating commission	Until next general election but not less than 2 years	Retention election	6
Connecticut				
Superior court	Nominating commission	8 years	Commission reviews, governor renominates, legislature reappoints	8
Delaware				
Superior court	Nominating commission	12 years	Reappointment by governor	12
District of Columbia				
Superior Court[c]	Nominating commission	15 years	Reappointment by judicial tenure committee or President	15
Florida				
Circuit court	Nonpartisan election	6 years	Nonpartisan election	6
Georgia				
Superior court	Nonpartisan election	4 years	Nonpartisan election	4
Hawaii				
Circuit court	Nominating commission	10 years	Reappointment by commission	10
Idaho				
District court	Nonpartisan election	4 years	Nonpartisan election	4
Illinois				
Circuit court	Partisan election[f]	6 years	Retention election	6

By State and name of court, as of June 1, 2001

State/name of court(s)	Initial Selection		Retention	
	Method[a]	Term	Method	Term (in years)
Indiana				
Circuit court	Partisan election[g]	6 years	Partisan election[g]	6
Superior court	Partisan election[h]	6 years[i]	Partisan election[j]	6
Iowa				
District court	Nominating commission	Until next general election but not less than 1 year	Retention election	6
Kansas				
District court	Nominating commission[k]	Until next general election	Retention election[l]	4
Kentucky				
Circuit court	Nonpartisan election	8 years	Nonpartisan election	8
Louisiana				
District circuit	Partisan election[m]	6 years	Partisan election	6
Maine				
Superior court	Appointed by governor	7 years	Reappointment by governor	7
Maryland				
Circuit court	Nominating commission	Until next general election but not less than 1 year	Nonpartisan election	15
Massachusetts				
Trial Court of the Commonwealth	Nominating commission	To age 70	X	X
Michigan				
Circuit court	Nonpartisan election	6 years	Nonpartisan election	6
Recorder's Court of Detroit	Nonpartisan election	6 years	Nonpartisan election	6
Minnesota				
District court	Nonpartisan election	6 years	Nonpartisan election	6
Mississippi				
Circuit court	Nonpartisan election	4 years	Nonpartisan election	4
Chancery court	Nonpartisan election	4 years	Nonpartisan election	4
Missouri				
Circuit court	Partisan election[n]	6 years[o]	Partisan election[p]	6
Montana				
District court	Nonpartisan election	6 years	Nonpartisan election, but if unopposed, retention election	6

(cont.)

TABLE 3–1 (*cont.*)

By State and name of court, as of June 1, 2001

State/name of court(s)	Initial Selection Method[b]	Term	Retention Method	Term (in years)
Nebraska				
District court	Nominating commission	Until next general election but not less than 3 years	Retention election	6
Nevada				
District court	Nonpartisan election	6 years	Nonpartisan election	6
New Hampshire				
Superior court	Appointed by governor[q]	To age 70	X	X
New Jersey				
Superior court	Appointed by governor	7 years	Reappointment by governor	To age 70
New Mexico				
District court	Nominating commission	Until next general election	Partisan election the first time; after that, winner runs in retention election	6
New York				
Supreme court	Partisan election	14 years	Partisan election	14
North Carolina				
Supreme court	Partisan election[r]	8 years	Partisan election[s]	8
North Dakota				
District court	Nonpartisan election	6 years	Nonpartisan election	6
Ohio				
Common Pleas court	Nonpartisan election	6 years	Nonpartisan election	6
Oklahoma				
District court	Nonpartisan election	4 years	Nonpartisan election	4
Oregon				
Circuit court	Nonpartisan election	6 years	Nonpartisan election	6
Pennsylvania				
Common Pleas court	Partisan election	10 years	Retention election	10
Rhode Island				
Superior court	Nominating commission	Life tenure	X	X
South Carolina				
Circuit court	Nominating commission[t]	6 years	Reelected by legislature	6
South Dakota				
Circuit court	Nonpartisan election	8 years	Nonpartisan election	8

By State and name of court, as of June 1, 2001

State/name of court(s)	Initial Selection		Retention	
	Method[a]	Term	Method	Term (in years)
Tennessee				
Circuit court	Partisan election	8 years	Partisan election	8
Texas				
District court	Partisan election	4 years	Partisan election	4
Utah				
District court	Nominating commission	Until next general election but not less than 3 years	Retention election	6
Vermont				
Superior court	Nominating commission	6 years	Automatic retention unless legislature votes against it	6
Virginia				
Circuit court	Elected by legislature	8 years	Reelected by legislature	8
Washington				
Superior court	Nonpartisan election	4 years	Nonpartisan election	4
West Virginia				
Circuit court	Partisan election	8 years	Partisan election	8
Wisconsin				
Circuit court	Nonpartisan election	6 years	Nonpartisan election	6
Wyoming				
District court	Nominating commission	Until next general election but not less than 1 year	Retention election	6

[a]In States that use nominating commissions, the governor makes the appointment.

[b]Counties with populations less than 250,000 select and retain superior court judges in nonpartisan elections for 4-year terms.

[c]Local electors can choose either nonpartisan elections or gubernatorial appointment.

[d]Judge must be elected to a full term on a nonpartisan ballot at the next general election. If the election is not contested, the incumbent's name does not appear on the ballot.

[e]Initial appointment is made by the President of the United States and confirmed by the Senate. If the President does not wish to reappoint the judge, the District of Columbia Nomination Commission compiles a new list of candidates.

[f]Circuit court associate judges are appointed by the circuit judges in each circuit for 4-year terms, as provided by supreme court rule.

[g]In Vanderburgh County, initial selection and retention are by nonpartisan election.

[h]A nominating commission is used for the superior court judges of Lake and St. Joseph Counties. In Vanderburgh County the election is nonpartisan.

(cont.)

[i]In Lake and St. Joseph Counties each appointed judge serves until the next general election but not less than 2 years.

[j]Nonpartisan elections are used in Allen and Vanderburgh Counties. Retention elections are used in Lake and St. Joseph Counties.

[k]Seventeen of 31 districts use a nominating commission for district judge selection; the remaining 14 select district judges in partisan elections.

[l]Fourteen of 31 districts use partisan elections.

[m]Although party affiliation of judicial candidates appears on ballots, judicial primaries are open. This gives judicial elections a nonpartisan character.

[n]Nominating commissions are used for selecting circuit court judges in Jackson, Clay, and Platte Counties, and the City and County of St. Louis.

[o]An associate circuit court judge's term is 4 years; also in counties that use nominating commissions the appointed judge serves until the next general election but not less than 1 year.

[p]Retention elections are used in Jackson, Clay, and Platte Counties, and the City and County of St. Louis.

[q]Subject to approval by an elected five-member executive council.

[r]Five special judges of the superior court are appointed by the governor. Three are appointed for 4-year terms and 2 judges are appointed for 5-year terms.

[s]Special judges of the superior court are reappointed by the governor and serve 4-year terms.

[t]The Judicial Merit Selection Commission was established on July 1, 1997. The commission screens and then recommends a list of three judicial candidates to the legislature. The legislature votes on the list submitted by the commission. If all candidates on the list are rejected, the process begins again with the commission.

judges rely on the inquisitorial method, which has its roots in ecclesiastical courts. The French criminal trial is a good example of this method. The main figures at the trial are the investigating magistrate and the presiding judge. The magistrate is responsible for the investigation. He sends the material to the trial, where the judge dominates the proceedings and interrogates the defendant and the witnesses, who are the same for both the defense and the prosecution. Obviously, there is no "coaching" of witnesses. The interrogation of the judge resembles more a conversation than a cross-examination (Loh, 1984:497-498). The judges are much more active than in the United States: They play a greater role in building and deciding a case, they put the evidence together, and they go far beyond the "refereeing" role characteristic of common-law judges.

Juries   An ancient Welsh king, Morgan of GlaMorgan, established trial by jury in A.D. 725 and the origins of the American jury system can be traced back to civil and criminal inquiries conducted under old Anglo-Saxon law in England (Adler, 1995; Abramson, 2000; Ramirez, 1994; Vidmar, 2000; Wolf and Sarat, 1997). The original concept of the jury was most likely imported to England after the Norman Conquest. The Normans started the practice of placing a group of local people under oath (hence the term "juror") to tell the truth. Early jurors acted as sources of information on local affairs and they gradually came to be used as adjudicators in both civil and criminal cases.

Before the twelfth century, criminal and civil disputes were resolved by ordeal. It took many forms. There was ordeal by water. The accused person was bound by rope and dropped into a body of water. If the person floated, it was a sign of guilt; if he or she sank, it was a sign of innocence. There were also ordeal by fire—carrying heated stones or iron, and if the subsequent burn did not get infected in three days, the accused was declared innocent— and ordeal of the morsel that did or did not choke the accused. Civil disputes were often resolved by oaths on the assumption that a false oath would expose someone to the judgment of God.

The jury system came to American shores with the British settlers in 1607 (Simon, 1980:5). One of the important symbols during the struggle for independence, it is prominently referred to in three of the first ten amendments to the Constitution. As noted earlier, juries are used in about half of the criminal and civil cases in federal district courts. Although the Constitution provides the right to a jury trial for both criminal and civil cases involving more than $20, in the state trial courts juries render verdicts in fewer than 10 percent of all cases. But one-quarter to one-half of all the cases that go before a jury are settled out of court. Many of them involve liability claims, in which the impaneling of a jury may be another strategy in the insurance companies' bargaining process. Of the 3 million or so people called to jury duty annually, for an average of 10 days each, only 60 percent will serve on a jury (*Time*, 1981:45). Lately more and more Americans are evading jury duty and the widespread failure to respond to jury-service summons delays trials and inconveniences judges, lawyers and court administrators (Gerlin, 1995:B1).

At the state and federal levels, generally "only criminal trials make extensive use of juries" (Jacob, 1984:165). In some jurisdictions, the prosecutor also has the right to have a case tried by a jury. In such jurisdictions, the jury may be used even if the defendant prefers to have the case tried by a judge, although how the proceedings are carried out is determined by the trial judge. A prosecutor may seek a jury trial because of the belief that a jury is more likely to convict than a particular judge, that a jury is more likely to impose the desired sentence, or that a jury trial will attract more public attention to a defendant's heinous crime (U.S. Department of Justice, March, 1992:7). Though the right to a jury trial is often waived, juries are essential to the operation of American courts. The jury is used in all death penalty cases, and a fundamental law in the United States is that no person may be convicted of a capital crime except by the unanimous verdict of a 12-member jury. That is the law in all of the 38 states that have the death penalty, as well as in federal cases. There is, however, one exception. A jury of five is all that is required to sentence a member of the armed services to death in a court-martial (Bonner, 2001).

Though they invented the jury system, the British have been steadily dismantling it for decades. There are no juries in British civil cases, except those involving libel or police misconduct. Around 93 percent of the criminal cases are heard before panels of three lay magistrates. Unlike in the United States, there is no voir dire and cross-examination of juries and criminal cases do not require unanimous verdicts.

Juries are used predominantly in common-law countries (Friedman, 1998, 2002), although Russian law now permits accused criminals to request a trial by jury as of November 1993. The old tribunal method, which only involved a judge and two assistants, was unfairly biased against the defendants, who now are entitled to a fair trial (Stead, 1994). It is estimated that 80 percent of all jury trials worldwide take place in the United States (Hans and Vidmar, 1986:31). A prominent federal judge, Richard A. Posner (1995), comments that this unique fidelity to the jury system to a great extent is due to the legacy of American distrust of officials, which has its roots in colonial times, and to a lesser extent to the political power of trial lawyers. Although this distrust is present in federal courts in both civil and criminal cases, it is much more pronounced in the state courts where it is reinforced by the low professional quality and rampant politicization of many of the state judiciaries. The distrust toward the judiciary retards government funding at all levels that would help to obtain better officials, and the resulting poor performance of the officials further reinforces the distrust.

Juries are used exclusively in trial courts. Dispute processing in trial courts involves two basic types of issues: issues of law and issues of fact. Issues of law emerge as participants in the dispute seek to identify and interpret norms that will legitimize their behavior. In a sense, a trial is a contest of interpretation and legal reasoning. The judge has the authority to determine which interpretations of law are proper and acceptable, but a trial is more than a question of legal reasoning. It also provides the opportunity for a reconstruction, description, and interpretation of events (that is, issues of fact). The purpose of a trial is to answer the question of who did what to whom and whether such conduct is legal. The function of the jury is to listen to and decide among competing and conflicting interpretations of events. The jury acts as a referee in an adversary contest dealing with the presentation of differing versions of the same event. By a crude division of labor, the jury is the authority on facts; the judge is the authority on law. But judges also control the jury and the common law provides several mechanisms by which judges can and often do intervene to prevent juries from going overboard, including the discretion to exclude prejudicial evidence, the power to split trials into separate phases so that liability can be decided before jurors hear of the terrible pain suffered by the plaintiffs, the prerogative to instruct the jury in the law, the use of special verdicts to ensure that factual determinations are rational, the power to reduce jury awards, and the ability to order new trials when a jury reaches an absurd result (see, for example, Bogus, 2001).

One of the most important functions of a trial lawyer is jury selection (Kassin and Wrightsman, 1988:22–27). Some attorneys contend that by the time the jury has been chosen, the case has been decided. During the process of *voir dire* (literally, "to see, to tell"), prospective jurors are questioned first by the judge, then by the attorneys representing defense and prosecution. The purpose of the voir dire is threefold. First, it is used to obtain information to assist in the selection of jurors and to ferret out any juror bias (Lilley, 1994). Second, it enables the attorneys to develop rapport with potential jury members. Finally, there is an attempt by both sides to try to change the attitudes, values, and perspectives of jurors (Klein, 1984:154). If a juror admits to a racial, a religious, a political, or some other bias that would influence his or her decision, the lawyers whose client would be harmed can ask the judge to excuse the juror for cause.

But lawyers know, and many studies have indicated, that when people are questioned before an authority figure (the judge) and a number of strangers in crowded seating conditions and under stress, they tend to give socially acceptable answers and to conceal or deny their prejudices about litigants (Andrews, 1982:68). For example, national polls have shown that one-third or more of Americans consider a criminal defendant probably guilty ("The person wouldn't be on trial if there wasn't something to it"), but few would admit that in the courtroom (Hunt, 1982:82).

The hypothesis that the composition of the jury is the most important determinant of the trial's outcome is implicit in the practice of law (Saks and Hastie, 1978:48). Lawyers rely on their private judgments about how jurors are likely to be biased, and by using their peremptory challenges, they eliminate those who worry them most. Decisions to exclude or include a juror are based on a variety of considerations: gut reactions to the juror's looks and manner, advice passed down by other lawyers, and various maxims or rules of thumb. Examples of this legal folklore include admonitions that clergymen, schoolteachers, and wives of lawyers do not make desirable jurors because they are often sought out for advice and tend to be opinionated. Or, cabinetmakers should be avoided because they want everything to fit neatly together, and Germans or Scandinavians should be shunned because they are too exacting (Saks and Hastie, 1978:49). Body language also influences the selection process (Dimitrius and Mazzarella, 1998). For example, sweating; shaking; sincere, furrowed-brow look; running tongue over teeth; inappropriate familiarity (back-slapping, touching, invading personal space) are considered signs of dishonesty. Arms, legs or ankles crossed; short or rapid breath; stiff, rigid posture; pointing fingers are viewed as signs of anger and volatility.

Many lawyers assume that Catholics will favor a Catholic litigant and Jews a Jewish one; that union members will be anticorporation; that women, especially mothers of daughters, will be quicker to convict an alleged rapist than men. Some jurors are avoided because they are wearing a loud sport

jacket, white socks, or a hairpiece. In damage suits, some people are eliminated because they are fat, on the assumption that fat persons tend to dish
out overly generous portions. In criminal cases, legal cookbooks on jury
selection would recommend men, Republicans, upper-income groups,
bankers, engineers, and certified public accountants for the prosecution, and
women, Democrats, middle- and lower-income groups, social scientists, and
members of racial and ethnic groups such as Latinos or Jews for the defense
(Simon, 1980:35).

For centuries, folklore, intuition, and unsystematic past experience
provided the basis for jury selection. Scientific jury selection enabled this
process to move to a more sophisticated and predictable level (Hans,
1992:61–63). Since the early 1970s, lawyers have made increasing use of
social scientists in jury selection. Scientific jury selection was first used in the
winter of 1971–1972 in the conspiracy trial of the Berrigan brothers and other
antiwar activists in Harrisburg, Pennsylvania (Saks and Hastie, 1978:55).
They were accused of plotting to blow up the heating pipes of the Pentagon
and kidnap the Secretary of State. Scientific jury selection has been used in
the Angela Davis trial, in the conspiracy trial of John Mitchell and Maurice
Stans for allegedly impeding a Securities and Exchange Commission investigation of a fugitive financier, and in a score of other cases (Hunt, 1982).

In essence, scientific jury selection consists of three steps. First, a random sample is drawn from the population, and the demographic profile of
this sample is compared with that of the prospective jurors (Pope, 1989). If
the jurors were randomly selected, the profile should match. If there is substantial over- or underrepresentation of particular characteristics (ethnic
groups, age, occupation, and so forth), the jury pool can be challenged.
Second, after it is established that the prospective jurors represent the population at large, a random sample is drawn from the jury pool to determine
the demographic, personal, and attitudinal characteristics considered to be
favorable to one's own side. Third, after establishing the psychological and
demographic profile of a "favorable" juror, the social scientist can make recommendations for selection of individual jurors (Loh, 1984:400). This basic
procedure is often supplemented with additional information. For example,
in the Angela Davis trial, investigators for the defense questioned prospective jurors' neighbors and friends to learn about their attitudes. In another
case, a research firm representing a corporate defendant called all potential
jurors and questioned them, pretending to be conducting a random telephone survey.

An expansion of the technique is the use of a shadow jury. Some social
scientists feel that since the opposing attorneys present conflicting views of
the facts, jurors tend to make decisions based more on empathy than evidence. Thus, techniques of effective communication and persuasion need to
be called to the attention of lawyers. To this end, simulated or "shadow"
juries are used to gain feedback for lawyers on how to try their cases. The

pioneering work with shadow juries took place during the antitrust case brought by California Computer Products of Anaheim against IBM. The IBM attorneys hired the consulting firm Litigation Sciences to help in IBM's defense. The researchers recruited six people with backgrounds and attitudes similar to the real jury. The six shadow jurors sat in the courtroom each day during the course of the trial, and each evening they telephoned the researchers to report on their impressions of the day's proceedings. Because the plaintiffs presented their case first, the researchers learned how shadow jurors reacted to the arguments and what issues they considered important. Although the judge ruled in favor of IBM after the plaintiffs presented their side, IBM attorneys would have used the knowledge gained from the shadow jury in presenting their side of the case (Hans and Vidmar, 1986:89). In 1989, Litigation Sciences (which has grown to more than 100 sociologists, psychologists, marketers, graphic artists, and technicians) has helped Pennzoil Co. win a $10.5 billion jury verdict against Texaco Inc. Litigation Sciences' annual revenue is in excess of $25 million (Adler, 1989).

In addition to using shadow juries, some attorneys practice their arguments in front of simulated juries, with social scientists making suggestions about their persuasiveness. In 1980, the law firm representing MCI Communications in an antitrust suit against AT&T hired consultants to develop a profile of potentially favorable jurors. The consultants arranged mock juries made up of such people, in front of whom the MCI attorneys practiced their arguments. The researchers also videotaped MCI's witnesses and then advised them on how their testimony could be presented more succinctly and persuasively. MCI won the case and was awarded $600 million. Of course, with amounts like this at stake, the fees paid to social-science consultants—ranging from $50,000 to $500,000—may be a bargain (even in 1980 dollars) if they actually help (Hunt, 1982:72).

Such mock trials are the most useful early in a case. They can help a lawyer pinpoint the main issue of a case and assemble pertinent evidence around it, also showing jurors' probable reactions to arguments which might contradict their basic beliefs. Most mock trials are conducted by jury consulting or market research firms and contain abbreviated versions of all parts of a regular trial (Clifford, 1995).

There are serious reservations about the appropriateness of the use of scientific jury selection. Lawyers, when they are being candid, admit that their goal is not fairness but the selection of biases that benefit them. In the words of an attorney, "I don't want an impartial jury. I want one that's going to find in my client's favor" (Hunt, 1982:85). But critics of the method contend that it tends to undermine our adversarial system of justice. The techniques for surveying the community and assessing juror values during the voir dire are clearly designed to achieve juror partiality. It leads to an imbalance in the composition of the jury. Thus, it is an advantage only to rich defendants in criminal cases and the richer side in civil suits. One with greater resources will have more lawyers, better lawyers, a larger staff. Jury research is one more such advantage. The ability of the adversary system to guarantee a fair and impartial jury and trial is obviously tested when the adversaries possess unequal resources (Hans and Vidmar, 1986:94).

There is also the danger that prosecutors may start relying on scientific jury selection if they lose too many cases because of the defendants' use of experts. In that case, as Amitai Etzioni wrote, "Could any but the most affluent Americans compete with the state, once it began to apply these procedures to the prosecution?" (quoted in Andrews, 1982:73). Finally, there is the question of the public perception of the trial. There is a possibility that the legitimacy of the trial and subsequent verdict is undermined by the use of scientific methods in jury selection. The entire system of peremptory challenges may come under attack if these issues are not confronted by those who carry out jury research and by those who benefit from the results. If the judges released the list of prospective jurors to lawyers only one day before the trial, and not several days before, which is the current practice, many of the dangers and ethical problems inherent in scientific jury selection could be minimized. This would drastically reduce the time available for experts to conduct thorough background investigations of prospective jurors and the subsequent advantages for one party in the litigation.

In addition to problems of jury selection, there are other important issues concerning the involvement of jurors in dispute processing in courts (Duff and Findlay, 1997). The first is whether juries are effective checks on judicial power. There is really no way of determining whether juries ensure that judges will be more restrained in using their power than they would be otherwise. In a study by Harry Kalven and Hans Zeisel (1966), an attempt was made to determine the effectiveness of the jury in checking the judge's power by examining the percentage of cases in which the judges and juries involved in the same case agreed as to the appropriate verdict. The researchers found a high degree of agreement between judge and jury— approximately 75 percent. They also noted that in almost all criminal cases in which judge and jury disagreed, the jury tended to be more lenient. Whether the leniency of the jury can be construed as limiting the exercise of judicial power is open to question: It does, however, show that the participation of laypersons in the decision-making process does make a difference in the outcomes of court decisions.

Another issue deals with the question of representativeness of the jury. Three steps are involved in the selection of jurors: (1) the placement of names on a master list of prospective jurors, (2) the selection of names from this list and the summoning of these persons to the court to constitute a jury panel, and (3) the selection from the panel of persons to serve on juries. Ideally, a jury that is representative of the community it serves is one that provides judgment by peers. Studies show, however, that American juries, as well as juries in other countries, are not always representative, mainly because the sources from which potential jurors are drawn—typically voter registration lists—are not representative of the various ethnic, social, and economic groups in the community (Alker et al., 1976; Israel, 1998). Defense lawyers often complain that the urban poor, many of them minorities, are more mobile than the middle class and thus less easy for jury commissioners to find. Therefore, fewer are located and called for jury service. Yet, having even a few members of a minority group on a jury panel can help enormously, because racist discussions are less likely to occur in a mixed-race setting (Kennedy, 1998).

This is why states such as New York and Arizona are initiating changes in the jury selection procedures to enlarge the jury pool to include people receiving unemployment or welfare benefits (Barge, 1995). Also, even a small number of jurors can hold together to block a verdict they consider unjust (Pollock and Adler, 1992:4). Obviously, the representativeness of juries is important, not only because of the need to ensure legitimacy of the jury, but also because different kinds of people bring different attitudes and values to the jury. This is particularly true in racially sensitive cases, as best illustrated in the 1992 trial and acquittal of four white Los Angeles policemen in a police-brutality case involving the videotaped beating of a black motorist. Jury representativeness in racially charged cases has become more difficult in the wake of the rioting that followed the acquittals. Notorious, controversial, and racially charged trials also raise the possibility that jurors will lean toward a verdict that is likely to keep the peace. There is no way of determining to what extent, if any, jurors will be influenced by the possibility of mob violence in highly controversial cases (Geyelin and Brannigan, 1992; *U.S. News & World Report*, 1992).

The representativeness of the jury is further jeopardized by the courts' generally lenient policy toward "no-shows," excuses and deferments. For the nation as a whole, one author estimates the "no-show" rate around 55 percent (Adler, 1995). Although anyone can theoretically get a temporary postponement for "undue hardship or extreme inconvenience," certain groups may be excused permanently, if they wish. In most jurisdictions, for example, these include people who are over 70 years of age; active ministers and members of religious orders; men and women with the daily care of a child under 12 years of age; and active lawyers, law students, physicians, dentists, and registered nurses. Also excused are people who are engaged in teaching, supervisory, and administrative positions in schools and colleges, and those who are sole proprietors of a business. Elected public officials and members of the armed forces and fire and police departments are also exempted, as are those who can convincingly demonstrate that their presence is required in a particular business or occupation. In New York State, more than 20 occupations are exempted from jury duty including optometrists, podiatrists, embalmers, and people who fit artificial limbs (*New York Times*, 1995:A18) in spite of recent attempts to reduce the number of exemptions for professions (Rohde, 1998). There is also a trend to reduce the size of the jury in the wake of a 1970 Supreme Court ruling that the Constitution does not require that the jury be made up of 12 people. For other than capital offenses, Arizona allows an eight-member jury and Florida allows six, and other states are considering similar reductions (Hoffman, 1995).

As a result, jury panels are more likely to be composed of people who have the time or can (or want to) take time off from the place of employment. In many occupations and professions, the prospect of being absent for a prolonged period (average jury duty is 10 days) is not welcomed. Thus, it is not surprising that juries draw disproportionately from the lower-middle and middle classes. At the same time in a disproportionate number of cases upper- and middle-class persons are chosen as jury forepersons over lower-class persons (Deosaran, 1993). The make-up of a jury, a dozen persons randomly pulled together, is vividly described by a college professor who served as the jury foreman in a Manhattan murder trial as 12 idiosyncratic individuals thrown together in tight quarters for hours and days of sequestered deliberations—pushing civics into a realm normally reserved for extreme sports (Burnett, 2002).

Finally, there are serious concerns about the ability of jurors to comprehend the judge's instructions, which can be particularly important in capital trials (Luginbuhl, 1992) where juries making decisions must properly understand legal instructions if they are to perform their duties properly (Cho, 1994) so that they do not make up their mind about the sentence before the evidence is presented as many do (Coyle, 1995) and about their bias against business and their competence in civil cases. Studies show that jurors tend not to be biased against business, they are generally skeptical of plaintiff tort claims against businesses, they question more the motivations and actions of plaintiffs than the responsibilities of business, and they tend to be conservative, in most cases, in awarding damages (Hans and Lofquist, 1992). Regarding competence, some observers argue that many disputes are so complex that an average person is incapable of understanding either the nature of the dispute or the complicated issues involved. For example, to decide whether IBM had monopolized various markets claimed in Memorex's $900 million antitrust suit, jurors needed a detailed understanding of things like "reverse engineering," "cross elasticity of supply," and "subordinated debentures." (And just try to imagine the complexity of cyber jargon in the ongoing Microsoft antitrust cases in 2001 and 2002.) The trial lasted 96 days. The jury heard 87 witnesses and examined some 3,000 exhibits. As a result of the inability to comprehend such a multitude of complex issues, some jurors may become susceptible to appeals to their emotions or increased levels of stress may influence their disposition toward the case (Hafemeister and Ventis, 1994; Whittemore and Ogloff, 1995). Some commentators would limit the role of jurors and even eliminate juries in civil cases. Others assert that, to the contrary, juries generally do grasp the facts (Corboy, 1975:186–187), and data from hundreds of jury trials and jury simulations show that actual incompetence is a rare phenomenon (Hans and Vidmar, 1986:129). Further, in a report by the *New York Times* (2001) on a comprehensive study (as yet unpublished) of nearly 9,000 trials across the country, it was noted that judges award punitive damages as often as juries and generally in about the same proportion suggesting that juries may be far less arbitrary, irresponsible and incompetent than is widely believed. This study is expected to be controversial not only because it concludes that jurors may be more rational than they were believed to be, but also because it contradicts other research.

By way of constructive measures to increase the still debated jury competence, some researchers encourage note taking by jurors, allowing them to ask questions during the proceedings (Dilworth, 1995; Penrod and Heuer, 1997) and structuring cases around specific themes with strong jury appeal such as family or work which are presented with a minimum of legal language (Baum, 1994).

The Flow of Litigation

Several characteristics of the flow of litigation are significant. The processes by which cases are decided differ widely according to the type of dispute, the participants involved, and the stage of the judicial process at which the dispute is settled. In many instances, civil and criminal cases are quite different, and I shall review them separately.

Criminal Cases   A high degree of discretion is characteristic of every phase of criminal prosecution (see, for example, Stolzenberg, and D'Alessio, 2002). The process begins with an alleged crime and the arrest of the suspect. At this point, the police may or may not exercise the option of arresting the lawbreaker, as, for example, in cases of a traffic violation, prostitution, public drunkenness, or gambling. Once an arrest is made, however, the next step is to file charges against the prisoner and to set the amount of bail. Most defendants do not plead guilty at the time of arrest. Bail is simply a method to assure the court that the defendant will appear for later proceedings. Again, at this stage, judges can exercise a great deal of discretion in setting the amount of bail, which frequently results in many defendants having to wait in prison for trial. Individuals who are unable to pay their bail suffer consequences, such as being treated like convicted prisoners, spending a long time in jail before the case is decided (where some 21 percent of the prisoners report at least one episode of forced sexual contact and 7 percent claim that they have been raped since being incarcerated) (Lewin, 2001a:14), and losing their jobs while in prison, thus forfeiting their chances for probation— all of which makes it difficult for them to prepare a defense. The poor are very much at a disadvantage in this respect. In New York City, for example, a study showed that 25 percent of those arrested could not come up with the $25 that would have enabled them to be set free on bail before trial (President's Commission on Law Enforcement and Administration of Justice, 1967:131). Further, a 1996 law barring the Federal Legal Services Corporation from financing legal aid organizations that represent prisoners reduced the number of lawyers available to litigate on behalf of the inmates (Lewin, 2001:1).

Following bail, the next step depends on the prosecutor, the defendant, and at times, the judge. Although a date is set for a trial during the arraignment or preliminary hearing, only 10 percent of the cases nationwide go to trial. This is due, in part, to the inability of law enforcement agents to establish accurately the identity of the perpetrator on the basis of eyewitness testimony (Levi, 1998). The use of eyewitness identification is most prevalent in robberies. In other property crimes, such as burglaries and auto theft, the proof of identity is seldom by eyewitness. Personal crimes such as rapes and assaults usually involve parties who know each other (Loh, 1984:551).

There are four basic types of police identification practices. The first is a showup, which involves a confrontation between a suspect and a witness. It may take place either at the crime scene if the police are available or at the police station. The second is the lineup at the police station, which is basically a "multiple choice recognition test" where a witness is presented with several suspects (Tredoux, 1998). The third is a photographic identification, which may take place in either showup or lineup form. Finally, there is informal identification in the field, which may involve riding around in an unmarked police car in search of the suspect or an "accidental" encounter with him or her at the time of a bail hearing.

Following the initial identification of a suspect, the question of the accuracy of eyewitness evidence and testimony also comes up on the witness stand during a trial (Inbau et al., 1997:639–692; Kassin and Wrightsman, 1988:79–86; Williams et al., 1992). The unreliability of eyewitness identification and the fallibility of testimony on the witness stand are brought about by three general problems of human memory (Woocher, 1977). To start, the perception of an event is not merely a passive recording. People can perceive only a limited number of events at the same time, and the number remembered is even smaller. Even trained observers find it difficult to describe accurately such basic physical characteristics as height, weight, and age. Humans also find it difficult to judge time, and because of the amount and variety of activities that occur during an action-packed event such as a crime, there is a tendency to overestimate the length of time. Often, crimes take place under poor observation conditions, making subsequent recall difficult. The presence of stress and anxiety decreases perceptual abilities. As a result, witnesses often compensate for perceptual selectivity by reconstructing what has occurred from what they assume must have occurred. In essence, they state what they think should have taken place rather than what actually transpired. Finally, eyewitness accuracy is further reduced in situations of cross-racial identifications. People are poorer at identifying members of another race than of their own. For example, whites have greater difficulties recognizing black or oriental faces than they do recognizing white faces.

The second problem is that memory decays over time. People forget quickly and easily. When it comes to recall at the police station or at the witness stand, people have a tendency to fill gaps in memory by adding extraneous details so "things make sense." For example, a witness may recall an individual accurately but is completely wrong in remembering the circumstances under which he or she encountered that person. A salesperson may identify the defendant as having been in the store with the murder victim when, in reality, the defendant had been in that store on a few earlier occasions but was out of town at the time of the crime.

Finally, the way in which information is recalled from memory invariably reduces the accuracy of eyewitness testimony. The recall of witnesses is influenced by the subtle suggestions they receive under questioning by a police officer or a lawyer (Wasby and Brody, 1997). Many people also feel compelled to answer questions completely in spite of incomplete knowledge in an attempt to please their interrogators. So they rely on their imagination to supplement factual information. Lawyers are cognizant of these concerns, and try to use voir dire as a safeguard to identify and excuse prospective jurors who are unable or unwilling to critically evaluate eyewitness testimony (Narby and Cutler, 1994).

Even after positive identification of defendants, the majority of cases are settled by negotiations between the prosecutor and the defendant's lawyer. In these cases, the prosecutor is placed in a bargaining situation and may "trade" with the defendant for an admission of a lesser crime. The process is called *plea bargaining*. It can be traced back to earliest days of common law (Nasheri, 1998). There is evidence that plea bargaining was used prior to the American Civil War (Alschuler, 1995:144).

Today, in many cases involving plea bargaining, the prosecutor acts as a de facto judge and makes most of the decisions regarding the disposition of a case. If the defendant, on the advice of his or her lawyer, does not plead guilty, the person goes to trial. Contrary to popular belief, the ones who plead guilty do not, on the average, receive a lighter sentence than those who do not. It is really the criminal justice system that benefits by saving time and the expense of conducting a trial (Klein, 1984:77). Studies show that there is a growing reliance on plea bargaining, especially by federal prosecutors—in 1980, 18 percent of criminal cases handled by federal prosecutors were decided at trial; by 1987, only 9 percent ended in trials (Glaberson, 1989). Nowadays, it is estimated that roughly 90–95 percent of all criminal convictions are arrived at through plea bargaining (Palermo et al., 1998:112).

In felony convictions, for example, 91 percent of the defendants plead guilty. When a felony case does not result in a dismissal or a guilty plea and goes to trial, the chances are five in six that the defendant will be convicted (U.S. Department of Justice, March 1992:6). The growth in recent years in plea bargaining is considered a to be a sign of the increasing professionalization of the judicial system. Criminal convictions are usually upheld on appeal (Hanson and Ostrom, 1993).

Plea bargaining is not limited to criminal cases. A version of it can be found even in traffic courts. A recent investigation in the metropolitan St. Louis area discovered that accused speeders retain attorneys (who specialize in traffic cases) to get the charges "adjusted" to nonmoving offenses such as having a loud muffler or a burned-out headlight: offenses that do not result in point penalties for driving records (Osborne, 1992). Missouri drivers are allowed eight points in any 12-month period or 12 points in 18 months. A speeding conviction, depending on its severity, can cost the driver two or three points. Three speeding tickets can result in the loss of the driver's license. The city deals with about 300 traffic tickets per judge per hour. Prosecutors, who want to clear the docket, prefer plea bargaining, lawyers make money by charging about $100 to negotiate a city ticket, and the accused speeders are not faced with the loss of their driving privileges. There is a silent understanding among the plea-bargain participants that if an offender paid the lawyer, "that's punishment enough." Poor people and those who insist on pleading not guilty on their own are the ones who are likely to have their licenses suspended.

Plea bargaining, as a form of negotiated justice, is a baffling and controversial topic in the sociological literature (see, for example, Feeley, 1979; Mulcahy, 1994; Palermo, et al., 1998). There are many objections to plea bargaining, the most common being that criminals are allowed to obtain "cheap" convictions (that is, ones in which they do not pay for the real crimes they committed), that it is moving criminal justice into an administrative process rather than an adversarial one, and that it is generating cynicism about criminal justice among the accused, the system's participants, and the public at large.

In explaining the widespread use of plea bargaining, Arthur Rosett and Donald R. Cressey (1976:85–97) assert that court personnel, including prosecutors, "develop a group sense of justice," which differs from attitudes generally held in the community, and which is generally more humane and pragmatic than that of the public. They maintain that prosecutors use caseloads as their public excuse for bargaining (there is evidence that plea bargaining affects positively the courts' ability to move the felony docket efficiently [Holmes et al., 1992]) but rarely consider caseloads in deciding whether to deal with specific cases before them (such as, to prosecute on the basis of initial charges or to negotiate). The real reasons for plea bargaining, they argue, are the weaknesses in cases that could result in acquittals; the desire to adjust the charges to more reasonable levels, depending on the facts and the character of the defendant; and the desire to comply with the courthouse consensus on concepts of fairness and justice. For a typical defendant, it is often his or her own defense lawyer who initiates negotiations and urges a settlement by plea bargaining. In one study, for example, Abraham S. Blumberg (1979:223) found that over half of the 724 defendants entering guilty pleas indicated that their defense counsel first suggested the guilty plea, usually during the first or second meeting between lawyer and client. The situation is similar in other countries and in England, for example, attorneys often justify the use of plea bargaining based on their desire to avoid going to trial, their belief that most defendants are guilty and their desire to control crime (Mulcahy, 1994).

Another form of "negotiated justice" aimed at reducing a sentence is "cooperation with the Government" (Hoffman, 1992). It is becoming quite common for prosecutors, particularly in organized crime cases and extensive white-collar cases, to ask the defendant to testify against a former colleague or associate in return for a reduced sentence or, occasionally, freedom. People who profit most from informing are usually the worst offenders, and testifying has little to do with justice but a great deal to do with giving a reward for the conviction of one's associate. Often, the defendants have to gamble that prosecutors will fulfill their end of the bargain for a reduced sentence. Recent and highly publicized examples of defendant-witnesses include Michael R. Milken, who testified against former Wall Street colleagues, and Sammy Gravano, who informed against his former friend and employer, John Gotti, the convicted head of the Gambino crime family. In addition to legal questions (for example, should the judge or the prosecutor have the power to grant a "reward" for cooperation?), this practice raises some moral dilemmas, for it goes against a highly cherished American value: loyalty.

The final step in most criminal proceedings is sentencing the defendants who have been found guilty. Although sentencing decisions are made within a specific legal framework (see, for example, Savelsberg, 1992; Tonry, 1996), most jurisdictions permit the exercise of considerable discretion. The extent of judicial discretion allowed by legislation varies from state to state. As a result, the decisions handed down by judges vary within and across jurisdictions. This is the case, in particular, with white-collar crimes (Wheeler, Mann, and Sarat, 1988). Similarly, in some states, virtually no sentencing discretion is allowed in felony cases, whereas in others, judges may effectively determine not only the nature of punishment (probation, fine, or imprisonment) but also the extent of punishment (the length of a prison term).

There are five common structures for prison sentences, each illustrating a different combination of legislative provisions and judicial discretion:

(1) Both maximum and minimum terms of imprisonment are set by the judge at any point within legislative outer limits; (2) maximum terms are fixed by statute, but the judge may set a minimum at any point up to the maximum; (3) maximum and minimum terms are set by the judge, but the minimum cannot exceed some fraction, usually one-third, of the maximum; (4) the maximum term is set by the judge, but the minimum is fixed by statute; and (5) both maximum and minimum terms are fixed by statutory law allowing the judge no discretion. (Anderson and Newman, 1998)

Thus, judges do have some choice between different sentencing options for most crimes, and they tend to exercise it. Generally, the judge's decision is influenced by the recommendations of the prosecutor and probation officers. Other factors that might influence a judge's decision include the race, sex, age, and socioeconomic and criminal background of the defendant, and the type of lawyer involved (for example, privately retained or court appointed). The decision to plea-bargain is also a factor. Although legal norms set the framework for the process, they do not control whether violators will be actually subjected to these legal norms. Instead of the judge or the defense attorney, the prosecutor plays the key role in administering criminal justice. Negotiation, bargaining, and compromise play an important part in the litigation process. Consequently, in many instances, offenders consider trials dangerous because they incite the judge and the prosecutor to "throw the book" at the defendant.

Throughout the world in recent years there have been several developments in sentencing (see, for example, Tonry and Hatlestad, 1997). In the United States, they include the use of mandatory minimums, various forms of determinate sentencing such as "three strikes and you are out," truth-in-sentencing, and guidelines-based sentencing. These measures are aimed at ensuring that some time will be served for violent offenses, limiting judicial discretion in sentence variation for the same offenses, and increasing the predictability of penalties (see, for example, Stolzenberg and D'Alessio, 1997).

As a response to the growing preoccupation with violent crime, a number of states have adopted mandatory sentencing laws to fight high crime rates. These laws require a minimum amount of incarceration upon conviction and were designed for specific offenses such as rape, murder, drug trafficking, and dangerous weapons violations. Studies show that mandatory minimums have dramatically increased the number of offenders in prison and the prison terms are longer. But other than keeping offenders of the streets for a longer time—specific deterrence, which will be discussed in Chapter 5—mandatory sentencing provisions did not act as general deterrence and had no measurable impact on crime rates (O'Connell, 1995).

Other law and order initiatives such as the three-strikes and two-strikes (and you are out) sentencing measures mandating life without parole for repeaters of certain violent or drug-related crimes, first passed in Washington State in 1993 then in California in 1994, did not fare much better

(Cox, 1994; Garland, 2001; Stolzenberg and D'Alessio, 1997). They too fail to combat crime and recidivism and ignore questions of rehabilitation and reform. For example, a 2001 study by the Sentencing Project, a nonprofit research group, showed that in California, these laws had no significant effect on the state's decline in crime. In California, with three-strikes and two-strikes laws, crimes dropped 41 percent from 1993 to 1999, New York, with no such laws, showed the same decline for the same period (Lewin, 2001b). They also waste precious jail space on minor offenders (the majority of convictions at least in California are for property, drug and other nonviolent offenses), strain resources, contribute to the aging of the prison population, denigrate the independence of the judiciary and rob judges of the discretion needed to tailor sentences to offenders and their life situations (Broderick, 1994; Franklin, 1994). In recognition of these concerns, some smaller states such as Louisiana, Connecticut, Indiana and North Dakota in 2001 have quietly started to roll back some of their most stringent anticrime measures, including those imposing mandatory minimum sentences and forbidding early parole (Butterfield, 2001).

Truth-in-sentencing measures reflect continued attention to discretion and to the association between sentences and time served. Truth-in sentencing is intended to reduce the discrepancy between the sentence imposed upon those who are sent to prison and the actual time they serve. Data indicate that violent offenders released from state prisons in 1992 served 48 percent of the sentence they had received—an average of 43 months on an average sentence of 89 months (U.S. Department of Justice, 1995a).

In federal courts, the amount of discretion judges may exercise is limited by the controversial Sentencing Reform Act, which took effect on November 1, 1987 (Margolick, 1992). One of the primary objectives of the act was to eliminate the problem of unwarranted disparity—that is, that two similarly situated offenders could go into two different courtrooms, even in the same courthouse at the same time, and come out with two vastly different sentences. Under the guidelines, all crimes are ranked on a scale from 1 to 43; the greater the heinousness and severity, the higher the number. For example, murder is assigned a score of 43; hijacking, 38; and blackmail, 9. The base score is affected by a variety of aggravating and mitigating circumstances, such as acknowledgment of guilt and cooperation with the government. Since the instrumentation of the guidelines, the range of sentences has been noticeably reduced. Critics complain, however, that it is difficult to master the complex guidelines (with amendments, the manual is three inches thick), and at times it can be tricky. For instance, robbery has a base score of 20. But if a post office or a bank is robbed, the score goes up to 22. If a weapon was fired, it rises 7 more; if a gun was merely "used," it goes up by 6, and if the gun was "brandished, displayed or possessed," by 5. In spite of these and other criticisms, the act is working by reducing and checking the power of judges and effectively eliminating what was sardonically referred to as a "system of roulette" in sentencing. It also filters out variations based on the philosophies of particular judges and probation officers, docket pressures in some courts, and other criteria, such as race, sex, and socioeconomic background of the defendant, that have been considered decisive in the literature (see, for example, Albonetti, 1992). Not surprisingly, there is widespread dissatisfaction among federal judges with the sentencing guidelines and they loath to have much of their discretion in sentencing taken away (Reske, 1994).

Civil Proceedings

In civil cases, a dispute reaches the court when it is filed by the plaintiff's attorney. The attorney generally has the option to choose a court based on a number of considerations, such as the quality and known biases of judges, the delay that may be expected in hearing a case, and the relative convenience of the court for the litigant (Jacob, 1984:213–215). Generally, the litigant has little voice in the selection of courts. It is left to the attorney who handles the case.

Just as in the case of criminal proceedings, bargaining governs negotiating settlements in civil courts. For example, in personal injury cases, plaintiffs who are represented by lawyers usually win a greater settlement than those who attempt to handle their own negotiations (Ross, 1980). Courts are often instrumental in expediting the settlement of cases through pretrial conferences. At times, the judge may even suggest a particular amount that seems reasonable, based on his or her experience with similar cases.

If a satisfactory settlement cannot be reached, the case goes to trial. Only a small proportion of cases that are filed end up in trial. In some types of cases, such as automobile accidents, the plaintiffs generally prefer a jury trial in anticipation of a larger settlement.

At times, disputes are settled before civil cases that go to trial, and, in such instances, the trial is used to legitimize the outcome. This is particularly true in divorce suits. In such cases, a separation agreement has been reached by husband and wife, and then the wife generally takes action in court to formalize and legitimize the agreement.

LEGISLATURES

To begin the study of the organization of legislatures, we first need to look at what they do. A legislature is defined as a collection of individuals who are elected as members of the formal parliamentary bodies prescribed by national and state constitutions. The functions of the legislature, at both the federal and the state levels, are numerous. Of course, the hallmark of legislative bodies is their lawmaking function, and part of the next chapter will be concerned with how this function is carried out. Yet, lawmaking takes up only a portion of the legislature's time. Legislative bodies are also engaged in conflict and integrative functions.

Conflict-Management Functions   Although conflict management is part of both the administrative and the judicial subsystems, the legislature may be distinguished by the extent to which compromise, as a mode of conflict management, is institutionalized in the system. The emphasis is on conflict management rather than on conflict resolution for, in a sense, few political decisions are final (Boulding, 1956:103).

The conflict-management functions of legislative bodies can be seen in the context of their deliberative, decisional, and adjudicative activities (Jewell and Patterson, 1986:5–10). Frequently, legislative bodies deliberate without arriving at a decision or taking action. However, the deliberation process itself and the rules under which it takes place contribute to the reconciliation of divergent interests. In addition to formal debates, deliberation is carried on in the hearing rooms, in the offices of legislators, or in the lobbies or cloakrooms surrounding the chambers. At times, these informal deliberations are more important, for they provide an opportunity to incorporate a variety of viewpoints and interests.

Some adjudicative activities are routinely undertaken by legislative bodies and the principles of dispute resolution currently being applied in the judicial system also benefit the legislators (Melling, 1994). For example, the work of some legislative committees has been adjudicative, as when hearings before investigating committees have been, in effect, trials during the course of which sanctions have been applied. A most celebrated and classic illustration of the application of sanctions by the Senate for the violation of its norms is that of the late Senator Joseph McCarthy. As chairperson of the Permanent Subcommittee on Investigations of the Committee on Government Operations, McCarthy engaged in a communist witchhunt during 1953 and 1954, which focused mainly on the Department of State and the U.S. Army. In December 1954, the Senate voted to censure McCarthy for his conduct—not for indiscriminately accusing people of being communists and abusing the investigatory powers of Congress, but for attacking the integrity of the Senate itself.

Integrative Functions   Legislative bodies contribute to the integration of the polity by providing support for the judicial and executive systems. They provide this support through authorization, legitimization, and representation (Jewell and Patterson, 1986:10). A characteristic of any constitution is the specific delegation of authority to different components of government. In the United States, the legislative branch is given various kinds of authority over the executive branch. Perhaps the most important of these is the budgetary process through which legislative bodies authorize a particular agency or body to collect taxes and disburse funds. Legislative bodies also authorize the courts to establish jurisdiction, to create their organizational machinery, and to qualify their members. Moreover, legislatures oversee bureaucratic activities and attempt to balance them against prevailing special interests in a community.

The integrative functions are also promoted through legitimization of activities. Legislative actions are considered by most people as legitimate. For example, when Congress gives the IRS permission to collect more taxes, their exercise of authority is legitimized in the process, and the IRS has the right as well as the power to collect more taxes.

The Organization of Legislatures

Because of the similarities in organizational patterns, I shall consider the federal and state legislative bodies together. Congress consists of two separate bodies—the Senate and the House of Representatives. These two bodies differ in several respects and are eager to protect their privileges and power. The House members are apportioned among the states on the basis of population. After each census, the apportionment of representatives among the states normally changes: States with the fastest-growing populations gain representation, and those with little or no population growth or with declining populations lose representation. United States Senators are not affected by apportionment or districting. Each state is entitled to two senators. Unlike the situation in the House, where members come up for election at the same time, Senate terms are staggered, so that only one-third of the Senate is up for election every two years, which ensures a greater continuity of both formal and informal organizational arrangements.

Herbert Asher (1973) points out that behavior in both the Senate and the House is influenced by a set of informal rules and norms: (1) Newcomers to the legislative body serve a period of apprenticeship in which they accept their assignments, do their homework, and stay in the background while learning their jobs; (2) members become specialists in the work of the committees to which they are assigned; (3) members avoid personal attacks on each other; (4) members are willing to reciprocate by compromising and trading votes (supporting each other's proposals) when possible; and (5) legislators do nothing that will reflect adversely upon the integrity of the legislative body and Congress as a whole. The same informal norms and rules operate in state legislatures.

Avoidance of personal disputes, restriction of full participation in the legislative process to senior members, and the norm of reciprocity all function to minimize conflict within legislative bodies. The emphasis on specialization provides Congress with the opportunity to deal with the increasingly complex issues it must consider, though specialization may also create some organizational problems. In general, House members are more likely than Senators to specialize in the work of the committees on which they serve.

Senators, on the other hand, are more apt to draw the attention of the media and have presidential ambitions. This is due in part to the length of time they are elected to serve. The norm of protecting the integrity of the legislative body may, and often has, led to controversy between the Senate and the House, and between Congress as a whole and the president.

Participants in the Legislative Process

The legislative process encompasses a variety of participants. In this section, I have chosen to give attention to three sets of participants who are particularly relevant to legislative activity: legislators, executives, and lobbyists. These three sets of participants in the legislative process are examined separately.

Legislators   Who are the legislators who make laws? Are legislatures composed of men and women who represent a cross-section of the population? What groups are "overrepresented" and "underrepresented" in the legislature? Social scientists have carried out a number of investigations on the social origins and occupational backgrounds of political decision makers. A few of these studies have focused on legislators. In spite of substantial gaps in factual knowledge about legislative personnel, certain generalizations about the individuals who serve as legislators can be made.

Most legislators come from a middle-class or an upper-class background. A recent survey on the characteristics of legislators of the 1990s, based on 900 state lawmakers in 16 states, reveal that lawmakers have an average age of 50 years, 83 percent are married (as contrasted to 42 percent of the general population), have 2.4 children, are well educated and successful with a much higher than average income. They are predominantly males (70 percent) and white (89 percent). The average legislator was reared in a comfortable, stable family which provided a strong work ethic and values (Woo, 1994).

Contrary to popular beliefs, legislators are not representative of the population at large, and obviously not all citizens have an equal chance to be elected to legislative office. As a group, legislators have a much higher educational attainment than the general population. In part, this high educational level can be accounted for by their relatively high social origins. Protestant Anglo-Saxon males are substantially overrepresented among legislators. And the situation was similar in 2001 in the national legislatures of European Union nations (Daley, 2001). Women, blacks, and foreign-born Americans are conspicuously underrepresented. The religious composition of most state legislatures and both houses of Congress is predominantly Protestant (Ornstein et al., 1990:32–36).

The recruitment of legislators is very selective by occupational status. By and large, those in the professional and business occupations dominate the legislative halls in the United States at both the state and the national levels. The most obvious fact about the occupations of legislators is that lawyers are predominant (Ornstein et al., 1990:20–31). Well over one-half of the members of Congress are lawyers, and overrepresentation is also found at the state level, where they account for 20 percent of legislators. Although lawyers remain the largest occupational group among legislators, the profession's "share" of state legislative seats decreased by 6 percent since 1966. The president of the American Bar Association considers this decline a "bad sign"; in his words, "I don't think it's good for the country, and I don't think it's good for the profession" (Slonim, 1980:30). Those who echo this highly debatable view believe that the absence of a large number of lawyers "bodes ill for the quality of legislation," because lawmaking by laypeople lends itself to ambiguity.

In addition to lawyers, it is common to find state legislatures in which over one-third of the members are businesspeople. Those engaged in the insurance business, real estate, and banking and investment are particularly numerous. In the less urbanized states of the Midwest and the South, legislators engaged in farming are likely to be about as numerous as those engaged in either business or law. Farmers, however, are not often elected to Congress. Educators account for a small fraction of state legislators, and women are significantly underrepresented at both the federal and the state levels.

From the preceding discussion, it is evident that no legislature comes close to representing a cross-section of the population it serves. The political system inevitably has built-in biases, numerous devices for the containment of minority-group aspirations for office and for the advancement of dominant segments of the population. Some groups win often, others lose often.

The Executive   There are three main functions for the president and the governors in the legislative process. First, they serve as a source of ideas for the programs that legislative bodies consider; second, they function as catalytic agents; and third, they instrument the law.

Although the extent of executives initiating ideas for legislative programs varies among the states, and certainly between the state and national levels, in most instances executive recommendations are the principal items on the legislators' agenda. Legislative recommendations emerge from individual cabinet departments or from agencies and are sent to the president far in advance of presentation to Congress. The presidential initiative is a permanent and ubiquitous feature of the legislative process (see, for example, Jones, 1994).

The president and the governors also function as catalytic agents in the legislative process. They not only offer programs but also strive to structure support, both directly within legislative bodies and indirectly through interest groups, party leaders, and other political activists. They are also greatly concerned with the manipulation of public opinion.

The instrumentation of law constitutes a third executive contribution to the legislative process. The legislative process seldom ends when the executive has signed a bill into law. In many instances, the enactment of a law is not the most important step in making public policy. Much legislation is phrased in general terms to apply to a diversity of concrete situations. Law is interpreted and given new dimensions as it is applied under the direction of the executive. An awareness of the relationships between law instrumentation and lawmaking is reflected in legislative eagerness to oversee administrative behavior.

Lobbyists   Organizations and groups that attempt to influence political decisions that might have an impact on their members or their goals are called interest groups. Whom do interest groups represent? At the most general level, the interest-group system in the United States has a distinct bias favoring and promoting upper-class and predominantly business interests. Interest groups are usually regarded as self-serving—with some justification (Rozell and Wilcox, 1999). The very word "interest" suggests that the ends sought will primarily benefit only a segment of society. Still, not all the groups that attempt to influence legislative bodies profit directly such as large corporations or industry associations. There are quite a number of groups that claim to represent the public, such as the Sierra Club and the League of Women Voters or identified with causes that are deemed progressive such as consumer advocates, homeless advocates, children's advocates, gay rights advocates, animal rights advocates and so on (Seligman, 1995). [Note that the word "advocate" sounds much better than "lobbyist."] Other groups represent foreign governments, small or medium-size political groups, public and private universities, and various charitable organizations (Hopkins, 1992).

The legislative bodies are the natural habitat of political interest groups. These interest groups enter the legislative process through their lobbying activities. Lobbyists are individuals who are paid to try to influence the passage or defeat of a legislation. Lobbying is considered a professional undertaking, and full-time experienced lobbyists are considered essential by most interest groups. It is estimated that in Washington alone, as many as 4,500 groups are represented by lobbyists covering a wide range of activities such as labor, education, business, health, welfare, banking, and farming. There are over 17,000 registered lobbyists, or about 34 for each member of Congress, including 128 former members of Congress (Abramson, 1998:A22). They collectively spend over $2 billion a year in an effort to influence lawmakers although this figure is likely to decrease due to a recent Senate rule (based on voluntary compliance) forbidding senators, their aides and other Senate officers to accept privately paid travel to "recreational" events, gifts or meals in excess of $50.00, or more than $100.00 worth of gifts and meals from any person in a year (Clymer, 1995).

This is in addition to the 4,618 PACs—political action committees (groups that are not affiliated directly with a candidate or a political party)—whose annual expenditures are well in excess of $0.5 billion (Salant and Cloud, 1995). If these figures sound a bit excessive, recall that the average amount spent by a winning candidate for a seat in the House of Representatives is around $556,000 and the average cost of a seat in the U.S. Senate is over $4 million (Coleman, 1998:32; *Time,* 1994). And once again, the Senate resurrected a bill, which was buried in a series of procedural votes for about a year, to overhaul the nation's campaign finance laws. There are no signs that it will pass (Schmitt, 1998).

The lobbyist plays a variety of roles in the legislative process. As a contact person, the lobbyist's time and energies are devoted to walking the legislative halls, visiting legislators, establishing relationships with administrative assistants and others of the legislator's staff, cultivating key legislators on a friendship basis, and developing contacts on the staffs of critical legislative committees. As a campaign organizer, the lobbyist gathers popular support for his or her organization's legislative program. As an informant, the lobbyist conveys information to legislators without necessarily advocating a particular position. Finally, as a watchdog, the lobbyist scrutinizes the legislative calendars and watches legislative activity carefully. This way, the lobbyist can be alert to developments in the legislative bodies that might affect client groups (Jewell and Patterson, 1986).

Large-scale lobbying efforts directed toward the enactment or defeat of certain legislations are omnipresent features at both the state and the federal levels (Abramson, 1998; Godwin, 1988:73–100; Mahood, 1990:52–81). In all probability, a professional lobbyist will be an ex-congressperson, an ex-senator, an ex-governor, or a former government employee who once occupied a high position in the administration and, ideally, still living up to the "highest standards of probity" (to borrow a term from the British Parliament) to maintain credibility. Lobbying groups are willing to pay dearly, for example, for the services of an experienced ex-senator or House member, particularly a former chairman or senior member of a top committee. And there is no shortage of them. Twenty-two percent of Senators and Representatives who left Congress in the 1990s are listed in the 1998 edition of *Washington Representatives,* a directory of lobbyists. Overall, 12 percent of those who left Congress since 1970 are listed (Abramson, 1998:A22).

What these groups are buying, by and large, are prestige and access to the inner sanctum of government. In Washington especially, an ex-lawmaker has privileges that set him or her apart from other lobbyists—including access to the House and Senate chambers, members' private dining rooms, gymnasiums, and swimming pools. But there are some restrictions. A former senator who is a registered lobbyist must wait a year before visiting the Senate for the purpose of influencing his former colleagues. The

House has no such rule but forbids a former member to enter the chamber if he or she has an interest in an issue that is being debated. Still, there is really not much to prevent a lawmaker-turned-lobbyist from making his or her pitch elsewhere (Baker, 1995:151–170).

Supplementing his or her personal efforts, the lobbyist often turns to public relations firms to stir up grass-roots sentiment. As a result, a stream of phone calls, letters, and cables will deluge the offices of legislators. The efforts of the National Rifle Association (NRA) (see, for example, Spitzer, 1995), American Association of Retired Persons (AARP), or the tobacco industry (Abramson, 1998), among many other organizations, are illustrative of these practices. Contributions in conjunction with these efforts can also be discreetly used among certain legislators to muster support when needed.

At times, however, a "discreet contribution" may turn out to be outright bribery in an attempt to buy political favors in the form of special bills, the right vote on a particular piece of legislation, or assistance in winning government contracts. But bribery can lead to criminal prosecution of political figures, and 42 percent of the criminal indictments against congressional office holders since 1940 involved some sort of bribery charges A most notorious example of this was the FBI's sting operation known as ABSCAM. Agents posed as representatives of an alleged Arab sheik who wanted some Washington favors. Eight officials were persuaded to sponsor special bills or use their influence in the government in return for cash or other rewards. One senator was given stock certificates in a bogus titanium mine for his assistance in obtaining government contracts. Another representative was videotaped stuffing $20,000 in his pocket. Those involved in ABSCAM were convicted of various crimes and given fines and prison terms (Coleman, 1998:45). Fortunately, most lobbyists do not resort to such extreme and illegal measures as outright bribery, nor do they wish to test the limits of politicians' resistance to temptation. But lobbyists often give small personal presents, free samples of company products such as perfume, and free meals at expensive restaurants to create a receptive climate for their efforts.

There are several types of lobbying efforts and techniques that are deployed with varying degrees of efficiency, depending on the cause. First, there are activities directed at influencing legislation during the electoral process by supporting the election of a person to the legislative body whose program one favors. Second, there are activities directed at influencing legislation by "educational work." If one happens to oppose a particular legislative action, one can substitute the phrase "educational work" for "propaganda work." The educational propaganda may be specifically directed toward a particular bill, or it may be directed only at the establishment of a political or an economic philosophy that will condition subsequent legislation (Ripley, 1988:272–273).

ADMINISTRATIVE AGENCIES

Like the study of legislation, the investigation of regulatory and administrative agencies has been neglected by legal sociologists, who tend to focus their attention primarily upon courts and litigations. As a result, there is a paucity of research and theorizing on administrative and regulatory bodies in the sociological literature (Tomasic, 1985:111). These agencies deal with an important sociological process, *social control,* which is a leading concern in the study of law and society. This section will describe the context within which that control is exercised. In the United States government in the twentieth century, the most striking development was the growth and multiplication of administrative agencies and the extension of their power and activities (Calvi and Coleman, 1997; Cann, 2001). Today, numerous local, state, and federal administrative agencies have a tremendous impact on our lives. They are often called "the fourth branch of government." On the federal level, there are some 50 agencies in Washington alone (Weidenbaum, 1979:15). The average state probably has more than 100 administrative agencies with powers of adjudication or rulemaking or both (Davis, 1975a:8). Individuals are much more directly and much more frequently affected by the administrative process than by the judicial process. The pervasiveness of the effects of just the federal administrative process and the ubiquitousness of the government can quickly be appreciated by considering the following hypothetical scenario (see, for example, Seib, 1995).

A typical couple is awakened by the buzz of an electric clock or perhaps by a clock radio. This marks the beginning of a highly regulated existence. The clock or radio that wakes them up is run by electricity provided by a utility company, regulated by the Federal Energy Regulatory Commission and by state utility agencies. They listen to the weather report, generated by the National Weather Service, part of the Commerce Department. When they go into the bathroom, they use products, such as mouthwash and toothpaste, made by companies regulated by the Food and Drug Administration (FDA). The husband might lose his temper trying to open a bottle of aspirin that has the child-proof cap required by the Consumer Product Safety Commission (CPSC). In the kitchen, his wife reaches for a box of cereal containing food processed by a firm subject to the regulations of the United States Department of Agriculture (USDA) and required to label its products under regulations of the Federal Trade Commission (FTC). The husband, who is conscious of his weight, uses an artificial sweetener in his coffee. Since the banning of cyclamates by the FDA, he has switched to saccharine, but he is worried because that, too, is on the FDA's proposed ban list. Obviously, it does not help his ulcer.

As they get in their car to go to work, they are reminded by a buzzer to fasten the seat belts, compliments of the National Highway Traffic Safety Administration. They paid slightly more for the car than they wanted to, because it contains a catalytic converter and other devices stipulated by the Environmental Protection Agency (EPA). They also pay more for gas, because the car can use only unleaded gasoline, another government requirement. On the way to work, they drive at speeds regulated by state and municipal ordinances and subject to the federally mandated sixty-five miles per hour speed limit. They listen to the car radio, which is regulated by the Federal Communications Commission (FCC), as is the telephone that they use at home or at their place of work. Our typical wife works in an office, and during the course of the day she provides information about the financial activities of her company to the Securities and Exchange Commission (SEC), and she is also likely to fill out a variety of statistical forms for the Bureau of the Census. She finds out in the office that she has lost her retirement benefits; the small company where she works recently terminated its pension plan because of the onerous requirements imposed by the Internal Revenue Service (IRS) and the Department of Labor under the Employee Retirement Income Security Act (ERISA).

In the meantime, the husband begins his work in the factory under conditions negotiated by his union, which was chosen after a lengthy strike in an election supervised by the National Labor Relations Board (NLRB). The equipment he uses in his job and in the lavatory must meet the requirements of the Occupational Safety and Health Administration (OSHA). The material he uses at work was shipped to his company under the guidelines of the Interstate Commerce Commission (ICC) for rail and truck, the Civil Aeronautics Board (CAB) for air, and the Federal Maritime Commission for sea. One of their outside contractors is late for a meeting because FAA prohibits airplanes to take off without an ashtray in the lavatory—even on non-smoking flights. The search for a replacement ashtray delayed the TWA flight by 90 minutes (*St. Louis Post-Dispatch*, 2001).

They take off time from work to negotiate a mortgage on the house they are buying with financing from a savings and loan association regulated by a Federal Home Loan Board (FHLB) with a guarantee by the Federal Housing Administration of the Department of Housing and Urban Development (HUD). They also plan to go to a commercial bank (regulated by the Federal Reserve System) to get a loan for the furniture they will need. On the way home, they stop for a hamburger, which is the subject of 41,000 federal and state regulations, many of those stemming from 200 laws and 111,000 precedent-setting court cases (*U.S. News & World Report*, 1980:64).

At home, they decide to watch commercial television, the programming and advertising of which are regulated by the Federal Communications Commission. They light up a cigarette with a package label mandated by the Surgeon General in the Department of Health and Human Services. But they have to cut their television watching short because of a letter they have received from the Internal Revenue Service questioning their tax return for the previous year. After a while, the husband decides to clean his shotgun, regulated by the Alcohol, Tobacco, and Firearms Bureau of the Treasury Department. He has yet to find out that these regulations cost every consumer thousands of dollars a year.

The Organization of Administrative Agencies

Administrative agencies are authorities of the government other than the executive, legislative, and judicial branches, created for the purpose of administering particular legislation. They are sometimes called commissions, bureaus, boards, authorities, offices, departments, administrations, and divisions. They may be created by legislative acts, by executive orders authorized by statutes, or by constitutional provisions. The powers and functions of an agency are generally contained in the legislation that created it (Breyer and Stewart, 1998:6–9).

At the federal level, all the agencies derive their power from Congress, which created them under its constitutional authority to regulate interstate commerce. Congress long ago began delegating this authority when it became clear that the job was too complex and technical to be handled entirely by legislation in the amount of time available and with the limited expertise of the lawmakers. As economic activity became more complex, legislative bodies were unable or unwilling to prescribe detailed guidelines for regulation. Traditional agencies of government could no longer regulate big business (Friedman, 1986:441). Agencies were established and given considerable discretion in determining the applicability of often vaguely written legislation to specific situations such as mass transport and communication. These agencies were expected to provide certain advantages over the courts in the instrumentation of public policy. These advantages included speed, informality, flexibility, expertise in technical areas, and continuous surveillance of an industry or an economic problem.

In general, administrative agencies were created to deal with a crisis or with emerging problems requiring supervision and flexible treatment. For example, when Congress decided in the nineteenth century not to permit railroads to operate without close public control, it established, in 1887, the Interstate Commerce Commission—the first federal independent regulatory agency. Its assignment was to supervise the railroads to guarantee cheap, safe service and rates that would be fair to small towns all across the country. The phenomenal development of radio, with its concomitant crowding of airwaves, brought about the creation of the Federal Radio Commission—the forerunner of today's Federal Communications Commission. This agency was charged with allocating licenses to stations to be operated "in the public interest." More recently, when environmental issues became a serious national concern, two agencies—the Council on Environmental Quality, and the Environmental Protection Agency—were established.

There is substantial variation in the responsibilities, functions, and operations of the various agencies. Some, such as the Environmental Protection Agency and the Federal Trade Commission, are concerned with only a few activities of a large number of firms (Harris and Milkis, 1989), and others, such as the Interstate Commerce Commission, oversee a great many matters involving a relatively small number of firms (in this case, transportation). Many agencies in the first category have the official mission of protecting the interests of the general public in regard to health, safety, and activities in the marketplace. Most of the agencies in the second category are expected not only to perform public protection functions but also to safeguard and promote the health of specific occupations, industries, or segments of the economy subject to their jurisdiction.

Administrative agencies are just as subject to pressures of interest groups as are all other policymakers (Rozell and Wilcox, 1999). Although many of the agencies were originally established in response to protests by various consumer groups against dangerous practices by various industries, their orientation has changed over the years. The agencies gradually shifted their orientation and became the "captive" of the groups they were supposed to regulate. Often appointees were (and still are) selected from the very industries that the agencies were created to regulate. Agency heads frequently take high-level jobs in such industries after finishing their governmental service. There have also been frequent revelations of agency heads fraternizing with representatives of regulated industries and of their willingness to accept favors, such as industry-paid vacations. For these reasons, critics have often pointed out that some high-level agency members seem more interested in protecting the interests of airlines, drug companies, trucking firms, stockbrokers, and other industries that they are supposed to regulate than in protecting the interests of the public (Schwartz, 1959).

The activities of the Interstate Commerce Commission illustrate this tendency. Originally, it was set up to protect consumers against predatory practices by the railroad monopolies. By 1920, the agency was almost solely responsive to the railroads, against the interests of consumers, and against other forms of interstate transportation. In case after case, the ICC's rulings benefited the railroads. More recently, the ICC has struck a balance between the interests of railroads and trucking companies, but the interests of consumers are still virtually ignored. Witness, for example, the progressive discontinuation of passenger-train services.

Administrative agencies have also been criticized by conservatives as being uncontrollable monsters that threaten the civil liberties of businesspeople and the proper functioning of the economic system (Weidenbaum, 1979). In a somewhat contradictory fashion, conservatives have also depicted regulatory agencies as inefficient, bungling bureaucracies that do little more than waste the taxpayers' money. Liberals have often been able to muster enthusiasm over the creation of new agencies but have become disappointed with their performance. Agencies are often seen by liberals as becoming the captive of the regulated, and thus unwilling to pursue their public-interest obligations. At this juncture, it is interesting to note the differences in attitudes toward regulatory agencies in the United States and Japan. Public trust of agencies is high in Japanese society. Citizens believe that social order can be maintained and progress facilitated by administrative agencies and that public administrators are honest, free from corruption, serve the public, and loyal and competent in carrying out their technical responsibilities. In the United States, by contrast, there is endemic distrust of regulatory agencies reinforced by the impression that administrators have failed to solve a phalanx of complex social, economic and environmental problems (Jun and Muto, 1995).

On an ideological level, governmental regulation has also been controversial because it raises questions regarding the proper role of government in the economy. The conservative of the "free enterprise" position has generally called for a hands-off policy by government in regulating economic activity. According to this view, the same protections against regulation are to be given to corporations. The pursuit of business profits, moreover, is seen by economic conservatives as being in the best interests of the general public. We are all familiar with the cliché "What is good for General Motors is good for the country." Liberals, by contrast, are more likely to seek restrictions on the rights of businesspeople or corporations to protect what they consider to be the important rights of workers, consumers, and the general public. Perhaps a case could be made that the public is not so much interested in *less* regulation in the abstract as they are in having *effective* regulation, and having it confined to areas where there is consensus on the need for it (Foreman, 1991:13).

The Administrative Process

Administrative agencies affect the rights of individuals and businesses by exercising powers of investigation, rulemaking, enforcement, and adjudication. This combination of functions does not conflict with the doctrine of the separation of powers, the constitutional principle that the legislative, executive, and judicial functions of government should not exist in the same person or groups of persons. Notes Freedman: "Administrative agencies were deliberately created as instruments of blended powers. In many instances they were expressly created to combine legislative, executive, and judicial powers" (1978:17). Although a wide range of powers are delegated to an agency by the Enabling Act, there are checks on its activities (see, for example, Mashaw, 1994). The creator of an agency, which is generally the legislature, retains the power to destroy it or alter the rules governing it. The judiciary retains the power of final review of the determinations of administrative agencies, but this right is, as a practical matter, rather limited. The principal administrative processes include investigation, rulemaking, and adjudication. I shall consider these separately.

Investigation   The authority to investigate is given to practically all administrative agencies. Without information, administrative agencies would not be in the position to regulate industry, protect the environment, prosecute fraud, collect taxes, or issue grants. Most administrative actions in both formal and informal proceedings are conditioned by the information obtained through the agency's prior investigation. As regulation has expanded and intensified, the agency's quest for facts has gained momentum. Some agencies are created primarily to perform the fact-finding or investigative function. The authority to investigate is one of the functions that distinguishes agencies from courts. This authority is usually exercised to perform properly another primary function, that of rulemaking.

Statutes usually grant an agency the authority to use several methods to carry out its information-gathering function. Requiring reports from regulated businesses and conducting inspections are methods of accomplishing this information-gathering task. Necessary information is often available from the staff, from the agencies' accumulated records, and from private sources. If these resources prove inadequate, the agency may seek further information by calling in witnesses or documents for examination, or by conducting searches. The authority of an agency to investigate is intertwined with the objectives of administrative investigation. The purposes of investigations vary, ranging over the entire spectrum of agency activity. For example, if an agency is responsible for enforcing a statute, its investigations may set the groundwork for detecting violations and punishing wrongdoers. To illustrate: The Labor Department may seek to inspect employers' payroll records when checking for compliance with minimum wage laws.

Congress has traditionally conferred broad investigative powers upon the agencies. Important and typical are the provisions of the Federal Trade Commission Act, empowering the commission to (1) instruct corporations to file annual or special reports and answer specific questions in writing (this may account, in part, for the fact that the federal government is using 4,987 different kinds of information-gathering forms [*Time*, 1978:26]), (2) obtain access to corporate files for examination and reproduction of their contents, and (3) subpoena the attendance of witnesses and the production of documentary evidence (Gellhorn and Levin, 1997). It would be difficult to devise a broader authorization for fact gathering.

Rulemaking   Rulemaking is the single most important function performed by government agencies (Kerwin, 1999:xi). It defines the mission of the agency and essentially involves the formulation of a policy or an interpretation that the agency will apply in the future to all persons engaged in the regulated activity. As quasi-legislative bodies, administrative agencies issue three types of rules: procedural, interpretive, and legislative. Procedural rules identify an agency's organization, describe its methods of operation, and list the requirements of its practice for rulemaking and adjudicative hearings. Interpretive rules are issued by an agency to guide both its staff and regulated parties as to how the agency will interpret its statutory mandate. These rules range from informally developed policy statements announced through press releases to authoritative rulings binding upon the agency and issued usually after a notice and hearing. Legislative rules are, in effect, administrative statutes. In issuing a legislative rule, the agency exercises lawmaking power delegated to it by the legislature.

Kenneth Culp Davis considers rulemaking one of the greatest inventions of modern government and argues that the United States is entering the age of rulemaking (Davis, 1977:241). Rulemaking is any agency process for formulating, amending, or repealing a rule, and most rulemaking falls into the "notice and comment" category. The Administrative Procedure Act requires simply that the proposed rule be announced in advance and that interested parties should be afforded an opportunity to present their views. Rulemaking generally involves policy issues (value judgments), which depend upon the agency's knowledge about current practices, the impact of the proposed rule, the need for public protection against inadequate safeguards, and the possible burden (cost) of government regulation on private or public interests.

The rulemaking process, more often than not, is lengthy and complicated. Usually a lawyer's expertise is needed to master the procedural maze and technical requirements imposed by administrative agencies. Even so, an average person may initiate and participate in the process. Unlike legislatures and courts, access to administrative agencies is often direct. No middlemen stand between agencies and their clients (Jacob, 1995).

Adjudication   Administrative agencies, of all kinds and at all levels, must settle disputes or mediate among conflicting claims. Adjudication is the administrative equivalent of a judicial trial. It applies policy to a set of past actions and results in an order against (or in favor of) the named party.

Much of this adjudication is handled informally through the voluntary settlement of cases at lower levels in an agency. At these levels, agencies dispose of disputes relatively quickly and inexpensively, and they take an immense burden off the courts. Moreover, they are handled by individuals who are experts in technical areas. But this practice is not without criticism. Many individuals—in particular, lawyers pleading cases before the agencies—have expressed concern over the extent of judicial power vested in agencies. They complain that administrators violate due process of law by holding private and informal sessions, by failing to give interested parties an adequate hearing, and by basing their decisions on insufficient evidence.

These complaints stem, in part, from the institutional differences between agency and court trials. Agency hearings, unlike court hearings, tend to produce evidence of general conditions, as distinguished from the facts relating specifically to the respondent. This distinction is due to one of the original justifications for administrative agencies—the development of policy. Another difference is that in an administrative hearing, a case is tried by a trial examiner and never by a jury. As a result, the rules of evidence applied in jury trials, presided over by a judge, are frequently inapplicable in an administrative trial. The trial examiner decides both the facts and the law to be applied. Finally, the courts accept whatever cases the disputants present. As a result, their familiarity with the subject matter is accidental. By contrast, agencies usually select and prosecute their cases. Trial examiners and agency chiefs either are experts or at least have a substantial familiarity with the subject matter, since their jurisdictions tend to be restricted.

Partly in response to these complaints and differences, the Administrative Procedure Act of 1946 was passed, providing for broader judicial review of administrative decisions. The courts have always had the power to overturn the agencies' judgments on points of law, as in cases where an agency has exceeded its authority or misinterpreted the law, or simply been unfair. Under the 1946 act, however, the courts acquired more authority to examine questions of *fact*–that is, to go over the mass of technical evidence examined by the agencies. Though this tendency has not gone far, it sheds light on the problem of maintaining the balance between judicial control and administrative expertise. Judicial review of agency activities also deals with procedural safeguards, such as more formalized hearings and proper notice of action (Edley, 1990). But the role of the courts is essentially limited to procedural matters—advising agencies, sometimes repeatedly, to go about their business in a fairer manner and to pay serious attention to all affected interests. In technical, complex disputes, courts cannot decide major issues. They will not set tariffs, allocate airline routes, or control the development of satellite communications (Breyer and Stewart, 1998).

LAW ENFORCEMENT AGENCIES

The word *police* comes from the Greek world, *polis*, meaning "city." The word also includes the idea of the city's "government," and by more modern extension that of the state. The principal functions of the police are law enforcement, maintenance of order, and community service (see, for example, Dunham and Alpert, 2001; Langworthy and Travis, 1999). Like other components of the American legal system, the origins of the American police can be traced to early English history (Novak, 1989). In the ninth century, Alfred the Great started paying private citizens for arresting offenders. The population was broken down into units of ten families or "tithings," and each person was responsible for watching over the others. Subsequently, the unit was expanded tenfold to the "hundred," and one person, designated as the constable, was in charge of maintaining order. In time, the hundred was increased to include the country-wide "shire," under the control of an appointed "shire-reeve," who later on became known as the "sheriff." The first citywide police force was created by Sir Robert Peel in London in 1829. Police officers were uniformed, organized along military lines, and called "Bobbies" after their founder. The American colonists adopted the English system of law enforcement, and the first metropolitan police force was created in Philadelphia in 1833 (Loh, 1984:276).

In 1996, the latest year for which data are available, 18,769 publicly funded state and local law enforcement agencies were operating in the United States, employing some 922,000 people (Table 3–2) (fewer than the

TABLE 3–2   Employees in State and Local Law Enforcement Agencies

By type of agency, United States, 1996

	Number of Employees					
	Full-time			Part-time		
Type of Agency	Total	Sworn	Nonsworn	Total	Sworn	Nonsworn
Number	921,978	663,535	258,433	97,770	47,712	50,058
Local police	521,985	410,956	111,029	61,453	30,976	30,477
Sheriff	257,712	152,922	104,790	22,412	10,845	11,567
State police	83,742	54,587	29,155	1,303	132	1,171
Special police	56,229	43,082	13,147	12,003	5,202	6,801
Texas constable	2,310	1,988	322	599	557	42
Percent	100%	72.0%	28.0%	100%	48.8%	51.2%
Local police	100	78.7	21.3	100	50.4	49.6
Sheriff	100	59.3	40.7	100	48.4	51.6
State police	100	65.2	34.8	100	10.1	89.9
Special police	100	76.6	23.4	100	43.3	56.7
Texas constable	100	86.1	13.9	100	93.0	7.0

Note: These data are from the Directory Survey of Law Enforcement Agencies, a census of the nation's state and local law enforcement agencies conducted in 1996. The data were collected by U.S. Department of Justice, Bureau of Justice Statistics. The Directory Survey includes all state and local agencies employing at least one sworn officer with general arrest powers and collects data on the number of sworn and nonsworn personnel employed by each agency, including both full-time and part-time employees. The pay period that included June 28, 1996 was the reference date for all personnel data. The final database includes responses from 13,578 general-purpose local police departments, 3,088 sheriff's departments, 49 primary state police departments, 1,316 special police agencies, and 738 county constable offices in Texas. Hawaii does not have a State police agency; the Hawaii Department of Public Safety primarily provides court support services.

A local police department was defined as a general-purpose police department operated by a municipal, county, or tribal government. A state police department was defined as the general-purpose state policy agency operated by the state. Included among special police agencies are both state and local agencies policing special geographic jurisdictions such as airports, parks, transit systems, public schools, colleges and universities, and public housing. Also included are agencies with special enforcement responsibilities such as those pertaining to natural resource conversation or alcoholic beverage control and special investigative units such as those operated by prosecutor's offices. Texas constables are elected officials who are responsible for serving process out of the justice, county, and district courts. About one-third of constable offices also performed law enforcement functions. Of the approximately 760 county constable offices in Texas, 738 employed sworn personnel as of June 1996.

Source: U.S. Department of Justice, Bureau of Justice Statistics, *Census of State and Local Law Enforcement Agencies, 1996*, Bulletin NCJ–164618 (Washington, DC: U.S. Department of Justice, June 1998), p. 2.

number of lawyers) and with an operating budget close to $47 billion (Maguire and Pastore, 1998:45). The largest police department is in New York City; it has over 45,000 full-time employees. Three in four departments nationwide serve a population less than 10,000. Most local police departments are in small towns; most local police officers are not. About half of all officers work in jurisdictions with a population of 100,000 or more, and one in five officers works for a department that serves 1 million or more residents. Nationwide, annual local police department expenditures are about $115 per resident served. In cities of 1 million or more, that figure is about $160. On the average, local police departments cost $58,000 per officer to operate per year. In cities over 250,000, that figure is $66,000.

The caliber of police service is determined to a great extent by personnel policy and at the intake by recruiting standards (Leonard and More, 2000:379). Only a small percentage (about 6 percent) of local police departments require new recruits to have at least some college education. About 18 percent of state police departments have such a requirement. It is interesting to note that local police departments serving fewer than 2,500 residents require an average of 400 hours of training for new officers contrasted with 1,000 hours in state and large city police departments. In most smaller departments, personnel are provided little guidance regarding professional development and personal growth, and the concept of career development is typically viewed in terms of promotion to the next higher rank (Gibbons, 1995). Table 3–3 summarizes the entrance and maximum base salaries of police officers by population groups, geographic division, and metro status as of January 1, 2001.

In the United States there is no unified system of law enforcement. As Thomas F. Adams observes:

> A police system—if one were to exist—in the United States would be a rank ordering of all the local police agencies in sequence, according to their relative importance; then higher up the scale would be placed the many state agencies, and finally a rank ordering up through all of the federal agencies to a single head or committee. Such a system does not exist in the United States. (1973:69)

In a classic and often-cited work, Bruce Smith (1960) identified five types of public law enforcement systems in the United States, conforming roughly to the major levels of government: (1) the police agencies of the federal government; (2) the state police forces and criminal investigation agencies of the 50 states; (3) the sheriffs in more than 3,000 counties, plus a few county police forces that either duplicate the sheriff's police jurisdiction or displace it; (4) the police of 1,000 cities and more than 20,000 townships or New England towns, to which must be added an unknown number of magisterial districts and county districts in the South and the West; and (5) the police of 15,000 villages, boroughs, and incorporated towns, together with a small number of special-purpose forces serving public-quasi corporations and ad hoc districts. If we add to these the law enforcement activities of private police agencies, we end up with a number of systems of law enforcement, related in their functions and at times overlapping in their jurisdictions.

In addition, within these systems are specific police agencies. Some federal agencies have law enforcement powers, such as the Federal Bureau

TABLE 3–3 Entrance and Maximum Salaries, and Mean Number of Years to Reach Maximum Salary, for Police Officers in Cities of 10,000 Persons and Over

By population group, geographic division, and metro status, United States, as of Jan. 1, 2001

Classification	Entrance salary					Maximum salary					No. of years to reach maximum	
	No. of cities reporting	Mean ($)	First quartile ($)	Median ($)	Third quartile ($)	No. of cities reporting	Mean ($)	First quartile ($)	Median ($)	Third quartile ($)	No. of cities reporting	Mean
Total	1,274	29,192	24,328	28,838	33,008	1,250	39,907	33,234	39,318	46,087	1,011	7
Population group												
Over 1,000,000	3	33,381	30,852	33,206	35,823	3	49,966	47,700	51,197	52,847	3	9
500,000–1,000,000	6	34,032	30,841	31,554	37,258	6	47,534	45,474	46,168	50,571	6	8
250,000–499,999	14	30,087	28,887	29,426	30,366	14	43,204	39,262	41,434	45,765	13	10
100,000–249,999	66	31,392	25,006	29,874	35,994	65	42,904	35,022	42,078	49,456	54	8
50,000–99,999	154	32,211	26,263	31,452	36,094	154	43,314	37,110	43,448	49,181	125	7
25,000–49,999	325	30,522	25,512	?9,979	34,340	319	41,667	35,530	41,579	47,497	265	7
10,000–24,999	706	27,639	23,082	27,316	31,653	689	37,870	31,000	36,686	44,017	545	6
Geographic division												
New England	91	30,721	27,301	30,306	33,609	89	38,233	34,299	37,117	42,432	80	5
Mid-Atlantic	150	30,745	27,058	30,274	33,648	147	48,850	41,699	47,857	55,391	137	5
East North Central	267	30,588	27,528	30,538	33,610	267	40,690	35,106	41,418	46,257	242	6
West North Central	129	27,293	23,616	27,726	30,507	128	36,994	31,539	36,803	43,192	102	7
South Atlantic	169	24,475	21,735	23,400	26,000	163	35,655	31,120	34,650	39,504	87	10
East South Central	68	22,256	20,254	21,922	23,841	68	30,128	25,269	30,168	33,875	48	10
West South Central	148	24,400	21,419	24,046	27,242	138	32,612	27,877	32,000	37,440	99	7
Mountain	76	27,870	25,149	27,452	31,254	76	39,301	34,820	40,340	44,484	55	9
Pacific Coast	176	38,163	33,491	38,286	42,318	174	48,002	43,129	48,384	53,181	161	5
Metro status												
Central	242	28,890	24,240	28,327	32,558	237	39,347	34,085	38,786	44,204	200	8
Suburban	727	31,121	26,592	30,762	34,668	718	43,164	36,652	43,657	48,563	595	6
Independent	305	24,835	21,276	24,372	27,866	295	32,428	28,301	32,316	36,461	216	7

Source: Evelina R. Moulder, "Police and Fire Personnel, Salaries, and Expenditures for 2001," in *The Municipal Year Book 2002* (Washington, DC: International City/Country Management Association, 2002), p. 122, Table 3/6.

of Investigation, the Secret Service, the Bureau of Narcotics, Post Office Inspectors, the Bureau of Internal Revenue, the Bureau of Customs, the Immigration Border Patrol, and the Alcohol Tax Unit of the Treasury Department (Adams, 1973:86-93). The federal government also maintains the U.S. marshal as a law enforcement agent, appointed by the president to a four-year term, whose duties are to preserve order in the courtrooms, handle subpoenas and summonses, seize goods, transport prisoners, and serve as a disbursing officer (Souryal, 1995).

Law enforcement at the state level was established, for the most part, at the beginning of the twentieth century. Although their jurisdictions vary from state to state, police agencies perform a myriad of varied functions, such as enforcing traffic laws, investigating fires, combating occult and cult crime (Hicks, 1991), enforcing liquor laws, arresting juvenile offenders, and inspecting property. They also assist local police agencies by providing technical expertise in criminal identification and laboratory and community services.

No review of law enforcement agencies is complete without mention of the private police (Davis, Lundman, and Martinez, 1991; Shearing and Stenning, 1987; Simonsen, 1998). Special needs of private sectors of the community require the services of private police patrols and investigation agencies. Businesses, industries, residential complexes, and others use private agencies, such as Pinkerton's Incorporated, to guard property, apprehend thieves, investigate offenses, and detect fraud and embezzlement. There are approximately 8,500 such firms in the United States, the largest 10 employing more than 30,000 employees. In the early 1990s, annual spending for private security was over $64.5 billion (*U.S. News & World Report*, 1994:13), and private security agencies employed more than 1.5 million people, almost twice as many as in public law enforcement (Munk, 1994). It is anticipated that by the year 2000, public expenditures for law enforcement will reach $44 billion; they will be dwarfed by private security expenditures, which will reach $104 billion. The average annual rate of growth in private security is 8 percent, double that of public law enforcement (Cunningham, et al., 1991:1–2). Policy expenditures represent a substantial part of the municipal budget (see, for example, Leonard and More, 2000:380–381) and many budget-conscious communities are exploring the privatization of police as a way to contain costs, and it may be a trend to watch in the years to come (O'Leary, 1994). While on the subject of money, the annual cost of crime in the United States was in excess of $700 billion in the mid-1990s (*U.S. News & World Report*, 1994:13).

Finally, many large corporations have their own private police. As an example, General Motors over two decades ago already had more than 4,200 plant guards, a police force larger than the police departments in all but the five biggest cities in the country (Friedman, 1998, 2002). As a matter of interest, it is not unusual for urban universities to have a campus police department of several hundred officers, a police force larger than that of many medium-size towns in Western Europe. The rest of this section will be devoted to the structural features of municipal police departments.

The Organization of Law Enforcement Agencies

Municipal and other police organizations have evolved in response to changes in technology, social organization and political governance at all levels of society (Carter and Radalet, 1999; Reiss, 1992). They are structured along the lines of complex bureaucratic organizations (see Figure 3–2). A variety of specific organizational tables or patterns describe how the police divide up tasks. In every case, a formal and highly complex division of labor characterizes these systems (see, for example, Wilson and McLaren, 1972). In addition to their bureaucratic characteristics, law enforcement agencies are structured like quasi-military institutions, which gives these agencies their special character. Bittner notes: "Both institutions are instruments of force and for both institutions the occasions for using force are unpredictably distributed. Thus, the personnel in each must be kept in a highly disciplined state of alert preparedness. The formalism that characterizes military organization, the insistence on rules and regulations, on spit and polish, on obedience to superiors, and so on, constitute a permanent rehearsal for 'the real thing'" (1970:53).

This system of law enforcement is built on a subordinating chain of command (Bordua and Reiss, 1966; Loveday, 1998). Although all units of a particular department may be related to a central command, the overall chain of command is divided into units so that different precincts or squads are immediately responsible to a localized authority. The functional divisions of police departments follow the kinds of activities they handle, such as traffic patrol, investigative work, undercover work (for example, in vice and narcotics), crowd control, and uniformed patrol, whose officers are popularly referred to as "cops"—which is the abbreviation of the British designation "constable on patrol."

Police departments do not require special education. Most officers entering the force have no more than a high school education, although lately some college education without any specialized training has become the norm. Police training is pragmatic and brief and usually takes place in a police academy. Most officers come from lower-middle-class or working-class backgrounds (Jacob, 1995). For many, becoming a police officer is an opportunity for upward social mobility, and in some ethnic groups, such as the Irish, there is a high proportion of family members in law enforcement.

Among police officers, there is a high degree of cohesion and solidarity, much more so than in other occupational groups (Brown, 1988). They are by virtue of occupational expectations suspicious, and tend to be skeptical toward outsiders, and much of their outlook and conduct have an authoritarian character (Bartol, 1983). Their subculture includes a code of

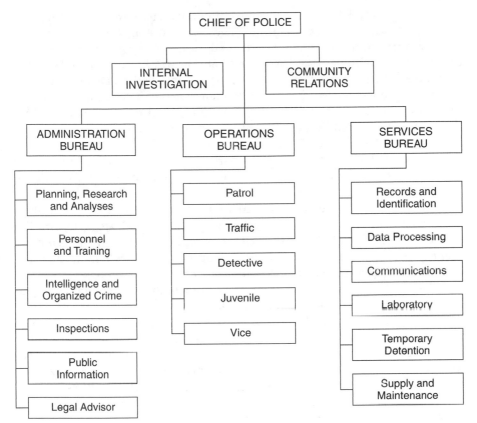

FIGURE 3–2   One form of a well-organized municipal police department.

silence, and fellow officers rarely incriminate each other. They socialize and make friends within the department, and some even conceal their police identity (Skolnick, 1994). In recent years, there has been a growing incidence of suicides among police personnel. Studies show that police suicides are caused by a variety of factors such as job stress, frustration, easy access to firearms, alcohol abuse and fear of separation from the police subculture (Violanti, 1995).

The activities of police both in the United States and in other parts of the world consist of routine patrol and maintaining order—such duties as attending to domestic disturbances, handling drunks, assisting motorists, traffic control, escorting dignitaries, and processing juveniles (Bayley, 1992: 523-527; Lyman, 1999; Skolnick and Bayley, 1988). Contrary to popular image, police officers, with the exception of detectives, spend about 20 percent of their time in criminal investigations (Brown, 1988:322).

The effectiveness of law enforcement agencies (as determined usually by arrest and clearance rates) depends on the size of the department and the way it is organized. Small departments often lack the training or equipment for proper handling of serious crimes. The experience of officers may be limited predominantly to traffic control and routine patrol, and in complex cases, the diversity in expertise is sorely absent (Glaberson, 1992). Whether or not departments are organized along professional criteria also has a bearing on their effectiveness. For example, in a study of a nonprofessionalized police department in a west coast city, James Q. Wilson (1968a) found that the nonprofessionalized department's members had no strong sense of urgency about police work and produced low rates of official actions on offenders. In the professionalized department, however, violations of the law were more likely to be detected, and offenders were more likely to be arrested, producing a higher crime rate.

In another well-known and influential study, Wilson (1968b) identified three styles of police work: the watchman style, the legalistic style, and the service style. Although elements of all three can be found in any law enforcement agency, different agencies tend to emphasize one style more than the others and, as a result, practice different law enforcement policies.

The *watchman* style emphasizes the responsibility for maintaining public order, as contrasted with traditional law enforcement (see, for example, Crank, 1994). The police officer in such an agency is viewed as a peace officer, ignoring or handling informally many violations of the law and paying much greater attention to local variations in the demand for law enforcement and maintenance of order. The role of peace officer is characterized by a great amount of discretion, since peacekeeping is poorly structured by law or by agency regulation. Underenforcement, corruption, and low arrest rates characterize watchman-style departments.

The *legalistic* style is just the opposite of the watchman style. Agencies characterized by this style tend to treat all situations, even commonplace problems of maintaining order, as if they were serious infractions of the law. Members of such agencies issue a high rate of traffic tickets, arrest a high proportion of juvenile offenders, and crack down on illicit enterprises. The police typically act as if there were a single standard of conduct rather than different standards for different groups. As a result, some groups, especially juveniles, blacks, and migrants, are more likely to be affected by law enforcement than others considered "respectable" by the police. Although this style of law enforcement is characterized by technical efficiency and high arrest rates, it also results in inequality in law enforcement, with complaints of harassment and police brutality by groups who are most often subjected to police scrutiny.

The *service* style combines law enforcement and maintenance of order. An emphasis is placed on community relations, the police on patrol work out of specialized units, and command is decentralized. The pace of work is more leisurely, and more promotional opportunities are available. This style differs from the watchman style in that the police respond to all groups and apply informal sanctions in the case of minor offenses. It differs from the legalistic style in that fewer arrests are made for minor infractions, and the police are more responsive to public sentiments and desires. In this sense, the service style is less arbitrary than the watchman style and more attuned to the practical considerations of public service than the legalistic style. There is little corruption, and complaints against police in service-style departments tend to be low. Such departments are also characterized by community-oriented policing (COP). The emphasis is on problem-solving policing where attention is focused on the problems that lie behind incidents, rather than on the incidents only (Moore, 1992; Zhao and Thurman, 1997). It aims at reducing alienation and distrust between police and minorities and between police and the poor—potentially explosive situations that can escalate a simple traffic stop into a riot. Community policing tries to improve neighborhood quality of life, involves citizens in crime fighting (in particular against drugs), and undertakes more concerted effort at crime prevention (Peak and Glensor, 1999; Thurman, et al., 2001). Although it is more expensive and labor intensive, more than 400 cities have already adopted community-oriented policing (Boyce, 1992). But the approach is not without criticisms and enthusiasm for it is being tempered by training needs, costs, and overall effectiveness (Joseph, 1994). Community policing, as a recent study contends, also colonizes community life and increases the capacity of police departments to shield themselves from criticism (Lyons, 1999).

Community policing is not limited to the United States. It is widely practiced in many European countries and it was more or less "invented" in Japan (Kristof, 1995). In Japan the police are highly respected and considered almost incorruptible. In every Japanese city, each neighborhood has its own *koban*, or police box. It is a one- or two-room office, staffed around the clock by police officers called "Honorable Walkabouts" for they spend much of their time strolling or bicycling around the neighborhood. They advise homeowners how to avoid burglaries, make teenagers rip up and throw away their cigarettes—"but in the trash can, not just on the ground"—issue a newsletter for the area, and visit homes at least once a year. The police have broad powers, they can stop people who look suspicious, they can ask them to come to the *koban* for a "discussion," to empty their pockets, or tell them to avoid the neighborhood. The police also have the right to detain people for up to three weeks for questioning, deprive them of sleep, and do their best to make them feel guilty and to confess. But despite appearances, Japanese police are much less powerful than their American counterparts—they are usually not allowed to infiltrate subversive organizations, to pay informers, tap telephones or to plea-bargain with defendants. Even though the crime rate is much lower, Japan spends a greater proportion of its GNP on the police than the United States does. New York City police, for example, have to answer more than twice as many emergency calls than the police in *all* of Japan. Adopting the Japanese style of policing in the United States would increase costs substantially. Placing police in *kobans* tends to cost more than keeping them in station houses. But Japan does have the lowest crime rate in the industrialized world and its high efficient model of policing deserves further scrutiny.

Police Discretion

A significant feature of law enforcement—indeed of the entire judicial process and the criminal justice system—is the discretionary power officials can exercise in specific situations (Gilbert, 1997). The exercise of discretion is integral to the daily routine of police officers in a large variety of activities ranging from routine traffic stops to responding to domestic violence calls (Campbell, 1999; Guyot, 1991:36–61; Kane, 1999; Williams, 1984). Police discretion is highly institutionalized in the American system of criminal justice (Reiss, 1992:74) and questions about police discretion increasingly appear in lawsuits against the police (Worrall, 1998). Albert J. Reiss and David J. Bordua (1967) point out that police discretion and disparity stem in large part from the general organization of modern police work. As a largely reactive force, primarily dependent on citizen mobilization, the police officer functions in criminal law much like a private attorney functions in civil law—determining when the victim's complaint warrants formal action and encouraging private settlement of disputes whenever possible. Among such private arrangements protected by the police are those of their own relationships with various categories of citizens, so that the degree to which formal legality is extended by police to different categories of individuals varies substantially. In view of the highly decentralized police operation, with minimal direct supervision, it is difficult to control such disparate treatment. Many of the decisions of police officers on the beat do not lend themselves to either command or review. As a result, police exercise a considerable amount of discretionary power, as reflected in disparities in the volume of arrests, parking tickets, and pedestrian stops. For example, James Q. Wilson's (1968:95) investigation of eight police agencies showed that, among other things, the arrest rates for moving traffic violations ranged from 11.4 to 247.7 per 1,000 population in the cities he studied, about the same as in the late 1990s.

Because of their discretionary power, "the police are among our most important policymaking administrative agencies. One may wonder whether any other agencies—federal, state, or local—make so much policy that so directly and vitally affects so many people" (Davis, 1975a:263). The police need to make policy with regard to nearly all their activities, such as deciding what types of private disputes to mediate and how to do it, breaking up sidewalk gatherings, helping drunks, deciding what to do with runaways, breaking up fights and matrimonial disputes, entering and searching premises, controlling juveniles, and managing race relations. The police exercise discretion in both reactive and proactive policing.

Reactive police work is a response to citizen mobilization. But even before a citizen can reach a police officer, discretionary power is exercised by police dispatchers at the communication center. A member of the dispatch crew answers the telephone call made to the police emergency number, interviews the caller to identify the nature and location of the reported problem, and decides whether to dispatch a patrol car. In a study of telephone calls to three departments, T. E. Bercal (1970) found that 20 to 40 percent of the calls are handled without dispatching a car. If the dispatcher decides to send a patrol car, the nature of the assignment (for example, burglary or robbery) and which car to assign must be determined. When a car is dispatched, the officer may informally turn down the assignment, or may procrastinate on the way, or even lie about having investigated the call (Rubinstein, 1973:87–123). If the officer follows up on the call, he or she often has to decide whether a crime has been committed. Albert J. Reiss (1971:73) found that in Chicago, whereas citizens considered 58 percent of their complaints as criminal matters, officers responding to those dispatches officially processed only 17 percent as criminal matters. One study found in domestic violence cases that over half of the offenders were gone upon police arrival (Kane, 1999:68). Harold E. Pepinsky (1976:21–22) suggests that police officers' decisions are determined mainly by the dispatcher's characterization of the incident and officers' experience with similar cases in their jurisdiction.

A great deal of police work is undertaken on the initiative of the police themselves without citizen mobilization (Reiss, 1971:88–114). The activities of traffic and tactical divisions are primarily proactive policing, as are the various nondispatched activities of detectives and vice divisions. In proactive policing, discretionary power is exercised in the context of whether or not to stop a suspicious pedestrian or automobile for investigation.

In both reactive and proactive policing, the use of discretion can take a number of forms: investigation, confrontation, disposition, and decisions about the use of force. Police officials have the option (although limited) of investigating some acts and not others. The police, for example, may elect to ignore or to actively pursue a citizen's complaint. In some cases, the police arrest a suspect, and in others—even though the act and circumstances may be similar—the individual is released. And some people are "roughed up" by the police, whereas others are handled with respect. All along the line, decisions are made by the police.

Kenneth Culp Davis (1975a:264) notes that the power of the police not to enforce the law in any particular circumstances is enormous. It can even be turned into an affirmative weapon. Jerome H. Skolnick, in *Justice without Trial* (1994), discusses an Oakland ordinance that permits holding every woman arrested for prostitution for eight days for a venereal check. The ordinance conferred no discretionary power on the police, but officers assumed a discretionary power not to enforce the ordinance against women who cooperated: They detained for testing only 38 percent of the women who were arrested. As one officer explained: "If a girl gives us a hard time . . . we'll put a hold on her. I guess we're actually supposed to put a hold on everybody, so there's nothing wrong in putting a hold on her . . . but you know how it is, you get to know some of the girls, and you don't want to give them extra trouble" (Skolnick, 1994:108). In this context, Davis (1975a:264) contends that because the ordinance requires holding every woman arrested, assumption of discretion not to enforce against 62 percent of those arrested was contrary to the terms of the ordinance. Here, discretion not to enforce was converted into an affirmative weapon: "If a girl gives us a hard time . . . we'll put a hold on her." This policy of enforcement discrim- inates against the innocent woman, because she is more likely to resist, and the experienced woman is more likely to cooperate. The discrimination appears clearly unjust.

There is, indeed, a thin line between discretion and discrimination in discretionary law enforcement. If the likelihood that an individual will be considered a criminal is dependent on the discretionary power of the police to respond to or to ignore a citizen's complaint, to arrest or to release a suspect, and the like, then the probability that any one person will be labeled a criminal increases or decreases depending on that person's cor- respondence to police conceptions of the criminal. Some individuals are more likely than others to have their behavior treated as a crime by the police and, consequently, are more likely to be labeled as criminal. For example, Nathan Goldman (1963:35–47) found that 65 percent of the black offenders arrested by the police were referred to the juvenile court, as con- trasted with 34 percent of the white youths apprehended. Similarly, Donald J. Black and Albert J. Reiss (1970:68) found that 21 percent of black teenagers, but only 8 percent of the white youths, encountered by the police were arrested. Although evidence is sketchy, there is reason to assume that young adults, poor citizens, minority members, migrants, and individuals who look disreputable by police standards are more likely to experience one or another form of police brutality and to be arrested than are more "respectable" citizens. They also tend to be less deferential toward officers, and in general, the police are likely to sanction suspects who fail to defer to police authority, whether legal grounds exist or not (Black, 1980:77).

Police discretion not to enforce the law is attributed to a number of conditions. These include the police belief that (1) the legislative body does not desire enforcement, (2) the community wants nonenforcement or lax enforcement, (3) other immediate duties are more urgent, (4) the offenders promise not to commit the act again, (5) there is a lack of adequate police manpower, (6) there is sympathy with the violator, (7) a particular criminal act is common within a subculture, (8) the victim is likely to get restitution without arrest, (9) nonenforcement can be traded for information, (10) the probable penalty is likely to be too severe, and (11) the arrest would unduly harm the offender's status (Davis, 1975a:264–265).

But as Kenneth Culp Davis (1975b:140) emphatically argues: "Police discretion is absolutely essential. It cannot be eliminated. Any effort to eliminate it would be ridiculous. Discretion is the essence of police work, both in law enforcement and in service activities. Police work without discretion would be something like a human torso without legs, arms, or head." Selective enforcement represents low-visibility interaction between individual officers and various citizens. The exercise of discretion is not guided by clear policy directives, nor is it subject to administrative scrutiny. For such reasons, selective enforcement can easily deteriorate into police abuse and discriminatory conduct. Although it cannot be eliminated, Joseph Goldstein (1960) proposes that an impartial civilian body should scrutinize the decisions as to which laws should be enforced. In that way, discretionary conduct would become more visible and might result in selective law enforcement that would then become a subject for open public dialogue. Discretionary law enforcement can also become an area in police-community relations (Clark, 1979:213–218; Thurman, et al., 2001).

SUMMARY

This chapter has been concerned with the organization of law in society in the context of judicial, legislative, administrative, and enforcement agencies.

Court cases generally begin with a dispute. Private-initiated, public-initiated, and public defendant disputes constitute, for the most part, the workload of American courts. There are 51 court systems in the United States—one federal court and 50 state court organizations. This dual hierarchy operates side by side. When disputes move from the trial to the appellate level, they are typically transformed and become almost exclusively disputes about law or about procedures.

Courts, as dispute-processing institutions, are composed of four distinct groups of participants—litigants, lawyers, judges, and juries. Litigants can be distinguished by the relative frequency with which they resort to court services. There are two types: the "one-shotters" and the "repeat players." The most important distinction that can be made among types of litigating lawyers is the manner in which they perceive their clientele. These types include public-interest lawyers, private-interest lawyers, criminal defense lawyers, and client-oriented attorneys. The judges are the most prestigious participants in court processes. In addition to basic adjudication functions and the control of the flow of litigation in the courtrooms, judges are responsible for administering their courts. Judges' personal backgrounds and values affect their decisions, which in turn are bases for their recruitment to the higher bench. Juries are used exclusively in trial courts. The principal issues surrounding the participation of jurors in the processing of disputes include their effectiveness on checking the power of judges; the use of the scientific method in jury selection; the degree of their representativeness of the community; and their competence. Although the flow of litigation is different in criminal and civil cases, a high degree of discretion at every level is characteristic of both.

Although the principal function of legislative bodies is lawmaking, they also engage in conflict-management and integrative functions. At the federal level and in most states, legislatures are comprised of two separate bodies—the House and the Senate—which differ in several respects. Differences exist between the House and the Senate in organization, procedure, and the regular activities of their members. The House operates under more formal rules than does the Senate. Behavior in both houses is influenced by a set of informal rules and norms. Much of the important work is done by standing committees and subcommittees.

The participants in the legislative process are legislators, executives, and lobbyists. The majority of legislators come from a middle-class or an upper-class background. The recruitment of legislators is selective by education, religion, and occupational status. Protestant Anglo-Saxon males are substantially overrepresented among legislators. Executives perform three main functions in the legislative process: They serve as a source of ideas; they function as catalytic agents; and they instrument the law. The lobbyist plays a variety of key roles in the legislative process, such as contact person, campaign organizer, and watchdog.

Administrative agencies, often called the fourth branch of government, reach into virtually every corner of American life. Administrative rules affect the food we eat, the cars we drive, the fuel we use, the clothes we wear, the houses we live in, the investments we make, the water we drink, and even the air we breathe. These agencies are authorities of the government other than the executive, legislative, and judicial branches, created for the purpose of administering particular legislations. Administrative agencies are just as subject to pressures of interest groups as are all other lawmakers. Administrative agencies have powers of investigation, rulemaking, and adjudication. Information is essential for administrative agencies to carry out their functions. Rulemaking is administrative lawmaking, and it consists of the power to make or alter rules and regulations. Adjudication is the administrative agency's equivalent of a judicial trial. Much of it is handled informally through the voluntary settlement of cases at lower levels in an agency. In case of disagreement, administrative decisions can be subjected to judicial review, and the courts have the power to overturn an agency's judgment, both on points of law and on questions of fact.

The police are expected and empowered to enforce the law. In the United States, there is no unified system of law enforcement. An important characteristic of law enforcement is the strongly bureaucratic and militaristic organization of the police. The effectiveness of law enforcement agencies depends on the way in which departments are organized. In professionalized departments, there is a greater tendency to detect violators and a higher arrest rate than in nonprofessionalized departments. Law enforcement is characterized by a high amount of discretion. Both in reactive and in proactive policing, the use of police discretion can take a number of forms: investigation, confrontation, disposition, and the decision to use force. There is a thin line between discretion and discrimination in a discretionary law enforcement.

SUGGESTED FURTHER READINGS

HENRY J. ABRAHAM, *The Judicial Process: An Introductory Analysis of the Courts of the United States, England, and France.* 7th ed. New York: Oxford University Press, 1998. A cross-cultural overview of court organizations, processes, and participants.

JEFFREY ABRAMSON, *We, the Jury: The Jury System and the Ideal of Democracy.* Cambridge, MA: Harvard University Press, 2000. A provocative scholarly analysis of the jury in predominantly criminal cases by a lawyer and political scientist.

STEPHEN J. ADLER, *The Jury: Trial and Error in the American Courtroom.* New York: Times Books, 1995. Could be considered as a companion to Abramson's book. It covers both criminal and civil cases, and it is primarily anecdotal.

GRAHAM D. BURNETT, *A Trial By Jury.* New York: Alfred B. Knopf, 2002. An insightful inside account of jury activities by a college professor who served as the jury foreman in a Manhattan murder trial.

STEVEN J. CANN, *Administrative Law.* 2nd ed. Thousand Oaks, CA: Sage Publications, Inc., 2001. A good and clearly presented overview of tools of the fourth branch of the government.

ROBERT A. CARP and RONALD STIDHAM, *Judicial Process in America.* 5th ed. Washington, DC: CQ Press, 2001. A comprehensive study of the American court system and its environment in which it functions. The book is intended for readers interested in the judicial process and behavior.

ROGER G. DUNHAM and GEOFFREY P. ALPERT, (EDS.), *Critical Issues in Policing, Contemporary Readings.* 4th ed. Prospect Heights, IL: Waveland Press, Inc., 2001. The newest edition of this popular anthology on policing offers a comprehensive and authoritative exploration into all aspects of the field.

DAVID GARLAND, *The Culture of Control: Crime and Social Order in Contemporary Society.* Chicago: University of Chicago Press, 2001. A good discussion of the reasons why America's get-tough approach to crime is not working.

SHELDON GOLDMAN and AUSTIN SARAT (EDS.), *American Court Systems: Readings in Judicial Process and Behavior.* 2nd ed., New York: Longman, 1989. A compendium of some of the best materials available on American courts.

DOROTHY GUYOT, *Policing As Though People Matter.* Philadelphia: Temple University Press, 1991. An excellent empirical study of a police department, with useful insights and generalizations on service, management, and change.

JOHN C. HUGHES, *The Federal Courts, Politics, and the Rule of Law*. New York: HarperCollins College Publishers, 1995. An exploration of dispute formation, resolution, federal court organization and extended impact litigation.

HERBERT JACOB, *Justice in America: Courts, Lawyers, and the Judicial Process*, 4th ed. Boston: Little, Brown, 1984. A timeless analysis of how justice is organized and administered in American courts by one of the most prolific authors on the topic.

CORNELIUS M. KERWIN, *Rulemaking: How Government Agencies Write Law and Make Policies*. 2nd ed. Washington, DC: CQ Press, 1999. A comprehensive overview of the various facets of administrative rulemaking.

V. A. LEONARD and HARRY W. MORE. *Police Organization and Management*, 9th ed. New York: Foundation Press, 2000. A landmark textbook and reference work that presents principles and procedures in the organization and management of the police enterprise.

DON J. LOFGREN, *Dangerous Premises: An Insider's View of OSHA Enforcement*. Ithaca, NY: Cornell University, 1989. An insightful and revealing narrative of the author's experience as an OSHA investigator written in nontechnical language.

WILLIAM T. LYONS, JR., *The Politics of Community Policing: Rearranging The Power to Punish*. Ann Arbor, MI: The University of Michigan Press, 1999. An in-depth examination of community policing in Seattle. The author explores the complex issues associated with the establishment and operation of community policing, an increasingly popular method for organizing law enforcement in the United States.

LARRY G. MAYS and PETER R. GREGWARE (EDS.), *Courts and Justice, A Reader*. 2nd. ed. Prospect Heights, IL: Waveland Press, Inc., 2001. Over thirty judiciously chosen articles on court functions, processes and problems.

QUINT THURMAN, JIHONG ZHAO and ANDREW GIACOMAZZI, *Community Policing in a Community Area: An Introduction and Exploration*. Los Angeles, CA: Roxbury Publishing Company, 2001. A recent primer on community policing with a good review of major trends, developments and theories and includes a number of good case studies.

MICHAEL TONRY and NORVAL MORRIS (EDS.), *Modern Policing*. Chicago: The University of Chicago Press, 1992. An outstanding collection of essays on policing.

CLIFFORD E. SIMONSEN, *Private Security in America: An Introduction*. Upper Saddle River, NJ: Prentice Hall, 1998. An insightful analysis and overview of the various aspects of private policing in the United States.

LISA STOLZENBERG and STEWART J. D'ALESSIO (EDS.), *Criminal Courts for the 21st Century*. Upper Saddle River, NJ: Prentice Hall, 2002. A collection of current articles on issues that face the criminal courts. A good source of ideas and references.

MICHAEL TONRY and KATHLEEN HATLESTAD (EDS), *Sentencing Reform in Overcrowded Times: A Comparative Perspective*. New York: Oxford University Press, 1997. A compendium on sentencing reform in the United States and Western Europe.

NEIL VIDMAR (ED.), *World Jury Systems*. New York: Oxford University Press, 2000. A timely compendium of informative articles on the jury systems and the challenges they face in various parts of the world. An excellent resource for the cross-cultural study of civil and criminal juries.

ROBERT V. WOLF and AUSTIN SARAT, *The Jury System*. Philadelphia, PA: Chelsa House Publishers, 1997. Traces the history of the jury system in the United States and discusses contemporary topics such as deliberation and verdicts with recommendations for reform.

REFERENCES

ABRAHAM, HENRY J. 1998. *The Judicial Process: An Introductory Analysis of the Courts of the United States, England, and France.* 7th ed. New York: Oxford University Press.

ABRAMSON, JEFFREY. 2000. *We, the Jury: The Jury System and the Ideal of Democracy.* Cambridge, MA: Harvard University Press.

ABRAMSON, JILL. 1998. "The Business of Persuasion Thrives in Nation's Capital," *New York Times* (September 29): A1, A22–23.

ADAMS, THOMAS F. 1973. *Law Enforcement: An Introduction to the Police Role in the Criminal Justice System.* 2nd ed. Englewood Cliffs, NJ: Prentice Hall.

ADLER, STEPHEN J. 1989. "Consultants Dope Out the Mysteries of Jurors for Clients Being Sued," *Wall Street Journal* (October 24): A1, A10. 1995. *The Jury: Trial and Error in the American Courtroom.* New York: Times Books.

ALBONETTI, CELESTA A. 1992. "An Integration of Theories to Explain Judicial Discretion," *Social Problems* 38 (2) (May): 247–266.

ALKER, HAYWARD R., JR., CARL HOSTICKA, and MICHAEL MITCHELL. 1976. "Jury Selection as a Biased Social Process," *Law & Society Review* 11 (1) (Fall): 9–41.

ALSCHULER, ALBERT W. 1995. "Plea Bargaining and Its History." Pp. 138–160 in Richard L. Abel (ed.), *The Law & Society Reader.* New York: New York University Press.

ANDERSON, PATRICK R. and DONALD J NEWMAN. 1998. *Introduction to Criminal Justice.* 6th ed. Boston: McGraw-Hill.

ANDREWS, LORI B. 1982. "Mind Control in the Courtroom," *Psychology Today* (March): 66–73.

ASHER, HERBERT. 1973. "The Learning of Legislative Norms," *American Political Science Review,* no. 67 (June): 499–513.

BAKER, ROSS K. 1995. *House and Senate.* 2nd ed. New York: W.W. Norton & Co., Inc.

BARGE, JEFF. 1995. "Reformers Target Jury Lists; Seeking Diversity, Jurisdictions May Call Benefit Recipients," *ABA Journal* 81 (January): 26–28.

BARTOL, C. R. 1983. *Psychology and American Law.* Belmont, CA: Wadsworth.

BAUM, DAVID B. 1994. "Creating a Theme," *Trial* 30 (3) (March): 66–70.

BAUM, LAWRENCE. 1998. *The Supreme Court.* 6th ed. Washington, DC: QC Press.

BAYLEY, DAVID H. 1992. "Comparative Organization of the Police in English-speaking Countries." Pp. 509–545 in Michael Tonry and Norval Morris (eds.), *Modern Policing.* Chicago: The University of Chicago Press.

BERCAL, T. E. 1970. "Calls for Police Assistance: Consumer Demands for Governmental Service," *American Behavioral Scientist* 13 (5–6) (May-August): 681–691.

BITTNER, EGON. 1970. *The Functions of the Police in Modern Society.* Chevy Chase, MD: National Institute of Mental Health.

BLACK, DONALD. 1973. "The Mobilization of Law," *Journal of Legal Studies* 2 (1) (January): 125–149. 1980. *The Manners and Customs of the Police.* New York: Academic Press.

BLACK, DONALD J., and ALBERT J. REISS, JR. 1970. "Police Control of Juveniles," *American Sociological Review* 35 (1) (February): 63–77.

BLUMBERG, ABRAHAM S. 1979. *Criminal Justice: Issues & Ironies.* 2nd ed. New York: New Viewpoints.

BOGUS, CARL. 2001. *Why Lawsuits Are Good for America: Disciplined Democracy, Big Business, and the Common Law.* New York: New York University Press.

BONNER, RAYMOND. 2001. "Push Is On for Larger Jury in Military Capital Cases," *New York Times* (September 4): A1, A9.

BORDUA, DAVID J., and ALBERT J. REISS, JR. 1966. "Command, Control, and Charisma: Reflections on Police Bureaucracy," *American Journal of Sociology* 72 (1) (July): 68–76.

BOULDING, KENNETH E. 1956. *The Image.* Ann Arbor: University of Michigan Press.

BOYCE, JOSEPH N. 1992. "Community Style Policing Takes Hold in Cities Like Takoma Park, Md.," *Wall Street Journal* (August 5): A1, A6.

BREYER, STEPHEN G., and RICHARD B. STEWART. 1998. *Administrative Law and Regulatory Policy.* 4th ed. New York: Aspen Law & Business.

BRODERICK, VINCENT L. 1994. "The Delusion of Mandatory Sentencing: The Wrong Approach to Fighting Crime," *Trial* 30 (8) (August): 62–67.

BROWN, MICHAEL K. 1988. *Working the Street: Police Discretion and the Dilemmas of Reform.* New York: Russell Sage Foundation.

BURNETT, GRAHAM D. 2002. *A Trial By Jury.* New York: Alfred B. Knopf.

BUTTERFIELD, FOX. 2001. "States Easing Stringent Laws on Prison Time," *New York Times* (September 2): A1, A5.

CAMPBELL, ELAINE. 1999. "Toward a Sociological Theory of Discretion," *International Journal of the Sociology of Law* 27:79–101.

CALVI, JAMES V., and SUSAN COLEMAN. 1997. *American Law and Legal Systems.* 3rd ed. Upper Saddle River, NJ: Prentice Hall.

CANN, STEVEN J. 2001. *Administrative Law.* 2nd ed. Thousand Oaks, CA: Sage Publications, Inc.

CARTER, DAVID L. and LOUIS A. RADELET. 1999. *The Police and The Community.* 6th ed. Upper Saddle River, NJ: Prentice Hall.

CARP, ROBERT A., and RONALD STIDHAM. 2001. *Judicial Process in America.* 5th ed. Washington, DC: CQ Press.

CASPER, JONATHAN. 1972. *Lawyers before the Warren Court.* Urbana: University of Illinois Press.

CHO, SUSIE. 1994. "Capital Confusion: The Effect of Jury Instructions on the Decision to Impose Death," *Journal of Criminal Law and Criminology* 85 (2) (Fall): 532–561.

CLARK, ROBERT S. 1979. *Police and the Community: An Analytic Perspective.* New York: New Viewpoints.

CLIFFORD, ROBERT A. 1995. "Mock Trials Offer Virtual Reality: Simulated Juries Can Be Used Most Effectively Early in the Litigation Process to Develop the Theory of the Case," *The National Law Journal* 17 (26) (February 27): 88.

CLYMER, ADAM. 1995. "Senate Votes 98–0 for Strict Limits on Lobbyist Gifts— Compliance Voluntary," *New York Times* (July 29): A1, A9.

COHN, ALVIN W. 1976. *Crime and Justice Administration.* Philadelphia: Lippincott.

COLEMAN, JAMES W. 1998. *The Criminal Elite: The Sociology of White Collar Crime.* 4th ed. New York: St. Martin's Press.

CORBOY, PHILIP H. 1975. "From the Bar." Pp. 179–195 in Rita James Simon (ed.), *The Jury System in America: A Critical Overview.* Beverly Hills, CA: Sage Publications.

COX, GAIL DIANE. 1994. "Voters Tough on Criminals: Law and Order Initiatives Sweep the Polls, While Tort Reform and Others Lose," *National Law Journal* 17 (12) (November 21): A6.

COYLE, MARCIA. 1995. "Death Juries Get It Wrong—Study: Survey Reports They Mishear Judges' Instructions," *National Law Journal* 17 (28) (March): 6.

CRANK, JOHN P. 1994. "Watchman and Community: Myth and Institutionalization in Policing," *Law and Society Review* 28 (2) (May): 325–351.

CUNNINGHAM, WILLIAM C., JOHN J. STRAUCHS, and CLIFFORD W. VAN METER. 1991. "Private Security: Patterns and Trends," National Institute of Justice, Research in Brief. Washington, DC: U.S. Department of Justice (August).

DALEY, SUZANNE. 2001. "France's Most Courted: Women to Join the Ticket," *New York Times* (February 8): 1, 8.

DAVIS, KENNETH CULP. 1975a. *Administrative Law and Government.* 2nd ed. St. Paul, MN: West Publishing Company. 1975b. *Police Discretion.* St. Paul, MN: West Publishing Company. 1977. *Administrative Law: Cases—Text—Problems.* 6th ed. St. Paul, MN: West Publishing Company.

DAVIS, MELISSA G., RICHARD J. LUNDMAN, and RAMIRO MARTINEZ, JR. 1991. "Private Corporate Justice: Store Police, Shoplifters, and Civil Recovery," *Social Problems* 38 (3) (August): 395–411.

DEOSARAN, RAMESH. 1993. "The Social Psychology of Selecting Jury Forepersons," *British Journal of Criminology* 33 (1) (Winter): 70–80.

DILWORTH, DONALD C. 1995. "Arizona Commission Proposes Far-Reaching Changes in Jury Procedures," *Trial* 31 (2) (February): 17–20.

DIMITRIUS, JO-ELLAN and MARK MAZZARELLA. 1998. *Reading People: How to Understand People and Predict Their Behavior, Anytime, Anyplace.* New York: Random House.

DUNHAM, ROGER G. and GEOFFREY P. ALPERT (EDS.). 2001. *Critical Issues in Policing, Contemporary Readings.* 4th ed. Prospect Heights, IL: Waveland Press, Inc.

DUFF, P., and M. FINDLAY. 1997. "Jury Reform: Of Myths and Moral Panics," *International Journal of the Sociology of Law* 25 (4) (December): 363–384.

EDLEY, CHRISTOPHER R. 1990. *Administrative Law: Rethinking Judicial Control of Bureaucracy.* New Haven: Yale University Press.

EISENSTEIN, JAMES, and HERBERT JACOB. 1977. *Felony Justice.* Boston: Little, Brown.

FEELEY, MALCOLM M. 1979. "Perspectives on Plea Bargaining," *Law & Society Review* (Special Issue on Plea Bargaining) 13 (2) (Winter): 199–209.

Foreman, Tucker C. (ed.). 1991. *Regulating for the Future: The Creative Balance.* Washington, DC: Center for National Policy Press.

FRANKLIN, DANIEL. 1994. "The Right Three Strikes," *Washington Monthly* 26 (9) (September): 25–30.

FREEDMAN, JAMES O. 1978. *Crisis and Legitimacy: The Administrative Process and American Government.* Cambridge: Cambridge University Press.

FRIEDMAN, LAWRENCE M. 1986. *A History of American Law.* 2nd ed. New York: Simon & Schuster/Touchstone Book. 1998. *American Law: An Introduction.* 2nd ed. New York: W. W. Norton & Co., Inc. 2002. *American Law in the Twentieth Century,* New Haven: Yale University Press.

GALANTER, MARC. 1974. "Why the `Haves' Come Out Ahead: Speculations on the Limits of Legal Change," *Law & Society Review* 9 (1) (Fall): 95–160.

GARLAND, DAVID. 2001. *The Culture of Control: Crime and Social Order in Contemporary Society.* Chicago: University of Chicago Press.

GELLHORN, ERNEST and RONALD M. LEVIN. 1997. *Administrative Law and Process in a Nutshell.* 4th ed. St. Paul, MN: West Publishing Company.

GERLIN, ANDREA. 1995. "Jury-Duty Scofflaws Try Patience of Courts," *Wall Street Journal* (August 9): B1, B6.

GEYELIN, MILO, and MARTHA BRANNIGAN. 1992. "Jury Selection in Racially Charged Cases Becomes More Difficult after Rioting," *Wall Street Journal* (May 5): B1, B10.

GIBBONS, GARY F. 1995. "Career Development in Smaller Departments," *FBI Law Enforcement Bulletin* 64 (2) (February): 16–19.

GILBERT, MICHAEL J. 1997. "The Illusion of Structure: A Critique of the Classical Model of Organization and the Discretionary Power of Correctional Officers," *Criminal Justice Review* 22 (1) (Spring): 49–64.

GLABERSON, WILLIAM. 1989. "Study Sees More U.S. Plea Bargains," *New York Times* (October 29): Y19. 1992. "With Au Pair Acquitted in Murder, the Focus Turns to the Police," *New York Times* (July 12): 20. 2001. "Lawyers' Study Says States Should Pay for Court Races," *New York Times* (July 23): 1.

GODWIN, R. KENNETH. 1988. *One Billion Dollars of Influence: The Direct Marketing of Politics.* Chatham, NJ: Chatham House Publishers, Inc.

GOLDMAN, NATHAN. 1963. *The Differential Selection of Juvenile Offenders for Court Appearance.* New York: National Council on Crime and Delinquency.

GOLDMAN, SHELDON, and AUSTIN SARAT (eds.). 1989. *American Court Systems: Readings in Judicial Process and Behavior.* 2nd ed. New York: Longman.

GOLDSTEIN, JOSEPH. 1960. "Police Discretion Not to Invoke the Criminal Process: Low Visibility Decisions in the Administration of Criminal Justice," *Yale Law Journal* 69 (March): 543–594.

GUYOT, DOROTHY. 1991. *Policing As Though People Matter.* Philadelphia: Temple University Press.

HAFEMEISTER, THOMAS L., and W. LARRY VENTIS. 1994. "Juror Stress: Sources and Implications," *Trial* 30 (10) (October): 68–73.

HANS, VALERIE P. 1992. "Jury Decision Making." Pp. 56–76 in Dorothy K. Kagehiro and William S. Laufer (eds.), *Handbook of Psychology and Law.* New York: Springer-Verlag.

HANS, VALERIE P., and WILLIAM S. LOFQUIST. 1992. "Jurors' Judgments of Business Liability in Tort Cases: Implications for the Litigation Explosion Debate," *Law & Society Review* 26 (1): 85–115.

HANS, VALERIE P., and VEIL VIDMAR. 1986. *Judging the Jury.* New York: Plenum.

HANSON, ROGER A., and BRIAN J. OSTROM. 1993. "Litigation and the Courts: Myths and Misconceptions," *Trial* 29 (4) (April): 40–45.

HARRIS, RICHARD A., and SIDNEY M. MILKIS. 1989. *The Politics of Regulatory Change: A Tale of Two Agencies.* New York: Oxford University Press.

HICKS, ROBERT D. 1991. *In Pursuit of Satan: The Police and the Occult.* Buffalo, NY: Prometheus Books.

HOFFMAN, JAN. 1992. "In Courtrooms, the Stoolie Is Pushed to Squeal Louder," *New York Times* (August 2): E18. 1995. "Why a Jury Can Be 12, Even 6, but Not 5," *New York Times* (June 11): E6.

HOLMES, MALCOLM D., HOWARD C. DAUDISTEL, and WILLIAM A. TAGGART. 1992. "Plea Bargaining Policy and State District Court Caseloads: An Interrupted Time Series Analysis," *Law & Society Review* 26 (1): 139–159.

HOPKINS, BRUCE R. 1992. *Charity, Advocacy, and the Law.* New York: John Wiley.

HUGHES, JOHN C. 1995. *The Federal Courts, Politics, and the Rule of Law.* New York: HarperCollins College Publishers.

HUNT, MORTON. 1982. "Putting Juries on the Couch," *New York Times Magazine* (November 28):70–87.

INBAU, FRED E., JAMES R. THOMPSON, JAMES B. ZAGEL, and JAMES P. MANAK. 1997. *Criminal Law and Its Administration.* 6th ed. Westbury, NY: The Foundation Press, Inc.

ISRAEL, MARK. 1998. "Ethnic Bias in Jury Selection in Australia and New Zealand," *International Journal of the Sociology of Law* 26: 35–54.

JACOB, HERBERT. 1984. *Justice in America: Courts, Lawyers, and the Judicial Process.* 4th ed. Boston: Little, Brown. 1995. *Law and Politics in the United States.* 2nd ed. Ft. Washington, PA: HarperCollins College Publishers. 1997. "The Governance of Trial Judges," *Law & Society Review* 32 (1): 3–30.

JEWELL, MALCOLM E., and SAMUEL C. PATTERSON. 1986. *The Legislative Process in the United States.* 4th ed. New York: Random House.

JONES, CHARLES O. 1994. *The Presidency in a Separated System.* Washington, DC: The Brookings Institution.

JOSEPH, THOMAS M. 1994. "Walking the Minefields of Community-Oriented Policing," *The FBI Law Enforcement Bulletin* 63 (9) (September): 8–13.

JUN, JOND S. and HIROMI MUTO. 1995. "The Hidden Dimensions of Japanese Administration: Culture and Its Impact," *Public Administration Review* 55 (2) (March-April): 125–134.

KALVEN, HARRY, JR., and HANS ZEISEL. 1966. *The American Jury.* Boston: Little, Brown.

KANE, ROBERT J. 1999. "Patterns of Arrest in Domestic Violence Encounters: Identifying a Police Decision-Making Model," *Journal of Criminal Justice* 27 (1): 65–79.

KASSIN, SAUL M., and LAWRENCE S. WRIGHTSMAN. 1988. *The American Jury on Trial.* New York: Hemisphere Publishing Corporation.

KENNEDY, RANDALL. 1998. *Race, Crime, and the Law.* New York: Random House/Vintage.

KERWIN, CORNELIUS M. 1999. *Rulemaking: How Government Agencies Write Law and Make Policies.* 2nd ed. Washington, DC: CQ Press.

KLEIN, MITCHELL S. G. 1984. *Law, Courts, and Policy.* Englewood Cliffs, NJ: Prentice Hall.

KRISTOF, NICHOLAS D. 1995. "A Neighborly Style of Police State," *New York Times* (June 4): E5.

LANGWORTHY, ROBERT H., and LAWRENCE F. TRAVIS. 1999. *Policing in America, A Balance of Forces.* 2nd ed. Upper Saddle River, NJ: Prentice Hall.

LEONARD, V. A. and HARRY W. MORE. 2000. *Police Organization and Management.* 9th ed. New York: Foundation Press,

LILLEY, LIN S. 1994. "Techniques for Targeting Juror Bias," *Trial* 30 (11) (November): 74–80.

LEVI, AVRAHAM M. 1998. "Are Defendants Guilty If They Were Chosen in a Lineup?," *Law and Human Behavior* 22 (4) (August): 389–408.

LEWIN, TAMAR. 2001a. "Little Sympathy or Remedy for Inmates Who Are Raped," *New York Times* (April 15): 1, 14. 2001b. "3–Strikes Law Is Overrated in California, Study Finds," *New York Times* (August 23): 1, 8.

LOH, WALLACE D. 1984. *Social Research in the Judicial Process: Cases, Readings, and Text.* New York: Russell Sage Foundation.

LOVEDAY, BARRY. 1998. "Improving the Status of Police Patrol," *International Journal of the Sociology of Law* 26: 161–196.

LUGINBUHL, JAMES. 1992. "Comprehension of Judges' Instructions in the Penalty Phase of a Capital Trial," *Law and Human Behavior* 16 (2) (April): 203–218.

LYMAN, MICHAEL D. 1999. *The Police: An Introduction.* Upper Saddle River, NJ: Prentice Hall.

LYONS, WILLIAM T., JR. 1999. *The Politics of Community Policing: Rearranging The Power to Punish.* Ann Arbor, MI: The University of Michigan Press.

MAGUIRE, KATHLEEN AND Ann L. PASTORE (EDS.). 1998. *Bureau of Justice Statistics. Sourcebook of Criminal Justice Statistics—1997.* Albany, NY: The Hindelang Criminal Justice Research Center/U.S. Department of Justice, Office of Justice Programs, Bureau of Justice Statistics. NCJ–171147.

MAHOOD, H. R. 1990. *Interest Group Politics in America: A New Intensity.* Englewood Cliffs, NJ: Prentice Hall.

MARGOLICK, DAVID. 1992. "Chorus of Judicial Critics Assail Sentencing Guides," *New York Times* (April 12): A1, A20.

MASHAW, JERRY L. 1994. "Improving the Environment of Agency Rulemaking: An Essay on Management, Games, and Accountability," *Law and Contemporary Problems* 57 (2) (Spring): 185–257.

MATTHEWS, DONALD R. 1954. *The Social Background of Political Decision-Makers.* New York: Random House. 1960. *U.S. Senators and Their World.* Chapel Hill: University of North Carolina Press.

MAYS, LARRY G. and PETER R. GREGWARE (EDS.), 2001. *Courts and Justice, A Reader.* 2nd ed. Prospect Heights, IL: Waveland Press, Inc.

MELLING, TOM. 1994. "Dispute Resolution Within Legislative Institutions," *Stanford Law Review* 46 (6) (July): 1677–1715.

MOORE, MARK HARRISON. 1992. "Problem-Solving and Community Policing." Pp. 99–158 in Michael Tonry and Norval Morris (eds.), *Modern Policing.* Chicago: The University of Chicago Press.

MULCAHY, AOGAN. 1994. "The Justification of 'Justice': Legal Practitioners' Accounts of Negotiated Case Settlements in Magistrates' Courts. (United Kingdom)," *British Journal of Criminology* 34 (4) (Autumn): 411–430.

MUNK, NINA. 1994. "Rent-a-Cops," *Forbes* 154 (8) (October 10): 104–106.

NARBY, DOUGLAS J., and BRIAN L. CUTLER. 1994 "Effectiveness of Voir Dire as a Safeguard in Eyewitness Cases," *Journal of Applied Psychology* 79 (5) (October): 724–730.

NASHERI, HEDIE. 1998. *Betrayal of Due Process. A Comparative Assessment of Plea Bargaining in the United States and Canada.* Lanham, MD: University Press of America, Inc.

NEW YORK TIMES. 1995. "Toward Democratic Jury Service" (June 14): A18. 2001. "A Study's Verdict: Jury Awards Are Not Out of Control" (August 6): A1.

NOVAK, WILLIAM J. 1989. "Intellectual Origins of the State Police Power: The Common Law Vision of a Well-Regulated Society," Working Papers Series 3. Legal History Program. Institute for Legal Studies. Madison, WI: University of Wisconsin 3: 2 (June): 1–112.

O'CONNELL, JOHN P., JR. 1995. "Throwing Away the Key (and State Money): Study Reveals Ineffectiveness of Mandatory Sentencing Policies," *Spectrum: The Journal of State Government* 68 (1) (Winter): 28–32.

O'LEARY, DENNIS. 1994. "Reflection on Police Privatization," *The FBI Law Enforcement Bulletin* 63 (9) (September): 21–26.

ORNSTEIN, NORMAN J., THOMAS E. MANN, and MICHAEL J. MALBIN. 1990. *Vital Statistics on Congress, 1989–1990.* Washington, DC: Congressional Quarterly Inc.

OSBORNE, RANDAL. 1992. "The Fixers," *Riverfront Times* (St. Louis). (June 17–23): 1, 14–15.

PALERMO, GEORGE B., MAXINE ALDRIDGE WHITE, LEW A. WASSERMAN, and WILLIAM HANRAHAN. 1998. "Plea Bargaining: Injustice for All?," *International Journal of Offender Therapy and Comparative Criminology* 42 (2) (June): 111–123.

PALMER, MICHAEL and SIMON ROBERTS. 1998. *Dispute Processes: ADR and the Primary Forms of Decision Making*. London: Butterworths.

PEAK, KENNETH J., and RONALD W. GLENSOR. 1999. *Community Policing and Problem Solving: Strategies and Practices*. 2nd ed. Upper Saddle River, NJ: Prentice Hall.

PENROD, STEVEN D., and LARRY HEUER. 1997. "Tweaking Commonsense: Assessing Aids to Jury Decision Making." *Psychology, Public Policy, and Law* 3 (2–3) (June-September): 259–284.

PEPINSKY, HAROLD E. 1976. *Crime and Conflict: A Study of Law and Society*. New York: Academic Press.

PHILIPS, SUSAN U. 1998. *Ideology in the Language of Judges: How Judges Practice Law, Politics, and Courtroom Control*. New York: Oxford University Press.

PINKELE, CARL F., and WILLIAM C. LOUTHAN (EDS.). 1985. *Discretion, Justice, and Democracy: A Public Policy Perspective*. Ames: The Iowa State University.

POLLOCK, ELLEN JOAN, and STEPHEN J. ADLER. 1992. "Justice for All? Legal System Struggles to Reflect Diversity, but Progress Is Slow," *Wall Street Journal* (May 8): 1, 4.

POPE, MAURICE. 1989. "Upon the Country—Juries and the Principle of Random Selection," *Social Science Information* 28 (2): 265–289.

POSNER, RICHARD A. 1995. "Juries on Trial," *Commentary* 99 (3) (March): 49–53.

PRESIDENT'S COMMISSION ON LAW ENFORCEMENT AND ADMINISTRATION OF JUSTICE. 1967. *The Challenge of Crime in a Free Society*. Washington, DC: U.S. Government Printing Office.

RAMIREZ, DEBORAH A. 1994. "A Brief Historical Overview of the Use of Mixed Jury," *American Criminal Law Review* 31 (3) (Summer): 1213–1224.

REISS, ALBERT J., JR. 1971. *The Police and the Public*. New Haven: Yale University Press. 1992. "Police Organization in the Twentieth Century." Pp. 51–97 in Michael Tonry and Norval Morris (eds.), *Modern Policing*. Chicago: The University of Chicago Press.

REISS, ALBERT J., JR., and DAVID J. BORDUA. 1967. "Environment and Organization: A Perspective on the Police." Pp. 25–55 in David J. Bordua (ed.), *The Police: Six Sociological Essays*. New York: John Wiley.

RESKE, HENRY J. 1994. "Judges Irked by Tough-on-Crime Laws," *ABA Journal* 80 (October): 18.

RIPLEY, RANDALL B. 1988. *Congress. Process and Policy* 4th ed. New York: W. W. Norton & Co., Inc.

ROHDE, DAVID. 1998. "Jury Duty in Manhattan Lightens a Bit After Changes," *New York Times* (August 27): A21.

ROSETT, ARTHUR, and DONALD R. CRESSEY. 1976. *Justice by Consent: Plea Bargains in the American Courthouse*. Philadelphia: Lippincott.

ROSS, H. LAURENCE. 1980. *Settled Out of Court*. 2nd ed. Chicago: Aldine.

ROZELL, MARK J., and CLYDE WILCOX. 1999. *Interest Groups in American Campaigns, The New Face of Electioneering*. Washington, DC: CQ Press.

RUBINSTEIN, JONATHAN. 1973. *City Police*. New York: Farrar, Straus & Giroux.

SAKS, MICHAEL J., and REID MASTIE. 1978. *Social Psychology in Court*. New York: Van Nostrand Reinhold.

SARAT, AUSTIN, and WILLIAM L. F. FELSTINER. 1995. *Divorce Lawyers and Their Clients: Power and Meaning in the Legal Process*. New York: Oxford University Press.

SALANT, JONATHAN D., and DAVID S. CLOUD. 1995. *Congressional Quarterly Weekly Report* 53 (15) (April 15): 1055–1060.

SAVELSBERG, JOACHIM J. 1992. "Law That Does Not Fit Society: Sentencing Guidelines as a Neoclassical Reaction to the Dilemmas of Substantivized Law," *American Journal of Sociology* 97 (5) (March): 1346–1381.

SCHMIDHAUSER, JOHN R. 1979. *Judges and Justices.* Boston: Little, Brown.

SCHMITT, ERIC. 1998. "Senate Revives Bill to Overhaul Laws on Finance Campaigns," *New York Times* (September 10): A21.

SCHWARTZ, BERNARD. 1959. *The Professor and the Commissions.* New York: Knopf.

SEIB, GERALD F. 1995. "You Can Get Away From Washington—But Not Government," *Wall Street Journal* (June 21): A1, A5.

SELIGMAN, DANIEL. 1995. "Advocates Unlimited," *Fortune* 131 (4) (March 6): 217.

SHEARING, CLIFFORD D., and PHILIP C. STENNING (EDS.). 1987. *Private Policing.* Beverly Hills, CA: Sage Publications.

SIMON, RITA J. 1980. *The Jury: Its Role in American Society.* Lexington, MA: Lexington Books, DC Heath.

SIMONSEN, CLIFFORD E. 1998. *Private Security in America: An Introduction.* Upper Saddle River, NJ: Prentice Hall.

SKOLNICK, JEROME H. 1994. *Justice without Trial: Law Enforcement in Democratic Society.* 3rd ed. New York: MacMillan.

SKOLNICK, JEROME H., and DAVID H. BAYLEY. 1988. *Community Policing: Issues and Practices around the World.* Washington, DC: National Institute of Justice.

SLONIM, SCOTT. 1980. "Survey Finds Fewer Lawyer-Legislators," *American Bar Association Journal* 66 (January): 30.

SMITH, BRUCE. 1960. *Police Systems in the United States.* 2nd ed. New York: Harper & Row, Pub.

SOURYAL, SAM S. 1995. *Police Organization and Administration.* 2nd ed. Cincinnati, OH: Anderson Publishing Company.

SPITZER, ROBERT J. 1995. *The Politics of Gun Control.* Chatham, NJ: Chatham House Publishers, Inc.

STEAD, DEBORAH. 1994. "Crime and Punishment—And Now Trial By Jury," *Business Week* (January 17): 20–22.

ST. LOUIS POST-DISPATCH. 2001. "Smoking Away" (April 15): A2.

STOLZENBERG, LISA and STEWART J. D'ALESSIO. 1997. "'Three Strikes and You're Out': The Impact of California's New Mandatory Law on Serious Crime Rates," *Crime & Delinquency* 43 (4) (October): 457–469.

STOLZENBERG, LISA and STEWART J. D'ALESSIO (EDS.). 2002. *Criminal Courts for the 21st Century.* Upper Saddle River, NJ: Prentice Hall.

THURMAN, QUINT, JIHONG ZHAO and ANDREW GIACOMAZZI. 2001. *Community Policing in a Community Area: An Introduction and Exploration.* Los Angeles, CA: Roxbury Publishing Company.

TIME, 1978. "Paper Chase: The Battle Against Red Tape" (July 10): 26. 1981. "We, the Jury, Find the . . ." (September 28): 44–56. 1994. "Follow the Money" (November 7): 25.

TOMASIC, ROMAN. 1985. *The Sociology of Law.* London: Sage Publications.

TONRY, MICHAEL. 1996. *Sentencing Matters.* New York: Oxford University Press.

TONRY, MICHAEL and KATHLEEN HATLESTAD (EDS.). 1997. *Sentencing Reform in Overcrowded Times: A Comparative Perspective.* New York: Oxford University Press.

TREDOUX, COLIN G. 1998. "Statistical Inference on Measures of Lineup Fairness," *Law and Human Behavior* 22 (2) (April): 217–238.

U.S. DEPARTMENT OF JUSTICE. 1992a. "State and Local Police Departments, 1990," *Bureau of Justice Statistics Bulletin* (February). 1992b. "Prosecutors in State Courts, 1990," *Bureau of Justice Statistics Bulletin* (March). 1995a. "Prison Sentences and Time Served for Violence," *Bureau of Justice Statistics, Selected Findings* 4 (April). 1995b. "National Assessment Program: 1994 Survey Results," *National Institute of Justice* (May).

U.S. NEWS & WORLD REPORT. 1980. "Your Hamburger: 41,000 Regulations" (February 1): 64. 1992. "The Justice System: Getting a Fair Trial" May 25: 36–38. 1994. "Outlook" (May 9): 13.

VIDMAR, NEIL (ED.). 2000. *World Jury Systems.* New York: Oxford University Press.

VIOLANTI, JOHN M. 1995. "The Mystery Within: Understanding Police Suicide," *FBI Law Enforcement Bulletin* 64 (2) (February): 19–24.

VOLCANSEK, MARY L., and JACQUELINE LUCIENNE LAFON. 1988. *Judicial Selection: The Cross-Evolution of French and American Practices.* New York: Greenwood Press.

WASBY, STEPHEN L. and DAVID C. BRODY. 1997. "Studies of Repressed Memory and the Issue of Legal Validity," *Law and Human Behavior* 21 (6) (December): 687–692.

WEIDENBAUM, MURRAY L. 1979. *The Future of Business Regulation: Private Action and Public Demand.* New York: AMACOM, A Division of American Management Associations.

WHEELER, STANTON, KENNETH MANN, and AUSTIN SARAT. 1988. *Sitting in Judgment: The Sentencing of White-Collar Criminals.* New Haven and London: Yale University Press.

WHITTEMORE, KAREN E., and JAMES R. P. OGLOFF. 1995. "Factors That Influence Jury Decision Making: Disposition Instructions and Mental State at the Time of the Trial," *Law and Human Behavior* 19 (3) (June): 283–304.

WICE, PAUL B. 1978. *Criminal Lawyers: An Endangered Species.* Beverly Hills, CA: Sage Publications.

WILLIAMS, GREGORY HOWARD. 1984. *The Law and Politics of Police Discretion.* Westport, CT: Greenwood Press.

WILLIAMS, KIPLING D., ELIZABETH F. LOFTUS, and KENNETH A. DEFFENBACHER. 1992. "Eyewitness Evidence and Testimony." Pp. 141–166 in Dorothy K. Kagehiro and William S. Laufer (eds.), *Handbook of Psychology and Law.* New York: Springer-Verlag.

WILSON, JAMES Q. 1968a. "The Police and the Delinquent in Two Cities." Pp. 9–30 in Stanton Wheeler (ed.), *Controlling Delinquents.* New York: John Wiley. 1968b. *Varieties of Police Behavior.* Cambridge: Harvard University Press.

WILSON, O. W., and ROY C. MCLAREN. 1972. *Police Administration.* 2nd ed. New York: McGraw-Hill.

WOLF, ROBERT V. and AUSTIN SARAT. 1997. *The Jury System.* Philadelphia, PA: Chelsea House Publishers.

WOO, LILLIAN C. 1994. "Today's Legislators: Who They Are and Why They Run?," *State Legislatures* 20 (4) (April): 28–32.

WOOCHER, FREDERIC D. 1977. "Did Your Eyes Deceive You?: Expert Psychological Testimony on the Unreliability of Eyewitness Identification," *Stanford Law Review* 29: 969–1030.

WORRALL, JOHN L. 1998. "Administrative Determinants of Civil Liability Lawsuits Against Municipal Police Departments: An Exploratory Analysis," *Crime & Delinquency* 44 (2) (April): 295–313.

ZHAO, JIHONG and QUINT C. THURMAN. 1997. "Community Policing: Where Are We Now?," *Crime & Delinquency* 43 (3) (July): 345–357.

4
Lawmaking

Routinely and seemingly mechanically, at the local, state and federal levels, legislative, administrative, and judicial bodies grind out annually tens of thousands of new laws. But, in spite of the piecemeal appearance, each law is unique. Each has its own distinct set of precipitating factors, special history, and *raison d'être*. Still, some generalizations are possible about how laws are formed, the sociological factors that play a role in lawmaking, and the social forces that provide an impetus for making or altering laws. This chapter focuses on the more important sociological theories of lawmaking; the ways in which legislatures, administrative agencies, and courts make laws; the roles of vested interests, public opinion, and social science in the decision-making process; and the sources of impetus for laws.

PERSPECTIVES ON LAWMAKING

The creation and instrumentation of laws are routine and ongoing processes (Cheney, 1998), and theoretical perspectives dealing with the many facets of lawmaking abound in the sociological literature (Chambliss, 1984:16–17; Chambliss and Zats, 1993; Hagan, 1980; Monahan and Walker, 1998:125–380; Tomasic, 1985:101–106; Zander, 1999). Students of lawmaking have used a number of them in attempts to explain how laws are created or defeated. I will consider briefly four such theories to illustrate the diversity of perspectives—the rationalistic model, the functional view, conflict theory, and a "moral entrepreneur" thesis.

The *rationalistic* model proposes that laws (in particular, criminal laws) are created as rational means of protecting the members of society from social harm. In this perspective, crimes are considered socially injurious. This is the most widely accepted but also the most simplistic theory of lawmaking (Goode, 1997). One of the principal difficulties with this perspective is that it is the lawmakers and powerful interest groups who define what activities may be harmful to the public welfare. Value judgments, preferences, and other considerations obviously enter into the process of definition (for example, why are certain types of behaviors, like prostitution or gambling—which will be discussed in the following chapter—labeled as criminal?).

The *functionalist* view of lawmaking, as formulated by Paul Bohannan (1973), is concerned mainly with how laws emerge. Bohannan argues that laws are a special kind of "reinstitutionalized custom." Customs are norms or rules about the ways in which people must behave if social institutions are to perform their functions and society is to endure. Lawmaking is the restatement of some customs (for example, those dealing with economic transactions and contractual relations, property rights in marriage, or deviant behavior) so that they can be enforced by legal institutions.

This view proposes that failure in other institutional norms encourages the reinstitutionalization of the norms by the legal institution. As noted earlier, this perspective implies a consensual model of lawmaking in a society. From the functionalist perspective, laws are passed because they represent the voice of the people. Laws are essentially a crystallization of custom, of the existing normative order. Although there are conflicts in society, they are relatively marginal, and they do not involve basic values. In this view, conflict and competition between groups in a society actually serve to contribute to its cohesion and solidarity.

The *conflict* perspective cites value dissensus, unequal access to economic goods and the resulting structural cleavages of a society as the basic determinant of laws. Specifically, the origin of law is traced to the emergence of an elite class. These elites, it is suggested, use social-control mechanisms such as laws to perpetuate their own advantageous positions in society. In the event of conflict over the prescription of a norm, conflict theorists would argue that the interest group(s) more closely tied to the interests of the elite group would probably win the conflict. To define who the elites or the powerful groups of the society are, conflict theorists often employ structural indices of power. For example, William J. Chambliss (1964), as shown in Chapter 1, claims that the groups in England having the most power to create the vagrancy laws were those representing the dominant economic interests at the time.

The *"moral entrepreneur"* theory attributes the precipitation of key events to the "presence of an enterprising individual or group. Their activities can properly be called *moral enterprise*, for what they are enterprising about is the creation of a new fragment of the moral constitution of society, its code of right and wrong" (Becker, 1963:146). The role of moral entrepreneurs in lawmaking is splendidly illustrated by Howard S. Becker's study (1963:121–146) of the development of criminal law designed to repress the use of marijuana. He notes that the Marijuana Tax Act of 1937 had its forerunners in earlier criminal statutes such as the Volstead Act (alcohol) and the

Harrison Act (opium and derivatives). The Narcotics Bureau of the Treasury Department was unconcerned with marijuana in its earlier years. It argued, instead, that the regulation of opiates was the real problem. However, shortly before 1937, the Narcotics Bureau redefined marijuana use as a serious problem. As a consequence, this agency acted in the role of moral entrepreneur, in that it attempted to create a new definition of marijuana use as a social danger. For example, the bureau provided information to the mass media on the dangers of marijuana, including "atrocity stories" that detailed gruesome features of marijuana smoking. Finally, in 1937 the Marijuana Tax Act was passed, ostensibly as a taxation measure but with the real purpose of preventing persons from smoking marijuana. But it had another little-known component to it. The campaign against marijuana was also colored by the fact that Harry Anslinger, the first drug tsar, was appointed by Andrew Mellon, his wife's uncle. Mellon, the Treasury Secretary, was banker to DuPont, and the sales of hemp threatened that firm's efforts to build a market for synthetic fibers. Spreading scare stories about cannabis was a way to give hemp a bad name. Obviously, moral outrage is always more effective when backed by vested interests (*Economist*, 2001:4).

Another good example of the role of moral entrepreneurs in lawmaking is in the context of birth control. In a fascinating book, *Devices and Desires, A History of Contraceptives in America*, Andrea Tone (2001) points out that it was not until the mid-1800s that contraceptive technology jumped beyond methods in use for centuries, such as making condoms out of animal intestines. After Charles Goodyear invented the vulcanization of rubber in 1839, rubber manufacturers began supplying not just condoms but douching syringes, "womb veils" (or diaphragms and cervical caps), and what amounted to IUDs. By the 1870s, pharmacies were graphically advertising and selling chemical suppositories, vaginal sponges and medicated tampons. The easy availability of birth control devices alarmed Anthony Comstock, a one-time salesman in New York City who believed that they assisted vice trade by divorcing sex from marriage and childbearing. In 1873, joined by like-minded allies, he successfully lobbied for Congressional passage of a bill that branded contraception obscene and prohibited its distribution across state lines or through the mails. Subsequently, versions of the Comstock law were enacted in 24 states.

Further, it should be noted that the passing of a law may also symbolize the supremacy of the groups that support it. The creation of a law is a statement that the illegal behavior is disreputable. Where groups differ significantly in prestige and status, or where two groups are competing for status, each sees the law as a stamp of legitimacy. They will seek to use it to affirm the respectability of their own way of life. According to Gusfield:

> The fact of affirmation through acts of law and government, expresses the public worth of one set of norms, or one subculture vis-à-vis those of others. It

demonstrates which cultures have legitimacy and public domination, and which do not. Accordingly it enhances the social status of groups carrying the affirmed culture and degrades groups carrying that which is condemned as deviant. (1967:178)

These are the currently prominent theories on lawmaking in the law and society literature. None of these theories can account for the creation of all laws. On the basis of research evidence, however, some models come closer to providing a general explanation than do others. But how much closer they come depends on one's theoretical perspective. Some would argue that "the paradigm that is most compatible with the facts is one that recognizes the critical role played by social conflict in the generation of . . . law" (Chambliss, 1976:67). Others, in a similar vein, would argue for the explanatory power of *their* respective theoretical stances. Because a large number of laws are made by the legislative, administrative, and judicial bodies each day, it is always possible to select a few examples that illustrate almost any conceivable theoretical position. At best, the theories I have discussed explain in part how laws are made. Probably all these theories are at least partially correct, but it is doubtful that any single theory fully explains the creation of law, although one or another may account for the formation of any particular law or kind of law. With these considerations in mind, let us now turn to an examination of the processes of legislative, administrative, and judicial lawmaking.

LEGISLATION

The main legal task of legislative bodies is to make law. The term "legislation" describes the deliberate creation of legal precepts by a body of government that gives articulate expression to such legal precepts in a formalized legal document. Legislation, as such, must be distinguished from normative pronouncements made by the courts. The verbal expression of a legal rule or principle by a judge does not have the same degree of finality as the authoritative formulation of a legal proposition by a legislative body. Furthermore, although both adjudication and legislation involve the deliberate creation of laws by a body of government, it should be remembered that the judiciary is not a body set up primarily for the purpose of lawmaking. As pointed out earlier, its main function is to decide disputes under a preexisting law, and the law-creating function of the judges should be considered incidental to their primary function of adjudication.

There are several other differences that should be kept in mind between legislative and judicial lawmaking. Judge-made law stems from the decision of actual controversies. It provides no rules in advance for the decision of cases but waits for disputes to be brought before the court for decision. Legislators, by contrast, formulate rules in anticipation of cases. A judicial decision is based on a justification for applying a particular rule, whereas a statute usually does not contain an argumentative or justificatory statement; it simply states: This is forbidden, this is required, this is authorized. An opinion supporting a court decision is normally signed by the judge who wrote it. By contrast, a statute carries no signature (Fuller, 1968:89–93). In general, legislators have much more freedom to make significant changes and innovations in the law than do the courts. The accumulation of precedents and the growth of an evermore complex body of principles have inevitably narrowed the scope of most judicial innovations. Legislators are also more responsive to public and private pressures than judges. Whereas judges deal with particular cases, legislators consider general problem areas with whole classes of related situations. At times, the attention of legislative bodies is drawn to a problem by a particular incident, but the law it eventually passes is designed for general applicability. For example, when Congress passed the Federal Kidnapping Law of 1932, the kidnapping and death of the Lindbergh baby were fresh in their minds, but the law that was enacted was designed to deal with a whole class of such possible occurrences. Thus, it may be concluded that legislators are solely responsible for formulating broad new rules and for creating and revising the institutions necessary to put them into effect.

Legislative lawmaking, at times, represents a response to some kind of problem, one acute enough to intrude on the well-being of a large number of individuals and their organizations or on the well-being of the government itself, one conspicuous enough to attract the attention of at least some legislators. But, legislation can also be generated, among other ways, by apprehension, social unrest, conflict, and technological innovation.

Federal pure food and drug laws resulted from an exposure of the practices of food and drug manufacturers and processors (Friedman and Macaulay, 1977:610–613). More recently, internal security laws were the outgrowth of apprehension over the activities of American communists; manpower retraining and area redevelopment legislation to provide for more rigorous control over the testing of drugs was passed in the wake of disclosures of the effects of thalidomide, a drug that caused numerous babies to be born malformed; and legislation to establish a system of communication satellites was passed shortly after the successful experiment with Telstar. The list of legislation passed in response to the emergence of new problems or to the successful dramatization of old ones could be extended infinitely.

But neither legislators' recognition of a social problem nor their recognition of a group's particular claims for action is certain to lead to legislation. The probability of some form of legislative response increases when (1) powerful interest groups mobilize their members to seek legislative action; (2) the unorganized public becomes intensely concerned with an issue, as in the controversy over thalidomide, or conversely, is indifferent to the particular measures advocated by an interest group; and (3) there is no pressure to maintain the status quo or opposition to the proposed legislation.

Typically, the introduction of a legislative plan is preceded by a series of prelawmaking "stages" of activity. The first stage is the *instigation and publicizing* of a particular problem (such as nuclear waste disposal). Typical instigators include the mass media (such as special TV programs like *60 Minutes* or a series of articles or editorials in major newspapers or news magazines), a representative who highlights an issue through investigative hearings, or an author (as we shall see later in this chapter) who documents and dramatizes a social problem. The second stage is *information-gathering*. It entails collecting data on the nature, magnitude, and consequences of a problem; alternative schemes for solving the problem and their costs, benefits, and inherent difficulties; the likely political impact of each scheme; and the feasibility of various compromises. The third stage is *formulation*, or devising and advocating a specific legislative remedy for the problem. The fourth stage is *interests-aggregation*, or obtaining support for the proposed measure from other lawmakers through trade-offs and compromises (that is, if you support my proposal, I will support yours); the championing of one interest group over others; or mediating among conflicting groups. The fifth stage is *mobilization*, the exertion of pressures, persuasion, or control on behalf of a measure by one who is able, often by virtue of his or her institutional position, to take effective and relatively direct action to secure enactment. Whether an issue goes beyond the first three stages usually depends on the support it receives from individuals, groups, or governmental units that possess authority and legitimacy in the policy area, and on the support that the proponents of a proposal are able to muster from key figures in the legislature. The last stage is *modification*, the marginal alteration of a proposal, sometimes strengthening it, and sometimes granting certain concessions to its opponents to facilitate its introduction (Price, 1972:4–5).

These six stages, although they show a certain sequential character and complementarity, do not simply represent the components the legislative process must "necessarily" include. They also illustrate, for example, the norms that govern the legislative process (for example, the airing of an issue and the attempt to accommodate diverse interests). They further illustrate the thoroughly political character of the legislative lawmaking process.

ADMINISTRATIVE LAWMAKING

Administrative agencies engage in lawmaking through rule making and through the adjudication of cases and controversies arising under their jurisdiction. They pursue both civil remedies and criminal sanctions to promote compliance with regulatory and administrative laws (Kerrigan, et al., 1993). Administrative lawmaking plays an increasingly important role in modern society (Evan, 1990:89–96), and its consequences are felt in all walks of life. The intent of this section is to examine the fundamental processes involved in that kind of lawmaking in the context of administrative rule making and adjudication.

Administrative Rule Making

Administrative rule making refers to the establishment of prospective rules (Bryner, 1987; Pierce, 1995; West, 1985). *A rule is a law made by an administrative agency.* Through rule making, a particular administrative agency legislates policy. Under the requirements of the Federal Administrative Procedure Act, general notice of proposed rule making must be published in the *Federal Register* (the daily compendium of new, revised, and proposed rules). The fact that the register grew from 20,000 pages in 1968 to well over 53,000 in 1988 (Ornstein et al., 1990:160) and in excess of 75,000 pages in 1998 is indicative of the considerable increase in administrative rule making. The notice must specify the location of the proceedings, the legal authority under which the rules are being proposed, and the substance of the proposed rules. After such a notice is given, interested parties are to be provided with the opportunity to participate in the rule-making proceedings through the presentation of written data. At the discretion of the agency, oral presentation may be made. Unless notice or a hearing is required by the statutes governing the agency's operation, notice of rule making can be withheld if the agency considers it to be impractical, unnecessary, or contrary to the public interest. This provision potentially excludes a number of administrative rule-making proceedings from any possibility of public participation (Davis, 1977:241–269).

The flexibility of agencies in rule-making procedures is much greater than in administrative adjudication. Formal hearings are not held unless required by statute. Administrators are free to consult informally with interested parties and are not bound by the more rigid requirements of adjudicative hearings. The number of parties that may participate is also potentially far greater than in adjudicative proceedings, where only those directly affected by an administrative order have standing (that is, are directly involved in litigation).

Much of the immense code of federal regulations is composed of the substantive rules of administrative agencies. The Internal Revenue Code, for example, is part of this compendium of regulations, which consists of a seemingly endless number of rules interpreting statutes that have been passed by Congress. At this point, it should be noted that administrative agencies issue a variety of pronouncements less formal and binding than their "legislative" regulations which are designed to clarify the laws they are administering (see, for example, Schwartz, 1995). Some of these are described as "interpretative regulations" (for example, the IRS regularly issues interpretations of the Internal Revenue Code, such as under what circumstances a college professor may deduct his or her office at home as a business expense). Moreover, in response to inquiries, agencies sometimes issue "advisory rulings," which interpret the law with reference to particular types of situations such as the disposal of certain types of potentially hazardous wastes. In addition, some agencies also publish instructions, guides, explanatory pamphlets, and so forth.

Regulatory agencies state many of their regulatory policies through rule making. For example, the Food and Drug Administration determines policies governing the labeling, availability, shelf-life and safety of drugs by rule making. Rate-setting proceedings (for example, the limits on fees brokerage houses may charge for certain class of services) of regulatory bodies are also considered to be rule making. Outside of the regulatory realm, departments such as Commerce and Defense are constantly stating their general policies through the issuance of rules ranging from banking practices to dress codes in the military.

Administrative Adjudication

The second way in which agencies create rules is through their adjudicative powers, given to them by congressional grants of authority. *Administrative adjudication is the process by which an administrative agency issues an order.* Adjudication is the administrative equivalent of a judicial trial. As I pointed out in Chapter 3, adjudication differs from rule making in that it applies only to a specific, limited number of parties involved in an individual case before the agency. Administrative orders have retroactive effect, as contrasted with the prospective effect of rule making. In rule making, the agency is apprising in advance those under its jurisdiction of what the law is. When an agency opens proceedings with the intention of issuing an order, it must eventually interpret existing policy or define new policy to apply to the case at hand. The parties involved do not know how the policy is going to be applied until after the order is issued, giving the agency decision retroactive effect. Adjudicative lawmaking tends to produce inconsistencies because cases are decided on an individual basis. The rule of *stare decisis* (requiring precedent to be followed, which will be discussed in the context of judicial lawmaking) need not prevail (West, 1985:53–55), and the high turnover of top-level administrators often results in a lack of continuity.

Since many agencies have both the power to issue regulations and the power to adjudicate cases, they can choose between the two methods of lawmaking. When an agency believes that the time has come to formulate a policy decision in an official text, it can draft and issue a regulation (for example, when the Securities and Exchange Commission (SEC) formulates law by writing rules that describe what disclosures must be made in a prospectus). But when an agency prefers to wait until the contours of a problem become clearer, it can continue to deal with the problem on a case-by-case basis, formulating a series of decisional rules couched in terms that ensure continuing flexibility (for example, individual workers' compensation claims). Furthermore, an agency, unlike a court, does not have to wait passively for cases to be brought before it. Its enforcement officials can go out looking for cases that will raise the issues its adjudicating officials want to rule on. And because the agency can decide for itself what enforcement proceedings to initiate, it can choose cases that present the issues in such a way that the court will be likely to uphold the agency's ruling if an appeal is taken.

JUDICIAL LAWMAKING

Over the years there has been a steady increase in judicial lawmaking in the United States (Canon and Johnson, 1999; Glazer, 1975; Glendon, 1994; Rabkin, 1989). In many instances, legislators and administrators are willing to let judges take the heat for controversial actions, such as allowing or disallowing abortion or ordering busing to desegregate schools. Similarly, it is often politically expedient to allow courts to handle such sensitive jobs as reapportioning legislatures, regulating employment practices, supervising land use or urban planning, and managing school systems (Stone, 1979:76). In addition, "an increasing number of judges hold the belief that law and the courts are the most appropriate and effective means of redressing the perceived ills of our society" (Rusthoven, 1976:1340). As a result, the judiciary in recent years has assumed a powerful role in our society. As Henry J. Abraham aptly remarks: "It is simply a fact of life that in the United States all social and political issues sooner or later seem to become judicial!" (1994:21).

Although traditional cases still occupy most of the court's time, the scope of judicial business has broadened. Courts have tended "to move from the byways onto the highways of policy making" (Horowitz, 1977:9). In fact, Nathan Glazer argues that we have developed an "Imperial Judiciary"—that is, the courts now have so much power, play such a great role in lawmaking, that they pose a threat to the vitality of the political system. Glazer contends that too much power has moved from the elected, representative branches of government to the largely nonelective judiciary, and the courts "are now seen as forces of nature, difficult to predict and impossible to control" (1975:110). Judicial activity is now extended, for example, to welfare, prison, and mental-hospital administration, to education and employment policy, to road and bridge building, to automotive safety standards, and to management of natural resources. Some activist judges are called by May Ann Glendon (1994) as "romantic judges" who follow their passions of "do-gooding" and use due process and equal protection to justify making law rather than interpreting it. These judges are bold, creative, compassionate and result-oriented who do not let tradition, precedent or nonromantic readings of the Constitution get in the way.

In recent years, courts altered laws requiring a period of instate residence as a condition of eligibility for welfare, laid down elaborate standards for food handling, hospital operations, inmate employment, and education, and ordered some prisons closed. Courts have established comprehensive programs of care and treatment for the mentally ill confined in hospitals. They have ordered the equalization of school expenditures on teachers' salaries, decided that bilingual education must be provided for Mexican-American children, and eliminated a high school diploma as a requirement for a firefighter's job. Courts have enjoined the construction of roads and bridges on environmental grounds and suspended performance requirements for automobile tires and air bags.

In some now classic, broad-ranging and often cited examples such as *Brown v. Board of Education* (347 U.S. 483 [1954]), the judiciary set a precedent in establishing new policies in interracial relations with its decisions forbidding official segregation in public schools. The judiciary also established a new set of laws for processing criminal cases, requiring that indigents be given attorneys at public expense in all but minor cases (*Gideon v. Wainwright*, 372 U.S. 355 [1963]); defendants must be warned that whatever they say to the police may be used against them, and that they will be permitted attorneys during police interrogation if they request them (*Miranda v. Arizona*, 348 U.S. 436 [1966]); and juveniles must be given some of the same rights as adult offenders in hearings that may lead to their imprisonment (*In re Gault*, 387 U.S. 1 [1967]). Reapportionment of national, state, and local legislative bodies has followed the decisions in *Baker v. Carr* (369 U.S. 186 [1962]) and *Reynolds v. Sems* (377 U.S. 533 [1964]), which required that all legislative districts be approximately the same size. The courts have been, "to put it mildly, very busy, laboring in unfamiliar territory" (Horowitz, 1977:5).

Judicial activism is not without criticism (Bryden, 1993; Leo and Thomas, 1998). There are questions about the policy-making role of judges in the American system of governments. The role of judges is to apply the law, and the policy-making activities carried out by the Supreme Court in interpreting the Constitution in view of social changes is considered an impermissible expansion of the powers granted to the judicial branch. The increase in judicial activism, it is argued, created a legislative body that is not accountable to the American people (Graglia, 1994).

Prior to discussing when and how judges make law, it is important to review the salient features of the adjudicative process. Adjudication is focused. The typical question before the judge is simply: Does one party have a right? Does another party have a duty? This should be contrasted with the question before legislators and administrators: What are the alternatives? Adjudication is also piecemeal, and the lawsuit is a good illustration of incremental decision making. Furthermore, courts must act when litigants present their cases before them. In the end, a judgment cannot be escaped. Moreover, fact-finding in adjudication is poorly adapted to the ascertainment of social facts. The unrepresentative character of the litigants makes it difficult to generalize from their situation to a wider context. Finally, adjudication makes no provision for policy review. Judges base their decisions on behavior that antedates the litigation. Consequential facts—those that relate to the impact of a decision on behavior—are equally important but much neglected. This results in an emphasis on rights and duties rather than on alternatives (Horowitz, 1977:33–56).

All these statements suggest that judicial lawmaking is different from legislative or administrative lawmaking. There are three types of judicial lawmaking: by precedents, by interpretation of statutes, and by interpretation of the Constitution. I shall examine these three types separately.

Lawmaking by Precedents

Judicial formulation of rules is based frequently on the principle that judges should build on the precedents established by past decisions, known as the doctrine of *stare decisis* ("stand by what has been decided"), which is both expeditious and a deeply rooted common-law tradition (Carr and Stidham, 1996:295–296). By contrast, civil-law countries, such as France and Germany, have a codified legal system where the basic law is stated in *codes*. These are statutes enacted by the national parliament, which arranges whole fields of law (family law, housing law, and so forth) in an orderly, logical, and comprehensive way. The judges follow the basic principles of law found in acts of parliament. In common-law countries, such as England and the United States, judges base their decisions on *case law*, a body of opinion developed by judges over time in the course of deciding particular cases. The doctrine of precedent, the notion that the judge is bound by what has already been decided, is a strictly common-law doctrine (Friedman, 1998, 2002).

In the common-law system, following precedents is often much easier and less time-consuming than working out all over again solutions to problems that have already been faced. It enables the judge to take advantage of the accumulated wisdom of preceding generations. It minimizes arbitrariness and compensates for weakness and inexperience. It conforms to the belief that "like wrongs deserve like remedies" and to the desire for "equal justice under the law." More important, the practice of following precedents enables individuals (with the assistance of attorneys) to plan their conduct in the expectation that past decisions will be honored in the future. Although certainty, predictability, and continuity are not the only objectives of law, they are certainly important ones. Many disputes are avoided, and others are settled without litigation simply because individuals are familiar with how the courts will respond to certain types of behavior.

But judicial formulations of rules are frequently revised and restated by the courts in cases presenting the same or similar problems. A judge may also be confronted with a case for which there are simply no precedents. For example, consider a problem that judges first had to face during the 1920s when farmers began to complain that airplanes were disturbing the peace and frightening their livestock. Obviously, there were no precedents dealing with the rights and duties of landowners and of individuals who flew aircraft over their land. To make a decision, judges searched through property-law cases for any analogies that seemed applicable. Through the selection of appropriate and desirable analogies (which is, indeed, a value judgment), judges make law in instances when they are not guided by precedents. In general, in view of the way courts deal with legal rules laid down in earlier decisions (by rephrasing, qualifying, broadening, narrowing, or changing such rules, or by analogies), a precedent must be considered as a weaker and less authoritative source of law than a statute.

The Interpretation of Statutes

In interpreting statutes, judges determine the effects of legislative decisions. For many, a legislative decree is not a law until enforced and interpreted by the courts (Jacob, 1984:37). In the vast majority of cases involving the application of statutes, the courts have no trouble determining how to apply the statute. Most cases fall squarely inside or outside the law's provisions.

In some cases, however, the intent of a legislature is ambiguous. Some statutes contain unintentional errors and ambiguities because of bad drafting of the law. Other statutes are unclear because those who pushed them through the legislature sought to avoid opposition by being vague or silent on potentially controversial matters. An important reason for the lack of clarity in many instances is that the proponents have not been able to foresee and provide for all possible future situations. This provides the courts with an opportunity to engage in lawmaking. For example, antitrust statutes permit much judicial lawmaking, for Congress has set up only the most general guidelines. Exactly what constitutes a restraint of trade or monopolization are questions that the court determines. In doing so, courts not only make law but also set explicit policy to guide other businesses and government agencies.

On rare occasions, judges find that all their efforts to discover the legislative intent of a statute are in vain. It is simply not clear how the statute applies to the case before them. In those cases, the judges must do just what they do when faced with a case for which there are no precedents. They must perform a creative act of lawmaking. In all probability, this is exactly what the legislature, unwilling to prescribe details for an unknown future, counted on them to do. It is the duty of judges to infer a purpose that is applicable to a particular case from what they know of the legislature's broader purposes and of the shared purposes and aims of the community.

The Interpretation of Constitutions

In addition to the U.S. Congress which plays a major role in constitutional interpretation (Davidson, 1993), the courts are regularly called upon to interpret the Constitution (Baum, 1998; McCann and Housemann, 1989; Wellington, 1991). Every controversial statute and a variety of controversial executive actions are challenged in the courts on grounds of unconstitutionality (Jacob, 1984:38). For example, in an attempt to avert a threatened strike, the president orders federal officials to seize and operate the nation's steel mills. The steel companies challenge his power to do so under Article II of the Constitution, which deals with the powers and duties of the president. Or an overzealous sheriff in a small town breaks into the offices of a business firm and searches for evidence of illegal sales without a search warrant. When the firm's owners are brought to trial for unlawful operations, they challenge the admission of the evidence offered against them on the grounds that it has been illegally obtained and that admitting it would violate the "due process" clause of the Fourteenth Amendment, which is supposed to protect individuals against irregular official procedures.

The opportunities to interpret constitutional provisions arise more often in federal than in state courts, because the national Constitution is considered more ambiguous in many of its key provisions. State constitutions, by contrast, are much more detailed documents and leave much less room for judicial interpretations. Usually both state and federal courts ratify the decision of the governmental officials by finding the challenged legislation or executive action constitutional. At times, however, they declare the law or action unconstitutional. When deciding on the constitutionality of a government action, the courts have to decide what meaning they wish to give to the Constitution and which social objectives to pursue. For example, the Supreme Court "has given quite different interpretations to the 'due process of law' clauses of the Fifth and Fourteenth Amendments, ranging from a guarantee of property against governmental intervention to a guarantee of civil rights against official abuse" (Jacob, 1984:38).

Judicial lawmaking is usually directed at other government agencies rather than at private individuals. Courts interpret statutes and constitutional provisions, and in so doing they permit or prohibit the action of other government agencies. For example, courts have prohibited racial discrimination by government agencies in schools, parks, and elections, but they have not prohibited racial discrimination (on constitutional grounds) by private individuals (for example, obtaining professional services such as dental, medical, or legal). Most judicial lawmaking efforts are concerned with the regulatory activities of agencies (Shapiro, 1968). There are, however, some issues that are rarely decided in courts. Foreign affairs (because they are considered political and not judicial issues) are generally beyond the scope of court action. For example, when the American participation in the

Vietnam conflict was challenged, the Supreme Court, by a six to three vote, refused to rule on its constitutionality. Moreover, courts are seldom involved in matters such as the appropriation of funds or the levying of taxes.

INFLUENCES ON THE LAWMAKING PROCESSES

Lawmaking is a complex and continuous process, and it exists as a response to a number of social influences that operate in society. The forces that influence lawmaking cannot always be precisely determined, measured, or evaluated. At times, a multitude of forces are in operation simultaneously. Although a variety of forces can exert influence on the lawmaking process, in this section I shall consider only the roles of vested interests, public opinion, and the social sciences—the ones most prominently discussed in the law and society literature.

Interest Groups

The interest-group thesis contends that laws are created because of the special interests of certain groups in the population (Mahood, 1990). The image of society reflected by this view stresses cultural differences, value clashes, inequities and social conflict (Hajnal and Clark, 1998). Examples of interest-group influence in lawmaking abound (Rozell and Wilcox, 1999). Laws governing the use of alcohol, regulations concerning sexual conduct, abortion bills, pure food and drug legislation, antitrust laws, and the like are all documented instances of interest-group activity (Quinney, 1970:49–94). Even alterations in existing statutes are not immune from influence by those who see some threat or advantage in the proposed changes. For example, Pamela A. Roby (1969) demonstrated, in a study of the New York State Penal Code regarding prostitution, that the changes originally proposed in this law were drastically altered by the time the new statute took effect. Throughout the legislative process, various groups (for example, the police, the New York Hotel Association, the Civil Liberties Union, and the mayor's office) were all involved in shaping the legislation to fit their interests or views. Often, interest groups also act as a communication network for social movements, facilitating the dissemination of their ideas in a manner that helps to legitimize movements, exert public pressure for legal change, attract some politicians to the movements' objectives, and effect policy change (Yarnold, 1992:115).

The nature of the interaction between interest groups and lawmakers varies to an extent based on the branch of the government. Judges, although they are not immune to interest-group pressures, are generally not lobbied in the same way as legislators or administrators. To reach the courts, a lawyer must be hired, formal proceedings must be followed, and grievances must be expressed in legal terminology. Minorities and the poor find the courts attractive because they are more readily available. To influence legislators, a group must be economically powerful or able to mobilize a large number of voters (Jacob, 1984:150). No such prerequisites are needed in the courts. If a group has enough money to hire an attorney, it can seek court action to further its interests. Further, interest groups may also turn to courts because they assume that the judicial branch may be more sympathetic to their objectives than the other two branches (Carp and Stidham, 2001:122). As a result, minority groups are often among the most active lobbies in courts. The NAACP, for example, has instituted and won numerous cases in its efforts to improve the legal protection of blacks. The technique is not new, of course, but in recent decades, urban interests, feeling underrepresented in state and national legislatures, have turned increasingly to the lawsuit.

The techniques used by interest groups to influence courts are different from those used to influence legislative or administrative bodies. Notes Jacob: "The principal techniques are: to bring conflicts to a court's attention by initiating test cases, to bring added information to the courts through *amicus curiae* (friend of the court) briefs, and to communicate with judges indirectly by placing information favorable to the group's cause in legal and general periodicals" (1984:151). By instituting test cases, interest groups provide judges with opportunities to make policies by which they overcome the otherwise passive nature of the judicial process. Often, such briefs communicate relevant social-science research findings to a particular case (Roesch et al., 1991). By providing information through *amicus curiae* briefs, interest groups expand the confines of the judicial process and build coalitions with other groups (McGuire, 1994). For example, the American Civil Liberties Union with other interest groups that share similar goals file many such briefs with the Supreme Court in cases that raise questions of constitutional liberty. The final technique is to publish decisions in legal periodicals. Judges generally read these journals to keep abreast of legal scholarship and sometimes even cite them as authority for their ruling. Publication in these journals gets one's views before the courts and before their attentive public.

Interactions between interest groups and legislative and administrative lawmakers are more overtly political in nature. Many interest groups maintain Washington and state capital offices staffed with people who keep track of developments in the legislative and administrative branches and attempt to influence their activities. Some groups pay for the services of law firms in dealing with legislators or administrators. These firms provide expertise in such areas as antitrust and tax regulations and use their personal contacts with important lawmakers on behalf of their clients.

A number of specific conditions can be identified that enhance the potential influence of interest groups on lawmakers (Ripley, 1980). In many instances, there may not be two competing groups on an issue. When only one point of view is presented, the group is likely to get much of what it wants. For example, when banking interests push for a higher ceiling for usury laws in a state, they are more likely to succeed if there is no organized opposition. Similarly, if the groups on one side of a controversy are unified and coordinated on the principal issues they want to push (or if they can minimize their disagreements), they will enhance their chances of success. For instance, the walnut growers are represented by a single highly organized group and are thus likely to get what they want. By contrast, chicken farmers are dispersed and have no effective single group to speak for them. Consequently, they have difficulty in achieving their legislative ends. If certain key members of legislative bodies (such as a subcommittee chairperson) believe in the interest group's position, the probability of success is greatly enhanced. The visibility of an issue is another consideration in influencing lawmakers. When the issue is not too visible, or when interest groups seek single distinct amendments to bills (such as to alter soybean export quotas in addition to others proposed by farming interests), as contrasted with large legislative packages, the chances for success increase. Conversely, as the visibility of issues increases and public attention grows (such as draft registration or wage-price controls), the influence of interest groups tends to diminish. Interest groups are likely to have greater influence on issues that coincide with the interests of the groups they purport to represent. For example, the AFL-CIO may be very influential in matters concerning working conditions, but they are likely to receive less attention from lawmakers when they advocate higher tariffs for imported goods or when they make attempts to guide foreign policy. Finally, interest groups are likely to have greater influence on amendments than on entire pieces of legislation. This is because amendments are generally technical and less understood by the public.

In general, the effectiveness of interest groups in influencing lawmakers is related to such considerations as their financial and information resources, their offensive or defensive positions, and the status of the group in the eyes of lawmakers. Financial resources determine the ability of an interest group to support court suits, lobbying, public relations, and other activities (Abramson, 1998). Interest groups that support the status quo have an advantage over groups trying to bring change, because whereas the latter must overcome several obstacles in the lawmaking process, the former may frustrate change at any of several points in the process. But the influence of an interest group depends mainly on its status as perceived by lawmakers. An interest group is particularly influential in situations where a lawmaker shares the same group affiliation (for example, when farm groups talk to legislators who are farmers), where the group is considered important to the legislator's constituency, and where the group is recognized as a legitimate and reliable source of information. In addition, a group's competence to influence lawmaking is enhanced by its ability to bring about social or economic disruptions. Threats of disorder, disruption, and violence have been, at times, effective bargaining weapons of relatively powerless groups. Similarly, the threat of a decline in the supply of such necessities as food, medical services, and energy have been used to influence lawmakers. For example, energy-supply problems have been employed to justify the removal of price controls on oil and natural gas. There is little doubt that the ability of an interest group to create a crisis, whether a social disorder, an economic slowdown, or the reduction of supply of a needed product or service, gives it considerable clout in the lawmaking process.

Public Opinion

When the relationship between law and popular will was refined in the nineteenth century, theorists of law and society were concerned with the origins of law and the development of legal institutions (see Chapter 2). Legal development was viewed as a sequence of events. First, practices and sentiments occur in a group of people, without their awareness that they are the "right" ones or the "only" ones. Eventually, particularly on occasions of deviance from prior practice, *a* way of acting or believing becomes *the* way of acting or believing. Custom becomes law.

It is easier to substantiate the association between popular sentiments and law in so-called primitive societies (Llewellyn and Hoebel, 1941:10–15). As a society becomes more complex, there is a less direct correspondence between public opinion and the law. In a primitive society, one comes to know intimately the law of one's tribe. It is highly unlikely that today one can know, let alone tinker with, much of the law that could affect one's life. As a result of such limited awareness, there is a fair amount of selectivity involved in the expression of opinions toward the law. Some questions, therefore, arise in the discussion of the influence of public opinion on lawmaking. One concerns the timing of the relationship between public opinion and lawmaking. At what point does the accumulation of practice and belief make the reflection of those practices and beliefs in law an inevitability? For example, how many marijuana violations cause the law relating to marijuana to be changed?

A related question concerns the identification of those individuals whose opinion is expressed in lawmaking and the means of translating those opinions into legal outcomes. The *people* may mean a numerical majority, an influential elite, blacks, women, the poor, the middle class, the young, the aged, migrant workers, students, college professors, and so forth. Popular views may be similar throughout all segments of the population, but on many important issues opinions will differ.

A more meaningful way of looking at the influence of public opinion on lawmaking would be to consider the diverse opinions of many "publics" (that is, segments of society) bearing on specific concerns such as sentencing offenders for particular crimes (Walker and Hough, 1988). These opinions are expressed through a multitude of channels, such as the media, political parties, and the various types of interest groups. Care should be exercised, however, not to overestimate the catalytic part played by public opinion in lawmaking, which is conditioned by economic forces. As Friedman states:

The "public opinion" that affects the law is like the economic power which makes the market. This is so in two essential regards: Some people, but only some, take enough interest in any particular commodity to make their weight felt; second, there are some people who have more power and wealth than others. At one end of the spectrum stand such figures as the president of the United States and General Motors; at the other, migrant laborers, babies, and prisoners at San Quentin. (1975:163)

The differential influence of public opinion on lawmaking processes is a well-known phenomenon and is recognized by lawmakers. Lawmakers are aware that some people are more equal than others because of money, talent, or choice. Notes Friedman:

They know that 100 wealthy, powerful constituents passionately opposed to socialized medicine outweigh thousands of poor, weak constituents, mildly in favor of it. Most people do not shout, threaten, or write letters. They remain quiet and obscure, unless a head count reveals they are there. This is the "silent majority"; paradoxically, this group matters only when it breaks its silence— when it mobilizes or is mobilized by others. (1975:164)

Lawmakers also know that most people have no clear opinions on most issues with which judicial, administrative, and legislative bodies must deal. This means that they have a wide latitude within which to operate. Thus, for example, when a legislator claims to be representing the opinion of his or her district, he or she is, on most issues, representing the opinion of only a minority of the constituents, because most do not know or care about the issue at hand and do not communicate their views on it.

In spite of these considerations, public opinion does exert an influence on the lawmaking process (Carp and Stidham, 2001:296–304). Dennis S. Ippolito and his associates (1976) identify three types of influences that press lawmakers into formulating certain decisions. These three types are direct, group, and indirect influences.

Direct influences refer to constituent pressures that offer rewards or sanctions to lawmakers. Rewards for compliance and sanctions for noncompliance may be votes in an election or reelection campaign, financial assistance, and other forms of pressure that could possibly range from the representative's standing in lawmaking bodies to prestige in his or her own particular community. But this kind of influence is not confined to legislators. Members of the judiciary are also pressured by partisan publications to make certain decisions consistent with opinions and interests that run throughout the jurisdiction of a particular court.

The second type of influence is distinctly that of organized interest groups representing a special constituency. Political parties, interest groups, and citizen action groups are continually influencing the lawmaking process. In the area of administrative law, for example, special-interest groups press regulatory agencies for rules and regulations that are in keeping with their own immediate interests. Public opinion in these and other areas is represented by organization leaders. The motivation behind joining such groups is the perceived need for expressing a point of view in a manner that will influence lawmakers. In this context, public opinion becomes organized around a specific issue or an immediate objective (for example, pros and cons of gun control or abortion). Through the process of organizing, interests are made specific, and public-opinion backing is sought in the attempt to gain an advantage in pressing for change or redress through the legal machinery.

The third type of public-opinion model is that which influences the lawmaking process indirectly. Here a lawmaker acts in the capacity of an "instructed delegate." The decisions made are on behalf of the desires of a particular constituency, for example, residents living around an airport who oppose expansion of facilities. Ippolito (1976:3) and his colleagues state that indirect influence occurs when legislators act in accordance with constituent preferences because they either share such preferences or believe such preferences should prevail over their own judgment. This type of influence is indicative of the importance attached to public-opinion polls.

Public-opinion polls seek to determine the aggregate view people hold in a community on current important issues. Polling is flourishing in the United States. Today, there are more than half a dozen well-established commercial firms that take public-opinion polls. Among the most respected are the Gallup, Harris, Yankelovich, and Sindlinger polls, the Opinion Research Corporation poll, and the Roper and Cambridge Research Reports poll. They often work jointly with major TV networks such as CBS, CNN or NBC or newspapers and magazines such as the *New York Times, U.S. News & World Report, Time,* or *Newsweek.* In addition, there are a variety of smaller, specialized public and private and university polling organizations. Scores of surveys have been commissioned by federal agencies and by various state bodies. A typical sample size for national polls is around 1,500 respondents. Pollsters claim that with a sample of that size, there is a 95 percent probability that the results obtained are no more than three percentage points off the figure that would be obtained if every adult in the country were interviewed.

Opinion polls clearly influence what lawmakers do (Lipset, 1976). On a variety of domestic issues, for example, public opinion led or prompted lawmakers toward passage of a program that might have otherwise been delayed for months or years. Legislation concerning minimum wages, social security, and medical programs are examples of issues on which public opinion has preceded and prompted legislative action. However, in other instances, such as civil liberties and civil rights, public opinion has either lagged behind government policy or tended to support measures that are repressive of constitutional rights. For example, since the mid-1950s the Supreme Court has played a leading role in interpreting and formulating policies on civil rights that were more progressive than the views reflected in public-opinion polls

(Simon, 1974). It should be noted, however, that whether the United States Supreme Court does—or should—reflect majority public opinion has been a recurring controversy in American legal thought (Marshall, 1989).

Generally, the use of polls in lawmaking is encouraged. For example, Irving Crespi suggests that lawmakers could be more effective if they learned to draw upon the full fruits of survey research. Direct evidence—unfiltered by the interpretations of special interests or lobby groups—of the wants, needs, aspirations, and concerns of the general public needs to be accounted for in lawmaking activities. In lawmaking processes, Crespi argues that there should be first an attempt to determine the views of both the general public and that segment of the public that would be directly affected by a particular law. It could then make public opinion part of the formative stages of the lawmaking process, and not simply a force to be coped with after the fact. Says Crespi: "The difference between treating public attitudes and opinions as a relatively minor variable instead of an influence that should be authoritative is ultimately the difference between technocratic and democratic government" (1979:18).

Lawmaking and Social Science

Lawmakers have long been aware of the contribution that social scientists can make to the lawmaking process. For example, the Brandeis brief of 1908, defending the constitutionality of limited working hours for women, is considered an early landmark for the use of social science in lawmaking (Zeisel, 1962:142). The ideas of the economist John R. Commons (1934) influenced the way most states in the United States deal with compensation for industrial accidents and unemployment. In the major U.S. Supreme Court decision of *Brown* v. *Board of Education of Topeka* (347 U.S. 483 [1954]), the court drew upon a spectrum of the social sciences—ranging from discrete psychological experiments to broad-ranging economic and social inquiry—in reversing an earlier ruling that had established the separate-but-equal standards in racial matters. The Court ruled that racial segregation in elementary schools is psychologically harmful. In a footnote—the famous footnote 11—the Court also cited a number of social-science studies summarizing evidence showing that segregation retards black children's educational development.

In an era increasingly dominated by scientific and technical specialists, it is not surprising that lawmakers reflect the quest for specialization and expertise. Experts abound in a variety of fields (Smith, 1992), and there is a growing reliance on social scientists and the research data they generate in diverse areas ranging from school desegregation studies (Wolf, 1976) to consumer surveys in trademark suits. With the aid of social scientists, ad hoc committees of legislative bodies have, at times, also produced important studies on matters such as insurance, investment banking, and public utilities (Zeisel, 1962).

Efforts to bring social science to bear on lawmaking processes involve the use of quantitative social-science data and the reliance on the social scientist as an expert witness in specific legal cases. Social-science data may be collected and analyzed for academic purposes and later utilized by one or more sides of a dispute as it was, for example, in *Brown* v. *Board of Education*. Social-science research may also be reactive in the sense that it is initially requested by parties in a dispute. In such instances, the materials may address facts in the case (for example, research on sex discrimination in the jury selection for the Attica trial) or initiate an intervention in a lawmaking process (for example, the disparate effects of wage garnishment on blacks). Social-science research may also be undertaken in a proactive fashion. In such a situation, a social scientist may undertake an investigation (such as the social impact of mandatory day care for companies with more than 500 employees) with the anticipation of subsequent use of the results by lawmakers (Berk and Oppenheim, 1979:125).

Social scientists can also participate in the lawmaking process as expert witnesses who testify typically for one of the litigants or appear before a legislative body. The demand for such service is evidenced by the various directories of expert witnesses and a growing body of literature on the intricacies of testifying in court or in front of legislative bodies (Brodsky, 1991). At times, social scientists are asked to directly assist either the court or the legislator in the preparation of background documents pertinent to a particular issue or to serve on presidential commissions intended for policy recommendations.

Although social science influences what lawmakers do, there are controversies surrounding the role of social scientists in lawmaking. Consider, for example, the controversy that broke out in the late 1960s over reinterpretations of the Equal Educational Opportunity Report, commonly known as the Coleman Report, after its principal author, James S. Coleman (1966, 1967). In the late 1960s, Coleman's data on pupil achievement were the basis for a number of important court decisions calling for school busing. With the use of extensive busing to achieve "racial balance" in public schools, social-science findings about the effects of integration on black children have been hotly debated (Howard, 1979:104). In reviewing the studies on busing, David J. Armor (1972) has questioned the assumption that school integration enhances Blacks' educational achievement, aspirations, self-esteem, or opportunities for higher education. He contends that it is possible that desegregation actually retards race relations. Other scholars, such as Thomas F. Pettigrew and Robert L. Green (1976), have accused Armor of presenting a distorted and incomplete review of a politically charged topic. Incidentally, the entire controversy could have been avoided, for Coleman had not found any race effect as such in his analysis of student-body characteristics and educational achievement. Instead, he had found a social class effect. At the time of his testimony, this fact was not made clear to the court.

Daniel Patrick Moynihan (a ranking member of the U.S. Senate in the late 1990s from New York state) proposes two general reasons why social scientists have been criticized for their involvement in lawmaking processes. First, he points out that social science is basically concerned with the prediction of future events, whereas the purpose of the law is to order them. Notes Moynihan: "But where social science seeks to establish a fixity of *relationships* such that the consequences of behavior can be known in advance—or, rather, narrowed to a manageable range of possibilities—law seeks to dictate future performance on the basis of past *agreements*" (1979:16). For example, it is the function of the law to order alimony payments; it is the function of social science to attempt to estimate the likelihood of their being paid, of their effect on work behavior and remarriage in male and female parties, or similar probabilities. The second reason he suggests is that "social science is rarely dispassionate, and social scientists are frequently caught up in the politics which their work necessarily involves" (1979:19). Social scientists are, to a great extent, involved with problem solving, and the identification of a "problem" usually entails a political statement that implies a solution. Moynihan states: "Social scientists are never more revealing of themselves than when challenging the objectivity of one another's work. In some fields almost *any* study is assumed to have a more-or-less-discoverable political purpose" (1979:19). Furthermore, there is a distinct social and political bias among social scientists. As a result, the social sciences attract many people who are more interested in shaping the future than preserving the past. Moynihan feels that this orientation coupled with "liberal" tendencies and the limited explanatory power of social sciences results in a weakening of influence on lawmakers. He points out, for example, that after examining a number of recent studies concerning the effects of rehabilitation programs on criminals, no consistent effects could be shown one way or the other. Moynihan notes: "Seemingly, all that could be established for certain about the future behavior of criminals is that when they are in jail they do not commit street crimes" (1979:20). Similarly, there are still controversies concerning the deterrent effects of the death penalty (see for example, Wolfgang, 1998). Obviously, when social science data yield uncertain results, the root causes of major problems remain elusive. When well-intentioned social scientists dispute about alternatives, it is not surprising that lawmakers are, at times, skeptical about social science and social scientists.

SOURCES OF IMPETUS FOR LAW

An impetus is a fundamental prerequisite for setting the mechanism of lawmaking in motion. Demands for new laws or changes in existing ones come from a variety of sources. In the following pages, several of the more widely analyzed and prominent sources of impetus for law creation are considered.

These sources, which are not mutually exclusive, include detached scholarly diagnosis, a voice from the wilderness, protest activities, social movements, public-interest groups, and the mass media.

Detached Scholarly Diagnosis

The impetus for law may come from a detached scholarly undertaking. From time to time, academicians may consider a given practice or condition as detrimental in the context of existing values and norms. They may communicate their diagnoses to their colleagues or to the general public through either scholarly or popular forums. In some cases, they may even carry the perceived injustice to the legislature in search of legal redress. Perhaps the best way to illustrate how an impetus for law can be provided by a member of an academic community is to refer to my study on wage garnishment (a legal process that enables a creditor upon a debtor's default to seize his or her wages from the employer before the debtor is paid), carried out some years ago.

I investigated the impact of wage garnishment on low-income families. The findings indicated that existing wage garnishment laws at that time in Missouri were more counterproductive than functional as a collection device. Approximately 20 percent of the debtors were dismissed by their employers upon the receipt of the first garnishment suit. Such an action was detrimental not only to the debtor, but also to his or her family, creditor, and employer, and to society at large.

As a result of the deleterious and unintended consequences of garnishment (i.e., broken homes or engaging in illegal behavior), I proposed a simple procedure in the study to provide the debtor whose wages were subject to garnishment with legal safeguards so he or she will not be dismissed from a job or be forced into bankruptcy. At the same time, a provision was made also to enable creditors to maintain an effective collection method.

On the basis of my data and recommendations, House Bill 279 was designed and introduced in the 75th General Assembly of the State of Missouri. Under the proposed bill, the service of the writ would be made upon the defendant only, and the employer of the defendant would not be involved in the litigation process. Upon entry of the judgment, the court may order the debtor to make payments to the clerk of the court, which would be disbursed in turn by the clerk. In settling the amount of these payments, the court would take into consideration the circumstances of the defendant, including his or her income and other obligations or considerations bearing on the issue. If the debtor fails to obey the order of the court, *then, and only then,* may the creditor summon the employer as a garnishee. The primary intention of the bill was to prohibit employers from discharging employees upon the receipt of the first garnishment suit, thus saving thousands of jobs for low-income individuals annually in Missouri. It was estimated that on the national level, approximately 500,000 individuals are fired each year as a direct result of the practice of wage garnishment. The societal implications of the proposed changes were obvious (Vago, 1968:7–20). Today, wage garnishment is regulated nationally. This is the result of the Consumer Credit Protection Act (PL 90–32), passed in 1968. The act protects consumers from being driven into bankruptcy by excessive garnishment of wages by limiting the amount of wages subject to garnishment to 25 percent of the employee's weekly disposable income although it still plays a role in the 1.2 million personal bankruptcies filed annually (Kilborn, 2001). It also forbids the firing of an employee because of wage garnishment.

There have been a number of attempts by university professors in a variety of disciplines to provide an impetus for lawmaking as an outgrowth of their investigations. For example, publications by David Caplovitz, such as *The Poor Pay More* (1963) and *Consumers in Trouble: A Study of Debtors in Default* (1974), resulted in proposals for much-needed reform of the consumer credit laws. In *Genetic Fix* (1973), Amitai Etzioni examines the implications of "human engineering" and suggests that the Mondale Bill (the establishment of a scientific review committee in the form of a Health-Ethics Commission) should be used as a model for safeguarding such activities. Marc F. Plattner's influential article "Campaign Financing: The Dilemmas of Reform" (1974) stimulated further reexamination of existing procedures in this domain. Martin S. Feldstein (1975a, 1975b) is concerned with changes in unemployment insurance and social security laws, as the titles of his articles indicate: "Unemployment Insurance: Time for Reform" and "Toward a Reform of Social Security." Anthony Downs, in *Urban Problems and Prospects* (1976), calls a series of specific solutions on housing, community schools, and transportation dilemmas to the attention of lawmakers. The list could go on *ad infinitum*. But the point has been argued and illustrated that detached scholarly diagnoses can, indeed, stimulate lawmaking. The source of impetus, however, is not limited to ivory towers. It can have other origins, as the following sections will demonstrate.

A Voice from the Wilderness

Through their writings, many people outside of academe succeed, or even excel, in calling public attention to a particular problem or social condition. There is a long list of those whose literary efforts stimulated changes in the law. For our purposes, it will suffice to call attention to a few better-known such ventures.

Around the turn of the twentieth century, there was a fair amount of concern in the United States about the quality of food products. In particular, numerous scandals had arisen over the quality of meat products. It was alleged that during the Spanish-American War, American soldiers were forced to eat cans of "embalmed beef." A number of horrible practices of manufacturers were revealed in the mass media, but a federal food and drug law had still not passed when, in 1906, Upton Sinclair published *The Jungle*, a novel about life in Chicago, centering on the stockyards.

The first half of the book deals with a vivid description of conditions in the Chicago meatpacking plants. To illustrate:

> Tubercular pork was sold for human consumption. Old sausage, rejected in Europe and shipped back "mouldy and white," would be "dosed with borax and glycerin, and dumped into the hoppers, and made over again for home consumption." Meat was stored in rooms where "water from leaky roofs would drip over it, and thousands of rats would race about on it." The packers would put out poisoned bread to kill the rats; then the rats would die, and "rats, bread and meat would go into the hoppers together." Most horrifying of all was the description of the men in the "cooking rooms." They "worked in tankrooms full of steam," in some of which there were "open vats near the level of the floor." Sometimes they fell into the vats "and when they were fished out, there was never enough of them left to be worth exhibiting—sometimes they would be overlooked for days, till all but the bones of them had gone out to the world as Durham's Pure Leaf Lard." (Quoted by Friedman and Macaulay, 1977:611–612)

When it was published, the book created a furor. A copy was sent to President Roosevelt, who, in turn, appointed two investigators whose report confirmed Sinclair's findings. It is hard to say to what extent Sinclair's book provided an impetus for the passage of the Pure Food and Meat Inspection Law in 1906, but it is indisputable that it played an important role in it.

In the domain of environmental protection laws, it would be difficult not to consider the book *Silent Spring*, by Rachel Carson (1962). It was the first time that the environmental threat posed by pesticides was announced to a wide audience. Others in the same vein included Richard Falk's *This Endangered Planet* (1971), Fairfield Osborn's *Our Plundered Planet* (1948), and *Moment in the Sun*, by R. and L. T. Reinow (1967).

Even a short list of influential authors would be incomplete without a reference to Ralph Nader. He was an unknown young lawyer at the time he published his book, *Unsafe at Any Speed* (1965), which alerted the public to the automobile industry's unconcern for safety in the design and construction of American cars. This book is a model of the kind of muckraking journalism that, at times, initiates the rise of public concern over a given issue. As a result of his book, and General Motors' reaction to it, Nader became front-page news, and his charges took on new weight. More than anyone else, he has contributed to and provided the impetus for the passing of a substantial number of auto safety provisions. Since 1966, Nader "has been responsible almost entirely through his efforts for the passage of seven major consumer-related laws—the Traffic and Motor Vehicle Safety Act (1966), Natural Gas Pipeline Safety Act (1968), Wholesale Meat Act (1967), Radiation

Control Act (1968), Wholesale Poultry Products Act (1967), Coal Mine Health and Safety Act (1969), and the Occupational Health and Safety Act (1970)" (Buckhorn, 1972:226).

There are other ways of transforming "private troubles into public issues" (Spector and Kitsuse, 1973:148). For example, we are all familiar with Rosa Parks, a black seamstress who, on December 1, 1955, sat down in the back of a city bus in Montgomery, Alabama, then refused to relinquish her seat to a white man when the "noncolored" section became overcrowded. Her action launched the famous black boycott of the buses that created a new era in the civil rights struggle and provided considerable impetus for civil rights legislation. And let's not forget Carrie Nation's efforts to demonstrate the advantages of Prohibition by chopping up saloons with her celebrated hatchet.

Protest Activity

Protest activity involves demonstrations, sit-ins, strikes, boycotts and more recently various forms of electronic civil disobedience or "hacktivism" (Harmon, 1998) that dramatically emphasize, often with the help of the media, a group's grievances or objectives. Often, such strategies, along with rioting or other use of violence, have been considered tools of those who are unable or unwilling to engage in the more conventional lawmaking or who regard it useless (Gamson, 1990). It should be noted at the outset that "the relationship among law, protest, and social change is neither unidirectional nor symmetrical—nor always predictable. One major function of protest may be to secure changes in the law as a means of inducing change in social conditions. Another may be to bring about change directly without the intervention of the law. Still a third may be to bring about legal change which ratifies or legitimizes social change accomplished by other means. These functions are not mutually exclusive" (Grossman and Grossman, 1971:357). But the impact of protest activities on law creation is clearly evident, for "the law in general, and the Court in particular, lacks a self-starter or capacity for initiating change on its own" (Grossman and Grossman, 1971:358).

Racial minorities, poverty organizations, antiwar groups, and opponents of nuclear power have been among those who have employed protest techniques in recent years in attempts to create laws in favor of their objectives. Much of this activity is designed to generate favorable media coverage and through this, the support of organizations and persons important in the eyes of lawmakers. But the young, the poor, and minority groups have not been the only ones to use protest techniques such as strikes and boycotts. Strike action has long been a central tactic of organized labor, including the unions of public employers in pursuing political and economic goals. In the mid-1970s, physicians used the strike weapon as a method of seeking governmental relief from medical malpractice insurance costs. Boycotts have been used by consumers protesting high prices. The national meat boycott of 1973 is an important example of such consumer action. It helped to generate enough pressure to force President Nixon to place a ceiling on meat prices. The controls, however, caused a meat shortage as farmers cut back on their supply.

To what extent protest activities provide an impetus for lawmaking is difficult to say. But "few major social movements or great changes have occurred without the unrest and disorder which, if one approves is called protest or civil disobedience, and if one disapproves, it is called breaking the law, violence, or worse. Violence in particular is as much a part of enforcing the law as it is of seeking changes in the law" (Grossman and Grossman, 1971:358).

Social Movements

Over the years, there have been many examples of social movements that have culminated in proposals for or the actual creation of new laws and social policies (Almeida and Stearns, 1998; Santoro and McGuire, 1997; Tarrow, 1998; Yarnold, 1992:109–128). By definition, a social movement is a type of collective behavior whereby a group of individuals organize to promote certain changes or alterations in certain types of behavior or procedures. Invariably, the movement has specified stated objectives, a hierarchical organizational structure, and a well-conceptualized and precise change-oriented ideology. The movement consciously and purposefully articulates the changes it desires through political, educational, or legal channels (see, for example, McAdam and Snow, 1997).

A good example is the movement to legalize abortion. People had for some time regarded illegal abortion as dangerous, but efforts to prevent it (and thus end the death or serious injury of women) were unsuccessful. Then, a combination of women's rights and medical groups began to demand the legalization of abortion. Medical spokespersons argued that abortion is rightfully a medical decision to be made by a physician and his or her patient. Women's leaders argued that a woman has an unassailable right over her own body and ought to be able to choose whether or not to terminate the pregnancy. At the same time, no significant groups in society had a stake either in a high birthrate or in providing expensive illegal abortions. On the contrary, the general consensus was that the economic interests of the nation were concerned with the issues of overpopulation. Furthermore, with modern medical techniques, a legal abortion is classified as minor surgery, both cheap and safe.

With relative speed, in the 1960s states began to repeal or greatly liberalize laws against abortion. Within this climate of opinion, the Supreme Court completed the process in 1973 by declaring state laws against abortion unconstitutional except in the case of the last three months of pregnancy, and in regulating the physicians who perform the operation. The landmark 1973 decision that established a woman's right to abortion is still the law of the land, although it was narrowed in 1989 by a Supreme Court decision that sharply restricts the availability of public funds for abortion and requires physicians to test for the viability of a fetus at 20 weeks (*Newsweek*, 1989:14). Still, it remains a classic example of a social movement. Of course, there are many others, including ecology, civil rights, feminism, "crime without victims," and "law and order movements." It should be pointed out that not all social movements are successful in bringing about changes through laws. As a matter of fact, at any given moment, hundreds of groups with hundreds of messages are trying to get public attention. Most fail as evidenced by the various "deviance liberation" movements, such those of prostitutes rights movements, both in this country and in Europe (Poel, 1995). In the United States, winning public attention, thus public support, is becoming a highly professional activity. Groups that can afford to hire or that can recruit public relations and advertising experts have a considerable advantage over other groups in getting a public hearing for their grievances. It is interesting to note that, regardless of the expertise available to them, all groups share the problem of developing an effective strategy to attract attention in a way that will not at the same time provoke outrage and opposition.

Public Interest Groups

Lawmakers are fully cognizant of the fact that private interests are much better represented than public interests (see, for example, Maloney, et al., 1994). There are literally hundreds of organizations and individuals in Washington and in state capitals who represent one or more private interests on a full- or part-time basis (Godwin, 1988; Mahood, 1990). They range from extremely well-financed organizations, such as the American Petroleum Institute, involved in worldwide affairs and supported by thousands of engineers, lawyers, and public relations experts, to small, single-issue groups, such as the Sportsman's Paradise Homeowners Association. Some, such as oil companies, regulate refinery output to maintain prices, and they lobby government representatives for favorable tax policies. Others, such as United States Shipbuilders and the National Maritime Union, win direct and indirect subsidies from Congress in the guise of national defense requirements. Power utilities are legal monopolies whose rate structures are decided by utility commissions that are, in turn, the focus of tremendous pressures to allow expansion and higher rates for the benefit of managers and investors. There are over 17,000 entries in the current *Encyclopedia of Associations*. Most of them represent specific private interests.

By contrast, the number of groups that claim to represent public interests is quite small. The most notable among these include John Gardner's Common Cause, the Sierra Club, Public Interest Research Groups (PIRGs) and the various Centers for Law in the Public Interest focusing on public safety and other local problems (Reske, 1994). These groups have been instrumental in the initiation of a series of changes in the law designed to benefit and protect the public.

The Common Cause organization, founded in 1970, had an annual budget of over $6 million and around 300,000 dues-paying members in mid-2001 and remains viable despite a reduction in both membership and budget since the early 1980s. It "has fought pitched battles on issues of the deepest concern to the American people—the Vietnam war, environmental pollution, racial injustice, poverty, unemployment, and women's rights" (Gardner, 1973:18). The organization is dedicated to "opening up the system" through the reform of campaign financing, open meeting laws, and disclosure laws. For example, in 1973, it initiated proposals for legislations that included making highway trust funds available for mass transit use, an unequivocal press-shield law, and "tax equity" (Wieck, 1973:21).

Spurred by the belief that the world faces an ultimate ecocatastrophe unless immediate and successful efforts are made to halt the abuse and deterioration of the environment, Sierra Club members "are no longer the outdoor recreationists of yesterday, but rather today's environmental politicos, in the vanguard of society's newest social movement" (Faich and Gale, 1971:282). The Sierra Club and similar organizations have been active in recent years in providing the impetus for a series of laws dealing with the protection of the environment. Some of these include the Air Pollution Control Act of 1967, the Clear Air Act of 1970, and the Clean Water Act of 1972, in addition to the formation of a number of new federal agencies both to monitor compliance with the numerous existing pollution and environmental protection laws and to help establish new policies.

Modeled after Nader's Center for Responsive Law, but independent of it, are the various public-interest research groups that now, after only a few years of organizing, include close to 400,000 student members at over 150 schools in twenty-four states. These groups are both funded and directed by students and are composed of a small professional staff of lawyers, scientists, and organizers, aided by hundreds of volunteer student researchers. For example, in the late 1990s, the Missouri Public Interest Research Group (MOPIRG) drafted a new consumer code to protect poor people in St. Louis and distributed a handbook on tenants' rights in Missouri. MOPIRG also participated in a study of the Educational Testing Service and is working with St. Louis unions to secure better enforcement of the occupational safety and health laws. Just recently it has been instrumental in setting up a small claims court in Missouri. In other states as well, the Public Interest Research Groups are active in pointing out deficiencies in the system and proposing legal solutions for their improvement through research, public information, and law reform.

Impetus for law may also come from the various quasi-public specialized interest groups. They may represent certain economic interests, such as consumer groups, organized labor, or the National Welfare Rights organization. Or they may represent certain occupational interests, such as the American Medical Association, which not only exercises considerable control over the practice of medicine in this country, but also actively takes stands, raises money, and lobbies in favor of specific positions on such issues as abortion, euthanasia, drugs, and alcohol. The same can be said for the American Association of University Professors (though not on the same issues). Still others include groups representing what may be called moral interests, such as temperance, various types of antidrug concerns, various forms of "child saving" (for example, delinquency control), sexual deviance, the "work ethic," and antipornography. The important point to remember is that all these organizations can agitate for changes in the law and can provide the needed impetus for it.

For a group to effectively promote its interests and to provide an impetus for lawmaking, it naturally must have access to lawmakers. But access to lawmakers depends, at least in part, on the socioeconomic status of the group. Groups with the most financial resources, the most prestigious membership, and the best organization are likely to have the greatest access to legislators. It takes a substantial amount of money to maintain lobbyists in Washington and throughout the state capitals. Moreover, lawmakers, on the local as well as the higher levels, may be more sympathetic to groups that represent interests of the middle and upper classes than to groups representing poor people, welfare recipients, and the like. Generally, groups with "mainstream" views, seeking only small changes in the status quo, may be given more sympathetic hearing than those advocating large-scale radical changes.

The Mass Media

The mass media (newspapers, magazines, and radio and television stations) function in part as an interest group. Each component of the mass media is a business, and like other businesses, it has a direct interest in various areas of public policy. For example, the media have had a general objective of securing legislation, such as freedom of information and open meeting laws, that facilitates their access to the news, and legislation or court decisions that allow them to protect the confidentiality of news sources. Associations like the National Association of Broadcasters are regularly concerned with the activities of the Federal Communications Commission, which controls their licensing of television and radio stations.

The mass media also function as conduits, although not altogether impartial ones, for others who would shape policy. Wealthier groups, for example, purchase media time or space in an effort to align public opinion behind their causes. Through the media, these groups may reach the ear of legislators and administrators by publicly exposing problems and proposals about which they might not otherwise hear, or in some instances, about which they might not want to hear.

The mass media, especially the news media, are able to generate widespread awareness and concern about events and conditions—to bring matters before the public so that they become problematic issues. For example, columnist Jack Anderson, the irreverent muckraker, repeatedly sniffs out malodorous secrets that vested interests—oil companies, the Pentagon, the various juntas in Latin American countries, the distributors of chemical defoliants—do not want aired.

The Watergate case is a classic demonstration of the number of ways in which the mass media influence current events. Without dogged investigations by the mass media, the scandal probably would have remained buried. Without the blitz of mass-media coverage, the issues probably would not have achieved as rapid, widespread, or deep an impact on the public. Many of the most scandalous incidents of the Watergate affair have involved the improper solicitation and employment of campaign funds. Outraged segments of public opinion demanded the prevention of future "Watergates." The legislative response to this outcry was the passage of a bill in April 1974 that would drastically alter the way in which presidential and congressional campaigns are funded. This is illustrative of situations in which, as a result of investigative reporting, the mass media provide a direct impetus for legislation. A more recent example of the role of mass media in influencing current events is seen in the context of the Iran-Contra scandal. Special congressional committees have been impaneled to look into the precipitating events leading to the scandal, and the Attorney General has opened a criminal investigation into the possibility that millions of dollars raised through secret U.S. arms sales to Iran had been diverted to the Contra supply effort in an attempt to topple Nicaragua's government, which was controlled by the leftist Sandinista Party. It is likely that these events will result in a series of laws dealing with the discretionary power of government agencies and officials (*St. Louis Post-Dispatch*, 1987:1B).

Since public opinion is an important precursor of change, the mass media can set the stage by making undesirable conditions visible to a sizable segment of the public with unparalleled rapidity. Through the exposure of perceived injustices, the mass media play a crucial role in the formation of public opinion. Ralph Turner and Lewis M. Killian (1987) discuss six processes considered essential in understanding how the mass media can influence public opinion. First, the mass media *authenticate* the factual nature of events, which is decisive in the formation of public opinion. Second, the mass media *validate* opinions, sentiments, and preferences. It is reassuring to hear one's views confirmed by a well-known commentator. It also enables a person to express his or her views more effectively by borrowing the commentator's words. A third effect of the mass media is to *legitimize* certain behaviors and viewpoints considered to be taboo. Issues that were discussed only in private can now be expressed publicly, since they have already been discussed on television (for example, legal rights of homosexuals). Fourth, the mass media often *symbolize* the diffuse anxieties, preferences, discontents, and prejudices that individuals experience. By giving an acceptable identification for these perplexing feelings, the mass media often aid their translation into specific opinions and actions. By providing symbols—the "me" generation, Yuppies, law and order, the new morality—the mass media create a number of objects toward which specific sentiments can be directed. Fifth, the mass media *focus* the preferences, discontents, and prejudices into lines of action. Finally, the mass media *classify into hierarchies* persons, objects, activities, and issues. As a result of the amount of consideration, preferential programming, and placement of items, they indicate relative importance and prestige.

The generalization that the views of individuals whose prestige and influence are established carry more weight than the views of others applies to public opinion. As a result, the "influences stemming from the mass media first reach 'opinion leaders,' who in turn, pass on what they read or hear to those of their everyday associates for whom they are influential" (Katz, 1957:61). Opinion leaders are usually leaders in only one sphere of activity. They tend to be different from the rest of the public in that they are more highly educated and are engaged in more prestigious occupations. They are also more powerful, active, and influential in specific community, interest-group, or political affairs. Consequently, their opinions are considered much more influential and, therefore, are targeted by much of the media efforts.

In addition to investigative reporting and the shaping of public opinion, the mass media can pressure or challenge lawmakers into taking action on an issue or into changing their stand on a question. Influential newspapers such as the *New York Times* and the *Washington Post* can make or break legislators by the use of the editorial pages. Endorsement by a major newspaper can greatly facilitate a candidate's chances for being elected. Conversely, opposition to a candidate on the editorial page can influence the outcome of an election. Legislators are quite aware of the power of the press, and as a result, editorial recommendations are given serious consideration. Similarly, articles in various influential weekly or monthly publications such as *Commentary, Daedalus, Encounter, Monthly Review, Economist, The Nation, New Leader, New Republic, Public Interest, Progressive, Social Policy,* and the diverse specialized professional and legal journals can agitate for change.

Finally, an indirect way by which the mass media can furnish an impetus for lawmaking is through the provision of a forum for citizens' concerns. For example, the "letters to the editor" page in newspapers is a traditional outlet for publicizing undesirable conditions. Such letters can accomplish several objectives. First, the letter can alert the community that an issue is before a lawmaking body; second, it can persuade the reader to take a position; third, it can make clear that there are responsible and articulate people in the community who are concerned with the issue; and fourth, it can enlist the active support of others. Similarly, many radio and television stations have local talk shows and public-affairs programs that can be used to air grievances and to seek redress.

SUMMARY

This chapter has been concerned with the complex and continuous process of lawmaking in society. A number of theoretical perspectives to account for lawmaking have been reviewed. They include the rationalistic model, the functional view, conflict theory, and the "moral entrepreneur" thesis. None of these theories can account for the creation of all laws. At best, they explain in part how laws are made.

Three general types of lawmaking processes—legislative, administrative, and judicial—were analyzed. Legislators are solely responsible for formulating broad new roles and for creating and revising the institutions necessary to put them into effect. Legislative lawmaking basically consists of finding major and minor compromises to ideas advanced for legislation by the executive, administrative agencies, interest groups, and various party agencies and spokespersons. Administrative lawmaking consists of rule making and adjudication. Rule making is essentially legislation by administrative agencies. Adjudication differs from rule making in that it applies only to a specific, limited number of parties involved in an individual case and controversy before the agency. Judicial lawmaking is an accelerating trend in the United States. Three types of judicial lawmaking were examined—by precedent, by interpretation of statutes, and by interpretation of the Constitution. Judicial lawmaking is generally directed at other government agencies rather than at private individuals.

Interest groups, public opinion, and social science all exert an influence on the lawmaking process. Interest groups influence judicial lawmaking by initiating test cases, by providing additional information to the courts through *amicus curiae* briefs, and by communicating indirectly with judges by placing information in legal and general periodicals. Interactions between interest groups and legislative and administrative lawmakers are more overtly political in nature. The notion that laws reflect public opinion can be misleading. Some groups are more influential than others, and the differential influence of public opinion on lawmaking processes is a well-known phenomenon. Still, public opinion does exert an influence on lawmakers through rewards and sanctions (for example, voting for or against a particular legislator); through interest groups; and through the use of public opinion polls. Lawmakers are aware of the contributions social scientists can make to the lawmaking process. These contributions are based on social-science research and expressed to lawmakers either directly in the form of expert testimony or indirectly through the use of research findings as they bear upon a particular piece of legislation or judicial and administrative decision. But the participation of social scientists in the lawmaking process is not without controversies. There are questions about the use of research results, their validity and reliability, and the political bias of social scientists. In spite of the controversies, it was noted that social-science evidence cannot be kept out of the lawmaking process.

Demands for lawmaking come from a multitude of sources. Ideas for change are born in the minds of a few people who are ready and willing to articulate their dissatisfaction. They represent diverse interests and causes and channel their discontent through different means. Once in a while, a scholarly investigation generates concern over a social condition or practice and points to a legal solution. At times, a novel can detect or warn about a deleterious situation that affects the public. The impetus for lawmaking can also come from institutionalized forces, such as lobbying activities and public-interest groups. Occasionally, the creation of laws has been stimulated by organized protest activities or social movements. Finally, the mass media can set the stage for lawmaking by calling attention to an issue.

SUGGESTED FURTHER READINGS

GARY C. BRYNER, *Bureaucratic Discretion: Law and Policy in Federal Regulatory Agencies.* New York: Pergamon Press, 1987. Four case studies on administrative lawmaking.

BRADLEY C. CANON and CHARLES A. JOHNSON. *Judicial Policies; Instrumentation and Impact.* 2nd ed. Washington, DC: CQ Press, 1999. An insightful book on the impact and consequences of judicial activities.

WILLIAM J. CHAMBLISS and MARJORIE S. ZATZ (eds.). *Making Law: The State, the Law, and Structural Contradictions.* Bloomington: Indiana University Press, 1993. A collection of 16 articles on the various facets of lawmaking.

TIMOTHY D. CHENEY, *Who Makes the Law; The Supreme Court, Congress, the States, and Society.* Upper Saddle River, NJ: Prentice Hall, 1998. A brief primer on law creation and instrumentation.

LON L. FULLER, *Anatomy of the Law.* New York: Praeger, 1968. See in particular Part 2, "The Sources of Law."

JOHN W. GARDNER, *In Common Cause* (rev ed.). New York: W. W. Norton & Co., Inc., 1973. An interesting and provocative account of a group serving the public interest.

NATHAN GLAZER, "Towards an Imperial Judiciary?" *Public Interest* (41) (Fall) 1975: 104–123. A classic, intriguing, and still controversial article on the increase in judicial lawmaking.

JOHN HAGAN, "The Legislation of Crime and Delinquency: A Review of Theory, Method, and Research," *Law & Society Review* 14 (3) (Spring), 1980: 603–628. A review of more than 40 influential early studies drawn from the crime and delinquency legislation literature.

RICHARD A. HARRIS and SIDNEY M. MILKIS, *The Politics of Regulatory Change: A Tale of Two Agencies.* New York: Oxford University Press, 1989. A fascinating account of how regulatory policies are made and unmade.

SEYMOUR MARTIN LIPSET, "The Wavering Polls," *Public Interest* (43) (Spring) 1976: 70–89. An essay on the advantages and limitations of public-opinion polls and their implications on lawmaking.

MICHAEL W. MCCANN and GERALD L. HOUSEMAN (eds.), *Judging the Constitution: Critical Essays on Judicial Lawmaking.* Glenview, IL.: Scott, Foresman/Little, Brown, 1989. Fifteen original and provocative essays by authors of different backgrounds and philosophies on judicial lawmaking.

JOHN MONAHAN and LAURENS WALKER, *Social Science in Law: Cases and Materials,* 4th ed. Westbury, NY: The Foundation Press, Inc., 1998. See in particular Chapter 4 on the various types of lawmaking and the social forces behind them.

MARK J. ROZELL and CLYDE WILCOX, *Interest Groups in American Campaigns, The New Face of Electioneering.* Washington, DC: CQ Press, 1999. A concise resource on the large and growing influence that interest groups have on the political process at all levels in the American society.

ROMAN A. TOMASIC (ed.), *Legislation and Society in Australia.* Sydney: George Allen and Unwin, 1980. A series of case studies and theoretical articles on the making and instrumentation of law in Australia.

MICHAEL ZANDER, *The Law-Making Process* (5th ed.). London: Butterworths, 1999. A fascinating discussion of lawmaking in England using a variety of original texts from a number of different sources.

REFERENCES

ABRAHAM, HENRY J. 1994. *The Judiciary: The Supreme Court in the Governmental Process.* 9th ed. Madison, WI: Brown & Benchmark Publishers.

ABRAMSON, JILL. 1998. "The Business of Persuasion Thrives in Nation's Capital," *New York Times* (September 29): A1, A22–23.

ALMEIDA, PAUL and LINDA BREWSTER STEARNS. 1998. "Political Opportunities and Local Grassroots Environmental Movements: The Case of Minamata," *Social Problems* 45 (1) (February): 37–57.

ARMOR, DAVID J. 1972. "The Evidence on Busing," *Public Interest* 25 (Summer): 90–126.

BAUM, LAWRENCE. 1998 *The Supreme Court.* 6th ed. Washington, DC: QC Press.

BECKER, HOWARD S. 1963. *Outsiders.* New York: Free Press.

BERK, RICHARD A., and JERROLD OPPENHEIM. 1979. "Doing Good Well: The Use of Quantitative Social Science Data in Adversary Proceedings," *Law and Policy Quarterly* 1 (2) (April): 123–146.

BOHANNAN, PAUL. 1973. "The Differing Realms of the Law." Pp. 306–317 in Donald Black and Maureen Mileski (eds.), *The Social Organization of the Law.* New York: Seminar Press.

BRODSKY, STANLEY L. 1991. *Testifying in Court.* Washington, DC: American Psychological Association.

BRYDEN, DAVID P. 1993. "A Conservative Case for Judicial Activism," *Public Interest* 111 (Spring): 72–87.

BRYNER, GARY C. 1987. *Bureaucratic Discretion: Law and Policy in Federal Regulatory Agencies.* New York: Pergamon Press.

BUCKHORN, ROBERT F. 1972. *Nader, The People's Lawyer.* Englewood Cliffs, NJ: Prentice Hall.

CANON, BRADLEY C., and CHARLES A. JOHNSON. 1999. *Judicial Policies; Instrumentation and Impact.* 2nd ed. Washington, DC: CQ Press.

CAPLOVITZ, DAVID. 1963. *The Poor Pay More*. New York: Free Press. 1974. *Consumers in Trouble: A Study of Debtors in Default*. New York: Free Press.

CARP, ROBERT A., and RONALD STIDHAM. 2001. *Judicial Process in America*. 5th ed. Washington, DC: CQ Press.

CARSON, RACHEL L. 1962. *Silent Spring*. Boston: Houghton-Mifflin.

CHAMBLISS, WILLIAM J. 1964. "A Sociological Analysis of the Law of Vagrancy," *Social Problems* 12 (1) (Summer): 67–77. 1976. "The State and Criminal Law." Pp. 66–106 in William J. Chambliss and Milton Mankoff (eds.), *Whose Law, What Order? A Conflict Approach to Criminology*. New York: John Wiley. 1984. *Criminal Law in Action*. 2nd ed. New York: John Wiley.

CHAMBLISS, WILLIAM J. and MARJORIE S. ZATZ (EDS.). 1993. *Making Law: The State, the Law, and Structural Contradictions*. Bloomington: Indiana University Press.

CHENEY, TIMOTHY D. 1998. *Who Makes the Law; The Supreme Court, Congress, the States, and Society*. Upper Saddle River, NJ: Prentice Hall.

COLEMAN, JAMES S. 1966. "Equality Schools or Equal Students," *Public Interest*, no. 7 (Summer): 70–75. 1967. "Toward Open Schools," *Public Interest*, 9 (Fall): 20–27.

COMMONS, JOHN R. 1934. *Institutional Economics*. New York: MacMillan.

CRESPI, IRVING. 1979. "Modern Marketing Techniques: They Could Work in Washington, Too," *Public Opinion* 2 (3) (June-July): 16–19, 58–59.

DAVIDSON, ROGER H. 1993. "The Lawmaking Congress," *Law and Contemporary Problems* 56 (4) (Autumn): 99–119.

DAVIS, KENNETH CULP. 1977. *Administrative Law: Cases-Text-Problems*. 6th ed. St. Paul, MN: West Publishing Company.

DOWNS, ANTHONY. 1976. *Urban Problems and Prospects*. 2nd ed. Chicago: Markham Publishing Company.

ECONOMIST. 2001. "High Time: A Survey of Illegal Drugs" (July 28): 1–16.

ETZIONI, AMITAI. 1973. *The Genetic Fix*. New York: MacMillan.

EVAN, WILLIAM M. 1990. *Social Structure and Law: Theoretical and Empirical Perspectives*. Newbury Park, CA: Sage Publications.

FAICH, RONALD G., and RICHARD P. GALE. 1971. "The Environmental Movement from Recreation to Politics," *Pacific Sociological Review* 14 (July): 270–287.

FALK, RICHARD. 1971. *This Endangered Planet*. New York: Random House.

FELDSTEIN, MARTIN S. 1975a. "Toward a Reform of Social Security," *Public Interest* 40 (Summer): 75–95. 1975b. "Unemployment Insurance: Time for Reform," *Harvard Business Review* 53 (March-April): 51–61.

FRIEDMAN, LAWRENCE M. 1975. *The Legal System: A Social Science Perspective*. New York: Russell Sage Foundation. 1998. *American Law: An Introduction*. 2nd ed. New York: W. W. Norton & Co., Inc. 2002. *American Law in the Twentieth Century*, New Haven: Yale University Press.

FRIEDMAN, LAWRENCE M., and STEWART MACAULAY. 1977. *Law and the Behavioral Sciences*. 2nd ed. Indianapolis: Bobbs-Merrill.

FULLER, LON. 1968. *Anatomy of the Law*. New York: Praeger.

GAMSON, WILLIAM. 1990. *The Strategy of Social Protest*. 2nd ed. Belmont, CA: Wadsworth.

GARDNER, JOHN W. 1973. *In Common Cause*. Rev. ed. New York: W. W. Norton & Co., Inc.

GLAZER, NATHAN. 1975. "Towards an Imperial Judiciary?" *Public Interest* 41 (Fall): 104–123.

GLENDON, MARY ANN. 1994. *A Nation Under Lawyers: How the Crisis in the Legal Profession Is Transforming American Society.* New York: Farrar, Straus, and Giroux.

GODWIN, R. KENNETH. 1988. *One Billion Dollars of Influence: The Direct Marketing of Politics.* Chatham, NJ: Chatham House Publishers, Inc.

GOODE, ERICH. 1997. *Deviant Behavior.* 5th ed. Upper Saddle River, NJ: Prentice Hall.

GRAGLIA, LINO A. 1994. "Do Judges Have a Policy-making Role in the American System of Government?," *Harvard Journal of Law & Public Policy* 17 (1) (Winter): 119–130.

GROSSMAN, JOEL B., and MARY H. GROSSMAN (EDS.). 1971. *Law and Social Change in Modern America.* Pacific Palisades, CA: Goodyear.

GUSFIELD, JOSEPH R. 1967. "Moral Passage: The Symbolic Process in Public Designations of Deviance," *Social Problems* 15 (2) (Fall): 175–188.

HAGAN, JOHN. 1980. "The Legislation of Crime and Delinquency: A Review of Theory, Method, and Research," *Law & Society Review* 14 (3) (Spring): 603–628.

HAJNAL, ZOLTAN L., and TERRY NICHOLS CLARK. 1998. "The Local Interest-Group System: Who Governs and Why?," *Social Science Quarterly* 79 (1) (March): 227–242.

HARMON, AMY. 1998. "'Hacktivists' of All Persuasions Take Their Struggle to the Web," *New York Times* (October 31): A1, A5.

HOROWITZ, DONALD L. 1977. *The Courts and Social Policy.* Washington, DC: Brookings Institution.

HOWARD, A. E. DICK. 1979. "The Road from 'Brown'," *Wilson Quarterly* 3 (2) (Spring): 96–107.

IPPOLITO, DENNIS S., THOMAS G. WALKER, and KENNETH L. KOLSON. 1976. *Public Opinion and Responsible Democracy.* Englewood Cliffs, NJ: Prentice-Hall.

JACOB, HERBERT. 1984. *Justice in America: Courts, Lawyers, and the Judicial Process.* 4th ed. Boston: Little, Brown.

KATZ, ELIHU. 1957. "The Two-Step Flow of Communication: An Up-to-Date Report on an Hypothesis," *Public Opinion Quarterly* 21 (1) (Spring): 61–78.

KERRIGAN, LAURA J. ET AL., 1993. "Project: The Decriminalization of Administrative Law Penalties: Civil Remedies, Alternatives, Policy and Constitutional Implications," *Administrative Law Review* 45 (4) (Fall): 367–434.

KILBORN, PETER T. 2001. "Out of a Swamp of Debt, a Rocky Path," *New York Times* (April 1): 1, 16.

LEO, RICHARD A. and GEORGE C. THOMAS III (EDS.). 1998. *The Miranda Debate: Law, Justice, and Policing.* Boston: Northeastern University Press.

LIPSET, SEYMOUR MARTIN. 1976. "The Wavering Polls," *Public Interest* 43 (Spring): 70–89.

LLEWELLYN, KARL N., and E. ADAMSON HOEBEL. 1941. *The Cheyenne Way: Conflict and Case Law in Primitive Jurisprudence.* Norman: University of Oklahoma Press.

MAHOOD, H. R. 1990. *Interest Group Politics in America: A New Intensity.* Englewood Cliffs, NJ: Prentice Hall.

MALONEY, WILLIAM A., GRANT JORDAN and ANDREW M. MCLAUGHLIN. 1994. "Interest Groups and Public Policy: The Insider/Outsider Model Revisited," *Journal of Public Policy* 14 (1) (January-March): 17–39.

MARSHALL, THOMAS R. 1989. *Public Opinion and the Supreme Court.* Boston: Unwin Hyman.

MCADAM, DOUG and DAVID A. SNOW (EDS.) 1997. *Social Movements: Readings on Their Emergence, Mobilization, and Dynamics.* Los Angeles, CA: Roxbury Publishing Company.

MCCANN, MICHAEL W., and GERALD L. HOUSEMAN (EDS.). 1989. *Judging the Constitution: Critical Essays in Judicial Lawmaking*. Glenview, IL: Scott, Foresman/Little, Brown.

MCGUIRE, KEVIN T. 1994. "Amici Curiae and Strategies for Gaining Access to the Supreme Court," *Political Research Quarterly* 47 (4) (December): 821–838.

MONAHAN, JOHN, and LAURENS WALKER. 1998. *Social Science in Law: Cases and Materials*. 4th ed. Westbury, NY: The Foundation Press, Inc.

MOYNIHAN, DANIEL PATRICK. 1979. "Social Science and the Courts," *Public Interest* 54 (Winter): 12–31.

NADER, RALPH. 1965. *Unsafe at Any Speed: The Designed-in Dangers of the American Automobile*. New York: Grossman.

NEWSWEEK. 1989. "The Future of Abortion: The Court Drills a Crack in the Foundation of *Roe*," (July 17): 14–27.

ORNSTEIN, NORMAN J., THOMAS E. MANN, and MICHAEL MALBIN. 1990. *Vital Statistics on Congress, 1989-1990*. Washington, DC: Congressional Quarterly Inc.

OSBORN, FAIRFIELD. 1948. *Our Plundered Planet*. Boston: Little, Brown.

PETTIGREW, THOMAS F., and ROBERT L. GREEN. 1976. "School Desegregation in Large Cities," *Harvard Educational Review*, no. 46 (February): 1–53.

PIERCE, RICHARD J. JR. 1995. "Seven Ways to Deossify Agency Rule Making," *Administrative Law Review* 47 (1) (Winter): 59–95.

PLATTNER, MARC F. 1974. "Campaign Financing. The Dilemmas of Reform," *Public Interest* 37 (Fall): 112–130.

POEL, SARI VAN DER. 1995. "Solidarity as Boomerang, The Fiasco of the Prostitutes' Rights Movement in the Netherlands," *Crime, Law & Social Change* 23:41–65.

PRICE, DAVID E. 1972. *Who Makes the Law? Creativity and Power in Senate Committees*. Cambridge, Mass.: Schenkman.

QUINNEY, RICHARD. 1970. *The Social Reality of Crime*. Boston: Little, Brown.

RABKIN, JEREMY. 1989. *Judicial Compulsions*. New York: Basic Books.

REINOW, R., and L. T. REINOW. 1967. *Moment in the Sun*. New York: Dial Press.

RESKE, HENRY J. 1994. "Ralph Nader's New Project: Law Centers to Help the Small Group Instead of the Little Guy," *ABA Journal* 80 (May): 32–33.

RIPLEY, RANDALL B. 1980. *Congress: Process and Policy*. 4th ed. New York: W. W. Norton & Co., Inc.

ROBY, PAMELA. 1969. "Politics and Criminal Law: Revision of the New York State Penal Law on Prostitution," *Social Problems* 17 (1) (Summer): 83–109.

ROESCH, RONALD, STEPHEN L. GOLDING, VALERIE P. HANS, and N. DICKON REPPUCCI. 1991. "Social Science and the Courts: The Role of Amicus Curiae Briefs," *Law and Human Behavior* 15 (1) (February): 1–11.

ROZELL, MARK J., and CLYDE WILCOX. 1999. *Interest Groups in American Campaigns, The New Face of Electioneering*. Washington, DC: CQ Press.

RUSTHOVEN, PETER J. 1976. "The Courts as Sociologists," *National Review* (December 10): 1339–1341.

SANTORO, WAYNE A., and GAIL M. MCGUIRE. 1997. "Social Movement Insiders: The Impact of Institutional Activists on Affirmative Action and Comparable Worth Policies," *Social Problems* 44 (4) (November): 503-519.

SCHWARTZ, BERNARD. 1995. "'Shooting the Piano Player'? Justice Scalia and Administrative Law," *Administrative Law Review* 47 (1) (Winter): 1–57.

ST. LOUIS POST-DISPATCH. 1987. "Warning on Contras" (JANUARY 26): 1B.

SHAPIRO, MARTIN. 1968. *The Supreme Court and Administrative Agencies.* New York: Free Press.

SIMON, RITA JAMES. 1974. *Public Opinion in America: 1936–1970.* Skokie, IL: Rand McNally.

SMITH, ANNE KATES. 1992. "Opinions with a Price: More-Complex Court Cases Mean Jobs for Expert Witnesses," *U.S. News & World Report* (July 20): 64–66.

SPECTOR, MALCOLM, and JOHN I. KITSUSE. 1973. "Social Problems: A Reformulation," *Social Problems* 21 (2) (Fall): 145–159.

STONE, MARVIN. 1979. "Should Judges Make Law?," *U.S. News & World Report* (June 4): 76.

TARROW, SIDNEY. 1998. *Power in Movement: Social Movements and Contentious Politics.* 2nd ed. Cambridge, England: Cambridge University Press.

TOMASIC, ROMAN. 1985. *The Sociology of Law.* London: Sage Publications.

TONE, ANDREA. 2001. *Devices and Desires, A History of Contraceptives in America.* New York: Hill & Wang.

TURNER, RALPH, and LEWIS M. KILLAN. 1987. *Collective Behavior.* 3rd ed. Englewood Cliffs, NJ: Prentice Hall.

VAGO, STEVEN. 1968. "Wage Garnishment: An Exercise in Futility Under Present Law," *Journal of Consumer Affairs* 2 (1) (Summer): 7–20.

WALKER, NIGEL, and MIKE HOUGH (EDS.). 1988. *Public Attitudes to Sentencing: Surveys from Five Countries.* Aldershot, England: Gower.

WELLINGTON, HARRY H. 1991. *Interpreting the Constitution: The Supreme Court and the Process of Adjudication.* New Haven: Yale University Press.

WEST, WILLIAM F. 1985. *Administrative Rulemaking: Politics and Processes.* Westport, CT: Greenwood Press.

WIECK, PAUL R. 1973. "The John Gardner Brigade," *New Republic,* no. 168: 21–22.

WOLF, ELEANOR P. 1976. "Social Science and the Courts: The Detroit Schools Case," *Public Interest* 42 (Winter): 102–120.

WOLFGANG, MARVIN E. 1998. "We Do Not Deserve to Kill," *Crime & Delinquency* 44 (1) (January): 19–31.

YARNOLD, BARBARA M. 1992. *Politics and the Courts: Toward a General Theory of Public Law.* New York: Praeger.

ZANDER, MICHAEL. 1999. *The Law-Making Process.* 5th ed. London: Butterworths.

ZEISEL, HANS. 1962. "Social Research on the Law: The Ideal and the Practical." Pp. 124–143 in William M. Evan (ed.), *Law and Sociology: Exploratory Essays.* New York: Free Press.

5
Law
and
Social Control

Over the years, a great deal has been written on social control and the topic occupies a central position in the sociological literature (see, for example, Bernard, Vold and Snipes, 2001). Social control refers to the methods used by members of a society to maintain order and promote predictability of behavior. There are many different forms of social control, and law is only one of them. The emphasis in this chapter is on social control through laws that are activated when other forms of control mechanisms are ineffective or unavailable. The chapter examines the processes of informal and formal social control, the use of criminal sanctions, the effectiveness of the death penalty, and civil commitment to regulate behavior. Part of the chapter is concerned with crimes without victims (drug addiction, prostitution, and gambling), white-collar crime, and the control of dissent. The chapter concludes with a consideration of administrative law as a means of control in the context of licensing, inspection, and the threat of publicity.

There are two basic processes of social control: the internalization of group norms and control through external pressures (Clinard and Meier, 2001). In the first instance, social control is the consequence of socialization, the process of learning the rules of behavior for a given social group. Individuals develop self-control by being taught early what is appropriate, expected, or desirable in specific situations. People acquire a motivation to conform to the norms, regardless of external pressures. Most students do not cheat because of the fear of being caught, and most people pay their taxes, most of the time. There is conformity to norms because individuals have been socialized to believe that they should conform, regardless of and independent of any anticipated reactions of other persons.

Mechanisms of social control through external pressures include both negative and positive sanctions. Negative sanctions are penalties imposed on those who violate norms. Positive sanctions, such as a promotion, a bonus, and encouragement, are intended to reward conformity. These positive and negative sanctions are forms of social control. Some types of social control are formal or official, and others are informal or unofficial in character. Typical reactions to deviance and rule breaking may generate both informal and formal sanctions. Although there is a considerable amount of overlapping between informal and formal mechanisms of social control, for analytical purposes they will be discussed separately.

INFORMAL SOCIAL CONTROLS

Methods of informal social controls are best exemplified by folkways (established norms of common practices such as those that specify modes of dress, etiquette, and language use) and mores (societal norms associated with intense feelings of right or wrong and definite rules of conduct that are simply not to be violated—for example, incest). These informal controls consist of techniques whereby individuals who know each other on a personal basis accord praise to those who comply with their expectations and show displeasure to those who do not (Shibutani, 1961:426). These techniques may be observed in specific behaviors such as ridicule, gossip, praise, reprimands, criticisms, ostracism, and verbal rationalizations and expressions of opinion. Gossip, or the fear of gossip, is one of the more effective devices employed by members of a society to bring individuals into conformity with norms. Unlike formal social controls, these informal controls are not exercised through official group mechanisms, and there are no specially designated persons in charge of enforcement.

Informal mechanisms of social control tend to be more effective in groups and societies where relations are face-to-face and intimate and where the division of labor is relatively simple. For example, Emile Durkheim argues that in simple societies, such as tribal villages or small towns, legal norms more closely accord with social norms than in larger and more complex societies. Moral disapproval of deviance is nearly unanimous in such communities (Shilling and Mellor, 1998); and as Daniel Glaser (1971:32) notes, "Tolerance of behavioral diversity varies directly with the division of labor in a society." In simple societies, laws are often unwritten, necessitating the direct teaching of social norms to children. Socialization in such simple societies does not present children with contradictory norms that create confusion or inner conflict. Intense face-to-face interaction in such societies produces a moral consensus that is well known to all members; it also brings deviant acts to everyone's attention quickly.

There is substantial evidence in the sociological literature to support the contention that informal social control is stronger in smaller, traditional, more homogeneous communities than in larger, more modern and heterogeneous communities (Hanawalt, 1998). In a classic and influential study of deviance in the seventeenth-century Massachusetts Bay Colony, Kai T.

Erikson found that the small size and the cultural homogeneity of the community helped control behavior, since everyone in the community pressured potential deviants to conform to dominant norms. There was a substantial amount of surveillance by neighbors in the community watching for acts of deviance. Moral censure immediately followed any observed act of deviance (Erikson, 1966:169–170). Even today, reaction to certain crimes (for example, rape or murder) in a small, homogeneous, and close-knit community may be so intense and immediate that justice for a defendant in a criminal case may be difficult, since public pressure on the legal system to exact harsh and immediate punishment may make the provision of due process rights doubtful. In such instances, it may be necessary to change the location of the trial to minimize public pressure. Such a change of venue order is more likely to take place in small communities than in larger ones where the court would not assume that the defendant cannot receive a fair trial because of prejudice (Friendly and Goldfarb, 1967:96–101).

Undoubtedly, informal social controls operate more effectively in smaller communities where people know each other and regularly interact. In such communities, law enforcement agents can probably expect better cooperation. As the President's Commission on Law Enforcement and Administration of Justice (1967a:6) points out: "A man who lives in the country or in a small town is likely to be conspicuous, under surveillance by his community so to speak, and therefore under its control. A city man is often almost invisible, socially isolated from his neighborhood and therefore incapable of being controlled by it. He has more opportunities for crime."

The greater effectiveness of informal social control mechanisms in small communities is demonstrated by Sarah L. Boggs's often-cited study of formal and informal social controls in central cities, suburbs, and small towns in Missouri. Boggs found that residents of large cities were more apt than suburban or small-town residents to feel that crime was likely to occur in their community. City residents were also more likely to think that their neighbors would not report a burglary that they observed, and more urban residents knew of a crime or a suspicious incident in their community within the previous year. Most people in all areas felt that their own neighborhood was safe, but fewer felt that way in the cities. When they were asked *what* it was that made their neighborhood safe, 83 percent of those in rural areas and small towns said that it was informal controls; 70 percent in suburbs and 68 percent of those in the cities attributed safety to informal controls. When they said that their neighborhood was kept safe by informal social controls, the people meant that they felt secure because of the character of the community and its residents—"good, decent, law-abiding, middle-class citizens" (Boggs, 1971:323). Safety in a neighborhood was also attributed to the social network in the community that might lead to bystander intervention in a crime. Respondents who lived in suburbs and large cities were more likely than those who lived in rural areas and small towns to attribute safety to such formal control agents as the police (Boggs, 1971:234). Boggs concluded that people in cities were most inclined to expect crime but least likely to feel that they could rely on their neighbors rather than the police to protect their community. As a result, they were more likely to take precautions, such as purchasing weapons or a watchdog, than their counterparts who lived in suburbs, small towns, and rural areas.

Similar conclusions about the role of informal social-control mechanisms can be drawn from studies dealing with developing nations. For example, in comparing a low-crime-rate community and a high-crime-rate community in Kampala, Uganda, Marshall B. Clinard and Daniel J. Abbott found that the areas with less crime showed greater social solidarity, more social interaction among neighbors, more participation in local organizations, less geographical mobility, and more stability in family relationships. There was also greater cultural homogeneity and more emphasis on tribal and kinship ties in the low-crime community, helping to counteract the anonymity of recent migrants to the city. The stronger primary group ties among residents of the low-crime area made it more difficult for strangers in the community to escape public notice. To prevent theft, residents of an area must feel that it is wrong, share some responsibility for protecting their neighbors' property, be able to identify strangers in the area, and be willing to take action if they observe a theft (Clinard and Abbott, 1973:149).

These and other studies (see, for example, Garofalo and McLeod, 1989) show that if there is intense social interaction on an intimate face-to-face basis, normative consensus, and surveillance of the behavior of members of the community, informal social control will be strong to the extent that legal or formal controls may be unnecessary. This contention is reinforced by Roberto Mangabeira Unger's (1976) argument, which was discussed in Chapter 2. To reiterate, Unger contends that bureaucratic law emerges when state and society become differentiated and there is a felt need for an institution standing above conflicting groups. This occurs when the community disintegrates, that is, when individuals may no longer be counted on to act in set ways without overt guidance. Such a disintegration comes about as the division of labor creates new opportunities for power and wealth, which, in turn, undercut old hierarchies determined by birth. This process is accompanied by an increased reliance on formal social controls.

Finally, the role of neighborhood committees (for example, little old ladies employed by the state to monitor their neighbors), such as those found in China, should be considered. The Chinese call them "KGB with little feet" (Ignatius, 1989). The "old lady" network, established in the 1950s as a bridge between the party and the people, remains in today China's the most effective means of grass-roots social control. In 2002, there were 1 million neighborhood committees in cities and villages around the country, employing 6.4 million retirees, virtually all women. In Beijing, there is, on the average, one old lady keeping watch on every 20 families. Their primary task is to seek out and resolve squabbles among neighbors. They report everything they see to higher-ups, investigate disturbances, routinely stop strangers, and pry into couples' plans for having children. In the summer of 1989, they were active in circulating photos of fugitive prodemocracy activists and helped to mobilize residents to attend mass rallies and public executions. This technique of community-based surveillance is modeled after the one introduced in the former Soviet Union in the 1920s which was based on the principle of denouncement. People were encouraged, and rewarded, to report on friends and relatives who were suspected of engaging in activities contrary to the interests of the government. Various versions of this technique were subsequently used in Nazi Germany and other totalitarian regimes.

FORMAL SOCIAL CONTROLS

Although there is no clear-cut dividing line, formal social controls are usually characteristic of more complex societies with a greater division of labor, heterogeneity of population, and subgroups with competing values and different sets of mores and ideologies. Formal controls arise when informal controls alone are insufficient to maintain conformity to certain norms. Formal controls are characterized by systems of specialized agencies, standard techniques, and general predictability of universal sanctions. The two main types are those instituted by the state and authorized to use force, and those imposed by agencies other than the state, such as the church, business and labor groups, universities, and clubs.

Formal social controls are incorporated in the institutions in society and are characterized by the explicit establishment of procedures and the delegation of specific bodies to enforce them (laws, decrees, regulations, codes). Because they are incorporated in the institutions of society, they are administered by individuals who occupy positions in those institutions. Generally, anyone who attempts to manipulate the behavior of others through the use of formal sanctions may be considered an agent of social control (Clinard and Meier, 2001).

Social institutions are organized for securing conformity to established modes of behavior and consist of established procedures for satisfying human needs. These procedures carry a certain degree of compulsion. They involve mechanisms of imposing conformity. Nonpolitical institutions may resort to a variety of penalties and rewards to ensure compliance (see, for example, Vaughan, 1998). For example, an organization may fire an employee; a church may withhold religious services at a wedding or a burial, or even excommunicate a member; a league owner may fine or suspend a professional athlete for infractions of rules. These same organizations may also use formal rewards to ensure conformity. To illustrate, through bonuses and promotion, an organization often rewards those who make an outstanding contribution. Dedicated church members may be commended for exemplary service, and professional athletes are often enticed by financial rewards.

It should be noted at the outset that control through law is seldom exercised by the use of positive sanctions or rewards. A person who, throughout his or her life, obeys the law and meets its requirements seldom receives rewards or commendations. State control is exercised primarily, but not exclusively, through the use or threat of punishment to regulate the behavior of citizens. The next two sections focus on the use of criminal sanctions, with particular emphasis on the death penalty debate and civil commitment to control certain types of behavior.

Criminal Sanctions

The social control of criminal and delinquent behavior exemplifies the most highly structured formal system (the criminal justice system) used by society. In 2000, the number of Americans under the control of the criminal justice system exceeded 6.5 million, 3.1 percent of adults in the United States, including some 2 million inmates in federal and state prisons and local jails—three times as many as in 1980—and another 3.5 million convicted criminals on probation and parole (Currie, 1998, *New York Times*, 2001a). By 2001, America's prison population rose another 2 percent. One person in 142 is behind bars, up from one in 218 a decade ago with some 4.5 million on probation (Hallinan, 2001). America not only has more people in prison than anywhere else, but a higher incarceration rate (it recently passed Russia). To put this in some kind of perspective, there are some 7 million students enrolled full-time in four-year colleges and universities nationwide, and if current trends continue, the number of Americans behind bars and on probation will very soon match and then possibly exceed this number. While comparing prisons and higher education, it is worth noting that states collectively spend more to construct prisons than universities, and they spend $40 billion a year, roughly $20,000 per prisoner, on keeping offenders behind bars. In this context, America's schools are losing the budget battle to prisons by a factor of more than two to one.

The laws, enacted by legislators and modified by court decisions, define criminal and delinquent behavior and specify the sanctions imposed for violations. Over time, there has been an increasing reliance on law to regulate the activities and, thus, the lives of people. As the law has proliferated to incorporate more types of behavior, many changes in penalties for certain crimes have also occurred. These increases inevitably result in more social control and in further changes in the control methods. As more behaviors are defined as criminal, more acts become the interest of the police, the courts, and the prison system.

The term "legalization" is used to describe the process by which norms are moved from the social to the legal level. Not all social norms become laws; in fact, only certain norms are translated into legal norms. Why is it that the violation of certain norms, but not others, is chosen to be incorporated into the criminal code? Austin T. Turk (1972) suggests that there are certain social forces involved in the legalization and creation of legal norms: moral indignation, a high value on order, response to threat, and political tactics.

As discussed in Chapter 4, laws may be created by the actions of "moral entrepreneurs" who become outraged over some practice they regard as reprehensible, for example, smoking marijuana. Others prefer order and insist on provisions to regulate life and to make society as orderly as possible. They promulgate laws to ensure order and uniformity, as in the case of traffic regulation. Some people react to real or imaginary threats and advocate legal-control measures. For instance, some people may assume that the availability of pornographic material not only is morally wrong but also directly contributes to the increase of sex crimes (although rape and child molestation undoubtedly predate erotic books and pornographic magazines and videocassettes). In this instance, it would appear certain that these people would attempt to legally prohibit the sale of pornographic material (Irving, 1992). The final source of legalization of norms is political, where criminal laws are created in the interest of powerful groups in society. This source is identified with the conflict perspective that I have considered in the preceding chapters.

The process of legalization of social norms also entails the incorporation of specific punishments for specific kinds of criminal law violators. Rusche and Kirchheimer note: "Every system of production tends to discover punishments which correspond to its productive relationships" (1968:5). Michel Foucault (1977) tells us that before the industrial revolution, life was considered cheap and individuals had neither the utility nor the commercial value that is conferred on them in an industrial economy. Under those circumstances, punishment was severe and often unrelated to the nature of the crime (for example, death for stealing a chicken). When more and more factories appeared, the value of individual lives, even criminal ones, began to be stressed. Beginning in the last years of the eighteenth century and the early years of the nineteenth century, efforts were made to connect the nature of a given punishment to the nature of the crime.

Fitting the punishment to the crime is a difficult and at times controversial and politically sensitive task. The definition of crime and the penalty for it and the components of the culture of control (Garland, 2001) vary over time and from one society to another. For example, in rural areas in Communist China, it is not uncommon to burn down the houses or to confiscate the property of those who violate birth control laws. In the words of a villager: "If you have more than one child, they will come and rip the engine out of your boat or destroy your house on the land" (Tyler, 1995: 6).

By contrast, in a democracy the power to define crime and punishment rests with the citizenry. This power is largely delegated to elected representatives. Their statutes are often broad and subject to various interpretations. As Chapter 3 demonstrated, legislative enactments allow judges, prosecutors, and juries considerable flexibility and discretion in assessing guilt and imposing punishment.

But what does it mean to punish an individual who violates a criminal law? Edwin H. Sutherland and Donald R. Cressey (1974:298) provide the following definition of the ingredients of punishment as a form of social control: "Two essential ideas are contained in the concept of punishment as an instrument of public justice. (a) It is inflicted by the group in its corporate capacity upon one who is regarded as a member of the same group. . . . (b) Punishment involves pain or suffering produced by design and justified by some value that the suffering is assumed to have."

Punishment of lawbreakers has several purposes. Paul W. Tappan (1960:241–261) offers the now established objectives of punishment. He suggests that punishment is designed to achieve the goal of *retribution* or *social retaliation* against the offender. This means punishment of the offender for the crime that has been committed and, to an extent, punishment that (in principle) matches the impact of the crime upon its victim (for instance, a person or an organization). The state is expected to be the agent of vengeance on behalf of the victim. Punishment also involves *incapacitation* (for example, a prison term), which prevents a violator from misbehaving during the time he or she is being punished. Increasingly, judicially created public humiliations are also being introduced in courtrooms as alternatives to incarceration and to satisfy a "retributive impulse" (Karp, 1998:277). They are considered as "shaming penalties"—after punishments like the stocks favored by seventeenth-century Puritans—and they take a mea culpa message to the community. For example, the names of men who solicit prostitutes are identified in local papers or radio shows and Kansas City, Missouri, in 1997 started the now popular "John TV," in which the names, mug shots, birth dates and hometowns of men arrested for trying to buy sex, and women arrested trying to sell it, are broadcast on the municipal cable channel; drunken drivers carry signs on their cars announcing their problem and urging other drivers to report their erratic driving to the police; convicted shoplifters must take out advertisements in local papers running their photographs and stating their crimes; and the courts ordered people convicted of assault or child molestation to put signs in their yards announcing their transgression (Belluck; 1998; Hoffman, 1997).

Further, punishment is supposed to have a *deterrent* effect, both on the lawbreaker and on potential deviants. *Individual or specific deterrence* may be achieved by intimidation of the person, frightening him or her against further deviance, or it may be effected through reformation, in that the lawbreaker changes his or her deviant behavior. *General deterrence* results from the warning offered to potential criminals by the example of punishment directed at a specific wrongdoer. It aims to discourage others from criminal behavior by making an example of the offender being punished.

The theory of deterrence is predicated on the assumption that individuals weigh the costs and rewards associated with alternative actions, and select behavior that maximizes gains and minimizes cost. Thus, crime takes place when law breaking is perceived as either more profitable (rewarding) or less costly (painful) than conventional activities. In this context, the purpose of punishment is to prevent crime (Bailey and Peterson, 1994). The concept of deterrence is often used to designate punishment in the form of threats directed at offenders or potential offenders so as to frighten them into law-abiding conduct. The effectiveness of these threats is conditioned by the operation of three variables: (1) the severity of the punishment for an offense, (2) the certainty that it would be applied, and (3) the speed with which it would be applied (Friedland, 1989). Research generally supports the view that certainty of punishment is more important than severity for achieving deterrence, but there is little research data as yet on the swiftness of punishment. For example, in a study of a series of criminal offenses, Charles R. Tittle (1969) found strong and consistent negative relationships between certainty of punishment and crime rates for different states, as measured by the ratio between felony admissions to state prisons and the total crimes known to the police in different states. Those states with the lowest crime rates had a proportionately larger number of incarcerated persons. On the other hand, severity of punishment bore no marked relationship to crime rates. Tittle's findings led him to conclude that measures to improve the efficiency of police work probably would have significant effects on crime rates but that increasing the severity of punishment would be of limited effectiveness.

However, sociologists have recognized that punishment may deter only some crimes and some offenders. For example, William J. Chambliss (1975) makes a distinction between crimes that are instrumental acts and those that are expressive. Illustrations of *instrumental* offenses include burglary, tax evasion, embezzlement, motor vehicle theft (note that 15 percent of all auto thefts reported are fraudulent and made by the owner to collect on his or her insurance [Cooke, 1989:68]), and other illegal activities directed toward some material end. Examples of *expressive* acts are murder, assault, and sex offenses, where the behavior is an end in itself. Chambliss hypothesizes that the deterrent impact of severe and certain punishment may be greater on instrumental crimes because they generally involve some planning and weighing of risks. Expressive crimes, by contrast, are often impulsive and emotional acts. Perpetrators of such crimes are unlikely to be concerned with the future consequences of their actions.

Chambliss further contends that an important distinction can be made between individuals who have a relatively high commitment to crime as a way of life and those with a relatively low commitment. The former would include individuals who engage in crime on a professional or regular basis. They often receive group support for their activities, and crime for them is an important aspect of their way of life (such as prostitutes or participants in organized crime). For them, the likelihood of punishment is a constant feature of their life, something they have learned to live with, and the threat of punishment may be offset by the supportive role played by their peers. On the other hand, a tax evader, an embezzler, or an occasional shoplifter does not view this behavior as criminal and receives little, if any, group support for these acts. Fear of punishment may well be a deterrent for such low-commitment persons, particularly if they have already experienced punishment (for example, a tax evader who has been audited and then subjected to legal sanctions).

On the basis of these two types of distinctions—instrumental and expressive acts, and high- and low-commitment offenders—Chambliss contends that the greatest deterrent effect of punishment will be in situations that involve low-commitment individuals who engage in instrumental crimes. Deterrence is least likely in cases involving high-commitment persons who engage in expressive crimes. The role of deterrence remains questionable in situations that involve low-commitment individuals who commit expressive crimes (such as murder), which can be illustrated by the arguments used for or against the death penalty.

Discord over the Death Penalty

As the most severe form of punishment, the death penalty is the most obvious, controversial, and emotional issue in the concept of deterrence (see, for example, Bedau, 1998; Sarat, 2001). Historically, property offenses rather than violent crimes accounted for the majority of executions. In the eighteenth century, the death penalty was imposed in England for more than two hundred offenses, including poaching and smuggling. Executions were performed in public. They were a popular spectacle. The public applauded a skillful execution of a criminal much as aficionados today cheer the matador who skillfully slays a bull (Foucault, 1977). The standard methods of execution included hanging, beheading, disemboweling, and quartering. The increased severity and frequency of executions during this period were associated with the growth of urbanization and wealth. Notes Loh: "Capital statutes 'served the interests of private property and commerce' against those who might seek to undermine them" (1984:194). Although the colonies inherited many of the capital punishments from England, by the middle of the nineteenth century most of them were repealed and the death sentence was imposed primarily for murder and, to a lesser extent, rape.

In the 1972 decision *Furman v. Georgia*, capital punishment was declared unconstitutional by the U.S. Supreme Court. The Court held that the discretionary application of the death penalty to only a small fraction of those eligible to be executed was capricious and arbitrary and hence unconstitutional.

However, a number of states since responded to the Court ruling by legislating modifications in state laws that make the death penalty mandatory for certain offenses, such as multiple killings; killing in connection with a robbery, rape, kidnapping, or hostage situation; murder for hire; killing a police officer or prison guard; and treason. Some of these revised statutes were held to be constitutional by the Supreme Court in 1976 when it voted 7–2 in *Gregg v. Georgia* to reinstate the death penalty. Over the past two and a half decades 38 states, most recently New York State, have passed capital punishment laws and several other states are considering similar statutes as well. By contrast, 47 percent of the world's countries had abolished capital punishment in law or practice by the end of 1993 (Worsnop, 1995) and South Africa was added to this list in mid-1995 (*U.S. News & World Report*, 1995:14). In China, however, the death penalty is still widely practiced, and during the current wave of executions, as many as 191 people were executed in a single day and in 2001, an estimated 5,000 to 10,000 were subjected to the death penalty (Smith, 2001).

In the United States, there is even a 54-page Execution Protocol, prepared by the U.S. Bureau of Prisons. Work on the protocol began in 1993, when federal rules for executions were finalized, and it was released in April 2001 (*St. Louis Post-Dispatch,* 2001). It is a detailed, comprehensive, almost macabre document, that spells out with exquisite, minute-by-minute precision every detail of an execution ranging from the length of the last meal to the surrender of the body to the coroner. It also deals with detailed contingency plans for handling disturbances that might be caused by protesters and sympathizers both within and outside of the facility.

A U.S. Department of Justice report (1995a:11) shows that since 1930, when national reporting began, 4,085 executions were carried out in the United States. For illustrative purposes, Table 5–1 shows the number of inmates awaiting execution in 1998 and the method used. [In October 2001, Georgia joined other states and the highest court struck down the use of the electric chair, saying the ghastly injuries inflicted, and the risk of "excruciating pain" violate the state constitution's ban on cruel and unusual punishment and it leaves Alabama and Nebraska as the only states with the electric chair as the sole method of execution.] All were convicted of murder. Of the 3,387 prisoners under death sentence, 1,611 or 47.5 percent were white, 1,420 or 42.1 percent black, and the 10.4 percent consisted of native Americans, Asians, and Hispanics. Studies show that other things being equal, killers of white people are more likely to receive death sentences than killers of blacks. [For racial differences in sentencing, see Culver, 1992; Eckholm, 1995; Gross and Mauro, 1989; Lewin, 1995; Miethe and Moore, 1986; and Radalet and Pierce, 1985.] Women represented 1.3 percent of death-row inmates. Prisoners executed in 1998 spent an average of 7 years and 11 months awaiting execution (but it has taken 11 years, on the average, to establish reversible error in capital cases). There have been more than 700 executions—including 2 federal executions in 2001—since 1976, when the death penalty was reinstated.

TABLE 5–1   Prisoners under Sentence of Death

By race, ethnicity, jurisdiction, and the method of execution by states, on Apr. 1, 1998

					Race, ethnicity			
Jurisdiction	Total	White	Black	Hispanic	Native American	Asian	Unknown	Method
United States[a]	3,387	1,611	1,420	265	45	25	21	
Federal statutes	18	4	12	1	0	1	0	
U.S. military	8	1	5	0	0	2	0	
Alabama	163	91	68	2	0	1	1	E
Arizona	121	86	13	18	4	0	0	GC
Arkansas	39	19	19	1	0	0	0	LI
California	494	203	179	82	13	9	8	GC
Colorado	4	1	2	1	0	0	0	LI
Connecticut	5	2	3	0	0	0	0	E
Delaware	17	7	10	0	0	0	0	LI, H
Florida	368	203	127	35	1	1	1	E
Georgia	119	64	54	1	0	0	0	E
Idaho	19	19	0	0	0	0	0	LI
Illinois	156	53	97	6	0	0	0	LI
Indiana	45	27	17	1	0	0	0	E
Kansas	1	1	0	0	0	0	0	—
Kentucky	30	23	7	0	0	0	0	E
Louisiana	72	17	50	0	0	0	5	LI
Maryland	17	3	14	0	0	0	0	GC
Mississippi	60	28	32	0	0	0	0	GC, LI
Missouri	87	47	40	0	0	0	0	LI
Montana	6	6	0	0	0	0	0	H, LI
Nebraska	11	9	1	0	1	0	0	E
Nevada	92	45	37	8	0	1	1	LI
New Hampshire	0	X	X	X	X	X	X	LI
New Jersey	15	8	7	0	0	0	0	LI
New Mexico	4	3	0	1	0	0	0	LI
New York	0	X	X	X	X	X	X	—
North Carolina	199	85	103	2	5	0	4	GC, LI
Ohio	180	87	88	3	2	0	0	E
Oklahoma	127	69	41	3	11	3	0	LI
Oregon	23	19	1	2	1	0	0	LI
Pennsylvania	216	69	133	12	0	2	0	LI
South Carolina	73	34	38	0	1	0	0	E
South Dakota	2	2	0	0	0	0	0	LI
Tennessee	96	63	29	1	2	1	0	E
Texas	425	169	168	80	4	3	1	LI
Utah	11	7	2	2	0	0	0	LI, FS
Virginia	46	23	21	1	0	0	1	E
Washington	19	15	3	0	0	1	0	LI, H
Wyoming	0	X	X	X	X	X	X	LI

E—Electrocution; FS—Firing Squad; GC—Gas Chamber; H—Hanging; LI—Lethal Injection.
[a]Detail will not add to total because prisoners sentenced to death in more than one state are listed in the respective state totals, but each prisoner is counted only once for the national total.

The dilemma of whether to kill the killers comes up only in a small fraction of homicides (see, for example, Smith and Zahn, 1998). The criteria for capital murder vary from state to state and from case to case. In general, there must be "aggravating circumstances." These can be as specific as the murder of a police officer or a prison guard; as common as homicide committed along with a lesser felony such as burglary; or as vague as Florida's law citing "especially heinous, atrocious or cruel" killing. Some 10 percent of homicides qualify, representing about 2,300 murders in 2001. Those killings are the ones the threat of capital punishment is meant to prevent.

What are the preventive effects of capital punishment? The arguments for the death penalty are mostly anecdotal but, at times, can become visceral. Proponents of the death penalty contend that it is a deterrent to others and that it protects society. It constitutes retribution for society and the victim's family and serves to protect police officers and prison guards. It also removes the possibility that the offenders will repeat the act. There is little empirical evidence in support of the death penalty as a deterrent. Were it not for the work of Isaac Ehrlich, the deterrence debate would be very much one-sided. Using econometric modeling techniques to construct a "supply-and-demand" theory of murder, Ehrlich (1975), in a now classic and frequently cited article subtitled "A Question of Life and Death," argued that the death penalty prevents more murders than do prison sentences. He speculates that because of the 3,411 executions carried out from 1933 to 1967, enough murderers were discouraged so that some 27,000 victims' lives were saved. As might be expected, his conclusions drew immediate criticisms.

A variety of concerns were raised. Among others, Ehrlich did not compare the effectiveness of capital punishment with that of particular prison terms. When data from 1965 to 1969 are omitted, the relationship between murder rates and executions is not statistically significant (Loh, 1984:258). While considering the increases in homicides in the 1960s, he failed to account for the possible influences of rising racial tensions, the Vietnam War, and increased ownership of handguns. Moreover, for deterrence to be effective, murderers need to take into consideration the probable costs of their action. Emotions and passions at play can make a cost-benefit analysis unlikely. Most murderers, in Chambliss's words, are low-commitment individuals, often under the influence of drugs or alcohol, who are unlikely to assess rationally the consequences of their action. For them, the death penalty remains a highly questionable deterrent.

Aside from ethical and moral considerations, there are many arguments against the death penalty. For serial killers and particularly for female serial killers, capital punishment is not a deterrent (Fisher, 1997; Kelleher and Kelleher, 1998). Almost every study of capital punishment has shown that there is no material difference in the rate of homicides in states that have capital punishment and states that do not (Sellin, 1959:28). The homicide rate per 100,000 in Michigan, which did not have the death penalty in the 1950s, was 3.49. In Indiana, which did have the death penalty, the homicide rate for the same period was 3.50. Similarly, Minnesota and Rhode Island, states with no death penalty, had proportionately as many killings as their respective neighbors that had capital punishment, Iowa and Massachusetts. A study of different types of police killings for 1976–1989 involving 1,204 officers found no evidence that police are afforded an added measure of protection against death by capital punishment (Bailey and Peterson, 1994). Studies in Canada, England, and other countries also found nothing to suggest that the death penalty is a more effective deterrent than long prison sentences. Although a cause-and-effect relationship cannot be inferred between capital punishment and murder rates, Lawrence M. Friedman (1998:214) speculates that capital punishment may work efficiently in some societies "which use it quickly, mercilessly, and frequently. It cannot work well in the United States, where it is bound to be rare, slow, and controversial."

Opponents of the death penalty argue that prison terms without parole would deter as many potential murderers as capital punishment. Data indicate that the certainty of being punished is negated by the fact that the death penalty is seldom imposed and that juries are less willing to convict when the penalty is death. Trials of capital cases are also more costly and time-consuming than trials for other cases, and maintenance costs for inmates in death row are higher than for inmates in the rest of the prison. An exhaustive system of judicial review is required in capital cases. Today, no death-row inmate will be executed until his or her case has been brought to the attention of the state's highest court, a federal district court of appeals, and the U.S. Supreme Court. In 1995, there were 20 federally founded centers for death-row appeals at an annual cost of $20 million although their numbers are likely to decline because of budget considerations (St. Louis Post-Dispatch, 1995). The total costs for trials and appeals are estimated to range between $3 million (Malcolm, 1989) and $5 million (Economist, 1990). By one study, each execution in North Carolina cost $2.16 million more than life imprisonment. California spent over $1 billion between 1977 and 1996 on its death penalty— but executed only five men during this period (Costanzo, 1997:61). A New York Times (1995a:F2) article mordantly remarks that it is because "quite simply, lawyers earn more than guards and it's lawyers who fly into action after a death sentence—with appeals, appeals and more appeals." Another way of illustrating the cost of the death penalty: The 1995 reinstatement of capital punishment in New York State is expected to cost over a five-year period the same as hiring 250 police officers and building prisons for 6,000 inmates.

Imprisoning one inmate for 50 years in most states would require less than $1 million. This negates the argument that prison is too costly and there are good fiscal reasons for executing murderers. There is also the possibility that an innocent person will be executed. A recent study shows that some 139 innocent people were sentenced to death between 1900 and 1985 in the United States. Of those, 29 were actually executed (Haines, 1992:130). Other studies show that one innocent person has been convicted for every 20 executions carried out since the turn of the century (*St. Louis Post-Dispatch,* 1985:6B). In their 1992 book, *In Spite of Innocence,* the authors (Radelet, et al., 1992) review more than 400 cases in which innocent people were convicted of capital crimes in the United States. In the past decade, eight men have been sentenced to die for murder in Illinois only to be later found innocent and released (Tuft, 1998). The greatest fear of opponents and supporters of death penalty—the execution of the innocent—was the topic of a three-day national conference on Wrongful Convictions and the Death Penalty, held at Northwestern University in November 1998, and attended by more than 1,000 lawyers, law students, professors and 28 of the 73 men and 2 women have been released from death rows across the country since 1972. Each was wrongfully convicted of murder and sentenced to death. It was also documented at the conference that for every seven executions in the United States since 1976, one condemned inmate has been freed (or one innocent is almost killed) after serving years on death row (Terry, 1998). Furthermore, federal judges have found constitutional errors in about 40 percent of the cases they have reviewed since 1976 (Smolowe, 1992:42).

The death penalty is also more likely to affect the poor and minority group members than more affluent whites (Berlow, 2001). This has to do in part with the quality of legal help available to murder defendants. Those with court-appointed lawyers are more likely to be sentenced to death than those represented by private attorneys. Court-appointed lawyers in most states are not required to stay on a homicide case after a conviction. Issues for appeal are likely to be raised by different court-appointed attorneys, if at all, for the poor. Defendants with more money get better legal defense. In a study carried out in Texas in 2000, it was found that people represented by court-appointed lawyers were 28 percent more likely to be convicted than those who hired their own lawyers. If convicted, they were 44 percent more likely to be sentenced to death (*New York Times,* 2001b).

Nevertheless, the debate on the penological effectiveness of capital punishment continues despite the paucity of empirical evidence in support of its alleged deterrent effect. Aside from the moral need for eliminating the death penalty, the evidence shows that capital punishment does not deter murder. Some even argue that it actually encourages homicide in certain circumstances. The threat of the death penalty raises the stakes of getting caught, and anyone who is subject to the death penalty has little to lose by killing again and again. Criminals who already face death for a previous crime are more likely to kill in order to avoid being captured or to silence possible witnesses. The death penalty is viewed by police as "the enemy of law enforcement" and ranks last as a way of reducing violent crime (Morgenthau, 1995).

Yet, there is a growing advocacy of the death penalty in the United States. Public-opinion surveys show that those who are in favor of capital punishment for persons convicted of murder increased from 38 percent in

1972 to a high of 77 percent in 1996 then dropped to 64 percent in 2000 (Maguire and Pastore, 2001:538).

A study shows that even inmates, especially the most violent ones, favor capital punishment for some crimes—when applied to others but not to their own criminal activity (Stevens, 1992). At this point, it should be noted that the majority of murders are committed by family members or acquaintances of the victim, and in more than half of all homicides handguns are used. There is a dramatic increase in gun-related violence (Bruce and Wilcox, 1998; Spitzer, 1995:68) and a former Attorney General of the United States correlated homicide rates with the prevalence of guns, and reported the highest rate of homicide in states where gun controls are lax and gun ownership is common (Clark, 1971:82–84), and 70 percent of the 24,526 homicides in 1993 were committed by guns (*New York Times*, 1995b:A6). Some startling figures to support this conclusion: In 1984, "handguns killed 48 people in Japan, 8 in Great Britain, 34 in Switzerland, 52 in Canada, 58 in Israel, 21 in Sweden, 42 in West Germany, 10,728 in the United States" (*Forbes*, 1985:28) (and close to 13,000 in 1998). Controlling handguns might be a more effective—but far less popular in view of the fact that in 1998, 31 states permitted adults to carry a concealed handgun—method of reducing homicide rates than capital punishment. But current sentiments seem to be in favor of concealed-weapons laws, and a University of Chicago economist, John Lott (2000), in a highly controversial and much debated book, *More Guns, Less Crime: Understanding Crime and Gun Control Laws*, claims that if more law-abiding citizens were allowed to carry guns, murder rates and crime would go down. The book claims to be the most comprehensive look ever at the effects of gun control laws on crime. Using data from all 3,054 counties in the United States from 1977 to 1994, he has found that, for each year that a concealed-handgun law is in effect, the local murder rate declines by 3 percent, robberies by over 2 percent and rape by 2 percent. Two groups most vulnerable to violent crime—women and blacks—benefit most from concealed-weapon laws. The book touched off furious protests from gun-control lobbyists and criminologists who question the methodologies used and suspect the conclusions (Ratnesar, 1998) and gun availability continues to be a topic of contentious debate among social scientists and policy makers (see, for example, Stolzenberg and D'Alessio, 2000).

An alternative to the death sentence may be life without parole. Thirty-one states have adopted a life prison term with no chance of parole for certain offenses (Malcolm, 1989). Life without parole can also short-circuit lengthy and expensive appeals over a death sentence, some of which can go on for a decade or longer. Florida's Supreme Court now devotes one-third of its time to capital cases. Yet, 40 percent of death sentences are overturned on appeal anyway. Life without parole, by contrast, has been consistently upheld on appeal. And, contrary to popular impressions, convicts ineligible for parole have not posed special problems of discipline or control. Capital punishment appears to be more popular than ever, possibly a result of the public perception of an increase in violent crime, but as a deterrent it remains ineffective and expensive (*Economist*, 1995:19–21). As Franklin Zimring concludes "no one on either side can defend the current system, which is hypocritical and unprincipled" (Zimring quoted by Kaplan, 1995:29).

Civil Commitment

The formal control of deviant behavior is not limited to criminal sanctions (see, for example, Arrigo, 2002). There is another form of social control through laws that operate extensively, but not exclusively (Duff, 1997), in the United States—the civil commitment (Forst, 1978:1) through medicalization of deviance (Conrad, 1996:69). Medicalization refers to the process of defining behavior as a medical problem or illness and mandating the medical profession to provide treatment for it. Examples of this would include drug abuse, alcoholism, and viewing violence as a genetic or psychological disorder.

Statutes governing civil commitment exist in every state, although with some variations in the criteria for involuntary hospitalization (Appelbaum, 1992). Civil commitment is a noncriminal process that commits disabled or otherwise dependent individuals, without their consent, to an institution for care, treatment, or custody, rather than punishment. It is based on two legal principles: (1) the right and responsibility of the state to assume guardianship over individuals suffering from some disability and (2) police power within constitutional limitations to take the necessary steps to protect society. Procedurally, the civil commitment is different from criminal commitment. In civil commitment, certain procedural safeguards are not available, such as a right to a trial by jury, which involves confronting witnesses against the defendant, and to avoid testifying against oneself. Moreover, the formal moral condemnation of the community is not an issue in civil commitment. Forst notes: "This situation may arise if the behavior is intentional but not morally blameworthy, as in a civil suit for damages, or if the behavior would have been morally blameworthy, but because of mental impairment, criminal culpability is either mitigated or negated. In the latter instance, the civil issue is not the person's *behavior* but his *status*" (1978:3). In this view, a heroin addict, a mental defective, or a sex offender is not held morally responsible for these actions. The general consensus is that the individual deserves treatment, not punishment, even though the treatment may entail the deprivation of his or her liberty in a mental institution without due process.

In the United States, about one in 12 people will spend some part of his or her life in a mental institution. On any given day of the year, nearly half a million Americans are in confinement in mental wards; in fact, nearly half of all hospital beds in the United States are occupied by people suffering from mental disorders. But civil commitment for mental illness and incompetence is only one of the many types of civil commitments used to control deviant behavior. Other types include the incarceration of juveniles in training schools or detention homes; the commitment of chronic alcoholics and alcohol-related offenders; the commitment of drug addicts; and the institutionalization, through the civil law, of sex offenders (variously known as sexual psychopaths, sexually dangerous persons, or mentally disordered sex offenders) and those who are considered "dangerous" to either themselves or the community as initially perceived by family members or the authorities (Dallaire, et al., 2000). Martin L. Forst (1978:7) contends that the various types of civil commitments "constitute one of the primary forms of social control through law in American society." He further notes that this form of social control is more extensive than the social control exercised by the traditional criminal commitment.

The use of civil commitment as a form of social control is not limited to adults. Difficult, disruptive, disobedient adolescents—the ones who may have been sent to military schools or juvenile detention centers—are now being placed in mental hospitals. Commitment of children under 18 years of age has increased from 82,000 in 1980 to more than 112,000 in 1986, the last year for which data are available (Darnton, 1989:66). Most of the increase in admissions was to private hospitals; roughly 43,000 adolescents were admitted to free-standing private psychiatric hospitals in 1986, compared with 17,000 in 1980 and 6,452 in 1970. About 80 percent of these children are from white middle- and upper-class families. At times, they are seriously disturbed, but others are simply rebellious teenagers fighting with their parents over anything—from the music they listen to, to the boyfriend or girlfriend they choose. Regardless of the reason, they are often held behind locked doors, virtually without civil rights. In the name of therapy, they are subjected to a strict regimen of rewards and punishments.

Problem adolescents are being shifted from a legal to a medical forum. Because of the movement to treat teenage deviance with medicine, private psychiatric beds for young adults is the fastest-growing segment of the hospital industry. These teenagers are often diagnosed with common behavioral problems, such as "conduct disorder," "oppositional defiant disorder," and the popular "adolescent adjustment reaction." These terms sound impressive, but they cover a variety of teenage activities: running away, aggression, persistent opposition to parental values and rules, and engaging in "excessive" sexual activity (usually as defined by the parent). Not surprisingly, many adolescents are committed to mental hospitals not because they are troubled but because they are troubling to someone else (Darnton, 1989:67–68).

In the legal arena, the causes of criminal behavior and the responsibility for such behavior lie within the individual. But in a legal system that posits individual causation, complications arise in attempts to control individuals who are threatening yet have broken no law (see, for example, Peay,

1998). One way to control such individuals is to define their conduct as a mental disorder. Greenaway and Brickey state: "This definition has the combined effect of imputing irrationality to the behavior and providing for the control of the individual through ostensibly benign, but coercive psychiatric intervention" (1978:139). Thus, it is not surprising to find that many state mental hospitals include people who have committed trivial misdemeanors or who have not been convicted of any crime at all, but have been sent there for "observation." The police and courts may refer individuals whose behavior appears odd for psychiatric examination, and if they are found to be "insane," they can be confined in a mental hospital against their will for long periods, in some cases for life.

There are diverse explanations for the increased use of civil commitment as a mechanism of social control. Forst states:

> There are those (the positive criminologists) who view the increase as a beneficial shift from the traditional emphasis on punishing people to rehabilitating them . . . Another explanation for the increased use of civil commitments (the divestment of the criminal law) is that the civil commitment serves as a substitute for, or a supplement to, the criminal law in order to socially control undesirable forms of behavior. (1978:9–10)

The use of civil commitment is not without criticisms. Some critics advocate the abolition of all civil commitment laws because the constitutional rights of the individuals subjected to them are violated, in spite of the number of recent laws designed to protect the rights of the mentally ill. Others oppose it because it allows people to avoid the punishment they deserve. Although the issue remains controversial, the use of civil commitment as a form of social control is on the increase.

CRIMES WITHOUT VICTIMS

The United States invests enormous resources in controlling victimless crimes where harm occurs primarily to the participating individuals themselves (Schur, 1965:170). For 2001, there were around 14 million arrests recorded in the FBI *Uniform Crime Report*. Many of these arrests involved crimes without victims. For example, roughly 100,000 arrests were made for prostitution; 1.5 million for drunkenness and violation of liquor laws (driving under the influence of alcohol is excluded); well over 1 million for drug abuse violations; and around 17,000 for gambling (Federal Bureau of Investigation, 2002).

The criminalization of some acts that have no victims stems from the fact that society regards those acts as morally repugnant and wishes to restrain individuals from engaging in them. Many of those arrested for victimless crimes are never prosecuted: Arrest and overnight lockup are used simply as a means of exerting social control over the drunk or the prostitute without going through the bothersome lengths of creating a convincing prosecution case. For example, habitual drunks may build up formidable "criminal" records by being repeatedly arrested, even though they may never have harmed anyone except, possibly, themselves (La Fave, 1965:439). One study found that two-thirds of repeatedly arrested alcoholics have been charged with nothing more than public intoxication and related offenses, such as vagrancy, throughout their long "criminal" careers (Pittman, quoted by Landsman, 1973:288).

There is an extensive victimless crime literature dealing with drug addiction, prostitution, gambling, abortion, homosexuality, suicide, alcoholism, heterosexual deviance, pornography, and such obscene and lewd "offenses" as women going topless on public beaches (Winerip, 1992) or breast-feeding in public (and at what age should children be weaned when it is practiced—fill in the blank) (Lewin, 2001). These are crimes *mala prohibita* (that is, behaviors made criminal by statute, but there is no consensus as to whether these acts are criminal of themselves). They are acts against public interest or morality and appear in criminal codes as crimes against public decency, order, or justice. Crimes like rape or murder are *mala in se* (that is, evils in themselves with public agreement on the dangers they pose) (Rich, 1978:27).

Victimless crimes are also differentiated from other crimes by the element of consensual transaction or exchange. These crimes are also differentiated from other kinds of crimes by the lack of apparent harm to others and by the difficulty in enforcing the laws against them as a result of low visibility and the absence of complainants. In other words, they are plaintiffless crimes—that is, those involved are willing participants who, as a rule, do not complain to the police that a crime has been committed. Although many people do not consider these activities "criminal," the police and the courts continue to apply laws against such groups as drug users, prostitutes, gamblers, homosexuals, and pornography distributors—laws that large sections of the community do not recognize as legitimate and simply refuse to obey. This situation is further compounded (and muddied) by recent technological breakthroughs such the use of computers to create pornographic images. Is there a line between "fake" pornography, where digital simulations are used to create images and "real" pornography with "live" subjects? The two are virtually indistinguishable from each other, and the criminalization of foul figments of cyber technology that does not involve human subjects raises some interesting First Amendment questions (Liptak, 2001).

The formal controls exerted on these types of behavior are expensive and generally ineffective. Still, they serve certain functions. Robert M. Rich (1978:28) notes that persons who are labeled as criminals serve as an example to community members. When the laws are enforced against lower-class and minority-group members, it allows the ones in power (middle- and upper-class people) to feel that the law is serving a useful purpose because it preserves and reinforces the myth that low-status individuals account for most of the deviance in society. Finally, the control of victimless crimes, in the forms of arrests and convictions, strengthens the notion in the community that the police and the criminal justice system are doing a good job in protecting community moral standards. Let us now consider law as a means of social control for certain victimless crimes such as drug addiction, prostitution, and gambling.

Drug Addiction

Although there have been several major periods of antidrug sentiments, crusades and drug scares, the nonmedical use of drugs, such as opium and heroin, only relatively recently became a criminal act in the United States (Reinerman, 1996). Before 1914, there had been only sporadic attempts to regulate the use of drugs. Although some states attempted to control drug use by passing laws to provide for civil commitment to institutions for drug addicts and outlawing the use of particular narcotic substances, it was not until 1914 that any systematic attempt was made to regulate drug use in the United States. In 1914, the Harrison Act was passed. It was the first attempt to deal comprehensively with the narcotics and dangerous drugs known at that time. It was essentially a tax measure, or more aptly, a series of prohibitive taxes. Drug use was restricted to medical purposes and research by licensed individuals and facilities. But in the act's interpretation, in court rulings in specific cases, and in supplementary laws, criminal sanctions were provided for the unauthorized possession, sale, or transfer of drugs. The states, too, have enacted a variety of antinarcotic laws. In the United States, penalties for violating drug laws have become more severe in recent years with increased and mandatory jail sentences for the sale and possession of many controlled substances, such as heroin, cocaine, and crack (Benjamin and Miller, 1992; Inciardi and McElrath, 2001; Treaster, 1992). In 1996, more than 1.5 million people were arrested for drug offenses; the nation's prisons, which in 1980 housed fewer than 30,000 drug offenders, harbored nearly 300,000 less than 2 decades later (Massing, 1998a:48). Drug offenders comprised a third of all persons convicted of a felony in state courts and the average prison sentence for persons convicted of drug trafficking was 6 years and 2 months, of which they served 1 year and 11 months (U.S. Department of Justice, 1995b:19–20).

In 2002, the United States had the highest substance abuse rate in any industrialized nation. The American market absorbs well over 60 percent of the world's production of illegal drugs. An estimated 20 million Americans are regular users of marijuana (and once again, started to rise rapidly among the young since 1998), 5–10 million are cocaine abusers, and estimates for heroin addicts range from 200,000 to 900,000, with about half of them in New York City alone (Abadinsky, 1997; Goode, 1998; Walker 1993:574). Studies by the National Institute of Drug Abuse indicate that one-third of all college students will use cocaine at least once before they graduate (Meyer, 1989:1, 30). There is substantial evidence that the best predictor of cocaine use is heavy early marijuana use (Grabowski, 1984:vii). Close to 80 percent of all Americans will try an illicit drug by their mid-20s. Although the use of narcotics has decreased slightly since the early 1990s, drugs are now far more available at cheaper prices and in greater purity and variety.

The illegal drug industry is simple and profitable. Its simplicity makes it fairly easy to organize and its profitability makes it hard to stop. At every level, its pricing is determined by the level of risk of enforcement: the risk of seizure and jail, and the uncertainty that arises because traders cannot rely on the laws to enforce the bargains. For example, a Pakistani farmer receives about $90 for a kilo of opium. The wholesale price in Pakistan is almost $3,000. The American wholesale price is $80,000, on the street, at 40 percent purity, the retail price is $290,000 a kilogram. As for cocaine, the leaf needed to produce a kilo costs between $400 and $600. By the time it leaves Colombia, the price has gone up to about $1,800. On the streets in the United States, after changing hands for a few times, the retail price of a kilo of cocaine comes to about $110,000, and in Europe, substantially more. The vast gap between the cost of production and the price paid by the end users obviously plays a role in the failure of drug policies. The producers see a modest return—the real profit is embedded mainly in the distribution chain, which is very hard to control effectively.

The sheer volume of available drugs and the dollar amounts involved in their trade in the United States are phenomenal: some 3,900 tons of imported marijuana at a retail price of $84 per ounce; more than 12 tons of heroin at a street value of $290,000 per kilogram; and 2,500 tons of cocaine at $110,000 a kilo, retail (*Economist*, 2001:7). In view of these numbers, it is interesting to note that, for example, in 1993 the various federal agencies participating in the Federal-wide Drug Seizure System (FDSS) (FBI, DEA, U.S. Customs Service and U.S. Coast Guard) seized 3,345 pounds of heroin, 238,053 pounds of cocaine and 752,114 pounds of marijuana—leaving the borders rather porous (U.S. Department of Justice, 1995b:12).

The American cocaine market alone is worth over $100 billion a year. By contrast, for example, the 1995 budget, which has not significantly changed over the years, devoted to antidrug programs is around $13.2 billion (U.S. Department of Justice, 1995b:10). More than two-thirds of it is going to measures that have consistently proved to be ineffective: police training for South America, swarms of planes and boats, radar balloons and drug agents at the borders, more jails, and battalions of police officers (Treaster, 1992). Less than a third is earmarked for treatment, rehabilitation, education, prevention, and international aid. With more than 2 million Americans now behind bars and up to 80 percent of them involved with powerful drugs like cocaine and heroin, rehabilitation programs offer a potent weapon for decreasing addiction, crime, and the spiraling cost of incarceration. Yet only a fraction of inmates—about 2 percent—undergo serious rehabilitation. It has been shown that every $1.00 invested in drug treatment saved $7.00 in future costs of crime and incarceration (Treaster, 1995). This conclusion is reinforced by a recent book by Michael Massing (1998b), *The Fix*, in which he contends that the hard-core users of heroin and cocaine are disproportionately poor, unemployed and members of minority groups. Although hard-core users are only one-fifth of total users, they consume three-fourths of the cocaine and heroine used in this country and are responsible for most of the pathological behavior that elicits public and governmental responses. If we could provide appropriate treatment to anyone in this population who wanted it, Massing maintains, the whole drug problem would diminish, as would the crime and illness associated with it.

Legally, psychoactive drugs are classified into three basic categories—legal drugs (alcohol, caffeine, nicotine); prescription drugs (amphetamines, barbiturates, tranquilizers), which must be prescribed by a physician; and illegal drugs (marijuana, heroin, hallucinogens), which may not be sold under any circumstances. Cocaine and morphine make up a subcategory. They have limited medical use and high potential for abuse. The categories are not based on the potential harm or addictive quality of the drugs. Under the Federal Controlled Substance Act of 1970, marijuana and heroin are classed together, although heroin is physically addictive and marijuana is not.

Marijuana has reached a kind of a low-profile status, and it is no longer a symbol of rebellion or creativity. Its use on college campuses is down, and prices have leveled off. Unlike most other drugs, 50 percent of the marijuana consumed in the United States is produced domestically, and in some states, such as Hawaii, Oregon, and California, it is the biggest cash crop; and for the country as a whole, it was already worth $18.6 billion in 1985 (Glassman, 1986:12). State marijuana laws have also changed radically in recent years. In most states, the possession of a small amount of marijuana is no longer a felony. The huge majority of the some 451,000 annual marijuana arrests (a number that has been fairly constant since 1975) are for possession—with charges regularly dropped. Several states treat possession as they do a traffic violation, and a person found with an ounce or less is subject to a small fine.

Although there has been an increase in the arrest rates for the sale, transportation, and possession of illegal drugs, and more severe mandatory prison terms for conviction, the criminal law has not been successful at effectively controlling illicit drug use in the United States. Some of the by-products of the tremendous legal efforts to control drugs resulted in the formation of elaborate illegal organizations for the supply of illicit drugs. Many users turn to other criminal activities to support their habit. Drug laws have contributed to a situation in which politicians and police ignore drug traffic—usually because of payoffs. Since drug use is a victimless crime, the lack of complainant makes enforcement difficult. In enforcement, the police frequently use entrapment and illegal search and seizure tactics (Sheley, 1985:122). Furthermore, there is a potential for conflict and recrimination in the control of the flow of illegal drugs. The principal consumer countries are affluent and industrialized; the principal drug-producing countries are poor and basically agricultural. Cocaine and heroin traffic in the Western Hemisphere is a particularly serious example of how this conflict of interests plays out (Martin and Romano, 1992:51–67). Consuming and producing countries vehemently accuse and blame each other and, depending on which side they are on, advocate either demand-side or supply-side solutions—controlling the demand of users in the United States for cocaine, as opposed to controlling the supply from South America. The concerns of the United States are fairly unambiguous. Cocaine imports have increased tenfold during the last decade, distribution patterns have become more sophisticated, and the abuse of cocaine and its derivative "crack" has become a serious problem (Rengert, 1998). The position of producing countries is also clear-cut. Elites there view antidrug campaigns with hostility because they impose significant new burdens and create formidable new challenges (Rensselaer, 1989). There are powerful vested economic interests profiting from drugs, and in the past decade, Colombia alone has lost 23 judges, 63 journalists, four presidential candidates, and more than 3,000 soldiers and police officers in its attempt moderate drug production (Samper, 1995).

In short, there is little prospect of effective control of drugs through the criminal law in the United States. Some even argue that the War on Drugs, at a cost of $16 billion annually, has corrupted the institutions of the nation and no law enforcement agency has escaped the effects of the profit and racism that drive the drug trade and its criminalization (Baggins, 1998). The various punitive approaches—attacking drug production abroad, interdiction (seizing drugs in transit) and domestic law enforcement (arresting and incarcerating sellers and buyers)—have failed (Massing, 1998a; 1998b).

There are two controversial alternatives, however. The first is a consideration of drug addiction and drug use more as a medical than a legal problem with an emphasis on comprehensive treatment, as is done, to some extent, in Great Britain and the Scandinavian countries (De Kort and Korf, 1992).

The second is the legalization or decriminalization of drugs. As the influential *Economist* (2001) argues, drugs are dangerous, but so is the illegality that surrounds them. Because it is illegal, it cannot be regulated. Governments cannot insist on minimum quality standards for cocaine; or warn asthma sufferers to avoid ecstasy; or demand that distributors take responsibility for the way their products are sold. With alcohol and tobacco, such restrictions are possible; with drugs, not. In legitimate commerce, the sale of drugs would be controlled, taxed, and supervised. Educational campaigns would proclaim their dangers. Through legalization, drugs would poison fewer customers, kill fewer dealers and bystanders, bribe fewer enforcement people, and raise more public revenue. Initially, there may be more users and more addicts. The recommendation of the *Economist* (2001:16) is simply "to set it free." The article contends that governments allow their citizens to engage in a variety of self-destructive things: to go bungee-jumping, to ride motorcycles and jet skies, to own guns, to drink alcohol, and to smoke cigarettes. Some of them are far more dangerous than taking drugs. It concludes that trade in drugs may be immoral or irresponsible, but it should no longer be illegal. A nice controversial position to debate.

Prostitution

If there is one area in the criminal law that arouses the most anxiety concerning public morals, it is sexual conduct. The range of sexual conduct covered by the law is so great and extensive that the law makes potential criminals of most teenagers and adults—especially with the increased availability and variety of cyber-sex. One of the justifications for such a complete control of sexual behavior is to protect the family system. A number of state laws control acts that would otherwise endanger the chastity of women before marriage, such as the variety of laws on rape (statutory and forcible), fornication, incest, and sexual deviance of juveniles. The criminal laws on adultery are also designed to protect the family by preventing sexual relations outside of marriage (Quinney, 1975:83–84). In addition, a complex set of federal and state laws control the advertising, sale, distribution, and availability of contraceptives; the performance of abortion; voluntary sterilization; and artificial insemination (Weinberg, 1979). Because of the complexity and extensiveness of legal controls on sexual conduct and related matters, this section will be limited to a discussion of the legal controls of female prostitution. In the United States, estimates of women who make some or all of their living as prostitutes range from half a million (Clinard and Meier, 2001) to a million (Aday, 1990:108).

It is now recognized that laws throughout the world against prostitution discriminate against women (see, for example, Davis, 1993; Kempadoo and Doezema, 1998; Scambler and Scambler, 1997). Many women's groups here and abroad maintain that a woman should have the right to engage in sexual relations for pay if she so desires (Poel, 1995). However, law enforcement authorities do not yet share that position, and there is still a tendency to regard only the women as offenders and not their clients.

State laws vary on prostitution (Meier and Geis, 1997:27–65). In many states, solicitation is considered a misdemeanor punished by a fine or a jail sentence of up to one year. Frequent arrests, however, may result in a charge of felony. There are three broad categories of arrests for prostitutes: (1) for accosting and soliciting; (2) on a charge of "common prostitution," which can be subsumed under disorderly conduct or vagrancy; and (3) detention under health regulations (La Fave, 1965:457–463). Law enforcement of prostitution is sporadic, and much of the control is limited to containment. There is a fair amount of discretion involved in the control of prostitutes. At times, there is practically no enforcement, and at other times, police conduct special campaigns directed at streetwalkers in certain neighborhoods. In general, most of the police control of prostitutes is aimed at the individual practitioners and streetwalkers. The high-class call girls are relatively immune to legal control (Rich, 1978:63).

Laws against prostitution are attempts to control private moral behavior through punitive social control measures. The influential and ubiquitous Wolfenden Report expresses rather eloquently the rationale for the continued legal control of prostitution.

> If it were the law's intention to punish prostitution per se, on the grounds that it is immoral conduct, then it would be right that it should provide for the punishment of the man as well as the woman. But that is not the function of the law. It should confine itself to those activities which offend against public order and decency or expose the ordinary citizen to what is offensive or injurious; and the simple fact that prostitutes do parade themselves more habitually and openly than their prospective customers, and do by their continual presence affront the sense of decency of the ordinary citizen. In so doing they create a nuisance which, in our view, the law is entitled to recognize and deal with. (1963:143–144)

The report also notes that prostitution has prevailed for many centuries, and it cannot be really controlled by criminal law. As long as there is a demand for the services of prostitutes and there remain women who choose this form of livelihood—even when there is no economic necessity for it—the Wolfenden Report concludes that "no amount of legislation directed towards its abolition will abolish it" (1963:132). Still, from time to time, community leaders and law enforcement agents would like to "clean up" some areas of the cities, and through these efforts, they persist in trying to suppress prostitution through the law (Lowman, 1992).

One day, perhaps, they will learn from history and will recognize that such efforts are futile in a free-enterprise society. A growing number of critics argue that the criminal statutes improperly and unwisely extend the coverage of criminal law to harmless matters of private morality, such as commercial sex between consenting adults. Prostitution is legal (with some restrictions) in Canada. Similarly, in many European countries in 2002, prostitutes ply their trade legally, pay taxes, and receive health and retirement benefits. The Netherlands, where the sex industry is now a $1 billion business or 5 percent of the Dutch economy, just recently legalized brothels, and the 30,000 or so sex workers now have a chance to get the basic labor rights, insurance policies and disability payments enjoyed by other citizens. Many prostitutes now are also setting themselves up as self-employed businesswomen with accountants, banks and health insurance companies as clients (Daley, 2001). In Germany, the law required for years now that cities with populations of 500,000 or more to designate 10 percent of their area as an "amusement" zone, with prostitution included among the amusements (*Wall Street Journal*, 1986a:16).

Influential critics, such as Gilbert Geis (1979), would revise these prohibitions to narrow the kinds of behavior they proscribe to acts that are clearly harmful to society. Prostitution is not considered one of them. The decriminalization of prostitution would, in essence, extend the practice of official tolerance already operative in many places (Adler and Adler, 1975:224). It would allow the police to deal with more important matters, and it would probably help lower the number of sex crimes. Opponents of decriminalization argue for increased legal control of prostitution, since they believe it leads, for example, to other crimes, such as drug addiction, blackmail, assault, and even murder.

Gambling

Some 70 percent of the American public gamble (Lesieur, 1992:43) and certain forms of casino gambling are legal in many parts of the country. Today more than 90 percent of Americans live within 200 miles of a legal casino where people legally bet some $640 billion a year and lose about $51 billion of that amount (O'Brien, 1998). As the legal gambling business has spread across the country, a fast-spinning revolving door has also developed, creating a situation in which a state senator with no casino experience has, in an instant, become president of a major casino, a law-enforcement official from a state attorney general's office has gone on to become the chief executive of the nation's most profitable casino, and where top gambling officials from one state after another have resigned to pursue lucrative casino careers. Legalized gambling has become a growth industry and created a robust new market for politically connected executives, lobbyists, and consultants who "speak the language" of the regulators (Pulley, 1998).

Legal and illegal gambling exist practically side-by-side and participants often cross the line. In the victimless-crime literature, illegal gambling, just like drug use and prostitution, is considered a consensual transaction and a plaintiffless crime (see, for example, Cozic and Winters, 1995). The players are willing participants who generally do not notify the police that a crime has been committed. Enforcement activity therefore must be initiated by the police, who then act as the complainant on the behalf of the community. By contrast, enforcement activity for other crimes, such as burglaries or muggings, usually occurs in response to citizen complaints.

Historically, the prohibition and regulation of gambling has largely been a function of the state. Federal involvement with gambling began in the late nineteenth century, when Congress put an end to the operation of corrupt lotteries by denying them mailing privileges and the ability to transact business across state lines. The next significant federal action dealing with gambling occurred in 1949, when Congress enacted legislation to eliminate the gambling ships that had been operating off the coast of California. Other actions dealt with the interstate transportation and transmission of wagering information and gambling paraphernalia. The Organized Crime Control Act of 1970 further extended jurisdiction over interstate gambling and made it a federal offense to operate certain illegal gambling businesses. Congress also has affected gambling activities through the exercise of its taxing powers by levying excise and occupational taxes on gambling operations, and a stamp tax on gambling devices, and by subjecting gambling winnings to the federal income tax (Commission on the Review of the National Policy Toward Gambling, 1976:5).

Local police departments have the primary responsibility for gambling enforcement, although the role of state-level agencies is growing. The Commission on the Review of the National Policy Toward Gambling (1976:44–46) identifies a number of control techniques used by law enforcement agencies. The commission notes that the most frequent source of gambling arrests is the direct observation of illegal gambling activity. Such arrests are primarily "nonserious," involving individual street players or low-level employees of gambling organizations. Arrests at higher levels—for example, large bookmakers or numbers offices—are rarely, if ever, made in this manner. They require investigation leading to a probable cause for search and arrest warrants. The use of informants in gambling control is widespread. Most police departments rely on this technique, as well as on undercover investigators who can often accumulate evidence against individuals and on operations by placing bets. In recent years, the use of electronic surveillance, authorized by Congress in 1968 under Title III of the Omnibus Crime Control and Safe Streets Act, became particularly widespread in the control of illegal gambling. Electronic surveillance is best suited for the use of gambling investigation because of the dependence of gambling operations on telephones. One of the devices that is used is the pen register, which records phone numbers dialed from a particular telephone. By attaching a pen register to the telephone line of a gambling location, police can often identify additional locations and individuals involved in illegal gambling operations.

Of the tens of thousands of individuals arrested annually in the United States for gambling offenses, a relatively small proportion are convicted. Of those convicted, a very small percentage receive jail or prison sentences, or substantial fines. For example, during the six-year period from 1969 to 1974, there were 36,207 arrests for gambling in Chicago. Only 6 percent of those arrested were convicted. But there are exceptions to the generally low conviction rates for gambling. For example, approximately 70 percent of persons appearing in Connecticut Circuit Courts on gambling charges between 1970 and 1974 were convicted (Commission on the Review of the National Policy Toward Gambling, 1976:46–47).

The criminal law is ineffective in controlling and preventing people from engaging in illegal gambling. The parties involved in gambling do not complain about it, and a typical gambling transaction is probably more easily, rapidly, and privately consummated than is any other kind of illegal consensual transaction. It is much easier to place a bet with a bookie than to buy cocaine or have an encounter with a prostitute. Aside from the difficulties of detection, the criminal sanction for illegal gambling exerts little deterrent force. Generally, the penalties for those who are convicted tend to be light. Public opinion does not consider gambling as particularly wrongful, a sentiment both affected by and reflected in the lenience with which gambling offenders are treated (Packer, 1968:348). There seems to be an ambivalence in attitudes toward gambling. It is reflected in a resistance to proposals to reduce or eliminate reliance on criminal sanctions, accompanied by an equivalent resistance to any but the most sporadic attempts at enforcement.

Illegal gambling provides the largest source of revenue to organized crime. In fact, gambling laws are now justified as necessary to combat organized crime (Sheley, 1985:121). In most urban areas, bookmakers associated with crime syndicates specialize in bets on horse racing, professional football and basketball, boxing, hockey, and baseball. Increasingly, they are also involved in college football and basketball. Syndicates also run "numbers games," which involve placing a bet on the possible occurrence of certain numbers, such as the last three digits of the U.S. treasury balance (Light, 1977). A complicated hierarchical organization is required to distribute the forms and to collect and pay off bets. Organized-crime syndicates employ "writers," "runners," or "sellers," terms to indicate the persons who accept numbers bets directly from bettors. Bets collected by them are given to a "pickup man," who forwards them to the next level in the hierarchy, the "bank." In larger operations, bets may be carried from the pickup man to another intermediary, the controller. Tickets with winning numbers are redeemed by cashiers or delivered by runners. In addition to bookmaking and numbers games, gambling syndicates also operate illegal casinos, "sponsor" backgammon tournaments, and provide opportunities for wagers to be made on a variety of activities—even the outcomes of political elections.

Attempts to control illegal gambling consume a large amount of law enforcement time and resources. The problem is further compounded by online gambling. As of 2002, no state nor the federal government yet has passed a law specifically targeted to online Internet gambling. Hence, to combat or regulate online gambling, state and federal law enforcement authorities must turn to laws passed to deal with more traditional types of gambling. In some cases these laws are badly suited to the new technology, while in others the language is surprisingly broad enough to encompass online gambling.

Ostensibly, control of gambling activities also includes fighting organized crime, maintaining a favorable public image of the police department, keeping undesirable activities or persons out of a city, and maintaining public order. The objective of controlling organized crime is reflected both in the intent of some gambling searches and in the view of the police that illegal gambling is related to organized crime. The objectives of preserving the department's public image and of maintaining public order are related, in that where open gambling, such as street cards and dice, is permitted to continue, citizens are likely to conclude that the police are either corrupt or derelict in their duty. In some instances, however, "meeting the quota" has become a principal stimulant for the control of illegal gambling by the police. In such instances, officers produce what may be called "symbolic" gambling arrests—that is, gambling arrests that meet the quota, thus fulfilling the department's stated policy of continuing enforcement activity.

An additional problem with gambling control is that most of the corruption of police and of the courts is associated with these offenses. Few police officers are willing to accept bribes from murderers, burglars, or other criminals whose acts are blatantly harmful and have identifiable victims. However, many police officers tend to feel that gambling is not particularly serious and that, in any case, it is impossible to eradicate. Hence, organized crime is often readily able to buy police protection for its activities. The Knapp Commission found corruption in the New York Police Department to be "at its most sophisticated among plainclothesmen assigned to enforce gambling laws" (Commission on the Review of the National Policy Toward Gambling, 1976:40). Participation in organized payoffs—a "pad"—netted individual New York plainclothes officers $300 to $1,500 a month. In return for protection, gambling establishments paid as much as $3,500 a month. Similarly, it was found that in Philadelphia, police throughout the city accept protection money from gamblers. It should be noted, however, that police corruption exists not only in gambling enforcement but in other areas as well. Investigations have also uncovered misconduct related to the enforcement of narcotics, prostitution, liquor establishments, construction-site regulations, and traffic. (See, for example, Chambliss, 1978.) These forms of police corruption are largely an urban problem.

One response to the difficulty and wastefulness in trying to enforce laws against gambling is to remove completely the criminal label. As the Knapp Commission recommended: "The criminal law against gambling should be repealed. To the extent that the legislature deems that some control over gambling is appropriate, such regulation should be by civil rather than criminal process. The police should in any event be relieved from any responsibility for the enforcement of gambling laws or regulations" (Wynn and Goldman, 1974:67). Although a number of similar suggestions have been made, the question of the decriminalization of gambling still remains a hotly debated and controversial issue. One of the concerns fueling this controversy is the estimate that some 1–2 percent of the adult population are probably pathological gamblers (people who chronically fail to resist impulses to gamble and for whom gambling interferes with other aspects of life) and an additional 2–3 percent are problem gamblers (Lesieur, 1992:49). Other estimates go even higher suggesting that 5 percent of the adult population, or some 10 million people, are compulsive gamblers.

A 2001 survey of 315 senior citizens (a relatively small sample size) who frequented riverboat casinos and bingo parlors to escape boredom suggested that they were particularly prone to develop gambling problems and 11 percent showed signs of being pathological or compulsive gamblers (Young and Stern, 2001). The number of older adults who had placed a bet nearly doubled from 1975 to 1998, a period in which legalized gambling exploded. The rate of increase was much higher than for other age groups. Elder adults remain a prime target for the industry. Casinos, in particular, court those over 65 and older with cheap buffets, free drinks, free transportation, money-back coupons and other discounts.

For those under twenty-one, estimates go as high as 15 percent. In the mordant words of one authority on gambling, "Compulsive gambling disorders may be for Generation X what cocaine and crack were for their parents' generation" (O'Brien, 1998). With further legalization of gambling, activities thought to be associated with pathological and problem gambling (excessive borrowing, family problems, difficulties at work, psychiatric disorders, crime, and so on) would probably increase.

WHITE-COLLAR CRIME

White-collar crimes are essentially crimes of privilege (Shover and Wright, 2001), being of the suite rather than of the street. The term "white-collar crime" was coined by Edwin H. Sutherland (1949:9) and first used in an address to the American Sociological Association (ASS) in 1939. He criticized proponents of social disorganization and social pathology theories of crime and introduced class and power dimensions. "White-collar crime" he proposed, "may be defined approximately as a crime committed by a person of respectability and high status in the course of his occupation." He documented the existence of this form of crime with a study of the careers of 70 large, reputable corporations, which together had amassed 980 violations of the criminal law, or an average of 14 convictions apiece. Behind the offenses of false advertising, unfair labor practices, restraint of trade, price-fixing agreements, stock manipulation, copyright infringement, and outright swindles were perfectly respectable middle- and upper-middle-class executives (Croall, 1989; Reichman, 1989). Check fraud alone represents a $10 billion loss for banks today (Holland, 1995:96).

Gilbert Geis (1978:279; 1994) argues that "white-collar crimes constitute a more serious threat to the well-being and integrity of our society than more traditional kinds of crime" and workplace injuries, unnecessary surgeries and illegal pollution consign far more people to the cemeteries than the offenses of traditional criminals. Moreover, as the President's Commission on Law Enforcement and Administration of Justice (1967b:104) concludes, "white-collar crime affects the whole moral climate of our society. Derelictions by corporations and their managers who usually occupy leadership positions in their communities, establish an example which tends to erode the moral base of the law." It raises questions about the equity of law and provides justification for other types of law violations.

The now classic textbook case of the $23 million "unauthorized loan" is illustrative of the question of equity of law dealing with white-collar crime. The defendants were charged with setting up a check-kiting operation: the art of repeatedly taking checks written on one account and quickly depositing them into another, and vice versa, staying a step ahead of the clearing system and thus creating a false impression of the balances in the accounts. Once false balances have been created, a kiter can take out money against them, and that is just what perpetrators of this scheme did, leaving Marine Midland Bank holding the bag for a loss in excess of $23 million. The two already wealthy individuals found themselves indicted for the felony of grand larceny and the misdemeanor of scheming to defraud. And because larceny requires an intent to deprive an owner of his or her property *permanently*, the defendants' repayment—as well as their ability to repay—played an important role in defense. Their attorneys argued that it was a *temporary* borrowing; they never intended to deprive the bank permanently of the funds. They insisted that they had no intention of keeping the money—so that what they were doing did not qualify as larceny. The jurors apparently agreed. The defendants were found innocent of the felony charge of grand larceny, which carries a possible seven-year prison sentence, because they claimed they intended to return the money *and* had the ability to pay. They were convicted only of a misdemeanor count of scheming to defraud, for which the maximum sentence is one year. The defendants unsuccessfully appealed the conviction (Cony and Penn, 1986).

The full extent of white-collar crime is difficult to assess. Many illegal corporate activities go undetected, and many wealthy individuals are able to evade taxes for years without being found out. White-collar crimes ("crimes in the suites" that are often dubbed crimes of the middle class [Weisburd et al., 1991]) are generally considered somehow less serious than the crimes of the lower class ("crimes of the streets"), and there is often strong pressure on the police and the courts not to prosecute at all in these cases—to take account of the offenders' "standing in the community" and to settle the matter out of court. For example, a bank that finds its safe burglarized at night will immediately summon the police, but it may be more circumspect if it finds that one of its executives has embezzled a sum of money. To avoid unwelcome publicity, the bank may simply allow the offender to resign after making an arrangement for him or her to pay back whatever possible.

The concept of white-collar crime generally incorporates both occupational and corporate crimes (Coleman, 1998:5). Some individuals commit crimes in connection with their occupations. For example, physicians may give out illegal prescriptions for narcotics, make fraudulent reports for Medicare payments, and give false testimony in accident cases. Lawyers may engage in some illegalities, such as securing false testimony from witnesses, misappropriating funds in receivership, and various forms of ambulance chasing to collect fraudulent damage claims arising from accidents. Corporate crimes are considered those illegal activities that are committed in the furtherance of business operations but that are not the central purpose of business. A convenient distinction between occupational and corporate crimes may be in the context of immediate and direct benefit to the perpetrator. In occupational crimes, generally the benefit is for the individual who commits a particular illegal activity—for example, the physician who receives money for giving out illegal prescriptions. In corporate crime, the benefit is usually for the organization (see, for example, Pearce and Tombs, 1998). For example, an executive bribes a public official to secure favors for his or her corporation. In this instance, the benefit would be for the corporation and not directly for the individual. The desire to increase profits is a crucial factor in a wide range of corporate crimes. The remainder of this section will focus on what is strictly called corporate crime. It is distinguished from ordinary crime in two respects: the nature of the violation and the fact that administrative and civil law are more likely to be used as punishment than the criminal law.

In the United States, corporate crime did not exist until the nineteenth century. The reason for it is simply that there were no laws against dangerous or unethical corporate practices. Before the nineteenth century, corporations were free to sell unsafe products, to keep workers in unsafe conditions, to pollute the atmosphere, to engage in monopolistic practices, to overcharge customers, and to make outrageously false advertising claims for their products. By the end of the nineteenth century and the beginning of the twentieth century, increasingly laws were passed that attempted to regulate some of the more flagrant business practices that prevailed at the time. Examples include the Sherman Anti-Trust Act (1890) and the Pure Food and Drug Act (1906). Since that time, a vast array of laws has been passed to regulate the various facets of potentially harmful corporate activities.

The extensive nature of corporate crime is unquestioned today; it has been revealed by many government investigative committees. In a study of the 582 largest publicly owned corporations in the United States, over 60 percent had at least one enforcement action completed against them in 1975 and 1976 (U.S. Department of Justice, 1979:XIX). The average number of actions initiated against these corporations for illegal activities (such as price fixing, foreign payoffs, illegal political contributions, manufacture of unsafe foods and drugs) was 4.2.

It is estimated that corporate crimes in the form of faulty goods, monopolistic practices, and similar law violations annually cost consumers between $174 billion and $231 billion (U.S. Department of Justice, 1979:16). The loss to taxpayers from reported and unreported violations of federal regulations by corporations is between $10 billion and $20 billion. About $1.2 billion goes unreported in corporate tax returns each year. Price fixing among corporations costs the consumer well over $65 billion a year (Simon, 2002). The loss alone from the electrical price-fixing conspiracy of the 1960s was nearly $2 billion, far greater than the total burglary losses during any given year. In 1979, nine major oil companies were sued by the Justice Department for illegal overcharges of more than $1 billion. The companies were accused of charging too much for products derived from natural gas liquids and artificially increasing consumer costs. In contrast, the largest robbery in the United States thus far involved the June 26, 1990, heist of $11 million in cash from an armored car in Rochester, New York. Previously, the much-publicized Sentry armored car robbery of about $10.5 million in New York City in 1982 had been the largest robbery loss so far. But these cases are atypical; the typical robbery involves armed theft of about $250, burglary of about $350, larceny of about $125 and bank robbery of about $2,000.

Undoubtedly, corporate crimes impose an enormous financial burden on society. In addition, it has been estimated that each year 200,000 to 500,000 workers are needlessly exposed to toxic agents such as radioactive materials and poisonous chemicals because of corporate failure to obey safety laws. Nearly half of all deaths among asbestos insulation workers are directly caused by exposure to that substance (Coleman, 1998:70–71). Many of the 2.5 million temporary and 250,000 permanent worker disabilities from industrial accidents each year are the result of managerial acts that represent culpable failure to adhere to established standards (Geis, 1978:279). Corporate crimes cause injuries to people on a larger scale than the so-called street crimes. Far more people are killed annually through corporate criminal activities than by the 20,000 or so individual criminal homicides; even if death is an indirect result, the person still died (U.S. Department of Justice, 1979:16).

Corporate crime is controlled by a variety of regulatory agencies. The control of corporate activities may be *prospective*, as in licensing, when control is exercised before deviant acts occur; *processual*, as in inspection where control is continuous; and *retrospective*, as when a lawsuit is brought for damages after deviance has occurred. These types of controls will be discussed further in the final section of this chapter. In addition, if a business concern defies the law, the government may institute, under civil law, an injunction to "cease and desist" from further violations. If further violations occur, contempt of court proceedings may be instituted. Fines and various forms of assessments are also used in attempts to control deleterious corporate activities, as, for example, in cases of levying fines on water and air polluters. At times, the government can also exercise control through its buying power by rewarding firms that comply and withdrawing from or not granting governmental contracts to those who do not (Nagel, 1975:341–352).

But, as Christopher D. Stone (1978:244–245) points out: "Whether we are threatening the corporation with private civil actions, criminal prosecutions, or the new hybrid 'civil penalties,' we aim to control the corporation through threats to its profits." Although corporations are subjected to federal sentencing guidelines (Podgor, 1994) which are rather controversial (Hemphill, 1993), corporate offenders are rarely criminally prosecuted and even more rarely imprisoned. A large proportion of these offenders are handled through administrative and civil sanctions, and the penalty is monetary. In a sense, the penalty imposed for violating the law amounts to little more than a reasonable licensing fee for engaging in illegal activity. Essentially, it is worthwhile for a large corporation to violate the laws regulating business. Typically, the fines are microscopic. For example, until 1955 the greatest fine a judge could levy against a company for violating the Sherman Anti-Trust Act was $5,000. In 1955 it was increased to $50,000, and in 1976 it was further increased to $250,000. This is not much of a deterrent to a company like General Electric or General Motors.

Controlling corporations through the law becomes, as Stone (1978:250) puts it, a "misplaced faith on negative reinforcement." Although there are now sophisticated detection and record-keeping technologies, forensic accountants and other legal specialists (Lindquist, 1995), the law constitutes only one of the threats that the corporation faces in dealing with the outside world. Often, paying a fine is considered part of doing business. For a businessperson, reducing the profits by a lawsuit does not involve the same loss of face as losses attributable to other causes. For example, being sued by the antitrust division, although "a mess," is "understandable." It is not a question of improving such behavior but a realization by businesspeople that it could happen to anyone. In financial reports, losses through lawsuits are explained in footnotes as nonrecurring losses.

Although there are signs of increased enforcement by federal agencies and local authorities (see, for example, Benson and Cullen, 1998; Calavita and Pontell, 1994), the current legal controls on corporate crime are inefficient. The government's response to corporate violations cannot be compared to its response to ordinary crime. Generally, penalties imposed on corporations are quite lenient, particularly in view of the gravity of the offenses committed, as compared with the penalties imposed on ordinary offenders. Few members of corporate management ever go to prison, even if convicted; generally they are placed on probation or requested to carry some kind of community service (Podgor, 1994). If they go to prison, it is almost always for a very short time period. For example, a study found that of the 56 federally convicted executives, 62.5 percent received probation, 28.6 percent were incarcerated, and the rest had their sentences suspended. The average prison sentence for all those convicted averaged 2.8 days (U.S. Department of Justice, 1979:xii). Gilbert Geis (1978, 1994) points out that it is, indeed, ironic that the penalties for corporate crime are the least severe, even though they are given to the very persons who might be the most affected by them, or who might "benefit" the most from them. In other words, if these offenders are potentially the most deterred, an increase in punishment and the intensity of enforcement might result in the greatest benefit to society. As it stands now, however, the penalty for corporate crime is far less than the harm caused and, unlike those who commit violent crimes, perpetrators of corporate crime are not subjected to the "three strikes and you are out" mandatory sentencing guidelines.

SOCIAL CONTROL OF DISSENT

A universal, omnipresent and pervasive governmental activity is the control of dissent. Political trials, surveillance and suppression of information and free speech are rampant in most countries (see, for example, Christenson, 1998). Some examples: In Islamic countries fundamentalists regularly ban books. (The most blatant recent case is that of the writer Salman Rushdie, who is being threatened with death because of his book *The Satanic Verses*. Ayatollah Ruhollah Khomeini called it blasphemy against Islam and in 1989 offered a million-dollar reward for the writer's execution. The offer was raised to $2.8 million by hard-liners in late 1998, although the Iranian government officially rescinded the reward in an attempt to improve relations with the West (*St. Louis Post-Dispatch*, 1998) and Rushdie is still in hiding— although with sporadic public appearances for book tours and talk shows under the watchful eyes of security guards in 2000 and 2001. In Islamic countries, also, the press is state-controlled, and dissidents, at best, are jailed. In African and Asian countries, journalistic fealty to the ruling dictatorship is demanded (see Singapore, for example); and the abuse of psychiatry to intimidate and torture dissidents in the former Soviet Union was well documented and loudly deplored by the West.

In China, the democracy movement continues to be suppressed in the aftermath of the 1989 Tiananmen crackdown (Branegan, 1998; Fein, 1992) and the abuse of psychiatry as a form of social control for dissent once again appears to be increasing. For example, the government has forcibly imprisoned members of Falun Gong in psychiatric hospitals. Falun Gong, a popular movement that advocates channeling energy through deep breathing and exercises, has been the target of government crackdowns with abuses reminiscent of the Cultural Revolution decades earlier. Hundreds of Falun Gong members have been taken to psychiatric institutions and drugged, physically restrained, isolated or given electric shocks (*New York Times*, 2001: 14wk). There is also a development of a network of new police psychiatric hospitals—called Ankangs which means "peace and happiness"—built in recent years. Chinese law includes "political harm to society" as legally dangerous mentally ill behavior. Law enforcement agents are instructed to take into psychiatric custody "political maniacs," defined as people who make anti-government speeches, write reactionary letters or otherwise express opinions in public on important domestic and international affairs contrary to the official government position. Currently, there are 20 Ankangs, with plans to build many more.

The United States is no exception. Although it has a history of welcoming dissent in the abstract, it punishes it in the concrete (Lieberman, 1972:74). Law supports the government as the legitimate holder of power in society. The government in turn is legitimately involved in the control of its citizens. The principal objectives of the government are to provide for the welfare of its citizens, to protect their lives and property, and to maintain order within society. To maintain order, the government is mandated to apprehend and punish criminals. In a democratic society, there are questions, however, about the legitimacy of a government that stifles dissent in the interest of preserving order. In principle, in a democratic society, tradition and values affirm that dissent is appropriate. At the same time, for social order to prevail, a society needs to ensure that existing power relationships are maintained over time. Furthermore, those in positions of power who benefit from the existing power arrangement use their influence to encourage the repression of challenges to the government. Consequently, governments generally opt for the control and repression of dissent.

One way of controlling dissent is through the various selection processes used to place individuals into desirable social positions (Oberschall, 1973:249–250). In most political systems, the leaders have ways of controlling the selection and mobility of people through patronage systems, the extension of the government bureaucracy, and co-optation in its many forms. Loyalty and conformity are generally the primary criteria for advancement. Another form of control in this context is the dismissal of individuals who do not comply with the stated expectations and voice "unpopular" opinions. In some instances, the leaders can directly control the supply and demand of certain services and skills. For example, "by exercising influence on budgets, examinations, student stipends, and university expansion, a government can within a couple of years reduce the total number of students in higher education for the purpose of quashing a troublesome student movement and floating population of unemployed graduates that it has brought into being and subsidized" (Oberschall, 1973:250).

Control can also be achieved through the manipulation of the structure of material benefits (Janowitz, 1976; Mandel, 1975). For example, Frances Fox Piven and Richard A. Cloward (1993) contend that welfare programs serve as a social-control mechanism in periods of mass unemployment by diffusing social unrest and thus reducing dissent. They argue that public assistance programs are used to regulate the political and economic activity of the poor. In periods of severe economic depression, the legitimacy of the political system is likely to be questioned by the poor. The possibility of upsetting the status quo of power and property relationships in society increases. Demands grow for changing the existing social and economic arrangements. Under this threat, public assistance programs are initiated or expanded by the government. They cite case after case from sixteenth-century Europe to mid-twentieth-century America, documenting their thesis that social welfare has, throughout the ages, been used as a mechanism of social control and a way by the government to diffuse social unrest through direct intervention. They note, however, that when economic conditions improve, the relief rolls are cut back in response to pressures from those who employ the poor so as to ensure an adequate supply of low-wage labor.

Another option for the government to use in the control of dissent is its coercive social-control apparatus to deal with crime, enforce the law, and keep social interaction peaceful and orderly. As compared with other mechanisms, "a coercive response to social disturbances is the cheapest and most immediately available means of control to the authorities" (Oberschall, 1973:252). The government is expected by the citizens, and is required by law, to protect life and property and to arrest the perpetrators of illegal activities. In addition to these coercive responses to dissent, the government has in its arsenal a variety of less overt, though equally effective, control mechanisms. For example, David Wise (1978:399–400) points out that the Central Intelligence Agency, although prohibited by law from doing so, has engaged in domestic operations to monitor and control the activities of Americans. For 20 years, the CIA opened 215,000 first-class letters, screened 28 million letters, and photographed the outside of 2.7 million letters. During the Nixon era, in Operation Chaos, the CIA followed antiwar activists, infiltrated various antiwar groups, undertook illegal break-ins and wiretaps, indexed 300,000 names in its "Hydra" computer, and compiled separate files on 7,200 Americans.

From 1955 to 1975, the Federal Bureau of Investigation investigated 740,000 "subversive" targets—including the renowned sociologist Talcott Parsons of Harvard's Social Relations Department (Diamond, 1992:37). The FBI has also engaged in illegal break-ins, installed taps on telephones, falsified the credit ratings of some individuals on the subversive list, obtained their tax returns, staged arrests by local police on narcotic pretexts, made anonymous phone calls to friends or family members of some targets telling them of immoral or radical conduct, provided distorted information to civil rights and antiwar organizations in an attempt to create dissension and disruption within the group, and tried to disrupt marriages of suspected dissidents by sending anonymous letters to husbands, wives, or newspaper gossip columnists (*Newsweek*, 1979:45). As late as 1972, the FBI had close to 7,500 "ghetto informants" on its payroll and still maintains a network of 1,500 "domestic intelligence" informants whom it pays $7.4 million a year (Wise, 1978:400).

The Internal Revenue Service, with more than 106,000 employees in 1998 (Worsham, 1998:17), is the most feared and powerful of all federal agencies. As possibly the most powerful instrument of social control in the United States, the IRS decides on a wide range of matters that are far removed from the collection of taxes (Burnham, 1989, 1996). The power of the IRS is based on several factors. It is the largest federal law enforcement agency. It has a computerized national database unmatched by any other agency. To collect information it deems necessary, the IRS has the power to order—without warrant—banks, employers, and others to provide data about a taxpayer. (Other law enforcement agencies *must* obtain a warrant to get such information.) It also has the authority to impose civil penalties. If a taxpayer feels that the penalty is not justified, the penalty can be challenged. However, because of the special nature of civil tax law, the legal burden of proving one's innocence almost always rests on the taxpayer. This is in contrast to the criminal law, where the burden of proving a suspect's guilt rests with the government. The IRS can also make a "jeopardy assessment"—that is, without prior approval of a judge, the IRS can seize the assets of any taxpayer suspected of contemplating flight. All these powers are stated in the some 2,200 pages of the Revenue Code of the United States. It is worth noting that the IRS regulations interpreting the law require an additional 7,600 pages.

The average American may never have any dealings with the FBI, the CIA, or similar organizations, but he or she comes in contact at least once a year with the IRS, on April 15. The tax system in the United States essentially rests on voluntary compliance. At the heart of the tax system is the citizens' trust and belief that the government will not use the vast powers of the IRS to punish citizens for their political views. That confidence was rudely shattered by the events of Watergate.

The congressional investigations that followed showed that one harassing tactic of the Nixon administration directed at its "enemies" was to subject them to frequent tax audits. The IRS, under pressure by the Nixon administration, established a secret section that eventually became known as the Special Services Staff (SSS). Operating under what was called "red seal" security, and situated in the basement of IRS headquarters in Washington, the SSS acted like a clandestine intelligence unit, in close liaison with the FBI, and compiled files on 8,585 persons and 2,873 organizations (Wise, 1978:326). The Special Service Staff was "given responsibility for investigating and collecting intelligence on 'ideological, militant, subversive, radical and similar type organizations' and individuals (and) . . . 'non-violent' groups and individuals, including draft-card burners, peace demonstrators and persons who 'organize and attend rock festivals which attract youth and narcotics' " (Wise, 1978:327). The IRS, like the FBI, became an instrument for social control, making its own judgments about what political views and cultural preferences were acceptable.

The Army Intelligence Unit and the highly secret National Security Agency have both been actively involved in the surveillance of dissenters. The National Security Agency for years was reading and listening in on international communications. In the 1960s, for example, Western Union, RCA, and ITT made available copies of international cables to the National Security Agency (NSA) in "Operation Shamrock." Later, when some of the communications companies switched to storing their cables on magnetic tape, NSA transported the tapes daily to its headquarters in Maryland for copying and then back to New York the same day. When these round trips became too burdensome, the CIA, in the guise of a television tape-processing company, provided the NSA with office space to copy the tapes in New York.

The government, through these various intelligence agencies, has, indeed, created a system of institutionalized social control of dissent. The government has shown a strong tendency to closely watch the activities of people who threaten it by collecting, concealing, suppressing and manipulating information (Moynihan, 1998). Obviously, the government has to exert some control over its citizens, but in exerting control, care needs to be exercised to protect individuals' rights as guaranteed by the Constitution. There is a thin line between governmental control of dissent and the creation of a police state. The technology is also a new disturbance to the delicate balance between the privacy rights of citizens and the growing power of technology to help government to invade privacy.

This control technology is ubiquitous in the modern state. To illustrate the potentials of just one aspect of that technology, there are millions of computers in use in the federal government providing electronic access to more than 35 billion records. There is even a monitoring technology which records keystrokes on a personal computer (Schwartz, 2001). Social security numbers have become national "identifiers," and the protections of the 1974 Privacy Act are eroded because the information in the database can be used with little notice or recourse. "Computer matches"—the cross-checking of records by one agency against another—are conducted routinely (Havemann, 1986). This is how the government is withholding the income tax refunds of student loan and other loan defaulters. The technology is available now to create an electronic dossier on every citizen in the United States (Ramirez, 1992; *Time*, 1991).

Horror stories already abound. For example, for almost 30 years, a state legislative committee spied on 20,000 Californians, documenting their personal habits, social lives and political and professional relationships and they have yet to release the 80 cartons of information gathered (Kennedy, 1998). From time to time, target groups are even required to pay a fee for being tracked. For example, the United States Immigration and Naturalization Services (INS) has started to instrument a $90.00 fee for international students during the summer of 2001 to help pay for the technology that will track them. They too will have a nationwide computer database.

The rationale is to try to minimize the risk of terrorism by keeping close surveillance on foreign students. Perhaps it is time to start thinking about some effective controls and checks to be devised and imposed upon the users of this technology so they do not overstep the boundaries as happened in the Nixon era.

ADMINISTRATIVE LAW AND SOCIAL CONTROL

A broadly and popularly held misconception about the law is that it consists almost entirely of criminal law, with its apparatus of crime, police, prosecutors, judges, juries, sentences and prisons. Another misconception is that all law can be divided into criminal law and civil law. But the resources of legal systems are far richer and more extensive than either of these views implies (Summers and Howard, 1972:198). This section is concerned with how distinctive legal ways can be used to control what Robert S. Summers and George G. Howard (1972:199) call "private primary activity." They use this concept to describe various pursuits, such as production and marketing of electricity and natural gas; provision and operation of rail, air, and other transport facilities; food processing and distribution; construction of buildings, bridges, and other public facilities; and radio and television broadcasting. But these activities are not confined to large-scale affairs such as electrical production and provision of air transport. The list can be expanded to include provision of medical services by physicians, ownership and operation of motor vehicles by ordinary citizens, construction of residences by local carpenters, and the sale and purchase of stocks and bonds by private individuals. Private primary activities not only are positively desirable in themselves, but also are essential for the functioning of modern societies. These activities generate legal needs that are met through administrative control mechanisms.

Today, all kinds of services are needed, such as those provided by physicians, transport facilities, and electric companies. But an incompetent physician might kill rather than cure a patient. An unqualified airline pilot might crash, killing everyone on board. A food processor might poison half a community. In addition to incompetence or carelessness, deliberate abuses are also possible. An individual may lose his or her entire savings through fraudulent stock operations. A utility company might abuse its monopoly position and charge exorbitant rates. An owner of a nuclear waste disposal facility may want to cut corners, thus exposing the public to harmful radiation.

Private primary activities, Summers and Howard (1972:199) note, can cause harm, avoidable harm. At the same time, such activities can have great potential for good. Airplanes can almost be made safe, and stock frauds by fly-by-night operators can be reduced. Legal control of these activities is then justified on two grounds: the prevention of harm and the promotion of good. For example, in the case of radio and television broadcasting, laws can be concerned with both the control of obscenity and the problem of balanced programming, such as covering public affairs, in addition to entertainment and sports. Control is exerted on private primary activity through administrative laws, primarily in the context of licensing, inspection, and the threat of publicity.

Licensing

The power of administrative law goes beyond the setting of standards and the punishing of those who fail to comply. Horack notes: "The belief that law enforcement is better achieved by prevention than by prosecution has contributed to the emergence of administrative regulation as a primary means of government control" (quoted by Summers and Howard, 1972:202). Requiring and granting licenses to perform certain activities is a classic control device. Licensing is pervasive, and by one estimate, at least 5,000 different licenses have been granted to more than 5,000 occupations (Simon et al., 1992:542). With so many groups being licensed in one state or another, licensing as a form of social control affects a substantial portion of the labor force. Nowadays a license may be required to engage in an occupation, to operate a business, to serve specific customers or areas, or to manufacture certain products. Physicians and lawyers must obtain specific training and then demonstrate some competence before they can qualify for licenses to practice. Here, licensing is used to enforce basic qualifying standards. Airplane companies just cannot fly any route they wish, and broadcasters are not free to pick a frequency at will. Underlying all regulatory licensing is a denial of a right to engage in the contemplated activity except with a license.

The control of professions and certain activities through licensing is justified as protection for the public against inferior, fraudulent, or dangerous services and products. But, under this rubric, control has been extended to occupations that, at the most, only minimally affect public health and safety. In some states, licenses are required for cosmetologists, auctioneers, weather-control practitioners, taxidermists, junkyard operators, and weather-vane installers. Hawaii licenses tattoo artists; New Hampshire, lightning-rod salespeople. In Delaware, 86 occupations are licensed, including circus exhibitors, bowling-alley operators, florists, and billiard-parlor owners. Until recently, it was a misdemeanor for someone without a license to repair a watch in North Carolina. The penalty was a six-month jail sentence, the same as for practicing medicine without a license (*U.S. News & World Report*, 1979:70). In addition to requiring a license to practice these occupations, control is exerted through the revocation or suspension of the license. For example, under administrative law, the state may withdraw the right to practice from a lawyer, a physician, or a beautician, and it may suspend a bar or restaurant owner from doing business a few days, a year, or even permanently. A recent study by Roger L. Goldman and Steven Puro (2001) on the police points out that a very common approach to addressing misconduct in police departments is the revocation of the offending officer's license or state certificate which is obtained after the completion of a state mandated training. They note that revocation of license is more effective than termination, which does not really prevent an officer from obtaining employment in another department. This little-known way of handling police misconduct by the general public has been successfully adopted by 43 states.

Local, state, and federal administrative controls through licensing are widely used mechanisms of social control. Administrative laws generally specify the conditions under which a license is required, the requirements that must be met by applicants, the duties imposed upon the licensees, the agency authorized to issue such licenses, the procedures in revoking licenses and the grounds that constitute cause for revocation, and the penalties for violations.

Inspection

Administrative law grants broad investigatory and inspection powers to regulatory agencies. Periodic inspection is a way of monitoring ongoing activities under the jurisdiction of a particular agency. Such inspections determine whether cars and trains can move, planes fly (see, for example, Wald, 1998), agricultural products can meet quality standards, newspapers can obtain second-class mailing privileges, and so forth. Similar procedures are used to prevent the distribution of unsafe foods and drugs, to prohibit the entry of diseased plants and animals into the country, or to suspend the license of a pilot pending a disciplinary hearing.

In a variety of industries, government inspectors operate on the premises. For example, when a Food and Drug Administration inspector finds botulism in soup, the manufacturer will withdraw the product from grocers' and manufacturers' shelves and destroy all cans—because of the unstated but understood FDA threat to prosecute through the Justice Department (Gellhorn and Levin, 1997).

Inspections constitute a primary tool of administrative supervision and control. For instance, the nation's banks are overseen by the Federal Reserve Board and the Federal Deposit Insurance Corporation through visits by their inspectors for examination of the bank's records. A housing official may inspect buildings to determine compliance with building codes. In some instances, inspection takes place occasionally, such as when ensuring compliance with building codes. In other instances, inspection is continuous, as in food inspection. Both forms of inspection, sporadic and continuous, also exert pressure for self-regulation and contribute to the maintenance of internal controls specified by the law. At times, these inspections may also lead to proposals for corrective legislation governing regulatory standards.

Threat of Publicity

In small communities where people tend to know each other, adversely publicizing wrongdoers can have a significant effect on changing their behavior. Such a system of social control normally would not work in an urban industrial society for individual deviance. Large companies selling widely known brand name products might, however, be greatly influenced by the threat of well-circulated publicity. For example, the publicity surrounding secret Ford Motor Company internal documents on defective and recalled Pintos, which showed that needed structural fuel tank improvements at the cost of about $11 per car could have prevented 180 fiery deaths a year, resulted in a significant drop in market share for the company (Fisse and Braithwaite, 1993).

Perhaps the most potent tool in any administrator's hands is the power to publicize (Gellhorn and Levin, 1997). A publicity release detailing the character of a suspected offense and the offender involved can inflict immediate damage. For instance, just before Thanksgiving in 1959, the Secretary of Health, Education, and Welfare destroyed practically the entire cranberry market by announcing at a press conference that some cranberries were contaminated by a cancer-producing agent. The effectiveness and power of publicity as a control mechanism were more recently confirmed by the announcement that botulism in a can of soup had killed a man. The publicity led to the bankruptcy of Bonvivant Soup Company (Gellhorn and Levin, 1997). It should be noted, however, that this power of control is not confined to public officials. For example, the demise of the Corvair is directly attributable to Ralph Nader's book *Unsafe at Any Speed* (1965) and his subsequent efforts.

In many areas, publicity serves a highly useful, if not indispensable, control function. The 1970 federal air-pollution legislation, for example, provides for making known to the public the extent to which each automobile manufacturer is complying with the auto emission standards of the Environmental Protection Agency. Quite often, polluting companies agree to cease and desist orders of administrative agencies out of fear of the consequences of adverse publicity (Nagel, 1975:347). Furthermore, in the enforcement of legislation protecting consumers against the manufacture and sale of impure food and drugs, the ability of administrative agencies to inform the public that a product may contain harmful ingredients can play an important role in preventing consumption of the product under investigation until the accuracy of this suspicion can be determined.

In some cases, however, firms that have a monopoly on their products, such as local gas and electric companies, are not likely to be hurt by adverse publicity. Agencies are, at times, also reluctant to stigmatize firms because adverse publicity is considered a form of informal adjudication, although it is often used and justified by the notion that people have a right to know.

SUMMARY

This chapter has considered law as a mechanism of formal social control. Law comes into play when other forms of social control are weak, ineffective, or unavailable. Individuals and groups are led to behave in acceptable ways through the processes of socialization and external pressures in the form of sanctions from others. Mechanisms of social control through external pressures may be formal and informal, and include both negative and positive sanctions. Informal social controls are exemplified in the functions of folkways and mores. Informal social controls tend to be effective when there is intense social interaction on an intimate face-to-face basis, normative consensus, and surveillance of the behavior of members of the community. Formal social controls are characteristic of more complex societies with a greater division of labor and different sets of mores, values, and ideologies. Formal social controls arise when informal controls are insufficient to maintain conformity to certain norms. Laws are one type of formal social control. Other types of formal social controls rely on both penalties and rewards, whereas control through the law is exercised primarily, but not exclusively, by the use of punishments to regulate behavior.

The social control of criminal and delinquent behavior represents the most highly structured formal system used by society to attempt to control deviant behavior. The concept "legalization" describes the process by which norms are moved from the social to the legal level. It also entails the incorporation of specific punishments for special kinds of criminal law violators. The goals of punishment include retribution or social retaliation, incapacitation, and both specific and general deterrence. Punishment is a deterrent in situations that involve low-commitment individuals who engage in instrumental crimes. The death penalty, as the most severe form of punishment, remains controversial, and there is no agreement on its deterrent effect.

Formal control of deviant behavior is not limited to criminal sanctions. The use of civil commitment as a mechanism of legal control is more widespread. In civil commitment, there are no procedural safeguards available for the defendant. Civil commitment operates through the process of defining deviant behavior as a mental disorder, and it includes the involuntary commitment of alcoholics, drug addicts, sex offenders, and troublesome teenagers. It allows mental health professionals, particularly psychiatrists, to exercise considerable judicial power by placing individuals in institutions without the guarantee of a trial.

The United States invests enormous resources in controlling victimless crimes. These are crimes *mala prohibita* and are differentiated from other crimes by the element of consensual transaction or exchange. Those who are involved in these crimes are willing participants, who, as a rule, do not complain to the police that a crime has been committed. It was shown that the legal control of victimless crimes, such as drug addiction, prostitution, and gambling, tends to be generally expensive, and ineffective, and often leads to the corruption of law enforcement agents.

White-collar crimes constitute a greater threat to the welfare of society than more traditional kinds of crime. The notion of white-collar crime incorporates both occupational and corporate crimes. Some persons commit crimes in connection with their occupation; others do it while promoting the interest of a corporation for which they work. Corporate crime is a relatively recent phenomenon in the United States. The three broad types of legal control of corporate activities are prospective, processual, and retrospective. In general, laws dealing with corporate crime are ineffective and the sanctions are insufficient to act as effective deterrents. Corporations tend to consider law violation and the resulting fine as part of their regular business expenses.

The social control of dissent is accomplished through the various selection processes, the manipulation of the structure of material benefits, and the use of coercive control mechanisms. In the past, the American government has relied heavily on the operations of various intelligence agencies to create a system of institutionalized social control of dissent.

Control through administrative law is exercised in the context of licensing, inspection, and the use of publicity as a threat. A license is an official permit to engage in certain types of activities. In addition to requiring a license to practice certain occupations or carry out certain activities, control can also be exercised through the revocation or suspension of the license in instances of noncompliance. Inspection allows a way of monitoring ongoing activities under the jurisdiction of a particular agency. It may be sporadic or continuous, and both forms exert pressure for self-regulation and contribute to the maintenance of internal controls specified by law. The threat of adverse publicity is considered a powerful administrative control mechanism. Since most large companies are sensitive to adverse publicity, administrative agencies can use the threat of such publicity to ensure compliance with the law. In the next chapter, the law as a method of conflict resolution will be considered.

SUGGESTED FURTHER READINGS

Bruce A. Arrigo, *Punishing the Mentally Ill: A Critical Analysis of Law and Psychiatry.* Albany: State University of New York Press, 2002. An excellent up-to-date analysis of the use of law to control the mentally ill.

Hugo Adam Bedau (ed.), *The Death Penalty in America: Current Controversies.* New York: Oxford University Press, 1998. The interdisciplinary perspectives offered in this compendium provide important and unique insights on the full effects of American capital punishment provisions.

JOHN M. BRUCE and CLYDE WILCOX (EDS.), *The Changing Politics of Gun Control*. Blue Ridge Summit, PA: Rowman and Littlefield, 1998. A collection of essays on both sides of the gun debate.

DAVID BURNHAM., *Above the Law: Secret Deals, Political Fixes, And Other Misadventures of the U.S. Department of Justice*. New York: Scribner, 1996. The title says it all.

RON CHRISTENSON, *Political Trials; Gordian Knots in the Law*. 2nd ed. Somerset, NJ: Transaction Publishers, 1998. An interesting book on dissent and how political trials engage society's conflicting values and loyalties.

JAMES W. COLEMAN, *The Criminal Elite: The Sociology of White Collar Crime*, 4th ed. New York: St. Martin's Press, 1998. A comprehensive study of white-collar crime that brings together the growing body of data on the subject and presents it in an integrated theoretical framework.

MARK COSTANZO, *Just Revenge; Costs and Consequences of the Death Penalty*. New York: St. Martin's Press, 1997. A comprehensive empirical analysis of the pros and cons of capital punishment.

ELLIOTT CURRIE, *Crime and Punishment in America*. New York: Metropolitan Books/Henry Holt and Company, 1998. A good analysis of current inefficient punishment policies with recommendations for alternatives.

NANETTE J. DAVIS (ED.), *Prostitution: An International Handbook on Trends, Problems, and Policies*. Westport, CT: Greenwood Press, 1993. A series of cross-cultural articles on prostitution and government policies.

MARTIN L. FORST, *Civil Commitment and Social Control*. Lexington, MA: Heath, 1978. A lucid and informative discussion of civil commitment as a form of social control through law, based on empirical investigation.

JACK P. GIBBS (ED.), *Social Control: Views from the Social Sciences*. Beverly Hills, CA: Sage Publications, 1982. A collection of classic papers from scholars in several fields regarding the notion of control—social, psychological, political—in their disciplines. Several conceptual, theoretical and empirical issues are identified and discussed.

ALLAN V. HORWITZ, *The Social Control of Mental Illness*. New York: Academic Press, 1982; *Creating Mental Illness*, Chicago: University of Chicago Press, 2002. Both books deal, albeit from a slightly different perspective, with series of case studies on the social control of mental illness in the theoretical framework of Donald Black's *The Behavior of Law*.

BARBARA A. HANAWALT, *'Of God and Ill Repute'—Gender and Social Control in Medieval England*. New York: Oxford University Press, 1998. A fascinating exploration of both formal and informal mechanisms of social control in medieval England.

JAMES A. INCIARDI AND KAREN MCELRATH (EDS.), *The American Drug Scene: An Anthology*. 3rd ed. Los Angeles, CA: Roxbury Publishing Company, 2001. A collection of articles on patterns, problems, perspectives, and policies relating to both legal and illicit drug use.

MICHAEL D. KELLEHER and C. L. KELLEHER, *Murder Most Rare: The Female Serial Killer*. Westport, CT: Praeger Trade/Greenwood Publishing Group, Inc., 1998. An eye-opener on the lethal careers of female serial killers and the paucity of effective deterrents for them.

JOHN LOTT, *More Guns, Less Crime: Understanding Crime and Gun Control Laws*. 2nd ed. Chicago: University of Chicago Press, 2000. A passionate and provocative argument for concealed-weapon laws, a position that gun-control lobbyists and most criminologists consider dangerous.

ROBERT F. MEIER and GILBERT GEIS, *Victimless Crime? Prostitution, Drugs, Homosexuality, Abortion.* Los Angeles, CA: Roxbury Publishing Company, 1997. An exploration of the role and function of law in the four areas indicated in the title.

HERBERT L. PACKER, *The Limits of Criminal Sanction.* Stanford, CA: Stanford University Press, 1968. A stimulating and provocative and still timely discussion on the limits of law in social control.

ROBERT N. RICH, *Crimes without Victims: Deviance and the Criminal Law.* Washington, DC: University Press of America, Inc., 1978. A comprehensive classic discussion of the origins of, and problems involved in, dealing with a variety of victimless crimes. The book provides useful background information on victimless crimes.

AUSTIN SARAT, *When the State Kills: Capital Punishment and the American Condition.* Princeton, NJ: Princeton University Press, 2001. A recent well-researched addition to the death penalty controversy.

GRAHAM SCAMBLER and ANNETTE SCAMBLER (EDS.), *Rethinking Prostitution: Purchasing Sex in the 1990s.* New York: Routledge, 1997. A collection of informative and provocative articles on the various facets of prostitution.

NEAL SHOVER and JOHN PAUL WRIGHT (EDS.), *Crimes of Privilege, Readings in White Collar Crime.* New York: Oxford University Press, 2001. An examination of the current state of knowledge about and the debate over white-collar crime.

DAVID R. SIMON, *Elite Deviance.* 7th ed. Boston: Allyn & Bacon, 2002. A good discussion of the various forms of immorality, corruption, political and corporate deviance, and occupational crimes.

DWAYNE M. SMITH and MARGARET A. ZAHN (EDS.), *Homicide, A Sourcebook of Social Research.* Thousand Oaks, CA: Sage Publications, Inc., 1998. A useful reference for anyone involved in or interested in homicide research.

U.S. DEPARTMENT OF JUSTICE, *Illegal Corporate Behavior.* National Institute of Law Enforcement and Criminal Justice. Law Enforcement Assistance Administration. Washington, DC: U.S. Government Printing Office, October 1979. The first large-scale comprehensive investigation of the nature, extent, and control of corporate crime in the United States. Marshall B. Clinard directed the project. Although more than two decades old, the insights are still valuable.

DAVID WISE, *The American Police State: The Government against the People.* New York: Vintage Books, 1978. A detailed and informative classic account of the illegal activities of the government to repress dissent.

REFERENCES

ABADINSKY, HOWARD. 1997. *Drug Abuse: An Introduction.* 3rd ed. Chicago: Nelson-Hall Publishers.

ADAY, DAVID P., JR. 1990. *Social Control at the Margins: Toward a General Understanding of Deviance.* Belmont, CA: Wadsworth.

ADLER, FREDA, and HERBERT M. ADLER. 1975. *Sisters in Crime: The Rise of the New Female Criminal.* New York: McGraw-Hill.

APPELBAUM, PAUL S. 1992. "Civil Commitment from a Systems Perspective," *Law and Human Behavior* 16 (1) (February): 61–74.

ARRIGO, BRUCE A. 2002. *Punishing the Mentally Ill: A Critical Analysis of Law and Psychiatry.* Albany: State University of New York Press.

BAGGINS, DAVID SADOFSKY. 1998. *Drug Hate and the Corruption of American Justice.* Westport, CT: Praeger Publishers/Greenwood Publishing Group, Inc.

BAILEY, WILLIAM C. and RUTH D. PETERSON. 1994. "Murder, Capital Punishment, and Deterrence: A Review of the Evidence and an Examination of Police Killings," *Journal of Social Issues* 50 (2) (Summer): 53–75.

BEDAU, HUGO ADAM (ED.). 1998. *The Death Penalty in America: Current Controversies.* New York: Oxford University Press.

BELLUCK, PAM. 1998. "Forget Prisons, Americans Cry Out For the Pillory," *New York Times* (October 4): WK5.

BENJAMIN, DANIEL K., and ROGER LEROY MILLER. 1992. *Undoing Drugs.* Washington, DC: Drug Policy Foundation.

BENSON, MICHAEL L. and FRANCIS T. CULLEN. 1998. *Combating Corporate Crime: Local Prosecutors at Work.* Boston: Northeastern University Press.

BERLOW, ALAN. 2001. "The Broken Machinery of Death," *American Prospect* (July 30): 16–17.

BERNARD, THOMAS J., GEORGE B. VOLD, and JEFFREY B. SNIPES. 2001. *Theoretical Criminology.* 5th ed. New York: Oxford University Press.

BOGGS, SARAH L. 1971. "Formal and Informal Crime Control: An Exploratory Study of Urban, Suburban, and Rural Orientations," *Sociological Quarterly* 12 (1) (Summer): 319–327.

BRANEGAN, JAY. 1998. "China—Photo-Op Diplomacy," *Time* (July 6): 36–37.

BRUCE, JOHN M. and CLYDE WILCOX (EDS.). 1998. *The Changing Politics of Gun Control.* Blue Ridge Summit, PA: Rowman and Littlefield.

BURNHAM, DAVID. 1989. "The Abuse of Power: Misuse of the IRS," *New York Times Magazine* (September 3): 24–61. 1996. *Above the Law: Secret Deals, Political Fixes, And Other Misadventures of the U.S. Department of Justice.* New York: Scribner.

CALAVITA, KITTY and HENRY N. PONTELL. 1994. "The State of White-Collar Crime: Saving the Savings and Loans," *Law & Society Review* 28 (2) (May): 297–324.

CHAMBLISS, WILLIAM J. 1975. "Types of Deviance and the Effectiveness of Legal Sanctions." Pp. 398–407 in William J. Chambliss (ed.), *Criminal Law in Action.* Santa Barbara, CA: Hamilton Publishing Company. 1978. *On the Take: From Petty Crooks to Presidents.* Bloomington: Indiana University Press.

CHRISTENSON, RON. 1998. *Political Trials; Gordian Knots in the Law.* 2nd ed. Somerset, NJ: Transaction Publishers.

CLARK, RAMSEY. 1971. *Crime in America.* New York: Pocket Books.

CLINARD, MARSHALL B., and DANIEL J. ABBOTT. 1973. *Crime in Developing Countries: A Comparative Perspective.* New York: John Wiley.

CLINARD, MARSHALL B., and ROBERT F. MEIER. 2001. *Sociology of Deviant Behavior.* 11th ed. Fort Worth: Harcourt Brace Jovanovich College Publishers.

COLEMAN, JAMES W. 1998. *The Criminal Elite: The Sociology of White Collar Crime.* 4th ed. New York: St. Martin's Press.

COMMISSION ON THE REVIEW OF THE NATIONAL POLICY TOWARD GAMBLING. 1976. *Gambling in America.* Washington, DC: U.S. Government Printing Office.

CONY, ED, and STANLEY PENN. 1986. "Tale of a Kite," *Wall Street Journal* (August 11): 1, 10.

CONRAD, PETER. 1996. "The Medicalization of Deviance in American Culture." Pp. 69–77 in Earl Rubington and Martin S. Weinberg (eds.), *Deviance: The Interactionist Perspective*. 6th ed. Boston: Allyn and Bacon.

COOK, PHILIP J. 1989. "The Economics of Criminal Sanctions." Pp. 50–78 in Martin Lawrence Friedland (ed.), *Sanctions and Rewards in the Legal System: A Multidisciplinary Approach*. Toronto: University of Toronto Press.

COSTANZO, MARK. 1997. *Just Revenge; Costs and Consequences of the Death Penalty*. New York: St. Martin's Press.

COZIC, CHARLES P. and PAUL A. WINTERS (EDS.). 1995. *Gambling*. San Diego, CA: Greenhaven Press.

CROALL, HAZEL. 1989. "Who Is the White-Collar Criminal?" *British Journal of Criminology* 29 (2): 157–174.

CULVER, JOHN H. 1992. "Capital Punishment, 1977–1990: Characteristics of the 143 Executed," *Sociology and Social Research* 76 (2) (January): 59–61.

CURRIE, ELLIOTT. 1998. *Crime and Punishment in America*. New York: Metropolitan Books/Henry Holt and Company.

DALEY, SUZANNE. 2001. "New Rights for Dutch Prostitutes, But No Gain," *New York Times* (August 12): 1.

DALLAIRE, BERNADETTE, MICHAEL MCCUBBIN, PAUL MORIN and DAVID COHEN. 2000. "Civil Commitment Due to Mental Illness and Dangerousness: The Union of Law and Psychiatry within a Treatment-Control System," *Sociology of Health and Illness* 22 (5) (September): 679–699.

DARNTON, NINA. 1989. "Committed Youth," *Newsweek* (July 31): 66–72.

DAVIS, NANETTE J. (ED.). 1993. *Prostitution: An International Handbook on Trends, Problems, and Policies*. Westport, CT: Greenwood Press.

DE KORT, MARCEL, and DIRK J. KORF. 1992. "The Development of Drug Control in the Netherlands: A Historical Perspective," *Crime, Law, and Social Change* 17 (2) (March): 123–144.

DIAMOND, SIGMUND. 1992. *Compromised Campus: The Collaboration of Universities with the Intelligence Community, 1945–1955*. New York: Oxford University Press.

DUFF, PETER. 1997. "Diversion From Prosecution Into Psychiatric Care. Who Controls the Gates?," *British Journal of Criminology* 37 (1) (Winter): 15–34.

ECKHOLM, ERIK. 1995. "Studies Find Death Penalty Often Tied to Victim's Race," *New York Times* (February 24): A1, A11.

ECONOMIST. 1990. "The Politics of Death" (March 24): 25–26. 1995. "The Waiting Game" (April 1): 19–21. 2001. "High Time: A Survey of Illegal Drugs" (July 28): 1–16).

EHRLICH, ISAAC. 1975. "The Deterrent Effect of Capital Punishment: A Question of Life or Death," *American Economic Review* 65:397–417.

ERIKSON, KAI T. 1966. *Wayward Puritans: A Study in the Sociology of Deviance*. New York: John Wiley.

FEDERAL BUREAU OF INVESTIGATION. 2002. *Uniform Crime Reports for the United States, 2001*. Washington, DC: U.S. Department of Justice.

FEIN, ESTHER. 1992. "Working to Nourish Democracy Where Minds Are Being Starved," *New York Times* (August 16): E9.

FISHER, JOSEPH C. 1997. *Killer Among Us*. Westport, CT: Praeger Trade/Greenwood Publishing Group, Inc.

FISSE, BRENT, and JOHN BRAITHWAITE. 1993. "The Impact of Publicity on Corporate Offenders: The Ford Motor Company and the Pinto Papers." Pp. 627–640 in Delos H. Kelly (ed.), *Deviant Behavior: A Text-Reader in the Sociology of Deviance.* New York: St. Martin's Press.

FORBES. 1985. "Startling Statistics" (November 4): 28.

FORST, MARTIN L. 1978. *Civil Commitment and Social Control.* Lexington, MA: Heath.

FOUCAULT, MICHEL. 1977. *Discipline and Punish: The Birth of the Prison.* Trans. Alan Sheridan. New York: Pantheon.

FRIEDLAND, MARTIN LAWRENCE (ED.). 1989. *Sanctions and Rewards in the Legal System: A Multidisciplinary Approach.* Toronto: University of Toronto Press.

FRIEDMAN, LAWRENCE N. 1998. *American Law: An Introduction.* 2nd ed. New York: W. W. Norton & Co., Inc.

FRIENDLY, ALFRED, and RONALD L. GOLDFARB. 1967. *Crime and Publicity: The Impact of News on the Administration of Justice.* New York: The Twentieth Century Fund.

GARLAND, DAVID. 2001. *The Culture of Control: Crime and Social Order in Contemporary Society.* Chicago: University of Chicago Press.

GAROFALO, JAMES, and MAUREEN MCLEOD. 1989. "The Structure and Operations of Neighborhood Watch Programs in the United States," *Crime & Delinquency* 35 (3): 326–344.

GEIS, GILBERT. 1978. "Deterring Corporate Crime." Pp. 278–296 in M. David Ermann and Richard J. Lundman (eds.), *Corporate and Governmental Deviance: Problems of Organizational Behavior in Contemporary Society.* New York: Oxford University Press. 1979. *Not the Law's Business: An Examination of Homosexuality, Abortion, Prostitution, Narcotics, and Gambling in the United States.* New York: Schocken Books. 1994. "Corporate Crime: 'Three Strikes You're Out?,'" *Multinational Monitor* 15 (6) (June): 30–31.

GELLHORN, ERNEST and RONALD M. LEVIN. 1997. *Administrative Law and Process in a Nutshell.* 4th ed. St. Paul, MN: West Publishing Company.

GLASER, DANIEL. 1971. "Criminology and Public Policy," *American Sociologist* 6 (6) (June): 30–37.

GLASSMAN, JAMES K. 1986. "Going to Seed," *New Republic* (August 25): 11–13.

GOLDMAN, ROGER L. and STEVEN PURO. 2001. "Revocation of Police Officer Certification: A Viable Remedy for Police Misconduct?" *Saint Louis University Law Journal* 45 (2) (Spring): 541–580.

GOODE, ERICH. 1998. *Drugs in American Society,* 5th ed. Boston: McGraw-Hill College.

GRABOWSKI, JOHN (ED.). 1984. *Cocaine: Pharmacology, Effects, and Treatment of Abuse.* NIDA Research Monograph 50. National Institute on Drug Abuse. Washington, DC: U.S. Government Printing Office.

GREENAWAY, WILLIAM K., and STEPHAN L. BRICKEY (EDS.). 1978. *Law and Social Control in Canada.* Scarborough, Ontario: Prentice-Hall of Canada, Ltd.

GROSS, SAMUEL R., and ROBERT MAURO. 1989. *Death and Discrimination: Racial Disparities in Capital Sentencing.* Boston: Northeastern University Press.

HAINES, HERB. 1992. "Flawed Executions, the Anti-Death Penalty Movement, and the Politics of Capital Punishment," *Social Problems* 39 (2) (May): 125–138.

HALLINAN, JOSEPH. 2001. *Going Up the River: Travels in a Prison Nation.* New York: Random House.

HANAWALT, BARBARA A. 1998. 'Of God and Ill Repute'—Gender and Social Control in Medieval England. New York: Oxford University Press.

HAVEMANN, JUDITH. 1986. "Federal Computers Are Putting a Glitch Into Laws on Privacy," St. Louis Post-Dispatch (July 12): B1.

HEMPHILL, THOMAS A. 1993. "Penalties for Polluters: Finding a Fair Formula," Business and Society Review (Fall): 29–32.

HOFFMAN, JAN. 1997. "Crime and Punishment: Shame Gains Popularity," New York Times (January 16): A1, A11.

HOLLAND, KELLEY. 1995. "Bank Fraud, The Old Fashioned Way," Business Week (September 4): 96.

IGNATIUS, ADI. 1989. "China's Golden Girls Monitor Neighbors," Wall Street Journal (August 1): A10.

INCIARDI, JAMES A. and KAREN MCELRATH (EDS.). 2001. The American Drug Scene: An Anthology. 3rd ed. Los Angeles, CA: Roxbury Publishing Company.

IRVING, JOHN. 1992. "Pornography and the New Puritans," New York Times Book Review (March 29): 1, 24–27.

JANOWITZ, MORRIS. 1976. Social Control of the Welfare State. New York: Elsevier North-Holland.

KAPLAN, DAVID A. 1995. "Anger and Ambivalence," Newsweek (August 7): 24–29.

KARP, DAVID R. 1998. "The Judicial and Judicious Use of Shame Penalties," Crime & Delinquency 44 (2) (April): 277–294.

KELLEHER, MICHAEL D. and C. L. KELLEHER. 1998. Murder Most Rare: The Female Serial Killer. Westport, CT: Praeger Trade/Greenwood Publishing Group, Inc.

KEMPADOO, KAMALA and JO DOEZEMA. 1998. Global Sex Workers: Rights, Resistance, and Redefinition. New York: Routledge.

KENNEDY, SHAWN. 1998. "California Weighs Release of Spying Records," New York Times (April 5): 18Y.

LA FAVE, WAYNE R. 1965. Arrest: The Decision to Take a Suspect into Custody. Boston: Little, Brown and the American Bar Foundation.

LANDSMAN, STEPHEN. 1973. "Massachusetts' Comprehensive Alcoholism Law—Its History and Future," Massachusetts Law Quarterly 58 (3) (Fall): 273–290.

LESIEUR, HENRY R. 1992. "Compulsive Gambling," Society 29 (4) (May-June): 43–50.

LEWIN, TAMAR. 1995. "Who Decides Who Will Die? Even Within States, It Varies," New York Times (February 23): A1, A13. 2001. "Breast-Feeding: How Old Is Too Old?," The New York Times (February 18): 5WK.

LIEBERMAN, JETHRO K. 1972. How the Government Breaks the Law. Baltimore: Penguin.

LIGHT, IVAN. 1977. "Numbers Gambling among Blacks: A Financial Institution," American Sociological Review 42 (6) (December): 892–904.

LINDQUIST, ROBERT J. 1995. "Private Investigators with Accounting Acumen: Forensic Accountants Can Aid Attorneys in Recognizing and Ferreting Out White-Collar Crime," The National Law Journal 17 (23) (February 6): B13.

LIPTAK, ADAM. 2001. "When Is a Fake Too Real? It's Virtually Uncertain," New York Times (January 28): WK3.

LOH, WALLACE D. 1984. Social Research in the Judicial Process: Cases, Readings, and Text. New York: Russell Sage Foundation.

LOTT, JOHN. 2000. More Guns, Less Crime: Understanding Crime and Gun Control Laws. 2nd ed. Chicago: University of Chicago Press.

LOWMAN, JOHN. 1992. "Street Prostitution Control," *British Journal of Criminology* 32 (1) (Winter): 1–17.

MAGUIRE, KATHLEEN and ANN L. PASTORE (EDS.). 2001. *Bureau of Justice Statistics. Sourcebook of Criminal Justice Statistics—2000.* Albany, NY: The Hindelang Criminal Justice Research Center/U.S. Department of Justice, Office of Justice Programs, Bureau of Justice Statistics. NCJ-171147.

MALCOLM, ANDREW H. 1989. "Capital Punishment Is Popular, but So Are Its Alternatives," *New York Times* (September 10): E4.

MANDELL, BETTY REID (ED.). 1975. *Welfare in America: Controlling the "Dangerous Classes."* Englewood Cliffs, NJ: Prentice Hall.

MARTIN, JOHN M., and ANNE T. ROMANO. 1992. *Multinational Crime: Terrorism, Espionage, Drug & Arms Trafficking.* Newbury Park, CA: Sage Publications.

MASSING, MICHAEL. 1998a. "Winning the Drug War Isn't So Hard After All," *New York Times Magazine* (September 6): 48–50. 1998b. *The Fix.* New York: Simon & Schuster.

MEIER, ROBERT F. and GILBERT GEIS. 1997. *Victimless Crime? Prostitution, Drugs, Homosexuality, Abortion.* Los Angeles, CA: Roxbury Publishing Company.

MEYER, THOMAS J. 1986. "1 in 3 College Students Tries Cocaine, Study Finds; Bennett Urges President to Crack Down on Drugs," *Chronicle of Higher Education* (July 16): 1, 30.

MIETHE, TERANCE D., and CHARLES A. MOORE. 1986. "Racial Differences in Criminal Processing: The Consequences of Model Selection on Conclusions about Differential Treatment," *Sociological Quarterly* 27 (2): 217–237.

MORGENTHAU, ROBERT M. 1995. "What Prosecutors Won't Tell You: Capital Punishment Is the Enemy of Law Enforcement," *New York Times* (February 7): A25.

MOYNIHAN, PATRICK DANIEL. 1998. *Secrecy: The American Experience.* New Haven, CT: Yale University Press.

NADER, RALPH. 1965. *Unsafe at Any Speed.* New York: Grossman.

NAGEL, STUART S. 1975. *Improving the Legal Process.* Lexington, MA: Heath.

NEW YORK TIMES. 2001. "Contortions of Psychiatry in China" (March 25): 14WK. 1995a. "Can New York Live With It?" (February 26): F2. 1995b. "Handgun Use Rose in 1993, Report Shows" (July 10): A6. 2001a. "U.S. Prison Population Rises but Slows in 2000" (August 26): A1. 2001b. "O'Connor Questions Death Penalty" (July 4): A1.

NEWSWEEK. 1979. "Another Dirty Trick by the FBI," (September 24): 45.

O'BRIEN, TIMOTHY L. 1998. "Gambling: Married to the Action, for Better or Worse," *New York Times* (November 8): WK3.

OBERSCHALL, ANTHONY. 1973. *Social Conflict and Social Movements.* Englewood Cliffs, NJ: Prentice Hall.

PACKER, HERBERT L. 1968. *The Limits of Criminal Sanction.* Stanford, CA: Stanford University Press.

PEARCE, FRANK, and STEVE TOMBS. 1998. *Toxic Capitalism: Corporate Crime and the Chemical Industry.* Brookfield, VT: Ashgate.

PEAY, JILL. (ED.). 1998. *Criminal Justice and the Mentally Disordered.* Brookfield, VT: Ashgate.

PIVEN, FRANCES FOX, and RICHARD A. CLOWARD. 1993. *Regulating the Poor: The Functions of Public Welfare.* Updated ed. New York: Vintage Books.

PODGOR, ELLEN S. 1994. "Corporate and White Collar Crime: Simplifying the Ambiguous," *American Criminal Law Review* 31 (3) (Spring): 391–401.

POEL, SARI VAN DER. 1995. "Solidarity as Boomerang, The Fiasco of the Prostitutes' Rights Movement in the Netherlands," *Crime, Law & Social Change* 23:41–65.

PRESIDENT'S COMMISSION ON LAW ENFORCEMENT and ADMINISTRATION OF JUSTICE. 1967a. *The Challenge of Crime in a Free Society*. Washington, D.C.: U.S. Government Printing Office. 1967b. *Crime and Its Impact—An Assessment*. Washington, DC: U.S. Government Printing Office.

PULLEY, BRETT. 1998. "From Illegal Gambling's Regulators to Casinos' Men," *New York Times* (October 28): A1, A20.

QUINNEY, RICHARD A. 1975. *Criminology: Analysis and Critique of Crime in America.* Boston: Little, Brown.

RADELET, MICHAEL L., and GLENN L. PIERCE. 1985. "Race and Prosecutorial Discretion in Homicide Cases," *Law & Society Review* 19 (4): 587–621.

RADELET, MICHAEL L., HUGO ADAM BEDAU and CONSTANCE E. PUTNAM. 1992. *In Spite of Innocence: Erroneous Convictions in Capital Cases.* Boston: Northeastern University Press.

RAMIREZ, ANTHONY. 1992. "The FBI's Latest Idea: Make Wiretapping Easier," *New York Times* (April 19): 2E.

RATNESAR, ROMESH. 1998. "Who Should Carry A Gun?" *Time* (July 6): 29.

REICHMAN, NANCY. 1989. "Breaking Confidences: Organizational Influences on Insider Trading," *Sociological Quarterly* 30 (2): 185–204.

REINERMAN, CRAIG. 1996. "The Social Construction of Drug Scares," Pp. 77–89 in Earl Rubington and Martin S. Weinberg (eds.), *Deviance: The Interactionist Perspective.* 6th ed. Boston: Allyn and Bacon.

RENGERT, GEORGE F. 1998. *The Geography of Illegal Drugs.* Boulder, CO: Westview Press.

RENSSELAER, W. LEE, III. 1989. *The White Labyrinth: Cocaine and Political Power.* New Brunswick, NJ: Transaction Publishers.

RICH, ROBERT M. 1978. *Crimes without Victims: Deviance and the Criminal Law.* Washington, DC: University Press of America, Inc.

RUSCHE, GEORG, and OTTO KURCHHEIMER. 1968. *Punishment and Social Structure.* New York: Russell and Russell.

SAMPER, ERNESTO. 1995. "Colombia's War on Drugs," *Wall Street Journal* (June 30): A16.

SARAT, AUSTIN. 2001. *When the State Kills: Capital Punishment and the American Condition.* Princeton, NJ: Princeton University Press.

SCAMBLER, GRAHAM and ANNETTE SCAMBLER (EDS.). 1997. *Rethinking Prostitution: Purchasing Sex in the 1990s.* New York: Routledge.

SCHUR, EDWIN M. 1965. *Crimes without Victims, Deviant Behavior, and Public Policy.* Englewood Cliffs, NJ: Prentice Hall.

SCHWARTZ, JOHN. 2001. "U.S. Refuses to Disclose PC Tracking," *New York Times* (August 25): A1.

SELLIN, THORSTEN. 1959. *The Death Penalty: Report for the Model Penal Code Project of the American Law Institute.* Philadelphia: Executive Office of American Law Institute.

SHELEY, JOSEPH F. 1985. *America's "Crime Problems": An Introduction to Criminology.* Belmont, CA: Wadsworth.

SHIBUTANI, TAMOTSU. 1961. *Society and Personality: An Interactionist Approach to Social Psychology.* Englewood Cliffs, NJ: Prentice Hall.

SHILLING, CHRIS and PHILIP A. MELLOR. 1998. "Durkheim, Morality and Modernity: Collective Effervescence, *Homo Duplex* and the Sources of Moral Action," *The British Journal of Sociology* 49 (2) (June): 193–209.

SHOVER, NEAL and JOHN PAUL WRIGHT, (EDS.). 2001. *Crimes of Privilege, Readings in White Collar Crime*. New York: Oxford University Press.

SIMON, DAVID R. 2002. *Elite Deviance*. 7th ed. Boston: Allyn & Bacon.

SIMON, LEONORE, BRUCE SALES, and LEE SECHREST. 1992. "Licensure of Functions." Pp. 542–563 in Dorothy K. Kagehiro and William S. Laufer (eds.), *Handbook of Psychology and Law*. New York: Springer-Verlag.

SMITH, CRAIG S. 2001. "Torture Hurries New Wave of Executions in China," *New York Times* (September 9): A1, A8.

SMITH, DWAYNE M., and MARGARET A. ZAHN (EDS.). 1998. *Homicide, A Sourcebook of Social Research*. Thousand Oaks, CA: Sage Publications, Inc.

SMOLOWE, JILL. 1992. "Must This Man Die?" *Time* (May 18): 41–44.

SPITZER, ROBERT J. 1995. *The Politics of Gun Control*. Chatham, NJ: Chatham House Publishers, Inc.

ST. LOUIS POST-DISPATCH, 1985. "25 Innocent People Executed, ACLU Says" (November 14): 6B. 1995. "Centers For Death-Row Appeals Run Out Of Time" (September 3): 4C 1998. "Group Still Wants Rushdie Murdered, Raises Reward" (October 13): A6. 2001. "McVeigh Execution Is Planned to the Smallest Detail" (April 8): A5.

STEVENS, DENNIS J. 1992. "Research Note: The Death Sentence Inmate Attitudes," *Crime & Delinquency* 38 (2) (April): 272–279.

STOLZENBERG, LISA and STEWART J. D'ALESSIO. 2000. "Gun Availability and Violent Crime. New Evidence from the National Incident-Based Reporting System," *Social Forces* 78 (4) June: 1461–1482.

STONE, CHRISTOPHER D. 1978. "Social Control of Corporate Behavior." Pp. 241–258 in M. David Ermann and Richard J. Lundman (eds.), *Corporate and Governmental Deviants: Problems of Organizational Behavior in Contemporary Society*. New York: Oxford University Press.

SUMMERS, ROBERT S., and GEORGE G. HOWARD. 1972. *Law: Its Nature, Functions and Limits*. 2nd ed. Englewood Cliffs, NJ: Prentice Hall.

SUTHERLAND, EDWIN H. 1949. *White Collar Crime*. New York: Dryden Press.

SUTHERLAND, EDWIN H., and DONALD C. CRESSEY. 1974. *Criminology*. 9th ed. Philadelphia: Lippincott.

TAPPAN, PAUL W. 1960. *Crime, Justice, and Correction*. New York: McGraw-Hill.

TERRY, DON. 1998. "Survivors Make the Case Against Death Row," *New York Times* (November 16): A12.

TIME. 1991. "NOWHERE TO HIDE" (NOVEMBER 11): 34–40.

TITTLE, CHARLES R. 1969. "Crime Rates and Legal Sanctions," *Social Problems* 16 (4) (Spring): 409–423.

TREASTER, JOSEPH B. 1992. "Echoes of Prohibition: 20 Years of War on Drugs, and No Victory Yet," *New York Times* (June 14): E7. 1995. "Drug Therapy: Powerful Tool Reaching Few Inside Prisons," *New York Times* (July 3): 1, 9.

TUFT, CAROLYN. 1998. "In the Past 10 Years, 8 in Illinois Were Sentenced to Die, Later Found Innocent," *St. Louis Post-Dispatch* (April 12): A7.

TURK, AUSTIN T. 1972. *Legal Sanctioning and Social Control*. Rockville, MD: National Institute of Mental Health.

TYLER, PATRICK E. 1995. "Population Control in China Falls to Coercion and Evasion," *New York Times* (June 25): 1, 6.

UNGER, ROBERTO MANGABEIRA. 1976. *Law in Modern Society: Toward a Criticism of Social Theory*. New York: Free Press.

U.S. DEPARTMENT OF JUSTICE. 1979. *Illegal Corporate Behavior.* National Institute of Law Enforcement and Criminal Justice. Law Enforcement Assistance Administration. Washington, DC: U.S. Government Printing Office (October). 1991. "Capital Punishment 1990," Bureau of Justice Statistics. Bulletin (September). 1995 "Drugs and Crime Facts, 1994," Bureau of Justice Statistics (June).

U.S. *NEWS & WORLD REPORT.* 1979. "Red-tape: It's Bad at Grass Roots, Too," (September 24): 69–72. 1989. "The Return of a Deadly Drug Called Horse" (August 14): 31–32. 1995. "South Africa Eliminates 'The Noose'" (June 19): 14.

VAUGHAN, DIANE. 1998. "Rational Choice, Situated Action, and the Social Control of Organizations," *Law & Society Review* 32 (1): 23–57.

WALD, MATTHEW L. 1998. "F.A.A. Asks, Can Airliners Get Too Old To Fly Safely," *New York Times* (October 2): A20.

WALKER, SAMUEL. 1993. "Reform the Law: Decriminalization." Pp. 569–579 in Delos H. Kelly (ed.), *Deviant Behavior: A Text Reader in the Sociology of Deviance.* New York: St. Martin's Press.

WALL STREET JOURNAL. 1986A. "No Longer Amused, Frankfurt Decides to Relocate Its Red-Light District" (July 28): 16. 1986b. "Reagan Starts Drive against Drug Abuse, May Seek More Tests of U.S. Employees" (July 31): 46.

WEINBERG, ROY D. 1979. *Family Planning and the Law.* 2nd ed. New York: Oceana Publications, Inc.

WEISBURD, DAVID, STANTON WHEELER, ELIN WARING, and NANCY BODE. 1991. *Crimes of the Middle Classes: White Collar Offenders in the Federal Courts.* New Haven: Yale University Press.

WINERIP, MICHAEL. 1992. "Where Life Is a Beach and Topless Is Now Legal, Trail Blazers Are Timid," *New York Times* (August 2): 19.

WISE, DAVID. 1978. *The American Police State: The Government against the People.* New York: Vintage Books.

WOLFENDEN REPORT. 1963. *Report of the Committee on Homosexual Offenses and Prostitution.* Briarcliff Manor, NY: Stein & Day.

WORSHAM, JAMES. 1998. "Can the IRS Be Fixed?" *Nation's Business* (May): 16–23.

WORSNOP, RICHARD L. 1995. "Death Penalty Debate: Will Support for Executions Continue to Grow?," *CQ Researcher* 5 (9) (March 10): 195–212.

WYNN, JOAN RANSOHOFF, and CLIFFORD GOLDMAN. 1974. "Gambling in New York City: The Case for Legalization." Pp. 66–75 in Lee Rainwater (ed.), *Social Problems and Public Policy, Deviance and Liberty.* Chicago: Aldine Publishing Co.

YOUNG, VIRGINIA and ERIC STERN. 2001. "Elderly Are Called Prone to Gambling Problems," *St. Louis Post-Dispatch* (August 6): 1, 7.

6
Law and Dispute Resolution

One of the major functions of law is the orderly resolution of disputes. The intent of this chapter is to examine the questions of why, how, and under what circumstances laws are used in disagreements between individuals, between individuals and organizations, and between organizations.

A NOTE ON TERMINOLOGY

There are a number of different terms used in the sociological and legal literature to describe the role of law in controversies. Terms such as "conflict resolution" (see, for example, Aubert, 1963; and Ford Foundation, 1978; Kriesberg, 1982, 1998), "conflict regulation" (see, for example, Wehr, 1979), "conflict management" (see, for example, Lewicki et al., 1992; Lord and Adelman, 1978; and Thomas, 1992), "dispute processing" (see, for example, Felstiner, 1974, 1975; Palmer and Roberts, 1998; and Thomas, 1992), "dispute settlement" (see, for example, Gulliver, 1969; Miceli, 1998), and "dispute resolution" (see, for example, Bradney and Cownie, 2000; Goldberg et al., 1999; Kawashima, 1969; Leeson and Johnston, 1988; Susskind and Cruikshank, 1987; and Ury et al., 1988) or simply "disputing" (Abel, 1995) are often used more or less interchangeably.

Some scholars, such as Richard L. Abel (1973), William L. F. Felstiner (1974, 1975), Michael Palmer and Simon Roberts (1998), and Paul Wehr (1979), contend that disputes are processed in society rather than settled, and conflicts are managed or regulated rather than resolved. Third-party intervention, whether through legal or nonlegal means, represents for them only the settlement of the resolution of the public component of the dispute or conflict, rather than the alleviation of the underlying forces or tensions that have created that conflict. Richard L. Abel (1973:228) epitomizes this position and chides anthropologists and sociologists who "have tended to write as though 'settlement' must be the ultimate outcome of disputes, 'resolution' the inevitable fate of conflicts." Then he adds that "it has recently become almost commonplace to observe that the outcome of most conflicts and disputes are other conflicts and disputes, with at most a temporary respite between them" (Abel, 1973:28).

Other authors point out that the actual dispute is preceded by several stages. For example, Laura Nader and Harry F. Todd (1978:14–15) contend that there are three distinct phases or stages in the disputing process: the grievance or preconflict stage, the conflict stage, and the dispute stage. The *grievance* or *preconflict* stage refers to situations that an individual or a group perceives to be unjust and considers grounds for resentment or complaint. The situation may be real or imaginary, depending on the aggrieved parties' perception. This condition may erupt into conflict or it may wane. If it is not resolved in the preconflict or grievance stage, it enters into the *conflict* stage, in which the aggrieved party confronts the offending party and communicates his or her resentment or feelings of injustice to the person or group. The conflict phase is dyadic; that is, it involves only two parties. If it is not deescalated or resolved at this stage, it enters into the final, *dispute* stage when the conflict is made public. The dispute stage is characterized by the involvement of a third party in the disagreement. P. H. Gulliver (1969:14) suggests that "no dispute exists unless and until the right-claimant, or someone on his behalf, actively raises the initial disagreement from the level of dyadic argument into the public arena, with the express intention of doing something about the denied claim." Ideally, then, a grievance is monadic, involving one person or a group; a conflict is dyadic; and a dispute is triadic, since it involves the participation of a third party, who is called upon as an agent of settlement.

The legal approach to dispute resolution entails the transition from a dyad of the conflicting parties to the triad, "where an intermediary who stands outside the original conflict has been added to the dyad" (Aubert, 1963:26). The stages discussed by Nader and Todd are not always clear-cut or sequential. A person may file a lawsuit without ever confronting the offender, or one party may quit or concede at any stage in the disagreement.

When disagreements formally enter the legal arena (that is, trial), from the perspective of the law, disputes are authoritatively settled rather than processed through the intervention of third parties (that is, judges), and conflicts are resolved rather than simply managed or regulated. The use of the terms "conflict resolution" and "dispute settlement" is thus, in this sense, justified. In this chapter, I shall use these concepts interchangeably, and at the same time, I will repeatedly emphasize, in different contexts, that the law resolves or settles only the legal components of conflicts and disputes, rather than ameliorating the underlying causes. The law, in brief, deals with disagreements that have been translated into legal disputes or conflicts. A legal resolution of conflict does not necessarily lead to a reduction of tension or antagonism between the aggrieved parties as evidenced by many, for example, of the 2.3 million or so Americans who annually get divorced (see, for example, Sarat and Felstiner, 1995).

METHODS OF DISPUTE RESOLUTION

Disputes are ubiquitous in every society at every level, and there is a wide variety of methods for their management (see, for example, Lauderdale and Cruit, 1993; Plett and Meschievitz, 1991). Most societies use fairly similar methods; the differences among them consist in the preference given to one method over others. Cultural factors and the availability of institutions for settling disputes will usually determine such preferences. There are two principal forms of resolving legal disputes throughout the world. *"Either* the parties to a conflict determine the outcome themselves by negotiations, which does not preclude that a third party acting as a mediator might assist them in their negotiations. *Or,* the conflict is adjudicated, which means that a third, and ideally impartial, party decides which of the disputants has the superior claim" (Ehrmann, 1976:82). These forms are used (and are sometimes intertwined) for the settlement of civil, criminal, and administrative suits. For nonlegal disputes, there are a variety of other means for settlement.

A noted anthropologist, Simon Roberts (1979:57–59), points out that in some societies, direct interpersonal violence constitutes an approved method of dispute settlement. Such interpersonal violence may be a way of retaliation for violence already suffered or a reaction to some other form of perceived injustice. Occasionally, physical violence may be channeled into a restricted and conventionalized form, such as dueling. In Germany before the Second World War, for example, dueling was a popular form of dispute settlement among university students, members of the officer corps in the military, and the nobility in general. Duels took place under controlled conditions and according to specific rules. The participants wore protective clothing, and usually the first sign of bloodletting marked the end of the dispute. It was often a question of honor to challenge the insulting party to a duel, who was, by convention, compelled to accept it. In the event of an insult or injustice, all the offended party had to do was to slap the offender. This act was a challenge to a duel, and the parties involved promptly settled on the time and place. Dueling scars on one's face represented symbols of courage and high status.

Another form of physical violence is feuding (Gulliver, 1979:1). It is a state of recurring hostilities between families or groups, instigated by a desire to avenge an offense (insult, injury, death, or deprivation of some sort) against a member of the group. The unique feature of a feud is that responsibility to avenge is carried by all members of the group. The killing of any member of the offender's group is viewed as appropriate revenge, since the group as a whole is considered responsible. Nicholas Gubser (1965) describes a feud that lasted for decades within a Nunamiut Eskimo community caused by a husband's killing of his wife's lover. When a man is killed, in Gubser's words,

> The closely related members of his kindred do not rest until complete revenge has been achieved. The immediate relatives of the deceased . . . recruit as much support from other relatives as they can. Their first action, if possible, is to kill the murderer, or maybe one of his closest kin. Then, of course, the members of the murderer's kindred are brought into the feud. These two kindreds may snipe at each other for years. (1965:151).

At times, the feud can turn into a full-scale battle when, in addition to the families, the communities are drawn into a dispute. This happened from time to time in the famous feud triggered by a romantic interlude between the Hatfields of Virginia and the McCoys of Kentucky. The feud broke out in 1882 and lasted for several years.

Disagreement, at times, is channeled into rituals. For example, the parties to the dispute may confront each other before the assembled community and voice their contentions through songs and dances improvised for the occasion. In the form of a song, the accuser states all the abuse he or she can think of; the accused then responds in kind. A number of such exchanges may follow until the contestants are exhausted, and a winner emerges through public acclaim for the greater poetic or vituperative skill.

In some societies, shaming is used as a form of public reprimand in the disapproval of disputing behavior. Ridicule directed at those guilty of antisocial conduct is also used to reduce conflict. At times, the singing of rude and deflating songs to, or about, a troublesome individual is also reported as a means of achieving a similar end. Ridicule, reproach, or public exposure may also take the form of a "public harangue," in which a person's wrongdoings are embarrassingly exposed by being shouted out to the community at large (Roberts, 1979:62).

In attempts to resolve disputes, parties may choose to resort to supernatural agencies. The notion that supernatural beings may intervene to punish wrongdoers is rather widespread. This notion is often accompanied by the belief that harm may be inflicted by witches or through the practice of sorcery. In some societies, witchcraft and sorcery are seen as a possible cause of death and of almost any form of illness or material misfortune. Jane Fishburne Collier (1973:113–120), for example, identifies a variety of witchcraft beliefs among the Zinacantecos in Mexico. They include witches who send sickness, ask that sickness be sent, perform specific actions (such as causing the victim to rot away), control weather, talk to saints, or cause sickness by an evil eye. Notes Collier: "Witchcraft beliefs underlie all of the reasons given for actions during a hearing" (1973:122). Consequently, in such societies the procedures for identifying witches or sorcerers responsible for particular incidences or misfortunes assume great importance in the handling of conflict (Roberts, 1979:64).

Of course, not all disputes are handled by violence, rituals, shaming, ostracism, or resorting to supernatural agencies. Some of these methods can be "domesticated" (Cobb, 1997) and most societies have access to a number of alternative methods of dispute resolution. These alternatives differ in several ways, including whether participation is voluntary, presence or absence of a third party, criteria used for third-party intervention, type of outcome and how it may be enforced, and whether the procedures employed are formal or informal (Administrative Conference of the United States, 1987:12–13). Before considering them, let us look at two other popular ways of coping with disputes: "lumping it" and avoidance.

"Lumping it" refers simply to inaction, to not making a claim or a complaint. Galanter says: "This is done all the time by 'claimants' who lack information or access or who knowingly decide gain is too low, cost too high (including psychic cost of litigating where such activity is repugnant)" (1974:124–125). In "lumping it," the issue or the difficulty that gave rise to the disagreement is simply ignored and the relationship with the offending party continues. For example, a college professor may not want to press a particular claim (say, for a higher increment) against the administration and continues his or her relationship with the university. A somewhat different form of withdrawal from conflict situations that seems likely to result in dispute is described by Carol J. Greenhouse (1989:252–273) in her study of Baptists in a southern town. The findings indicate that Baptists in the community consider disputing a profoundly unchristian act because the Bible states clearly that Jesus is the judge of all people. The implication is that to partake in a dispute is to stand as judge over another person. This would be an indication of lack of faith and a preemption of Jesus' power (1989:256).

Avoidance refers to limiting the relationship with other disputants sufficiently so that the dispute no longer remains salient (Felstiner, 1974:70). Albert O. Hirschman (1970) calls this kind of behavior "exit," which entails withdrawing from a situation or terminating or curtailing a relationship. For example, a consumer may go to a different store rather than press grievances. In consumer-transaction disputes, for example, "the exit option is widely held to be uniquely powerful: by inflicting revenue losses on delinquent management" (Hirschman, 1970:21), it can be considered not only expedient in dispute settlement but also a way of imposing sanctions. Avoidance entails a limitation or a break in the relationship between disputants, whereas "lumping it" refers to the lack of resolution of a conflict, grievance, or dispute for the reason that one of the parties prefers to ignore the issue in dispute, generally basing the decision on feelings of relative powerlessness or on the social, economic, or psychological costs involved in seeking a solution. Avoidance is not always an alternative, especially in situations when the relationship must continue—for example, with certain companies that have monopolies, such as gas or electric companies, or with the Social Security Administration or the Welfare Department. An important aspect of avoidance is the reduction of social interaction or its termination. Lumping behavior entails the ignoring of the issue in dispute while continuing the relationship.

Primary Resolution Processes

The primary dispute resolution mechanisms can be depicted on a continuum ranging from negotiation to adjudication. In negotiation, participation is voluntary and disputants arrange settlements for themselves. Next on the continuum is mediation, in which a third party facilitates a resolution and otherwise assists the parties in reaching a voluntary agreement. At the other end of the continuum is adjudication (both judicial and administrative), in which parties are compelled to participate, the case is decided by a judge, the parties are represented by counsel, the procedures are formal, and the outcomes are enforceable by law. Close to adjudication is arbitration, which is more informal and in which the decision may or may not be binding. Negotiation, mediation and arbitration are the principal components of what is referred to as "alternative dispute resolution" (ADR) in legal parlance (Palmer and Roberts, 1998). The movement is spreading to other parts of the world and in France, for example, recourse to ADR carries with it a fashionable progressive American connotation, and ADR is regularly promoted by the French authorities and legal scholars alike as a means of relieving the burden of the courts, of rendering dispute resolutions that are faster, simpler and cheaper, and of "de-dramatizing" disputes to render their resolutions more satisfactory to the parties (Gaillard, 2000).

Since dispute resolutions are bread and butter issues in the legal profession, not surprisingly there is now mounting evidence that law firms are becoming uneasy about the spreading use of alternative means because the money and time saving potential for disputants can be considerable by discouraging potential litigation (France, 1995). Let us now consider these processes and some of their variants in some detail.

Negotiations in disputes take place when disputants seek to resolve their disagreements without the help of neutral third parties. Negotiation is a two-party arrangement in which disputants try to persuade one another, establish a common ground for discussion, and feel their way by a process of give-and-take toward a settlement. It involves the use of debate and bargaining (Raiffa, 1997). A basic requirement for successful negotiation is the desire of both parties to settle a dispute without escalation and without resort to neutral third parties. Aubert states: "The advantage of negotiated solutions is that they need not leave any marks on the normative order of society. Since the solution does not become a precedent for later solutions to similar conflicts, the adversaries need not fear the general consequences of the settlement" (1969:284). When interests are contradictory to the extent that gains and losses must cancel each other out, negotiations are inadequate in resolving the conflict, and in such situations, parties may bring the case to court for legal settlement. In industrialized countries, such as the United States, lumping behavior, avoidance, and negotiation are the most frequent responses to dispute situations (Best and Andreasen, 1976).

Mediation is a dispute resolution method that interposes a disinterested and noncoercive third party, the mediator, between the disputants. Unlike litigation, where the ultimate decision is imposed by the judge, the mediator does not make the final decision. Rather, the terms of settlement are worked out solely by and between the disputants. It can be an effective way of resolving a variety of disputes if both parties are interested in a reasonable settlement of their disagreement (Fitzpatrick, 1994). Mediation begins with an agreement. It is nonadversarial, and the basic tenet is cooperation rather than competition. The role of the mediator in the dispute is that of a guide, a facilitator, and a catalyst.

A mediator may be chosen by the disputants or appointed by someone in authority. A mediator may be selected because the person has status, position, respect, power, money, or the alleged power to invoke sanctions in behalf of a deity or some other superhuman force. (There is some empirical evidence that lawyers playing the role of mediators are considered effective by clients in dispute resolutions (Croson and Mnookin, 1997)). A mediator may have none of these but simply be a designated agent of an organization set up to handle specific disputes. Bringing disputes to a mediator may be the choice of both parties or of one but not the other party to a conflict, or it may be the result of private norms or expectations of a group which "require" that disputes be settled as much as possible within the group.

Mediation essentially consists of influencing the parties to come to an agreement by appealing to their own interests. The mediator may use a variety of techniques to accomplish this objective.

> He may work on the parties' ideas of what serves them best . . . in such a way that he gets them to consider the common interests as more essential than they did previously, or their competing interests as less essential. He may also look for possibilities of resolution which the parties themselves have not discovered and try to convince them that both will be well served by his suggestion. The very fact that a suggestion is proposed by an impartial third party may also, in certain cases, be sufficient for the parties to accept it. (Eckhoff, 1978:36)

Ideally, both parties should have confidence in the mediator, be willing to cooperate, listen to his or her advice, and consider the mediator as impartial. A mediator may also use warnings, promises, or flattery in attempts to reconcile differences between the parties. Eckhoff points out:

> The conditions for mediation are best in cases where both parties are interested in having the conflict resolved. The stronger the common interest is, the greater reason they have for bringing the conflict before a third party, and the

more motivated they will be for cooperating actively with him in finding a solution, and for adjusting their demands in such a way that a solution can be reached. (1978:36)

The use of mediators is widespread in the more than 300 neighborhood justice resolution centers in the United States (U.S. Department of Justice, 1986:2). The initial idea for such centers came from Richard Danzig (1973). Using the example of resolving intratribal disputes by conciliation in Liberia, he suggested the establishment of neighborhood community moots. Such moots involve community members with shared values who might be able to resolve more effectively than courts those disputes that affect the disputants and the neighborhood, such as family and housing disputes and minor criminal charges. Although there is a great variation among centers in the types of cases they handle, almost all tend to concentrate on disputes between persons with an ongoing relationship. Participation in mediation is voluntary. The majority of disputants are referred to the centers by judges, police, prosecutors, and court clerks. Mediators include lawyers, law students, undergraduates, and laypeople. Before acting as mediators, they receive training in mediation techniques. These neighborhood centers are listed in the ABA's Dispute Resolution Project Directory, which is updated annually (American Bar Association, 2002).

There are many advantages of such neighborhood justice centers (McGillis, 1982). These nonjudicial forums can increase access to justice because of their low cost (or no cost), convenient hours, and location. Mediation provides a better process than other forums for handling disputes because participants are able to explore the underlying problems contributing to the dispute without legal formalities, time limits, and lawyers acting as intermediaries in the discussion. The reliance on informal alternatives also frees the courts to attend to more serious cases (Wright and Galaway, 1989) and is being used with increasing frequency in victim-offender mediation for nonviolent offenses in attempts to work out a restitution program as an option to a prison sentence (Reske, 1995).

Related to mediation is the *ombudsman* process, which combines mediatory and investigatory functions in dispute resolution. In the classic Scandinavian model, the ombudsman is a public official designated to hear citizen complaints and carry out independent fact-finding investigations to correct abuses of public administration. In a traditional sense, ombudsmen are independent agents of the legislature and they can criticize, publicize and make recommendations, but they cannot reverse administrative actions (Rosenbloom and Goldman, 1998:474–476).

The system is widely used as an alternative to courts in other countries. In Denmark, for example, courts are very rarely used by the consumer (Blegvad, 1983:207). Instead the ombudsman negotiates with the firms in disputes on behalf of clients. In the United States, Alaska, Hawaii, Iowa and

Nebraska have used ombudsmen at the state level and more and more corporations, hospitals, and universities are beginning to rely on the process to correct organizational abuses and resolve internal disputes. Some newspapers and radio stations, in the format of "action lines," also perform the role of ombudsman in disputes. A major criticism against the ombudsman process is that the person acting as mediator often represents the vested interest of a particular agency, which suggests bias in favor of his or her employer. For example, the hospital ombudsman may be partial to the hospital and biased against the client (Marshall, 1985:108).

Arbitration is another way of involving a third party in a dispute. Unlike mediation, in which a third party assists the disputants to reach their own solution, arbitration requires a final and binding decision to be made for the disputants by a third party. Disputants agree beforehand both to the intervention of a neutral third party and to the finality of his or her decision. Unlike in courts, the proceedings in arbitration can remain private and participants can opt for simplicity and informality. Arbitration and other nonjudicial methods tend to reduce the cost of dispute resolution (Fine, 1988) because of the lack of opportunity to appeal the arbitrator's decision and especially when attorneys are not hired. It is also faster than adjudication because participants can proceed as soon as they are ready rather than waiting for a trial date to be set.

Nowadays, almost all collective bargaining contracts contain a provision for final and binding arbitration. Arbitration clauses are showing up more often in business contracts and even in executive employment letters (*New York Times*, 1986:1F). The conduct of commercial arbitrators (such as the American Arbitration Association, with offices in major cities) is governed by a code of ethics. Many private organizations, professional groups, and trade associations have their own formal arbitration machinery for the settlement of disputes among members. Similarly, labor-management disputes are often brought before arbiters, designated in advance, whose decisions are binding by mutual consent of the disputants and ultimately enforceable by private sanctions and by the courts. In general, willingness to submit disputes to private but formal arbitration is characteristic of parties who have a commitment to long-term relationships (Sarat, 1989).

Arbitration is increasingly considered as an alternative to judicial and administrative processes. Compulsory arbitration, especially for small claims, can free courts for more substantial disputes, and depending upon the issues involved, it may reduce the cost to litigants and be a more effective way of solving problems. For example, in Philadelphia, a case that is under $10,000 is automatically assigned by the court to arbitration. Three arbitrators are selected by the deputy court administrator from a panel of lawyers. They make their decisions on the pleadings supplemented by oral arguments by the attorneys for the parties. It is estimated that the average arbitrated case costs one-fifth less per day than it would in the Philadelphia court system. Similar systems of compulsory arbitration exist in England, Germany, and in the Scandinavian countries.

Adjudication is a public and formal method of conflict resolution and is best exemplified by courts. Courts have the authority to intervene in disputes whether or not the parties desire it and to render a decision and to enforce compliance with that decision. In adjudication, the emphasis is on the legal rights and duties of disputants, rather than on compromises or on the mutual satisfaction of the parties. Adjudication is also more oriented toward zero-sum decisions than the other mechanisms I have noted. Courts require disputants to narrow their definitions of issues in the identification of the nature of their problems. Felstiner states: "Adjudication as a consequence tends to focus on 'what facts' and 'which norms' rather than on any need for normative shifts" (1974:70). In other words, courts deal with issues and facts. Consequently, they can deal only with disagreements, grievances, or conflicts that have been transformed into legal disputes. For example, in a divorce case, the court may focus on one incident in what is a complex and often not very clear-cut series of problems. It results in a resolution of a legal dispute but not necessarily of the broader issues that have produced that conflict.

Although courts occasionally seek compromise and flexibility, generally the verdict of the court has an either-or character: The decision is based upon a single definite conception of what has actually taken place and upon a single interpretation of legal norms. When a conflict culminates in litigation, one of the parties must be prepared for a total loss. Aubert says: "One aspect of legal decisions that is closely linked to their either/or character is the marked orientation toward the past" (1969:287). The structure of legal thinking is also oriented toward comparisons between actions and sanctions rather than toward utility and effectiveness. Because of this orientation, and because of the use of precedents, there is a fair amount of predictability in how similar cases will be settled by courts. But since the courts are dealing only with the legal issues, they do not take into consideration the possibility that the applicable legal facts and norms may have been influenced by different social conditions and that, in many instances, courts are treating only the symptoms rather than the underlying causes of a problem. With these limitations, the courts work "to clean up all the little social messes (and the occasional big ones) that recurrently arise between the members of the society from day to day" (Hoebel, 1954:280).

Hybrid Resolution Processes

In both the public and private sectors, the intervention of a third party—a person, a government agency, or other institution—can often facilitate dispute resolution among conflicting parties (Ross and Conlon, 2000) and there are currently several "hybrid" dispute-resolution processes in use.

The term "hybrid" is employed because these processes incorporate features of the primary processes discussed in the preceding section. The main ones include rent-a-judge, med-arb, and minitrial.

The *rent-a-judge* process is basically a form of arbitration (Goldberg et al., 1985:280–309). In the process, the disputants, in an attempt to avoid the use of a regular court, select a retired judge to hear and decide a pending case as an arbitrator would. The same procedure is used as in court, and the decision of the judge is legally binding. Unlike in arbitration, the "referee's" decision can be appealed for errors of law or on the ground that the judgment was against evidence, though such appeals are rare. In California, where this system of private judging is quite prevalent, former judges have decided on hundreds of cases. The system is considered both an alternative to adjudication and a sort of "rich-man's justice" that undermines public methods of dispute resolution and threatens constitutional values.

There are other hybrid processes of dispute resolution that have been used with considerable success (Goldberg et al., 1999). One is *med-arb*, in which the issues that were not solved by mediation are submitted to arbitration, with the same person serving first as mediator, then as arbitrator. Med-arb has been used often in contract negotiation disputes between public employers and their unionized employees. Another is the *minitrial*, which has been repeatedly utilized in a number of big intercorporate disputes. In this method, attorneys for each disputant are given a short time (not more than a day) in which to present the basic elements of their case to senior executives of both parties. After the presentation, the senior executives try to negotiate a settlement of the case, usually with the aid of a neutral advisor. If there is no settlement, the advisor gives the parties his opinion of the likely outcome if the dispute were litigated. This dose of reality at times helps to break the deadlock.

In this section, I have distinguished among a number of procedures used for settling disputes. Some are public, some private. Some are official, some unofficial. Some are formal, some informal. These procedures overlap, and each has its limitations and advantages. They are related in different ways to outcomes and consequences. A number of procedures may also be used for the settlement of a single dispute. Table 6–1 summarizes the salient features of the more widely used procedures.

Obviously, no one procedure is applicable to every kind of problem. A number of considerations appear relevant in the selection of a particular method. One is the relationship between the disputants; that is, is there an ongoing relationship between the disputants, such as business partners, or is the dispute the result of a single encounter, such as an automobile accident? When an ongoing relationship is involved, it is more productive for the parties to work out their difficulties through negotiation or mediation, if necessary. An advantage of mediation is that it encourages the restructuring of the underlying relationship so as to eliminate the source of conflict rather than dealing only with the manifestation of conflict. Another consideration is the nature of the

TABLE 6–1 Partial List of Characteristics of the Major Primary and Hybrid Dispute-Resolution Processes

Negotiation	Mediation	Arbitration	Adjudication	Rent-a-Judge	Minitrial
Voluntary	Voluntary	Voluntary unless contractual or court ordered	Nonvoluntary	Voluntary	Voluntary
Nonbinding	Nonbinding	Binding, usually no appeal	Binding, subject to appeal	Binding but subject to appeal and possibly review by trial court	Nonbinding
No third-party facilitator	Party-selected facilitator	Party-selected third-party decision maker	Imposed third-party neutral decision maker	Party-selected third-party decision maker, usually a former judge or lawyer	Third-party neutral advisor
				Flexible as to timing, place, and procedures	
Informal and unstructured	Informal and unstructured	Procedurally less formal than adjudication	Highly procedural; formalized and structured by predetermined, rigid rules		Less formal than adjudication and arbitration
Presentation of proofs usually indirect or nonexistent	Presentation of proofs less important than attitudes of each party	Opportunity for each party to present proofs supporting decision in its favor	Opportunity for each party to present proofs supporting decisions in its favor	Opportunity for each party to present proofs supporting decisions in its favor	Opportunity and responsibility for each party to present proofs supporting decisions in its favor
		Compromise result possible	Win/lose outcome	Win/lose outcome (judgment of court)	
Mutually acceptable agreement	Mutually acceptable agreement sought	Reason for result not usually required	Expectation of reasoned statement	Findings of fact and conclusion of law possible but not required	Mutually acceptable agreement sought
Agreement usually included in contract or release sought	Agreement usually embodied in contract or release	Consistency and predictability balanced against concerns for disputants' relationship	Process emphasizes attaining substantive consistency and predictability results	Adherence to norms, laws, and precedent	Agreement usually embodied in contract or release
Emphasis on disputants' relationship	Emphasis on disputants' relationship		Public process; lack of privacy of submissions		Emphasis on sound, cost-effective, and fair resolution satisfactory to both parties
Highly private process	Private process	Private process unless judicial enforcement sought		Private process unless judicial enforcement sought	Highly private process

dispute. If a precedent is required, such as in civil rights cases, litigation in the form of class action may be appropriate. The amount at stake in a dispute also plays a role in deciding on the type of dispute-resolution procedure. Small, simple cases might end up in small-claims courts, whereas more complex issues might require court-ordered arbitration, such as in contract negotiation disputes between public employers and unions. Speed and cost are other relevant factors. For example, arbitration may be speedier and less costly than a court trial. Finally, consideration must be given also to the power relationship between the parties. When one party in a dispute has much less bargaining strength than the other, as in the case of a pollution victim faced by a powerful corporation, an adjudicatory forum in which principle, not power, will determine the outcome may be desirable. In the remainder of this chapter, I shall consider why some disputants turn to legal mechanisms of conflict resolution, under what circumstances they choose the law rather than some other procedures, and the limitations of the law in resolving conflicts.

DEMANDS FOR COURT SERVICES IN DISPUTE RESOLUTION

Increasingly Americans turn to the courts to tell them how to live their lives and there is an explosion in legalisms (Rosen, 2001). As former Chief Justice Warren E. Burger aptly remarked a while ago, "our society is drowning in litigation" (quoted by Cross, 1992:647). Indeed, litigation is becoming a national pastime, and more and more people are telling their troubles to a judge. The President's Council on Competitiveness (1991) laments that in 1989, almost 18 million new civil cases were filed in state and federal courts—one for every 10 adults. Between 1960 and 1990, the number of lawsuits filed in federal courts increased from about 90,000 to more than 250,000 and exceeded 276,000 by the end of 1993 (Administrative Office of the U.S. Courts, 1995) and topped 300,000 at the end of the decade. Between 1977 and 2001, the legal industry grew 483 percent, compared with 78 percent for the auto industry and 97 percent for the food industry. During the same period, there were substantial augmentations in the number of court employees, judges, and lawyers. At the millennium, there was one lawyer for every 260 Americans. Because of questionable comparability of data, this is a rough comparison, but Japan has a lawyer-population ratio of about 1:10,000 (Stumpf and Culver, 1992:63). The ratio in Germany is approximately 1:2,500; in England 1:1,400; and in Sweden 1:5,200. These ratios demonstrate how the United States, which has about 5 percent of the world's population, accounts for more than two-thirds of all the lawyers.

The increase in district court cases, dramatic as it has been, is dwarfed by the growth of caseloads in appeals courts—from 3,765 in 1960 to 29,580 in 1983. This is an increase of 686 percent (Posner, 1996:65). By the end of 1993, the caseloads in appeals courts came close to 49,000 (Administrative Office of the U.S. Courts, 1995:1). The same conditions prevail in state courts. For example, since

1960, the number of lawsuits has more than tripled in Massachusetts and doubled in Los Angeles County. Although New York City's population has not grown, its civil court caseload rose 50 percent from 1978 to 1984 (Lauter, 1986:46) and another 40 percent by 2001. This extraordinary rise in civil litigation coincidentally comes at a time when the courts are already inundated with criminal cases.

A decade ago already, the cost of tort litigation was estimated to be between $280 billion and $300 billion annually (Epp, 1992:25) and these are rather conservative figures. By 2001, it exceeded $500 billion. Tort litigation primarily involves claims or damages related to personal injury. About 47 percent of all torts involve lawsuits between individuals, 37 percent between individuals and business, and the rest between individuals and government agencies or hospitals (U.S. Department of Justice, 1995). A rather controversial study, carried out by a University of Texas finance professor, Stephen P. Magee (1989) and his associates, finds that predatory and frivolous lawsuits reduced the gross national product to 10 percent below its potential during the 1980s—at a price tag of about $1 million per attorney. Legal fees, damage awards, and increased insurance premiums account for about $80 billion, representing a small fraction of the GNP. Most costs are indirect, such as time wasted in filing questionable suits; the loss of potential engineers, physicians, and scientists to the legal profession; and the withholding of certain products from the market to reduce the potential for liability action. The so-called tort tax is responsible for about 30 percent of the price of a stepladder and 95 percent of the cost of childhood vaccines. Influential reports by the Institute for Legal Studies (Epp, 1992; Galanter, 1992) attempt to refute these allegations and conclude that the case of economic growth versus the number of lawyers rests on frivolous claims. The controversy continues (Cross, 1992; Galanter, 1993).

There are several explanations for the increase in civil litigation over time. Americans today tend to accept that being sued is the price of freedom, they seem more fascinated by litigation than people perhaps in any other society, and the legal system is more prone to frivolous lawsuits (a rather value-laden term) as a result. In a sense, it is a form of entertainment and a favorite indoor activity to see due process take its course on television (Zobel, 1994). Some even argue that lawsuits are good for America (Bogus, 2001). For instance, product liability litigation has saved countless lives, brought critical information to light (along with labels that warn us about most everything that could be potentially harmful), forced manufacturers to make products safer, and driven off the market unreasonably dangerous products when regulatory agencies or Congress lacked the political will to do so. From time to time, however, such litigations can get out of control. For example, toothbrushes seem like innocent little things. Inexpensive and simple to use, they make life a lot more pleasant for everybody. But in 1999, a couple of lawyers filed a class action suit against several manufacturers arguing that toothbrushes are actually dangerous. When used improperly, the lawyers said, they can lead to discomfort, receding gums, and sensitive teeth—conditions that could, in extreme cases, cost a few thousand dollars to repair. If the plaintiffs' attorneys had been able to convince a jury that they were right, the defendants could have been hit with a judgment of $1 billion or more. The case was thrown out of court and dampened temporarily the proliferation of a new breed of dubious class action suits (France, 2001:122).

Some economists contend that litigation is related to the proportion of lawyers in the population and the relative expenditure on civil justice (Chinloy, 1989:8, 88–89, 90). Basically, the more lawyers there are, the greater is the quantity of litigation. Lawyers are better informed about the legal system than the client, and as a result, there is an asymmetric exchange of information between them. Thus, an increase in the supply of lawyers can increase the demand for legal services and litigation. A comparable argument is applicable to medical care. Physicians are specialized and have more information on diagnosis and procedure than patients do. The same kind of asymmetric relationship exists as between lawyers and clients, and in both cases, there is an economic incentive to suggest intervention. The increase in the number of lawyers also increases competition and reduces a variety of costs, such as the cost of retaining an attorney and lower contingency fees. The cost to the litigant decreases while the total cost of tort action goes up. The increase in the supply of lawyers results in more litigation, increasing the demand for lawyers. This spiral is fueled by incentives in the American legal system that encourage litigation, such as the lack of penalty to litigants. An effective way to moderate the quantity of litigation in this context would be to evoke the so-called English rule (Polinsky and Rubinfeld, 1998) (used in England and Japan, among other places), under which the defendant recovers costs against an unsuccessful plaintiff.

In addition to the hypothesis that the supply of lawyers accounts for the increase in court cases, it is possible that there has been an increase in the number of individuals who have, at one time or another, been involved in litigation. An expansion in the volume of litigation may result even from a small increase in the total number of litigants. Such an expansion may be attributed to changes in the social and political conditions that facilitate the translation of conflicts and disputes into lawsuits. Although litigation requires a substantial investment of time and money, in recent years a number of attempts have been made to reduce or redistribute such costs through, for example, the provision of free legal services. Because of the greater availability of inexpensive or free legal services to individuals who were formerly unable to afford to bring disputes to court, the amount of litigation also may have increased (Goldman and Sarat, 1989:41).

Another explanation for the increase in the number of cases reaching the courts may be that although the number of litigants has not increased, the relatively few individuals or organizations (that is, repeat players) who typically use courts to settle disputes have in recent years simply found more occasion to do so. This resulted in a kind of assembly-line litigation aided by all-butautomated computerized litigation packets that are now available for products ranging from handguns to tires (France, 2001).

The increase in litigation is also related to the increase in the range and variety of legally actionable or resolvable problems.

> As the scope of law expands, as more legal rights and remedies are created, the amount of litigation increases as a result of the new opportunities for court action. As new rights are created, litigation may be necessary to clarify the way in which those rights will be defined and understood by the courts. Furthermore, the creation of new rights may direct the attention of organized interest groups to the judiciary. Interest groups may come to perceive litigation as a viable strategy for stimulating group mobilization to achieve the group's political goals. (Goldman and Sarat, 1989:41)

At the same time, it is also plausible that litigation is not viewed by the parties as an effort to settle a conflict; "instead it is a tactical engagement in a sustained war" (Barton, 1975:575). In such a situation, resolving the legal issue or the conflict becomes secondary to creating publicity for a cause or to obtaining a delay of decision through procedural grounds (see, for example, Skerry, 1998). An example of this is a situation in which general minority rights have priority over the resolution of a specific disagreement, such as alleged discrimination in hiring or promotion. It is also part of the so-called entitlement mentality evidenced by general demands rather than specific claims and epitomized by what one author refers to as the "rights talk" (Glendon, 1991). It is perhaps most pronounced in instances of prisoners' lawsuits where inmates claim that prisons have violated their rights to:

- an orthopedically correct wooden gymnasium floor
- wear sunglasses
- own Soap on a Rope
- have *Rolling Stone* magazine delivered to isolation cells
- practice martial arts
- have two hot meals
- low cholesterol diet and prescription dandruff shampoo (filed by a death row inmate in California in addition to 15 other similar suits)
- silky women's lingerie, makeup and jewelry (by a 47-year-old male inmate)
- unlimited refills of Kool-Aid
- larger pieces of cake because the ones served in the prison cafeteria are too small (Manning, 1995)

Prisoner's lawsuits have been steadily increasing since the 1964 Supreme Court decision permitting prisoners to sue state correctional officials when conditions of confinement failed to meet constitutional standards. The Court had in mind complaints involving excessive force, inadequate medical treatment, and freedom of religious expression. Instead, the courts often ended up with a

variety of frivolous suits, and now prisoners' lawsuits make up around 20 percent of all civil cases before the federal courts (*Newsweek*, 1995:6). This kind of
court use has been dubbed as "recreational litigation," and fewer than 1 percent
of such suits result in a verdict for the prisoner, and most are dismissed for
causes that counsel would have foreseen. Note that constitutional right to an
attorney does not apply to such civil cases (Dilworth, 1995). Finally, because of
the huge price tag, some states have already passed laws that penalize inmates
if a judge rules their lawsuits frivolous. The state can delay a parole hearing by
two months or raid half of the inmate's prison bank account (Bell, 1995). But
care must be exercised that frivolous lawsuits are not turned into a serious
denial of rights.

Sheldon Goldman and Austin Sarat (1989:41–43) identify three generic
factors that may explain litigation. The first they call *social development*.
Variation in the frequency of litigation is a function of changes in the level of
complexity, differentiation, and skill of the society in which courts operate.
Social development and changes in the structure of society bring about
increased reliance on courts to process disputes. In less developed societies,
as a result of stable and enduring contacts among individuals, disputes are
easier to resolve informally. Consequently, courts play a less important role
in disputes. In more complex societies, on the other hand, relationships are
typically more transitory in nature, disputes often take place between
strangers, and under such circumstances, informal dispute processing is
impractical. Furthermore, in developed societies, there is no longer a single
dominant ethos or a set of customs that results from heterogeneity, secular-
ization, and the closer interaction among different subgroups with specific
norms (Barton, 1975:574). For example, corporate executives and environmentalists offer radically different ethical norms for the same activities, such
as potentially hazardous waste disposal.

The second generic factor that explains why disputes are translated into
demands for court services is subjective cost-benefit calculations on the part of
disputants. For some disputants, the decision to use courts is a relatively objective, well-thought-out decision, since they must calculate a "risk" factor and
weigh what they may lose against the possible benefits of doing nothing or of
using different methods of conflict resolution. For others, however, resorting to
courts may be an act "that has value because of its cathartic effect, even though
it may not produce tangible, material benefits" (Goldman and Sarat, 1989:42).
In such a situation, vindictiveness, spite, or the desire for a "moral" victory out-
weighs the financial considerations. Moreover, the disputants' decision to use
the court decreases the pressure upon them to resolve disputes by using nonlegal resources that they can mobilize. Informal and private settlements seem
less likely where the parties have the option for legal recourse (Turk, 1978:224).

The third generic factor in litigation is the creation of more legally actionable rights and remedies by legislatures and courts. Goldman and Sarat state:
"The greater the reach and scope of the legal system, the higher its litigation

rate will be" (1989:42). To some extent, the expanded use of courts is attributable to the expansion of rights and remedies stemming from Supreme Court decisions. The growing scope of law increases litigation implicitly or explicitly by expanding the jurisdiction of the courts. The creation of new rights is likely to stimulate litigation designed to vindicate or protect those rights. For example, the "criminal rights explosion" of the 1960s followed the logic that the creation of new rights would stimulate subsequent litigations that, in turn, would create new rights that would require further litigation.

Thus, with the creation of new norms, courts actually (although unintentionally) promote disputing, since these new norms may lead to claims that otherwise would not have been asserted. For example, the 1973 Supreme Court decision in *Roe v. Wade* invalidating statutes prohibiting abortions led to a series of disputes concerning such issues as whether the federal government had to pay for abortion through its Medicaid program and whether hospitals receiving federal funds had to make facilities for abortions available. Moreover, in clarifying certain norms, courts may make other normative conflicts salient and thus more likely to be disputed. Thus, the abortion decision has also led to disputes over whether parents must consent to a minor's abortion and whether a husband can veto his wife's decision to terminate a pregnancy (Lempert, 1978:97–98). Even laws intended for other purposes can be used as dispute facilitators. For example, the racketeering law which was passed in 1970 as a weapon for fighting organized crime has been used against militant antiabortion groups. A class-action suit filed by the National Organization for Women on behalf of some 900 abortion clinics claimed that antiabortion leaders and their organizations, Operation Rescue National and the Pro-Life Action League, violated the Racketeer Influenced and Corrupt Organizations statue (RICO) by conducting a nationwide conspiracy to intimidate abortion providers and patients. A jury recently ruled in favor of the plaintiff and allows abortion clinics to seek additional damages for the costs of added security (*Economist*, 1998:32).

In addition, since the mid-1950s the courts have discovered a slate of new constitutional rights, protections, and entitlements for whole groups of people—for example, disenfranchised voters, women, Hispanics, prisoners, children, and mental patients. Each of these new rights in turn creates potentially conflict-laden situations conducive to further litigation. At the same time, questions are being raised by critics about the "rights industry" running amok and its impact on major institutions (Morgan, 1984).

Variations in Litigation Rates

There are two general ways of measuring judicial involvement in dispute settlement (Galanter, 1988; Kritzer, 1988; Lempert, 1978). It can be measured by the percentage of disputes that courts play some part in resolving, and by the percentage of the adult population who take disputes to courts. With both measures, there are some difficulties. As Richard Lempert (1978:99) points out, there are several ways in which courts contribute to dispute settlement:

1. Courts establish norms that influence or control the private settlement of disputes. For example, norms established in an appellate opinion resolving one dispute can lead other disputants to resolve their conflict without legal intervention.
2. Courts ratify private settlements and provide guarantees of compliance. For example, in divorce cases where the parties have already reached an agreement, courts ratify that agreement which carries with it the probability of sanctions should it be breached.
3. Courts can escalate the cost of disputing, thereby increasing the likelihood of private settlement.
4. Courts provide opportunities to disputants to learn about each other's cases, thus increasing the probability of private settlement by decreasing mutual uncertainty.
5. Court staff act as mediators to encourage consensual private settlement.
6. Courts resolve certain issues in the case, leading disputants to agree on others.
7. Courts authoritatively resolve disputes.

Thus, at times, it is difficult to determine the extent to which courts contribute to dispute settlement. The clearest case is when disputes are adjudicated and a settlement is imposed after a full trial. But many cases do not end up at trials. A settlement may be reached during a pretrial conference or through informal negotiations where the judge is a participant. Judges also exert informal pressure, even after litigation has commenced, and attorneys usually listen to the recommended solutions. Settlement is also encouraged by the mounting financial costs. Under the uniquely American rule that each side pays his or her own way (the "English rule," for example, as noted earlier, forces the loser to pay for fees and court costs for both sides), the plaintiff's lawyers who make big enough nuisances of themselves will usually get an out-of-court settlement. Defendants calculate that it is cheaper to settle than to try a case, even if there is a good likelihood that they will win. Thus, attempts to explore the dispute-settlement functions of courts over time must consider the different roles courts play and the influences they exert. Lempert notes: "Exploration is complicated by difficulties in measuring the various ways that courts contribute to dispute settlement, and these difficulties are compounded if the measures must allow comparisons over time" (1978:100).

Complications arise also in attempts to measure longitudinally the percentage of the adult population who use court services in disputes. The figures may be inaccurate to the extent that certain individuals or organizations are "repeat players" (Galanter, 1974). Moreover, many courts do not keep adequate records for long periods of time. Where records are kept, the record-keeping procedures vary. Historically, a number of minor courts, such as justice of the peace and magistrate courts, did not keep records. Over time, the court systems had changed through reorganization, and new courts were established and others eliminated. There were also changes in the jurisdiction of many courts. Consequently, there are some questions about the validity and reliability of longitudinal studies that deal with rates of litigation over time. In view of these precautions, let us turn briefly to some studies that have challenged the idea that the dispute-processing function of the courts has increased in recent years as a result of social and economic changes.

In modern societies such as the United States, the use of courts as a forum for conflict resolution is on the increase as a result of societal developments toward increased complexity, heterogeneity, and the prevalence of impersonal and contractual relations. [Where else would a state—Missouri—sue an employee who objected to wearing a tie to work? After multiple trials and appeals, the employee lost.] There is even an argument suggesting that computers have made a major contribution to increases in litigation by making it feasible to engage in protracted, and occasionally frivolous, litigation (Gerson, 1994). Although data are available to support these contentions, some authors contend that social, economic and technological developments do not necessarily lead to higher rates of litigation. For example, Lawrence M. Friedman (1973:338) argues that there is no evidence that nineteenth-century America witnessed proportionately less interpersonal litigation than mid-twentieth-century America, despite more cohesive kin and residential systems. Similarly, over time in Spain, the litigation rate "has remained remarkably constant and at a relatively low rate . . . the process of economic change does not seem to have affected the rate of litigation" (Jose Toharia, quoted by Grossman and Sarat, 1978:59).

A comparable conclusion was reached by Vilhelm Aubert (1969) in his study of the Norwegian legal system. He notes that the demand for dispute resolution during the last 100 years has remained stable or has even decreased throughout a period characterized by vast social changes and great economic progress, whereas the demand for most other kinds of services has multiplied at a very rapid rate. Aubert concludes that "the pure legal model plays a modest part in actual instances of conflict resolution in Norway today" (1969:302). Similarly, Joel B. Grossman and Austin Sarat conclude that "industrialization is a useful predictor of levels of legal activity but not litigation rates; legal activity but not litigation rates appears to be greater in more industrialized areas" (1975:343). Their study was based on litigation rates in federal courts in the United States from 1902 to 1972.

In a study of the civil load of two trial courts in California between 1890 and 1970, Lawrence M. Friedman and Robert V. Percival sampled civil case files of the superior courts in two counties. They found that highly developed economic systems do not show growth in their litigation. On the contrary, rates tend to decline in the face of rapid economic growth. Although they are careful about the generalizability of their data, they conclude that "the dispute settlement function in the courts is declining" (1976:296). They attempt to explain the decline in litigation by suggesting that uncertainty—

a prime breeder of litigation—has declined in the law and that rules are more "settled" now than in 1890. The routine administrative function has replaced the dispute settlement functions in these courts. It is plausible that the court itself—its style, its mode of operation—discourages its use for dispute settlement. In reanalyzing the data used by Friedman and Percival, Richard Lempert comes to the opposite conclusion: Although "the mix of judicial business has changed over the years" and there is "little reason to believe that courts today are functionally less important as dispute settlers than they were in 1890 . . . over all, I do not believe that we can conclude from the Friedman and Percival data that the dispute settlement function of courts . . . has diminished over time" (1978:133). Lempert further comments that the conclusion about the diminution in the dispute settlement activity of trial courts is overstated because Friedman and Percival neglect the mediative activity of trial judges and court personnel (1978:131). This neglect is attributable, in part, to the difficulty, if not the impossibility, of measuring activities of courts over time.

In addition to these studies contending that social and economic developments, with their concomitant increases in the complexity and impersonality in social relations, do not lead to higher rates of litigation, there is also a substantial amount of differentiation in the use of courts in disputes among other nations. Americans are more likely to turn to the civil court system than are people in similar situations in other countries (Kritzer, 1991:407). Henry W. Ehrmann (1976:83–84) points out that litigiousness, the propensity to settle disputes through the judicial process, is a cultural factor of some importance. Studies that have attempted to compare such attitudes cross-culturally have used as a measure the index of civil cases initiated per unit of population. Some of the findings of cross-cultural studies run counter to widely held assumptions about the litigiousness of various nations. Indians do not exhibit a propensity for litigation and never resort to legal measures when alternative means to resolve a dispute are available, and there is a decrease in India in court cases since the pre-independence period (Moog, 1993).

In citing a study by Brian Able-Smith and Robert Stevens suggesting that "in England 'the law' plays a less important role than in almost any other western country," Ehrmann (1976:84) provides figures to show an extraordinarily high litigation rate for Great Britain, "higher than that for Western Germany, whose population is frequently described as being addicted to solving conflicts by lawsuits." The litigation rate per 100,000 population in Great Britain was 3,605 in 1969, and 2,085 in the former West Germany during the same year. Enormous differences exist also in the rate of litigation between Denmark and other Scandinavian countries. Resort to the judiciary in disputes is about 10 times higher in Denmark than in Norway, Sweden, or Finland. Ehrmann finds it difficult to explain the differences between these countries, especially in view of the fact that Norway has about three times as many attorneys per 100,000 population as Denmark.

It is also difficult to explain the relatively high litigation rates for Japan in relation to some Western European countries and in view of the contention that the courts are still not a highly valued site for conflict resolution. The litigation rate for Japan was 980 per 100,000 population in 1986—but still ten times lower than in California (Tanase, 1995:58). Comparable rates for Scandinavian countries for the same year were 683 for Sweden, 493 for Finland, and 307 for Norway. In an often-quoted article, "Dispute Resolution in Japan," Takeyoshi Kawashima (1969) discusses specific social attitudes toward disputes that are reflected in the judicial process. Traditionally, the Japanese prefer extrajudicial, informal means of settling a controversy. Litigation in Japan presupposes and admits the existence of a dispute and leads to a decision that makes clear who is right and wrong in accordance with legal standards. This is contrary to the attitude in favor of a compromise that does not assign a moral fault to disputants. This attitude is related to the nature of social groups in Japan, which are hierarchical in the sense that differences in social status are reflected in degrees of deference and authority; the relations among individuals in social groups are intimate and diffuse. Legal intervention in disputes would upset the harmonious social relationships. As a result, Kawashima contends, the Japanese not only hesitate to resort to a lawsuit but also are quite ready to settle a dispute through informal means of dispute resolution, such as mediation and conciliation. The use of law is further discouraged by the lack of easy availability of lawyers and judges. Donald Black (1989:84) notes that the number of judges and lawyers per capita has declined in Japan since the 1920s. In fact, the total number of judges has not increased since 1890. Today, there is only one judge for every 60,000 persons, compared with one for every 22,000 a century ago. This is due to Japan's decision to place statutory limitations on the number of judges and prosecutors in its system (Westermann and Burfeind, 1991:162). The number of lawyers is much smaller in Japan than in the United States—some 12,000 as contrasted with a very conservative estimate of about 950,000 in the late 1990s. (It is worth noting that the population of Japan is less than half that of the United States.) A typical, uncomplicated civil case can take five or ten years to be heard (*Economist*, 1993:62).

Moreover, in Japan the individual who asserts legal rights and insists on judicial intervention

> is thought to be "inflexible" and selfish. . . . Introduction of a lawyer into a business conference is thought to be an unfriendly act . . . equal to an explicit threat of litigation. . . . When acts such as drafting a contract or the bringing of a suit are unavoidable, the contract is made as short and flexible as possible, or the act of suit is viewed as deplorable, even by the plaintiff. . . . The law . . . goes directly contrary to the Japanese feeling that the relations (even business relations) should be based upon a warm subjective relationship which can solve every practical problem by mutual compromise and accommodation, regardless of formal rights and obligations. The most notable practical result of this attitude is a paucity of litigation in Japan. (Strick, 1977:209)

Undoubtedly, it is difficult to reconcile the differences between these arguments and the relatively high rate of litigation in Japan. It is possible that the attitudes toward the law as a means of conflict resolution are changing and that in urban areas there is a greater reliance on the judiciary to settle disputes. However, I have no data to support these contentions, and the puzzle has yet to be solved empirically.

Complete and reliable data are lacking also for the United States. However, the differences that exist between two neighboring states, Massachusetts and New Hampshire, are startling. In Massachusetts, the litigation rate for 1971 per 100,000 was 1,814, and in New Hampshire for the same year 345. The differences point to the likely fact that the socioeconomic characteristics of a state or the particularities of its historic court system will have an effect on people's inclination to take their disputes to the courts (Ehrmann, 1976:84). But why the difference in litigation rates between two neighboring New England states should be that enormous remains unexplained.

Even within a state, differences in litigation rates exist among cities of comparable size and characteristics. In a study of four Wisconsin cities, Herbert Jacob (1969:92) suggests that "political culture may be a significant explanatory device for accounting for the differences in litigation rates." A traditional political culture is characterized by a relatively low level of bureaucratization in government and a reluctance to invoke governmental processes. There is a greater reliance on private dispute-settling processes in a traditional culture than in a more modern one with a more highly bureaucratized government. In traditional political cultures, people make greater efforts to settle disputes between themselves as neighbors and friends, and they have greater opportunities to settle conflicts within the confines of established private relationships. In a modern political culture, personal relationships are more strained, individuals deal with each other more on a contractual basis, and they have, as a result, less confidence in using private dispute-settling procedures. At the same time, they are more willing "to invoke the public processes of government for solving their problems, be they a neighborhood-development program needing a city council decision or a creditor-debtor conflict which requires the services of a court" (Jacob, 1969:92). Jacob provides some evidence for his contention that the use of courts will be greater in more modern political cultures. In his study on debtors, he found that the process of taking a debtor to court to collect a loan occurs more frequently in modern political cultures. But, beyond that, available data do not permit one to make further generalizations concerning the impact of political culture on the "propensity to sue" (Kritzer, 1988) although it may play a role in encouraging excess consumption and subsequent inability to pay for the goods and services (see, for example, Ritzer, 2001).

Finally, in the past few years the term *litigation explosion* has received considerable fresh publicity in the wake of the publication of Walter Olson's controversial book by the same title (1991). He contends that there is a "revolution" in civil litigation which he views as the "civil war in very, very slow motion." But is there really such an "explosion," or is it a myth? It depends on whom one asks. The estimated number of lawsuits filed each year varies from 18 to 30 million, but no one really knows the precise numbers (Jacobs, 1995). It is difficult to collect data from the antiquated record-keeping systems in courthouses around the country. Records are still filed in thousands of county seats and most kept on paper. With civil cases, each jurisdiction has its own system of cataloging the number of people suing and the kind of claim, making comparisons between courts difficult. Close to half of the states lump all civil claims together, making it difficult to tell how many are medical malpractice or product liability disputes. There is not enough incentive for local courts to spend money on anything but salaries and administration, and as a consequence there is a paucity of comparative statistical data. Federal court records are, fortunately for researchers, more sophisticated. With these caveats, let us return to the question of litigation explosion.

Richard A. Posner (1996) talks about the caseload "crisis" of federal courts. He notes that civil cases increased from 48,886 to 210,503, more than 330 percent, from 1960 to 1983 (1996:65). Appeals, as indicated earlier, increased 686 percent for the same time period. This trend continued well into the 1990s as evidenced by comparable increase in civil filings in federal courts (Administrative Office of the U.S. Courts, 1995). Federal litigation has increased much faster than the population, and this is a significant fact. But there are 50 state court systems in addition to federal courts where some 95 percent of cases are filed. State court cases number in the millions. Is there a litigation explosion in state courts similar to that in federal courts? A study of court filings in 25 states by the National Center for State Courts contends that the litigation explosion is a myth and that litigation rates actually declined between 1981 and 1984, the most recent year with available data (Lauter, 1986:46). The states that have shown an increase are the ones with large population growth, such as California, Florida, and Texas. A surprising finding was that even in small-claims courts, where simplified legal procedures are supposed to ease barriers to filing suits, filings have been decreasing. But in spite of the decline, there were some 13.6 million suits filed in state courts in 1984.

But filing a case does not necessarily mean that it is judicially resolved. Most cases do not reach the trial stage. This is particularly true in accident and personal injury matters. Insurance companies tend to settle most claims out of court. In California, for example, fewer than 1 percent of filed accident claims go to trial; the rest are settled along the way (Friedman, 1985:18).

Thus, what is important are not the numbers, but the types of cases filed. In recent years, whole new areas of litigation opened up, such as malpractice, product liability, and employment discrimination. Social Security cases have burgeoned as the government has attempted to restrict benefits, and suits in which the government is seeking to collect money from individuals have grown 6,600 percent since 1975 (Lauter, 1986:46). Disputants in traditional cases such as contract disputes, consumer matters, landlord-tenant quarrels, and real estate are slowly discovering alternative mechanisms of dispute resolution. There is a change in the types of cases as courts respond to social and legal developments over the years. But there are still questions that researchers cannot answer with certainty: What kinds of cases come to court? Who wins? How often do juries award damages, including punitive ones? And how much do plaintiffs get in cases settled before trial?

PREREQUISITES FOR THE USE OF COURTS IN DISPUTE RESOLUTION

Courts provide a forum for the settlement of a variety of private and public disputes. The courts are considered a neutral and impartial place for dispute processing. Other than criminal cases, legal disputes are processed in civil courts. Individuals and organizations who want to use the courts for dispute processing must meet certain legal requirements. At the minimum, plaintiffs must be able to demonstrate justiciability and standing (Jacob, 1969:17–19).

Justiciability means that the conflict is viable to trial and courts. The court must be mandated to provide a remedy. In the United States, most disputes are justiciable in one court or another, although the jurisdiction of particular courts varies. For example, federal courts are not permitted to grant divorces or adoptions or to probate wills. Various state courts exist for these and most other cases excluded from the federal judiciary. The potential litigant must turn the grievance into a legal dispute and must determine, with or without the aid of an attorney, whether the complaint is justiciable. Essentially, justiciability refers to real and substantial controversy that is appropriate for judicial determination, as differentiated from disputes or differences of a hypothetical or an abstract character. Furthermore, in some instances, the courts may not be authorized to intervene in certain types of disputes. For example, the Wagner Act forbade court intervention in most labor disputes.

Standing is a more severe limitation to litigation than justiciability. The theory behind standing is that individuals should be able to bring lawsuits only if their personal legal rights have been violated. For example, a taxpayer may not sue the government to prevent the expenditure of funds for an objectionable purpose because the ordinary taxpayer's stake in the expenditure is minimal. If one disapproves what the CIA or the Army Corps of Engineers is doing, one is supposed to take it up with Congress, not with the courts. Similarly, a mother-in-law cannot sue for a divorce: Such proceedings must be initiated by the husband or wife. It should be noted though that since the late 1960s, the doctrine of standing has been broadened by activist courts (see Judicial Lawmaking in Chapter 4) eager to solve the nation's problems (Frum, 1993). Various public interest groups, as it will be discussed later, have used the court against private companies and government agencies.

Herbert Jacob (1969:18) points out that the limits to justiciability and standing are not social accidents. They are related to political compromises achieved over the distribution of powers and functions between various branches of the government and interest groups who had favorable access to one branch of government or another. The jurisdiction of courts in most cases is determined by legislation. The decision to present one kind of dispute or another in a court is a political one. For example, civil rights groups in the 1960s worked for the passage of laws that, among other things, gave federal courts broadened jurisdiction over disputes affecting civil rights, because they considered federal courts to be more favorably disposed to them than state courts or administrative agencies. The use of courts for collection purposes (in creditor-debtor disputes) or the settlement of complex public-policy disputes are also the product of legislative compromises brought about by interest-group pressures.

However, justiciability and standing are not the only limitations to the use of courts in disputes. There is also the old legal axiom *de minimus non curat lex*: The law will not concern itself with trifles. Trivial matters may not be litigated. For example, a court may refuse to hear a suit to recover a $10 overcharge even if the cause appears just (Lempert and Sanders, 1986:137). In addition, untold numbers of disputes arise over which the courts have clear jurisdiction and someone has standing to sue. But using the court is dependent on a number of considerations. These considerations are superimposed on the legal barriers to litigation.

Resort to court services in disputes is voluntary for the plaintiffs; for defendants, participation in a legal dispute is involuntary. The plaintiffs approach the courts with different expectations and often through different circumstances from those of the defendants. Jacob notes: "Whereas the initiation of court action may promise relief to the plaintiff, it threatens deprivation for the defendant. Since the plaintiff initiates court action he can exert a certain degree of control over it, but the action often descends without warning upon defendants" (1969:19).

Economic resources for both plaintiffs and defendants are important in their decision to pursue a suit through trial and appeal. With the exception of magistrate courts and individuals who qualify for legal-aid services, plaintiffs are unlikely to use the courts unless they have sufficient funds to hire an attorney and bear the costs of litigation. The litigant must bear court fees for filing cases, for calling witnesses, and for compensating the jury. Disputants must also be able to afford the costs of delay, which occur when disputes are submitted to the courts. For example, automobile accident cases involving large sums of money do not reach the court dockets for several years in many large American cities. In the interim, the plaintiff has expenses. Often the cost of waiting must be calculated against the benefits of a quick settlement for only part of the claim. Obviously, for many people economic resources play an important role in the use of court services and may be decisive in out-of-court settlements.

Before initiating a lawsuit, individuals must recognize the relevance of court services to their problems. Jacob (1969:20) notes that the use of the judiciary varies with education, for better-educated individuals are more likely to differentiate between the courts and other agencies and to be aware of their various services. Perception of the courts also varies with other factors, such as integration into a social group in which court usage has previously occurred or where it is relatively prevalent. Says Jacob: "Thus it may be that certain ethnic groups of communities are more litigious than others. Members of such groups are more likely to perceive court action as relevant to their problems and consequently they become more frequent consumers of court services" (1969:20).

Socioeconomic status is also related to the use of the judiciary in disputes. Those who cannot afford a lawyer and the necessary court fees are less likely to litigate than those who have sufficient funds. Moreover, social status is related to the kind of court services that are used. In general, the poor are more likely to be defendants and recipients of court-ordered sanctions. Middle-class litigants are less likely to be subjected to court sanctions and more likely to benefit from the use of court services in their own behalf from the legitimization of their private agreements or from out-of-court negotiations.

A TYPOLOGY OF LITIGANTS

As I noted in Chapter 3, the use of courts varies also by the types of litigants. Marc Galanter advances a typology of litigants by the frequency of the utilization of courts. Those who have only occasional recourse to the courts are called one-shotters, and those who are engaged in many similar litigations over time are designated as repeat players. Illustrations for the former include the wife in a divorce case and the auto injury claimant. The latter is exemplified by insurance or finance companies. Based on this typology, Galanter proposes a taxonomy of litigation by the configuration of parties. He comes up with four types of litigation—one-shotter versus one-shotter, repeat player versus one-shotter, one-shotter versus repeat player, and repeat player versus repeat player.

The largest number of cases involving disputes between one-shotters are divorces and insanity commitments. Disputes between one-shotters are "often between parties who have some intimate tie with one another, fighting over some unsharable good, often with overtones of 'spite' and 'irrationality' " (Galanter, 1974:108). The courts are used when an ongoing relationship is ruptured and the law is invoked *ad hoc* and instrumentally by the parties. When such disputes take place between neighbors or business partners, there may be a strong interest in vindication, and the court decisions are seldom appealed.

The second type of litigation, repeat players versus one-shotters, is exemplified by suits initiated by finance companies against debtors, landlords against tenants, and the IRS against taxpayers. Except for personal injury cases, insanity hearings, and divorces, the great bulk of litigation is found in disputes between repeat players and one-shotters. Here, the law is used for routine processing of claims by parties for whom the making of such claims is a regular business activity. In many instances, courts authorize repeat players to borrow the government's power for their private purposes. Repeat players may use that power to achieve many objectives, such as to collect debts, oust tenants, or prohibit some harmful activity. In such a case, the plaintiff comes to court with a grievance. If the court considers the complaint a legitimate one, it issues a judgment or an injunction. The judgment authorizes the plaintiff to make use of the government's police power to effectuate it. Thus, a real estate agent may, for example, call on the sheriff to oust a tenant, to reclaim some property, to sell property belonging to a defendant, or to seize the defendant's wages or property. When the court issues an injunction on behalf of the plaintiff, it orders the defendant not to engage in the activity about which the plaintiff complained. If the defendant persists, he or she may be fined or imprisoned.

The third combination of litigants is one-shotters versus repeat players. Illustrations of this include tenant versus landlord, injury victim versus insurance company, student versus university, defamed versus publisher, and client versus welfare agency. Outside of the personal injury area, litigation in this combination is not routine. It usually represents the attempt of some one-shotters to invoke outside help to create leverage on an organization with which the individual has a dispute.

The fourth type of litigation is repeat players versus repeat players. Examples of this include litigation between union and management, purchaser and supplier, regulatory agency and firms of regulated industry, and church/state litigations focusing on value differences (who is right) rather than interest conflicts (who gets what). With these types of litigation in the background, let us now turn to certain types of conflicts between individuals, between individuals and organizations, and between organizations where one of the disputants resorts to the judiciary in an attempt to resolve the conflict.

DISPUTES BETWEEN INDIVIDUALS

Although most controversies between individuals never come to the attention of courts, the handling of interpersonal differences is a traditional function of courts. Most individual disputes involve one-shotters. For those individuals whose disagreements come before a court, the experience is likely to be the most intimate they will have had with the government, and the manner in which the dispute is handled is likely to have a marked affect on their attitudes toward the government. Judicial resolution of individual disputes also affects the distribution of values. Some people gain, others lose; some individuals are honored, others are stigmatized; and as with all types of disputes, a court decision seldom resolves the underlying conditions for the conflict.

Individual disputes include private litigation as opposed to organizations, criminal defendants, or state agencies. These disputes generally deal with the distribution of economic resources and a variety of noneconomic problems.

Economic disputes include various claims associated with contests over wills, trusts, and estates, landlord-tenant controversies, and disputes over property, titles, and sales. The greatest distinction between economic and noneconomic individual disputes is that the former directly involve a conflict over the control of economic resources, whereas the latter, although often involving money, do not necessarily stem from economic conflicts. Noneconomic conflicts include allegations of slander and libel, custody cases, divorce proceedings, insanity commitments, and malpractice suits.

Courts often make an effort to encourage disputants to settle their differences by agreement, since this is a less costly way to reestablish an equilibrium, which any conflict is likely to disturb. Settlements may even be encouraged after the disputants have brought their complaint to a court. Such efforts may be initiated by the judge in pretrial hearings or in open court. The success of such efforts depends to a great extent on the skills of the judge and on the nature of the disputes. When the parties are unable or unwilling to resolve their disputes by agreement, and when they have decided against letting matters rest, formal adjudication must take over and will normally end in a decision that claims to be binding on the parties (Ehrmann, 1976:83).

In the adjudication of individual disputes, one party wins and the other loses. Robert B. Seidman (1978:213–214) points out that in situations in which parties want to, or must, cooperate after the dispute, both must leave the settlement procedures without too great a sense of grievance. If, however, there are opportunities for avoidance (that is, parties need not live or work together), then the disputants may continue their antagonism. Compromises tend to resolve the disputes in the sense that they reduce any continuing antagonism. Win-or-lose situations, however, will not ameliorate antagonism.

Therefore, disputants who wish to maintain an ongoing relationship will generally engage in compromise settlements. Businesspeople do not sue customers whose trade they want to keep. Married couples who want to stay together do not sue each other; instead, they consult marriage counselors who look for compromises.

The structure of social relationships thus plays a role in the decision as to whether to take a dispute to court. When continuing relations are important to the individuals involved in the dispute, they are generally more predisposed to resolve their differences through nonlegal means. In a now classic paper, Stewart Macaulay describes the avoidance of the law as a way of building and maintaining good business relations. Businesspeople prefer not to use contracts in their dealings with other businesspeople. Says Macaulay: "Disputes are frequently settled without reference to the contract or potential or actual legal sanctions. There is a hesitancy to speak of legal rights or to threaten to sue in these negotiations" (1969:200). Similar sentiments prevail in other countries. For example, "For a Korean, it is not decent or 'nice' to insist on one's legal right. When a person hauls another person into court, he is in fact declaring war on him. . . . He has lined himself up on the side of the bureaucrats to use the power of the state to oppress his fellow man. Thus, a Korean cannot think of law as anything other than oppressive. . . . This reluctance to maintain one's legal right is particularly pronounced in the area of property" (Hahm, quoted by Friedman and Macaulay, 1977:1026).

How the either-or court decision would mitigate against continuing relations is further illustrated by Jane Fishburne Collier in her work on the Zinacanteco Indians of Southern Mexico. She points out that Indians who wish to preserve a valued relationship will seek a settlement procedure that promotes reconciliation.

> Cases end when an appropriate settlement has been found. In Zinacanteco eyes, an ideal settlement involves reconciliation: Both sides agree to forget their differences and drink together, or the guilty person begs pardon and is forgiven through acceptance of a bottle of rum. Settlements often involve agreements to pay money or repair damages, though such agreements are seen as a part of the reconciliation process. A case that ends without reconciliation and drinking is considered less than satisfactory. (Collier, 1973:38)

However, continuing relationships are but part of a broader issue of whether to litigate in individual disputes. Nader and Todd point out: "It is not enough to state that because litigants wish to continue their relation they will seek negotiated or mediated settlement with compromise outcomes" (1978:17). In some instances, ties within the family itself may give rise to disputes over inheritance among brothers or sisters, or arguments between males and females over the males' attempts to control the behavior of their unmarried sisters. At the same time, social relations may act not as an impetus to conflict but as a constraint on escalation. For example, Barbara B. Yngvesson (1978:59), in her study of a small Scandinavian fishing village, notes that "disputes are focused less on *acts than on people*. What was done is *less important than who did it*. An act considered normal when done by a kinsman or fellow community member may generate an entirely different response when done by an 'outsider.' "

Thus, it is no longer sufficient to generalize that a preference for continuing relations will turn disputants to some kind of compromise or reconciliation mechanism rather than to litigation. In a variety of instances, disputants resort to legal rather than nonlegal ways, with the full awareness of the risks involved in their attempts to settle their disputes.

Practically an unlimited variety of economic and noneconomic disputes take place between individuals and end up before a judge for decision. Some recent highlights of our litigious society: People argue over cows in the corn and pigs in the garden (Karsten, 1998). A Panama City, FL, waitress is suing her employer, Hooters. After winning a contest (not specified in the suit) that offered a Toyota for a prize, she says, she was blindfolded and presented with . . . a toy Yoda. A young woman brushed her teeth for two weeks with Crest Baking Soda toothpaste. She claims it misaligned and scarred her teeth, and she is suing both the manufacturer and the store that sold it to her. A New Jersey couple whose home caught fire after a Pop-Tart was left unattended in the toaster is suing Kellogg and Black & Decker for damages (*Time*, 2001:15).

Affluent litigants may want possession of boats, silverware, or family dogs. Married couples want a divorce, and unmarried ones argue over property rights. A client may sue his or her attorney for legal malpractice, and attorneys' malpractice insurance rates have been going up both directly and indirectly. Higher deductibles and exclusions for some kinds of exposure have contributed to indirect rises (Hazard, 1994). A patient may institute charges against a physician for medical malpractice. For example, a woman in New York sued her physician for an off-center belly button stemming from unsuccessful plastic surgery. (A jury awarded her $854,000 for damages incurred by having her belly button two inches off center.) In the context of medical malpractice, there are obvious litigation excesses—those who sue and collect are often not victims of negligence and almost 60 percent of malpractice rewards go to lawyers (*New York Times*, 1995:14E).

A clergyman is charged with clerical malpractice and the plaintiff alleges that his advice to remain married to her husband caused her "severe trauma, insomnia, and a chronic lower-back problem" (*Saturday Review*, 1979:7). (As a result of this suit, an insurance company began to offer malpractice coverage for the clergy; for about $20 a year, $300,000 of protection will be provided. Today, several insurance companies offer such protection. In 1986, there were some 2,000 cases involving the clergy, and more than $100 million has been awarded to those suing them [*New York Times*, 1986b:1F].) It should be noted however that nowadays churches, just like any other organizations, who fire ministers for adultery or other misconduct risk a countersuit for wrongful termination, defamation or emotional distress (Rosen, 2001:49). Even judges are not immune today; nearly 3,300 nationwide have decided that they, too, need malpractice insurance. This lack of judicial immunity is the cause of approximately 300 insurance claims that have been filed by judges annually since 1984 (Hagerdon, 1989).

The American Tort Reform Association (1992) complains about "scapegoat litigation" in the wake of the rash of corporate bankruptcies and the collapse of the savings and loan industry in the late 1980s. They contend that creditors and regulators are suing lawyers and investment bankers for alleged malpractice because they are the only solvent targets left. Such litigation, they claim but do not explain how, will result in higher prices and a reduction in the gross national product by an average of $17.8 billion annually between 1992 and 1996. A Maryland man sued a marriage counselor, alleging emotional distress because the counselor had an affair with his wife. He put a $10 million price tag on the suit for alienation of affection (Stumpf and Culver, 1992:1). A Colorado man has filed claims against his parents for the sum of $350,000, charging that they gave him inhumane and inadequate care as a child, making it impossible for him to fit into society as an adult. A black man in Omaha,

Nebraska, sued the makers of a Compton's Encyclopedia CD-ROM for $40 million, claiming that he and his children suffered emotional distress when, during a search, he mistakenly typed in the word nigger—instead of Niger—and the program called up several references (*Time*, 1995). A former St. Louis University law student bit the left buttock of the president of the student bar association of another law school in a bar. After graduation, she sued him for damages and a jury awarded her $2,500 in actual and $25,000 in punitive damages (Poor, 1990). A Florida man has filed suit against a nightclub, claiming he suffered whiplash when a topless dancer knocked him out with her breasts. To compensate for pain and suffering, mental anguish and loss of capacity for enjoyment of life, among other things, he is seeking more than $15,000 in damages (*Vancouver Sun*, 1998). To conclude this litany of illustrations with another Florida case, a 15-year-old girl in West Palm Beach has sued her prom date for standing her up. She sought compensation of $49.53 for the shoes, flowers, and hairdo that went to waste when her date failed to appear (Page, 1989). Such cases may strike many people as frivolous and amusing. They may be, but at the same time they are illustrative of the spectrum of individual disputes that end up in court.

Data on patterns of outcomes in individual disputes are scarce. In adjudication, courts are supposed to decide disputes by reference to the facts of who did what to whom, and by identifying, interpreting, and applying appropriate legal norms. Sheldon Goldman and Austin Sarat (1989:514) suggest that this requires that judges remain neutral with regard to both the issues of the case and its result. They use the notion of result impartiality in referring to the extent cases are decided independently of the personal attributes of the parties involved. Impartiality is displayed when both parties in a dispute are given the same opportunities and are shown the same considerations. It requires that the judge not be influenced by an interest in the outcome or by attitudes toward the disputants and the particular situations in which they are involved.

To study the question of impartiality, it is necessary to examine a number of decisions involving similar situations to discover whether over time different kinds of disputants are equally likely to gain favorable results. For impartial results, the pattern of decision should be random and should not consistently favor one type of litigant over another. For example, if courts in custody cases at times rule for the mother and at other times for the father, it may be concluded that they show equal regard for both sexes. However, if they consistently favor mothers over fathers, regardless of the facts or the applicable law, then the results would not be impartial.

Goldman and Sarat point out, however, that the difficulty with this way of determining result impartiality is that it does not take into account other factors responsible for variation from the standard of randomness that go beyond the attitudes and values of the judges. A most obvious factor is that, even if courts are impartial in their procedures, they may still produce biased results if the laws that they apply favor one type of litigant. This is particularly true in custody cases, since most state divorce laws still favor the mother.

The outcome of court decisions may also be influenced by the type of attorney that disputants are able to retain. Availability of resources to disputants directly affects the quality of legal talent they can hire. Access to a skillful attorney increases the likelihood of a favorable court decision, since courts assume that in individual disputes both parties can marshal the resources and legal skills needed to present a case effectively.

To an extent, these considerations can be useful in predicting the outcomes of individual disputes. In some instances, however, both parties may be able to afford delays and the services of highly trained attorneys, and to have convincing legal arguments on their side. In such instances, the determination of the outcome of the case will have to wait until the judge hands down the verdict.

DISPUTES BETWEEN INDIVIDUALS AND ORGANIZATIONS

In this section, I will discuss disputes between individuals and organizations. The first part of the section will consider individuals as plaintiffs and organizations as defendants. The second part will deal with legal disputes initiated by organizations against individuals. I will use the term "organization" to cover a broad range of social groups that have been deliberately and consciously constructed to achieve certain specific goals—hospitals, credit agencies, universities, General Motors, regulatory agencies, the American Medical Association, public-interest law firms, and so forth.

Disputes between individuals and organizations may take place over a variety of issues, many of which may be included in four general categories: (1) disputes over property and money (economic disputes); (2) claims for damages and restitution; (3) issues of civil rights; and (4) disputes concerning organizational actions, procedures, and policy. These broad categories of disputes are, of course, not mutually exclusive.

Economic disputes are exemplified by the following types of actions: suits for unpaid rent; eviction; claims for unpaid loans and installment purchases; foreclosures and repossessions; and suits on contracts and insurance policies.

Claims for damages and restitution most frequently involve automobile accidents and lawsuits against insurance companies. However, other forms of injury—for example, airplane accidents, faulty appliances, and medical and academic malpractices—also give rise to claims. Damage suits may also be initiated to compensate for losses sustained from the failure to honor a contract or to perform a service properly. Slander and libel actions also fall within this category. Although money may change hands as a result of these actions, the actions themselves seek compensation for alleged improper behavior and its consequences. It should be noted that economic disputes and claims for damages and restitution also occur in individual disputes as well as in disputes between individuals and organizations.

Civil rights disputes include claims of discrimination by race, sex, or national origin in matters of employment, hiring, promotion, retention, pay, housing, and admission policies. Other issues that may lead to civil rights disputes include other discriminatory practices, such as the exclusion of handicapped people and setting arbitrary age or educational limits.

The final category of disputes includes challenges to a variety of actions, procedures, and policies of organizations. Decisions of zoning boards or tax assessors may be challenged as a violation of statutes or of administrative procedures. Plaintiffs may seek a reversal of particular decisions, or a voiding of statutes or injunctions prohibiting the continued application of particular policies. In organizations that distribute benefits, such as the program of Aid to Families with Dependent Children (AFDC), food stamps, aid to the disabled, and Medicaid, there are disputes about the appropriate form of benefits, conflicting and inconsistent eligibility rules on employment and training incentives, and disputes about how administrators should deal with beneficiaries. In business organizations, disputes over policies governing warranties, replacement of defective products, or unethical collection practices also come to courts.

Usually, organizations are plaintiffs in the first category of disputes and defendants in the other three. In general, as Marc Galanter (1975) concludes, organizations are more successful as both plaintiffs and defendants than are individuals. They enjoy greater success against individual antagonists than against other organizations. Individuals fare less well contending against organizations than against other individuals. For example, in 2000 the retail-store chain Wal-Mart was hit with 4,851 suits filed by individuals and currently it has about 9,400 cases open. Dozens of lawyers now specialize in suing Wal-Mart; many share documents and other information via the Internet. The allegations range from falls on slippery floors and icy parking lots to claims of being injured in shoppers' stampedes triggered by bargain hunting to employment discrimination practices. In the vast majority of cases (no exact numbers are available) Wal-Mart wins by aggressively fighting cases even when it would be cheaper for the company to settle (*Bellingham Herald*, 2001). It is interesting to note that Wal-Mart is sued more often than any other American entity except the U.S. government, which was sued more than 7,500 times in 2000.

Galanter's conclusion is supported by the Wal-Mart example and reinforced by Donald Black's (1976:92, 1989:41–46) contention that law and organization are inversely related: Law is greater toward less organization. Over one-half of the plaintiffs in civil cases in the United States are organizations, and two-thirds of the defendants are individuals. Organizations win more often than individuals. In small-claims courts, as well, more organizations sue individuals than the other way around. In these instances, the plaintiffs nearly always win. For example, David Caplovitz (1974:222) found that legal actions against debtors in his sample of 1,331 cases, drawn from four cities, resulted in creditor victories in all but 3 percent of the cases. Moreover, if an organization loses its case against an individual, it is more likely to appeal, and, if it does, it is more likely to win a reversal.

Black also points out that "although any group is more likely to bring a lawsuit against an individual than vice versa, then, the likelihood of a lawsuit by a group increases with its organization. On the other hand, the likelihood of a lawsuit by an individual against a group decreases with the organization of the group" (1976:93). In other words, a large organization such as the Internal Revenue Service is more likely to sue an individual than the reverse. Organization, as Black notes, provides an immunity from law and "an offense committed by an organization or its representatives is less serious than an offense by an individual on his own, and the more organized the organization, the less serious it is" (Black, 1976:94).

Although organizations have a greater chance of winning and a higher frequency of initiating lawsuits, it does not mean that individuals do not sue organizations. On the contrary, individuals are taking their disputes with organizations to courts at an unprecedented rate. Workers increasingly seek compensation in courts for health damages, allegedly suffered in hazardous working environments. There is a rapid growth of suits by consumers claiming harm from defective products or harm suffered while on company premises. For the remainder of this section, I shall consider disputes initiated by individuals and organizations separately. For the former, I shall illustrate the use of law as a method of dispute resolution in academe, and for the latter, I shall discuss the use of courts as collection agencies in the field of consumer credit.

Law as a Method of Dispute Resolution in Academe

In 2002, law remains a potent force in institutions of higher learning in the United States. More and more, disputes that develop on campuses in America are resolved outside the groves of academia. Students, faculty members, academic administrators, and their institutions are becoming litigants in steadily growing numbers. Over the years, a substantial amount of literature emerged on legal guidelines in institutions of higher learning (see, for example, O'Reilly and Green, 1992), about the offenses committed in academe in the name of political correctness and multiculturalism (Kors and Silverglate, 1998), and law's pronounced presence on the campus reverberates on most activities (Kaplin and Lee, 1995:1). Some examples: A college basketball player sues his institution for admission to a bachelor's degree program so he can maintain eligibility for intercollegiate sports. Another student sues her institution for $125,000 after an instructor gave her a B+ grade, which she claimed should have been an A−. As an unintended consequence of growing legalism on campus, due to concerns with probable complications, adverse administrative reactions, lengthy justifications, a myriad of memos, grievance committees and even with the possibility of litigation, many faculty members are reluctant to fail a student or to assign a D or even a C+. (And it would be a professional suicide for an untenured assistant professor to assign a low grade or dare fail a student in a "chip on the shoulder" course.) Acknowledging intellectual diversity and divergent performance on the grade sheet is a pedagogical fact of life—although fewer and fewer professors do it because of the fear of consequences and giving in to administrative and student intimidation.

Faculty members are similarly active. In one case, a tenured professor sought an injunction after the college reduced his laboratory space from 1,000 to 300 square feet. Others have sued (successfully) claiming that the Teachers Insurance and Annuity Association-College Retirement Equities Fund (TIAA-CREF) illegally discriminated on the basis of sex. These and other types of lawsuits on campus will be considered in the context of faculty-administration, student-faculty, and student-administration relations.

The *faculty-administration* relationship in postsecondary institutions is defined by an increasingly complex web of legal principles and authorities. The essence of this relationship is contract law, but "that core is encircled by expanding layers of labor relations law, employment discrimination law, and, in public institutions, constitutional law and public employment statutes and regulations" (Kaplin and Lee, 1995:150). The growth in the number and variety of laws and regulations governing faculty-administration relations provides a fertile ground for grievances and coincides with an increase in the number of lawsuits stemming from that relationship.

Many legal disputes center on the meaning and interpretation of the faculty-institution contract. Depending on the institution, a contract may vary from a basic notice of appointment to a complex collective bargaining agreement negotiated under federal or state labor laws. In some instances, the formal document does not encompass all the terms of the contract, and other terms are included through "incorporation by reference"—that is, by referring to other documents, such as the faculty handbook, or even to past custom and usage at an institution. In the context of contract interpretation, legal disputes arise most often in the context of contract termination and due notice for such termination.

A number of suits instituted by faculty members to redress their grievances against university administrations have focused on faculty-personnel decisions, such as appointment, retention, promotion, and tenure policies; pecuniary matters affecting women and minority groups; and sex discrimination. (Faculty members who sue their institutions over sex discrimination have had only a 1-in-5 chance of winning their cases [*Chronicle of Higher Education*, 1989:A14].) As a result of civil rights legislation, hiring procedures must follow clearly established affirmative action guidelines. Many traditional practices of departments and universities are being questioned, such as the use of "the old boy network" and other selection processes not in compliance with these guidelines. Similarly, termination procedures must also follow specific guidelines and deadlines, and in recent years faculty members have increasingly resorted to lawsuits on the grounds of procedural matters.

Other potentially conflict-laden situations in academe arise from *student-faculty* relations. Students are increasingly considering themselves buyers of education, treating education like other consumer items; concomitantly, there is a growing emphasis on the proper return for their educational dollars. Well over a generation ago, Ladd and Lipset already commented: "In fact, the students are the 'consumers,' the buyers, the patrons of a product sold by the faculty through a middle-man, the university system. In economic class terms, the relationship of student to teacher is that of buyer to seller, or of client to professional. In this context, the buyer or client seeks to get the most for his money at the lowest possible price" (1973:93).

Because students are purchasers of education, they expect "delivery" of a product. In this context, the question of academic malpractice becomes important. Although the legal definition of academic malpractice is yet to be codified, it is generally considered as improper, injurious, or negligent instruction or action that has a "negative effect" on the student's academic standing, professional licensing, or employment (Vago, 1979:39). Although the concept of academic malpractice is rather amorphous, several patterns have emerged. A faculty member may be charged with malpractice by a student who perceives a particular course as "worthless," or by a student who contends that he or she did not obtain any "relevant" information or that for some reason it did not fit into the student's general educational outlook, requirement, or area of concentration. In such instances, individual professors are charged, and the object of the lawsuit is usually the recovery of tuition monies, and occasionally an intent to seek punitive damages, since the legal doctrine of *respondeat superior* (that is, the sins of the employee are imputed to the employer) is usually invoked. Several cases have been also litigated in which students have claimed contract damages for an institution's failure to provide bargained-for services. In a most extraordinary case, for example, the defendant-student has alleged in a counterclaim that Columbia University

> had represented that it would teach the defendant wisdom, truth, character, enlightenment, understanding, justice, liberty, honesty, courage, beauty, and similar virtues and qualities; that it would develop the whole man, maturity, well-roundedness, objective thinking and the like; and that because it failed to do so it was guilty of misrepresentation, to the defendant's pecuniary damage. (Vago, 1979:41)

In this case, the trial court granted the university's motion for summary judgment, which was sustained on appeal.

Disputes resulting from a failure of a student to pass an internal examination may also culminate in attempts to involve the courts. In such a situation, a student may question the expertise and competency of professors to evaluate examinations, or a department may be accused of following improper procedures during examinations. Questions of expertise and competency usually arise in the area of alleged academic overspecialization. (That is, is someone qualified to evaluate an examination in social psychology when his or her professed specialty is the sociology of law?) Issues of improper procedures often arise in the context of due process involving the department's or the university's failure to list specific guidelines for examination procedures, or to live up to those guidelines, or to provide clearly written guidelines and appeal procedures. But when it comes to strictly academic decisions made by faculty members about a student's academic career, the right of judges to overturn such decisions is limited. According to a 1985 Supreme Court ruling, "When judges are asked to review the substance of a genuinely academic decision . . . they should show great respect for the faculty's professional judgment," and courts are not "suited to evaluate the substance of the multitude of academic decisions that are made daily by faculty members" (Palmer, 1985:33).

The student's failure to pass a professional examination is another ground for lawsuits. Here the charge is usually that a given department "failed" to properly prepare the student to successfully take an external examination, such as a bar examination, and thus provided a "defective product." In a well-publicized case, a court ruled against a graduate of the Southern University Law School who claimed the university was responsible for his failure to pass—on three occasions—the state bar examination. The court held that it was against Louisiana law to sue a state agency and that the university is such an agency; the court also noted that a properly drafted contract suit may have stated a "remediable" course of action (Vago, 1979:41).

Student-administration relations provide a third area for potential conflict in academe. Increasingly, suspension and dismissal procedures, the rights of students to organize, alleged censorship activities over student publications, and sex discrimination are being challenged by students in courts.

Although institutions of higher learning have the right to dismiss, suspend, or otherwise sanction students for misconduct or academic deficiency, this right is determined by a body of procedural requirements that must be observed in such actions. Under the due process clause, students are entitled to a hearing and notice before disciplinary action is taken. In general, several court rulings indicate a judicial trend toward increased protection of student rights, in both public and private institutions, in suspension and dismissal cases (Kaplin and Lee, 1995:371–604).

First Amendment rights have been increasingly cited in student-administration disputes. Under the First Amendment, students have a legal right to organize and to use appropriate campus facilities. In some instances, however, postsecondary institutions retain the authority to revoke or withhold recognition, and to regulate the organizational use of campus facilities. When a mutually acceptable and satisfactory balance between the organization's rights and the institution's authority cannot be attained, the organizing students may turn to the courts to settle their dispute with the administration, as has been the case, for example, with various gay rights organizations.

The First Amendment principles also apply to student publications. The chief concern here is censorship and administrative control over publications. In one case, for example, financial support for the campus newspaper was terminated on the grounds that the paper printed prosegregation articles and that it urged the maintenance of an all-black university. The court of appeals held that the administration's action violated the student staff's First Amendment rights. Other currently controversial issues include questions of obscenity and libel in the context of student publications.

Lawsuits against university administrations on the basis of alleged sex discrimination, particularly in athletics, are also becoming more numerous (Kaplin and Lee, 1995:564–569). These involve, for example, the use of university sports facilities and locker rooms; funding for women's athletic programs; segregated versus unitary (integrated) athletic teams; scheduling games and practice time; the provision of equipment and supplies; travel and per diem allowance; publicity; and the provision of coaches, housing, and dining facilities.

The growing frequency and diversity of lawsuits as a method of conflict resolution in academe has important implications for contemporary higher education. Postsecondary institutions are the parties that are most adversely affected by successful litigation. The economic and social costs of such litigations can be enormous. The need for universities to develop and maintain effective mechanisms of internal conflict management is obvious. The following section will consider disputes initiated by organizations against individuals in the domain of consumer credit.

The Courts as Collection Agencies

Disputes between individuals and organizations, where organizations are the plaintiffs, most often are triggered by disagreements over property and money. Such disputes are most prevalent in the creditor-debtor relationship, where the creditor is usually an organization such as a finance and loan company, car dealership, department store, or hospital. In such situations, there is a gross power disparity between the debtor and the organization, the debtor is relatively ignorant of the technical aspects of the product, and the stakes are small in dollars but large in their impact on the debtor (Goldberg et al., 1999).

Kagan comments: "If the extension of credit is the lifeblood of a dynamic commercial society, the forcible collection of unpaid debts is its backbone" (1984:324). When a debtor defaults on his or her contractual obligation to make payments, the standard legal remedy is for the creditor to sue in civil court. The purpose is to establish the legality of the debt and its amount. Of course, creditors "hope to collect the debt by invoking the power of the court, but even if they do not collect, a judgment against the debtor is still of value for income tax purposes. Bad debts are worth 50 cents in deductions on every tax dollar" (Caplovitz, 1974:191).

If the creditor is successful in the suit, he or she obtains a judgment against the debtor. Once obtained, there are a variety of legal remedies available for collecting the judgment, including garnishment, liens, and the forced sale of the debtor's property. As I noted earlier, a garnishment is a court order directing someone who owes or possesses money due to the debtor (such as an employer) to pay all or some of that money to the court, which then turns it over to the creditor (Vago, 1968, 1971). A lien establishes a creditor's claim on property (such as a house or a car). A forced sale involves seizure and sale at an auction of the debtor's property. The proceeds then are turned over to the creditor to satisfy the judgment.

Before going to court, a creditor may resort to a number of social pressures and sanctions of varying severity, ranging from impersonal routine "reminders" and dunning letters or telephone appeals to get the debtor "in" to make some kind of "arrangement" with him and to remind or threaten him or her, to personal visits to the debtor's home in an attempt to elicit payments or at least promises. At times, creditors resort to unusual extrajudicial methods of collection. For example, a London firm is using a rather unconventional method of extracting money from debtors—smell: "Smelly Tramps, Ltd. is just what it sounds: a motley crew of ragged, foul-smelling tramps, who specialize in dunning particularly evasive debtors. The tramps are really otherwise respectable chaps, dressed in disgusting clothes and treated with a special stomach churning chemical" (*Economist*, 1979:104). Their technique is simply to sit around the victim's office or home until he or she signs a check. Not to be outdone, a debt-collecting firm in Bombay, India, is employing six eunuchs who threaten to remove their saris if the defaulters do not pay up. The eunuchs' arrival at a debtor's home or office usually ensures he pays his debt rather than be embarrassed in front of colleagues or neighbors (*Vancouver Sun*, 1999:E3).

Another unusual and ingenious dunning technique has been successfully used by Paragon Cable of New York on customers who were reluctant to pay their cable-television bill. Instead of cutting off service completely, Paragon filled each of its 77 channels with C-SPAN's programming. Collection of overdue balances has improved dramatically since the company started its constant bombardment by the public-affairs network specializing in live broadcasts of the proceedings of the U.S. Senate and the House of Representatives (*U.S. News & World Report*, 1995:14).

When such dunning efforts fail and creditors have exhausted nonlitigation alternatives, they are likely to sue. A characteristic of most civil suits for debt is that the plaintiff usually wins by default. Most defendants are not represented by counsel. In fact, many of them are not present when their cases are heard. Their absence is treated as an admission of the validity of the claim, and a default judgment is entered against them. Such judgments are rendered in over 90 percent of consumer cases (Caplovitz, 1974:220–221).

There are a number of reasons why defendants fail to respond to summons and to appear in court. Some recognize the validity of the creditor's claim and see no point in attempting to contest it or cannot afford an attorney to do so (Kagan, 1984). Others may simply find it impossible to leave work (with consequent loss of pay), travel to court, and spend most of the day waiting for their cases to be called. The fact that most courts are open from 9 A.M. to 5 P.M., hours when most debtors are at work, further contributes to default judgments. At times, the wording of a summons is so complicated and obtuse that many debtors simply cannot grasp what is at stake, or that they must appear if they are to avoid a default judgment. Others simply do not know that they are being sued. Instead of properly serving the summons, process servers in some areas (because of the inability to locate debtors or the fear of going into certain neighborhoods) destroy it and claim it has been served. Although accurate statistics on the frequency of such "sewer service" do not exist, it is evidently commonplace in many cities (Caplovitz, 1974:193–195). These individuals learn the hard way about suits against them—when a garnishment or eviction notice is served.

A similar situation but with much greater consequences existed in South Africa until late 1995. A creditor would go to court complaining that he had not been paid. A judge would then issue a judgment against the debtor and a request for payment. If the debtor did not pay within 10 days, the judge would hold the debtor in contempt of the court and send him or her to jail for up to three months. But many debtors, just like in the United States, were never even aware of the court proceedings. In some cases, debtors were illiterate and did not comprehend what was going on. Often, the first sign of trouble was when the police van showed up to take them to prison. The imprisonment of debtors has been very common, almost always involving the poor. In the late 1980s, for example, one-tenth of South Africa's prison population has been incarcerated because of debt. It should be noted, however, that by one criterion—payment of outstanding obligations—the system of imprisoning debtors was rather effective. Most people paid off their creditors within days. Studies showed that while the average contempt sentence was 31 days, the average debtor spent only 9 days in jail. Most of the time, the incarceration of the debtor set off a family-wide scramble to come up with the money (Daley, 1995).

Although I have focused on suits for debts, there are a number of other important types of actions initiated by organizations against individuals. Real estate companies regularly initiate legal action in the form of evictions against unknown thousands of tenants. The Internal Revenue Service continuously files suits against individuals (and at times organizations) for back taxes or for tax evasion. Radio and television stations regularly use the courts to settle disputes with former announcers or disc jockeys who have decided to join competing stations, contrary to the desires of their former employers. In the final section, I shall consider disputes between organizations.

DISPUTES BETWEEN ORGANIZATIONS

There are two general types of organizational conflicts: (1) conflict between groups within the organization and (2) conflict between organizations. For example, interorganizational conflict within a university includes disputes between the faculty and administration over issues of collective bargaining, unionization, faculty freedom, and staff reduction based on alleged financial exigencies (Kaplin and Lee, 1995; Westin and Feliu, 1988). Interorganizational conflict is exemplified by disputes between the university and the community over matters of zoning, land use, and tax-exempt status, or between the university and the federal government concerning compliance with federal regulations, such as occupational safety, pollution, and civil rights.

Although the emphasis in this section is on interorganizational disputes, the generalizations that will be made are, of course, applicable to intraorganizational disputes. Such disputes may arise between private firms, between private firms and government, between government agencies, and between public-interest groups and private firms or government, or both. After a brief consideration of the various types of interorganizational disputes, I will examine in greater depth the activities of public-interest law firms in environmental disputes. At this point it should be noted that although most environmental offenses are processed by regulatory agencies and corrected by civil and administrative remedies, there is an increased "criminalization" of environmental wrongs (see, for example, Situ and Emmons, 2001) and the trend is likely to continue.

Disputes between organizations cover a wide spectrum of participants and controversies. Businesspeople may take their disagreements to court over contract interpretation, trademarks, or alleged patent infringements. The federal government is involved as a plaintiff in suits to acquire land needed for federal projects (highways, dams, parks, buildings) which the acquiring agency is unable to purchase through negotiation, in actions to force private companies to comply with contracts with federal agencies, and in suits brought under the antitrust statutes. Disputes between the government and private firms arise over matters of licensing and regulation, labor relations, Sunday closing laws, and governmental contracts. The government is often the defendant in cases involving zoning and land use, location of public housing projects, and tax reassessment.

In recent decades, complex public-policy disputes and regulatory disputes stemming from the government's regulation of the economic and social systems have become more pronounced. The regulation of economic activities has become pervasive, and it involves important decisions about the distribution of goods and services.

Social-policy disputes develop when the government pursues broad national objectives that may involve or impinge upon many interests and groups, such as racial equality and economic opportunity, environmental protection, income security, and public health and safety. Examples of agencies with such objectives are the Occupational Safety and Health Administration, the Equal Employment Opportunity Commission, and the Environmental Protection Agency. In fact, all large-scale social welfare programs—cash transfers, food stamps, housing, health, and education—generate similar complex public-policy disputes (Ford Foundation, 1978:3).

Regulatory disputes frequently involve difficult technical questions, whereas social-policy disputes raise difficult political and value questions. In both types of disputes, information about important variables is often incomplete or inaccurate, effects of alternative choices are hard to ascertain, and often there are no easy answers to cost-benefit questions or to questions of trade-offs among various interests. The various regulatory agencies discussed in Chapter 3, in addition to major policy issues, also process large numbers of routine disputes. For example, the Civil Aeronautics Board (CAB), in addition to allocating airline routes (large complex disputes), in any given year will also handle thousands of passenger and shipper complaints, tariff applications, and referrals. The Securities and Exchange Commission (SEC), in addition to a number of formal hearings annually, also rules on thousands of registration statements.

In many instances, the formal quasi-adjudicative procedures used by regulatory agencies are ill-suited to resolving large and complex disputes. Delays in settling disputes are frequent, and the situation is further compounded by the fact that some agencies traditionally engaged in economic regulations are now being asked to consider environmental claims as well. The regulatory process, in a sense, encourages conflict, rather than acting to reconcile opposing interests. When agencies grant licenses, set rates, or determine the safety of drugs, they often allow the parties to the proceedings to have a full adversary hearing with impartial decision makers, formal records, and rights of cross-examination and appeal. This leads the parties to approach the agency as if they were in a lawsuit.

Public-Interest Law Firms in Environmental Disputes

Since the mid-1960s, the types of activities associated with Ralph Nader and his consumer organizations and Centers for Law in the Public Interest (Reske, 1994), with the Sierra Club and its environmental programs, and with a new institutional form embodied in law firms that characterize their activities as partly or wholly "public interest" law and "cause lawyering" (Sarat and Scheingold, 1998) have proliferated. Law students founded the National Association for Public Interest Law (NAPIL) in 1986 to create more opportunities for students and lawyers interested in this area of the law. There are 131

NAPIL chapters, and three-fourths of ABA-accredited law schools have them (Vargas and Bushnell, 1995). NAPIL also offers the Fellowships for Equal Justice to encourage law students to go into public-interest law but cannot because of their large law school debt. Undoubtedly, more law students would enter public-interest law if there were a comprehensive, nationally funded loan forgiveness program for students entering the public-interest field where they make less than half of what their classmates earn in large firms (Hoye, 1995).

Public-interest law is the term frequently used to describe the activities of the foundation-supported law firms that represent environmentalists and consumer and like groups, as well as test-case litigation in civil rights and poverty controversies. It is generally oriented toward causes and interests of groups, classes, or organizations, rather than individuals (Handler, 1976:99). Although public-interest law firms engage in activities such as lobbying, reporting, public relations, and counseling, litigation is by far their most important activity. Education, employment discrimination, consumer problems, and environmental problems are the four areas that account for the largest proportion of their activities.

Educational controversies include school financing, legal rights of students and parents, bilingual education, special education, the political activity of teachers and various forms of politically "incorrect" activities (Leatherman, 1994). Employment discrimination activities consist of class-action suits against private and public discriminators and the government agencies responsible for enforcing fair employment laws. A typical lawsuit seeks to establish affirmative action plans for minorities or women in hiring and promotion. Consumer matters include attacks on import restrictions to lower costs to the consumer and to improve quality, product safety, and guarantee and warranty practices.

After civil liberties, environmental defense generates the highest volume of cases for public-interest law firms (Aron, 1989:26). Private groups often use the courts to pursue better environmental quality (Naysnerski and Tietenberg, 1992). For example, a group of environmental lawyers is exploring novel legal strategies to adopt against global warming (Seelye, 2001). Public environmental enforcement can occur at the federal level through administrative proceedings, or through either civil or criminal judicial action. Several of the foundation-supported firms, such as the Natural Resources Defense Council and the Environmental Defense Fund, concentrate exclusively on this area, whereas other firms, such as the Center for Law and Social Policy, devote substantial resources to this type of work (Trubek, 1978:151). Public-interest lawyers have been active in a variety of environmental domains. They have challenged dams and other water resources projects, raised questions about nuclear power plants, attacked the pricing policies of electric utilities, stopped the use of dangerous pesticides, and sought to improve enforcement of such major environmental statutes as the National Environmental Policy Act, the Clear Air Act, and the Federal Water Pollution Control Act. Accounts of environmental policy disputes regularly fill the daily press (see, for example, Almeida and Stearns, 1998). Disputes include such questions as "Shall we expand or contract our programs for flood control and stream channelization? Should we relax or tighten the rules governing air pollution? Should we build a dam on a scenic stream, or allow nuclear energy plants to damage aquatic life in the natural bodies of water they use for cooling?" (Trubek, 1978:152).

Environmental disputes typically fall into two broad categories—enforcement and permitting cases. Enforcement disputes come about when a public-interest group raises questions about a party's compliance with certain state or federal law setting specific environmental standards, such as air or water quality. Permitting cases involve disputes over the planned construction of new facilities, such as a dam or an airport. Environmental disputes are also different from more traditional disputes in several ways: Irreversible ecological damages may be involved; at least one party to the dispute may claim to represent broader public interest—including the interests of inanimate objects, wildlife, and unborn generations; and the instrumentation of a court decision may pose special problems (what will happen to the community if the major employer is forced to close a factory responsible for water pollution) (Goldberg et al., 1985:403–404).

The background of the actors in environmental disputes may also be different. Unlike those involved in many other disputes involving racial discrimination in schools, housing, or employment, environmentalists do not come from oppressed groups. In fact, they tend to draw most of their support from the white middle class. More often than not, their commitment is born of ideology rather than of pressing social or economic need. Consequently, environmental disputes seem to lack the immediacy of disputes in other areas. Often, they go on for years. Unlike in other disputes, delay favors the dissidents, and environmentalists prefer to postpone as long as possible decisions involving, for example, permits to construct new facilities.

Over the years, there has been a steady growth in the number of environmental disputes in the United States as well as in all other advanced industrialized countries (Heidenheimer et al., 1990:308–344). This phenomenon can be attributed to the significant increase in public awareness that our civilization causes substantial and possibly irreparable damage to the natural environment and to the growing significance of public action affecting the environment. Consequently, the recognition of the costs society pays for environmental damage and the failure of companies to internalize environmental costs lead to a proliferation of regulatory laws designed to protect the natural environment. Many environmental controversies are about the extent to which the government should regulate private-sector decisions that are considered contributive factors in environmental degradation (Rabe, 1991). At the same time, the government itself is also a potential cause of environmental damages. Public programs of many types, from flood control to mineral leasing, have a potential for environmental damage.

Environmental disputes are further complicated by the establishment of a number of mission-oriented government agencies, such as the Army Corps of Engineers and the various highway departments. These agencies are set up to carry out programs: build dams, construct highways, or develop nuclear power. Such activities may cause environmental harm, but if an agency recognizes this harm, it will be forced to curtail its own activities and thus undermine, at least in part, the justification for its existence. At the same time, since these activities are perfectly lawful, they tend to magnify the advantages of those organized groups that favor development and to increase the obstacles facing environmental groups that set out to challenge agency decisions (Trubek, 1978:157). Much environmental advocacy occurs in complex policy disputes. In many such disputes, the resources available to environmental advocates may be insufficient to ensure that their concerns receive the degree of attention from decision makers that they would if the full extent of their demands were reflected in their representational resources.

SUMMARY

Starting with the basic premise that disagreements are ubiquitous in social relationships, this chapter has reviewed and analyzed the role of law as a method of dispute resolution. It was demonstrated that there is no consensus in the sociological and legal literature on the terminology concerning the role of law in controversies. The concepts of conflict resolution and dispute settlement were used interchangeably to show how the law resolves the legal components of conflict and disputes. It was repeatedly emphasized that the law does not deal with the underlying causes of conflict and does not reduce tension or antagonism between the aggrieved parties.

Nonlegal methods of dispute resolution include violence, rituals, shaming and ostracism, supernatural agencies, "lumping it," avoidance, negotiation, mediation, and arbitration. In industrialized countries, such as the United States, lumping behavior, avoidance, and negotiation are the most frequent responses to dispute situations. Adjudication is a public and formal method of dispute resolution and is best exemplified by courts. Court decisions have an either-or character, and the adversary nature of court proceedings forces disputes into the mold of a two-party conflict.

As a result of social developments, the increased availability of legal mechanisms for conflict resolution, and the creation of legally actionable rights and remedies, there is a growing demand for court services in dispute resolution. Data indicate that litigation rates in the United States have increased substantially during the last two decades. There are some authors, however, who challenge the notion that the dispute-processing function of the courts has increased in recent years as a result of social and economic changes. There are obvious difficulties in measuring litigation rates over time, and similar problems exist in cross-cultural studies of litigation rates.

Courts provide a forum for the settlement of a variety of private and public disputes. To qualify for the use of court services, at the minimum plaintiffs must be able to demonstrate justiciability and standing. Those who have only occasional recourse to the courts are called one-shotters, and those who are engaged in many similar litigations over time are designated as repeat players. There are four combinations of litigations: one-shotter versus one-shotter, repeat player versus one-shotter, one-shotter versus repeat player, and repeat player versus repeat player.

Most individual disputes involve one-shotters. Such disputes include private litigation as opposed to organizations, criminal defendants, or state agencies. Because litigation is costly and time-consuming, courts often make an effort to encourage disputants to settle their differences by agreement. A preference for continuing relations will not, in general, deter individuals from litigation. Those disputants who are better organized and have more expandable resources fare better in litigations.

Disputes between individuals and organizations may take place over economic issues, claims for damages and restitution, issues of civil rights, and issues concerning organizational actions, procedures, and policy. In general, more organizations are plaintiffs and more individuals are defendants, and organizations tend to be uniformly more successful than individuals.

For disputes initiated by individuals against organizations, law as a method of conflict resolution in academe was used as an illustration. Faculty and student-initiated lawsuits against the university were considered in the context of faculty-administration, student-faculty, and student-administration relations.

Disputes between individuals and organizations where organizations are the plaintiffs were analyzed in the context of creditor-debtor relationships. When nonlegal methods of collection fail, creditors are likely to enlist the courts in the collection process. Of the legal devices available for collecting the judgments, garnishment of wages is used most frequently. A characteristic of most civil suits for debts is that the plaintiff usually wins by default.

Disputes between organizations cover a wide spectrum of participants and controversies. In interorganizational disputes, the activities of public-interest law firms in environmental disputes were examined. In general, the party that is better organized with greater resources and greater capacity to generate data will have a higher probability of influencing the outcome of the dispute.

SUGGESTED FURTHER READINGS

NAN ARON, *Liberty and Justice for All: Public Interest Law in the 1980s and Beyond*. Boulder, CO: Westview Press, 1989. A good and still timely description of public-interest law and the mission of public-interest lawyers.

JEROLD A. AUERBACH, *Justice without Law?* New York: Oxford University Press, 1983. An outstanding review of nonjudicial methods of dispute resolution in a historical context.

CARL BOGUS, *Why Lawsuits Are Good for America: Disciplined Democracy, Big Business, and the Common Law*. New York: New York University Press, 2001. The author argues litigation serves a variety of protective and productive functions and that law is a careful, conservative, and self-correcting system. A perspective not often found in the social sciences.

ANTHONY BRADNEY and FIONA COWNIE. *Living Without Law: Alternative Dispute Resolution in Practice*. Brookfield, VT: Ashgate, 2000. A review of nonconflictual forms of dispute resolution from the perspective of legal anthropology.

STEPHEN B. GOLDBERG, FRANK E. A. SANDER, and NANCY H. ROGERS, *Dispute Resolution: Negotiation, Mediation, and Other Processes*. 3rd ed. Gaithersburg, MD: Aspen Law & Business, 1999. An analysis and application of various conventional and not-so-conventional techniques of dispute processing.

WILLIAM A. KAPLIN and BARBARA A. LEE, *The Law of Higher Education*. 3rd ed. San Francisco, CA: Jossey-Bass Publishers, 1995. A comprehensive 1000-page plus guide to legal implications of administrative decision making in an increasingly legalistic and litigious academic climate.

LOUIS KRIESBERG, *Constructive Conflicts: From Escalation to Resolution*. Lanham, MD: Rowman & Littlefield Publishers, Inc. 1998. A comprehensive analysis of all kinds of conflicts and their resolutions from a variety of perspectives that supplements and compliments the legal approach.

PAT LAUDERDALE and MICHAEL CRUIT. *The Struggle for Control: A Study of Law, Disputes, and Deviance*. New York: State University of New York Press, 1993. A detailed examination of nine land disputes in Costa Rica as expressions of underlying structural problems.

LAW & SOCIETY REVIEW 15 (3–4) 1980–1981. A special issue on dispute processing and civil litigation.

ROY J. LEWICKI, STEPHEN WEISS, and David Lewin, "Models of Conflict, Negotiation and Third Party Intervention: A Review and Synthesis," *Journal of Organizational Behavior* 13 (3) (May) 1992. A seminal review article identifying 44 major models in the area of conflict, negotiation, and third-party processes such as mediation and arbitration.

MIRIAM K. MILLS, ED., *Alternative Dispute Resolution in the Public Sector*. Chicago: Nelson-Hall, 1991. A collection of symposium papers on conflict-resolution approaches in labor relations, environmental issues, rule making, and related conflicts.

WALTER K. OLSON, *The Litigation Explosion*. New York: Dutton, 1991. A discussion of the changes that took place after America deregulated the business of litigation in the 1970s.

MICHAEL PALMER and SIMON ROBERTS, *Dispute Processes: ADR and the Primary Forms of Decision Making*. London: Butterworths, 1998. An up-to-date cross-cultural overview of ADR.

KONSTANZE PLETT and CATHERINE S. MESCHIEVITZ, eds., *Beyond Disputing: Exploring Legal Culture in Five European Countries*. Baden-Baden, Germany: Nomos Verlagsgesellschaft, 1991. A collection of articles on dispute processing in five Western European countries.

REFERENCES

ABEL, RICHARD L. 1973. "*A Comparative Theory of Dispute Institutions in Society*," Law & Society Review 8 (2) (Winter): 217–347.

RICHARD L. ABEL (ED.). 1995. *The Law & Society Reader*. New York: New York University Press.

ADMINISTRATIVE CONFERENCE OF THE UNITED STATES. 1987. *Sourcebook: Federal Agency Use of Alternative Means of Dispute Resolution.* (Office of the Chairman).

ADMINISTRATIVE OFFICE OF THE U.S. COURTS. 1995. *Federal Judicial Workload Statistics.* Washington, DC: The Administrative Office of the U.S. Courts.

ALMEIDA, PAUL and LINDA BREWSTER STEARNS. 1998. "Political Opportunities and Local Grassroots Environmental Movements: The Case of Minamata," *Social Problems,* 45 (1) (February): 37–57.

AMERICAN BAR ASSOCIATION. 2002. *Dispute Resolution Program Directory.* Washington, DC: American Bar Association.

AMERICAN TORT REFORM ASSOCIATION. 1992. "Scapegoat Litigation Will Drain U.S. Economy an Average of $17.8 Billion Annually," press release (August 5).

ARON, NAN. 1989. *Liberty and Justice for All: Public Interest Law in the 1980s and Beyond.* Boulder, CO: Westview Press.

AUBERT, VILHELM. 1963. "Competition and Dissensus: Two Types of Conflict and Conflict Resolution," *Journal of Conflict Resolution* 7 (1): 26–42. 1969. "Law as a Way of Resolving Conflicts: The Case of a Small Industrialized Society." Pp. 282–303 in Laura Nader (ed.), *Law in Culture and Society.* Chicago: Aldine.

BARTON, JOHN H. 1975. "Behind the Legal Explosion," *Stanford Law Review* 27 (February): 567–584.

BELL, KIM. 1995. "Prisoners Can Now Lose More Than Their Lawsuits," *St. Louis Post-Dispatch* (July 6): 1, 9.

BELLINGHAM HERALD, THE. 2001. "Lawsuits a Volume Business at Wal-Mart" (August 19): E1, E.3.

BEST, ARTHUR, AND A. ANDREASEN. 1976. *Talking Back to Business: Voiced and Unvoiced Consumer Complaints.* Washington, DC: Center for the Study of Responsive Law.

BLACK, DONALD. 1976. *The Behavior of Law.* New York: Academic Press. 1989. *Sociological Justice.* New York: Oxford University Press.

BLEGVAD, BRITT-MARI. 1983. "Accessibility and Dispute Treatment: The Case of the Consumer in Denmark." Pp. 203–219 in Maureen Cain and Kalman Kulcsar (eds.), *Disputes and the Law.* Budapest: Akademiai Kiado.

BOGUS, CARL. 2001. *Why Lawsuits Are Good for America: Disciplined Democracy, Big Business, and the Common Law.* New York: New York University Press.

BRADNEY, ANTHONY and FIONA COWNIE, 2000. *Living Without Law: Alternative Dispute Resolution in Practice.* Brookfield, VT: Ashgate.

CAPLOVITZ, DAVID. 1974. *Consumers in Trouble: A Study of Debtors in Default.* New York: Free Press.

CHINLOY, PETER. 1989. *The Cost of Doing Business: Legal and Regulatory Issues in the United States and Abroad.* New York: Praeger.

COBB, SARA. 1997. "The Domestication of Violence in Mediation," *Law & Society Review* 31 (3): 397–440.

CHRONICLE OF HIGHER EDUCATION. 1989. " 'In' Box" (January 25): A14.

CROSON, RACHEL and ROBERT H. MNOOKIN. 1997. "Does Disputing Through Agents Enhance Cooperation? Experimental Evidence," *Journal of Legal Studies,* XXVI (June): 331–348.

COLLIER, JANE FISHBURNE. 1973. *Law and Social Change in Zinacantan.* Stanford, CA: Stanford University Press.

CROSS, FRANK B. 1992. "The First Thing We Do, Let's Kill All the Economists: An Empirical Evaluation of the Effect of Lawyers on the United States Economy and Political System," *Texas Law Review* 70 (3) (February): 645–683.

CURRAN, BARBARA A. 1986. "American Lawyers in the 1980s: A Profession in Transition," *Law & Society Review* 20 (1): 19–52.

DALEY, SUZANNE. 1995. "Court Tells South Africa to Stop Imprisoning Debtors." *New York Times* (October 1): A4.

DANZIG, RICHARD. 1973. "Toward the Creation of a Complementary, Decentralized System of Criminal Justice," *Stanford Law Review* 26 (1): 1–54.

DILWORTH, DONALD C. 1995. "Prisoners' Lawsuits Burden Federal Civil Courts," *Trial* 31 (5) (May): 98–100.

ECKHOFF, TORSTEIN. 1978. "The Mediator: The Judge and the Administrator in Conflict-Resolution." Pp. 31–41 in Sheldon Goldman and Austin Sarat (eds.), *American Court Systems: Readings in Judicial Process and Behavior*. San Francisco: W. H. Freeman & Company Publishers.

ECONOMIST. 1979. "The Odour of Solvency," 273 (7101) (October 6): 104. 1993. "Paper Stockade: Lawyers in Japan," 328 (7823) (August 7): 60–62. 1998 "Abortion and Extortion," 347 (8065) (April 25): 32.

EHRMANN, HENRY W. 1976. *Comparative Legal Cultures*. Englewood Cliffs, NJ: Prentice Hall.

EPP, CHARLES R. 1992. "'Honey, They Shrunk the Economy!' An Empirical Examination of the Claim that Lawyers Impair Economic Growth." Working Paper DPRP 11–2 (March). Madison: University of Wisconsin, Institute for Legal Studies.

FELSTINER, WILLIAM L. F. 1974. "Influences of Social Organization on Dispute Processing," *Law & Society Review* 9 (1) (Fall): 63–94. 1975. "Avoidance as Dispute Processing: An Elaboration," *Law & Society Review* 9 (4) (Summer): 695–706.

FINE, ERIKA S. (ED.). 1988. *Containing Legal Costs: ADR Strategies for Corporations, Law Firms, and Government*. New York: Butterworth.

FITZPATRICK, ROBERT B. 1994. "Nonbinding Mediation of Employment Disputes," *Trial*, 30 (6) (June): 40–44.

FORD FOUNDATION. 1978. *New Approaches to Conflict Resolution*. New York: Ford Foundation.

FRANCE, MIKE. 1995. "More Businesses Ask: Can We Talk, Not Sue?," *National Law Journal*, 17 (28) (March 13): B1. 2001. "The Litigation Machine," *Business Week* (January 29): 116–123.

FRIEDMAN, LAWRENCE M. 1973. *A History of American Law*. New York: Simon & Schuster. 1985. *Total Justice*. New York: Russell Sage Foundation.

FRIEDMAN, LAWRENCE M., and STEWART MACAULAY. 1977. *Law and the Behavioral Sciences*. 2nd ed. Indianapolis: Bobbs-Merrill.

FRIEDMAN, LAWRENCE M., and ROBERT V. PERCIVAL. 1976. "A Tale of Two Courts: Litigation in Alameda and San Benito Counties," *Law & Society Review* 10 (1 and 2): 267–302.

FRUM, DAVID. 1993. "Free to Sue," *Forbes* 151 (11) (May 24): 90–91.

GAILLARD, EMMANUAL. 2000. "Alternative Dispute Resolution (ADR) A La Francaise," *New York Law Journal* (June 1): 1–3.

GALANTER, MARC. 1974. "Why the 'Haves' Come out Ahead: Speculations on the Limits of Legal Change," *Law & Society Review* 9 (1): 95–160. 1975. "Afterword: Explaining Litigation," *Law & Society Review* 9 (2): 347–368. 1988. "Beyond the Litigation Panic." Pp. 18–30 in Walter Olson (ed.), *New Directions in Liability Law*. New York: The Academy of Political Science. 1992. "The Debased Debate on Civil Justice." Working Paper DPRP (May). Madison: University of Wisconsin, Institute for Legal Studies.

1993. "News From Nowhere: The Debased Debate on Civil Justice," *Denver University Law Review* 71 (1): 77–113.

GERSON, STUART M. 1994. "Computers Generate Litigation Explosion," *National Law Journal* 16 (31) (April 4): A17.

GLABERSON, WILLIAM, 2001. "A Study's Verdict: Jury Awards Are Not Out Of Control," *New York Times* (August 6): A1.

GLENDON, MARY ANN. 1991. *The Rights Talk: The Impoverishment of Political Discourse.* New York: Free Press.

GOLDBERG, STEPHEN B., FRANK E. A. SANDER, and NANCY H. ROGERS. 1999 *Dispute Resolution: Negotiation, Mediation, and Other Processes.* 3rd ed. Gaithersburg, MD: Aspen Law & Business, 1999.

GOLDMAN, SHELDON, and AUSTIN SARAT (EDS.). 1978. *American Court Systems: Readings in Judicial Process and Behavior.* San Francisco: W. H. Freeman & Company Publishers.

GREENHOUSE, CAROL J. 1989. "Interpreting American Litigiousness." Pp. 252–273 in June Starr and Jane F. Collier (eds.), *History and Power in the Study of Law: New Directions in Legal Anthropology.* Ithaca, NY: Cornell University Press.

GROSSMAN, JOEL B., and AUSTIN SARAT. 1975. "Litigation in Federal Courts: A Comparative Perspective," *Law & Society Review* 9 (2): 321–346.

GUBSER, NICHOLAS J. 1965. *The Nunamiut Eskimos: Hunters of Caribou.* New Haven: Yale University Press.

GULLIVER, P. H. 1969. "Introduction to Case Studies of Law in Non-Western Societies." Pp. 11–23 in Laura Nader (ed.), *Law in Culture and Society.* Chicago: Aldine. 1979. *Disputes and Negotiations: A Cross-Cultural Perspective.* New York: Academic Press.

HAGERDON, ANN. 1989. "Judges, Immune No More, Seek Malpractice Insurance," *Wall Street Journal* (July 26): 1B.

HANDLER, JOEL F. 1976. "Public Interest Law: Problems and Prospects." Pp. 99–115 in Murray L. Schwartz (ed.), *Law and the American Future.* Englewood Cliffs, NJ: Prentice Hall.

HAZARD, GEOFFREY C. 1994. "Liability Coverage May Become Impossible to Obtain Under Traditional Procedures," *National Law Journal* 16 (28) (March): A17.

HEIDENHEIMER, ARNOLD J., HUGH HELCO, and CAROLYN TEICH ADAMS. 1990. *Comparative Public Policy: The Politics of Social Choice in America, Europe and Japan.* New York: St. Martin's Press.

HIRSCHMAN, ALBERT O. 1970. *Exit, Voice, and Loyalty: Responses to Decline in Firms, Organizations, and States.* Cambridge: Harvard University Press.

HOEBEL, E. ADAMSON. 1954. *The Law of Primitive Man: A Study in Comparative Legal Dynamics.* Cambridge: Harvard University Press.

HOYE, WILLIAM P. 1995. "High Cost of Doing Good; More Law Grads Would Enter Public Service with Loan-Forgiveness Plan," *ABA Journal* 81 (January): 96–97.

JACOB, HERBERT. 1969. *Debtors in Court: The Consumption of Government Services.* Chicago: Rand McNally.

JACOB, MARGARET A. 1995. "Reliable Data About Lawsuits Are Very Scarce," *Wall Street Journal* (June 9): B1, B2.

KAGAN, ROBERT A. 1984. "The Routinization of Debt Collection: An Essay on Social Change and Conflict in Courts," *Law & Society Review* 18 (3): 323–371.

KAPLIN, WILLIAM A. and BARBARA E. LEE. 1995. *The Law of Higher Education.* 3rd ed. San Francisco, CA: Jossey-Bass Publishers.

KARSTEN, PETER. 1998. "Cows in the Corn, Pigs in the Garden, and 'the Problem of Social Costs': 'High' and 'Low' Legal Cultures of the British Diaspora Lands in the 17th, 18th, and 19th Centuries," *Law & Society Review* 32 (1): 63–92.

KAWASHIMA, TAKEYOSHI. 1969. "Dispute Resolution in Japan." Pp. 182–193 in Vilhelm Aubert (ed.), *Sociology of Law*. Harmondsworth, England: Penguin Books, Ltd.

KORS, ALAN CHARLES and HARVEY A. SILVERGLATE. 1998. *The Shadow University: The Betrayal of Liberty on America's Campuses*. New York: The Free Press.

KRIESBERG, LOUIS. 1982. *Social Conflicts*. Englewood Cliffs, NJ: Prentice Hall. 1998. *Constructive Conflicts: From Escalation to Resolution*. Lanham, MD: Rowman & Littlefield Publishers, Inc.

KRITZER, HERBERT M. 1988. "Political Culture and the 'Propensity to Sue'," Working Papers Series 9. Institute For Legal Studies. University of Wisconsin 9 (1) (July): 1–50. 1991. "Propensity to Sue in England and the United States of America: Blaming and Claiming in Tort Cases," *Journal of Law and Society* 18 (4) (Winter): 400–427.

LADD, EVERETT C., JR., and SEYMOUR MARTIN LIPSET. 1973. *Professors, Unions and American Higher Education*. Domestic Affairs Study 16. Washington DC: American Enterprise Institute for Public Policy Research.

LAUDERDALE, PAT and MICHAEL CRUIT. 1993. *The Struggle for Control: A Study of Law, Disputes, and Deviance*. New York: State University of New York Press.

LAUTER, DAVID. 1986. "Report Says Litigation Explosion Is a 'Myth'," *National Law Journal* (April 28): 46.

LEATHERMAN, COURTNEY. 1994. "A Public-Interest Law Firm Aims to Defend the Politically Incorrect," *The Chronicle of Higher Education* 41 (13) (November 23): A18–A20.

LEESON, SUSAN M., and BRYAN M. JOHNSTON. 1988. *Ending It: Dispute Resolution in America*. Cincinnati: Anderson Publishing Company.

LEMPERT, RICHARD. 1978. "More Tales of Two Courts: Exploring Changes in the 'Dispute Settlement Function' of Trial Courts," *Law & Society Review* 13 (1) (Fall): 91–138.

LEMPERT, RICHARD, and JOSEPH SANDERS. 1986. *An Invitation to Law and Social Science*. New York: Longman.

LEWICKI, ROY J., STEPHEN WEISS, and DAVID LEWIN. 1992. "Models of Conflict, Negotiation and Third Party Intervention: A Review and Synthesis," *Journal of Organizational Behavior* 13 (3) (May): 209–252.

LORD, WILLIAM, LEONARD ADELMAN, PAUL WEHR, ET AL. 1978. *Conflict Management in Federal Water Resource Planning*. Boulder: Institute of Behavioral Science, University of Colorado.

MACAULAY, STEWART. 1969. "Non-Contractual Relations in Business." Pp. 194–209 in Vilhelm Aubert (ed.), *Sociology of Law*. Harmondsworth, England: Penguin Books, Ltd.

MCGILLIS, DANIEL. 1982. "Minor Dispute Processing: A Review of Recent Developments." In Roman Tomasic and Malcolm M. Feeley (eds.), *Neighborhood Justice: Assessment of an Emerging Idea*. New York: Longman.

MAGEE, STEPHEN P., WILLIAM A. BROCK, and LESLIE YOUNG. 1989. *Black Hole Tariffs and Endogenous Policy Theory: Political Economy in General Equilibrium*. Cambridge: Cambridge University Press.

MANNING, CARL. 1995. "Legal Party's Over, Inmates Told: Attorney General Clamps Down on Frivolous Suits," *St. Louis Post-Dispatch* (September 6): 1B.

MARSHALL, TONY F. 1985. *Alternatives to Criminal Courts*. Hampshire, England: Gower.

MICELI, THOMAS J. 1998. "Settlement Strategies," *The Journal of Legal Studies*, XXVII (2) (June): 473–482.

MOOG, ROBERT. 1993. "Indian Litigiousness and the Litigation Explosion," *Asian Survey* 33 (12) (December): 1136–1151.

MORGAN, RICHARD E. 1984. *Disabling America: The "Rights Industry" in Our Time*. New York: Basic Books.

NADER, LAURA, and HARRY F. TODD, JR. (EDS.). 1978. "Introduction." Pp. 1–40 in *The Disputing Process—Law in Ten Societies*. New York: Columbia University Press.

NAYSNERSKI, WENDY, and TOM TIETENBERG. 1992. "Private Enforcement of Federal Environmental Law," *Law Economics* 68 (1) (February): 28–48.

NEW YORK TIMES. 1986A. "Staying out of Court," August 31, 1F. 1986b. "Suing the Clergy," (September 2): 1F. 1995. "Wrong Direction on Malpractice," (July 16): 14E.

NEWSWEEK. 1995. "Slammer Suits," (August 7): 6.

OLSON, WALTER K. 1991. *The Litigation Explosion*. New York: Dutton.

O'REILLY, ROBERT C., and EDWARD T. GREEN. 1992. *School Law for the 1990s: A Handbook*. New York: Greenwood Press.

PAGE, CLARENCE. 1989. "Filing Suit Means Never Saying 'Sorry'," *St. Louis Post-Dispatch*, (August 19): 3B.

PALMER, MICHAEL and SIMON ROBERTS. 1998. *Dispute Processes: ADR and the Primary Forms of Decision Making*. London: Butterworths.

PALMER, STACY E. 1985. "Supreme Court Curbs Judges' Right to Overturn Academic Decisions." *Chronicle of Higher Education* (December 18): 1–33.

PLETT, KONSTANZE, and CATHERINE S. MESCHIEVITZ (EDS.). 1991. *Beyond Disputing: Exploring Legal Culture in Five European Countries*. Baden-Baden, Germany: Nomos Verlagsgesellschaft.

POLINSKY, MITCHELL and DANIEL L. RUBINFELD. 1998. "Does the English Rule Discourage Low-Probability-of-Prevailing Plaintiffs?," *Journal of Legal Studies*, XXVII (January): 141–160.

POOR, TIM. 1990. "Lawyer Sues Lawyer For Buttock Bite," *St. Louis Post-Dispatch* (April 19): 6.

POSNER, RICHARD A. 1996. *The Federal Courts: Challenge and Reform*. Cambridge: Harvard University Press.

PRESIDENT'S COUNCIL ON COMPETITIVENESS. 1991. *Agenda for Civil Justice Reform in America: A Report from the President's Council on Competitiveness*. Washington, DC: The Council (August).

RABE, BARRY G. 1991. "Impediments to Environmental Dispute Resolution in the American Political Context." Pp. 143–163 in Miriam K. Mills (ed.), *Alternative Dispute Resolution in the Public Sector*. Chicago: Nelson-Hall.

RAIFFA, HOWARD. 1997. *Lectures on Negotiation Analysis*. Cambridge, MA: PON Books.

RESKE, HENRY J. 1994. "Ralph Nader's New Project: Law Centers to Help the Small Group Instead of the Little Guy," *ABA Journal*, 80 (May): 32–33.

RESKE, HENRY J. 1995. "Victim-Offender Mediation Catching On: Advocates Say Programs, Typically for Nonviolent Offenders, Benefit Both Parties," *ABA Journal* 81 (February): 14–16.

RITZER, GEORGE. 2001. *Explorations in the Sociology of Consumption: Fast Food, Credit Cards and Casinos*. Thousand Oaks, CA: Sage Publications.

ROBERTS, SIMON. 1979. *Order and Dispute: An Introduction to Legal Anthropology*. New York: St. Martin's Press.

ROSEN, JEFFREY, 2001. "In Lieu of Manners," *New York Times Magazine* (February 4): 49–51.

ROSS, WILLIAM H. and DONALD E. CONLON. 2000. "Hybrid Forms of Third-Party Dispute Resolution: Theoretical Implications of Combining Mediation and Arbitration, *Academy of Management Review* 25 (2) (April): 416–427.

ROSENBLOOM, DAVID H. and DEBORAH G. GOLDMAN. 1998. *Public Administration: Understanding Management, Politics, and Law in the Public Sector.* 4th ed. New York: The McGraw-Hill Companies, Inc.

SARAT, AUSTIN. 1989. "Alternatives to Formal Adjudication." Pp. 33–40 in Sheldon Goldman and Austin Sarat (eds.), *American Court Systems: Readings in Judicial Process and Behavior.* 2nd ed. New York: Longman.

SARAT, AUSTIN and WILLIAM L. F. FELSTINER. 1995. *Divorce Lawyers and Their Clients: Power and Meaning in the Legal Process.* New York: Oxford University Press.

SARAT, AUSTIN and STUART SCHEINGOLD (EDS.). 1998. *Cause Lawyering: Political Commitments and Professional Responsibilities.* New York: Oxford University Press.

SATURDAY REVIEW. 1979. "Getting Hot under the Collar" (June 9): 7.

SEELYE, KATHARINE Q. 2001. "Global Warning May Bring New Variety of Class Action," *New York Times* (September 6): A1, A6.

SEIDMAN, ROBERT B. 1978. *The State, Law and Development.* New York: St. Martin's Press.

SITU, YINGYI and DAVID EMMONS. 2001. *Environmental Crime: The Criminal Justice System's Role in Protecting the Environment.* Thousand Oaks, CA: Sage Publications, Inc.

SKERRY, PETER. 1998. "The Affirmative Action Paradox," *Society* 35 (6) (September–October): 8–16.

ST. LOUIS POST-DISPATCH, 2001. "Employee who objected to wearing a tie to work loses battle against state," (April 1): D9.

STRICK, ANNE. 1977. *Injustice for All.* New York: Penguin Books.

STUMPF, HARRY P., and JOHN H. CULVER. 1992. *The Politics of State Courts.* New York: Longman.

SUSSKIND, LAWRENCE, and JEFFREY CRUIKSHANK. 1987. *Breaking the Impasse: Consensual Approaches to Resolving Public Disputes.* New York: Basic Books.

TANASE, TAKAO. 1995. "The Management of Disputes: Automobile Accident Compensation in Japan." Pp. 58–83 in Richard L. Abel (ed.), *The Law & Society Reader.* New York: New York University Press.

THOMAS, KENNETH W. 1992. "Conflict and Conflict Management: Reflections and Update," *Journal of Organizational Behavior* 13 (3) (May): 265–274.

TIME. 1995. "Last Call at the Bar" (March 20): 14. 2001. "Crowded Courts" (August 13): 15.

TRUBEK, DAVID M. 1978. "Environmental Defense I: Introduction to Interest Group Advocacy in Complex Disputes." Pp. 151–194 in Burton A. Weisbrod, Joel F. Handler, and Neil K. Komesar (eds.), *Public Interest Law: An Economic and Institutional Analysis.* Berkeley and Los Angeles: University of California Press.

TURK, AUSTIN T. 1978. "Law as a Weapon in Social Conflict." Pp. 213–232 in Charles E. Reasons and Robert M. Rich (eds.), *The Sociology of Law: A Conflict Perspective.* Toronto: Butterworths.

URY, WILLIAM L., JEANNE M. BRETT, and STEPHEN B. GOLDBERG. 1988. *Getting Disputes Resolved: Designing Systems to Cut the Costs of Conflict.* San Francisco: Jossey-Bass.

U.S. DEPARTMENT OF COMMERCE. 1989. *Statistical Abstract of the United States. 1989.* Washington, DC: Bureau of the Census.

U.S. DEPARTMENT OF JUSTICE. 1986. "Toward the Multi-Door Courthouse-Dispute Resolution Intake and Referral," National Institute of Justice Reports, SNI 198 (July): 2–7. 1995. "Tort Cases in Large Counties," Bureau of Justice Statistics, Special Report, (April).

U.S. NEWS & WORLD REPORT. 1995. "Graveling the Deadbeats" (July 31): 14.

VAGO, STEVEN. 1968. "Wage Garnishment: An Exercise in Futility under Present Law," *Journal of Consumer Affairs* 2 (1) (Summer): 7–20. 1971. "The Legal Problems of Low Income Consumers—Some Methodological Considerations," *Journal of Legal Education* 23 (1): 165–170. 1979. "Consumer Rights in Academe," *Social Policy* 9 (5) (March–April): 39–43.

VANCOUVER SUN. 1998. "Man Sues Nightclub for Whiplash From Stripper," (July 3): A15. 1999. "Global Capitalism Update: A Eunuch Approach to Collecting Bad Debts." (May 29): E3.

VARGAS, HECTOR and GEORGE E. BUSHNELL, JR. 1995. "Toiling in the Vineyards: Young Leaders in Public Service Work Give Meaning to 'Professionalism,'" *ABA Journal* 81 (March): 6–7.

WEHR, PAUL. 1979. *Conflict Regulation.* Boulder, CO: Westview Press.

WESTERMANN, TED D., and JAMES W. BURFEIND. 1991. *Crime and Justice in Two Societies, Japan and the United States.* Pacific Grove, CA: Brooks/Cole.

WESTIN, ALAN F., and ALFRED G. FELIU. 1988. *Resolving Employment Disputes without Litigation.* Washington, DC: The Bureau of National Affairs, Inc.

WRIGHT, MARTIN, and BURT GALAWAY (EDS.). 1989. *Mediation and Criminal Justice.* London: Sage Publications.

YNGVESSON, BARBARA B. 1978. "The Atlantic Fishermen." Pp. 59–85 in Laura Nader and Harry F. Todd, Jr. (eds.), *The Disputing Process—Law in Ten Societies.* New York: Columbia University Press.

ZOBEL, HILLER B. 1994. "In Love with Lawsuits," *American Heritage* 45 (7) (November): 58–65.

7
Law and Social Change

For decades now, law and society theorists were often preoccupied with attempts to explain the relationship between legal and social change in the context of development of legal institutions (see, for example, Anleu, 2000). These theorists, some of whom were discussed in Chapter 2, viewed the law as both an independent and a dependent variable in society and emphasized the interdependence of the law with other social systems. In light of the theoretical concerns raised earlier in the book, this chapter will further examine the interplay between law and social change. The law will again be considered as both a dependent and an independent variable—that is, as both an effect and a cause of social change. The chapter will also analyze the advantages and the limitations of the law as an instrument of social change, and will discuss a series of social, psychological, cultural, and economic factors that have an influence on the efficacy of law as an agent of change.

The first step in understanding the relationship between law and social change is conceptual. What is social change? The term "change," in everyday usage, is often employed loosely—as demonstrated in the rhetoric of the 2000 presidential campaign—to refer to something that exists that did not exist previously, or to the demise or absence of something that formerly existed. But not all change is social change. Many changes in life are small enough to be dismissed as trivial, although at times they may add up to something more substantial and consequential. In its most concrete sense, social change means that large numbers of people are engaging in group activities and relationships that are different from those in which they or their parents engaged in previously. Society is a complex network of patterns of relationships in which all the members participate in varying degrees. These relationships change and behavior changes at the same time. Individuals are faced with new situations to which they must respond. These situations reflect such factors as new technologies, new ways of making a living, changes in place of residence, and innovations, new ideas, and new social values. Thus, social change means modifications in the way people work, rear a family, educate their children, govern themselves, and seek ultimate meaning in life. It also refers to a restructuring of the basic ways people in a society relate to each other with regard to government, economics, education, religion, family life, recreation, language, and other activities (Vago, 1999).

Social change is a product of a multitude of factors and, in many cases, the interrelationships among them. In addition to law and legal cultures (Gibson and Caldeira, 1996), there are many other mechanisms of change, such as technology, ideology, competition, conflict, political and economic factors, and structural strains (see, for example, McMichael, 2000). All the mechanisms are in many ways interrelated. One should be very careful not to assign undue weight to any one of these "causes" in isolation. Admittedly, it is always tempting and convenient to single out one "prime mover," one factor, one cause, one explanation, and use it for a number of situations. This is also the case with legal change: It is extremely difficult, perhaps impossible, to set forth a cause-and-effect relationship in the creation of new laws, administrative rulings, or judicial decisions. Although there are exceptions, as will be alluded to in this chapter, one should be somewhat skeptical and cautious concerning one-factor causal explanations in general, and in particular about such explanations for large-scale social changes.

RECIPROCITY BETWEEN LAW AND SOCIAL CHANGE

The question of whether law can and should lead, or whether it should never do more than cautiously follow changes in society, has been and remains controversial. The conflicting approaches of the British social reformer Jeremy Bentham and the German legal scholar Friedrich Karl von Savigny have provided the contrasting classical paradigms for these propositions. At the beginning of industrialization and urbanization in Europe, Bentham expected legal reforms to respond quickly to new social needs and to restructure society. He freely gave advice to the leaders of the French Revolution, since he believed that countries at a similar stage of economic development needed similar remedies for their common problems. In fact, it was Bentham's philosophy, and that of his disciples, that turned the British Parliament—and similar institutions in other countries—into active legislative instruments bringing about social reforms partly in response to and partly in stimulation of felt social needs. Writing at about the same period, Savigny condemned the sweeping legal reforms brought about by the French Revolution that were threatening to invade Western Europe. He believed that only fully developed popular customs could form the basis of legal change. Because customs grow out of the habits and beliefs of specific people, rather than expressing those of an abstract humanity, legal changes are codifications of customs, and they can only be national, never universal.

Over six generations later, the relationship between law and social change remains controversial. Still, "there exists two contrasting views on the relationship between legal precepts and public attitudes and behavior. According to the one, law is determined by the sense of justice and the moral sentiments of the population, and legislation can only achieve results by staying relatively close to prevailing social norms. According to the other view, law, and especially legislation, is a vehicle through which a programmed social evolution can be brought about" (Aubert, 1969:69). At one extreme, then, is the view that law is a dependent variable, determined and shaped by current mores and opinions of society. According to this position, legal changes would be impossible unless preceded by social change; law reform could do nothing except codify custom. This is clearly not so, and ignores the fact that throughout history, legal institutions have been found to "have a definite role, rather poorly understood, as instruments that set off, monitor, or otherwise regulate the fact or pace of social change" (Friedman, 1969:29). The other extreme is exemplified by jurists in the former Soviet Union, such as P. P. Gureyev and P. I. Sedugin (1977), who saw the law as an instrument for social engineering. Accordingly, "during the period of the transition from capitalism to socialism, the Soviet state made extensive use of legislation to guide society, establish and develop social economic forms, abolish each and every form of exploitation, and regulate the measure of labour and the measure of the consumption of the products of social labour. It used legislation to create and improve the institutions of socialist democracy, to establish firm law and order, safeguard the social system and state security, and build socialism" (Gureyev and Sedugin, 1977:12).

These views represent the two extremes of a continuum representing the relationship between law and social change. The problem of the interplay between law and social change is obviously not a simple one. Essentially, the question is not, Does law change society? or Does social change alter law? Both contentions are likely to be correct. Instead, it is more appropriate to ask under what specific circumstances law can bring about social change, at what level, and to what extent. Similarly, the conditions under which social change alters law need to be specified.

In general, in a highly urbanized and industrialized society like the United States, law does play a large part in social change, and vice versa, at least much more so than is the case in traditional societies or in traditional sociological thinking (Nagel, 1970:10). There are several ways of illustrating this reciprocal relationship. For example, in the domain of intrafamily relations, urbanization, with its small apartments, has lessened the desirability of three-generation families in a single household. This social change helped to establish social security laws that in turn helped generate changes in the labor force and in social institutions for the aged. Changes in landlord-tenant relations brought about changes in housing codes, resulting in changes in tenancy relations. As a result of technological change, the relation of personal-property owners to other individuals has become more impersonal and frequently more likely to lead to injury. As a result, there have been alterations in the legal definition of fault, which in turn has changed the American insurance system. Finally, in the context of employer-employee relations, much of American labor history before the 1930s pointed toward the enactment of precedents and statutes guaranteeing the right to unionize, and once the Wagner Act was passed, the percentage of the labor force in unions did drastically increase, although it has since reached a plateau (Nagel, 1970:11) and started to decline in recent years.

Although there is an obvious and empirically demonstrable reciprocal relationship between law and social change, for analytical purposes I will briefly consider this relationship as unilateral. To this end, in the next section I will examine the conditions under which social change induces legal change; then, in the following section, I will discuss law as an instrument of social change.

SOCIAL CHANGES AS CAUSES OF LEGAL CHANGES

In a broad historical context, social change has been slow enough to make custom the principal source of law. Law could respond to social change over decades or even centuries. Even during the early stages of the industrial revolution, changes induced by the invention of the steam engine or the advent of electricity were gradual enough to make legal responses valid for a generation. Notes Friedmann: "But today the tempo of social change accelerated to a point where today's assumptions may not be valid even in a few years from now" (1972:513). In the often-quoted dramatic words of Alvin Toffler (1970:11), "Change sweeps through the highly industrialized countries with waves of ever accelerating speed and unprecedented impact." In a sense, people in modern society are caught in a maelstrom of social change, living through a series of contrary and interacting revolutions in demography, urbanization, bureaucratization, industrialization, science, transportation, agriculture, communication, biomedical research, education, and civil rights. Each of these revolutions has brought spectacular changes in a string of tumultuous consequences, and transformed people's values, attitudes, behavior, and institutions.

These changes further transformed the social and economic order of society. Contemporary society is characterized by a great division of labor and specialization in function. In modern society,

> interpersonal relations have changed; social institutions, including the family, have become greatly modified; social control previously largely informal has become formalized; bureaucracy, that is, large-scale formal organizations, has proliferated both in the private and public sectors; and new risks to the individual have emerged including the risk of disrupted income flow through

unemployment, of industrial accidents, and of consumer exploitation; and increased chronic illness and physical impairments have accompanied the extension of life. (Hauser, 1976:23-24)

The emergence of new risks to the individual as a result of the attenuation of the various family functions, including the protective function, has led to the creation of legal innovations to protect the individual in modern society. Illustrations of such innovations include provisions for worker's compensation, unemployment insurance, old-age pensions, Medicare, and various forms of categoric and general provisions for "welfare" (Hauser, 1976:24).

Many sociologists and legal scholars assert that technology is one of the great moving forces for change in law (see, for example, Volti, 1995). Law is influenced by technology in at least three ways:

> The most obvious . . . is technology's contribution to the refinement of legal technique by providing instruments to be used in applying law (e.g., fingerprinting or the use of a lie detector). A second, no less significant, is technology's effect on the process of formulating and applying law as a result of the changes technology fosters in the social and intellectual climate in which the legal process is executed (e.g., televised hearings). Finally, technology affects the substance of law by presenting new problems and new conditions with which law must deal. (Stover, quoted by Miller, 1979:14)

Illustrations of technological changes leading to legal changes abound. The advent of the automobile and air travel brought along new regulations. The automobile, for example, has been responsible for an immense amount of law: traffic rules, rules about drunk driving, rules about auto safety, drivers' license laws, rules about pollution control, registration, and so on. New devices in crime detection (fingerprinting and electronic snooping, among a host of others) resulted in changes in the law, such as the kinds of evidence admissible in court. The computer makes possible our present systems of credit, merchandising, manufacturing, transportation, research, education, dissemination of information, government, and politics. The computer and easy access to cyberspace, especially the Internet, also have inspired legislation on both the federal and the state levels to safeguard privacy, to protect against abuse of credit information and computer crime [although not too efficiently, as evidenced by the phenomenal increase in, for instance, identity thefts (see, for example, Lee, 2001)], and to require an employer to tell a job applicant who is rejected the source and nature of any adverse report on his or her credit or past record or opinions that caused the rejection.

Change in law may be induced by a voluntary and gradual shift in community values and attitudes. People may come to think that poverty is bad and laws should be created to reduce it in some way. People may come to condemn the use of laws to further racially discriminatory practices in voting, housing, employment, education, and the like, and may support changes that forbid the use of laws for these purposes. People may come to think that businesspeople should not be free to put just any kind of foodstuff on the market without proper governmental inspection, or fly any plane without having to meet governmental safety standards, or show anything on television that they wish. So laws may be enacted as appropriate, and regulatory bodies may be brought into being as necessary. And people may come to think that the practice of abortion is not evil, or that the practice of contraception is desirable, or that divorce and remarriage are not immoral (Glendon, 1989; Jacob, 1988). Hence, laws governing these practices may undergo repeal or revision.

Changes in social conditions, technology, knowledge, values, and attitudes, then, may induce legal change. In such instances, the law is reactive and follows social change. It should be noted, however, that changes in law are one of many responses to social change. But the legal response in some respects is important, since it represents the authority of the state and its sanctioning power. A new law in response to a new social or technological problem may aggravate that problem or alleviate and help to solve it. Often, the legal response to social change, which inevitably comes after a time lag, induces new social changes. For example, laws created in response to air and water pollution brought about by technological changes may result in unemployment in some areas, where polluting firms are unwilling or unable to install the required pollution-abatement controls. Unemployment, in turn, may result in relocation, may affect the crime rate in the community, or may bring about coercive pressures from the disaffected. These correlations and chain reactions can be extended practically indefinitely. Thus, law can be considered as both reactive and proactive in social change. In the next section, the proactive aspect of law as an initiator of social change will be considered.

LAW AS AN INSTRUMENT OF SOCIAL CHANGE

There are numerous historical and cross-cultural illustrations in which the enactment and instrumentation of laws have been used deliberately to induce broad social changes in society (see, for example, Fernandes and Varley, 1998). With the advent of Roman jurists, the notion of law as an instrument of social change became clearly conceptualized. Says Nisbet: "The conversion of Rome from republic to empire could not have been accomplished except by means of explicit legal decree buttressed by the doctrine of imperial sovereignty" (1975:173). Since Roman times, great ages of social change and mobility almost always involved great use of law and of litigation. There are several illustrations of the idea that law, far from being simply a reflection of social reality, is a powerful means of *accomplishing* reality—that is, of fashioning it or making it. It is generally acknowledged that, in spite of the ideas of Marx, Engels, and Lenin that law is an epiphenomenon of bourgeois class society doomed to vanish with the advent of the Revolution, the former Soviet Union succeeded in making enormous changes in society by the use of laws (Dror, 1968). In Spain, during the 1930s, law was used to reform agrarian labor and employment relations (Collier, 1989:201–222). More recently, the attempts by Nazi Germany and later on by Eastern European countries to make wholesale social changes through the use of laws—such as nationalization of industry, land reform and introduction of collective farms, provision of free education and health care, and elimination of social inequities—are illustrative of the effectiveness of law to induce change (Eorsi and Harmathy, 1971). In China, when the Communist Party came into power in 1949, virtually all vices that are ubiquitous in Western countries—prostitution, gambling, pornography, drug trafficking, and usury—were eliminated by government decree along with business operations that were dependent on profits from such activities (Brady, 1981). China also managed to moderate through law its population growth and as a result devote more of its resources to economic development and modernization (Tyler, 1995). They established an effective women's health system that discourages large families through patient education, contraceptive choice and heavy taxes for couples who choose to have an additional child (Rosenthal, 1998).

Recognition of the role of law as an instrument of social change is becoming more pronounced in contemporary society. Says Friedmann: "The law—through legislative or administrative responses to new social conditions and ideas, as well as through judicial reinterpretations of constitutions, statutes or precedents—increasingly not only articulates but sets the course for major social changes" (1972:513). Thus, "attempted social change, through law, is a basic trait of the modern world" (Friedman, 1975:277). In the same vein, Yehezkel Dror (1968:673) contends that "the growing use of law as a device of organized social action directed toward achieving social change seems to be one of the characteristics of modern society." Many authors, such as Joel B. Grossman and Mary H. Grossman (1971:2), consider law as a desirable, necessary, and highly efficient means of inducing change, preferable to other instruments of change.

In contemporary societies, the role of law in social change is of more than theoretical interest. In many areas of social life, such as education, race relations, housing, transportation, energy utilization, the protection of the environment, and crime prevention, the law and litigation are important instruments of change (Aron, 1989:85–114; Reed, 1998; Visher and Weisburd, 1998). In the United States, the law has been used as the principal mechanism for improving the political and social position of Blacks. Since the 1960s, the courts and Congress have dismantled a racial caste system embedded in the law and in practice for generations. The old order was swept away by legislation, including the Civil Rights Act of 1964 and the Voting Rights Act of 1965, as well as by the commitment of billions of dollars to social welfare programs. In a relatively short time, these policies have produced notable effects. For example, the immediate results of the Voting Rights Act of 1965 were dramatic, particularly in states that had successfully resisted earlier attempts to end voting discrimination. The percentage of potential black voters registered in Alabama increased from 23 to 52 percent between 1964 and 1967. By 1969, it had gone up to 61 percent. In Mississippi, the increase was most significant, from 7 percent in 1964 to 60 percent in 1967, and 67 percent by 1969. Between the 1964 and 1968 presidential elections, overall black registration in the South increased by nearly one million voters. About 75 percent of the increase came in the six states that were fully covered by the act—Alabama, Georgia, Louisiana, Mississippi, North Carolina, and South Carolina. This effectively doubled the number of registered Blacks in those states (Logan and Winston, 1971:27). The 1965 law, through its impact on black registration and voting, also had profound consequences for black political power. In 1965, there were some 70 elected black officials in the South. By 1969, their number had risen to 400. In 1981, there were approximately 2,500 elected black officials in 11 southern states, including a black mayor in Atlanta (Scher and Button, 1984:45). It would be erroneous to assume, however, that similar changes took place in other domains. For instance, since 1964, the median family income of Blacks has vacillated between 54 and 62 percent of the figure for whites.

Similarly, in the former Eastern-bloc countries, the law was a principal instrument in transforming society after the Second World War from a bourgeois to a socialist one. Legal enactments initiated and legitimized rearrangements in property and power relations, transformed basic social institutions such as education and health care, and opened up new avenues of social mobility for large segments of the population. Legislation guided the reorganization of agricultural production from private ownership to collective farms, the creation of new towns, and the development of a socialist mode of economic production, distribution, and consumption. These changes, in turn, affected values, beliefs, socialization patterns, and the structure of social relationships.

There are several ways of considering the role of law in social change. In an influential article, "Law and Social Change," Dror (1968) distinguishes between the indirect and direct aspects of law in social change. Dror (1968:673) contends that "law plays an important indirect role in social change by shaping various social institutions, which in turn have a direct impact on society." He uses the illustration of the compulsory education system, which performed an important indirect role in regard to change. Mandatory school attendance upgraded the quality of the labor force, which, in turn, played a direct role in social change by contributing to an increased rate of industrialization and modernization. He emphasizes that law interacts in many cases directly with basic social institutions, constituting a direct relationship between law and social change. For example, laws prohibiting racial discrimination in education have a direct influence on social change by enabling previously excluded groups to attend schools of their choice. He warns, however, that "the distinction is not an absolute but a relative one: in some cases the emphasis is more on the direct and less on the indirect impact of social change, while in other cases the opposite is true" (Dror, 1968:674).

Dror argues that law exerts an indirect influence on social change in general by influencing the possibilities of change in various social institutions. For example, the existence of a patent law protecting the rights of inventors encourages inventions and furthers change in the technological institutions, which, in turn, may bring about other types of social change.

For all modern societies, every collection of statutes and delegated legislation is "full of illustrations of the direct use of law as a device for directed social change" (Dror, 1968:676). A good example of social change directly induced by law was the enactment of Prohibition in the United States to shape social behavior. (It was also one of the more conspicuous failures, showing that there are limits to the efficacy of law to bring about social change, as I will discuss later.) Other illustrations of comparable magnitude include the abolition of slavery in the United States and the passage of the 1964 Civil Rights Act (Horowitz and Karst, 1969).

Another way of considering the role of law in social change is in the context of Leon H. Mayhew's (1971:195) notion of the possibility of either redefining the normative order or creating new procedural opportunities within the legal apparatus. He designates the former as an "extension of formal rights," illustrated by the pronouncement of the Supreme Court that defendants accused of serious crimes have the right to legal representation. The latter is termed the "extension of formal facilities," and is exemplified by the establishment of a system of public defenders who provide the required legal representation. The extension of formal rights and of formal facilities has definite implications for the criminal justice system in the form of greater protection of individual rights.

A rather different perspective on law in social change is presented by Lawrence M. Friedman. He describes two types of change through law: "planning" and "disruption." Planning "refers to architectural construction of new forms of social order and social interaction. Disruption refers to the blocking or amelioration of existing social forms and relations" (Friedman, 1973:25). Planning through law is an omnipresent feature of the modern world. Although it is most pronounced in socialist countries (for example, five-year plans of social and economic development), all nations are committed to planning to a greater or lesser extent. Both planning and disruption operate within the existing legal system and can bring about "positive" or "negative" social change, depending on one's perspective.

Although revolution is the most distinct and obvious form of disruption, milder forms are everywhere. Judicial review is frequently disruptive. American courts have smashed programs and institutions from the Missouri Compromise to the Alaska pipeline. Activist reformers have played a sensational role in American life in the last decade. Ralph Nader is the most well-known example . . . He stimulates use of legal process as a lever of social change. Much of his work is technically disruptive; it focuses on litigation and injunctions, on stopping government dead in its tracks, when it fails to meet his ethical and policies standards. Legal disruption can . . . include lawsuits; particularly after *Brown v. Board of Education,* reformers have frequently gone to court to upset many old and established arrangements. (Friedman, 1975:277)

Social change through litigation has always been an important feature in the United States. Whether the change produced by such action is considered "destructive" or "constructive," the fact remains that law can be a highly effective device for producing social change. For example, when the California Supreme Court destroyed the legal basis for the system of financing schools in the state, Friedman (1973:27) succinctly observed: "Many a *coup d'etat* in small countries have achieved less social change than this quiet *coup d'etat* in the courts."

Friedman considers social change through litigation an American phenomenon and raises the question, Will this spread to other countries? His response is that creative disruption of the judicial type presupposes a number of conditions that rarely coincide and are apparently not present in other countries to the same degree. These conditions include an activist legal profession, financial resources, activist judges, a genuine social movement, and what he describes as "the strongest condition"—that is, in the United States, "elites—the power holders—must accept the results of disruptive litigation, like it or not" (Friedman, 1975:278). Clearly, no socialist or authoritarian country will tolerate anything like the American form of judicial review. Their legal structures are not designed to accommodate these patterns.

The Efficacy of Law as an Instrument of Social Change

As an instrument of social change, law entails two interrelated processes: the institutionalization and the internalization of patterns of behavior. Institutionalization of a pattern of behavior refers to the establishment of a norm with provisions for its enforcement (such as desegregation of public schools), and internalization of a pattern of behavior means the incorporation of the value or values implicit in a law (for example, integrated public schools are "good"). Evan notes: "Law . . . can affect behavior directly only through the process of institutionalization; if, however, the institutionalization process is successful, it, in turn, facilitates the internalization of attitudes or beliefs" (1965:287).

Often law is an effective mechanism in the promotion or reinforcement of social change. However, the extent to which law can provide an effective impetus for social change varies according to the conditions present in a particular situation. William M. Evan (1965:288–291) suggests that a law is likely to be successful to induce change if it meets the following seven conditions: (1) The law must emanate from an authoritative and prestigious source; (2) the law must introduce its rationale in terms that are understandable and compatible with existing values; (3) the advocates of the change should make reference to other communities or countries with which the population identifies and where the law is already in effect; (4) the enforcement of the law must be aimed at making the change in a relatively short time; (5) those enforcing the law must themselves be very much committed to the change intended by the law; (6) the instrumentation of the law should include positive as well as negative sanctions; and (7) the enforcement of the law should be reasonable, not only in the sanctions used but also in the protection of the rights of those who stand to lose by violation of the law.

The efficacy of law as a mechanism of social change is conditioned by a number of factors. One is the amount of information available about a given piece of legislation, decision, or ruling. When there is insufficient transmission of information about these matters, the law will not produce its intended effect. Ignorance of the law is not considered an excuse for disobedience, but ignorance obviously limits the law's effectiveness. In the same vein, law is limited to the extent that rules are not stated precisely, and not only because people are uncertain about what the rules mean. Vague rules permit multiple perceptions and interpretations. (What does the expression "all deliberate speed" mean?) Consequently, the language of the law should be free of ambiguity, and care should be exercised to prevent multiple interpretations and loopholes (Carter, 1998).

Legal regulations and the required behavior of people to whom the law is addressed must be clearly known, and the sanctions for noncompliance need to be precisely enunciated. The effectiveness of the law is directly related to the extent and nature of perception of officially sanctioned rules. Perceptions of rules, in turn, vary with their sources. Rules are more likely to be accepted if they reflect a notion of fairness and justice that is prevalent in society and when their source is considered legitimate (Jacob, 1995). It should be noted, however, that the contrast between legitimacy and legality at times remains confused. As Carl J. Friedrich (1985:202) observes: "Law must not be seen as operating only in one dimension of the state, but in the many dimensions of the community if we are to comprehend legitimacy as an objective pattern. Legitimacy is related to right and justice; without a clarification of what is to be understood by the rightness and justice of law, legitimacy cannot be comprehended either. Hitler's rule was legal but it was not legitimate. It had a basis in law but not in right and justice."

The responsiveness of enforcement agencies to a law also has an impact on its effectiveness. Law enforcement agents not only communicate rules, but also show that the rules are taken seriously and that punishment for their violation is likely. But for a law to be enforceable, the behavior to be changed must be observable. For example, it is more difficult to enforce a law against homosexual behavior than a law against racial discrimination in public housing. Moreover, law enforcement agents need to be fully committed to enforcing a new law. One reason for the failure of Prohibition, for example, was the unwillingness of law enforcement agents to instrument the law. Selective enforcement of a law also hinders its effectiveness. The more high-status individuals are arrested and punished, the greater will be the likelihood that a particular law will achieve its intended objective (Zimring and Hawkins, 1975:337–338). Laws regularly and uniformly enforced across class and group lines tend to be perceived as more binding than they would have been if they were seldom and selectively enforced, because enforcement establishes behavioral norms, and in time, as E. Adamson Hoebel (1954:15) puts it: "The *norm* takes on the quality of the *normative*. What the most do, others should do."

As a strategy of social change, law has certain unique advantages and limitations as compared with other agents of change. Although these advantages and limitations go hand in hand and represent the opposite sides of the same coin, for analytical purposes I will examine them separately. The following discussion will focus on some of the more obvious reasons why law can facilitate change in society.

ADVANTAGES OF LAW IN CREATING SOCIAL CHANGE

As I have emphasized earlier, identifying the perimeters of change and attributing change to a particular causal variable or a set of variables should always be undertaken with prudence. In many instances, the state of the art of social-change endeavors is not methodologically sophisticated enough to distinguish clearly among causal, necessary, sufficient, and contributory conditions to produce desired effects in society. Social change is a complex, multifaceted phenomenon brought about by a host of social forces. At times, change is slow and uneven and can be brought about by different factors to differing degrees. Change in society may be initiated by a number of means. Of these, the most drastic is revolution, aimed at fundamental changes in the power relation of classes within society. Others include rebellion, riot, coup d'etat, various forms of violent protest movements, sit-ins, boycotts, strikes, demonstrations, social movements, education, mass media, technological innovations, ideology, and various forms of planned but nonlegal social-change efforts dealing with various behaviors and practices at different levels in society.

Compared with this incomplete list of change-inducing forces, the law has certain advantages. Change efforts through law tend to be more focused and specific. Change through law is a deliberate, rational, and conscious effort to alter a specific behavior or practice. The intentions of legal norms are clearly stated, with a concomitant outline of the means of instrumentation and enforcement and sanction provisions. Essentially, change through law aims at rectifying, improving, ameliorating, or controlling behaviors and practices in precisely defined social situations—as identified by the proponents of a particular change. The advantages of law as an instrument of social change are attributed to the fact that law in society is seen as legitimate, more or less rational, authoritative, institutionalized, generally not disruptive, and backed by mechanisms of enforcement and sanctions.

Legitimate Authority

A foremost advantage of law as an instrument of social change is the general feeling in society that legal commands or prohibitions ought to be observed even by those critical of the law in question. To a great extent, this feeling of obligation depends on respect for legitimate authority (Andenaes, 1977:52).

The classic treatment of legitimate authority is that of Max Weber (1947). Weber defines "imperative coordination" as the probability that specific commands from a given source would be obeyed by given groups of persons. Obedience to commands can rest on a variety of considerations, from simple habituation to a purely rational calculation of advantage. But there is always a minimum of voluntary submission based on an interest in obedience. In extreme cases, this interest in obedience can be seen in the tendency for people to commit illegal acts when so ordered by authority (and for others to excuse such acts as not subject to ordinary morality). Examples of this include the defense used at the Nuremberg trials, at the Watergate hearings, and at the court-martial of Lt. William Calley for the My Lai massacre during the Vietnam War (Kelman and Hamilton, 1989). Obedience to authority can be based on custom, affectual ties, or a purely material complex of interests—what Weber calls "ideal motives." These purely material interests result in a relatively unstable situation and must therefore be supplemented by other elements, both affectual and ideal. But even this complex of motives does not form a sufficiently reliable basis for a system of imperative cooperation, so that another important element must be added, the belief in legitimacy.

Following Max Weber, there are three types of legitimate authority—traditional, charismatic, and rational-legal. *Traditional* authority bases its claims to legitimacy on an established belief in the sanctity of traditions and the legitimacy of the status of those exercising authority. The obligation of obedience is not a matter of acceptance of the legality of an impersonal order but, rather, a matter of personal loyalty. The "rule of elders" is illustrative of traditional authority. *Charismatic* authority bases its claim to legitimacy on devotion to the specific and unusual sanctity, heroism, or exemplary character of an individual and the normative patterns that are revealed or ordained. The charismatic leader is obeyed by virtue of personal trust in his or her revelation, or in his or her exemplary qualities. Illustrations of individuals with charismatic authority include Moses, Christ, Mohammed, and Gandhi.

Rational-legal authority bases its claims to legitimacy on a belief in the legality of normative rules and in the right of those elevated to authority to issue commands under such rules. In such authority, obedience is owed to a legally established impersonal order. The individuals who exercise authority of office are shown obedience only by virtue of the formal legality of their commands, and only within the scope of authority of their office. Legal authority is not entirely conceptually distinct from traditional authority, although the distinction is nonetheless worth having. In modern society, "legality" suggests a component of rationality that traditional authority seems to lack. Indeed, during the transition to modernity, especially in the sixteenth and seventeenth centuries, authority tends more and more to be rationalized in distinctively legalistic and voluntaristic terms. "Rational" people "voluntarily" make a "contract," which generates the impersonal legal order.

Theory and research show that legitimate authority can wield considerable influence over both actions and attitudes (see, for example, Tyler et al., 1988). It can be the result of both the coercive processes involved and the individual's internalized values regarding legitimate authority. There is a tendency on the part of individuals to assume that the law has the right to regulate behavior and then to justify conformity to the law. To an extent, obedience to the law stems from respect for the underlying process: "People obey the law, 'because it is the law.' This means they have general respect for procedures and for the system. They feel, for some reason, that they should obey, if Congress passes a law, if a judge makes a decision, if the city council passes an ordinance. If they were forced to explain why, they might refer to some concept of democracy, or the rule of law, or some other popular theory sustaining the political system" (Friedman, 1975:114).

Acceptance of legitimate authority can also minimize the possibility of cognitive dissonance (discrepancies between action and cognition) by interpreting or construing legally prohibited action as "wrong" or morally bad. The law, consequently, not only represents accepted modes of behavior but also enforces and reinforces those accepted modes of behavior (Vining, 1986). Further, it defines the "correct" way of behaving in our daily lives. This effect is ingrained and institutionalized and is present even without the sanctions that are part of the enforcement machinery. In fact, most people in most situations tend to comply with the law without consciously assessing the possibility of legal sanctions or punishment. The legal definitions of proper conduct become to a large extent subsumed in individual attitudes toward everyday life and become part of internalized values.

The Binding Force of Law

There are many reasons that law is binding (Honore, 1987). They range from an assertion that laws are ordained by nature to the belief that law results from the consensus of its subjects to be bound. The immediate and simplest answer is that law is binding because most people in society consider it to be. The awareness and consciousness of law by most people serve as the foundation for its existence. People generally submit their behavior to its regulations, although they may have many different reasons for doing so. Some may believe that in obeying the law, they obey the higher authority of the law: God, nature, or the will of the people (Negley, 1965).

Others consider the content of the law to command obedience, which, in turn, is seen as an obligation (Ladd, 1970). The law achieves its claim to obedience, and at least part of its morally obligatory force, from a recognition that it receives from those, or from most of those, to whom it is supposed to apply. In addition to agencies that encourage obedience through the application of law, other ingredients are normally present and essential. They include an inner desire of people to obey, reinforced by a belief that a particular law is fair and just because it is applied equally, a feeling of trust in the effectiveness and legitimacy of the government, and a sense of civic-mindedness. They also include self-interest and the knowledge that most people obey the law and recognize it as having a certain morally rightful claim upon their behavior, or at the very least, that they behave as though they felt that way. Essentially, people follow the law because they feel that, as one author (Tyler, 1990) succinctly puts it, it is the "right thing to do."

Even when laws go against accepted morality, they are often obeyed. The extermination of more than six million Jews in Nazi Germany, clearly the most extreme instance of abhorrent immoral acts, was carried out by thousands of people in the name of obedience to the law. Stanley Milgram (1975:xii) contends that the essence of obedience is that individuals come to see themselves as instruments for carrying out someone else's wishes, and they therefore no longer view themselves as responsible for their actions. In many instances, the acceptance of authority results in obedience. For example, Milgram, interested in the phenomena of obedience and authority, has shown that people from a wide range of backgrounds will do morally objectionable things to other people if they are told to do so by a clearly designated authority. Under the guise of conducting experiments on the "effects of punishment on memory," he found that about two-thirds of his laboratory subjects willingly behaved in a manner *they* believed was painful or harmful to others. Even though "victims" cried out in pain, feigned heart attacks, and

literally begged for the experiment to be terminated, most subjects continued to obey authority and deliver what they believed to be high levels of
electric shock (Milgram, 1975). The study, in addition to showing that under
certain conditions many people will violate their own moral norms and
inflict pain on other human beings, succinctly underlines the notion that
most people willingly submit to authority and, by extension, the law.

Another reason for the binding force of the law may be that people prefer order over disorder and predictability of behavior. Individuals are creatures of habit because the habitual way of life requires less personal effort
than any other and caters well to a sense of security. Obedience to the law
guarantees that way. It also pays to follow the law—it saves effort and risk,
a motivation sufficient to produce obedience. Obedience to the law is also
related to the socialization process. People in general are brought up to obey
the law. The legal way of life becomes the habitual way of life. From an early
age, a child increasingly gains insight into the meaning of parental orders
and regulations and becomes socialized. This process repeats itself in school
and in the larger society. All such discourse increasingly provides—or
should provide—for participation of the maturing person. The individual,
so to speak, shapes these regulations and makes them his or her own. In the
process, discipline is replaced by self-discipline.

Sanctions

Sanctions for disobedience to the law are surely among the primary
reasons that laws have binding force (Evan, 1990:72–73). As Hoebel eloquently states: "The law has teeth, teeth that can bite if need be, although
they need not necessarily be bared" (1954:26). Sanctions are related to legal
efficacy and are provided to guarantee the observance and execution of legal
mandates, to enforce behavior. The sanctions recognized and used by legal
systems are usually of a diversified character. In primitive societies, they
may take the form of cruel punishments or social ostracism. In developed
legal systems, the administration of sanctions is, as a general rule, entrusted
to the organs of political government. Among the means of coercive law
enforcement are punishment by fine or imprisonment; the imposition of
damage awards, which may be carried out by executions into the property
of the judgment debtor; the ordering by a court of specific acts or forbear-
ances at the threat of a penalty; and the impeachment and removal of a public officer for dereliction of duty. As Hans Kelsen (1967:35) notes, the
sanctions characteristic of modern legal systems go beyond the exercise of
merely psychological pressure, and authorize the performance of disadvan-
tageous coercive acts, namely, "the forceable deprivation of life, freedom,
economics and other values as a consequence of certain conditions."

Robert B. Seidman (1978:100) points out that "laws more or less consistent with the existing social order need not rely upon the threat of legal

sanction to induce behavior." However, not all laws are consistent with the existing social order, and an advantage of the law as an agent of social change is that potential violation of the law is often deterred by actual or perceived risk and by the severity of sanctions attached to noncompliance. Even the threat of sanctions can deter people from disobedience. Perhaps sanctions also play a part by inducing a moralistic attitude toward compliance (Schwartz and Orleans, 1970).

The types of sanctions used obviously vary with the purposes and goals of a law or legal policy. An essential distinction is whether the main purpose of a law is to prevent individuals from doing things that others in society oppose as being harmful or immoral, or whether the purpose of the law is to create new types of relationships between groups or individuals—essentially the difference between proscriptive and positive policy (Grossman and Grossman, 1971:70). The distinction is not always perfect. Positive policy-making often involves negative sanctions as well as positive rewards, although proscriptive policy-making usually involves only negative sanctions (Friedland, 1989). Rewards, such as federal contracts or subsidies, are frequently part of regulatory statutes attempting to change established patterns of economic behavior and have been used widely as an incentive for compliance with desegregation laws. Those who violate such laws not only lose prospective rewards but also may be liable for fines or criminal penalties. Grossman and Grossman point out: "Laws or statutes which seek positive societal changes of major proportion must rely as much on education and persuasion as on negative sanctions. For the carrot and stick approach to be successful, the latter must be visible and occasionally used" (1971:70).

The situation is different where the changes sought through the law are the reduction or the elimination of deviant behaviors. In such instances, the law does not provide rewards or incentives to dissuade individuals from committing such acts—only the possibility, if not the certainty, of detection and punishment. In such instances, the emphasis is on deterrence, punishment, and vengeance, and the objective is the elimination or the reduction of a particular type of behavior considered harmful.

There are, of course, additional discernible advantages of the law in creating social change. For example, the law as an instrument of change can effectively be involved in the context of John Stuart Mill's notion of the law:

> (i) to achieve common purposes which cannot be left to the forces of supply and demand—such as education; (ii) to protect the immature and helpless; (iii) to control the power of associations, managed not only by the persons directly interested but by delegated agencies; (iv) to protect individuals acting in concert in cases where such action cannot be effective without legal sanctions; (v) to achieve objects of importance to society, present and future, which are

beyond the powers of individuals or voluntary associations or which, if within their powers, would not normally be undertaken by them. (Ginsberg, 1965:230)

The list of conceivable advantages of the law as an instrument of social change is indeed incomplete. What has been said so far is intended simply to demonstrate that the law has a peculiar and unparalleled position among agents of social change. At the same time, it has certain limitations. A knowledge and an awareness of the limitations will help us to understand more fully the role of the law in social change, and they need to be taken into account for the use of the law in change efforts.

LIMITATIONS OF LAW IN CREATING SOCIAL CHANGE

In a period when alienation from virtually all social institutions proceeds swiftly, when there is widespread demoralization brought on by uncontrollable economic conditions, when people are suffering from a "crisis of confidence," it would seem a bit absurd to advance the idea that the law is an expression of the will of the people. For the great majority of individuals, the law originates externally to them and is imposed upon them in a manner that can be considered coercive. In reality, very few individuals actually participate in the formation of new laws and legislation. Consequently, one of the limitations of the law as an instrument of social change is the possibility of prevailing conflict of interest, which tends to determine which laws are promulgated and which alternatives are rejected. Other limitations bearing on the efficacy of the law as an instrument of social change include the divergent views on the law as a tool of directed social change and the prevailing morality and values. In the following pages, I will consider these limitations separately, and then examine a number of conditions conducive to resistance to change from sociological, psychological, cultural, and economic perspectives.

Conflicting interests arise out of scarcity. Access to scarce resources and highly cherished objects is limited in every society. In the struggle to achieve them, some individuals and groups win, others lose. Several decades ago, Max Weber had already recognized, as did Karl Marx before him, that many laws are created to serve special economic interests. Individuals with the control of ownership of material goods are generally favored by laws since "economic interests are among the strongest factors influencing the creation of law" (Weber, 1968:334). Weber further recognized that other special interests, in addition to the economic ones, influence the formation of law. Says Weber: "Law guarantees by no means only economic interest, but rather the most diverse interests ranging from the most elementary ones of protection of personal security to such purely ideal goods as personal honor or the honor of the divine powers. Above all, it guarantees political, ecclesiastical, familial and other positions of authority as well as positions of social preeminence of any kind" (1968:333).

There are two important insights contained in Weber's points. The first is that conflict of interest provides the framework in which laws are framed and change is brought about. Consequently, social stratification in a society will determine to a large extent the part laws will play in bringing about change based on the selectiveness and preferences exercised by those who promulgate those changes. The second point concerns the significance of the use of power to back up those changes. Studies of the legislative, judicial, and administrative processes in a society could lead very quickly to a discovery of not only who wills the power in society but also what interests are significant and influential in that group. Thus, the law as an instrument of a change can be viewed in the context of the organization of power and the processes by which interests are established in everyday social life; the resulting changes might very well be evaluated in those terms.

In a sense it is obvious, understandable, and even tautological that the powerful make and administer the laws in society. If anything gets done, it is because somebody had the power to do it. At the same time, those who are powerful and influential tend to use the law to protect their advantageous position in society, and for them "the law in effect structures the power (superordinate-subordinate) relationships in a society; it maintains the status quo and protects the various strata against each other" (Hertzler, 1961:421).

Many legislative enactments, administrative rulings, and judicial decisions reflect the power configurations in society. Some groups and associations are more powerful than others, and by virtue of being at the center of power, they are better able to reinforce their interests than those at the periphery. Even members of the legal profession are considered "professional go-betweens" for the principal political, corporate, and other interest groups, and hence serve to "unify the power elite" (Mills, 1957:289). Furthermore, as I noted in Chapter 3, many people are often apathetic about or unaware of an issue, but even when they are concerned, they are frequently unable to organize and thus successfully impose their preference on the legislature.

Curiously, however, those who are supposed to be coerced or oppressed by a system of laws imposed upon them by a ruling minority often seem unaware of their coercion or oppression. Indeed, they are frequently among the strongest partisans of the existing legal system. It may be argued that they have been "indoctrinated" by the ruling establishment, who uses its power to confuse them as to their true interests. But this requires that we distinguish between what people define as their interests and what their "true interests" are, a distinction that has given rise to a great deal of complex, subtle, and inconclusive polemics.

There are numerous instances of racial and ethnic minorities, workers, and farmers organizing to promote what they conceive to be their interests.

Blacks have been instrumental in the passage of a variety of civil rights laws (Scheingold, 1989). More recently, Spanish-Americans succeeded in introducing bilingual education into high schools in areas with a large proportion of Hispanics. Labor was instrumental in the enactment of a series of legislations dealing, for example, with occupational safety and health, flex-time work schedules, collective bargaining, and unemployment compensation. Similarly, farmers have succeeded in furthering their interests through legal measures dealing, for example, with migrant workers, farm subsidies, the importation of certain food items, such as citrus fruits, and favorable export provisions. Does this not mean that racial and ethnic minorities, workers, and farmers are also a part of the power structure? And if they are, does this not mean that the distribution of power in society is more widespread and complicated than is suggested by writers who speak of a simple division of society into "the powerful" and "the powerless"?

It is debatable whether the existence of conflicting interests could really be construed as pointing to a serious limitation of the law as an instrument of change. The points raised concerning the power of certain interest groups are valid, but the actual mechanics of change through the law would in any case preclude inclusion of large segments of the population. Large-scale participation of the citizenry in legal change, even in a democratic society, is seldom feasible. But lack of participation does not necessarily mean lack of representation. In the United States and most parts of Europe, people do have access (although of varying rates) to lawmakers and to the legal apparatus, and their aspirations for change through the law are often realized.

Law as a Policy Instrument

Another school of thought on the limits of the law as an instrument of social change is epitomized by Yehezkel Dror. He contends that "law by itself is only one component of a large set of policy instruments and usually cannot and is not used by itself. Therefore, focusing exclusive attention on law as a tool of directed social change is a case of tunnel vision, which lacks the minimum perspective necessary for making sense from the observed phenomena" (Dror, 1970:554). He suggests that it is necessary to redefine the subject of "law as a tool of directed social change" and to consider it as part of other social policy instruments, because the law is but one of many policy instruments that must be used in combination. In the context of social problems such as race relations, public safety, drug abuse, and pollution, "the necessity to use law as a policy instrument should be quite convincing" (Dror, 1970:555). This view certainly has merits. At times, change through the law can and should be construed as an ingredient of a larger policy. For example, the passage of the Economic Opportunity Act took place in the context of a broader policy that attempted to alleviate poverty in the United States.

However, the law is often used as an instrument of change outside of the context of a broad policy-making framework. This is typically the situation in reform-oriented litigation, where the object is to alter a particular institutionalized practice. For example, the 1973 Supreme Court decision to overrule state abortion statutes (Marshall, 1989:145), and its 1992 restrictions on abortion, were not carried out within specific policy considerations, and yet they obviously had a tremendous impact on women seeking to terminate pregnancy legally. Although judicial decisions are generally not rendered a policy instrument, because of the adversary nature of litigation, legislative and administrative reforms dealing with larger social issues should take place in a broader social policy-making framework. Such an approach would greatly enhance the efficacy of the law as an instrument of change. To this end, Dror advocates the establishment of interdisciplinary teams of lawyers, social scientists, and policy analysts to engage in relevant studies and prepare policy recommendations.

Morality and Values

The sociological literature recognizes, as James P. Levine (1970:592) notes, that the ability of the law to produce social change is probabilistic, contingent, and sequential. If a law is enacted or a court decision is rendered, it is probable that certain changes will follow, but the degree of change is contingent on certain prevailing circumstances. The law is sequential to the degree that it must precede certain desired changes, but because a large number of factors influence change, the time lag is not obvious. Moreover, a number of factors other than the law may have an effect on change in a particular area, which means that the cause-and-effect relationship between the law and change is very difficult to identify. Some of these factors are related to the prevailing morality and values in society.

Patrick Devlin (1965) argues that a society owes its existence less to its institutions than to the shared morality that binds it together. Although his thesis is only partly true, morality and values affect the efficacy of the law in social change. Obviously, society could not exist without accepting certain basic values, principles, and standards. On certain issues, such as violence, truth, individual liberty, and human dignity, a shared morality is essential. This does not mean, however, that all the values in our shared morality are basic and essential, or that decline in one value spells decline in all the rest. Moreover, not all our values are essential. Rules about property, for example, are not: Some principles about property are essential, but no society needs to have those very property principles that are characteristics of, for example, the United States—the principle of private ownership. A society could own all property in common without ceasing to count as a society.

In general, when the law is used as an instrument of social change, it needs the support of society. Says Schur: "A good illustration of the systematic ineffectiveness of unsupported law is provided by the utter failure of legislation designed to enforce private morality" (1968:132). Thus, an obvious limitation of the law in social change appears when it tries to deal with what may be called moral issues in society. Laws prohibiting adultery, for example, have existed for centuries, but adultery remains a favorite indoor sport in the United States and elsewhere. Similarly, laws dealing with homosexuality and prostitution have generally been ineffective (Kempadoo and Doezema, 1998). The well-known failure of the prohibition of alcohol through constitutional amendment and legislation to produce a truly "dry" society, or to keep most people from drinking, is another example of the limitation of the law to bring about social change in public "morals."

A comparable situation exists with regard to the prohibition of several kinds of drugs, especially marijuana (Kleinman, 1989). Interestingly, the marijuana laws have been called the "new prohibition," to underline the similarity to alcohol prohibition and the futility of legal control of consumption of those substances (Kaplan, 1971). Clearly, "behavior that is perceived of as satisfying important drives is more difficult to extinguish than behavior that satisfies less compelling drives" (Zimring and Hawkins, 1975:332). In fact, some argue that marijuana at least should be a source of pleasure, not pain or shame: "We should be free to cultivate and sell and buy this `euphoriant.' The only controls should be those imposed to protect from bogus or polluted merchandise. With the dreadful example of Prohibition before us, it seems nearly unthinkable that we should have done it again. . . . When will we learn that in a democracy it is for the people to tell the government, not for the government to tell the people, what makes them happy?" (Goldman, quoted in *Behavior Today*, 1979:8).

The link between law and morality in the making and unmaking of law raises two questions: (1) What needs to be done in considering a change in the law when moral opinion is divided? Are there criteria other than individual likes and dislikes to which appeal can be made? (2) How can the line be drawn between that part of morality or immorality which needs legal enforcement and that which the law ought to leave alone (Ginsberg, 1965:232)? In response to these questions, Morris Ginsberg suggests that the law ought to deal only with what can be ascertained on reliable evidence and with acts that can be precisely defined, and primarily with overt or external observable acts; and the law must, as far as possible, respect privacy. He contends that these are "principles of demarcation arising from the limitations inherent in the machinery of the law" (Ginsberg, 1965:238).

Thus, laws are more likely to bring about changes in what may be called external behavior. However, changes in external behavior are after a while usually followed by changes in values, morals, and attitudes. As Morroe Berger (1952:172) emphasizes: "While it is true that the province of law is `external' behavior, it is also true that in an urban, secular society an increasing number of relations fall within this province. Thus the range of behavior that can be called `external' is enlarged. At the same time, law can influence `external' acts which affect or constitute the conditions for the exercise of the private inclinations and tastes that are said to be beyond the realm of law." The fact that a change in attitude is only partial at first does not make it any the less of a change. This is contrary to the arguments advanced decades ago by William Graham Sumner (1906), which since have been echoed by many, that "stateways cannot change folkways."

Sumner contended that the law is limited to the regulation of individual behavior, and it cannot be used to alter attitudes, values, and morality. There are many examples both to support and to refute this contention. There are several instances where the promulgation of laws did not result in widespread acceptance by the population. For example, the U.S. Constitution asserted the equality of persons before the law without much effect upon increased opportunities for blacks or upon the prejudicial attitudes of many whites for generations. Similarly, the Indian Constitution purportedly outlawed discrimination against untouchables that has not significantly changed the values and attitudes of most Indians (Seidman, 1978:156).

On the other side of the debate regarding the power of law to change attitudes, there are several studies suggesting that law can, indeed, alter values and attitudes. For example, studies on the effects of desegregation in situations such as "armed forces units, housing projects, and employment situations indicate that change required by law has lessened prejudice" (Greenberg, 1959:26). Essentially, the purpose of the law is to change behavior, and in some measure the laws requiring whites to change their behavior in dealing with Blacks has changed attitudes (Harris, 1977:168). However, it should be noted that there is no simple way to describe white attitudes toward black people. Although there has been an enormous shift toward more favorable racial attitudes, resistance to change in race relations is still widespread. Some forms of change, such as acceptance of Blacks in work situations, are accepted. Other, more private kinds of change (for example, interracial marriage) are still resisted in many parts of the country. The idea of racial superiority is no longer characteristic of white attitudes. This conventional sign of racial doctrine seems to have changed for the better. This is reflected, in part, in the relative disuse of derogatory and stereotyped language. Until fairly recently, derogatory words and expressions were commonly used to describe blacks—and one hardly thought it was wrong to do so. Although such language is still used today, its use has greatly diminished.

But the law can change morality and values only under some conditions, and those conditions need to be specified. As Robert B. Seidman

(1978:156) notes, "The literature contains little more than speculations," and there is a great lack of empirical studies. In general, the law will more readily change morality and values where it first changes behavior. Such a change is usually followed by a justification of the new activity. To a great extent, however, the efficacy of the law depends much upon its adaptation to morality and values if it is intended to induce change (Fuller, 1969:38–91).

There is still much to be learned about when and under what conditions the law cannot "only *codify* existing customs, morals, or mores, but also . . . *modify* the behavior and values presently existing in a particular society" (Evan, 1965:286). In change efforts through the law, the prevalence and intensity of moral feelings and values need to be taken into account in both preserving and altering the status quo.

RESISTANCE TO CHANGE

In addition to the limitations of law as an instrument of social change discussed in the preceding section, the efficacy of the law (as well as other mechanisms of change) is further hindered by a variety of forces. In the modern world, situations of resistance to change are much more numerous than situations of acceptance. Members of a society can always find a justification in some more or less practical and rational terms for active resistance to change. Often change is resisted because it conflicts with traditional values and beliefs, prevailing customs (Banks, 1998) or a particular change may simply cost too much money, and sometimes people resist change because it interferes with their habits or makes them feel frightened or threatened. Although the law has certain advantages over other agents of change, for a greater appreciation of the role of law in change, it is helpful to identify some general conditions of resistance that have a bearing on the law. The awareness of these conditions is a prerequisite for a more efficient use of law as a method of social engineering.

The sociological literature recognizes a variety of tendencies to ward off change that directly or indirectly have an effect on law as an instrument of change. The intent of this section is to discuss briefly, rather than to analyze in depth, a series of forces that act as barriers to change. For the sake of clarity, I shall consider resistance to change through law in the context of social, psychological, cultural, and economic factors. The categories are only illustrative, and this distinction is made only for analytical purposes, for many of these factors operate in various combinations and intensities, depending on the magnitude and scope of a particular change effort. Obviously, there is a fair amount of overlapping among these factors. They are not mutually exclusive, and many of them, depending on the purpose, may be subsumed under different categories.

Social Factors

There are several factors that may be construed as potential barriers to change. They include vested interests, social class, ideological resistance, and organized opposition.

Vested Interests   Change may be resisted by individuals or groups who fear a loss of power, prestige, or wealth should a new proposal gain acceptance. There are many different types of vested interests for whom the status quo is profitable or preferable. Most British lawyers and judges insist on wearing the arcane court uniform of wigs and ceremonial robes that became fashionable and subsequently mandatory under King Charles II in the late seventeenth century (Schmidt, 1992) although there is a move led by the Lord Chancellor, head of the Britain's judiciary, to wear business attire for every day and save the knee breeches, silk stockings and buckled shoes for special occasions (*St. Louis Post-Dispatch*, 1998). Students attending state universities have a vested interest in tax-supported higher education. Divorce lawyers constitute a vested interest, and for a long time have fought efforts to reform the divorce laws. Physicians opposing various forms of "socialized medicine" constitute a vested interest. Residents in a community often develop vested interests in their neighborhood. They often organize to resist zoning changes, interstate highways, the construction of correctional facilities, or the busing of their children. In fact, nearly everyone has some vested interests—from the rich with their tax-exempt bonds to the poor with their welfare checks.

The acceptance of almost any change through law will adversely affect the status of some individuals or groups in society, and to the degree that those whose status is threatened consciously recognize the danger, they will oppose the change. For example, Gregory Massell (1973) reports that Soviet efforts in the early 1920s in central Asia to induce Moslem women to assert their independence from male domination was perceived by men as threatening to traditional status interests. The men reacted by forming counter-revolutionary bands and murdering some of the women who obeyed the new laws.

Social Class   Rigid class and caste patterns in general tend to hinder the acceptance of change. In highly stratified societies, people are expected to obey and take orders from those in superior positions of authority or power. The prerogatives of the upper strata are jealously guarded, and attempts to infringe upon them by members of lower socioeconomic groups are often resented and repulsed. For instance, under the traditional Indian and Pakistani rigid caste system, members of different castes could not draw water from the same well, go to the same schools, eat together, or otherwise mingle. In most cases, for the upper classes there is a tendency to cherish the old ways of doing things and to adhere to the status quo.

In the United States, those who identify themselves as working-class people tend more readily to agree that legal intervention is necessary to rectify deleterious social conditions, such as guaranteeing employment opportunities and providing adequate medical care (Beeghley, 1996). By contrast, middle- and upper-class people tend to oppose government intervention in these domains. For other government programs (such as aid to education), class-related differences tend to diminish.

Ideological Resistance   Resistance to change through law on ideological grounds is quite prevalent. A good example of this is the opposition of the Catholic Church to legislation and court decisions dealing with the removal of some of the restrictions on birth control and abortion. Specifically, in 1982, a French pharmaceutical company announced that it had developed a pill that would end pregnancy if taken within seven weeks of conception. Advocates of reproductive freedom hailed the news, because of the pill, know as RU-486, meant that abortions could be induced soon after contraception in a doctor's office, without surgery. By the early 1990s, RU-486 was available in France, Britain and Sweden. But protests by antiabortionists were driving its European manufacturers to quit making it, and opponents in the United States helped block its introduction here by threatening to boycott the products of any drug company that sold it. In the face of such intimidation and moral condemnation, virtually no American company was willing to supply it in commercial quantities. Since its approval for sale by the Food and Drug Administration in the fall of 2000, RU-486 has been distributed in the United States by a pharmaceutical company specializing in women's health that gets it from a producer in China (Tone, 2001).

Another illustration of ideological resistance (which goes hand in hand with vested interests) is that by the medical profession to anything suggesting socialized medicine, including the enactment of the Medicare Law of 1965 (Allen, 1971:278–279). In general, the basic intellectual and religious assumptions and interpretations concerning existing power, morality, welfare, and security tend to be rather consistent and adversely disposed to change (Vago, 1999:224).

Organized Opposition   Occasionally, widespread individual resistance to change may become mobilized into organized opposition, which can assume formal organizational structure (for example, the National Rifle Association opposing gun control or the National Association of Retired Persons protesting changes in Social Security benefits), or it may be channeled through a social movement (for instance, the recent pro-life activities) or political action committees or lobbyists. In modern societies, with the multiplicity of informal and formal organizations often in conflict with each other, a variety of new organizations have developed to combat specific threats to the status quo. For example, members of the John Birch Society decry a whole range of social changes from racial integration to the acceptance and legal protection of pornography. As with the John Birch Society, the reemergence of the Ku Klux Klan is based on public opposition to social change but focuses mainly on changing race relations. These and similar organizations have resisted change that was underway, and although most of them have fought a losing battle, their delaying effects have often been considerable. At times, however, when organized opposition to change through law is not forthcoming, the consequences can be disastrous. For instance, more than six million Jews were slaughtered in concentration camps during the Second World War in part because they did not organize resistance to the changes beginning in the early 1930s in Nazi Germany (Vago, 1999:239).

Psychological Factors

Goodwin Watson (1969:488) remarks that "all of the forces which contribute to stability in personality or in social systems can be perceived as resisting change." Any detailed discussion of these forces is obviously beyond the scope of this book. For the present purpose, I shall consider only habit, motivation, ignorance, selective perception, and moral development.

Habit   From a psychological perspective, habit is a barrier to change. Once a habit is established, its operation often becomes satisfying to the individual. People become accustomed to behaving or acting in a certain manner, and they feel comfortable with it. Once a particular form of behavior becomes routinized and habitual, it will resist change. Meyer F. Nimkoff (1957:62) suggests that the customs of a society are collective habits; in particular, where sentiment pervades custom, custom is slow to change when challenged by new ideas and practices. To cite but a single illustration, attempts to introduce the metric system have met with considerable resistance in the United States. We are accustomed to miles and feel uncomfortable with kilometers; we prefer a quart of something to a liter of something. When the law is used as an instrument of social change to alter established customs, it is more likely that the achievement of acceptable rates of compliance will require an active reorientation of the values and behaviors of a significant part of the target population (Zimring and Hawkins, 1975:331).

Motivation   The acceptance of change through law is also conditioned by motivational forces. Some motivations are culture-bound, in the sense that their presence or absence is characteristic of a particular culture.

For instance, religious beliefs in some cultures offer motivations to certain kinds of change, whereas in other cultures these motivations center on the preservation of the status quo. Other kinds of motivations tend to be universal, or nearly universal, in that they cut across societies and cultures (Foster, 1973:152). Examples of these motivations include the desire for prestige or for economic gain and the wish to comply with friendship obligations. Changes that may threaten the desire for economic gain or the attraction of prestige and high status will in general be considered threatening and likely resisted.

Ignorance   Ignorance is another psychological factor generally associated with resistance to change. At times, ignorance goes hand in hand with fear of the new. This is often true in the case of new foods. Not too long ago, many individuals assumed that citrus fruit brought an acid condition to the digestive tract. Once it was proved otherwise, resistance based on the acid matter faded. Ignorance can also be a factor in noncompliance with laws designed to reduce discriminatory practices. For example, employers often make observations about nonwhites as a group relative to whites and then on that basis hesitate to hire individual nonwhites (Beeghley, 1996). Ignorance is obviously an important factor in prejudice when a preexisting attitude is so strong and inflexible that it seriously distorts perception and judgment.

Selective Perception   Law, by design and intent, tends to be universal. The perception of the intent of the law, however, is selective and varies with socioeconomic, cultural, and demographic variables. The unique pattern of people's needs, attitudes, habits, and values derived through socialization determines what they will selectively attend to, what they will selectively interpret, and what they will selectively act upon. People in general will be more receptive to new ideas if they are related to their interests, consistent with their attitudes, congruent with their beliefs, and supportive of their values. Differing perceptions of the purpose of a law may hinder change. For example, in India the law provides for widespread distribution of family-planning information and supplies. But the use of contraceptive devices has been rejected by many Indian villagers because they perceive the law's intent to stop birth completely. In the United States, the early attempts to fluoridate city water supplies met with perceptions that a "communist conspiracy" was behind these efforts, and as a result they were resisted in many communities.

The way a law is written, as I noted earlier, also affects perception. For example, in their early stages most civil rights laws have been ambiguous and weak. The *Brown* decision is a good illustration. Calling for desegregation "with all deliberate speed" is too vague, too indefinite to bring about meaningful change. "Ambiguity always lends itself to individualized perceptions" (Rodgers and Bullock, 1972:199), and the individuals will interpret and perceive the meaning of the law in a way they consider most advantageous.

Moral Development   To a great extent, obedience to the law stems from a sense of moral obligation, which is the product of socialization. Only relatively recently, however, has there been some awareness of moral codes that are not necessarily linked to conventional external standards of right and wrong behavior, but represent internally consistent principles by which people govern their lives.

Perhaps the most extensive work on moral development was carried out by Lawrence Kohlberg (1964, 1967). He defines six stages in moral development. The first stage is described as an "obedience and punishment" orientation. This stage involves a "deference to superior power or prestige" and an orientation toward avoiding trouble. The second stage, "instrumental relativism," is characterized by naive notions of reciprocity. With this orientation, people will attempt to satisfy their own needs by simple negotiation with others or by a primitive form of equalitarianism. He calls these two stages "premoral." The third stage, "personal concordance," is an orientation based on approval and pleasing others. It is characterized by conformity to perceived majority beliefs. Such people adhere to what they consider to be prevailing norms. Stage four is the "law and order" stage. People with such orientations are committed to "doing their duty," and being respectful to those in authority. Stages three and four combine to form a conventional moral orientation.

Stages five and six indicate the internalized-principle orientation. Kohlberg calls stage five the "social contract" stage; it involves a legalistic orientation. Commitments are viewed in contractual terms, and people at this stage will avoid efforts to break implicit or explicit agreements. The final and highest stage of moral development is "individual principles." This emphasizes conscience, mutual trust, and respect as the guiding principles of behavior.

If the development theory proposed by Kohlberg is correct, the law is more or less limited depending on the stage of moral development of members of a society. In this context, David J. Danelski (1974:14–15) suggests that both qualitative and quantitative considerations are important. We would need to know the modal stage of the moral development of elites, of "average" citizens, and of deprived groups. If most members of a society were at the first and second stages, institutional enforcement would be essential to maintain order and security. Law would be least limited in a society in which most people were at the third and fourth stages of development. Law at the last two stages is probably more limited than at stages three and four, "but it might be otherwise if it is perceived as democratically agreed upon and consistent with individual principles of conscience. If it is not, it is likely to be more limited" (Danelski, 1974:15). The limits of law, in other words, appear to be curvilinear with respect to moral development.

Cultural Factors

When long-established practices or behaviors are threatened, resistance to change is usually strong, often on the basis of traditional beliefs and values. The status quo is protected and change resisted. For example, the Mormons, on the basis of traditional religious beliefs, opposed laws threatening their polygamous marriages. Similarly, in India, where malnutrition is a problem of considerable magnitude, millions of cows sacred to Hindus not only are exempt from being slaughtered for food but also are allowed to roam through villages and farm lands, often causing extensive damage to crops. Eating beef runs counter to long-held religious beliefs, and as a result it is unlikely that the raising of cattle for food will be acceptable in India. Other cultural factors also act often as obstacles to change. They include fatalism, ethnocentrism, notions of incompatibility, and superstition.

Fatalism   States Mead: "In many parts of the world we find cultures adhering to the belief that man has no causal effect upon his future or the future of the land; God, not man, can improve man's lot. . . . It is difficult to persuade such people to use fertilizers, or to save the best seed for planting, since man is responsible only for the performance, and the divine for the success of the act" (1953:201). Basically, fatalism entails a feeling of a lack of mastery over nature. People have no control over their lives and everything that happens to them is caused by God or evil spirits. Such a fatalistic outlook undoubtedly results in resistance to change, for change is seen as human-initiated rather than having a divine origin.

Ethnocentrism   Some groups in society consider themselves "superior," possessing the only "right" way of thinking about the world and of coping with the environment. Feelings of superiority about one's group are likely to make people unreceptive to the ideas and methods used in other groups. As a result, ethnocentrism often constitutes a bulwark against change. For example, such feelings of superiority by whites have hindered integration efforts in housing, employment, and education.

Incompatibility   Resistance to change is often due to the presence in the target group of material and systems that are, or considered to be, irreconcilable with the new proposal. When such incompatibility exists in a culture, change comes about with difficulty. An illustration is the marriage-age law enacted in Israel in an attempt to induce changes in the immigrant population through legal norms. The law sets 17 as the minimum age for marriage with the exception of pregnancy and imposes a criminal sanction on anyone who marries a girl below the age of 17 without permission of the district court. By setting the minimum age at 17, the law attempted to impose a rule of behavior that was incompatible with the customs and habits of some of the sections of the Jewish population of Israel that came from Arab and Oriental countries, where marriage was usually contracted at a lower age. The act had only limited effect, and communities that formerly permitted marriage of females at an early age continue to do so (Dror, 1968:678).

Superstition   Superstition is defined as an uncritical acceptance of a belief that is not substantiated by facts. At times, superstitions act as barriers to change. For example, in one situation in Zimbabwe (formerly Rhodesia), nutrition-education efforts were hampered because many women would not eat eggs. According to widespread belief, eggs cause infertility, make babies bald, and cause women to be promiscuous. Similarly, in the Philippines, it is a widely accepted idea that squash and chicken eaten at the same time produce leprosy. In some places, women are not given milk during late pregnancy because of the belief that it produces a fetus too large for easy delivery, and in other places, a baby may not be given water for several months after birth because water's "cold" quality will upset the infant's heat equilibrium. In some parts of Ghana, children are not given meat or fish because it is believed that they cause intestinal worms (Foster, 1973:103–104). Obviously, where such superstitious beliefs prevail, change efforts through law or other agents will meet some resistance.

Economic Factors

Even in affluent societies, limited economic resources constitute a barrier to changes that might otherwise be readily adopted. For instance, in the United States, almost everyone would readily accept the desirability of more effective controls on pollution, cheaper and more convenient systems of public transportation, effective welfare programs, and adequate health care for all. The fact that changes in these areas come very slowly is a matter not only of priorities but also of cost. Cost and limited economic resources in a society do in effect provide a source of resistance to change.

It is a truism that, like everything else, change through law has its costs. In most instances, the instrumentation of legislation, administrative ruling, or court decision carries a price tag. For example, the economic impact of federal regulations on institutions of higher education has been significant. The various affirmative action programs carry sanctions providing for the cutoff of *all* federal funding to institutions that do not comply with antibias laws. Compliance, in turn, results in increased administrative costs for postsecondary institutions, which are resisted in many academic circles and have contributed to the demands for modification of a variety of laws affecting higher education.

In addition to the direct cost of a particular change effort, the way costs and benefits are distributed also affects resistance. For example, when costs and benefits are widely distributed (as in Social Security), there is minimal resistance to programs. The cost to each taxpayer is relatively small, the benefits are so widely distributed "that they are almost like collective goods; beneficiaries will enjoy the benefits, but only make small contributions to their retention or growth" (Handler, 1978:15). Resistance will be forthcoming in situations where benefits are distributed while costs are concentrated. For example, automakers still resist (although not too successfully) legal attempts to impose more sophisticated pollution-control measures on cars.

Although a particular change through the law may be desirable (such as an effective and comprehensive universal health insurance plan in the United States), limited economic resources often act as barriers to such change efforts. Of the four sources of resistance to change, the economic factors are perhaps the most decisive. Regardless of the desirability of a proposed change, its compatibility with the values and beliefs of the recipients, and many other considerations, it will be resisted if the economic sacrifice is too great. Simply stated, regardless of how much people in a society want something, if they cannot afford it, chances are they will not be able to get it. As George M. Foster (1973:78) suggests: "Cultural, social and psychological barriers and stimulants to change exist in an economic setting . . . (and) economic factors . . . seem to set the absolute limits to change."

SUMMARY

Social change occurs constantly—although at varying rates—in contemporary societies, and it affects the lives of individuals in different ways. Changes in society are a product of a multitude of factors and, in many cases, of the interrelationships among them. In addition to law, there are a number of other mechanisms of social change. All these mechanisms are in many ways interrelated, and one should be careful not to assign undue weight to any one of these "causes" in isolation.

Law is both a dependent and an independent variable in social change. The relationship between law and change is still controversial. Some maintain that law is a reactor to social change; others argue that it increasingly is an initiator of change. These two views represent the extremes of a continuum dealing with the relationship between law and social change. In modern society, law does play a large part in social change, and vice versa.

Increasingly, law is being considered an instrument of social change. Today the role of law in change is of more than theoretical interest. In many areas of social life, such as education, race relations, housing, transportation, energy utilization, and the protection of the environment, the law has been relied on as an important instrument of change. Law influences social change directly and indirectly. It redefines the normative order, extends formal rights, and is used for planning purposes.

As compared with other agents of change, the law has several distinct advantages. The advantages of law as an agent of change are attributed to the perception that the law in society is legitimate, more or less rational, authoritative, institutionalized, generally not disruptive, and backed by mechanisms of enforcement and sanctions.

At the same time, the law has certain limitations in creating social change. It is not always able to resolve conflicting interests, and generally the powerful in society fare better than the less privileged and the unorganized. Law alone cannot deal effectively with social problems such as drug addiction, overpopulation, and corruption in government. These problems still defy adequate solution. Each is not a single problem but a complex of problems: Each generates a host of countervailing considerations—moral, economic, and otherwise—that compound the complexities. Further limitations flow from the inherent clumsiness of the instrument of the rule of law. One cannot easily foresee and take into account the situations to which a rule might apply. How many advocates of rent control for the poor could have anticipated the extent to which it would contribute to the perpetuation of the ghetto? How many legislators could have foreseen that subsidies to help farmers would result in reducing the number of farmers? The law is further limited by the divergencies in values and moral codes, the difficulty in enforcing some laws, the occasional lack of clarity of law, and the questionable diligence in enforcing certain laws.

In addition to these limits on the law in social change, a variety of social, psychological, cultural, and economic forces may provide direct or indirect resistance to change efforts. The social factors include vested interests, social class, moral sentiments, and organized opposition. Psychological resistance may be triggered by habit, motivation, ignorance, selective perception, and the complexities inherent in moral development. Cultural barriers to change include fatalism, ethnocentrism, notions of incompatibility, and superstition. But the economic factors are perhaps the most decisive. Cost and limited economic resources effectively set a limit to change.

SUGGESTED FURTHER READINGS

A. ALLOTT, *The Limits of Law*. London: Butterworths, 1980. A critical analysis of the role and limits of law in social change.

SHARYN I. ROACH ANLEU, *Law and Social Change*, Thousand Oaks, CA: Sage Publications, 2000. A survey of current theoretical debates and socio-legal research on the social conditions under which laws emerge and are changed; the extent to which law can be a resource to instrument social change; and the ways in which laws shape social institutions and practices and vice versa.

VILHELM AUBERT, "Law and Social Change in Nineteenth-Century Norway." Pp. 55–80 in June Starr and Jane F. Collier (eds.), *History and Power in the Study of Law: New Directions in Legal Anthropology.* Ithaca, NY: Cornell University Press, 1989. A discussion of a series of changes in Norway brought about by the law.

EDESIO FERNANDES and ANN VARLEY (EDS.), *Illegal Cities: Law and Urban Change in Developing Countries.* New York: St. Martin's Press, 1998. A collection of cross-cultural articles on the role of law in the process of urban change.

LAWRENCE M. FRIEDMAN, *American Law: An Introduction.* 2nd ed. New York: W. W. Norton & Company, Inc., 1998. See in particular the section on law and social change.

LAWRENCE M. FRIEDMAN, *American Law in the Twentieth Century.* New Haven: Yale University Press, 2002. A stimulating overview of some of the major legal and social changes in the United States.

MARY ANN GLENDON, *The Transformation of Family Law: State, Law, and Family in the United States and Western Europe.* Chicago: University of Chicago Press, 1989. A comparative and historical analysis of the social forces promoting legal changes in England, France, West Germany, Sweden, and the United States.

JOEL F. HANDLER, *Social Movements and the Legal System: A Theory of Law Reform and Social Change.* New York: Academic Press, 1978. An analysis of the conditions under which the law and the courts can be used to accomplish changes in the domains of environmental protection, consumer protection, civil rights, and social welfare.

PHILIP MCMICHAEL, *Development and Social Change.* 2nd ed. Thousand Oaks, CA: Pine Forge Press, 2000. A broad overview of social changes in the context of globalization with an abundace of case studies.

STEVEN VAGO, *Social Change.* 4th ed. Upper Saddle River, NJ: Prentice Hall, 1999. A comprehensive, up-to-date, and highly regarded text on social change.

REFERENCES

ALLEN, FRANCIS R. 1971. *Socio-Cultural Dynamics: An Introduction to Social Change.* New York: Macmillan.

ANDENAES, JOHANNES. 1977. "The Moral or Educative Influence of Criminal Law." Pp. 50–59 in June Louis Tapp and Felice J. Levine (eds.), *Law, Justice, and the Individual in Society: Psychological and Legal Issues.* New York: Holt, Rinehart & Winston.

ANLEU, SHARYN I. ROACH. 2000. *Law and Social Change.* Thousand Oaks, CA: Sage Publications.

ARON, NAN. 1989. *Liberty and Justice for All: Public Interest Law in the 1980s and Beyond.* Boulder, CO: Westview Press.

AUBERT, VILHELM (ED.). 1969. *Sociology of Law.* Harmondsworth, England: Penguin Books, Ltd.

BANKS, CINDY. 1998. "Custom in the Courts," *British Journal of Criminology* 38 (2) (Spring): 299–316.

BEEGHLEY, LEONARD. 1996. *The Structure of Social Stratification in the United States.* 2nd ed. Boston: Allyn and Bacon.

BEHAVIOR TODAY. 1979. "New Roundup" 10 (26) (July 9): 8.

BERGER, MORROE. 1952. *Equality by Statute.* New York: Columbia University Press.

BRADY, JAMES P. 1981. "A Season of Startling Alliance: Chinese Law and Justice in the New Order," *International Journal of the Sociology of Law* 9:41–67.

CARTER, LIEF H. 1998. *Reason in Law*. 5th ed. New York: Longman.

COLLIER, GEORGE. 1989. "The Impact of Second Republic Labor Reforms in Spain." Pp. 201–222 in June Starr and Jane F. Collier (eds.), *History and Power in the Study of Law: New Directions in Legal Anthropology*. Ithaca, NY: Cornell University Press.

DANELSKI, DAVID J. 1974. "The Limits of Law." Pp. 8–27 in J. Roland Pennock and John W. Chapman (eds.), *The Limits of Law*. New York: Lieber-Atherton.

DEVLIN, PATRICK. 1965. *The Enforcement of Morals*. New York: Oxford University Press.

DROR, YEHEZKEL. 1968. "Law and Social Change." Pp. 663–680 in Rita James Simon (ed.), *The Sociology of Law*. San Francisco: Chandler Publishing Company. 1970. "Law as a Tool of Directed Social Change," *American Behavioral Scientist* 13:553–559.

EORSI, GYULA and ATTILA HARMATHY. 1971. *Law and Economic Reform in Socialistic Countries*. Budapest: Akademiai Kiado.

EVAN, WILLIAM M. 1965. "Law as an Instrument of Social Change." Pp. 285–293 in Alvin W. Gouldner and S. M. Miller (eds.), *Applied Sociology: Opportunities and Problems*. New York: Free Press. 1990. *Social Structure and Law: Theoretical and Empirical Perspectives*. Newbury Park, CA: Sage Publications.

FERNANDES, EDESIO and ANN VARLEY (EDS.) 1998. *Illegal Cities: Law and Urban Change in Developing Countries*. New York: St. Martin's Press.

FOSTER, GEORGE M. 1973. *Traditional Societies and Technological Change*. 2nd ed. New York: Harper & Row, Pub.

FRIEDLAND, M. L. (ED.). 1989. *Sanctions and Rewards in the Legal System: A Multidisciplinary Approach*. Toronto: University of Toronto Press.

FRIEDMAN, LAWRENCE M. 1969. "Legal Culture and Social Development," *Law & Society Review* 4 (1): 29–44. 1973. "General Theory of Law and Social Change." Pp. 17–33 in J. S. Ziegel (ed.), *Law and Social Change*. Toronto: Osgoode Hall Law School, York University. 1975. *The Legal System: A Social Science Perspective*. New York: Russell Sage Foundation.

FRIEDMANN, WOLFGANG. 1972. *Law in a Changing Society*. 2nd ed. New York: Columbia University Press.

FRIEDRICH, CARL J. 1958. *The Philosophy of Law in Historical Perspective*. Chicago: University of Chicago Press.

FULLER, LON L. 1969. *The Morality of Law*. Rev. ed. New Haven: Yale University Press.

GIBSON, JAMES L. and GREGORY A. CALDEIRA. 1996. "The Legal Cultures of Europe," *Law & Society Review* 30 (1) (February): 55–85.

GINSBERG, MORRIS. 1965. *On Justice in Society*. Ithaca, NY: Cornell University Press.

GLENDON, MARY ANN. 1989. *The Transformation of Family Law: State, Law, and Family in the United States and Western Europe*. Chicago: University of Chicago Press.

GREENBERG, JACK. 1959. *Race Relations and American Law*. New York: Columbia University Press.

GROSSMAN, JOEL B. and MARY H. GROSSMAN (EDS.). 1971. *Law and Change in Modern America*. Pacific Palisades, CA: Goodyear.

GUREYEV, P. P. and P. I. SEDUGIN (EDS.). 1977. *Legislation in the USSR*. Trans. Denis Ogden. Moscow: Progress Publishers.

HANDLER, JOEL F. 1978. *Social Movements and the Legal System: A Theory of Law Reform and Social Change*. New York: Academic Press.

HARRIS, PATRICIA ROBERTS. 1977. "Freedom and the Native-Born Stranger." Pp. 160–174 in Norman A. Graebner (ed.), *Freedom in America: A 200-Year Perspective.* University Park: The Pennsylvania University Press.

HAUSER, PHILIP M. 1976. "Demographic Changes and the Legal System." Pp. 15–29 in Murray L. Schwartz (ed.), *Law and the American Future.* Englewood Cliffs, NJ: Prentice Hall.

HERTZLER, J. O. 1961. *American Social Institutions.* Boston: Allyn & Bacon.

HOEBEL, E. ADAMSON. 1954. *The Law of Primitive Man: A Study in Comparative Legal Dynamics.* Cambridge: Harvard University Press.

HONORE, TONY. 1987. *Making Law Bind: Essays Legal and Philosophical.* Oxford: Clarendon Press.

HOROWITZ, HAROLD W. and KENNETH L. KARST. 1969. *Law, Lawyers and Social Change.* Indianapolis: Bobbs-Merrill.

JACOB, HERBERT. 1988. *Silent Revolution: The Transformation of Divorce Law in the United States.* Chicago: University of Chicago Press. 1995. *Law and Politics in the United States.* 2nd ed. Ft. Washington, PA: HarperCollins College Publishers.

KAPLAN, JOHN. 1971. *Marijuana: The New Prohibition.* New York: Pocket Books.

KELMAN, HERBERT C. and V. LEE HAMILTON. 1989. *Crimes of Obedience: Toward A Social Psychology of Authority and Responsibility.* New Haven and London: Yale University Press.

KELSEN, HANS. 1967. *The Pure Theory of Law.* 2nd ed. Trans. M. Knight. Berkeley and Los Angeles: University of California Press.

KEMPADOO, KAMALA and JO DOEZEMA. 1998. *Global Sex Workers: Rights, Resistance, and Redefinition.* New York: Routledge.

KLEINMAN, MARK A. R. 1989. *Marijuana: Costs of Abuse, Costs of Control.* New York: Greenwood Press.

KOHLBERG, LAWRENCE. 1964. "Development of Moral Character and Ideology." Pp. 383–431 in L. Hoffman and M. Hoffman (eds.), *Review of Child Development Research,* Vol. I. New York: Russell Sage. 1967. "Moral Education, Religious Education, and the Public Schools: A Developmental Approach." Pp. 164–183 in T. Sizer (ed.), *Religion and Public Education.* Boston: Houghton Mifflin.

LADD, JOHN. 1970. "Legal and Moral Obligation." Pp. 3–45 in Roland Pennock and John W. Chapman (eds.), *Political and Legal Obligation.* New York: Lieber-Atherton, Inc.

LA PIERE, RICHARD T. 1965. *Social Change.* New York: McGraw-Hill.

LEE, JENNIFER. 2001. "Fighting Back When Someone Steels Your Name." *New York Times,* (April 8): B8.

LEVINE, JAMES P. 1970. "Methodological Concerns in Studying Supreme Court Efficacy," *Law & Society Review* 4 (1) (May): 583–592.

LOGAN, RAYFORD W., and MICHAEL WINSTON. 1971. *The Negro in the United States,* Vol. 2, *The Ordeal of Democracy.* Princeton, NJ: Van Nostrand Reinhold.

MARSHALL, THOMAS R. 1989. *Public Opinion and the Supreme Court.* Boston: Unwin Hyman.

MASSELL, GREGORY. 1973. "Revolutionary Law in Soviet Central Asia." Pp. 226–261 in Donald Black and Maureen Mileski (eds.), *The Social Organization of Law.* New York: Seminar Press.

MAYHEW, LEON H. 1971. "Stability and Change in Legal Systems." Pp. 187–210 in Bernard Barber and Alex Inkeles (eds.), *Stability and Social Change.* Boston: Little, Brown.

McMichael, Philip. 2000. *Development and Social Change* (2nd ed.). Thousand Oaks, CA: Pine Forge Press.

Mead, Margaret (ed.). 1953. *Cultural Patterns and Technical Change*. Paris: UNESCO.

Milgram, Stanley. 1975. *Obedience to Authority*. New York: Harper Colophon Books.

Miller, Arthur Selwyn. 1979. *Social Change and Fundamental Law: America's Evolving Constitution*. Westport, CT: Greenwood Press.

Mills, C. Wright. 1957. *The Power Elite*. New York: Oxford University Press.

Nagel, Stuart S. (ed.). 1970. *Law and Social Change*. Beverly Hills, CA: Sage Publications.

Negley, Glenn. 1965. *Political Authority and Moral Judgement*. Durham, NC: Duke University Press.

Nimkoff, Meyer F. 1957. "Obstacles to Innovation." Pp. 56–71 in Francis R. Allen, Hornell Hart, Delbert C. Miller, William F. Ogburn, and Meyer F. Nimkoff, *Technology and Social Change*. New York: Appleton-Century-Crofts.

Nisbet, Robert. 1975. *Twilight of Authority*. New York: Oxford University Press.

Reed, Douglas S. 1998. "Twenty-Five Years after *Rodriguez*: School Finance Litigation and the Impact of New Judicial Federalism," *Law & Society Review*, 32 (1): 175–220.

Rodgers, Harrell, R. Jr., and Charles S. Bullock III. 1972. *Law and Social Change: Civil Rights Laws and Their Consequences*. New York: McGraw-Hill.

Rosenthal, Elisabeth. 1998. "For One-Child Policy, China Rethinks Iron Hand," *The New York Times*, (November 1): Y1, Y16.

Scheingold, Stuart. 1989. "Constitutional Rights and Social Change: Civil Rights in Perspective." Pp. 73–91 in Michael W. McCann and Gerald Houseman (eds.), *Judging the Constitution: Critical Essays on Judicial Lawmaking*. Glenview, IL: Scott, Foresman/Little, Brown.

Scher, R. and J. Button. 1984. "Voting Rights Act: Instrumentation and Impact." Pp. 20–54 in Charles Bullock and Charles Lamb (eds.), *Instrumentation of Civil Rights Policy*. Monterey, CA: Brooks/Cole.

Schmidt, William E. 1992. "British Courts to Doff Wig? Verdict Asked," *New York Times* (August 23): 4Y.

Schur, Edwin M. 1968. *Law and Society: A Sociological View*. New York: Random House.

Schwartz, Richard D. and Sonya Orleans. 1970. "On Legal Sanctions." Pp. 533–547 in Richard D. Schwartz and Jerome A. Skolnick (eds.), *Society and the Legal Order*. New York: Basic Books.

Seidman, Robert B. 1978. *The State, Law and Development*. New York: St. Martin's Press.

St. Louis Post-Dispatch. 1998. "Britons Take off Jackets, Hang up Their Customs and Relax Dress Codes" (September 2): A2.

Sumner, William Graham. 1906. *Folkways*. Boston: Ginn.

Toffler, Alvin. 1970. *Future Shock*. New York: Random House.

Tone, Andrea. 2001. *Devices and Desires, A History of Contraceptives in America*. New York: Hill & Wang.

Tyler, Patrick E. 1995. "Population Control in China Falls to Coercion and Evasion," *New York Times* (June 25): 1, 6.

Tyler, Tom R. 1990. *Why People Obey the Law*. New Haven: Yale University Press.

TYLER, TOM R., JONATHAN D. CASPER, and BONNIE FISHER. 1988. *Maintaining Allegiance toward Legal Authorities: The Role of Prior Attitudes and the Use of Fair Procedures*. ABF Working Paper #8813. Chicago: American Bar Foundation.

VAGO, STEVEN. 1999. *Social Change*. 4th ed. Upper Saddle River, NJ: Prentice Hall.

VINING, JOSEPH. 1986. *The Authoritative and the Authoritarian*. Chicago: University of Chicago Press.

VISHER, CHRISTY A. and DAVID WEISBURD. 1998. "Identification of What Works: Recent Trends in Crime Prevention Strategies," *Crime, Law & Social Change* 28: 223–242.

VOLTI, RUDI. 1995. *Society and Technological Change*. 3rd ed. New York: St. Martin's Press.

WATSON, GOODWIN. 1969. "Resistance to Change." Pp. 488–498 in Warren G. Bennis, Kenneth D. Benne, and Robert Chin (eds.), *The Planning of Change*, 2nd ed. New York: Holt, Rinehart & Winston.

WEBER, MAX. 1947. *The Theory of Social Economic Organizations*. Ed. Talcott Parsons. Glencoe, IL: Free Press. 1968. *Economy and Society*, Vol. I. Ed. Roph Guenther and Claus Wittich. New York: Badminster Press.

ZIMRING, FRANKLIN and GORDON HAWKINS. 1975. "The Legal Threat as an Instrument of Social Change." Pp. 329–339 in Ronald L. Akers and Richard Hawkins (eds.), *Law and Control in Society*. Englewood Cliffs, NJ: Prentice Hall.

8
The
Legal
Profession

An examination of the legal profession and its role in society touches on important issues in sociological theory—issues involving power, social control, stratification, socialization, and the social organization of law work. This chapter analyzes the character of the legal profession and the social forces shaping it. It begins with a historical background of law, with an emphasis on the professionalization of lawyers and the evolution of the legal profession in America. Next, the chapter focuses on the legal profession today: what lawyers do and where, their income, and how they compete for business. The emphasis is then placed on the accessibility of legal services to the poor and the not so poor, followed by a portrayal of law schools and the training and socialization of lawyers into the profession. The section concludes with some comments on bar admission, bar associations as interest groups, and professional discipline.

BACKGROUND

The cultural history and the emergence of the legal profession and the legal professional have long fascinated scholars in history, law and sociology (see, for example, Pue and Sugarman, 1999). In primitive societies, as noted in Chapter 2, custom and law coincided. The laws of a primitive legal system are unwritten and comparatively undifferentiated. Such societies have courts and judges but no lawyers. The courts are temporary, and when a violation of a law has occurred, the defendant is not represented by a "lawyer." Each individual is his or her own "lawyer," and everyone more or less knows the law. Although some individuals may be wiser than others and more skilled in social affairs, this skill is not considered a *legal* skill.

The development of the legal profession has been intimately connected with the rise and development of legal systems. The origins of the legal profession can be traced back to Rome (Friedman, 1977:21). Initially, Roman law allowed individuals to argue cases on behalf of others; however, those persons were trained not in law but in rhetoric. They were called orators and were not allowed to take fees. Later on, by Cicero's time, there were jurists as well—individuals who were knowledgeable about the law and to whom people went for legal opinions. They were called *juris prudentes*, but these men learned in the law did not yet constitute a profession. Only during the Imperial Period did lawyers begin to practice law for a living and schools of law emerge. By this time, the law had become exceedingly complex in Rome. The occupation of lawyers arose together with a sophisticated legal system, and the complexity of that system made the Roman lawyer indispensable.

C. Ray Jeffery (1962:314–315) points out that by the Middle Ages, the lawyer had three functions—agent, advocate, and jurisconsult. The word "attorney" originally meant an agent, a person who acts or appears on behalf of someone else. In this role of agent, the lawyer appeared in court to handle legal matters in place of his client. In ancient Athens and Rome, an agent was allowed to appear in the place of another person. In France, however, a person had to appear in court himself, and in England, he needed special permission from the king to be represented in court by an agent. In France, by 1356, there were 105 *legistes* (men of law) representing clients in court (Jacoby, 1973:14).

The difference between an agent and an advocate appeared when the lawyer went to court with his client to assist the client in presenting his case. In addition to law, the advocate was trained in the art of oratory and persuasion. In England, the function of the agent was taken over by solicitors and attorneys; the advocate became the barrister (trial lawyer). The function of a lawyer as a jurisconsult was both as a legal advisor and as a writer and teacher. Although contemporary lawyers perform essentially the same functions, the modern legal profession is fundamentally different. Friedman notes: "It is organized. It is lucrative. It is closed except to those who have undergone training or apprenticeship. It holds a monopoly of courtroom work and the giving of 'legal' advice" (1977:21).

THE PROFESSIONALIZATION OF LAWYERS

Law is considered one of the three archetypical "learned" professions—the Church and medicine are the other two (Kritzer, 1990:5). But what is a profession, and what does the process of professionalization entail? In the sociological literature, professionalization implies the transformation of some nonprofessional occupation into a vocation with the attributes of a profession, and the specification of these could be discussed in great detail (see, for example, Macdonald, 1995). Foote captures the essential ingredients: "As a modicum, the possession (1) of a specialized technique supported by a body of theory, (2) of a career supported by an association of colleagues, and (3) of a status supported by community recognition may be mentioned as constituting an occupation as a profession" (1953:371–372). Also usually included in the discussion of professions are the ideas of a client-practitioner relationship and a high degree of autonomy in the execution of one's work tasks. Harold L. Wilensky (1964:143) has studied those occupations that are now viewed as professions, such as law, medicine, and the Church, and notes that they have passed through the following general stages in their professionalization:

1. Became full-time occupations
2. a. Training schools established
   b. University affiliation of training schools
3. a. Local professional associations started
   b. National professional associations evolved
4. State licensing laws
5. Formal codes of ethics established

Magali Sarfatti Larson (1977) provides additional insights into professionalization as the process by which producers of special services seek to constitute and to *control* a market for their expertise. Because marketable expertise is an important element in the structure of inequality, professionalization also appears as a collective assertion of special social status and as a collective process of upward mobility. She considers professionalization an attempt to translate one type of scarce resources—special knowledge and skills—into another—social and economic rewards. The attempt by professions to maintain scarcity implies a tendency toward monopoly: monopoly of expertise in the market and monopoly of status in a system of stratification. She contends: "Viewed in the larger perspective of the occupational and class structures, it would appear that the model of professional passes from a predominantly economic function—organizing the linkage between education and the marketplace—to a predominantly ideological one—justifying inequality of status and closure of access in the occupational order" (Larson, 1977:xviii). For Larson, the following elements in the professionalization process are inseparably related: differentiation and standardization of professional services; formalization of the conditions for entry; persuasion of the public that they need services only professionals can provide; and state protection (in the form of licensing) of the professional market against those who lack formal qualifications and against competing occupations. She contends that educational institutions and professional associations play a central role in attaining each of these goals.

A crucial element in the professionalization process is market control—the successful assertion of unchallenged authority over some area of knowledge and its professional instrumentation (Flores, 1988). Until the body of legal knowledge, including procedure, became too much for the ordinary person to handle, there was no need for a legal profession. Before the thirteenth century, it was possible for a litigant to appoint someone to do his or her technical pleading. This person was not a member of a separate profession, for apparently anyone could act in that capacity. The person who did the technical pleading eventually developed into, or was superseded by, the attorney who was appointed in court and had the power to bind his employer to a plea.

"The profession of advocate," writes Michael E. Tigar (1977:157), "in the sense of a regulated group of (law) practitioners with some formal training, emerged in the late 1200s." Both the English and the French sovereigns legislated with respect to the profession, limiting the practice of law to those who had been approved by judicial officers. The profession of full-time specialists in the law and in legal procedures appeared initially as officers of the king's court. The first professional lawyers were judges who trained their successors by apprenticeship. The apprentices took on functions in the courtroom and gradually came to monopolize pleading before the royal judges. In England, training moved out of the courtroom and into the Inns of Court, which were the residences of the judges and practicing attorneys. The attorneys, after several reorganizations of their own ranks, finally became a group known as barristers. Members of the Inns became organized and came to monopolize training in the law as well as control of official access to the government. Signs of the professionalization of lawyers began to appear.

In England, the complexity of court procedures required technical pleading with the aid of an attorney, and oral argument eventually required special skills. By the time of Henry III (1216–1272), judges had become professionals, and the courts started to create a body of substantive legal knowledge as well as technical procedure. The king needed individuals to represent his interests in the courts. In the early fourteenth century, he appointed sergeants of the king to take care of his legal business. When not engaged in the king's business, these fabled sergeants-at-law of the Common Pleas Court could serve individuals in the capacity of lawyers.

A crucial event in the beginning of the legal profession was an edict issued in 1292 by Edward I. During this period, legal business had increased enormously; yet, there were no schools of common law, and the universities considered law too vulgar a subject for scholarly investigation. The universities were, at that time, agencies of the church, and the civil law taught there was essentially codified Roman law, the instrument of bureaucratic centralization. Edward's order, which directed Common Pleas to choose certain "attorneys and learners" who alone would be allowed to follow the court and to take part in court business, created a monopoly of the legal profession.

The effect of placing the education of lawyers into the hands of the court cannot be overestimated. It resulted in the relative isolation of English lawyers from Continental, Roman, and ecclesiastical influences. Lawyer taught lawyer, and each learned from the processes of the courts, so that the law had to grow by drawing on its own resources and not by borrowing from others. But the court itself was no place for the training of these attorneys and learners. It did, however, provide aid in the form of an observation post, called the crib, in which students could sit and take notes, and from which occasionally they might ask questions during the course of a trial.

Training for lawyers was provided by the Inns of Court. A small self-selecting group of barristers gave informal training and monopolized practice before the government courts of London, as well as judgeships in those courts. Barristers evolved into court lawyers (that is, lawyers who acted as the mouthpiece of their clients in court proceedings). Originally they were called "story-tellers" (Latin *narrators*); they told their client's story in courts, and this is their essential function to this day. The barristers' monopoly of court activities helped create a second group within the legal profession, named the "solicitors" (or "fixers"), who advised clients, prepared cases for trial, and handled matters outside the courtroom (Simpson, 1988:148–156). This group arose to meet the needs of clients, because barristers were too involved as officers of the court to be very responsible to outsiders. The barristers outranked solicitors, both by virtue of their monopoly of access to the court and through their control of training. Originally, solicitors were drawn from the ranks of those who attended the Inns of Court, and later they came to be trained almost entirely by apprenticeships or through schools of their own. At first, in the Inns of Court, lawyers lived together during the terms of court, and for them the Inns represented law school, a professional organization, and a tightly knit social club, all in one.

Initially, universities such as Oxford and Cambridge saw little reason to include training such as it was practiced in the Inns in their teaching programs. (Until fairly recently, law was not regarded highly as a university subject. The number of law professors was small, and their prestige was rather low, since "law school was treated as the appropriate home for rowing men of limited intellect" [Simpson, 1988:158].) Only subjects such as legal history, jurisprudence, and Roman and ecclesiastical law were considered part of a liberal education to be provided by the universities (Kearney, 1970). University education was sought by "gentlemen," whereas legal training at the Inns of Court became the cheapest and the easiest route of social mobility for those who aspired to become gentlemen. Many sons of prosperous yeomen and merchants chose legal apprenticeship in an attempt to adopt a lifestyle associated with a gentleman. The appointment in 1758 of Sir William Blackstone to the Vinerian chair of jurisprudence at Cambridge marked the first effort to make English law a university subject. Blackstone thought it would help both would-be lawyers and educated people generally to have a "system of legal education" (as he called it), which would be far broader than the practical legal training offered in the Inns of Court. Blackstone may thus be considered the founder of the modern English system of university education in law (Berman, 1996:6–9).

By the end of the eighteenth century, law in England had become a full-fledged profession. Members of the profession considered the law a full-time occupation, training schools were established, universities began to offer degrees in law, and a professional association evolved in the form of a lawyers' guild. The practice of law required licensing, and formal codes of ethics were established. Knowledge of law and skills of legal procedures became a marketable commodity, and lawyers had a monopoly on them. The practice of law in royal courts was limited to members of the lawyers' guild, which in turn enhanced their political power, their monopoly of expertise in the market, and their monopoly of status in a system of stratification. Access to the profession became controlled, and social mobility for those admitted assured. By the end of the eighteenth century, the name "attorney" had been dropped in favor of the term "solicitor," with the formation of the Society of Gentlemen Practicers in the Courts of Law and Equity, which was their professional society until 1903, when the Law Society came into being. In the following section, I shall examine the rise of the legal profession in the United States

THE EVOLUTION OF THE AMERICAN
LEGAL PROFESSION

The American legal profession, like the American government, has its roots in English government organization. Colonial America was a transplant of English institutions, but with an emphasis on even greater decentralization. The practice of law in the pre-Revolutionary period was virtually monopolized by the upper class of merchants and planters, who did their best to emulate the English pattern of closed legal castes. In the South, wealthy planters tended to send their sons to the Inns of Court in London for legal training. In the northern colonies, bar associations developed in most of the populous places after 1750, beginning originally as social clubs, but gradually coming to control admission to practice. The colonial legislatures delegated to the courts the power of admission to practice before them. In the late eighteenth century, the local bar associations, in particular in New York and Massachusetts, were in turn delegated responsibility for recommending lawyers for admittance, amounting to de facto control; their numbers constituted a powerful political elite (Hurst, 1950:249–311).

Before the Revolution, lawyers were unpopular. Both the Puritans and the planters feared a secularized legal profession. The Puritans felt that the Bible was all the "law" needed and wished to combine their religion with law. The planters opposed lawyers because of the threat they posed to their political power. Lawyers became even more unpopular during the American Revolution than they had been before (Friedman, 1973:265). Since many lawyers were closely associated with the upper class in background and in interests, it was among this group that the British sympathizers were most concentrated. As a result, a substantial proportion of lawyers emigrated to England during wartime persecutions of Tories. The prevailing custom of the bar to limit practice to a small group of elites also contributed to lawyers' unpopularity, as did their efforts to collect wealthy creditors' claims in the period following the Revolution.

After the Revolution, the legal profession became more egalitarian, the distinction between barristers and attorneys—in imitation of the English system—disappeared with democratization of the legal profession, standards of admission to the bar became loosened, and bar associations crumbled and disappeared as their powers waned. Between 1800 and 1870, the power of admission to the bar was granted by local courts. In its most extreme form, this meant that admission in one court conferred no right to practice before others, although it was more usual for the right to practice in one court to enable one to practice before any other court in the same state. Centralized admission (more in theory than practice) was prevalent only in a handful of states and territories.

Neither college education nor a law degree was absolutely required for admission to the bar. The bar examination itself was usually oral and administered in a casual fashion. Legal education throughout the nineteenth century was similarly informal. The principal method of education was apprenticeship in a lawyer's office, during which the student performed small services, served papers, and copied legal documents. In his spare time, he read what law, history, and general books were available. Students in the offices of leading lawyers were often charged fees for apprenticeship.

The first law schools grew out of specialized law offices offering apprentice programs. They used many of the same techniques as the offices. The earliest such school was founded in Litchfield, Connecticut, in 1784. It proved successful and grew rapidly in size. In time, it gained national reputation and attracted students from all over the country. It offered a fourteen-month course, but the school gave no diploma. At that time, law degrees were of little worth. The system was not one of formal certification. The egalitarian caste of political power in nineteenth-century America extended to legal practice as well. The school taught law by the lecture method. The lectures were never published; to publish would have meant to perish, since students would have no reason to pay tuition and attend classes.

Along with other noteworthy developments in American higher education (Freeland, 1992), university law schools started to replace the Litchfield type as the principal alternative to office training, but legal training at the university level was still rare. A few university professorships of law were established as far back as 1779 at William and Mary, and 1793 at Columbia, as well as at Harvard in 1816 and at Yale in 1824. But attendance was spotty, and the courses given were short and informal, covering the same materials as apprenticeship programs and allowing students to drop in and out as suited their own convenience. Legal standards for passing the course were minimal, and only a single final oral examination was required at some universities. Even at Harvard in the mid-nineteenth century, the standards were very low, and "there were absolutely no examinations to get in, or to proceed, or to get out. All that was required was the lapse of time, two years, and the payment of the fees" (Friedman, 1998:242).

After 1870, a number of interrelated changes took place that established stratification within the legal profession and brought university law schools to an important position. A nationally prominent group of lawyers developed, and the bar (or the lawyers' union, although never called by that name) fought vigorously to protect the boundaries of the calling (Friedman, 1973:550). Simultaneously, university professors of law began to make claims for the scientific status of law. The bar association movement started and spread at the same time that farmers and workers were also organizing. The new establishment of bar associations led to efforts to restrict admission to the bar. In 1878, the American Bar Association was formed (Friedman, 1973:563). After 1878, boards of examiners normally controlled by the local bar associations replaced the state supreme courts as the examining authority. Statewide boards were established and financed themselves out of applicants' fees. The boards were almost invariably controlled by the state bar associations. Professional self-regulation had taken another important step forward (Stevens, 1971:458–459).

Starting in 1870, the teaching of law began with the use of the case method at Harvard University. Instead of using the older system of text reading and lectures, the instructor carried on a discussion of assigned cases designed to bring out their general principles. The proponent of the case method, Harvard Law Dean Christopher Columbus Langdell, believed that law was a general science and that its principles could be experimentally induced from the examination of case materials. He rejected the use of textbooks and instead used casebooks as teaching materials; these were collections of reports of actual cases, carefully selected and arranged to illustrate the meaning and development of principles of law. The teacher became a Socratic guide, leading the student to an understanding of concepts and principles hidden as essences among the cases. Langdell also made it more difficult for students to gain admission. If an applicant did not have a college degree, he had to pass an entrance examination. A student was required to show a knowledge of Latin by translating from Virgil or Cicero; on occasion, a skill in French was acceptable as a substitute for Latin. Langdell likewise made it harder for a student to get out. The length of legal education was increased to two years in 1871, then to three years in 1876. The lax oral examinations for the law degree were replaced by a series of written exams with increasingly formal standards. By 1896, Harvard required a college degree as a prerequisite for admission to law school (Friedman, 1973:530–532). Before that, in fact, there were more lawyers than college graduates in America (Stevens, 1983:73).

But the method remained attractive and suited the needs of the legal profession. It enabled the size of classes to expand, with one professor to every 75 students (Stevens, 1983:63). It exalted the prestige of law and legal training and affirmed that legal science stood apart as an independent entity distinct from politics, legislation, and ordinary people. Langdell provided grounds for certain important claims of the legal profession. Law, he maintained, was a science that demanded rigorous formal training. There was justification, then, for the lawyers' monopoly of practice. The bar association movement coincided with Langdell's rise to power. The two supplemented and complemented each other and further strengthened the lawyers' monopoly of practice.

The increased emphasis on professionalization and monopoly of the practice of law brought about concerted efforts to improve the quality of legal education, to raise admission standards, and to intensify the power of bar associations. Attempts to improve legal education meant, in practice, the adoption of the standards of the leading law schools. The adoption of formal education requirements for admission to bar exams further strengthened the schools, and by 1940, three years of law school study were required by 40 states. At the same time, efforts were made to incorporate the standards of the leading law schools into the bar exam prerequisites by calling for the requirement of two years of college as preparation before law studies in 1921, a requirement that was adopted by two-thirds of the states by 1940. By 1950, three years of college had become the norm, and by the 1960s, four years of college were required. A law student of today would find it hard to believe that until the 1950s, the number of lawyers who had not been in college exceeded the number of those who had been (Stevens, 1983:209). The Law School Admission Test (LSAT) was ready for general use in 1948. The American Bar Association, in 1929, established law school accreditation standards, and the bar-admitting authorities encouraged the ABA's accreditation efforts. Today, graduation from an ABA-approved law school satisfies the legal-education requirement for admission to the bar (after passing the bar exam) in all jurisdictions in the United States.

For much of its history, the profession was dominated by white males. Not a single woman was admitted to the bar before the 1870s, and very few blacks (Friedman, 1998, 2002). Women, particularly married women, were not considered suitable for the practice of law. They were seen as delicate creatures and, just like children and lunatics, lacked full legal rights. By allowing women to practice law, the traditional order of the family would be upset. In a notorious opinion of a justice of the U.S. Supreme Court in 1873, "the natural and proper timidity and delicacy which belongs to the female sex evidently unfits it for many of the occupations of civil life. . . . The paramount destiny and mission of women are to fulfill the noble and benign offices of wife and mother. This is the law of the creator" (Stevens, 1983:82). Not until 1878 did federal courts open the door to women attorneys. Law schools began to admit women in 1869, although in many places the courses of instruction were "open to the male sex only." In 1872, Charlotte E. Ray became the first black woman to graduate from an American law school (Smith, 1998). As of 1880, there were 75 women lawyers and 1,010 by 1900 (Stevens, 1983:83). By 1984, of the 649,000 lawyers, more than 83,000 were women (Curran, 1986:20, 25).

The profession explicitly discriminated against blacks (Abel, 1986). They were excluded from the American Bar Association until the 1950s and from many law schools. As recently as 1965, blacks made up 11 percent of the population but less than 2 percent of lawyers and only 1.3 percent of law students, half of them in all-black law schools. Even in 1977, only 5 percent of the country's law students were black (Friedman, 1998, 2002). By the 1990–91 academic year, this figure had risen slightly to 5.6 percent. Although law schools claim that they recruit aggressively for minorities, in 1992 blacks still made up just 3.4 percent of lawyers (Pollock and Adler, 1992:4) and in 2001 their representation was still around 4 percent.

Law firms were about as discriminatory as law schools. Many excluded Jews, Catholics, blacks, and women. Through the 1950s, most firms were solidly WASP (white Anglo-Saxon Protestant). Legal politicians argued that the profession was a means by which Jews, immigrants, and basically non-WASPs "might undermine the American way of life" (Stevens, 1983:100–101). By the 1960s, discriminatory hiring practices had started to decrease, but they have not yet fully disappeared. There are still signs of tokenism for blacks and women, and Jews are excluded from high-prestige fields (Heinz and Laumann, 1994). Income disparities and subtler forms of gender bias in promotion to top positions still persist (Keeva, 1995). A recent study shows that only 14 percent of the partners are women in the nation's top 250 law firms (Nossel and Westfall, 1998).

A 2001 survey of the 12 highest-grossing law firms in the United States by the New York Times (Glater, 2001a) finds that minority lawyers accounted for about 5 percent of the new partners in recent years at the seven firms that supplied such data. Some lawyers contend that while law schools have aggressively recruited minority students and many law firms have done the same for minority graduates, firms have been more reluctant to promote minority associates to partnership. One reason lawyers offer is that minority lawyers are less likely to have relationships with important clients or to have landed a significant amount of business for the firm. But some minority lawyers say that they are not given the same opportunities as white lawyers to work with important clients, often because they do not have mentors who ensure that they have access to the best work. Finally, minority lawyers also cite what they perceive to be a lack of opportunity for advancement within firms and as a result they opt for career opportunities in business, consulting firms, government jobs or corporate legal departments.

There are also complaints about alleged disparate treatment of male and female lawyers in court in demeanor and language (Curriden, 1995a). Minority female attorneys claim that they lack support by white women and minority men attorneys, face both race and sex discrimination, and have difficulties establishing networks (Quade, 1995). Sexual harassment continues to be a problem. In a survey of the Ninth U.S. Circuit Court (California and eight other western states), 60 percent of women lawyers alleged that they have been sexually harassed by men involved in the court system (Woo, 1992). There is evidence to suggest that women's integration into the legal profession remains marginal in spite of their growing proportions in the field. They are still underrepresented in law firm partnerships and move more slowly than men toward these positions. Further, women exit from the legal profession at a much higher rate than their male counterparts (Kay, 1997).

There have also been noticeable changes in the practice of law. Before the Civil War, much of legal business concerned land and commerce, representing primarily speculative interests in the West. After the middle of the nineteenth century, the most lucrative business came to center on the big corporations, beginning first with the railroads. After the Civil War, the position of general counsel for the railroads was the most highly esteemed legal position, and, during the same period, lawyers became closely involved with the major banks and began to sit on boards of directors. By the turn of the century, corporate law firms were edging to the pinnacle of professional aspiration and power (Auerbach, 1976:22). Lawyers were instrumental in the growth of corporations, devising new forms of charters, assisting companies to organize national business, while taking maximum advantage of variable state laws concerning incorporation and taxation. At the turn of the century, the emergence and proliferation of firms specializing in corporation law provided those lawyers who possessed appropriate social, religious, and ethnic credentials with an opportunity to secure personal power and to shape the future of their profession. But only lawyers who possessed what Gerald S. Auerbach (1976:21) calls "considerable social capital" could inhabit the world of the corporate-law firm.

Through corporate-law firms, the large modern-style law firm came into existence. Before the middle of the nineteenth century, law practice was individual or conducted in two-man partnerships. After 1850, partnerships dealing with business interests began to specialize internally, with one person handling the court appearances and the other taking care of office details. At the same time, business clients started to solicit opinions from law firms on legal aspects of prospective policies, a practice that gradually led to the establishment of permanent relationships between law firms and corporations. The size of major law firms began to grow. The prominence of the "Wall Street law firm," allied with major corporations, originated in the late nineteenth century, growing along with the corporations whose economic dominance they helped make possible. Notes Friedman: "By and large, the leading lawyers of the big Wall Street firms were solid Republicans, conservative in outlook, standard Protestant in faith, old English in heritage" (1973:553). It should be noted, however, that such large firms were, and are today, an exception. Close to half of all lawyers in private practice continue to practice alone, usually in a particular ethnic community, and this has undoubtedly been the case throughout history (Carlin, 1962). Generally, individual practitioners of law use the legal profession more as an avenue of social mobility than do their counterparts in large firms.

In addition to changes in the structure and functions of the profession, there have been substantial changes in its numbers. In 1850, there were approximately 24,000 lawyers in the United States. In the next 50 years, after the Civil War and the transformation of the American economy, there were significant changes in supply and demand. The number of lawyers increased to approximately 60,000 by 1880, and to 115,000 by 1900 (Halliday, 1986:62).

THE PROFESSION TODAY

Since the 1960s, law has become the fastest-growing of all professions in the United States. The number of lawyers increased from 285,933 in 1960 to 355,242 in 1970 and reached 649,000 in 1984 when already one out of every 364 people was a lawyer (Curran, 1986:20). (But only one attorney seems to be available for every 7,000 *poor* Americans, and the ratio is one to 14,000 in the Chicano community [Spangler, 1986:6].) By contrast, as noted in Chapter 6, the population-to-lawyer ratios are much higher in other countries. In the early 1980s, for example, there was one lawyer for 1,431 people in Belgium, one for 963 in Scotland, and one for 599 in Ontario, Canada (Lewis, 1986:82). China, with a population in excess of 1.2 billion, has about 30,000 lawyers (Galanter, 1992:13). Close to the end of the twentieth century there were over 950,000 lawyers in the United States (Gross, 1998:26), and their number has exceeded one million by the dawn of the twenty-first century. The number of lawyers in any society is a function of the social role assigned to lawyers (Friedman, 1977:24; Halliday, 1986). The role of lawyers in society is conditioned by a variety of factors, such as the degree of industrialization, bureaucratization, complexity of business transactions, expansion of legal entitlements, the growth of regulation, crime rates, and attitudes toward and availability of nonlegal methods of conflict resolution.

Attorneys have never been popular, and "lawyers, on the whole, have a terrible image" (Friedman, 1998, 2002). Plato spoke of their "small and unrighteous" souls, and Keats said, "I think we may class the lawyer in the natural history of monsters." Thomas More left lawyers out of his Utopia, and Shakespeare made his feelings known in that famous line from *Henry VI, Part II:* "The first thing we do, let's kill all the lawyers." Undoubtedly, the adversarial system is costly not only in money (a controversial economist [Magee, 1992] argues that lawyers cause a $600 billion reduction in our economy annually) but also in trust. Polls show that the public has limited confidence in the profession. For example, in a 1993 American Bar Association poll, 63 percent of people queried said lawyers make too much, 59 percent called them greedy, and 40 percent said the phrase "hone and ethical" does not apply (Shullins, 1994). In a recent Gallup poll, 46 percent of the respondents rated them as "low" or "very low" in honesty and ethical standards—just slightly above car salesmen if it is any consolation (Gross, 1998:26).

Headlines in professional and popular publications and book titles are anything but flattering. Some examples: "The Lawyer as Liar" (Uviller, 1994); "Why Lawyers Lie: The Truth Is Not the Highest Priority in a Criminal Trial" (Abrams, 1994). "The Law According to the Chequebook—The Duplicity of Lawyers" (Fotheringham, 1994); "Who Ya Gonna Call? 1–800–Sue Me" (*Newsweek*, 1995), *Beyond All Reason: The Radical Assault on Truth in American Law* (Farber and Sherry, 1997). Their perceived greediness is reflected in titles such as "How to Rob a Bank" (Frum, 1994) or "A King's Ransom" (Lerman, 1995) referring to Rodney King's lawyer, submitting a $1 million bill to the city of Los Angeles for his defense-related activities. In *Why Lawyers Behave As They Do,* Paul G. Haskell (1998) actually claims that the public is justified in its low opinion of the legal profession and explains the professional rules that govern how lawyers behave and which allow—or require—conduct that laypersons may find unethical. Finally, Richard Zitrin and Carol M. Langford (1999) in *The Moral Compass of the American Lawyer: Truth, Justice, Power, and Greed,* argue that the delivery of of legal and adjudicative services should not be governed solely by market forces and human acquisitiveness.

Similar attitudes prevail toward lawyers in other countries. For example, in the former Soviet Union (even though Lenin himself was trained as a lawyer and actually practiced for a short time), lawyers were considered one of the most unnecessary, parasitic, and exploitative groups, ranking in esteem with priests and capitalists (Cameron, 1978:50). In India, the profession "has lost the social and moral prestige," and lawyers "go all out for money with little qualms about the image and morality of the profession" (Gandhi, 1982:33). In England, lawyers always have had a bad press. They have been depicted as hypocrites; greedy social parasites; pettyfoggers, who, in the pursuit of their clients' interests, obfuscate real issues and use distinctions devoid of ethical merit; and being basically contemptuous of truth and unsympathetic and brutal in their behavior.

Although lawyer-bashing is a venerable tradition, in fairness to lawyers, much of their negative image is exaggerated, and they are probably not much worse than members of other professions. Some of the charges are due to guilt by association. They often deal with people in trouble: criminals, politicians, businesspeople, and those seeking a divorce. At times, they articulate strong partisan interests, and it is no surprise that they are the object of strong sentiments. Although lawyers play a useful role and are sometimes admired, they are rarely loved. Probably no other legitimate profession has been as subjected to extremes of homage and vilification as lawyers (Bonsignore et al., 1989:241).

There are four principal subgroups in the legal profession: lawyers in private practice, lawyers in government service, lawyers in private employment, and the judiciary. In the United States, 74 percent of lawyers are in private practice, 12 percent work for the government, 12 percent are in salaried positions in private industry, and the rest are in the judiciary, educational institutions, legal-aid programs, private associations such as unions, and other special-interest organizations. It is interesting to note, by contrast, that in Germany slightly over one-fifth of the bar are in private practice, and another fifth are employed by the judiciary. Proportionately, three times as many lawyers work for the government and twice as many are in private employment in Germany as in the United States (Rueschemeyer, 1973:32).

In career patterns, self-image, and sheer numbers, lawyers in private practice constitute the central group of the American legal profession from which other types of practice are branching out. These lawyers generally work as either individual practitioners or members of law firms. Of the lawyers in private practice, some 180,000 work as individual practitioners (Curran, 1986:28). The next section will consider the private practice of law in the context of solo and firm practitioners.

WHERE THE LAWYERS ARE

Law is big business in the United States, and legal work now accounts for over 2 percent of the gross national product, more than steel or electric power. Each year, thousands of young adults graduate from law school, pass the bar, and enter the profession. They engage in a variety of activities in diverse settings. Some go into private practice; others find jobs in government or private industry. A few even decide not to stay in law.

Private Practice

The majority of lawyers (roughly 74 percent) in the United States are in private practice. Contrary to the popular image that is reinforced by television, only a small proportion of lawyers engage in litigation. In private practice, lawyers perform a number of significant roles. One is *counseling*. Attorneys spend about one-third of their time advising their clients about the proper course of action in anticipation of the reactions of courts, agencies, or third parties. Another is *negotiating*, both in criminal and in civil cases. Plea bargaining is an example of negotiation and is widely used in criminal cases (Palermo et al., 1998). Pretrial hearings and conferences in attempts to reach a settlement and thus avoid a costly trial are illustrative of the negotiating role of lawyers in civil cases. *Drafting*, the writing and revision of legal documents such as contracts, wills, deeds, and leases, is the "most legal" of a lawyer's role, although the availability of standardized forms for many kinds of legal problems often limits the lawyer to filling in the blanks. *Litigating* is a specialty, and relatively few lawyers engage in actual trial work. Much of the litigation in the United States is generally uncontested in cases such as debt, divorce, civil commitment, and criminal charges. Some lawyers also engage in *investigating*. In a criminal case, for example, the defense attorney may search for the facts and gather background information in support of the client's plea. Finally, lawyers take part in *researching*—searching, for example, for precedents, adapting legal doctrine to specific cases, and anticipating court or agency rulings in particular situations. Much of such research activity is carried out by lawyers in large firms and appellate specialists. Experienced lawyers working in their specialty (or those working for a small fee) usually do little research (Klein, 1984:74–76).

The two extremes in private practice are represented by solo practitioners and big law firms, often referred to as Wall Street firms. In between, there are partnerships and small law firms of relatively modest size. There is now a growing trend of female attorneys setting up their own firms (Graham, 1995). Solo practitioners are generalists; they operate in small offices and are "the jacks-of-all-trades of the legal profession" (Jacob, 1995). Many of these lawyers engage in marginal areas of law, such as collections, personal injury cases, rent cases, and evictions. They face competition from other professionals, such as accountants and real estate brokers, who are increasingly handling the tax and real estate work traditionally carried out by the solo practitioner. Jerome E. Carlin (1962:209) points out that the pressures to make a living may force individual practitioners to submit to pressures to violate legal ethics, and in a later study he suggests that indeed this is the case (Carlin, 1966). Lawyers in solo practice often act, Carlin notes, as intermediaries between clients and other lawyers to receive referral fees. In such an instance, the individual practitioner may become a businessperson rather than a lawyer, thus defeating his or her original purpose of becoming a professional in the first place. As Carlin concludes:

> In considering the work of the individual lawyer in Chicago, one is drawn to the conclusion that he is rarely called upon to exercise a high level of professional skill. This arises in part from the generally low quality of his professional training, but even more from the character of the demands placed upon him by the kinds of work and clients he is likely to encounter. Most matters that reach the individual practitioner—the small residential closing, the simple uncontested divorce, drawing up a will or probating a small estate, routing filings for a small business, negotiating a personal injury claim, or collecting on a debt—do not require very much technical knowl-

edge, and what technical problems there are generally simplified by use of standardized forms and procedures. (1962:206–207)

Carlin notes that these lawyers attempt to justify their low status in the profession by emphasizing their independence and pointing out that they are general practitioners and thus knowledgeable about all facets of the law. This notion of autonomy, however, does not compensate for their feeling of insignificance in the overall legal structure and their frustration over not realizing their initial high ambitions, although they are professionals. Carlin (1962:206) suggests that these individual practitioners, like their counterparts in general practice in medicine, are "most likely to be found at the margin of (their) profession, enjoying little freedom in choice of clients, type of work, or conditions of practice."

Jack Ladinsky (1963), in a study of a sample of 207 Detroit-area lawyers, of whom 100 were solo and 107 were medium- to large-firm practitioners, reinforced Carlin's findings on individual practitioners. Ladinsky also found that individual practitioners come from minority religious and ethnic backgrounds, have parents of entrepreneurial or small-business status, and receive qualitatively and quantitatively inferior education more often than the lawyers in the law-firm practice he included in the study (1963:49). Ladinsky suggests that social background (religious preference of mother and occupation of father) is the strongest determinant of whether a lawyer goes into firm or solo practice. The quality of the law school is an important intervening variable. Ladinsky notes: "Social background describes two major career contingencies: level of technical skill and access to clients" (1963:53). Socioeconomic considerations and ethnic and cultural factors force solo lawyers toward local night school or Catholic university law schools. Ladinsky further points out that after graduation, relatively poor training and discrimination in firm recruitment make it difficult to get a prestigious firm job, and so solo lawyers end up doing low-paying, low-status work—that is, injury suits, divorce, petty criminal, and debt collection. They often develop a clientele of people of similar class, ethnic, and religious background.

There are also differences between individual and firm practitioners in acceptance of and compliance with ethical norms. Jerome Carlin (1966) found that the individual practitioner was the most likely to violate ethical norms (for example, soliciting kickbacks or making or arranging police payoffs), with the nature of the client and the type of case being important contributing factors in the violations. Since solo practitioners often represent individuals, as contrasted with corporations that are represented by larger firms, the quality of the lawyers involved adversely affects the legal representation that many individuals receive. Because these lawyers are often from minority groups, minority clients are the ones who are adversely affected. Moreover, many of the larger, more prestigious, and more ethical firms will not accept the kinds of cases the individual practitioner confronts, and in fact refer those cases to him or her, so that the organization of the bar is such that ethical violations and ineffective practice are almost built into certain situations.

In a survey of the Chicago Bar's attitudes toward a specific problem in professional ethics (ambulance chasing), Kenneth F. Reichstein (1965) documents essentially the same relationship between professional status and notions of professional ethics found by Carlin in New York. Even though selecting personal injury cases is prohibited by the canons of ethics, an elaborate social structure (that is, legitimating values, specialist practitioners, techniques, and so on) exists around this type of practice. Reichstein found that high-status lawyers (high income, corporate practice, large firm, and the like) were almost unanimous in strongly disapproving of personal injury practice (and those lawyers engaged in it), on the grounds that "it brings disrepute on the profession." On the other hand, low-status lawyers (low income, solo practitioners, lack of established clientele) were more likely to give qualified approval of personal injury practice. Low-status lawyers based their attitudes on the rationale that "it is necessary to make a living," or "it prevents poor people from being taken advantage of." Reichstein also notes that "deviance" in this case is in no small part a product of elite control of the rule-making and enforcement machinery of the organized bar, which will be discussed later in this chapter.

Practicing in large law firms is very different from solo practice. At the turn of the century, more than 75 law firms in the United States have over 200 lawyers—Chicago-based Baker & MacKenzie is the largest firm in the world, with over 1,900—along with hundreds of people in the supporting staff, including paralegals, business-trained administrators, librarians, and technicians generating close to $7 billion in annual revenues (*Lawyer's Almanac*, 2001). Many of these large firms are becoming national and international in scope by opening up offices in several cities in the United States and abroad. These firms shy away from less profitable business—individual legal problems such as wills and divorces—in favor of corporate clients. Unlike solo practitioners, firms maintain long-term relationships with their clients, and many are on retainers by large corporations. Large firms offer a variety of specialized services, with departments specializing in a number of fields such as tax law, mergers, antitrust suits, and certain types of government regulations. These firms deal generally with repeat players and provide the best possible information and legal remedies to their clients along with creative and innovative solutions for the clients' problems (Jacob, 1995).

Large firms have a pronounced hierarchical organization structure (Hagan, Huxter, and Parker, 1988; Nelson, 1988). Young lawyers are hired as associates. Beginning associates are seen as having limited skills, in spite of their elite education, and are assigned the task of preparing briefs and engaging in legal research under the supervision of a partner or a senior associate. In seven or eight years, they either become junior partners or leave the firm. For a new associate who has a strong desire to move into a partnership position, the competition with cohorts is very strong. Nowadays, it is almost as difficult for an associate in a good firm to attain partnership as it is for an assistant professor in sociology to get tenure and promotion.

Associates are on a fixed salary, whereas partners' incomes are based on profits. In most firms, law partners earn profits largely on hourly billings of associates: the more associates per partner, the higher the profits. How profits are divided among partners is usually decided by a small committee that looks at such factors as work brought in, hours billed, and seniority. The traditional rule is that associates should produce billings of about three times that of their salaries—a third goes to the associate, a third to overhead, and a third to the firm's profit. For example, an associate who earns $50,000 and whose time is billed at $75 an hour would have to put in 2,000 billable hours, or 38.5 billable hours a week, 52 weeks a year. That may not sound like much, but 2,000 billable hours usually means 50 hours or more at the office a week. (On the average, lawyers work 46.5 hours a week [Reidinger, 1986b:44].) At most firms, lawyers' time is billed in six-minute or fifteen-minute units, with each nonbusiness conversation, personal phone call, and vacation day cutting into billable hours. No wonder many associates are workaholics and spend evenings and weekends in their offices.

One of the most complete analyses of law firms is Erwin O. Smigel's (1964) *Wall Street Lawyer*. Although the Wall Street law firm is not typical of the majority of law firms in the United States because of its size and type of practice, the contrast between this type of law practice and that of the individual practitioner illustrates the immense diversity within the legal profession.

The law firms investigated by Smigel perform a variety of functions. They are spokespersons for much of big business in the United States. But they not only represent business; many members of the firms also serve as members of the boards of directors of corporations they represent. These law firms also act as recruiting centers for high-level government service. Members of the firm are appointed to important government positions and seek national political offices. Many of their members are also active in various capacities in national, state, and local governmental agencies. Wall Street lawyers also participate in civic and philanthropic activities, such as the Metropolitan Opera, various museums, and other cultural and charitable affairs.

The Wall Street law firms are large, ranging from 50 to several hundred lawyers on the staff. Over 70 percent of the lawyers attended Harvard, Yale, or Columbia Law School—the elite schools of the nation—and were top students. The Wall Street law firms actively recruit these top individuals, and would prefer all their lawyers to have these credentials. In addition, the firms also look for the "correct" family background, which is considered important in making contacts that will bring business in the future. As might be expected, Smigel found very few black or female attorneys in the Wall

Street firms. Similarly, relatively few Catholic lawyers were found in the Wall Street firms because of what are considered to be lower-class origins, poorer education, and immigrant parents. As compared with individual practitioners, the Wall Street lawyers have a superior education, both quantitatively and qualitatively. It should be noted, however, that not every graduate of prestigious law schools desires the kind of law practiced by the Wall Street lawyers. Smigel notes that many students feel that the specialization in the large law office is so great that they would soon become limited in their abilities. Others feel that they would be lost in such a setting, and their mobility opportunities impaired. Some law school graduates look upon the Wall Street firm as a postgraduate training period, using it as a springboard for future positions in industry and government.

The observations of Carlin and Ladinsky on solo practitioners and Smigel on large law firms are supplemented by the conclusions of John P. Heinz and Edward O. Laumann's (1994) seminal study of the Chicago Bar. They note that much of the "differentiation within the legal profession is secondary to one fundamental distinction—the distinction between lawyers who represent large organizations (corporations, labor unions, or government) and those who represent individuals. The two kinds of law practice are the two hemispheres of the profession." Most lawyers, they add, "reside exclusively in one hemisphere or the other and seldom, if ever, cross the equator" (1994:319). The two sectors of the profession are separated by the social origins of lawyers, the schools where they were trained, the types of clients they serve, office environment, frequency and type of litigation, values, and different circles of acquaintance; the two sectors "rest their claims to professionalism on different sorts of social power" (1994:384). Large cities, Heinz and Laumann conclude, have two legal professions—one that is recruited from more privileged social origins where lawyers serve wealthy and powerful corporate clients, and the other from less prestigious backgrounds where lawyers serve individuals and small businesses. Thus, "the hierarchy of lawyers suggests a corresponding stratification of law into two systems of justice, separate and unequal" (1994:385).

Government

Roughly 12 percent of the members of the bar in the United States are now employees of the federal, state, county, and municipal governments, exclusive of the judiciary. Malcom Spector (1972) suggests that taking positions in government agencies may be a strategy used by young lawyers for upward professional mobility. He considers employment with the government a mobility route into a more prestigious practice for the young lawyer handicapped by mediocre education or stigmatized by sex, religion, or ethnic background. Spector maintains that by pursuing a short-term career in a government agency, the young lawyer not able to initially break into "big

league" firms gains valuable trial experience, specialized knowledge of regulatory law, and government contacts that eventually might be parlayed into
a move to Wall Street or to private industry. Many of those entering public
service are recent law school graduates who find government salaries sufficiently attractive at this stage of their careers, and seek the training that such
service may offer as a prelude to private practice. Limitations on top salaries
discourage some from continuing with the government, although in recent
years, public service has become more attractive as a career.

The majority of lawyers serve by appointment in legal departments of a
variety of federal and state agencies and local entities. The various departments and regulatory agencies, such as the Justice and Treasury Departments
and the Interstate Commerce Commission, employ thousands of attorneys.
Others work in the various legal departments in cities. Still others are
engaged as public prosecutors. Federal prosecutors, the United States attorneys, and their assistants are appointed by the president and are subordinate
to the attorney general of the United States. State prosecutors, sometimes
known as district attorneys, are commonly elected by each county and are not
under the control of the state attorney general. As a rule, lawyers in government are directly engaged in legal work, since law training is infrequently
sought as preparation for general government service. However, a small but
important minority, which is considered an exception to this rule, consists of
those who have been appointed to high executive positions and those who
have been elected to political office.

Private Employment

About 12 percent of lawyers are in private employment. These lawyers
(often referred to as house counsels) are salaried employees of private business concerns, usually industrial corporations, insurance companies, and
banks. Large corporations such General Electric, AT&T, State Farm and
Liberty Mutual have huge legal departments with almost 500 lawyers
(*Lawyer's Almanac,* 2001).

The growth of corporations, the complexity of business, and the multitude of problems posed by government regulation make it desirable, if not
imperative, for some firms to have lawyers and legal departments familiar
with the particular problems and conditions of the firm. In view of the
increased complexity of business transactions and the growth of federal regulations, the proportion of the profession engaged in this kind of activity can
be expected to increase in coming years. In addition to legal work, lawyers
often serve as officers of the company, and may serve on important policy-
making committees, perhaps even on the board of directors. Although
lawyers in legal departments are members of the bar and are entitled to
appear in court, their lack of trial experience means that a firm will usually
hire an outside lawyer for litigation and for court appearances. Lawyers in

legal departments of business firms do not tend to move to other branches of legal work after a number of years. Many of these lawyers have been in private practice or in government service. There is some horizontal mobility between government work and private employment, but not to the same extent as between government and law firms (Jenkins, 1977).

Judiciary

A very small proportion of lawyers are federal, state, county, and municipal court judges. Except for some inferior courts, judges are generally required to be admitted to the bar to practice, but they do not practice while on the bench. There is so little uniformity that it is difficult to generalize further about judges, other than to point out three salient characteristics that relate to the ranks from which judges are drawn, to the method of their selection, and to their tenure.

Judges are drawn from the practicing bar and less frequently from government service or the teaching profession. In the United States, there is no career judiciary such as is found in many other countries, and there is no prescribed route for the young law graduate who aspires to be a judge—no apprenticeship that he or she must serve, no service that he or she must enter (Carp and Stidham, 2001:209–245). (This is in contrast to some other countries, such as Japan and France, where there are special schools for training judges. In Scandinavian countries, judicial training is acquired during a practical internship period following law school. In the former Soviet Union, judges often lacked formal legal training and were appointed on the basis of loyalty and Communist Party affiliation [Glendon et al., 1994].) The outstanding young law graduates who act for a year or two as law clerks to distinguished judges of the federal and state courts have only the reward of the experience to take with them into practice, not the promise of a judicial career. Although it is not uncommon for a vacancy on a higher court to be filled by a judge from a lower court, even this cannot be said to be the rule. The legal profession is not entirely unaware of the advantages of a career judiciary, but it is generally thought that they are outweighed by the experience and independence that lawyers bring to the bench. Many of the outstanding judges of the country's highest courts have had no prior judicial experience. Criticism has centered instead on the prevalent method of the selection of judges. There is also an increased awareness of the need for continuing education and practical training programs for new judges because attorneys are seated on the bench with less experience (Carnahan, 1992).

As I discussed in Chapter 3, in over two-thirds of the states, judges are elected, usually by popular vote and occasionally by the legislature. Since 1937, the American Bar Association has advocated a system (the Missouri Plan) under which the governor appoints judges from a list submitted by a special nominating board, and the judge then periodically stands unopposed for reelection by popular vote on the basis of his or her record. Such a system is now in effect in several states. In a small group of states, judges are appointed by the governor, subject to legislative confirmation. This is also the method of selection of federal judges, who are appointed by the president, subject to confirmation by the Senate. The selection of judges is not immune from political influence, pressure and controversy (Shuman and Champagne, 1997). Nor is it reflective of the racial and ethnic composition of the population. To illustrate: In 1992, of the 356 judges sitting on the states' highest courts, only 4.2 percent were black, and there was only one Hispanic. Of the 837 judges on the federal bench, 5.2 percent are black (Pollock and Adler, 1992:4). In the ensuing 10 years, the situation has not changed and the progress of minorities on the bench has been very slow at all levels.

A third characteristic is that judges commonly serve for a term of years rather than for life. For courts of general jurisdiction, it is typically four to six years, and for appellate courts, six to eight years. In a few state courts and in the federal courts, the judges sit for life. Whether on the bench for a term of years or for life, a judge may be removed from office only for gross misconduct and only by formal procedures.

LAWYERS AND MONEY

Almost two decades ago, a *Wall Street Journal* article (1986:23) already boasted that one out of every nine lawyers is a millionaire, and the rest have an average net worth of one-half million dollars. The fiscal position of lawyers since that time has undoubtedly improved. After physicians, who averaged $188,000 during 2000, lawyers as a group are the highest-paid professionals, with an average annual income of more than $138,000. To put these figures into some kind of perspective, a glance at average faculty salaries in 2000 at public universities shows that full professors earned on the average $82,535; associate professors $58,741 and assistant professors $49,100 (*Chronicle of Higher Education Almanac,* 2001:5), and the median family income (4-person families) was just under $60,000 and the per capita personal income was $21,809. Not surprisingly, a poll showed that almost one-half of the lawyers chose law because its income potential appealed to them (but only 21 percent wanted "to see justice done" and 23 percent had a desire to improve society) (Reidinger, 1986b:44). There is an unusually large range of income among lawyers, and a high proportion of income goes to elites. A study found that 5 percent of law-firm partners earned 35 percent of all income, whereas the bottom 19 percent of individual practitioners earned only 5 percent (York and Hale, 1973:16). There are several factors that account for the variation in lawyers' income. They include the type of practice (firm or solo); the type of clientele (corporations or individuals with "minor" problems); the reputation of the law school; achievement in law school; the age and length of practice; the degree of specialization; and the region and population of the place of practice (generally, the larger the community, the greater the average income).

In 2000, the median starting salaries of law school graduates in private practice ranged from a "low" of $56,000 in Dallas-Ft. Worth to a high of $85,000 in New York City. The average starting salary for the class of 1997 was $48,860 and the median was $41,000 (*Official Guide*, 2000:35). After six years with a firm, associates can expect to receive compensation ranging from a low of $50,000 to a high of well over $100,000 for the aforementioned cities, with a national average of over $70,000. In the mid-1990s, the individual partners in top law firms averaged around $435,000 and senior associates about $350,000 (Stevens, 1995a) and the figures are undoubtedly much higher today.

Some unusually high starting salaries in New York City got a great deal of publicity in the media in the late 1980s. Some firms offered new associates fresh from law school $65,000 and anywhere from $10,000 to $20,000 in additional bonuses if they had spent a year or two clerking for a judge. Investment firms were luring away highly qualified law school graduates with starting salaries in excess of $100,000 (Reidinger, 1986a:42). But there were few such openings and they were filled by top graduates of elite law schools. Still, such high initial salaries jolted the legal profession, especially the expanding megafirms that compete with each other for a relatively stable pool of top graduates. Shortly after the publicity, a ripple effect pushed up salaries at major firms across the country. This is good news for young associates who work in some cases up to nine years in the hope of joining the full partners, who split a firm's profit.

On the whole, lawyers in private employment do not fare as well as their colleagues in private practice. At the turn of the century, the average total compensation of recent law school graduates was $55,000. Chief legal officers in corporations averaged $299,000. Nonsupervisory attorneys received $91,000 on the average, and senior attorneys earned slightly over $135,000 (*Lawyer's Almanac*, 2001). For large corporations, it was not unusual for chief legal officers to have a total compensation package (salary, bonus, profit sharing, insurance, company car and various perks) well in excess of $1 million and a recent study of 215 large and medium size enterprises shows that in 1994 the average compensation package was $789,000 (Mansnerus, 1995a:F7). Even paralegal assistants had an average cash compensation of almost $38,000, noticeably higher than that of beginning assistant professors in sociology.

In general, the compensation of judges is lower than that of attorneys in private practice or private employment. Some examples: In 2000, salaries of associate justices of the highest courts ranged from $68,874 to $132,250, with a median salary of $100,518; for intermediate appellate court judges, salaries ranged from $79,413 to $124,200, with a median of $97,050 and for judges of general jurisdiction trial courts, the spread was $67,513 to $115,500, with a median of $88,663. For comparison, note that the income of state court administrators ranged from $55,277 to $122,893, with a median salary of $84,200 (*Lawyer's Almanac*, 2001). Although judges' compensation and salary increments come from the general revenue (tax) in the United States, in England there is a move underway that the full costs of court services in most cases should be met by the users. Essentially it means that litigants' fees will cover the judges' pay (*Economist*, 1994:59).

In private practice, there are several ways lawyers generate income. Some charge by the hour for services rendered. For top firms, the hourly rates billed by senior partners approximate $1,000, and many good firms average $450 an hour in 2001. That is also the range of going rates for established trial attorneys. In recent years, law-firm billing practices have come under close scrutiny. In addition to the amount, there are legal and ethical questions concerning billing practices. Such practices include "using a heavy pen," which means rounding up to the next time unit in measuring fractions of hours worked on a client's case. There is also "late time," adding to the bill extra hours that lawyers did not work. Another questionable practice is the "smell test," a crude way lawyers can tell whether a padded bill will seem exorbitant to the client. Of course, there is not a clear-cut line between aggressive billing practices and fraud. Ideally, legal billing should be as simple as paying for a housecall by a plumber. Both charge by the hour, and they expect to be reimbursed for expenses incurred. However, it is not as simple as it sounds. Since lawyers charge hundreds of dollars per hour and incur thousands in expenses, any imprecision can be costly to the client. Associates, for example, who are expected to bill from 1,800 to 2,400 hours (the latter means 6.57 hours of *actual* work 365 days a year) often introduce a modest multiplier in the charges (rounding off phone calls so a one-minute call costs the client a full time unit of six or fifteen minutes on the bill, or charging a full hour of work that includes lunch and a visit to the bathroom) (Moses and Schmitt, 1992). Through a process of legal alchemy known as double billing, lawyers can make two into four (take two hours of research spent on Client's A legal problem, which turns out to be the same as Client's B's problem.) While double billing is condemned by the American Bar Association, lawyers are not bound by ABA rulings, and are free to bill both clients for the same work. Associates are even told that any time spent thinking about a client's legal woes, even while eating or jogging, should be billed (Stracher, 2001).

In a highly controversial book, *Lawyers, Money, and Success: The Consequences of Dollar Obsessions*, Macklin Fleming (1997) notes that lawyers claim that the last hour worked in a 20-hour day is as productive as the first —and the client should happily pay the same rate for both. He contends that the modern law firm is a Ponzi scheme; to maintain its profit base, the firm must hire two new associates every time it adds a partner. The retainers charged by the partners must cover both these rainmakers' fees and the salaries of the lawyers who actually do the work.

In the United States, legal expenses can be as devastating as medical expenses. To most Americans, legal fees for justice seem almost criminal: about $3,000 for misdemeanors, $3,000 to $8,000 for nontrial felonies, and $6,000 and above for felony trials. Similarly, the legal fees in estate and probate provide the opportunity for large profits from legal work. Few people understand why a lawyer who fills out mostly standard forms for two hours at the closing of a $200,000 house deserves 1 percent, or $2,000, for his or her effort. In probate, legal fees are determined usually as a percentage of the worth of the transaction—in this case, the value of the estate. Typical charges are 7 percent for the first $7,000 of the estate, 5 percent for the next $4,000, 4 percent for the next $10,000, 3 percent for the next $60,000, and 2.5 percent for the remainder. Once again, the amount of the fee is not necessarily related to the amount of work expended by lawyers, especially in cases where the value of an estate exceeds several million dollars. Nowadays, it is not unusual to hear of lawyers receiving multimillion-dollar fees, especially in large class-action suits such as the one against the Manville Corporation, which was sued by those who were exposed to the asbestos it manufactured. Mergers provide another avenue for lucrative fees. In addition to fees, percentages, and hourly charges, some lawyers and law firms are on retainers. A wealthy individual or a corporation pays a certain sum a year to a lawyer or a firm for a predetermined amount of legal work, for example, a maximum of 80 hours of consultation.

Lawyers also take cases on a contingency-fee basis. This is an arrangement whereby a lawyer receives a percentage of any damages collected. This practice is limited to a great extent to the American legal system, and most countries emulate England which refuses to allow lawyers to work for contingency fees. Such fees in the United States are used primarily in medical malpractice, personal injury, and some product liability and wrongful death cases. If the plaintiff loses, there is no payment required for legal services; if he or she wins, the lawyer takes his or her expenses off the top, then gets a percentage of the remainder—from 10 to 15 percent on big airline-crash suits to 35 percent on smaller suits. For example, when an individual is awarded $100,000 in damages, the lawyer may get from $10,000 to $35,000. The system has its merits. It allows individuals to retain the services of an attorney who could not otherwise afford it. It encourages lawyers to screen out weak cases because they share the risk of litigation—if they do not win, they do not collect.

At the same time, the contingency-fee arrangement provides a motivation to seek high damages. Lawyers make substantial investments by hiring investigators, expert witnesses, and consultants to augment their chances of winning. Often, they invest a considerable amount of their time in cases that can drag on literally for years. But the payoff can be substantial. It is not unusual to hear of a jury award of about $15 million in a personal injury case (*U.S. News & World Report*, 1986:35–36). Although the average verdict award in specific personal injury cases is relatively modest (knee injury $189,184; vertebrate fracture $259,061; cervical strain $42,157), million-dollar verdicts are quite common. By 1995, there were 703 million-dollar verdicts as compared with 127 in 1980 and seven in 1970 and in the late 1990s, the verdicts in litigations against tobacco companies were in excess of $1 billion (*Lawyer's Almanac*, 2001). The average personal injury verdict was almost $70,000, and the highest award was over $100 million. By contrast, in many other countries, awards do not even approximate the dollar amount of many American judgments. Courts aim to award that sum of money which will put an individual back in as close a position as he or she would have been without the injury and it covers only actual treatment and treatment-related expenses such as transportation to a clinic. Not surprisingly, contingency-fee law made more overnight millionaires than just about any legal business one could name. An extensive survey of the richest lawyers in America found that the big fortunes were made predominantly in contingency-fee work, not the corporate law and transaction planning that have always represented the height of lucrative law practice (Olson, 1991a:45).

It should be noted that, in addition to actual damages, *punitive* damages further increase the dollar amount involved in litigation. Punitive damages are not intended to compensate plaintiffs but rather to punish defendants where their conduct has been outrageous, grossly negligent and close to criminal. Punitives may be awarded in many types of tort litigation, including medical malpractice, product liability, and insurance bad faith. In most states, however, the law gives little guidance to judges and juries in determining whether punitive damages should be assessed and in what amount (see, for example, Hastie et al., 1998) although it should be noted that in a recent nationwide study of nearly 9,000, it was found that judges and juries each awarded punitive damages in about 4 percent of the cases won by plaintiffs and generally in about the same proportions (Glaberson, 2001). Attorneys have little to lose by pressing a punitive-damages claim, and, if they win, it can be an immense windfall for the plaintiff. It is not unusual to have punitive damages sought in the tens of millions of dollars (*Business Week*, 1989). Although a fraction of civil cases end with punitive damages (*New York Times*, 1995a:B12), the threat of punitive damages has become an effective bargaining chip in settlement negotiations. In insurance cases, for instance, claim settlements average 10 percent higher when claimants seek punitive damages. In an attempt to moderate the size of excessive punitive damages, there is a nascent movement to split civil trials into two phases, one dealing with liability, the other with punitive damages. If the liability and punishment issues were tried separately, or bifurcated, the jury would hear evidence and render a verdict only on the defendant's liability, then return to hear evidence on punishment issues and render a second verdict, similar to the proceedings in criminal trials. Opponents of two-phase trials claim that they would be more time-consuming, further strapping already busy courts (Harlan and Geyelin, 1992).

Although the contingency-fee arrangement does influence the amount of effort lawyers devote to a given case (Kritzer et al., 1985), the high legal fees and high damage awards create a number of problems. Medical fees are increasing to cover the cost of malpractice insurance. Some obstetricians and surgeons are walking away from their practices rather than pay insurance premiums of $100,000 or more per year. States, cities, and school districts are faced with substantial increases in their liability insurance and have started to phase out high-risk services such as recreation programs. Corporations are passing on to the consumers the cost of higher insurance premiums for product liability. With certain products such as new chemical contraceptives, the fear of product liability suits has also driven many companies out of research directed toward the development of new birth control technology (Tone, 2001).

The general public is also unhappy with the prevalence of liability suits. In a public-opinion survey on the topic, seven out of ten people polled agreed with the statement that a major effect of liability suits is to give lawyers "much more money than they deserve" (Society, 1992:3). Almost two-thirds in the sample agreed that people often initiate frivolous lawsuits because the potential awards are substantial and they have practically nothing to lose. Much less than half of the 1,970 people surveyed (40 percent) said that a significant outcome of liability suits is the fair compensation of victims. About half agreed that individuals and companies act more responsibly because of the threat of litigation. Participants were divided over whether the number of malpractice, personal injury, and product liability suits is reasonable. Slightly over a third called them "mostly justified," and almost an equal number considered them "mostly unjustified." About 70 percent would limit punitive awards and would have a cap for lost wages and pain and suffering. Lawyers disagree with the results of the poll and argue that there is a discrepancy between public perception and reality. They contend that product liability suits are filed in only a small fraction of cases where people are injured, and that headlines showing large punitive awards are misleading because often those awards are sharply reduced by judges.

Several states are now considering measures to limit both the size of damage awards and lawyers' fees. Some states have already imposed caps on the size of medical malpractice awards to $250,000. A few states are also imposing controls on what a lawyer can charge. In general, the new laws allow the traditional fees for prosecuting minor lawsuits but reduce them sharply for certain big-money cases that are costly and complicated to bring. Lawyers, of course, do not like these limitations. They contend that the contingency fee is the victim's key to the courthouse. It allows the poor to obtain the same high-caliber legal services as the rich. Many of the cases require much expense and preparation. If the suit is lost, the lawyer gets nothing; therefore, the one-third contingency fee is most reasonable. But it does not seem that cutting contingency fees would reduce the number of malpractice and other damage suits filed. Because of the high level of competition for business, if top lawyers bow out, others will still handle these cases. In states without caps on verdict size, there will still be huge damage awards and log-jams in the courts.

COMPETITION FOR BUSINESS

The days of exorbitant legal fees for the profession are numbered. As a result of the confluence of the size of the profession, cost of legal products and services, downsizing, and the economic turndown in 2001, many lawyers are likely to enjoy less prestige, less interesting work, less security, and lower pay scales in the future. For years now, law schools have been churning out more lawyers than the profession can afford. The job market for lawyers is so tight that some are willing to take jobs as paralegals, especially in such markets as Los Angeles, New York and Washington, DC. In 1993, only about 70 percent of law school graduates found law-related jobs within six months of graduation (Samborn, 1995), and the situation has not improved substantially in subsequent years (*Official Guide*, 2000). (In Scandinavian countries, by contrast, the bar is declining in size, and there is also a decrease in the proportion of law students to other students in most European countries.) In the prescient and unflattering words of former U.S. Chief Justice Warren E. Burger, "We may well be on our way to a society overrun by hordes of lawyers, hungry as locusts. . . ." (*Time*, 1978:56). Not surprisingly, there is growing competition among lawyers for the consumer's dollars.

Two Supreme Court decisions have contributed to competition among lawyers for business. In 1975, the Court ruled that lawyers, like others in business, should not be allowed to fix prices. Until then, it had been standard procedure for lawyers' associations to issue "minimum-fee schedules," lists of the lowest fees members should charge for handling divorces, wills, and so on. Another important case gave lawyers the right to advertise. Two Arizona lawyers placed an ad for their firm in a local newspaper that violated the model code of professional responsibility formulated in 1969 by the American Bar Association and adopted in Arizona by the state's supreme court. The lawyers were censured for their ad. They appealed the case to the U.S. Supreme Court, which decided in 1977 that state laws and bar associations prohibiting lawyers' advertising were in conflict with the Constitution's guarantee of free speech.

Historically, bar associations have strongly opposed advertising by lawyers (Cebula, 1998; Olson, 1991a, 1991b). In the common-law tradition, a lawsuit was considered an evil, albeit a necessary one. Lawmakers and judges considered litigation wasteful, expensive, time-consuming, and an invasion of privacy. It was considered acrimonious, increasing hostility and resentment among people who could otherwise find an opportunity to cooperate. It hindered productive enterprise, and society discouraged litigation where it was not absolutely imperative. Lawyers were forbidden to "stir up" litigation. Any attempt to drum up business as ordinary tradesmen did was discouraged. Lawyers were expected to wait passively for clients and to temper any entrepreneurial urge to solicit them (Olson, 1991b:27).

The demise of opposition to advertising began with a simple idea. Lawsuits came to be considered an effective way to deter misconduct and to compensate wronged persons. There was also a need to increase the demand for legal services, in part because law schools kept turning out large numbers of newly minted attorneys. Many attorneys and law firms began to view law as business which requires the use of business marketing strategies (Savell, 1994). Of course, lawsuits are not the only products of lawyers. Much of their work can be seen as preventive, nonadversarial, or defensive, such as tax planning, contract negotiation, adoption, or document drafting. But all these activities can lead to a cycle of new demands and suspicions, for much of lawyering work contains an element of adversariness and assertiveness. Thus, an uncontested divorce can turn into a contested one, and advertising can entice aggrieved parties to seek out a lawyer to help them "to drop the spouse but keep the house."

At the prodding of the Supreme Court, bar associations have developed and subsequently refined guidelines to allow lawyers to advertise. Typically, these guidelines allow lawyers to indicate their education, specialties, public offices, teaching positions held, and memberships in professional organizations. They may also indicate other clients represented with those clients' permission, tell what credit arrangements are acceptable, and indicate fees for initial consultations and other services.

The number of lawyers currently advertising has risen sharply over the years. Effective advertising generates approximately $8.00 in revenue for each advertising dollar (Kennedy, 1994). Young, small-town, small-firm, or solo practitioners who earn less than $35,000 are the most likely to try it. Older, big-city lawyers still shy away from advertising: 30 percent of lawyers aged 24–34 have tried it, compared with 11 percent in the 55-and-older age bracket, and 14 percent in the 45–54 age group. Lawyers are more likely to advertise in cities with fewer than 50,000 residents and less likely in cities with 1 million or more. Large legal clinics advertise heavily, especially on television, with slogans such as "no frill will—$25." Large law firms are least likely to advertise (*ABA Journal*, 1986:44). But, by 1992, more than 900 law firms spent close to $83 million on television advertising alone. As one attorney (who hypes his practice regularly on television) sarcastically remarked, "Who wants to wait 30 years to become a household name?" (MacLachlan, 1989:1BP). Nowadays, late-night TV airs a steady drumbeat of messages inviting the audience to "dump their hubbies, stiff their creditors, and take their bosses to the cleaners" (Olson, 1991b:31).

Members of the legal profession have not unanimously welcomed the changes. There is concern that lawyer advertising has contributed to the low public image of attorneys (Podgers, 1995). The profession has traditionally considered unethical the more obvious forms of competition—advertising and soliciting clients. The underlying belief of traditionalists is that increased competition leads to a decreased quality of service. The implication is that high fees indicate high quality. In fact, the U.S. Supreme Court said that lawyers had wrongly overcharged clients for decades, under the rationale that the dignity of the profession required it (Green, 1975:55). Many people avoid going to lawyers because they do not have the necessary information about specialization and because they believe that lawyers charge too much. To reach a larger segment of the population, lawyers could advertise the types of cases they handle and lower their fees. However, most bar associations, although they are developing guidelines, still treat advertising as something that is just not done. Attempts to lower fees are usually met with the old arguments about ethics and the quality of service. As a result, with some exceptions, the fees are steadily increasing, and few lawyers allow themselves anything more than the traditional one-line listing in the yellow pages—name, address, and phone number.

After advertising, the next step in competition for business was solicitation. Until 1985, bar associations discouraged lawyers from drumming up litigation against a particular opponent, such as the Catholic Church or Xerox. In 1985, the Supreme Court, in *Zauderer v. Office of Disciplinary Council,* ruled that soliciting injury claims from the use of the Dalkon Shield, an intrauterine device, through advertisement is permissible. It created a precedent for lawyers recruiting litigants against all kinds of institutions and businesses. Lawyers now have the right to send letters to solicit the business of individuals known to have legal problems. Even in-person solicitation is no longer a taboo. From airplane disasters to mine accidents, the scene is characterized by a "ravenlike descent" of tort lawyers anxious to contact the victims or their relatives. For example, competition for business among lawyers was so intense in the 1989 Exxon oil spill in the Alaskan town of Valdez that it was referred to as "tanker chasing." A commentator vividly captures this scene: "Liability lawyers and prostitutes fresh from nearby Anchorage are said to prowl the dark, smoky bars in search of clients. Townspeople aren't as concerned about the prostitutes as they are about the lawyers" (Olson, 1991b:32). One of the consequences of this well-publicized incident was the creation of a code of conduct for accident scenes by the Trial Lawyers of America. More recently, in a decision that may open the door to new restrictions on advertising by lawyers, the U.S. Supreme Court in 1995 upheld a Florida rule that bars letters to accident victims or their relatives within thirty days of the accident (Freivogel, 1995:7A).

Some large law firms are becoming more competitive by adopting modern cost-management techniques and strategic planning. Others are starting to experiment with public relations firms to handle new contacts. Virtually every major law firm in the country has a partner for whom management has become a primary preoccupation. Many firms are also increasing the number and size of specialized departments, and there is a growth of "specialty firms," such as the type that specializes in labor law work on the side of management (Heinz and Laumann, 1994). The business of law in large firms, in fact, is turning out to be much like business in any field. Some even provide written service guarantees promising to resolve issues to the clients' satisfaction. Even if it means a reduction in legal fees (*New York Times*, 1995b:A13).

Competition for law business is not limited to the United States. In India, for example, the legal profession is "extremely crowded" (Nagpaul, 1994:66) and there is excessive and unrestrained competition among lawyers for clients. India has the longest written Constitution incorporating ideas of basic rights, equalities and social justice. Citizens are becoming more aware of their legal rights, the number of statues enacted annually are staggering, and the courts are increasingly used as a forum for dispute resolution. In this legal environment the author of an excellent study on lawyers bitterly complains that the profession has turned into a commercial business "bereft of all ideals, principles . . . there are no sacrosanct ground rules" and "the ruling passion of the Bar is greed and maximisation of economic gains" (Gandhi, 1982:153, 155–156). Many lawyers rely on "touts" or brokers to get business, and "touting" is a widely used, albeit highly unprofessional, activity. A tout may be a government clerk, a typist in the courtroom, a policeman, a village headman, or anyone with some prestige and visibility in the community. A tout befriends a potential client and refers him to a lawyer. He gets a commission from the lawyer, the seller of legal services, to whom he brings business. A tout may get up to 50 percent of the fee the lawyer collects from the client but receives no commission from the client. A tout works for only one lawyer, and good touts are sought after by lawyers. Successful lawyers have several touts "procuring" for them, and about two-thirds of criminal and one-third of civil cases are obtained through touts (Gandhi, 1982:108). In another study, it was noted that young lawyers were acting as touts for older, well-established attorneys primarily because they were unable to obtain professional work on their own (Nagpaul, 1994:69).

In this highly competitive climate, the clients are often cheated by unscrupulous touts and lawyers, who know they are vulnerable and expendable. The clients are helpless because they are ignorant of the law and unfamiliar with the legal arena. In rural areas in particular, most litigants are either illiterate or have a low level of formal education. They do not know where to find adequate and reasonable legal services and welcome the advances of touts with the promise of professional help. Once entrapped, they are passed on "among the various actors of the drama as a nutritious morsel and each has his mouthful of bite." Clients have no recourse, or even a chance to protest, because lawyers do not give them receipts for services rendered. Lawyers view clients as exclusive trading commodities and non-repeat business and extract whatever they can from them the first time. They are even reluctant to be seen with clients unless they a formal business arrangement. The touts associated with lawyers are equally ruthless and exploitative and, like lawyers, do not develop continuing relationships with the clients. Even the most notorious "shysters," "ambulance chasers," and "ticket-fixers" hungry for legal business in the United States do not come close to their counterparts in India when it comes to violating ethical codes and professional standards.

LEGAL SERVICES FOR THE POOR
AND THE NOT SO POOR

Well over a third of the U.S. population have at least one legal problem in a year, but only one in ten consults an attorney (Waldman, 1986). A frequently cited survey carried out for the American Bar Association Consortium on Legal Services and the public found that in general low and moderate income families do not seek legal help for their problems. Although 41 percent of the poor and 52 percent of moderate income families encountered at least one legal problem in 1992, 71 percent of the poor and 61 percent of moderate income families did not turn to attorneys for help with their legal problem. The legal problems faced by these people were mainly consumer issues and personal finance (Hansen, 1994). A main reason is that law and lawyers are expensive. Many people who need or want a lawyer have trouble paying the price. But as Friedman (1998) comments: "Justice is for sale; but in a just society it should not be totally for sale." Consequently, under a 1963 Supreme Court decision, people involved in a serious criminal case who tell the court that they are too poor to pay a lawyer must be represented, usually by public defenders on the state's payroll (who generally bear the stigma of ineptitude) (McIntyre, 1987) or by court-appointed attorneys. Such defendants are now involved in well over half of the felony cases in the country (U.S. Department of Justice, 1992:4). An editorial in *Harvard Law Review* (1994) calls for federal legislation to ensure that capital defendants receive legal assistance that meets the standards of effective assistance higher than those applied in other criminal cases. Almost a decade later, there is still a shortage of qualified lawyers in capital cases, which places inmates at risk of missing crucial filing deadlines, possibly preventing them from raising appeal issues. In addition two out of three appealed death sentences are set aside because of errors by defense lawyers. Increasingly, private law firms cannot afford or balk at spending up to a 1,000 potentially billable hours on a death penalty case, and often they lack competent attorneys for such pro bono work. This forces inmates to rely on incompetent and often overworked court-appointed lawyers who miss filing deadlines, fail to investigate cases or submit inadequate appeals (Hines, 2001).

At the same time, the practice of the court appointing attorneys for the defense is unpopular among lawyers. It is damaging to their pocketbook, for they receive only nominal compensation for their services and it interferes with their regular activities. Even though the compensation is modest, ranging from $15 to $20 per hour in Missouri to $40 per hour for courtroom work and $25 an hour for work out of court in New York City (Fritsch and Rohde, 2001:1), for example, from time to time states run out of money to pay court-appointed lawyers for defending indigents. In Missouri, when the state ran out of money to pay court-appointed lawyers and the legislature refused to appropriate any more, the Missouri Supreme Court upheld compulsory service without compensation rather than see the criminal justice system come to a halt. As a result, all lawyers in the state, including real estate and merger specialists, were faced with compulsory service in criminal courts. Obviously, many of these attorneys were not specialists in criminal proceedings, which had a bearing on the quality of legal help defendants received.

The plight of the indigent criminal defendants is further complicated in many instances by the absence of some basic legal work that their more affluent counterparts would have. For example, most lawyers appointed to represent the poor do not hire private investigators to look for witnesses or evidence. Most do not get expert witnesses, like psychiatrists or pathologists, to help challenge the prosecution's case. Most do not take the time to go to the scene of crime and some do not even make a jail or prison visit to discuss the case with their clients. In New York, for example, a defendant facing life in prison may get a lawyer who spends as little as 20 hours on the cases—half a week's work—and is paid as little as $693. For example, a recent study of 137 New York homicide cases completed by appointed lawyers in 2000 shows that in 42 of them—nearly one-third—the lawyers did less than a week preparation, raising questions about their effort and thoroughness. Only 12 spent at least 200 hours—five weeks or more—investigating and preparing their cases, a sign of "appropriate diligence, according to legal experts" (Fritsch and Rohde, 2001:27). The median for all cases was 72 hours, not quite two weeks' work.

At times, in part to maintain public confidence in the legal system (Podgers, 1994), lawyers provide legal services *pro bono publico* (for the public good) for indigents. From time to time, various bar associations have recommended that all lawyers engage in such endeavors. But many cannot afford it, and others, particularly those who work for large firms, are discouraged from doing so. Many large firms are reluctant to take on *pro bono* criminal-law work, divorce, housing disputes, and consumer problems because they would be regarded as unseemly by their corporate clients. A principal reason for the reluctance of large firms to represent "the poor, downtrodden, friendless, and despised" or to engage in public-interest causes is that that sort of legal work "would give offense to their regular clientele" (Heinz and Laumann, 1994:371).

In civil cases, the poor can gain access to lawyers through public or private legal-aid programs. As part on the War on Poverty program in the 1960s, the Office of Economic Opportunity established neighborhood law offices to serve the indigents. In 1974, much of legal-aid work was assumed by the Legal Services Corporation (LSC), which distributes money to 323 legal service organizations, with a total of 1,200 offices around the country in 1995. In general, an individual is eligible for free legal services if he or she has income less than $9,338 a year, and a family of four qualifies if its income is less than $18,938 (Pear, 1995:A9).

Because of the number of activist lawyers in the program who fought and antagonized city hall, the corporation soon became controversial. There were attempts by President Reagan in the early 1980s to phase the program out, but Congress balked. The LSC is under attack again, and there are renewed efforts in Congress to phase it out over the five years to save $1.6 billion. As a result of financial cutbacks, in several states including large ones such as New York, the quality of legal services continues to decline along with representation of indigent defendants and increasing caseloads for fewer and fewer attorneys (*New York Times*, 1998). Critics contend the LSC often advances a left-wing agenda of its own through lobbying and litigation at the expense of the poor, and there are other agencies that provide legal aid to the needy (MacLachlan, 1995; Pear, 1995). One such organization is the recently formed National Service Legal Corps (NSLC), which is setting up interdisciplinary teams of attorneys, paralegals, social workers, health providers, and educators in different states to work on a number of issues affecting the poor such as affordable housing, homelessness, environmental protection and community revitalization (Grange and Schwartz, 1995).

The work of Legal Services attorneys is concentrated in five main areas: family, consumer, housing, landlord-tenant, and welfare. To qualify, applicants must have proof of indigence and have a case that falls within the mandate of Legal Services. Of the 1.7 million cases handled by Legal Service lawyers in 1994, 33 percent involved family matters like child support, spouse abuse and divorce. Twenty-two percent involved housing, 16 percent welfare and other government benefits, and 11 percent consumer issues. The rest dealt with education, employment, individual rights and health care matters. Legal-aid attorneys cannot file class-action suits against the federal government or any state or local government and they cannot take any case on which they might recover attorneys' fees. Such fees are sometimes awarded in Social Security, civil rights, and domestic relations (i.e., palimony) cases. Litigations that involve contingency fees are not accepted, because private attorneys would handle them even for poor clients. It should be noted though that poor people are often unable to obtain private lawyers because the likely fees tend to be small and speculative (Pear, 1995).

A novel version of legal assistance for the poor is "Street Law." The concept is very simple. Volunteer lawyers set up folding tables for three hours at a main intersection on Saturday afternoon and dispense legal advice to anyone who wants it on everything from family issues to debt problems to landlord-tenant disputes. The program lets anyone speak to an attorney, free, for a few minutes. It is designed for quick advice and the consultations last for 10–15 minutes. Sponsored by Legal Assistance by Whatcom (LAW) Advocates (Bellingham, Washington), a nonprofit agency that offers legal assistance to low-income people, Street Law's goal is to help those who cannot afford to otherwise obtain legal help. The program started initially to help homeless people and street kids in the downtown area who would seldom end up in a law office. Since its inception in 1994, the program has helped hundreds of people at least to find out whether they have a legal issue to fight and, if so, how to proceed. These Saturday sessions, which are advertised in the local papers, also benefit lawyers because they are exposed to issues outside their normal specialties and often subjected to the kinds of cases they have not heard about since law school. On a personal note, I saw the lawyers sitting at their green folding tables with people lining up for advice on a balmy Saturday afternoon in August 2001, in Bellingham, Washington, and found the sight not only unusual but most impressive.

Some of those who lack both proof of indigence and the means (or the will) to hire a private attorney started to take matters in their own hands in the form of "pro se litigants" (*pro se* means "for oneself" in Latin.) It is a do-it-yourself approach and the growing volume of cases involving self-representation is beginning to put pressure on the courts. For example, clerks have to answer basic questions a lawyer would not need to ask. Judges say pro se litigants constantly ask them for help, raising questions of impartiality. Legal-aid advocates fear pro se litigants may not receive the same shot at justice because they are naive to the system (*St. Louis-Post Dispatch*, 2001). For those who do not wish to act on their own behalf, there are two relatively low-cost ways of obtaining legal services. They are legal clinics and prepaid legal plans.

A legal clinic is simply a high-volume, high-efficiency law firm. Because the cost per case is low, the firm can afford to set lower fees. Legal clinics build case volume primarily through advertising and publicity. They achieve efficiency by using systematic procedures, by relying heavily on standard forms, and by delegating much of the routine work to paralegals (nonlawyers trained to handle routine aspects of legal work). They concentrate on legal problems that are fairly common, such as wills, personal bankruptcy, divorces, and traffic offenses (Muris and McChesney, 1979).

Some clinics have established chain operations with hundreds of offices in various states and advertise heavily on late-night television, in TV guides, and neighborhood newspapers. Two-thirds of the clients have problems that do not require formal legal action. They are mostly money claims—rent deposits, suits by collections companies, and the like. When a case does not warrant the services of a lawyer, the client is informed how to go to small-claims court or how to negotiate with bill collectors. Of the cases that go beyond the first meeting, about half are divorces, wills, name changes, and adoptions. The fees are usually set in advance and are based on a published schedule. For example, they charge a flat fee of $300 (plus court costs) for a simple uncontested divorce, in contrast to $600 at a conventional firm. The offices are often located in shopping centers or other heavy traffic areas with easy access and plenty of parking. Attorneys are available during the day and the evening and on Saturdays. Credit cards are accepted, as are installment payments (Sullivan, 1979:9).

A second way of providing low-cost legal services is through prepaid legal plans, which work very much like medical insurance (Waldman, 1986). There are currently two basic ways used to finance such a plan. The organizer can sign up a group of people—a labor union or a credit union—and charge so many dollars per person per year. The other way is to sign up individuals one by one. Obviously, individuals who sign up are those who think they will be likely to use the service. Since more legal services will be used, the cost per person will be higher compared with the group method.

There are two general ways of selecting lawyers in prepaid legal plans. Either there is a designated lawyer or a group of lawyers from which a client may select, or a client may pick any lawyer he or she prefers. In the latter case, there are usually limits on how much of the fee will be covered by the plan. In recent years, unions have been the prime movers in organizing prepaid plans. For example, a plan set up by the United Auto Workers is probably the largest in the country. It covers over 150,000 Chrysler employees, retired workers, and their immediate families. Thus far, though, prepaid plans have not grown as fast as the proponents expected. Individuals in general consider the need for legal insurance less urgent than the need for medical insurance. Another impediment to widespread prepaid legal plans may be the legal clinic. If many more legal clinics are established, fees for routine services are likely to decline throughout the profession. As a result, there will be less of a need for protection against problems that may come up. In other countries, however, the idea of legal insurance seems more appealing. In Germany, prepaid legal plans are widely accepted, and about 40 percent of the households carry legal-expense insurance.

LAW SCHOOLS

In 2002 there were 182 law schools approved by the American Bar Association. Overall enrollment increased from 46,666 in the academic year 1963–64 to 125,184 in 1999–00—the peak enrollment of 129,580 students was reached in the academic year of 1991–92. There was a corresponding increase in the number of degrees awarded during the same time period—from 9,638 to 39,071—with the largest number of 40,236 students graduating in 1994 (American Bar Association, 1995:67; *Official Guide*, 2000:5). In addition, seven states have provisions for "reading law" programs allowing people to pursue an independent study of law under a lawyer's tutelage to obtain legal licenses. Most require up to four years of study under a member of the bar, along the line of the traditional apprenticeship programs, and some require a year in law school. Students are tested regularly and they follow a preset curriculum. The American Bar Association opposes these programs, and the lawyer-graduates

TABLE 8–1   Legal-Education and Bar-Admissions Statistics, 1963–2000

Academic Year	Number of Schools	First-Year Enrollment	First-Year Female Enrollment	Total JD Enrollment	Total JD Women Enrollment	LSAT Administrations	JD or LL.B. Awarded	Admissions to the Bar
1963–64	135	20,776	877	46,666	1,739	30,528	9,638	10,788
1964–65	135	22,753	986	51,079	2,056	37,598	10,491	12,023
1965–66	136	24,167	1,064	56,510	2,374	39,406	11,507	13,109
1966–67	135	24,077	1,059	59,236	2,520	44,905	13,115	14,644
1967–68	136	24,267	1,179	61,084	2,769	47,110	14,738	16,007
1968–69	138	23,652	1,742	59,498	3,554	49,756	16,077	17,764
1969–70	144	29,128	2,103	64,416	4,485	59,050	16,733	19,123
1970–71	146	34,289	3,542	78,018	6,682	74,092	17,183	17,922
1971–72	147	36,171	4,326	91,225	8,567	107,479	17,006	20,485
1972–73	149	35,131	5,508	98,042	11,878	119,694	22,342	25,086
1973–74	151	37,018	7,464	101,675	16,303	121,262	27,756	30,879
1974–75	157	38,074	9,006	105,708	21,283	135,397	28,729	30,707
1975–76	163	39,038	10,472	111,047	26,020	133,546	29,961	34,930
1976–77	163	39,996	11,354	112,401	29,343	133,320	32,597	35,741
1977–78	163	39,676	11,928	113,080	31,650	128,135	33,640	37,302
1978–79	167	40,479	13,324	116,150	35,775	125,757	33,317	39,068
1979–80	169	40,717	13,490	117,297	37,534	111,235	34,590	42,756
1980–81	171	42,296	15,272	119,501	40,834	112,750	35,059	41,997
1981–82	172	42,521	15,811	120,879	43,245	111,373	35,598	45,382
1982–83	172	42,034	16,136	121,791	45,539	118,565	34,846	42,905
1983–84	173	41,159	16,049	121,201	46,361	111,620	36,389	41,684
1984–85	174	40,747	16,236	119,847	46,897	104,621	36,687	42,630
1985–86	175	40,796	16,510	118,700	47,486	95,129	36,829	42,450
1986–87	175	40,195	14,491	117,813	47,920	91,921	36,121	40,247
1987–88	175	41,055	17,506	117,997	48,920	100,751	35,478	39,918
1988–89	174	42,860	18,395	120,694	50,932	115,407	35,701	46,528
1989–90	175	43,826	18,722	124,471	53,113	136,367	35,520	47,174
1990–91	175	44,104	18,592	127,261	54,097	138,087	36,385	43,286
1991–92	176	44,050	18,773	129,580	55,110	144,736	38,880	44,154
1992–93	177	42,793	18,325	128,212	54,644	140,054	40,037	43,257
1993–94	177	43,644	19,059	127,792	55,132	132,028	40,236	42,151
1994–95	179	44,298	19,312	128,983	55,803	128,533	39,710	49,757
1995–96	179	43,676	19,462	129,318	56,923	114,756	39,191	56,613
1996–97	179	43,245	19,402	128,623	57,123	105,313	39,920	56,629
1997–98	179	42,186	19,409	125,386	56,915	103,990	40,114	56,184
1998–99	181	42,804	20,319	125,627	57,952	104,326	59,455	55,481
1999–00	182	43,182	21,008	125,184	59,362	N.A.	39,071	N.A.

Sources for these figures include ABA's *Review of Legal Education in the United States,* Fall 2001.

are restricted to practice in their own states (Curriden, 1995b). Table 8–1 provides an overview of the most recent legal-education and bar-admission data.

For many years, the first degree in almost all law schools was the Bachelor of Law (LL.B.). A few gave their Juris Doctor (JD) to all students, whereas others reserved the JD for students graduating with honors. In recent years, all schools have changed to granting the JD. There is no difference in the nature of the course of study for the two degrees. The master's degree (LL.M.) usually involves a one-year program combining coursework and research beyond the JD; the Doctorate of Juridicial Sciences (S.J.D.) is a graduate academic research degree that involves substantial advanced academic publishable work; and the Master's in Comparative Law (M.C.L.) involves advanced work for foreign-educated lawyers. In addition, a number of law schools offer "joint degrees"; that is, a law school in conjunction with some other college or school offers a combined program leading to a joint degree, such as Juris-Doctor-Master of Public Administration degree. Some of the other popular joint degree programs combine law and medicine, law and psychology, law and hospital and health administration, and law and Russian and Eastern European Studies. Joint degrees give students career management flexibility and the additional degree is expected (or hoped) to open law-firm doors in a competitive legal-job market (Sangchompuphen, 1995).

Over the years, there have been substantial changes in the composition and characteristics of law students. Women have been dramatically underrepresented in the past both in law schools and in the profession. As late as 1970, women made up only 2.8 percent of the population of lawyers in the United States. More recently, women have been entering the profession in unprecedented numbers, and by 1984 almost 13 percent of lawyers were women (Curran, 1986:25). In 1970, 8.5 percent of law school students were women; in 2000, over 48 percent were women and they are poised to outnumber men in law school (Thomson, 2001). In 1995, a lawyer who once could not find work because of her sex has become the American Bar Association's first female president (New York Times, 1995c:A13).

Historically, minorities, like women, have been extremely underrepresented in the legal profession. In 1970, black lawyers made up slightly over 1 percent of all lawyers—3,845 of whom 600 were located in the South (Leonard, 1977:4–5). The various minority-recruitment programs instrumented by most law schools in the late 1960s have increased the enrollment of minority-group students substantially over earlier years. But these groups still do not have representations within the law school populations anywhere near the percentage of the total population. Between 1970 and 2000, the percentage of minority students enrolled in law schools increased from 3.3 to 10.9 percent. In 2000, close to 6 percent of all law students were black Americans, 3.2 percent Hispanic-Americans, 2.3 percent Asian-Americans, and 0.03 percent Native Americans. The number of minority-group law students remains disappointingly low, and there are discouraging indications that this group is the most likely to drop in numbers as the total registration slackens or even declines (McKay, 1976:272–273). There is also a scarcity of female and minority professors in law schools. For the first time in 1989, law school students around the country demonstrated and successfully exerted pressure on their institutions to hire more women and minority-group members as professors (Leatherman, 1989:A32). These and similar efforts in subsequent years resulted in major changes in the composition of law school faculties.

Lawyers in the United States, just like lawyers in other parts of the world (see, for example, Trubek and Cooper, 1999), established a monopoly on the instrumentalities of the law and the right to practice in the courts. Similarly, law schools have a monopoly on the training of lawyers. They are the gatekeepers for the legal profession. Entry into the profession is conditioned by socioeconomic status and academic standing. Robert Stevens (1973), in a sample of eight law schools studied in 1960, 1970, and 1972, reconfirms that law schools tend to draw students from more affluent families. Students in general come from better-educated and richer families than the general population, and there is increasing homogenization of the college background of law students. In 1960, Stevens found that law schools recruited primarily humanists; by 1970, however, they were recruiting social scientists. By 1970, the numbers majoring in social sciences had doubled to more than a majority (Stevens, 1973:574–575).

The number of applicants to law schools peaked in 1990. Since 1990–91, when a record of 99,300 applicants vied for 44,104 spots, there has been a steady decline of college graduates applying to the nation's accredited law schools. By 1996–97, the number of applicants had dropped 27 percent, to about 72,300, the sharpest drop in recent memory, but the number of openings had declined only slightly, to 43,245 (Mangan, 1998a). By contrast, applications to medical schools are up 3 percent, and there is an even higher percentage in business schools. The reasons for the decline in the number of law school applicants include limited job prospects, low morale at law firms after layoffs, and other lingering effects of the legal recession (Mangan, 1998a; Stevens, 1995b) and the continuing abasement of the prestige and economic status of the profession as evidenced, for example, by newspaper headlines such as "More Scorn and Less Money Dim Law's Lure" in the influential *New York Times* (Johnson, 1995). But this situation may be changing in view the emerging signs of economic distress in 2001 and early 2002. Now, as the job market deteriorates, law schools are drawing more attention, applications are on the increase along with the number of people taking the LSAT and the preparatory classes for it. But the number of applicants still remains well below the nearly 100,000 who sought entry to law schools at the depth of the last recession in 1991 (Glater, 2001c).

Although still more people apply to law school than can be accepted, about 70 percent of all applicants are accepted by at least one school.

Admission to law school is competitive. The higher the reputation of a law school, the greater the competition among students for the number of places. There are annual rankings of law schools by a number of popular magazines on a variety of criteria (see, for example, *U.S. News & World Report*, 2001). The status of a law school is related to the placement of its graduates. Graduates of law schools attached to elite colleges and universities (for example, Harvard, Yale, Columbia, and Chicago) are more likely to be employed in firms, whereas graduates of Catholic or commercial law schools are more likely to be found in solo practice (Ladinsky, 1967:222–232). The elite Wall Street firms have been most educationally selective in this regard, choosing not only from Ivy League law schools but also from a group whose backgrounds include attendance at elite prep schools and colleges (Smigel, 1964:73–74). Moreover, many lawyers graduating from high-status law schools do not practice in the lower-status specialties of criminal, family, poverty, and debtor-creditor law (Zemans, 1977). Since many students are motivated by a desire for financial rewards (Stevens, 1973:577), competition for admission in high-status law schools is further heightened. As a result, only a small proportion of applicants are accepted in elite national law schools. For example, in 1999–2000 academic year, *The Official Guide to U.S. Law Schools* (2000) shows that of the 5,813 applicants, 14 percent were accepted at Harvard, and of the 4,022 applicants, slightly more than 12 percent were accepted at Stanford. The percentage of those admitted at state schools is much higher. For example, Ohio Northern University admitted 75 percent and Mississippi College School of Law 69 percent. But in addition to the quality and reputation of the law school, other factors enter into a decision to apply to a particular school, such as the desire to practice in the school's state, job opportunities upon graduation, the school's orientation toward social sciences, availability and extent of financial aid, job opportunities for a spouse while in school, attraction to the community or area where the school is located, and, not the least, tuition.

Law school education is expensive. For the 1999–2000 academic year, tuition alone ranged from $2,000 to over $25,000. After adding food, housing, cost of books and personal expenses, the cost of a three-year law school education can well exceed $125,000 at the higher end. For example, the annual tuition at elite schools such as Harvard was $23,900, at Yale $25,550 and at Stanford $25,080 for the academic year 1999–2000. The minimum budget required at these schools is about $45,000 a year for a single student. At the lower end, tuition for in-state residents at the University of Alabama is $2,245 and at University of North Dakota School of Law $2,125. Law schools generally admit only those with a college degree, which itself restricts the profession to those who can afford seven years of education beyond high school. If one goes to a state university where the cost of an undergraduate degree is a reasonable $5,000 a year, the direct cost is $20,000. If the modest yearly "income" of $15,000 is added (the amount a student might have earned had he or she not gone to college), the total "cost" of college education is $80,000. Add to this the cost of law school and forgone earnings, another $80,000, and a law degree from a state university around the bottom of the tuition scale will cost at least $160,000. And this is a very conservative figure. For those who cannot afford such expenses, the alternative is to attend a less expensive college, then go to law school part-time at night. But this option will take longer and will provide a lower-quality legal education than full-time enrollment. Approximately 75 percent of law students rely on educational loans as their main source of financial aid for law school.

Admission to law school is determined to a great extent by the combined scores of grade point averages in college and Law School Admission Test (LSAT) scores. Although they do not like to publicize the fact, law schools are not above admitting students based on non-academic criteria such as alumni or substantial family donations. This process is referred to as "institutional interest," and in part justified by suggesting that it helps poorer students by bringing in extra money from donations (Myers, 1994). The LSAT is a nationally administered, standardized test taken by all law school applicants. Most people take the test only once; only about 18 percent take it twice and about 4 percent more than twice. In 1999–2000 the test alone cost $90 plus another $32 for handscoring. Virtually all law schools also require that applicants submit the Law School Data Assembly Service Report, a summary of their college transcript that the Law School Admission Council/Law School Admission Services prepares. The LSAT test and the basic transcript service for 12 months cost $177. There is also an application fee at most law schools, which can be as high as $75, making multiple applications an expensive proposition since the average applicant applies to 4.7 law schools. Letters of recommendation in support of one's application are generally submitted separately to law schools.

The LSAT has been used in various forms since 1948. The current version was administered the first time in June 1991. In the academic year 1999–2000, over 125,000 persons took the test, but only about half of them actually applied to a law school. The LSAT is a one-half-day standardized test. It consists of five 35-minute sections of multiple-choice questions designed to measure the ability to read with understanding and insight, the ability to structure relationships and to make deductions from them, the ability to evaluate reading, the ability to apply reasoning to rules and facts, and the ability to think analytically. There is also a 30-minute writing sample that is sent directly to the applicant's law school. The score is reported on a scale of 120 to 180, with 180 as the highest possible score (*Official Guide*, 2000). For tests administered before 1991, the scores ranged from 10 to 48. Applicants are advised not to take the LSAT for practice since all scores will be reported to every law school one applies for admission.

The test repeatedly came under criticism, and questions have been raised concerning the extent to which the LSAT can predict success in law school. Performance criteria of success in law school have traditionally been, and continue to be, grades obtained in formal course work. More and more studies conclude that the LSAT, or a combination of LSAT and grade point average, does not predict law school grades for practical purposes of selection, placement, or advisement for candidates seeking entrance into law school (Leonard, 1977:204). Even though there are questions about the validity and reliability of the LSAT to predict success in law school, all law schools require it as part of the admission process. It should be noted, though, that law schools are not alone in their dependence on some form of admissions (or exclusionary) device. Americans have come to expect testing. The fact that some definitive scientific answer about the best way or ways to measure human abilities and potentials is still remote will not stop the process.

Socialization into the Profession

The purpose of law school is to change people; to turn them into novice lawyers; and to instill "in them a nascent self-concept as a professional, a commitment to the value of the calling, and a claim to that elusive and esoteric style of reasoning called 'thinking like a lawyer' " (Bonsignore et al., 1989:271). Chambliss and Seidman sardonically but correctly note: "The American law school education is a classic example of an education in which the subject matter formally studied is ridiculously simple, but the process of socialization into the profession is very difficult" (1971:97). The study of law is a tedious although not a challenging undertaking. After the first year, the workload in law schools tends to be light. The popular conception of law students' life as a mixture of long hours, poring over casebooks, and endless discussions of the contents of those books is more myth than reality. For many students, law school is a part-time commitment, and by the fifth semester, they have the equivalent of a two-day workweek and discuss their studies rarely if at all. Says Stevens: "At least intellectually law school appears to be a part-time operation" (1973:653).

The key to an understanding of the socialization of law students is best found through an examination of their principal method of instruction, the case or Socratic method. As I noted earlier, the case method was initiated by Langdell in 1870 at Harvard, and it has since become the dominant form of instruction in American law schools.

This method of education "generally involves an intensive interrogation by the teacher of individual students concerning the facts and principles presumed to be operative" in a particular case. The method is intended to accomplish two objectives. The first is informational: instruction in the substantive rules of law. The second

> is to develop in the student a cognitive restructuring for the style analysis generally called "thinking like a lawyer." In that analysis, a student is trained to

account for the factual "details" as well as legal issues determined by the court to be at the core of the dispute which may allow an intelligent prediction of what another court would do with a similar set of facts. The technique is learner centered: students are closely questioned and their responses are often taken to direct the dialogue. (Bonsignore et al., 1989:275)

This method of learning the law through court decisions, appellate opinions, and attempts to justify those opinions predominates at virtually every law school in the country and has not changed since its introduction in 1870. Historically, as well as today, the first year of legal education is the most dramatic of the law school's three years. The curriculum of the first year has become as well established in the past century as the teaching method. Nearly all of the more than 43,000 people who begin their legal education every fall are required to take what are generally thought of as the basic subjects—contracts, torts, property law, criminal law, and civil procedure. And for all of them, the effects of that education are considered to be equally predictable and far-reaching. It is during the first year that law students learn to read a case, frame a legal argument, and distinguish between seemingly indistinguishable ideas; then they start absorbing the mysterious language of the law, full of words like *estoppel* and *replevin*. It is during the first year that a law student learns "to think like a lawyer," to develop the habits and perspectives that will stay with him or her throughout a legal career (Turow, 1977:60).

The ratio of the number of students to the number of faculty in law schools is markedly higher than that in any other field of graduate training. A 1-to-25 faculty-student ratio is common at the best law schools, compared with about a 1-to-6 ratio in graduate schools (Loh, 1984:735). The ratio is predicated on the assumption that law students, unlike other graduate students, are handled in large classes and that law professors, unlike other academicians, "have no research work to be done" (Manning, 1968:4). Although the emphasis on research is on the increase among law professors, students, especially during the first year, are taught in large classes. One striking advantage of the case method noted by educational administrators is its adaptability to large classes; indeed, there is an argument to be made for the proposition that the impersonality of the large class is helpful to the student called upon to perform under attack for the first time in his or her life. As stated by a law professor at Yale, "I prefer a hundred, I will work for a hundred and put on a good show; I'll go to sleep with ten or twelve. After you've taught a subject to a class of a hundred for two or three years, you can anticipate the questions and their timing. When I started, I was told, 'Pick four or five points and keep coming back to them; find the bright students and play them like a piano!' It works" (Mayer, 1967:83–84). This method requires the student to do his or her own work and to prepare regularly for classes. When a professor has a gift for posing hypothetical questions, and invents cases to supplement the real ones, the method can be extremely stimulating, pointing out to a student that the rule, as he or she has stated it, would produce a different result under other circumstances. The method also focuses attention on subtleties and provides a good background for logical reasoning.

Although the processes of legal education continue to produce lawyers to fill the present institutional roles calling for them, through methods that have worked and proved themselves consistently over the last century, a feeling of malaise and discontent has been growing among students and faculty at many of the nation's law schools. Many students deplore the Socratic method's inconclusiveness, its failure to encourage creativeness, and its lack of intellectual stimulation (Stevens, 1973:636–638). The class atmosphere is considered to be a hostile one, with the hostility directed from the icily distant law professor toward the student on the spot. Law professors often ignore the emotional level of communication. The impersonal nature of education and mistrustful relations between faculty and students culminate in an intense emotional climate in the classroom, which can pose a threat to the students' self-esteem, self-respect, and identity. Elevated levels of depression and anxiety are ubiquitous among law students (Carney, 1990). Many complain of a high level of stress which will stay with them during their professional careers (New York Times, 1995d:B15).

These unintended results of the Socratic method of teaching are generally rationalized by explaining that the method is meant to acclimate the students to "real life," "legal reasoning," or "thinking like a lawyer." But it is difficult to see the relationship between the psychic damage and those stated goals, "and one often gets the feeling that the recitation of 'thinking like a lawyer' has become more a talismanic justification for what is going on than an articulated educational program" (Packer and Ehrlich, 1972:30). In addition to the tendency of the Socratic method to provoke anxiety, hostility, and aggression in the classroom, the domination by the law professor as an authority figure suggests that another aspect of law school training is to enforce a respect for authoritative power (Bonsignore et al., 1989:277). Women seem to dislike the Socratic method more than men. Recent studies also find that men outperform women in law schools as measured by higher grades (Mansnerus, 1995b). Yet, the method has proved to be remarkably resilient, and in spite of all the criticism against it, there has been no serious competitor (Stevens, 1983:xiv).

Essentially, the objective of law school education is to indoctrinate students into the legal profession. Questions that challenge the basis of the system are seldom raised, and law students define the problems presented to them within the framework of the existing system. The socialization of law students tends to make them intellectually independent, but at the same time it restrains them from looking for radical solutions, "for throughout their law school education they are taught to define problems in the way they have always been defined" (Chambliss and Seidman, 1971:99). During law school, students change their political orientation in a conservative direction (Erlanger and Klegon, 1978). It is not surprising that "legal education seems to socialize students toward an entrepreneurial value position in which the law is presumed to be primarily a conflict-resolving mechanism and the lawyer a facilitator of client interests. The experience seems to move students away from the social welfarist value in which the law is seen as a social change mechanism, and the lawyer a facilitator of group or societal interests" (Kay, 1978:347).

Political values are often fused with the learning of law, and "students are conditioned to react to questions and issues which they have no role in forming or stimulating. Such teaching *forms* have been crucial in perpetuating the status quo in teaching *content*. For decades, the law school curriculum reflected with remarkable fidelity the commercial demands of law firm practice" (Nader, 1969:21). Students anticipate and law professors reinforce the notion that successful lawyers tend to be conservative and use conservative solutions. A financially successful lawyer needs clients who are able to pay fees. Businesspeople and rich people in general pay larger fees than wage earners and poor people. Successful lawyers represent successful clients, and such a lawyer "if not already attuned to the value-sets of his client, tends to adopt them" (Chambliss and Seidman, 1971:99).

In response to the escalating criticism of the socialization process of law students, there is a growing emphasis on interdisciplinary work in law schools, and on joint degrees such as law and sociology, law and psychiatry, law and business, and law and just about anything. There is also a call for globalization of legal education (Mangan, 1998b) and a trend toward "clinical" programs, which are becoming standard curricular features at more and more law schools (Schrag and Meltsner, 1998). The idea is to remove law students from classroom situations and place them during their second and third years in real situations, such as criminal defense offices and poverty-related neighborhood legal-aid offices. For many law students, clinical education is considered to be more "relevant" to perceived social needs, and they believe that it should contribute to providing better legal services for the poor and other unrepresented groups in society. Clinical education lends itself to being a separate activity and is by nature removed from the law school. Since active participation is fundamental in clinical education, in addition to learning "how to think like a lawyer" students learn "how to work like lawyers." It injects a sense of realism and gives the students a feel for the human factors in dealing with clients, judges, juries, and regulators—something difficult to impart in the classroom (*U.S. News & World Report*, 1992). However, in view of the prevailing academic ethos that rewards faculty more for publishing than for teaching, some universities look with disdain on innovations that seek to provide courses that are snobbishly referred to as "vocational training." Clinical education is also expensive: It is more economical to deploy senior faculty (who earn well in excess of $200,000 at top schools) to teach 150 students in a large lecture hall than to advise and supervise a handful in a time-consuming clinical program. Not surprisingly, other than some attempts at clinical education, law schools oppose the traditional curriculum, such as the establishment of comprehensive programs (similar to medical internships) to provide students with a more practical grounding in courtroom skills and other aspects of law practice (Jacobson, 1979:10).

BAR ADMISSION

The legal profession has defined the perimeters of the practice of law and carefully excluded all who cannot utter the password of bar membership. Recall the lockstep of the profession as it now operates. The process begins after college, when the performance of the aspiring lawyer is carefully measured by more or less standard grading processes, as further refined by the Law School Admission Test. Nowadays, only the strongest, as measured by those two criteria, have been allowed to enter the portals of legal education. There the refining process continues with study and examinations designed to test the same qualities that were measured on the LSAT. Finally, at the end of law school—again a graded performance—there is for nearly all a bar examination, which reviews fitness to practice by testing for the same qualities as did the LSAT and the law school examinations.

In the United States, the possession of a law degree does not entitle one to practice law. Since a lawyer is technically a court official, he or she must, in addition to legal training, be admitted to practice by a court. Historically, there were no criteria for admission to the bar, and it depended a great deal on the charity or leniency of a local judge. In most instances, to be admitted by one court was sufficient to practice before any court in a state, for each judge respected his or her colleagues' actions in admission proceedings. As a result, the standards of the most lenient judge in a state became the minimum standard for admission (Hurst, 1950:276–285).

The lack of standards attracted the attention of the American Bar Association and state bars. Their concern was twofold. Easy admission permitted the entry of unqualified and unscrupulous lawyers whose work blemished the reputation of all lawyers. Furthermore, easy entrance into the legal profession allowed more lawyers to compete for the available legal business and depressed the income of lawyers.

There were several efforts by the ABA and state bar associations to restrict entry into the legal profession. They obtained legislation to lengthen the required training before application for admission could be accepted. Most efforts to restrict entry into the bar, however, were focused on requiring applicants to pass a standardized bar examination. Bar examinations have had their desired impact in reducing admission to the legal profession and increasing the standards of the profession. Today, "no person who is not a member of the bar of another American or Common-Law jurisdiction should be admitted to practice until he has successfully undergone a written examination accomplished under terms and conditions equivalent to those applicable to all other candidates for bar admission" (American Bar Association, 1979:83).

Over time, bar examinations have had some unanticipated consequences. Since bar examinations follow a content pattern substantially identical to that borrowed from the law school curriculum, the pattern of the local bar examination, in turn, strongly inhibits change in educational programs. The extent to which a school introduces innovative programs or markedly deviates in its curriculum from traditional programs places its graduates at a competitive disadvantage in taking a bar examination. Moreover, because law schools are accredited according to, among other criteria, the number of students who pass the bar exam, and are often rated by students according to this standard, legal education has become very much examination oriented in many states. Subjects included in the examination are required of the students, and courses in those subjects are often molded according to the questions asked on the examinations.

More and more law school graduates, in preparation for the local bar examination, take cram courses and sit through six hours of daily lectures for six to 12 solid weeks, memorizing endless outlines and gimmicks of local examinationship—which will be erased from their minds within months after the examination date. And more and more of them take out "bar exam loans," averaging $5,000, to pass the fiscal bridge between commencement and the first paycheck, to pay for living expenses and for the $1,100 to $1,500 cost of bar review course (Anderson, 1995). Whatever improvement is made in law schools greatly increases the necessity of this type of cramming, unless the bar examinations change, too. Apparently, there is a payoff for intense preparation—the percentage of 1994 law school graduates who passed the bar exam was the highest in the past 25 years (Myers, 1995).

In addition to educational qualifications of would-be lawyers, bar associations restrict admission procedures to those who are morally fit to become lawyers. Applicants for admission to the bar must have "good moral character." But the definition of this standard is weak. Basically, it means that no one who has a serious criminal record can be admitted to the practice of law. In some cases, it has led to the refusal of a board of examiners to admit someone who has held (or still holds) unpopular political views, and during the McCarthy era the ABA urged that all those who would become lawyers should take a loyalty oath as a condition of practice (Green, 1976:5). Although the standards are vague, historically the U.S. Supreme Court often upheld the authority of state courts to refuse admission to individuals the state deemed unworthy to practice law. Admission is a privilege that a court may withhold. Through such actions, bar associations effectively control the entry of some individuals who could potentially damage the image of the legal profession.

BAR ASSOCIATIONS AS INTEREST GROUPS

In addition to restricting entry into the profession and seeking to control the activity of their members, bar associations are interest groups actively engaged in the promotion of activities that the bar considers vital to its interests.

Much of the bar's activity concerns the organization and personnel of the courts. Bar associations attempted repeatedly to devise and to promote court reorganization schemes. Much of this effort went into the elimination of nonprofessional elements from the judicial process. The bar has also been active in seeking to influence the selection of judges. On the state level, where judges are often elected on a partisan or nonpartisan ballot, the bar association has frequently lobbied for a change in selection procedures that would give the bar a greater voice. The bar also influences the selection of federal judges, and it is now a standard procedure for the attorney general of the United States to seek the ABA's opinion about political nominees when choosing a name for submission by the president to the Senate. The bar is also active in promoting legislation that will benefit lawyers and the administrations of justice. For example, the bar actively promoted legislation against the unauthorized practice of the law, which includes software programs and manuals for creating wills, contracts, or simple divorce papers (*Time*, 1998), in an attempt to safeguard its monopoly of legal services.

In addition to taking a leading part in shaping laws (especially on criminal and regulatory matters), structuring the legal system, and making recommendations for judicial positions, the national and state bar associations have often turned to politics to promote their professional and economic interests. Such efforts have resulted in, among other things, state regulations that limit the number of lawyers and raise the income of those who do practice. Associations of trial lawyers have also sought to influence state and national legislation or regulations that are regarded as affecting their economic interests. A recent example has been the opposition of trial lawyers to no-fault automobile insurance, whereby people in an automobile accident can collect from their own insurance companies without having to hire a lawyer, go to court, and establish liability—whose proponents say that it would save drivers some $40 billion annually in lower premiums (Passell, 1998). Other attempts of the bar to enhance the economic status of its members include the promotion of continued benefits for self-employed lawyers, permission for lawyers to practice before federal agencies without having to obtain special admission or take a special admission examination, promotion of a bill to remove ceilings on attorneys' fees in federal departments and agencies, opposition to bankruptcy reform that would remove lawyers from the proceedings, and opposition to the extension of the role of title companies in home closings at the expense of lawyers (Green, 1976:7). But because of the rising concern over the cost and quality of legal representation in the United States, there have been arguments of late that formally trained attorneys are not the best advocates in many situations. For example, in a recent book, *Legal Advocacy: Lawyers and Nonlawyers at Work,* Herbert M. Kritzer (1998) describes lawyers and nonlawyer advocates at work in four different legal situations: unemployment compensation claim appeals, Social Security disability appeals, state tax appeals, and labor grievance arbitrations and concludes that nonlawyers can be effective advocates and, in some legal settings, more effective than many lawyers.

Organized bar also opposes the spread of legal self-help materials and the growth of the self-help industry, which dispenses step-by-step guidance for solving common legal problems and translates legalese into plain English. Not surprisingly, publishers of self-help legal books and software are reporting brisk sales (Benjamin, 2001). These popular legal resources are useful for simple matters such as simple wills, no-fault divorces, landlord-tenant disputes, bankruptcies and other bread and butter issues that previously used to be the exclusive domain of lawyers. Even though many lawyers invoke the old maxim that a person who represents himself "has a fool for a client," Nolo Press, one of the more successful publishers of legal self-help material (100 or so titles annually), sells hundreds of thousands of books such as *How to Do Your Own Divorce in California.* There are also video clips that deal with legal topics and the ubiquitous Internet for those who are wired (try Nolo.com to see an illustration of the variety of legal products available in cyberspace).

Of course, the bar associations, like all professional associations (and unions), have, as one of their primary functions, the promotion of the social, political, and economic interests of their members. Ideally, at least, however, there is a fundamental difference between the legal profession and other professions. Fred Rodell of Yale is quoted as stating that "while law is supposed to be a device to serve society . . . it is pretty hard to find a group less concerned with serving society and more concerned with serving themselves than lawyers" (Green, 1976:19). Thus, it is not surprising that the most discernible common cause of bar associations is to represent the needs of their lawyers and those clients whose interests they regularly attend. Bar associations, in the final analysis, have been rather successful in preserving lawyers' monopoly on legal practice and the profession's lucrative role in society.

PROFESSIONAL DISCIPLINE

One of the characteristics of a profession is a code of ethics. A profession involves, among other things, a sense of service and responsibility to the community, and the conduct required of a professional is delineated in a code of ethics for that profession. A lawyer's code of ethics deals with his or her relations with clients, other lawyers, the court, and the public.

The legal profession has long been concerned with the ethical forms under which lawyers operate. In 1908, the American Bar Association published its *Canons of Ethics*. In 1969, it was revised and called the *Model Code of Professional Responsibility*. The standards of professional conduct promulgated by the code were adopted by most states. The code covered a variety of important rules from representation of conflicting interests and preservation of clients' confidences to matters of professional etiquette. In 1977, the ABA decided that the code was insufficient in view of the changing nature of the profession and established a commission to come up with a new, more realistic, and more practical set of ethical rules.

In 1983, the ABA adopted the *Model Rules of Professional Conduct and Code of Judicial Conduct* (The American Law Institute, 1989). It contains a series of guidelines and rules on matters such as fees, confidentiality of information, certain types of conflict of interest, safekeeping property, unauthorized practice of law, advertising, and reporting professional misconduct. Some of these were modified at the ABA's annual meeting in August 2001, in Chicago. For example, the House of Delegates approved a proposal allowing lawyers to disclose confidences when doing so prevents "reasonably certain death or substantial body harm" (Glater, 2001b:1). This update in the *Model Rules of Professional Conduct* in nearly 20 years is significant because it means that lawyers who may know of a defective product may now warn potential victims (although they are not compelled to do so). Formerly, breaking the code of confidentiality was limited to prevent the client from committing a criminal act that the lawyer believed was likely to result in imminent death or substantial bodily harm. The delegates at the 2001 meetings also supported a new rule that would prohibit a lawyer from having sex with a client unless a consensual sexual relationship predated the professional contact. In this context, it is interesting to note that the language is much stronger than the ethical guidelines for other professional associations such as university professors or accountants.

A serious weakness of the codes and model rules is that they are not binding on lawyers and the adoption of them is not required by local groups. The ABA exerts no control over state bars in this process. Furthermore, enforcement is not obligatory. Although the ABA advocates uniform standards in disciplinary procedures, it is unable to instrument uniform adherence.

Disciplinary authorities are supposed to make sure that only honest and competent people are licensed to practice law. In some states, the disciplinary committee operates under the auspices of the state court system. In others, the bar organization runs the disciplinary agency and investigates complaints but any sanctions are imposed by the courts. Although the procedures vary from state to state, the boards investigate complaints about alleged violations of professional rules of conduct.

In general, disciplinary sanctions, such as reprimand, suspension or disbarment, are imposed only for serious instances of misconduct, such as criminal acts, mishandling of a client's property, and flagrant violation of certain rules of professional conduct, such as breach of confidentiality. Some of these sanctions are in addition to possible criminal proceedings, which are handled separately by law-enforcement authorities, and they may publicized as a form of "risk prevention" (Davis, 1995). Of course, unhappy clients can always sue their lawyers, and an indirect form of punishment is the very high cost of attorneys' malpractice insurance (Hazard, 1994). Other rule violations rarely evoke formal disciplinary action, although there is informal discipline in the form of expressed disapproval, which carries its own practical penalties, such as questions about one's professional reputation (American Bar Association, 1986). It is interesting to note that, unlike psychiatrists and psychologists, who are ethically proscribed from sleeping with patients, the ABA still does not take an official position on lawyers engaging in sexual relations with clients. A *National Law Journal* article headline nicely captures this view in stating: "Draconian Sex Rules Premature" (Barker and Rhodes, 1992) although some states began to consider "attorney sex guidelines" barring most lawyer-client sex (Dilworth, 1993).

Generally, the highest ethical standards are found among attorneys who work for large firms (Carlin, 1966:47–48) and represent big-business clients in more traditional fields such as patents and admiralty. Those who represent individuals in cases that are characterized as "unsavory," such as personal injury plaintiffs' work, divorce, and criminal defense, tend to have lower ethical standards (Heinz and Laumann, 1994). These are usually lower-status solo practitioners who practice before state courts. As Herbert Jacob (1984:62) notes, the more contact such attorneys have with lower courts, the less likely they are to comply with legal ethics: "The culture of lower courts—waiting around, exchanging gossip, litigating petty criminal and civil cases" promotes unethical conduct.

Violations of legal ethics may be punished by a reprimand, a temporary suspension of the license to practice law, or the revocation of the license. Jerome E. Carlin (1966:170) found that only about 2 percent of the lawyers who violated ethical norms were even processed by the bar's disciplinary machine, and only 0.2 percent were officially sanctioned. In 1972, bar associations disciplined 357 lawyers, roughly one-tenth of 1 percent of practicing lawyers at that time (Garbus and Seligman, 1976:48). In 1984, 59,862 complaints were received by the disciplinary boards in 48 states. That number represents about 8 percent of all practicing attorneys. During the same year, 1,408 lawyers received public sanctions (disbarment, suspension, and public reprimand) and 1,833 received private sanctions (reprimand and formal admonition) (Austern, 1986:17). Although the bar spent more than $30 million for lawyer discipline, the enforcement of the ethical standards it has promulgated for the guidance of its members leaves something to be desired when only 5.4 percent of those who had complaints against them were subjected to either public or private sanctions. In 1994, the American Bar Association created a nationwide online database of disbarred and censured lawyers, some 25,000 to start with, to keep track of lawyers who move from state to state. The service is available to disciplinary authorities but not to consumer groups because in case of the slightest inaccuracy it could harm a lawyer's reputation and lead to potential lawsuits. Discipline boards and state bar associations welcome the service. Because each state regulates its own lawyers, discipline is complicated as lawyers become increasingly mobile and register in more than one state. Lawyers who are disciplined in one state can move to another, take the bar examination and start over without alerting authorities or potential clients of the infractions (Stevens, 1994).

How serious are lawyers about professional responsibility? In a 1985 poll conducted for the *ABA Journal*, Reskin (1985:41) finds that professional responsibility is important to most lawyers; most are familiar with ethical codes in effect in their jurisdiction. Lack of familiarity with the code of professional responsibility is highest (15 percent) among lawyers who are not in private practice—law professors and government, legal-aid, and corporate law department lawyers.

Ethics are emphasized and considered extremely important among partners, according to 66 percent of the respondents. The group that places the greatest accent on ethics consists of lawyers earning more than $75,000 from the practice of law (76 percent). Ethics are not discussed or emphasized especially among solo practitioners (22 percent) and lawyers not in private practice (27 percent). These findings are consistent with studies on lawyers' ethics (see, for example, Carlin, 1966, and Heinz and Laumann, 1994) that suggest that high-status lawyers in firms are more likely to adhere to the ethical norms of the profession than their lower-status counterparts in solo practice.

Lawyers have an obligation to report known or suspected ethical violations by other lawyers according to the ethics rules and standards of the governing bodies (Pitulla, 1995). But only seven out of 10 lawyers say that they would report a lawyer outside of their firm who acted unethically, and six out of 10 would report a colleague in their own firm. Because 71 percent say they have occasionally encountered dishonest opposing counsel, it is obvious that lawyers should be doing much more reporting. But they are not. Most complaints against lawyers are filed by clients or initiated by the bar council. It is rare that lawyers or judges report lawyer or judicial misconduct. The reasons for not reporting vary from "no use" because nothing would happen and it is not their responsibility to not wanting to ruin someone's career. About 40 percent of the lawyers who do not report misconduct fear that too much time would be taken up testifying in a disciplinary proceeding, do not know where to report the misconduct, or are afraid of being subjected to a lawsuit. Although lawyers claim that ethical conduct is important and the majority are willing to report violation of professional norms, in reality, they are reluctant to do it—which raises serious concerns about the efficacy of the internal modes of control of the profession.

There are also external modes of control of the profession, primarily from the federal government. Both the Federal Trade Commission and the Justice Department are concerned with the delivery of legal services in matters of monopolistic restrictions (curbing the provision of legal services to poor and moderate-income people) and practices constituting restraint of trade (such as real estate agents filling out legal forms in closing a deal, which is considered "unauthorized" practice of law). The Securities and Exchange Commission also has authority to discipline lawyers who practice before it and engage in fraudulent activities by temporarily suspending or disbarring them.

Finally, there is the delicate and difficult problem of monitoring judicial conduct. How can judges be protected from unfair attacks so they can maintain their judicial independence and have, at the same time, effective mechanisms for the retirement or removal of those who do not perform their duties properly? In some states, the only procedure for removal of judges before the end of their term is impeachment by a vote of legislators. In others, committees of judges are empowered to investigate judicial incompetence and compel the retirement of a judge found unable to carry out his or her duties (Flood, 1985:42).

The problem is further compounded by the failure of most lawyers to report judicial misconduct that they have witnessed (Reskin, 1985:41). So far, the most dramatic measure for rooting out judicial corruption has been Operation Greylord (Flood, 1985:42). The Federal Bureau of Investigation for three-and-a-half years investigated the largest court system in the country, with over 300 judges—the Cook County system, which includes Chicago. It uncovered a variety of corrupt practices by some judges, such as favorable rulings, case referrals, and lighter criminal sentences in return for bribes. Judges also gave permission to attorneys to solicit clients in the courthouse. The FBI relied on agents to represent attorneys and criminals to infiltrate the court, and in one instance a judge was wired to record conversations between corrupt lawyers and judges. As a result of the FBI investigation, several judges, lawyers, and court officials have been indicted for corruption; four judges so far have been convicted and one acquitted.

SUMMARY

In all societies, the legal profession has been intimately connected with the rise and development of legal systems. Primitive societies had courts and judges but no lawyers. In such societies, custom and law coincided. No special legal skills were required before a court. With the development of court procedures, a class of skilled advocates emerged. The origins of the legal profession can be traced back to Rome. Lawyers, in the sense of a regulated group of practitioners, emerged in the late 1200s. By that time, the body of legal knowledge, including procedure, had become too much for the ordinary person to handle alone. Technical pleadings required the aid of an attorney, and legal business increased tremendously. In the fourteenth and fifteenth centuries, a secular class of lawyers emerged in England, and the law administered by the royal courts became independent, in some important respects at least, from Roman and canon law. To a large extent, English lawyers received their training in the Inns of Court, at the hands of the legal profession itself, and not in the universities. Blackstone's appointment to the Vinerian Chair of Jurisprudence in 1758 marked the first effort to make English law a university subject.

Initially in the United States, legal education was modeled after the British system. Many of the early upper-class American lawyers obtained their training in the Inns of Court. In the late eighteenth and early nineteenth centuries, general courses in law were established in many American universities. However, these courses were in time superseded by the development of university law schools—a form of professional legal education that, strictly speaking, has no counterpart either in England or on the continent of Europe.

Lawyers have established a monopoly on legal business, and the profession of law has become the fastest-growing of all professions in the United States during the last two decades. Although members of the profession have never been popular, lawyers rank high in prestige in the United States. There are four principal subgroups in the legal profession: lawyers in private practice, in government service, in private employment, and in the judiciary. The American legal profession is highly stratified. Lawyers in private practice who are solo practitioners in general tend to have a lower status in the profession than their counterparts working in law firms. The relatively low status of solo practitioners is attributed to their socioeconomic background and to the quality of education they have received. Many solo practitioners use the legal profession as a form of social mobility. Employment with the government is often considered a mobility route into a more prestigious practice for young lawyers. The proportion of lawyers in private employment is on the increase, and they handle only the work of their corporate employer. Some larger corporations today have legal departments that compare in size and excellence with those of the largest law firms. In the United States, there is no career judiciary, and there is no prescribed route for the young law graduate to become a judge. Judges are elected or appointed.

There is substantial variation in income by types of lawyers. Those in law firms and in private employment generally earn more than their counterparts in solo practice or in the judiciary. Income is related to the type of practice, the type of clientele, the degree of specialization, the size of the firm, the quality of education and achievement in law school, the age and length of practice, and the size and location of the place of practice. In recent years, there has been a growing competition for legal business. Although the minimum fee schedules have been abolished (at least in principle) and lawyers are now able to advertise, the cost of legal services is still beyond the reach of many people.

Law and lawyers are expensive. In criminal cases, the poor are represented either by public defenders or by court-appointed attorneys. In civil cases, the poor can gain access to lawyers through public or private legal-aid programs. Others with less limited finances resort to legal clinics or prepaid legal plans as a way of obtaining legal representation.

Contemporary lawyers must submit to a long period of training before becoming eligible to practice. This, however, is a recent development in the United States. Throughout the nineteenth century, legal training was haphazard. Most lawyers received their training in the office of a practicing attorney. They worked for him as a clerk, and by doing so learned the trade themselves. University training of lawyers in the United States did not really begin until after 1870. Today there are 182 law schools approved by the American Bar Association. Entry into a law school requires a college degree, and applicants must have a high grade point average in addition to a moderately high LSAT score. The number of law students tripled during the past two decades, and the number of women in law schools increased almost twenty-fold. However, minority students still represent a smaller proportion in law schools than their percentage of the total population. Law school education still relies heavily on the case or Socratic method, which has remained virtually unchanged since its introduction. The method is meant to acclimate the students to "legal reasoning," or to "thinking like a lawyer," but lately it has been subjected to criticisms that, for example, it fails to encourage creativeness and that it lacks intellectual stimulation. It also provokes anxiety, hostility, and aggression in the classroom. Law schools seem to socialize students toward an entrepreneurial value position, and questions that challenge the basis of the legal system are seldom raised. During law school, students tend to change their political orientation in a conservative direction. In response to the growing criticism of the socialization process of law students, law schools in recent years began to emphasize interdisciplinary work and clinical programs. However, concerted efforts to reform curriculum are still opposed.

To maintain standards and to control entry into the bar, law school graduates are required to pass a standardized bar examination in the state where they wish to practice. Bar examinations have stifled changes in legal education. Many students are preoccupied with passing the bar, which forces law schools to mold courses according to the questions asked on the examinations. Bar associations further restrict admission procedures to those who are morally fit to become lawyers. Applicants for admission to the bar must have "good moral character." Bar associations also act as interest groups in promoting social, economic, and political activities that the bar considers vital to its interests. They often act like other interest groups in pressing for adoption of measures desired by their members.

In an attempt to improve the negative public image of lawyers, and to assist the courts in rendering justice, the legal profession adopted a code of ethics in 1908. Although violation of the code of legal ethics may be punished by reprimand, suspension from the bar, or disbarment, only a very small proportion of lawyers who violate the ethical standards are ever subjected to disciplinary action. Ethical codes seem to be more enforced when the profession, rather than the clients or society at large, is threatened.

SUGGESTED FURTHER READINGS

RICHARD L. ABEL and PHILIP S. C. LEWIS (EDS.), *Lawyers in Society: An Overview.* Berkeley, CA: University of California Press, 1995. A compendium of cross-cultural articles on the profession and practice of law by leading international authorities.

MAUREEN CAIN and CHRISTINE B. HARRINGTON (EDS.), *Lawyers in a Postmodern World; Translation and Transgression.* New York: New York University Press, 1994. A collection of articles exploring how lawyers create the forms of power they and others deploy.

JEROME E. CARLIN, *Lawyers on Their Own.* New Brunswick, NJ: Rutgers University Press, 1962. A now-classic study of individual practitioners in Chicago.

MACKLIN FLEMING, *Lawyers, Money, and Success: The Consequences of Dollar Obsessions.* Westport, CT: Quorum, 1997. A sobering critique of modern legal practice and a call for reform for economic injustices in the legal marketplace.

MARC GALANTER and THOMAS PALAY, *Tournament of Lawyers: The Transformation of the Big Law Firm.* Chicago: University of Chicago Press, 1991. A provocative study of the growth patterns of large corporate-law firms.

J. S. GANDHI, *Lawyers and Touts: A Study in the Sociology of the Legal Profession.* Delhi, India: Hindustan Publishing Corporation, 1982. A fascinating study of the various undesirable legal practices such as the exploitation of clients and the use of business agents or touts who procure clients for a share of the fee.

ROBERT GRANFIELD, *Making Elite Lawyers: Visions of Law and Beyond.* New York: Routledge, 1992. A fascinating empirical work on the conservatizing effects of legal education at Harvard on a broad cross section of students.

KERMIT L. HALL, *The Magic Mirror: Law in American History.* New York: Oxford University Press, 1989. An insightful, concise, and chronologically complete history of law in America.

PAUL G. HASKELL, *Why Lawyers Behave As They Do.* Boulder, CO: Westview Press, 1998. An account of why the public is justified in its low opinion of the legal profession.

JOHN P. HEINZ and EDWARD O. LAUMANN, *Chicago Lawyers: The Social Structure of the Bar.* Rev. ed. Evanston, IL: Northwestern University Press; Chicago: American Bar Foundation, 1994. A seminal study of the profession in Chicago based on 777 personal interviews with lawyers.

RICHARD D. KAHLENBERG, *Broken Contract: A Memoir of Harvard Law School.* New York: Hill & Wang, 1992. A 1989 Harvard Law School graduate paints a troubling picture of his alma mater. An eye-opening book for law school–bound students.

HERBERT M. KRITZER, *Legal Advocacy: Lawyers and Nonlawyers at Work.* Ann Arbor, MI: The University of Michigan Press, 1998. A comparative study of the work of lawyers and nonlawyers in several legal settings demonstrating that nonlawyers can be as effective as lawyers, or more so, in several different types of situations.

ANTHONY T. KRONMAN, *The Lost Lawyer: Failing Ideals of the Legal Profession.* Cambridge: The Belknap Press of Harvard University Press, 1993. See in particular the second part, which examines the realities of lawyering in three institutional settings—law schools, law firms and the court from a Weberian perspective.

SUZANNE NOSSEL and ELIZABETH WESTFALL, *Presumed Equal: What America's Top Women Lawyers Really Think About Their Firms.* Franklin Lakes, NJ: Career Press, 1998. An empirical study of women lawyers' career opportunities based on 1,225 interviews with women in 77 large firms—those with 50 or more female attorneys.

W. WESLEY PUE and DAVID SUGARMAN (EDS.), *Lawyers Culture and the Cultural Significance of Lawyers: Historical Perspectives.* Brookfield, VT: Ashgate, 1999. A collection of original essays by a group of international scholars on the cultural history of the legal professional.

AUSTIN SARAT and WILLIAM L. F. FELSTINER, *Divorce Lawyers and Their Clients: Power and Meaning in the Legal Process.* New York: Oxford University Press, 1995. An insightful analysis of the activities of divorce lawyers.

AUSTIN SARAT and STUART SCHEINGOLD (EDS.), *Cause Lawyering and the State in a Global Era.* New York: Oxford University Press, 2001. A compendium of interesting articles on a variety of causes and their lawyers.

PHILIP G. SCHRAG and MICHAEL MELTSNER, *Reflections on Clinical Legal Education.* Boston: Northeastern University Press, 1998. A review of the evolution of clinical legal education over the past three decades with topics on the structure and methods of clinical teaching programs, the process of supervision, the learning contract between professors and students, and the administration of legal clinics.

MARK SIMENHOFF, *My First Year as a Lawyer; Real-World Stories From America's Lawyers.* New York: Walker and Company, 1994. Eighteen lawyers share the stories of their first year of practice, discussing the challenges and rewards of the day-to-day work of novice attorneys.

J. CLAY SMITH, JR. (ED.), *Rebels in Law: Voices in History of Black Women Lawyers.* Ann Arbor, MI: The University of Michigan Press, 1998. A collection of essays that demonstrates the involvement of black women lawyers in important public issues of our time and shows them addressing the sensitive issues of race, equality, justice and freedom.

EVE SPANGLER, *Lawyers for Hire: Salaried Professionals at Work.* New Haven: Yale University Press, 1986. A now classic discussion of how salaried attorneys do their work in a variety of settings.

LOUISE G. TRUBEK and JEREMY COOPER, *Educating for Justice Around the World: Legal Education, Legal Practice and the Community.* Brookfield, VT: Ashgate, 1999. The book focuses on social values in legal education and practice and on the role of law and legal institutions in various parts of the world.

REFERENCES

ABA JOURNAL. 1986. "Lawyer Advertising Is on the Rise," 72 (April): 44.

ABEL, RICHARD L. 1986. "The Transformation of the American Legal Profession," *Law & Society Review* 20 (1): 7–17.

ABRAMS, FLOYD. 1994. "Why Lawyers Lie: The Truth Is Not the Highest Priority in a Criminal Trial," *New York Times Magazine* (October 9): 54.

AMERICAN BAR ASSOCIATION. 2001. Section of Legal Education and Admission to the Bar, *A Review of Legal Education in the United States, Fall, 2001*. Chicago: American Bar Association.

AMERICAN LAW INSTITUTE. 1989. *Professional Ethics and Responsibility*. Boston: The American Law Institute.

ANDERSON, LISA. 1995. "Bridging the Income Gap After Law School: Graduates Turn to Bar Exam Loans," *New York Times* (July 2): 14F.

AUERBACH, JEROLD S. 1976. *Unequal Justice: Lawyers and Social Change in Modern America*. New York: Oxford University Press.

AUSTERN, DAVID. 1986. "How Lawyers Police Themselves," *Trial* 22 (4) (April): 17.

BARKER, WILLIAM T. and C. HARKER RHODES, JR. 1992. "Draconian Sex Rules Premature," *The National Law Journal* 14 (43) (June 29): 17.

BENJAMIN, MATTHEW. 2001. "Legal self-help: Cheap counsel for simple cases," *U.S. News & World Report* (February 12): 54–56.

BERMAN, HAROLD J., WILLIAM R. GREINER and SAMIR N. SALIBA. 1996. *The Nature and Functions of Law*. 5th ed. Westbury, NY: The Foundation Press.

BONSIGNORE, JOHN J., ETHAN KATSH, PETER D'ERRICO, RONALD M. PIPKIN, STEPHEN ARONS, and JANET RIFKIN. 1989. *Before the Law: An Introduction to the Legal Process*. 4th ed. Boston: Houghton Mifflin.

BUSINESS WEEK. 1989. "Punitive Damages: How Much Is Too Much?" (March): 54–56.

CAMERON, GEORGE DANA, III. 1978. *The Soviet Lawyer and His System*. Ann Arbor, MI: Division of Research, Graduate School of Business Administration, The University of Michigan.

CARLIN, JEROME E. 1962. *Lawyers on Their Own*. New Brunswick, NJ: Rutgers University Press. 1966. *Lawyers' Ethics*. New York: Russell Sage Foundation.

CARNAHAN, DOUGLAS G. 1992. "Judges Need a Trade School," *The National Law Journal* 14 (32) (April 13): 15.

CARNEY, MICHAEL E. 1990. "Narcissistic Concerns in the Educational Experience of Law Students," *The Journal of Psychiatry & Law* 18 (1) (Spring–Summer): 9–34.

CARP, ROBERT A., and RONALD STIDHAM. 2001. *Judicial Process in America*. 5th ed. Washington, DC: CQ Press.

CHAMBLISS, WILLIAM J., and ROBERT B. SEIDMAN. 1971. *Law, Order, and Power*. Reading, MA: Addison-Wesley.

CEBULA, MARK A. 1998. "Does Lawyer Advertising Adversely Influence the Image of Lawyers in the United States? An Alternative Perspective and New Empirical Evidence," *The Journal of Legal Studies* 27 (2) (June): 503–518.

CHRONICLE OF HIGHER EDUCATION ALMANAC. 2001. "Average Pay of Full-Time Professors, Public Institutions" (August 28): 5.

CURRAN, BARBARA. 1986. "American Lawyers in the 1980s: A Profession in Transition," *Law & Society Review* 20 (1): 19–52.

CURRIDEN, MARK. 1995a. "Female Lawyers See Bias in Their Arrests: Cursing and Culottes Were Unacceptable to Authorities in Texas, Florida," *ABA Journal* 81 (March): 28–29. 1995b. "Lawyers Who Skip Law School: Seven States Allow Read-law Programs Despite ABA's Opposition," *ABA Journal* 81 (February): 28–30.

DAVIS, ANN. 1995. "Title Insurers Eye N.J. Lawyers Under Ethics Cloud: Newly Opened Disciplinary Process Lets Them Keep Tabs," *The National Law Journal* 17 (30) (March 27): A7.

DILWORTH, DONALD C. 1993. "New York Tightens Rules for Matrimonial Lawyers, May Extend Coverage to Others," *Trial* 29 (10) (October): 13–16.

EASTON, STEPHEN D. 1984. "Fewer Lawyers? Try Getting Your Day in Court," *Wall Street Journal* (November 27): 34.

ECONOMIST. 1994. "Paying the Judge: Legal Costs. Litigant's Fees Hiked to Pay Judges' Salaries in Great Britain" 330 (February 26): 59.

ERLANGER, HOWARD S., and DOUGLAS A. KLEGON. 1978. "Socialization Effects of Professional School: The Law School Experience and Student Orientations to Public Interest Concerns," *Law & Society Review* 13 (1) Fall: 11–35.

FARBER, DANIEL A., and SUZANNA SHERRY. 1997. *Beyond All Reason: The Radical Assault on Truth in American Law.* New York: Oxford University Press.

FLEMING, MACKLIN. 1997. *Lawyers, Money, and Success: The Consequences of Dollar Obsessions.* Westport, CT: Quorum.

FLOOD, JOHN. 1985. *The Legal Profession in the United States.* 3rd ed. Chicago: American Bar Foundation.

FLORES, ALBERT (ED.). 1988. *Professional Ideals.* Belmont, CA: Wadsworth.

FOOTE, NELSON N. 1953. "The Professionalization of Labor in Detroit," *American Journal of Sociology* 58 (4) (January): 371–380.

FOTHERINGHAM, ALLAN. 1994. "The Law According to the Chequebook—The Duplicity of Lawyers," *Maclean's* 107 (43) (October 24): 60–61.

FREELAND, RICHARD M. 1992. *Academia's Golden Age.* New York: Oxford University Press.

FRIEDMAN, LAWRENCE M. 1973. *A History of American Law.* New York: Simon & Schuster. 1977. *Law and Society: An Introduction.* Upper Saddle River, NJ: Prentice Hall. 1998. *American Law: An Introduction.* 2nd ed. New York: W. W. Norton & Company, Inc. 2002. *American Law in the Twentieth Century.* New Haven: Yale University Press.

FREIVOGEL, WILLIAM H. 1995. "Limits on Lawyers' Ads Upheld," *St. Louis Post-Dispatch* (June 22): 7A.

FRITSCH, JANE and DAVID ROHDE. 2001. "Legal Help Often Fails New York's Poor," *The New York Times,* (April 8): 1, 27.

FRUM, DAVID. 1994. "How to Rob a Bank, Sturdevant & Sturdevant Law Firm Sues Banks," *Forbes* 153 (5) (February 28): 62–63.

GALANTER, MARC. 1992. "The Debased Debate on Civil Justice." Working Paper DPRP 10–10. Madison: University of Wisconsin, Institute for Legal Studies.

GANDHI, J. S. 1982. *Lawyers and Touts: A Study in the Sociology of Legal Profession.* Delhi, India: Hindustan Publishing Corporation.

GARBUS, MARTIN, and JOEL SELIGMAN. 1976. "Sanctions and Disbarment: They Sit in Judgement." Pp. 47–60 in Ralph Nader and Mark Green (eds.), *Verdicts on Lawyers.* New York: Thomas Y. Crowell.

GLABERSON, WILLIAM. 2001. "A Study's Verdict: Jury Awards Are Not Out of Control," *New York Times* (August 6): A1.

GLATER, JONATHAN D. 2001a. "Few Minorities Rising to Law Partner," *New York Times* (August 7): A1, A6. 2001b. "Lawyers May Reveal Secrets of Clients, Bar Group Rules," *New York Times* (August 8): A1, A20. 2001c. "Law School Beckons as Economy Slows," *New York Times* (August 24): A1, A7.

GLENDON, MARY ANN, MICHAEL WALLACE GORDON, and CHRISTOPHER OSAKWE. 1994. *Comparative Legal Traditions.* 2nd ed. St. Paul, MN.: West Publishing Company.

GRAHAM, DEBORAH. 1995. "Law's New Entrepreneurs," *ABA Journal* 81 (February): 54–60.

GRANGE, LORI, and DAVID SCHWARTZ. 1995. "Lawyers Answer Public Service Call," *Human Rights* 22 (1) (Winter): 34–36.

GREEN, MARK J. 1975. "The High Cost of Lawyers," *New York Times Magazine* (August 10): 8–9, 53–56. 1976. "The ABA as Trade Association." Pp. 3–19 in Ralph Nader and Mark Green (eds.), *Verdicts on Lawyers*. New York: Thomas Y. Crowell.

GROSS, EDWARD. 1998. "Lawyers and Their Discontents," *Society as Needed* 36 (1) (November–December): 26–31.

HAGAN, JOHN, MARIE HUXTER, and PATRICIA PARKER. 1988. "Class Structure and Legal Practice: Inequality and Mobility among Toronto Lawyers," *Law & Society Review* 22 (1): 9–55.

HALLIDAY, TERENCE C. 1986. "Six Score Years and Ten: Demographic Transitions in the American Legal Profession, 1850–1980," *Law & Society Review* 20 (1): 53–78.

HANSEN, MARK. 1994. "A Shunned Justice System: Most Families Don't Turn to Lawyers or Judges to Solve Legal Problems, Survey Says," *ABA Journal* 80 (April): 18–20.

HARLAN, CHRISTI, and MILO GEYELIN. 1992. "Tennessee Backs Punitive Damage Change," *Wall Street Journal* (May 8): B5.

HARVARD LAW REVIEW. 1994. "The Eighth Amendment and Ineffective Assistance of Counsel in Capital Trials," 107 (8) (June): 1923–1940.

HASKELL, PAUL G. 1998. *Why Lawyers Behave As They Do*. Boulder, CO: Westview Press.

HASTIE, REID, DAVID SCHKADE and JOHN PAYNE. 1998. "A Study of Juror and Jury Judgments in Civil Cases: Deciding Liability for Punitive Damages," *Law and Human Behavior*, 22 (3) (June): 287–314.

HAZARD, GEOFFREY C. 1994. "Liability Coverage May Become Impossible to Obtain Under Traditional Procedures," *The National Law Journal* 16 (28) (March): A17.

HEINZ, JOHN P., and EDWARD O. LAUMANN. 1994. *Chicago Lawyers: The Social Structure of the Bar*. Rev. ed. Evanston, IL: Northwestern University Press; Chicago: American Bar Foundation.

HINES, CRYSTAL NIX. 2001. "Lack of Lawyers Blocking Appeals in Capital Cases," *New York Times* (July 5): A1, A5.

HURST, J. WILLARD. 1950. *The Growth of American Law*. Boston: Little, Brown.

JACOB, HERBERT. 1984. *Justice in America: Courts, Lawyers, and the Judicial Process*. 4th ed. Boston: Little, Brown. 1995. *Law and Politics in the United States*. 2nd ed. Ft. Washington, PA: HarperCollins College Publishers.

JACOBSON, ROBERT L. 1979. "Law Schools Are Cool to Chief Justice's Ideas on Reforming Curriculum," *Chronicle of Higher Education* 17 (18) (January 15): 10.

JACOBY, HENRY. 1973. *The Bureaucratization of the World*. Trans. Eveline L. Kanes. Berkeley and Los Angeles: University of California Press.

JEFFERY, C. RAY. 1962. "The Legal Profession." Pp. 313–356 in F. James Davis, Henry H. Foster, Jr., C. Ray Jeffery, and E. Eugene Davis, *Society and the Law: New Meanings for an Old Profession*. New York: Free Press.

JENKINS, JOHN A. 1977. "The Revolving Door between Government and the Law Firms," *Washington Monthly* 8 (11) (January): 36–44.

JOHNSON, DIRK. 1995. "More Scorn and Less Money Dim Law's Lure," *New York Times* (September 22): A1, A8.

KAY, FIONA M. 1997. "Flight from Law: A Competing Risks Model of Departures from Law Firms," *Law & Society Review.* 31 (2): 301–333.

KAY, SUSAN ANN. 1978. "Socializing the Future Elite: The Nonimpact of a Law School," *Social Science Quarterly* 59 (2) (September): 347–356.

KEARNEY, HUGH. 1970. *Scholars and Gentlemen: Universities and Society in Pre-Industrial Britain.* Ithaca, NY: Cornell University Press.

KEEVA, STEVEN. 1995. "Standing Up for Women," *ABA Journal* 81 (April): 118–119.

KENNEDY, DANIEL B. 1994. "The Payback: The Way to Gauge the Effectiveness of Advertising Is by the Business It Brings In," *ABA Journal* 80 (June) 62–65.

KLEIN, MITCHELL S. G. 1984. *Law, Courts, and Policy.* Englewood Cliffs, NJ: Prentice Hall.

KRITZER, HERBERT M. 1990. *The Justice Broker: Lawyers and Ordinary Litigation.* New York: Oxford University Press. 1998. *Legal Advocacy: Lawyers and Nonlawyers at Work.* Ann Arbor, MI: The University of Michigan Press.

KRITZER, HERBERT M., WILLIAM L. F. FELSTINER, AUSTIN SARAT, and DAVID M. TRUBEK. 1985. "The Impact of Fee Arrangement on Lawyer Effort," *Law & Society Review* 19 (2): 251–278.

LADINSKY, JACK. 1963. "Careers of Lawyers, Law Practice, and Legal Institutions," *American Sociological Review* 28 (1) (February): 47–54. 1967. "Higher Education and Work Achievement among Lawyers," *Sociological Quarterly* 8 (2): 222–232.

LARSON, MAGALI SARFATTI. 1977. *The Rise of Professionalism: A Sociological Analysis.* Berkeley and Los Angeles: University of California Press.

Lawyer's Almanac, 2001. 2001. Englewood Cliffs, NJ: Aspen Law and Business, A Division of Aspen Publishers, Inc.

LEATHERMAN, COURTNEY. 1989. "Law-School Students Protest Scarcity of Female and Minority Professors," *Chronicle of Higher Education* (April 19): A32–A33.

LEONARD, WALTER J. 1977. *Black Lawyers.* Boston: Senna and Shih.

LERMAN, STEVEN. 1995. "A King's Ransom, Excerpts from Rodney King Attorney's Bill," *Harper's Magazine* (April): 20–23.

LEWIN, TAMAR. 1983. "A Gentlemanly Profession Enters a Tough New Era," *New York Times* (January 16): 1F, 10F. 1986. "Leaving the Law for Wall Street, The Faster Track," *New York Times Magazine* (August 10): 14–19, 42, 50–53.

LEWIS, P. S. C. 1986. "A Comparative Perspective on the Legal Profession in the 1980s," *Law & Society Review* 20 (1): 79–91.

LOH, WALLACE D. 1984. *Social Research in the Judicial Process: Cases, Readings, and Text.* New York: Russell Sage Foundation.

MACDONALD, KEITH M. 1995. *The Sociology of Professions.* Thousand Oaks, CA: Sage Publications, Inc.

MACLACHLAN, CLAUDIA. 1989. "Admissible—Advertising by Lawyers Gets Respectable Here," *St. Louis Post-Dispatch* (March 20): 1BP, 20BP. 1995. "Legal Services Come Under Attack—Again," *National Law Journal* 17 (31) (April): A12.

MAGEE, STEPHEN P. 1992. "How Many Lawyers Ruin an Economy?" Letters to the Editor. *Wall Street Journal* (September 24): A17.

MANGAN, KATHERINE S. 1998a. "Students' Odds of Getting Into Law School Improve, But Their Qualifications Drop," *The Chronicle of Higher Education* (January 23): A41–42. 1998b. "Law Professors, Calling Their Institutions Complacent, Urge Curricular Changes," *The Chronicle of Higher Education* (January 16): A14.

MANNING, BAYLESS. 1968. "Introduction: New Tasks for Lawyers." Pp. 1–11 in Geoffrey C. Hazard, Jr. (ed.), *Law in a Changing America*. Englewood Cliffs, NJ: Prentice Hall.

MANSNERUS, LAURA. 1995a. "Good Job, Great Pay: Legal Officer for a Company," *New York Times* (February 10): B13.

MAYER, MARTIN. 1967. *The Lawyers*. New York: Harper & Row, Pub.

MCINTYRE, LISA J. 1987. *The Public Defender: The Practice of Law in the Shadows of Repute*. Chicago: University of Chicago Press.

MCKAY, ROBERT B. 1976. "Legal Education." Pp. 261–276 in Bernard Schwartz (ed.), *American Law: The Third Century*. South Hackensack, NJ: Fred B. Rothman & Company (published for New York University School of Law).

Model Rules of Professional Conduct and Code of Judicial Conduct. 1983. Chicago: American Bar Association.

MOSES, JONATHAN, and RICHARD B. SCHMITT. 1992. "Lawyer's Billing Practices Are Scrutinized," *Wall Street Journal* (April 6): B7.

MURIS, TIMOTHY J., and FRED S. MCCHESNEY. 1979. "Advertising and the Price and Quality of Legal Services: The Case for Legal Clinics," *American Bar Foundation Research Journal*, no. 1 (Winter): 179–207.

MYERS, KEN. 1994. "Sometimes It's Not What You Know: Law Deans Debate Admitting Students for the Wealth and Influence They Bring," *National Law Journal*, 17 (4) (September 26): A1. 1995. "Based on Results of Bar Exam, Class of 1994 is One of Brightest," *The National Law Journal* 17 (19) (January 9): A17.

NADER, RALPH. 1969. "Law Schools and Law Firms," *New Republic* (October 11): 21–23.

NAGPAUL, HANS. 1994. "The Legal Profession in Indian Society: A Case Study of Lawyers at a Local Level in North India," *International Journal of the Sociology of Law* 22: 59–76.

NELSON, ROBERT L. 1988. *Partners with Power: The Social Transformation of the Large Law Firm*. Berkeley and Los Angeles: University of California Press.

NEWSWEEK. 1995. "Who Ya Gonna Call? 1-800-Sue Me" (March 20): 36–37.

NEW YORK TIMES. 1995a. "Mere Fraction of Civil Cases End With Punitive Awards" (July 21): B12. 1995b. "Where Legal Help Comes Complete With Guarantee" (August 11): A13. 1995c. "Woman Heads Bar Association" (August 11): A13. 1995d. "Rising Concern About Stress in Lawyer's Lives" (March 10): B15. 1998. "The Crisis at Legal Aid" (September 1): A24.

NOSSEL, SUZANNE AND ELIZABETH WESTFALL. 1998. *Presumed Equal: What America's Top Women Lawyers Really Think About Their Firms*. Franklin Lakes, NJ: Career Press.

OFFICIAL GUIDE TO U.S. LAW SCHOOLS 2000. 2000. New York: Times Books/Random House, Inc.

OLSON, WALTER K. 1991a. *The Litigation Explosion*. New York: Dutton. 1991b. "The Selling of the Law," *American Enterprise* (January–February): 27–35.

PACKER, HERBERT L., and THOMAS EHRLICH. 1972. *New Directions in Legal Education*. New York: McGraw-Hill.

PALERMO, GEORGE B., MAXINE ALDRIDGE WHITE, LEW A. WASSERMAN, and WILLIAM HANRAHAN. 1998. "Plea Bargaining: Injustice for All?," *International Journal of Offender Therapy and Comparative Criminology* 42 (2) (June): 111–123.

PASSELL, PETER. 1998. "A Call for 'Auto Choice' and Lower Premiums," *New York Times* (August 30): BU1, BU19.

PEAR, ROBERT. 1995. "As Welfare Overhaul Looms, Legal Aid for Poor Dwindles." *New York Times* (September 5): A1, A9.

PITULLA, JOANNE. 1995. "Firm Commitments: Lawyers Cannot Ignore Duty to Report Ethics Violations by Colleagues," *ABA Journal* 81 (April): 108–109.

PODGERS, JAMES. 1994. "Chasing the Ideal: As More Americans Find Themselves Priced Out of the System, the Struggle Goes on to Fulfill the Promise of Equal Justice for All," *ABA Journal* 80 (August): 56–61. 1995. "Sorting Out Image, Ads, Ethics," *ABA Journal*, 81 (March): 94–95.

POLLOCK, ELLEN JOAN, and STEPHEN J. ADLER. 1992. "Justice for All? Legal System Struggles to Reflect Diversity, but Progress Is Slow," *Wall Street Journal* (May 8): 1, 4.

PUE, W. WESLEY and DAVID SUGARMAN (EDS.), 1999. *Lawyers Culture and the Cultural Significance of Lawyers: Historical Perspectives*. Brookfield, VT: Ashgate.

QUADE, VICKI. 1995. "There Is No Sisterhood: Non-white Women Lawyers Say They're Still at the Bottom of the Heap," *Human Rights* 22 (1) (Winter): 8–13.

REICHSTEIN, KENNETH J. 1965. "Ambulance Chasing: A Case Study of Deviation and Control within the Legal Profession," *Social Problems* 13 (1) (Summer): 3–17.

REIDINGER, PAUL. 1986a. "Salary Wars," *ABA Journal* 72 (August 1): 42. 1986b. "It's 46.5 Hours a Week in Law," *ABA Journal* 72 (September 1): 44.

RESKIN, LAUREN RUBENSTEIN. 1985. "Lawyers Are Serious about Professional Responsibility," *ABA Journal* 71 (December): 41.

RUESCHEMEYER, DIETRICH. 1985. *Lawyers and Their Society*. Cambridge: Harvard University Press.

SAMBORN, HOPE VINER. 1995. "Post-Law School Job May Be as Paralegal: Trend More Pronounced on East and West Coasts Where Work Tough to Find," *ABA Journal* 81 (March): 14–16.

SANGCHOMPUPHEN, TOMMY. 1995. "More Law Students Seek Joint Degrees to Boost Job Chances," *Wall Street Journal* (August 7): B8.

SAVELL, LAWRENCE. 1994. "I'm Bill Low. File With Me and Win, Win, Win!," *National Law Journal*, 17 (3) (September 19): A23.

SCHRAG, PHILIP G. and MICHAEL MELTSNER. 1998. *Reflections on Clinical Legal Education*. Boston: Northeastern University Press.

SHULINS, NANCY. 1994. "Survey Says Let's Bash All the Lawyers," *St. Louis Post-Dispatch* (April 30): 1D, 3D.

SHUMAN, DANIEL W., and ANTHONY CHAMPAGNE. 1997. "Removing the People from the Legal Process: The Rhetoric and Research on Judicial Selection and Juries," *Psychology, Public Policy, and Law* 3 (2–3) (June–September): 242–258.

SIMPSON, A. W. B. 1988. *Invitation to Law*. Oxford, England: Basil Blackwell.

SMIGEL, ERWIN O. 1964. *The Wall Street Lawyer*. New York: Free Press.

SMITH, CLAY J., JR. (ED.). 1998. *Rebels in Law: Voices in History of Black Women Lawyers*. Ann Arbor, MI: The University of Michigan Press.

SOCIETY. 1992. "Liability Suits" 29 (5) (July–August): 3.

SPANGLER, EVE. 1986. *Lawyers for Hire: Salaried Professionals at Work*. New Haven: Yale University Press.

SPECTOR, MALCOLM. 1972. "The Rise and Fall of a Mobility Route," *Social Problems* 20 (2) (Fall): 173–185.

St. Louis-Post Dispatch. 2001. "Do-It-Yourselfers Are Becoming More Common in Court," (March 25): A3.

STEVENS, AMY. 1994. "A List of Bad Lawyers to Go On Line," *Wall Street Journal* (August 26): B1. 1995a. "Fewer Partners, More Mergers Enriched Top Law Firms

Last Year Survey Shows," *Wall Street Journal* (June 24): B1. 1995b. "Law Schools See Sharp Decline in Applicants," *Wall Street Journal* (February 19): B1, B16.

STEVENS, ROBERT. 1971. "Two Cheers for 1870: The American Law School." Pp. 405–548 in Donald Fleming and Bernard Bailyn (eds.), *Law in American History.* Boston: Little, Brown. 1973. "Law Schools and Law Students," *Virginia Law Review* 59 (4) (April): 51–707. 1983. *Law School: Legal Education in America from the 1850s to the 1980s.* Chapel Hill: The University of North Carolina Press.

STRACHER, CAMERON. 2001. "How to Bill 25 Hours in One Day," *New York Times Magazine* (April 8): 74.

SULLIVAN, COLLEEN. 1979. "The Upstart Lawyers Who Market the Law," *New York Times* (August 26): A1, 9.

TIGAR, MICHAEL E. 1977. *Law and the Rise of Capitalism.* New York: Monthly Review Press.

THOMSON, SUSAN C. 2001. "Women Are Poised to Outnumber Men in Law School," *St. Louis Post-Dispatch* (September 18): 1, 9.

Time. 1978. "Those #*X!!! Lawyers,"(April 10): 56–66. 1998. "A Legal Press in Texas: A State Court Targets Self-Help Publisher Nolo Press for Making It Too Easy to Bypass Lawyers" (August 3): 29.

TONE, ANDREA. 2001. *Devices and Desires, A History of Contraceptives in America.* New York: Hill & Wang.

TRUBEK, LOUISE G. and JEREMY COOPER. 1999. *Educating for Justice Around the World: Legal Education, Legal Practice and the Community.* Brookfield, VT: Ashgate.

TUROW, SCOTT. 1977. "The Trouble with Law School," *Harvard Magazine* 80 (1) (September–October): 60–64.

U.S. DEPARTMENT OF JUSTICE. 1992. "Prosecutors in State Courts, 1990," *Bureau of Justice Statistics Bulletin* (March).

U.S. NEWS & WORLD REPORT. 1986. "Sky-High Damage Suits,"(January) 27, 35–43. 1989. "Applying a Scalpel to Doctors' Wallets," (December 4) 11. 1992. "Realism on the Docket" (March 23): 70–74. 2001. "Exclusive Rankings, Schools of Law" (April 9): 78–84.

UVILLER, RICHARD H. 1994. "The Lawyer as Liar," *Criminal Justice Ethics* 13 (2) (Summer–Fall): 2–7.

WALDMAN, PETER. 1986. "Pre-Paid Legal Plans Offer Consultations, Follow-Up Calls and Referrals at Low Cost," *Wall Street Journal* (February 11): 33.

WALL STREET JOURNAL. 1986. "Parties, Polls and Pejoratives: Lawyers Meet" (August 13): 23. 1989. "Average Lawyer Income Tops $100,000 Mark" (July 21): B1.

WILENSKY, HAROLD L. 1964. "The Professionalization of Everyone?" *American Journal of Sociology* 70 (2) (September): 137–158.

WOO, JUNDA. 1992. "Sexual Harassment Is Found in Study of Federal Courts in 9 Western States," *Wall Street Journal* (August 5): B3.

YORK, JOHN C., and ROSEMARY D. HALE. 1973. "Too Many Lawyers? The Legal Service Industry: Its Structure and Outlook," *Journal of Legal Education* 26 (1): 1–31.

ZEMANS, FRANCES K. 1977. *Law School and Law Practice: Credentials for Professional Status.* Chicago: American Bar Foundation.

ZITRIN, RICHARD and CAROL M. LANGFORD. 1999. *The Moral Compass of the American Lawyer: Truth, Justice, Power, and Greed.* New York: Random House, Inc.

9
Researching
Law
in Society

Empirical studies provide the background for many of the generalizations and conclusions reached about law and society in the previous chapters. The purpose of this chapter is to show how sociologists carry out such studies by describing some of the ways they research law and the methods they use to arrive at their findings. The chapter also demonstrates the relevance and applicability of sociological research to the formulation, instrumentation, and evaluation of social policy. The general comments on methodological tools for research on law are not intended to replace the more detailed technical discussions found in books on methods of social research (see, for example, Alford, 1998; Bernard, 2000; Morse and Field, 1995; Nock and Kingston, 1990; and Schutt, 2001). They are intended merely to provide an exposure to the strategies used in the study of the interplay between law and society and to highlight the methodological concerns and complexities inherent in such endeavors.

METHODS OF INQUIRY

Several methods can be applied in researching law in society, and more than a single method is usually involved in such a study. However, there are four commonly used methods of data collection in sociology: All other methods are variations and combinations of these four methods. The four methods that will be considered are the historical, the observational, the experimental, and the survey methods.

Actual research is much more complicated than these methods indicate. All research is essentially a process in which choices are made at many stages. The are several methods and they are combined in various ways in the actual research. Methodological decisions are made on such diverse matters as the kind of research design to be used, the type of research population and sample, the sources of data collection, the techniques of gathering data, and the methods of analyzing the research findings. The differences among the four methods are more a matter of emphasis on a particular data-collection strategy to obtain observable data for a particular research purpose than a clear-cut "either-or" distinction. For example, in the observational method, although the emphasis is on the researcher's ability to observe and record social activities as they occur, the researcher may interview the participants—a technique associated with the survey and experimental methods. Similarly, in the experimental method, the subjects are usually under the observation of the researcher and his or her collaborators. The information gained in such observations also plays a crucial role in the final analysis and interpretation of the data. Furthermore, historical evidence is often used in observational, survey, and experimental studies.

At all stages of sociological research, there is an interplay between theory and method (Morse and Field, 1995). In fact, it is often the theory chosen by the researcher that determines which methods will be used in the research. The selection of the method is to a great extent dependent on the type of information desired.

To study a sequence of events and explanations of the meanings of the events by the participants and other observers before, during, and after their occurrence, observation (especially participant observation) seems to be the best method of data collection. The researcher directly observes and participates in the study system with which he or she has established a meaningful and durable relationship, as did, for example, Jerome H. Skolnick (1994) in his study of police officers. Although the observer may or may not play an active role in the events, he or she observes them firsthand and can record the events and the participants' experiences as they unfold. No other data-collection method can provide such a detailed description of social events. Thus, observation is best suited for studies intended to understand a particular group and certain social processes within that group. When these events are not available for observation as they occurred in the past, the historical approach is the logical choice of method for collecting data.

If an investigator wishes to study norms, rules, and status in a particular group, intensive interviewing of "key" persons and informants in or outside the group is the best method of data collection. For example, in a well-known study, Jerome E. Carlin (1966) interviewed approximately 800 lawyers in New York City for his study of legal ethics and their enforcement. Those who set and enforce norms, rules, and status, because of their position in the group or relations with persons in the group, are the ones who are the most knowledgeable about the information the researcher wishes to obtain. Intensive interviews (especially with open-ended questioning) with these persons allow the researcher to probe for such information.

When an investigator wishes to determine the numbers, the proportions, the ratios, and other quantitative information about the subjects in his or her study possessing certain characteristics, opinions, beliefs, and other categories of various variables, then the best method of data collection is the survey. The survey relies on a representative sample of the population to which a standardized instrument can be administered.

Finally, the experiment is the best method of data collection when the researcher wants to measure the effect of certain independent variables on some dependent variables. The experimental situation provides control over the responses and the variables, and gives the researcher the opportunity to manipulate the independent variables. In the following pages, I will examine and illustrate these methods in greater detail.

Historical Methods

Sociologists generally are accustomed to studying social phenomena at one time—the present. But social phenomena do not appear spontaneously and autonomously. Historical analysis can indicate the possibility that certain consequences can issue from events that are comparable to other events of the past: history as something more than a simple compilation of facts. It can generate an understanding of the processes of social change and document how a multitude of factors have served to shape the present. The study of history also has an existential function. It informs us who we are, and that we are links that connect the past with the present and the future (Inciardi, Block, and Hallowell, 1977:27–28).

Historical research carried out by sociologists is a critical investigation of events, developments, and experiences of the past; a careful weighing of evidence of the validity of sources of information on the past; and the interpretation of the evidence. Historical research is important and valuable in sociology because the origins of the discipline have to be understood if contemporary theories and research are to be understood. As a substitute for direct data from the participants, contents from documents and historical materials are used as a method of data collection. These documents and materials can range from census data, archives of various types, official files such as court records, records of property transactions, records of poor relief administration, tax records, and business accounts to personal diaries, witness accounts, propaganda literature, and numerous other personal accounts and letters. The researcher uses these available data sources to carry out what is generally referred to as secondary analysis; that is, the data were not generated or collected for the specific purpose of the study formulated by the researcher. Of course, the usefulness of the historical method depends to a large extent on the accuracy and thoroughness of the documents and materials. With accurate and thorough data, the researcher may be able to gain insights, generate hypotheses, and even test hypotheses.

Official records and public documents have provided the data for sociological analyses attempting to establish long-term legal trends. For example, William J. Chambliss (1964), as I mentioned in Chapter 1, has shown how the vagrancy statutes changed in England according to emerging social interests. The first full-fledged vagrancy law, enacted in 1349, regulated the giving of alms to able-bodied, unemployed people. After the Black Death and the flight of workers from landowners, the law was reformulated to force laborers to accept employment at a low wage. By the sixteenth century, with an increased emphasis on commerce and industry, the vagrancy statutes were revived and strengthened. Eventually, vagrancy laws came to serve, as they do today, the purpose of controlling people and activities regarded as undesirable to the community. Similarly, Jerome Hall (1952) has shown, on the basis of historical records, how changing social conditions and emerging social interests brought about the formulation of trespass laws in fifteenth-century England.

The historical method is also used to test theories. For example, Mary P. Baumgartner (1978) was interested in the relationship between the social status of the defendant and the litigant and the verdicts and sanctions awarded them. She analyzed data based on 389 cases (148 civil and 241 criminal) heard in the colony of New Haven between 1639 and 1665. She found, not unexpectedly, that in both the civil and the criminal cases, individuals who enjoyed high status were more likely to receive favorable treatment by the court than their lower-status counterparts. Another example to test theories is Lawrence M. Friedman and Robert V. Percival's survey of the caseloads of two California trial courts at five points between 1890 and 1970 (1978). As I described in Chapter 6, the authors hypothesized that over time, trial courts have come to do less work in settling disputes and more work of a routine administrative nature. They concluded that the dispute-settlement function of the trial courts has declined noticeably over time, a conclusion that has since been repeatedly questioned. A third example is Susan W. Brenner's (1992:5–174) analysis, which traces the use of precedents from pre-Norman England to the present, demonstrates that their use has changed as new ways have been established for making them more available, and shows how they implicitly justify a legal system's reliance upon *stare decisis*.

In addition to relying on official documents, the historical method may also be based on narrations of personal experiences, generally known as the *life-histories* method. This technique requires that the researcher rely solely on a person's reporting of life experiences relevant to the research interest with minimal commentary. Often life histories are part of ethnographic reports. In such instances, they are referred to as "memory cases" (Nader and Todd, 1978:7). This method is useful to learn about events such as conflict or dispute that occurred in the past, particularly when there are no written records available. Obviously, this method has certain pitfalls, for life histories tend to be tainted by selective recall: Subjects tend to remember events that have impressed them in some way and tend to forget others. Although the life-history method has been little used in recent years, it serves several functions. First, it provides insights into a world usually over-looked by the objective methods of data collection. Second, life histories can serve as the basis for making assumptions necessary for more systematic data collection. Third, life histories, because of their details, provide insights into new or different perspectives for research. When an area has been studied extensively and has grown "sterile," life histories may break new grounds for research studies. Finally, they offer an opportunity to view and study the dynamic process of social interactions and events not available with many other kinds of data.

A notable difficulty of the historical method lies in the limited accuracy and thoroughness of the documents and materials involved. Because the data are "compiled" by others with no supervision or control by the researcher, the researcher is, in fact, at the mercy of those who record the information. The recorders use their own definitions of situations, define and select events as important for recording, and introduce subjective perceptions, interpretations, and insights into their recordings. For example, how do the recorders define a dispute? In many instances, a dispute enters officially into the court records when it is adjudicated, and a settlement is imposed after full trial. But as I noted in Chapter 6, not all disputes are adjudicated. Many are settled informally in pretrial conferences, or judges may intervene in other less formal ways as well. Therefore, a researcher must ascertain the reliability and validity of documents. They should be verified for internal consistency (consistency between each portion of the document and other portions) and external consistency (consistency with empirical evidence, other documents, or both). Although the historical method provides details, and in certain cases presents a processual view of events, often unmatched by other methods of data collection, it is desirable (when possible, of course) to combine this method with other data-collection methods.

Observational Methods

Observational methods can be divided into two types: those utilizing either human observers (participant observers or judges) or mechanical observers (cameras, tape recorders, and the like) and those directly eliciting responses from subjects by questioning (questionnaires, schedules, and interview guides). Observational methods can be carried out both in laboratory or controlled situations and in field or natural settings.

Participant observation has a long history of use in anthropological research. Thus, there is justification if the term conjures up the image of a social scientist living with some preliterate tribe, perhaps for several years. Indeed, much of our knowledge of primitive law comes from anthropologists who lived in traditional societies, such as Bronislaw Malinowski and E. Adamson Hoebel. Of course, for anthropologists, the opportunity to observe ongoing legal phenomena (outside of an institutional setting such as a court) depends on a combination of circumstances and luck: It means that the anthropologists have to be in the right place at the right time. Anthropological (and sociological) field researchers generally proceed by way of a kind of methodological eclecticism, choosing the method that suits the purpose and present circumstances at any given time. In summary: "Hence, unobtrusive measurement, life history studies, documentary and historical analysis, statistical enumeration, in-depth interviewing, imaginative role-taking, and personal introspection are all important complements of direct observation in the field worker's repertoire" (Williamson, Karp, and Dalphin, 1977:200).

Many of the observational techniques are used in laboratory or controlled situations. For example, comparatively little empirical research has been performed with actual juries because of the legal requirements of private deliberations. Consequently, mock trials in which jurors or juries respond to simulated case materials have become a primary research vehicle. The mock trial permits both manipulation of important variables and replication of cases (Davis, Bray, and Holt, 1977:327). Many of the laboratory jury studies deal with the deliberation processes preceding the verdict and how the verdict is reached by juries of diverse composition deliberating under various conditions (Loh, 1984:460–461). One method of analyzing deliberations is to audiotape or videotape the deliberations and then analyze their content (Kessler, 1975:73).

Observational methods have been used by sociologists extensively in field settings that involve direct contact with subjects and take place in relatively natural social situations (McCall, 1978:1) and they are often part what is called "action research," the way to integrate knowledge with action (Reason and Bradbury, 2001). For example, in attempts to find out and understand how the law typically works on a day-to-day basis, sociologists have focused on various aspects of the criminal justice system. The study of the public defender's office by David Sudnow (1965); studies of the police by Richard V. Ericson (1989), Maurice Punch (1989), and Jerome H. Skolnick (1994) among others; Frank W. Miller's (1969) study of prosecution; Donald J. Newman's (1966) study of conviction; and Abraham S. Blumberg's (1979) work on the entire criminal justice system, all point to the day-to-day working of law. These studies have also noted the role of discretion in the application or nonapplication of the law in legally equivocal and unequivocal situations. At each step in the criminal justice system, from the citizen's decision to lodge a complaint or to define the situation as one in which it is necessary to summon the police, to the judge's decision as to what sentence a convicted person should receive, decisions are made that are not prescribed by statutory law.

There are both advantages and limitations to observational methods. The advantages include the opportunity to record information as the event unfolds or shortly thereafter. Thus, the validity of the recorded information

͙͙e high. Often observations are made and information is recorded independently of the observed person's abilities to record events. At times, when verbal or written communication between the researcher and the subjects is difficult—for example, in studying primitive tribes—observation is the only method by which the researcher can obtain information. Finally, the observer need not rely on the willingness of the observed persons to report events.

There are also several limitations of observational research. The method is not applicable to the investigation of large social settings. The context investigated must be small enough to be dealt with exhaustively by one or a few researchers. In the case of fieldwork, there is a great likelihood that the researcher's selective perception and selective memory will bias the results of the study. There is also the problem of selectivity in data collection. In any social situation, there are literally thousands of possible pieces of data. No one researcher, in other words, can account for every aspect of a situation. The researcher inevitably pulls out only a segment of the data that exist, and the question inevitably arises as to whether the selected data are really representative of the situation. Finally, there is no way to easily assess the reliability and validity of the interpretations made by the researcher. As long as data are collected and presented by one or a few researchers with their own distinctive talents, faults, and idiosyncrasies, suspicion will remain concerning the validity of their rendering of the phenomena studied. Researchers often respond to these criticisms by suggesting that the cost of imprecision is more than compensated for by the in-depth quality of the data produced.

Experimental Methods

The prevailing method for testing causal relations by social scientists, especially psychologists, is the experiment. An experiment may be carried out in a laboratory or a field setting, and it ideally begins with two or more equivalent groups, with an experimental variable introduced into only the experimental group. The researcher measures the phenomenon under study before the introduction of the experimental variable and after, thus getting a measure of the change presumably caused by the variable.

There are two common ways of setting up experimental and control groups. One is the matched-pair technique. For each person in the experimental group, another person similar in all important variables (age, religion, education, occupation, or anything important to the research) is found and placed in the control group. Another technique is the random-assignment technique, in which statistically random assignments of persons to experimental and control groups are made—such as assigning the first person to the experimental group and the next to the control group, and so on.

Experiments in sociology face certain difficulties (see, for example, Orr, 1998). An experiment involving thousands of people may be prohibitively expensive. It may take years to complete a prospective study. Ethical and legal considerations prohibit the use of people in any experiments that may injure them. The scientific community reacts strongly in those infrequent instances where human subjects have been used in a hazardous or harmful manner (Mintz and Cohen, 1976). When people are unwilling to cooperate in an experiment, they cannot be forced to do so (although occasionally they are tricked into unconscious cooperation). Moreover, when individuals realize that they are experimental subjects, they begin to act differently and the experiment may be spoiled. Almost any kind of experimental or observational study upon people who know they are being studied will give some interesting findings, which may vanish soon after the study is terminated. Experiments with human subjects are most reliable when the subjects do not know the true object of the experiment. But the use of deception in social research poses the ethical question of distinguishing between harmless deception and intellectual dishonesty.

Moreover, the law does not allow experiments in the United States that involve elimination of a right that the due process clause guarantees under all circumstances. For example, there would be legal and ethical questions involved in the use of experimental methods in the study of legal services, welfare payments, or incarcerations. There are exceptions, however, such as the Wisconsin Welfare Experiment (DeParle, 1998) or the often-cited and controversial New Jersey Guaranteed Income Experiments, a rare example of government-sponsored policy experimentation. These experiments involve the systematic selection of experimental and control groups, the application of the policy under study to the experimental groups only, and a careful comparison of differences between the experimental and the control group after the application of the policy.

The New Jersey Guaranteed Income Experiments were designed to resolve some serious questions about the impact of welfare payments on the incentives for poor people to work. Debates over welfare reform have generated certain questions that social science could presumably answer with careful, controlled experimentation. Would a guaranteed family income reduce the incentive to work? If payments were made to poor families with employable male heads, would the men drop out of the labor force? Would the level of the income guarantee, or the steepness of the reductions of payments with increases in earnings, make any difference in working behavior? Since current welfare programs do not provide a guaranteed minimum family income, or make payments to families with employable males, or graduate payments in relation to earnings, these questions could be answered only through experimentation.

To assess the impact of guaranteed incomes on families with able-bodied men, the Office of Economic Opportunity sponsored a three-year social experiment involving 1,350 families in New Jersey and Pennsylvania. The research was undertaken by the University of Wisconsin's Institute of Research on Poverty. To ascertain the effects of different levels of guaranteed income, four guarantee levels were established. Some families were chosen to receive 50 percent of the Social Security Administration's poverty-line income, others 75 percent, others 100 percent, and still others 125 percent. To ascertain the effects of graduated payments in relation to earnings, some families had their payments reduced by 30 percent of their outside earnings, others 50 percent, and still others 70 percent. Finally, a control sample was observed—families who received no payments at all in the experiment but were matched in every way with families who were receiving payments.

The experiment began in 1968, and a preliminary report issued by the U.S. Office of Economic Opportunity (1970) showed that there were no differences between the outside earnings of families who were receiving guaranteed incomes (experimental groups) and those who were not (control group). More important, the experiment raised a series of questions (Rossi and Lyall, 1976). Do researchers have the right to withhold public services from some individuals simply to provide a control for experimentation? In the medical area, where the giving or withholding of treatment may result in death or injury, the problem is obvious, and many attempts have been made to formulate a code of ethics. In the area of social experimentation, what can be said to control groups who are chosen to be similar to experimental groups but are denied benefits so that they may serve as a basis for comparison? Setting aside the legal and moral issues, it will be politically difficult to provide services for some people and not for others. Moreover, as noted earlier, people behave differently when they know they are being watched. Students, for example, generally perform at a higher level when something—anything new and different—is introduced into the classroom routine. This "Hawthorne effect" may cause a new program or reform to appear more successful than the old, but it is the newness itself that produces improvement rather than the program or the reform. Another problem in such experimentation is that results obtained with small-scale experiments may differ substantially from what would occur if a large-scale nationwide program were adopted. In the New Jersey experiments, if only one family receives income-maintenance payments in a neighborhood, its members may continue to behave as the neighbors do. But if everyone in the nation is guaranteed a minimum income, community standards may change and affect the behavior of all recipient families (Kershaw, 1969).

On a smaller scale, experimental methods have been used, for example, in the study of jury deliberation (Hans, 1992; Simon, 1975), the evaluation of objections in the courtroom (Koehler, 1992), allocation of scarce criminal resources (Nagel and Neef, 1977), the impact of increasing or decreasing police patrol on crime (Zimring, 1989), and the determination of the effectiveness of pretrial hearings. In the last case, a controlled experiment was done to find out whether pretrial hearings were time savers or time wasters. Sociologists developed a design calling for a random assignment of cases by court clerks to one of two procedures: obligatory pretrial hearing in one group of cases and optional pretrial in the control group, where it was held only if one or both of the litigants requested it. The conclusion was that the obligatory pretrial hearing did not save court time; in fact, it wasted it (Zeisel, 1967:84). Persuaded by the experiment, the state of New Jersey changed its rules and made pretrial hearings optional.

Many experiments, such as those dealing with juror and jury behavior (Diamond, 1997; Kramer and Kerr, 1989) or with violence, are conducted in a laboratory situation. The widely publicized National Commission on the Causes and Prevention of Violence (1969), for example, relied heavily, although not exclusively, on the results of laboratory experiments for its final report. In one group of experiments, young children who were shown acts of violence and then later observed at play committed more acts of violence in their play than children who did not witness acts of violence. In another group of experiments, college students were told that they were participating in a "learning experiment" in which they must apply mild electric shocks at whatever level of intensity they wished to other "learners" if the "learners" made a mistake. The "learning experiment" was interrupted and some students were shown a violent film while others were shown a nonviolent one. When the "learning experiment" was resumed, the students who saw the violent film used slightly stronger shocks on their "learners" than those who had watched the nonviolent film.

Laboratory experiments, as important as they may be in revealing insights into human behavior, achieve rigorous and controlled observation at the price of unreality. The subjects are isolated from the outside and from their normal environment. The laboratory experiment has been criticized for its unnaturalness and questioned as to its generalizability. By contrast, experimental methods that are used in nonlaboratory settings increase the generalizability of results and lend greater credence to the findings, but concomitantly increase the difficulty of controlling relevant variables.

Survey Methods

Survey research aims for a systematic and comprehensive collection of information about the attitudes, beliefs, and behavior of people. The most common means of data collection are face-to-face interviews, self-administered questionnaires (for example, mail questionnaires), and telephone interviews. Typically, the questionnaire or the interview schedule is set up so that the same questions are asked of each respondent in the same order with exactly the same wording and the validity of surveys is dependent on the design of the questions asked (see, for example, Fink and Kosecoff, 1998; Fowler, 1995). A survey deals with a representative sample of a population. Probabilistic sampling is essential to survey studies. Survey studies tend to be larger than is typically the case in observational or experimental studies. Usually, data are collected at one time, although a survey approach can be used to study trends in opinion and behavior over time. Because of its ability to cover large areas and many respondents, the survey method has become the dominant method of data collection in sociology.

Survey methods, like other research methods, have their pitfalls. Probably foremost among them is the response rate or the nonresponse rate. Because one of the important reasons for conducting a survey is that it deals with a large representative sample from a population and thus permits inference from the sampled data to the population, it is essential that the sample maintain its representativeness, which may be affected severely when a substantial number of the respondents fail to participate in the study. The return rate for mail questionnaires is generally low; a 60 percent or higher return rate is considered rather good (see, for example, Mangione, 1995). Of course, for the interview survey, the expected response rate is higher than that of the questionnaire survey. In both cases, in addition to the subject's refusal to participate, other factors affect the response rate. They include the inability of the subject to understand the question, the possibility that the subject may have moved or died, and the physical or mental incapacitation of the participants. Although questionnaire and interview studies have a margin of error, they are still useful. For example, public officials seldom take a position on a public issue without first reviewing public-opinion polls, and legislators often delay casting a vote on an important bill until they receive the latest survey of voter opinion from their districts.

An illustration of the use of survey methods can be seen in the efforts of the Department of Justice to gain a more accurate measure of the extent of crime in the United States. For years both law enforcement agencies and sociologists have had to rely on official records compiled by such agencies as the Federal Bureau of Investigation to measure the amount of crime. However, there have been concerns about the accuracy of these reports, and many sociologists have suggested that officially recorded crime statistics are a far better indicator of police activity than they are of criminal activity.

For the past 30 years, the U.S. Department of Justice (1995a) has conducted sophisticated victimization surveys for the nation and several major cities in an attempt to supplement official crime records and to overcome some of the problems of accuracy therein. In victimization surveys, subjects in a large sample of the population are systematically interviewed to determine how many crimes have been committed against them. In addition to determining the volume of crime, the surveys are also used in developing a variety of information on crime characteristics and the effects of crime on the victims: victim injury and medical care, economic losses, time lost from work, victim self-protection, and reporting of crime to the police. There are three advantages of victimization surveys that make them superior to self-report studies and the FBI's *Uniform Crime Reports*. First, people are more willing to discuss crimes committed against them than the ones they have committed. Second, victimization surveys by design seek out information about crimes rather than waiting for victims to report them as is the case with the *Uniform Crime Reports*. Third, victimization surveys rely on more representative samples than the other sources of crime data. There are also some disadvantages to these surveys. They are rather expensive—costing about $75 per interview—and since they deal primarily with major cities, information is lacking for the majority of local areas in the United States.

At times, large-scale surveys are carried out at the behest of the Congress. For example, the Ninety-third Congress passed an amendment to an educational bill in 1974 requiring the Secretary of Health, Education, and Welfare to conduct a survey to determine the extent and seriousness of school crime. This extensive study included 4,014 school principals, 31,373 students, and 23,895 teachers in 642 junior and senior high schools throughout the country who received questionnaires from Washington (Toby, 1980). The study reconfirmed the general belief that schools are plagued with real crime and showed, unexpectedly, that the crime problem was worse in junior than in senior high schools. The findings prompted a series of hearings in Congress but surprisingly little in the way of systematic national effort to reduce school crime. In other instances, however, the results of such extensive surveys—such as the studies by James S. Coleman (1966) and his colleagues on the effects of a large number of variables on educational achievement, which will be discussed shortly—contribute significantly to policy decisions.

Survey methods have been widely used also in a variety of cross-cultural studies dealing with knowledge and opinion about law (Tomasic, 1985:116–126), evaluation of the effectiveness of the law, prestige of the law, and legal and moral attitudes (Podgorecki, 1974:83–124). Some of these studies reveal important and unexpected findings. For example, a European study asked people of Poland, the Netherlands, and Germany whether they thought people should obey the law. They found significant national variations; more Germans (66 percent) than Poles (45 percent) or Netherlanders (47 percent) answered yes to this general question (Friedman and Macaulay, 1977:216). Several surveys have also found that the public knowledge in a number of European countries concerning legal topics is considerably poorer than assumed by the legal authorities and by many scholars. But lack of knowledge about the law is not limited to European countries. For example, many respondents in an Oregon study did not know that Oregon law provides minors with the right to treatment for venereal disease, birth control information, and medical treatment without parental knowledge (Friedman and Macaulay, 1977:607–608).

THE IMPACT OF SOCIOLOGY ON SOCIAL POLICY

In every scientific field there is distinction between pure and applied science. *Pure* science is a search for knowledge, without primary concern for its practical use. *Applied* science is the search for ways of using scientific knowledge to solve practical problems. For example, a sociologist making a study of the social structure of a slum neighborhood is working as a pure scientist. If this is followed by a study of how to prevent crime in a slum neighborhood, the latter study is applied science.

Essentially, however, sociology is both a pure and an applied science. For unless a science is constantly searching for more basic knowledge, its practical applications of knowledge are not likely to be very practical. This explains, in part, why a substantial amount of sociological work is still generated for academic purposes and executed with disciplinary concerns in mind. Much of sociological knowledge remains within the boundaries of the discipline. Often, the consumers of this knowledge are other sociologists and their students. But, simultaneously with the continuing development of scientific knowledge, social scientists are also concerned with the generation and dissemination of knowledge and information with potential applied or policy-relevant implications (Lempert, 1991; Nagel, 1993). Social-science research has long been used to help resolve empirical issues that arise in litigation (Monahan and Walker, 1991, 1998), and sociological knowledge and methodology can be useful in the formulation and instrumentation of social policy and in the evaluation of current policies or proposed policy alternatives (Moynihan, 1989). Contemporary sociologists are attempting to contribute toward improving conditions of life in society in a number of ways, and providing policymakers with information needed to make informed decisions is a mandated activity in American sociology today (D'Antonio, 1992:4). Other fields, such as economics, are already playing a significant role in policy matters. There are attempts to reformulate legal concepts in the language and equations of the marketplace. Many good law schools in the country now employ at least one economist, and policy reforms in fields as diverse as antitrust law, environmental regulation and criminal sentencing bear the distinctive imprint of economic analysis (see, for example, Posner, 2001).

Theoretical knowledge can and should be translated into practical applications and the purpose of this section is to demonstrate how sociological knowledge and expertise can have an impact on social policy. But what is "social policy"? Although there is no consensus in the sociological literature on the term "social policy" (Cochran and Malone, 1995; Lavalette and Pratt, 1997; Morris, 1979:1–13), it generally refers to purposive legal measures that are adopted and pursued by representatives of government who are responsible for dealing with particular social conditions in society. The term "policy-making" refers to the process of identifying alternative courses of action that may be followed and choosing among them (Scott and Shore, 1979:XIV). Following Robert A. Scott and Arnold R. Shore (1979:13–33), the impact of sociology on social policy can be ascertained by looking at sociology's contributions to policy recommendations and sociology's contributions to enacted policy. The former deals with specific sociological research endeavors carried out on social problems that have been used for the development of specific policy recommendations for governmental programs to diminish and ameliorate those conditions, and the latter has had a direct impact on enacted policy.

Contributions of Sociology to Policy Recommendations

The proposition that law should be seen in a broad social context is now almost a truism. "Widespread acceptance of the view that law is at least in part concerned with policy making, coupled with realistic enthusiasm for empiricism has resulted in increasing use of social science materials in resolving many legal problems" (Monahan and Walker, quoted by Freeman and Roesch, 1992:571). Over the years, there have been many instances in which sociological knowledge, perspectives, concepts, theories, and methods have been useful in connection with the development of policy recommendations (see, for example, Mullard and Spicker, 1998). Perhaps the best-known illustrations of this are the various uses made of sociology in presidential commissions. These commissions include the Commission on Law Enforcement and Administration of Justice, the Commission on the Causes and Prevention of Violence, the Commission on Obscenity and Pornography, and the Commission on Population Growth and the American Future. Sociologists were active in these commissions, and disciplinary research and knowledge were incorporated in the recommendations.

Sociology played an important role in the Commission on Law Enforcement and Administration of Justice. Social-science concepts, theories, and general perspectives were of great utility to the commission in forming final recommendations, and "existing social science theories and data were drawn upon to formulate broad general strategies in the prevention and control of crime" (Ohlin, 1975:108). Sociologists also provided sensitizing concepts and theories that oriented the search for solutions of the crime problem. For example, studies of the correctional system and the operation of law enforcement in the courts raised doubts about the effectiveness of existing criminal justice policies and of rehabilitation and treatment efforts. On the basis of sociological data, the commission accepted the view that alternative systems of social control should be used in place of the criminal justice system when possible, recommended the possibility of decriminalizing certain offenses against moral or public order, and called for a reconsideration of consensual crimes, or "crimes without victims" (Ohlin, 1975:109).

James F. Short points out that sociologists made similar contributions to the work of the National Commission on the Causes and Prevention of Violence. The specific recommendations provided by sociologists were incorporated in the commission's progress report and "marked the high point of social science input to the Commission" (Short, 1975:84). Specific recommendations included the "relativity of attributions of legitimacy or illegitimacy to violence"; that the nature of violence is essentially social as opposed to biological or psychological; that there is a connection between perceived legitimacy of the law and effective legal control of violence; and that the notions of responsibility for violence and of "relative deprivation" often lie in the unresponsiveness of social institutions (Short, 1975:85).

One of the final recommendations of the Commission on Obscenity and Pornography resulted directly from sociological and other social science research on the personal, psychological, and social consequences of exposure to explicit sexual materials. The commission recommended that federal, state, and local laws prohibiting the sale, exhibition, and distribution of sexual material to consenting adults be repealed (Scott and Shore, 1979:17).

This recommendation was based upon extensive sociological investigation that provided

> . . . no evidence that exposure to or use of explicit sexual materials plays a significant role in the causation of social or individual harm such as crime, delinquency, sexual and nonsexual deviancy, or severe emotional disturbance—Empirical investigations thus support the opinion of a substantial majority of persons professionally engaged in the treatment of deviancy, delinquency and anti-social behavior, that exposure to sexually explicit material has no harmful causal role in these areas. (Report of the Commission, quoted by Scott and Shore, 1979:17)

A similar conclusion was reached by Berl Kutchinsky (1973) in his study of the effects of liberalizing pornography in Denmark. In fact, he found that concurrent with the increasing availability of pornography, there was a significant decrease in the number of sex offenses registered by the police in Copenhagen. He adds: "The unexpected outcome of this analysis is that the high availability of hard-core pornography in Denmark was most probably the very direct cause of a considerable decrease in at least one type of serious sex offense, namely, child molestation" (Kutchinsky, 1973:179). In a later study, Kutchinsky found a similar decrease in child molestation in Germany, which he attributed to an increased availability of pornographic material (U.S. Department of Justice, 1986:974). By contrast, the controversial report of the Attorney General's Commission on Pornography (U.S. Department of Justice, 1986) negates many of the conclusions of earlier studies and that of the 1970 commission report partly because, in the words of the commission chairman, "If we relied exclusively on scientific data for every one of our findings, I'm afraid all our work would be inconclusive" (*Newsweek*, 1986:18). No doubt many of the "proofs" in support of the report's conclusions were less than compelling (Dines, Jensen, and Russo, 1997).

Sociological research also had an appreciable impact on the substance of the final report of the President's Commission on Population Growth and the American Future. The commission recognized that although population growth played a minor role in the short run (30 to 50 years) as compared with technological, economic, and government policy considerations, "in the longer run, population growth would become increasingly important. The message for population policy, therefore, was that resource and environmental considerations implied prudence rather than crisis; that there were no benefits to be realized from continued growth, but that population was an indirect and ineffectual policy level for environmental problems" (Westoff, 1975:54).

Demographic research contributed importantly to other commission deliberations and recommendations. For example, it was shown that if women averaged 2.0 rather than 2.1 births, zero population growth could be achieved near the same level while immigration remains at the current volume. Notes Westoff: "Although not a world-shaking scientific discovery, this bit of demographic intelligence was extremely important in the debate over immigration policy and was influential in defeating a recommendation to reduce the volume" (1975:55).

But one of the most important applications of social-science research to policy formation resulted from the National Fertility Studies of 1965 and 1970. It makes a considerable difference in the nature of population policy whether the stabilization of population can be achieved largely through the prevention of unwanted births or whether more radical social changes are necessary to change the number of children desired. These two studies estimated that the elimination of unwanted pregnancy would result in a population growth rate that would be below replacement level. The policy significance of this finding cannot be overestimated. By concentrating on the improvement and distribution of methods of fertility control, a solution to the problems of population growth can be reached within politically acceptable means.

Sociological research also discovered an appalling amount of ignorance among the general public about population (for example, 60 percent did not know or could not guess the size of the United States population within plus or minus 50 million [it was approximately 287 million in January, 2002—just in case . . .]), which provided a ground for recommendations about population education. A research finding that only 20 percent of sexually active unmarried teenage girls report using any contraception regularly dramatized the recommendation that such information and service be provided to minors (Westoff, 1975:55–56). There were other contributions as well. Studies showing a negative relationship between income and unwanted births served as a rationale for governmental subsidization of family planning for the poor. An opinion poll taken by the commission has shown that about half of the American people felt that abortion is a private matter and should be decided solely between individuals and their physicians, a finding that was subsequently used to support a policy recommendation for liberal abortion (Scott and Shore, 1979:19).

On the basis of the involvement of sociologists in presidential commissions, Scott and Shore conclude that sociology has made a contribution to recommendations for policy in three ways:

> The first is through the use of sociological concepts that are said to provide new or unique perspectives on social conditions—perspectives that are based upon more than common sense and that may in fact be inconsistent with basic notions upon which existing policies are based. . . . Second, prescriptions for policy are sometimes suggested by the findings of sociological research undertaken primarily to advance scientific understanding of society. . . . The third is the use of sociological methods and techniques of research to obtain information about specific questions central to the deliberations of Commissions. (1979:20-21)

Of these three uses of sociology, the third is by far the most common (see, for example, Deutscher, 1999). However, it should be noted that there is no way of precisely determining the extent to which sociology can or does contribute to policy recommendations. For example, in many instances the methods of empirical research, not the knowledge and concepts of sociology, have been directly responsible for policy prescriptions. Obviously, conducting research is not a skill possessed exclusively by sociologists. Moreover, there is no way of distinguishing between the contributions of intelligent and insightful individuals who happen to be trained as sociologists and the contributions of sociological knowledge and perspective as such. Consequently, care needs to be exercised in crediting the discipline's knowledge in all cases in which sociology has had an impact on policy.

Despite these qualifications, it is fair to state that sociological knowledge can and at times does have an impact on developing recommendations for social policy. "For this reason," as Scott and Shore observe (1979:23), "sociologists can legitimately claim that their discipline has been and is relevant to the development of policy recommendations."

Contributions of Sociology to Enacted Policy

Although there is a growing influence of social science in law, measuring the impact of social-science research is a fairly difficult endeavor. Impact studies rely predominantly on citations for an indication of whether policymakers have used such research (Roesch et al., 1991:2-3). Counts of social-science publications and findings cited in legal decisions could possibly underrepresent the influence of research because policymakers are reluctant to cite them even when they have influenced their decisions. Because of their training in law, they have a preference for legal scholarship and precedent rather than for social-science methodology and statistics. Consequently, the extent of impact in some instances remains controversial; in certain cases, sociology is considered to have had a direct impact on enacted policy. A most widely cited illustration of this is the social-science contribution to the 1954 Supreme Court decision outlawing segregation in public schools. Other examples of impact on social policy include sociological studies that resulted in the reduction of delay in the courts, changes in testimony procedures, changes in the procedures to select judges, the provision for counsel to the indigent, various cross-cultural studies on sentencing with policy alternatives (Walker and Hough, 1988), and releasing indigent criminal defendants without bail pending trial. The last study, for example, showed that a careful screening and notifying of defendants released without any bond produced a higher percentage of court appearances than did the traditional bail bond system (Nagel, 1969:31–32).

A number of other examples may be cited to support the view that sociology has had an impact on enacted policy. They include the involvement of sociologists in programs to combat juvenile delinquency (U.S. Department of Justice, 1995b), to reduce school dropout rates, and to prevent narcotics addiction (in particular, studies dealing with attempts to reduce youth crime and delinquency problems contributed to legislation that became the Juvenile Delinquency and Youth Offenses Control Act of 1961 [Katz, 1978:137]); and sociological research on talent loss as a consequence of inadequate educational opportunities for minority groups and persons of low socioeconomic status led to the enactment of remedial measures, such as the establishment of new scholarships and loan resources, and the creation of federal programs like Outward Bound, Talent Search, and Vista. In each instance, sociologists have contributed research and conceptual skills toward the "formulation of programs and policies that were eventually enacted to ameliorate social conditions deemed harmful to society" (Scott and Shore, 1979:24).

In social-policy research, sociologists doing scientific work are often confronted with problems and issues that have an impact on many people whose lives may be substantially altered or changed. To illustrate, a study that had a significant impact on the lives of many people in the United States is the so-called Coleman Report. In 1964, the U.S. Office of Education was authorized by the Civil Rights Act to undertake a survey and to make a report to the president and Congress in two years concerning the lack of availability of equal educational opportunities for individuals by reason of race, color, religion, or national origin in public educational institutions at all levels in the United States. Subsequently, a social survey on a huge scale was carried out by a social-science team led by James S. Coleman, Ernest Q. Campbell (1966), and their associates. The survey included 570,000 school pupils, 60,000 teachers, and 4,000 schools. The final report is a 737-page document.

Following this monumental study, efforts at the national and regional levels involving financial support and structural changes on a large scale have been made for the purpose of achieving a better mix of students in schools and continuity of research activities in this area. One far-reaching policy outcome of the study was the decision of the federal government to instrument busing for the purpose of achieving integrated schools. The issue of busing, as I noted in Chapter 3, remains a controversial policy and has generated many protests, counterprotests, and even violence. Although the researchers involved in the original study may not agree with all the policies that have been formulated and instrumented, the study's policy influence has been substantial.

The preceding illustrations show some of the contributions of sociology to enacted policy. However, a great deal of applied sociological research has no discernible policy implications of any kind. Many of the recommendations are pragmatically useless (that is, too expensive to instrument) or are considered politically unrealistic or implausible by policymakers. Furthermore, policy questions are fundamentally political and not sociological questions. Often, policies are formulated and *then* relevant research is sought to support, legitimize, and dramatize (or even propagandize) these policies. Thus, it would be erroneous to assume that research generally precedes and determines policy actions. Furthermore, some sociologists feel that they should not be directly involved through research in the development and instrumentation of social policy, and this position is epitomized by Daniel P. Moynihan (1969:193), who contends that "the role of social sciences lies not in the formation of social policy but in the measurement of its results." In the next section, I shall consider evaluation research and impact studies.

EVALUATION RESEARCH AND IMPACT STUDIES

Evaluation of enacted policy is as old as policy itself. Policymakers always have made judgments regarding the benefits, costs, or effects of particular policies, programs, and projects (Nathan, 1988; Orr, 1998). Many of these judgments have been impressionistic, often influenced by ideological, partisan self-interest, and valuational criteria. For example, a tax cut may be considered necessary and desirable because it enhances the electoral chances of the evaluator's political party, or unemployment compensation may be deemed "bad" because the evaluator "knows a lot of people" who improperly receive benefits. Undoubtedly, much conflict may result from this sort of evaluation because different evaluators, employing different value criteria, reach different conclusions concerning the merits of the same policy.

Another type of evaluation has centered on the operation of specific policies of programs, such as a juvenile correctional reform (McGarrell, 1988), bootcamp (Zhang, 1998), or a welfare program. Questions asked may include: Is the program honestly run? What are its financial costs? Who receives benefits (payments or services) and in what amounts? Is there any overlap or duplication with other programs? What is the level of community reintegration of participants? What is the degree of staff commitment? Were legal standards and procedures followed? This kind of evaluation may provide information about the honesty or efficiency in the conduct of a program, but like the impressionistic kind of evaluation, it will probably yield little if anything in the way of hard information on the societal effects of a program. A welfare program, for instance, may be carried out honestly and efficiently, and it may be politically and ideologically satisfying to a given evaluator. However, such an evaluation will tell very little about the impact of the program on the poor, or whether it is achieving its officially stated objectives.

Since the late 1960s, a third type of policy evaluation is receiving increasing attention among policymakers. It is the systematic objective evaluation of programs to measure their societal impact and the extent to which they are achieving stated objectives. In 1967 and 1968, Congress altered some of the central pieces of President Johnson's Great Society legislation so that mandatory evaluation would be included in all programs, such as the Economic Opportunity Act. The intention was to monitor the progress of programs and to terminate those that did not seem to yield the desired level of results. There were also political benefits to be obtained by emphasizing evaluation. Low-cost experiments on social problems and rigid evaluation requirements could be used to subvert attempts to solve social problems through (expensive) direct social change or action programs. The contrast between the evaluation components required for War on Poverty programs and those required for such "welfare" programs as urban renewal, railroad subsidies, and agribusiness subsidies points this up dramatically. Notes Morehouse: "None of the older, well-established, and 'safe' domestic programs have evaluation requirements. . . . Program evaluation requirements were an important by-product of a general policy of bringing controversial programs under control" (1972:873).

For many, evaluation research quickly became a proper use of sociology in policy-related work (Babbie, 1998:333–355; Scott and Shore, 1979:43). Rapidly, this use of social research in policy analysis became widespread and an entire field of specialization has developed about methods and procedures for conducting evaluation research. Technically speaking, however, there are no formal methodological differences between evaluation and nonevaluation research. They have in common the same techniques and the same basic steps that must be followed in the research process. The difference lies in the following: (1) Evaluation research uses deliberately planned intervention of some independent variable, (2) the programs it assesses assume some objective or goal as desirable, and (3) it attempts to determine the extent to which this desired goal has been reached. As Edward A. Suchman (1967:15) puts it, "evaluative research asks about the *kind* of change the program views as desirable, the *means* by which this change is to be brought about, and the *signs* according to which such change can be recognized." Thus, the greatest distinction between evaluation and nonevaluation research is one of objectives.

Carol Weiss (1998:6–8) proposes several additional criteria that distinguish evaluation research from other types of research:

1. Evaluation research is generally conducted for a client who intends to use the research as a basis for decision making.
2. The investigator deals with his or her client's questions as to whether the client's program is accomplishing what the client wishes it to accomplish.
3. The objective of evaluation research is to ascertain whether the program goals are being reached.
4. The investigator works in a situation where priority goes to the program as opposed to the evaluation.
5. There is always a possibility of conflicts between the researcher and the program staff because of the divergences of loyalties and objectives.
6. In evaluation research there is an emphasis on results that are useful for policy decisions.

Social policy evaluation is essentially concerned with attempts to determine the impact of policy on real-life conditions. As a minimum, policy evaluation requires a specification of policy objectives (what we want to accomplish with a given policy), the means of realizing it (programs), and what has been accomplished toward the attainment of the objectives (impacts or outcomes). In measuring objectives, there is a need to determine not only that some change in real life conditions has occurred, such as a reduction in the unemployment rate, but also that it was due to policy actions and not to other factors, such as private economic decisions.

Thomas R. Dye (1998:337–348) suggests that the impact of a policy has several dimensions, all of which must be taken into account in the course of evaluation. These include the impact on the social problem at which a policy is directed and on the people involved. Those whom the policy is intended to affect must be clearly defined—that is, the poor, the disadvantaged, schoolchildren, or unwed mothers. The intended effect of the policy must then be determined. If, for example, it is an antipoverty program, is its purpose to raise the income of the poor, to increase the opportunities for employment, or to change their attitudes and behavior? If some combination of such objectives is intended, the evaluation of impact becomes more complicated, since priorities must be assigned to the various intended effects.

At times, as Friedman and Macaulay (1977:501) note, it is difficult to determine the purpose of a law or a program of regulation. They suggest that the determination of intent is complicated because many individuals with diverse purposes participate in the policy-making. Will consideration be given to the intention or intentions of the persons who drafted the statute or the judge who wrote the opinion creating the rule? To that of the majority of the legislature or court who voted for it? To that of the lobbyists who worked for the bill? To that purpose openly discussed or to the purpose that is implicit but never mentioned? They add that sometimes one can only conclude that a law has multiple and perhaps even conflicting purposes, but this is not to say that one can never be sure of the purpose of a law. However, one must be aware of the complexities of determining "purpose."

It should also be noted that a law may have either intended or unintended consequences or even both. A guaranteed-income program, for example, may improve the income situation of the benefited groups, as intended. But what impact does it also have on their initiative to seek employment? Does it decrease this, as some have contended? Similarly, an agricultural price support program intended to improve farmers' incomes may lead to overproduction of the supported commodities.

The difficulties of measurement of impact are most acute for those areas of conduct where the behavior in question is hard to quantify and where it is hard to tell what the behavior *would* have been without the intervention of the law. The laws against murder illustrate the difficulties here. There is a fairly good idea about the murder rate in most countries, but no information at all exists about the contribution that the *law* makes to this rate. In other words, there is no way of determining how high the murder rate would be if there were, for example, no capital punishment for murder.

Knowledge of a new law by members of the legal profession also plays a role in the study of impact. For example, the Magnuson-Moss Warranty Act of 1975 was heralded as a major piece of legislation intended to protect the consumers against defective products. Did the new law help consumers with specific complaints about faulty products? Not much, according to research findings. Two years after the passage of the new law, one study concluded that "most lawyers in Wisconsin knew next to nothing about the Magnuson-Moss Warranty Act" and "many had never heard of it" (Macaulay, 1979:118). The fact that many lawyers know little about laws that are intended to protect consumers obviously impairs the effectiveness of such laws. As this example shows, another problem confronting impact research is the assessment of knowledge of a particular law on the part of those who are involved in its interpretation and application.

The study of impact is further complicated by the fact that policies may have effects on groups or situations other than those at which they are directed. These are called spillover effects (Wade, 1972). These spillover effects may be positive or negative. An illustration of the negative effects is the testing of nuclear devices, which may provide data for the design of nuclear power plants but may also generate hazards for the population. An illustration of a positive spillover effect is that when tariffs are lowered at the request of American exporters to increase their sales abroad, consumers in the United States may benefit from lower prices caused by increased imports that lower tariffs stimulate. Obviously, in the evaluation of impact, attention must also be paid to the spillover effects.

A given legislation may also have impact on future as well as current conditions. Is a particular policy designed to improve an immediate short-term situation, or is it intended to have effects over a longer time period? For example, was the Head Start program supposed to improve the cognitive abilities of disadvantaged children in the short run, or was it to have an impact on their long-range development and earning capacity? The determination of long-term effects stemming from a policy is much more difficult than the assessment of short-term impacts. For example, it will be next to impossible to determine if the regulation of the price of natural gas at the wellhead, a policy that began in the 1950s, really contributed to the controversial energy shortage in the late 1970s, as some now contend. If so, this would be a long-term effect of a policy with a negative spillover effect.

A fairly rich literature of evaluation of actual and proposed programs of law has developed, using criteria derived from economics as its standard. This literature takes certain economic goals as its basic values and assesses legal programs as good or bad depending upon whether they most efficiently or rationally achieve the economic goals or make use of theoretically correct economic means. Of course, it is fairly easy to calculate the dollar costs of a particular policy when it is stated as the actual number of dollars spent on a program, its share of total government expenditures, how efficiently the funds are allocated, and so on. Other economic costs are, however, difficult to measure. For example, it is difficult to discover the expenditures by the private sector for pollution-control devices that are necessitated by air pollution control policy. Moreover, economic standards are hardly applicable to the measurement of social costs of inconvenience, dislocation, and social disruption resulting, for instance, from an urban renewal project. At the same time, it is also difficult to measure the indirect benefits of particular policies for the community. For example, the Social Security program may contribute to social stability as well as the retirement incomes of recipients. The problem of measurement is again apparent.

In addition to the difficulties inherent in the measurement of indirect costs and benefits, other complexities arise because the effects of a particular law may be symbolic (intangible) as well as material (tangible). Intended symbolic effects capitalize on popular beliefs, attitudes, and aspirations for their effectiveness. For example, taken at face value, the graduated income tax is a symbol of equality and progressiveness in taxation and draws wide support on that basis (Reed and Swain, 1997:70–112). In reality, the impact of income tax on many people, particularly the affluent, is noticeably reduced by provisions such as those for tax shelters. The result is that effective tax rates for the rich are substantially lower than commonly believed. What is symbolically promised is quite different from what materially results. There are other laws that appear to promise more symbolically than their instrumentation actually yields in material benefits. They include antitrust activity, regulation of public utility rates, and various antipoverty efforts. These endeavors attempt to assure people that policymakers are concerned with their welfare, although the real tangible benefits are limited.

These are some of the difficulties that need to be taken into consideration in measuring the impact of a particular law. There are several possible research approaches that can be used for measuring impact. One approach is the study of a group of individuals from the target population after it has been exposed to a program that had been developed to cause change. This approach is referred to as the *one-shot* study. Another possible approach is to study a group of individuals both *before and after* exposure to a particular program. Still another possibility would be the use of some kind of *controlled* experiment. But as I noted earlier in this chapter, in measuring the impact of law, one serious problem is the absence of control groups. As a result, one is rarely able to say with confidence what behavior would have been had a law not been passed or had a different law been passed. Outside of a laboratory setting, it is difficult to apply an experimental treatment to a group that one has matched in all significant respects to another group that does not receive the treatment, so as to control for all possible sources of distortion or error. This difficulty is further accentuated by ethical problems that often arise from such research methods as the random assignment of persons to different legal remedies.

The final consideration of evaluation research involves the utilization of results. As James S. Coleman (1972:6) states, "The ultimate product is not a `contribution to existing knowledge' in the literature, but a social policy modified by the research result." In many instances, however, those who mandate and request evaluation research fail to utilize the results of that research. These people may feel committed to particular ways of doing things despite evidence that a program is ineffective. This is particularly true in instances where programs were instigated by political pressures such as the various endeavors in model-city programs, war against poverty, corrections, and drug and alcohol rehabilitation. As public interest waned in the later stages of these programs, there was no real pressure to incorporate the results of evaluation studies into the ongoing activities (Vago, 1999:388–390). There are, of course, a number of other ways initiators of evaluation research can respond to the results. They include the manipulation of research outcomes for their own interests, rationalization of negative results, and in some instances where the findings are negative, dismissal of results.

It is evident that sociological expertise can be made relevant to social policy. Of course, it is a question of choice whether one would want to pursue primarily disciplinary or a policy-oriented applied sociology, although the two are not mutually exclusive. Sociology undoubtedly has a good potential to play an active, creative, and practical role on the formulation, instrumentation, and evaluation of social policy (Rogers, 1988). At the same time, as sociological knowledge and methods become relevant to and influential on policy, they become part of politics by definition. In such a situation, the contributions of sociology can become a tool for immediate political ends and propaganda purposes by justifying and legitimizing a particular position. Ideally, the objective should be to insulate, but not isolate, sociological contributions from the immediate vagaries of day-to-day politics, and to strike some sort of balance between political and sociological considerations, permitting neither to dominate.

SUMMARY

This chapter examined procedures that are useful for advancing our understanding of law in society and considered the impact of sociological research on law and the applicability of such research to social policy. Several methods can be applied in studying law in society, and more than a single method is usually involved in an investigation. The methods of sociological research include the historical, observational, experimental, and survey studies. Historical analysis relies on secondary sources collected for purposes other than the researcher's intentions. Thus, a notable difficulty of the historical method lies in the limited accuracy and thoroughness of the documents and materials involved. In addition to relying on official documents, the historical method may also be based on narrations of personal experiences, generally known as the life-histories method. Although there are difficulties with the use of historical methods, they provide an aid in understanding long-term developments and change processes involved in the study of law.

Observational methods utilize either human observers or mechanical devices and procedures to elicit responses directly from the subjects by questioning. Many of the observational techniques are used in laboratory situations as, for example, the studies on jury deliberations. Observational methods are also used by sociologists in field settings, which involve direct contact with subjects and take place in relatively natural social situations. Observational methods have been used extensively to study the various facets of the criminal justice system and the legal profession.

Experimental methods are used to test causal relationships, either in a laboratory or in a field setting. Experiments in sociology face certain difficulties such as ethical, legal, and financial considerations. Although there have been several large-scale experiments dealing with law and a large number of laboratory studies, questions of generalizability of results still plague the researchers. The use of experimental methods also raises questions about the legitimacy of "manipulating" human subjects.

Survey methods are widely used in sociological research, and they generally involve a reasonably representative cross section of the population under study. Survey studies tend to be larger than is typically the case in observational and experimental studies, and data may be collected at one point in time or over time. Policymakers tend to rely on the results of surveys more than on other methods of sociological inquiry.

Sociology, like all sciences, may be either pure or applied. Pure sociology searches for new knowledge, whereas applied sociology tries to apply sociological knowledge to practical problems. Although this distinction is often used in the sociological literature, sociology is both a pure and an applied science. Sociological knowledge and expertise have demonstrable relevance to and influence on social policy in terms of the discipline's contributions to policy recommendations and to enacted policy. Sociological knowledge, methods, and concepts have been used in a number of presidential commissions as grounds for policy recommendations, and a number of sociological studies have had a direct impact on enacted policy, such as the Coleman study on school desegregation.

There is an increasing involvement of sociologists in evaluation research and impact studies. There are specific requirements for the evaluation of many federal programs and activities designed to induce change in some area. The object of evaluation research is to determine how successful a particular change effort is in achieving its goals. Impact studies are concerned with the intent of those who formulated a legal rule or policy, whether or not a legal rule was responsible for the change, knowledge of a law by its interpreters, and spillover effects. Evaluation research allows policymakers to determine the effectiveness of a program, whether it should be continued or phased out, and what in-course adjustments, if any, are needed to make it more effective. In some cases, however, when the results of the evaluation are negative, the client might attempt to dismiss or rationalize the findings.

SUGGESTED FURTHER READINGS

ROBERT R. ALFORD, *The Craft of Inquiry: Theories, Methods, Evidence.* New York: Oxford University Press, 1998. A lucid presentation of basic explanatory approaches to sociology.

IRWIN DEUTSCHER, *Making a Difference: The Practice of Sociology.* Somerset, NJ: Transaction Publishers, 1999. A contribution to the debate over the extent to which health, educational, and social programs initiated over the years have been successful in intimate, human terms.

ARLENE FINK and JACQUELINE KOSECOFF, *How to Conduct Surveys, A Step-by-Step Guide.* Thousand Oaks, CA: Sage Publications, Inc., 1998. A useful book on the basics of survey research.

MICHAEL LAVALETTE and ALAN PRATT (EDS.), *Social Policy: A Conceptual and Theoretical Introduction.* Thousand Oaks, CA: Sage Publications, Inc., 1997. A collection of articles on the diverse theoretical approaches and pragmatic concerns in policy analysis.

WALLACE D. LOH, *Social Research in the Judicial Process: Cases, Readings, and Text.* New York: Russell Sage Foundation, 1984. An excellent and detailed treatment of empirical legal studies and the application of social research in the judicial process.

R. LUCKHAM (ED.), *Law and Social Inquiry: Case Studies of Research*. Uppsala, Sweden: Scandinavian Institute of African Studies, 1981. An enlightening collection of nine articles discussing the problems of sociolegal research in different parts of the world.

JOHN MONAHAN and LAURENS WALKER, *Social Science in Law: Cases and Materials*, 4th ed. Westbury, NY: The Foundation Press, Inc., 1998. See, in particular, Chapters 2 and 3 on the use of social-science research methods in law.

STUART S. NAGEL (ED.), *Research in Law and Policy Studies*. Greenwich, CT: Jai Press, Inc. Vol. 2, 1988, Vol. 3, 1990. A collection of interdisciplinary and cross-cultural empirical studies on various facets of law and society.

STUART S. NAGEL WITH LISA A. BIEVENUE, *Social Science, Law, and Public Policy*. Lanham, MD: University Press of America, Inc., 1992. An excellent analysis of the various social-science measures applicable to law and public policy.

MAURICE MULLARD and PAUL SPICKER, *Social Policy in a Changing Society*. New York: Routledge, 1998. A succinct review of the uses and paradigms of policy analysis.

PETER REASON and HILARY BRADBURY (EDS.), *Handbook of Action Research, Participative Inquiry and Practice*. Thousand Oaks, CA: Sage Publications, 2001. A collection of articles on how to integrate knowledge with action and how to collaborate with co-researchers representing other disciplines in the field.

ROBERT A. SCOTT and ARNOLD R. SHORE, *Why Sociology Does Not Apply: A Study of the Use of Sociology in Public Policy*. New York: Elsevier, 1979. A provocative essay on the role of sociology in social policy. The book was used to provide some of the background information for parts of this chapter.

RUSSELL K. SCHUTT, *Investigating the Social World, The Process and Practice of Research*. 3rd ed. Thousand Oaks, CA: Pine Forge Press, 2001. A widely used popular text on social research with an extensive coverage of the basics.

RITA J. SIMON, *The Jury: Its Role in American Society*. Lexington, MA: Lexington Books, Heath, 1980. A review of much of the major research that has been done on the American jury between 1950 and 1979.

THOMAS J. SULLIVAN, *Applied Sociology: Research and Critical Thinking*. New York: Macmillan, 1992. A primer on the basics of sociological research and its applications to policy concerns.

REFERENCES

ALFORD, ROBERT R. 1998. *The Craft of Inquiry: Theories, Methods, Evidence*. New York: Oxford University Press.

BABBIE, EARL. 1998. *The Practice of Social Research*. 8th ed. Belmont, CA: Wadsworth Publishing Company.

BAUMGARTNER, MARY P. 1978. "Law and Social Status in Colonial New Haven, 1639–1665." Pp. 153–174 in Rita J. Simon (ed.), *Research in Law and Sociology*, Vol. 1. Greenwich, CT: Jai Press, Inc.

BERNARD, H. RUSSEL. 2000. *Social Research Methods: Qualitative and Quantitative Approaches*. Thousand Oaks, CA: Sage Publications, Inc.

BLUMBERG, ABRAHAM S. 1979. *Criminal Justice: Issues & Ironies*. 2nd ed. New York: New Viewpoints.

BRENNER, SUSAN W. 1992. *Precedent Inflation*. New Brunswick, NJ: Transaction Publishers.

CARLIN, JEROME E. 1966. *Lawyers' Ethics: A Survey of the New York City Bar.* New York: Russell Sage Foundation.

CHAMBLISS, WILLIAM J. 1964. "A Sociological Analysis of the Law of Vagrancy," *Social Problems* 12 (1) (Summer): 67–77.

COCHRAN, CHARLES L. and ELOISE F. MALONE. 1995. *Public Policy: Perspectives and Choices.* New York: McGraw-Hill, Inc.

COLEMAN, JAMES S. 1972. *Policy Research in Social Science.* Morristown, NJ: General Learning Press.

COLEMAN, JAMES S., ERNEST Q. CAMPBELL, CAROL J. HOBSON, ET AL. 1966. *Equality of Educational Opportunity.* Washington, DC: U.S. Government Printing Office.

D'ANTONIO, WILLIAM V. 1992. "Sociology's Lonely Crowd—Indeed!" *Footnotes,* May, 3–4.

DAVIS, JAMES H., ROBERT M. BRAY, and ROBERT W. HOLT. 1977. "The Empirical Study of Decision Processes in Juries: A Critical Review." Pp. 326–361 in June Louin Tapp and Felice J. Levine (eds.), *Law, Justice, and the Individual in Society: Psychological and Legal Issues.* New York: Holt, Rinehart & Winston.

DEPARLE, JASON. 1998. "Wisconsin Welfare Experiment: Easy to Say, Not So Easy to Do," *New York Times* (October 18): Y1, Y20.

DEUTSCHER, IRWIN. 1999. *Making a Difference: The Practice of Sociology.* Somerset, NJ: Transaction Publishers.

DIAMOND, SHARI SEIDMAN. 1997. "Illuminations and Shadows From Jury Simulations," *Law and Human Behavior* 21 (5) (October): 561–573.

DINES, GAIL, ROBERT JENSEN and ANN RUSSO. 1997. *Pornography: The Production and Consumption of Inequality.* New York: Routledge.

DYE, THOMAS. 1998. *Understanding Public Policy.* 9th ed. Upper Saddle River, NJ: Prentice Hall.

ERICSON, RICHARD V. 1989. "Patrolling the Facts: Secrecy and Publicity in Policework," *British Journal of Sociology* 40 (2): 205–226.

FINK, ARLENE and JACQUELINE KOSECOFF. 1998. *How to Conduct Surveys, A Step-by-Step Guide.* Thousand Oaks, CA: Sage Publications, Inc.

FOWLER, FLOYD J., JR. 1995. *Improving Survey Questions, Design and Evaluation,* Thousand Oaks, CA: Sage Publications, Inc.

FREEMAN, RICHARD J., and RONALD ROESCH. 1992. "Psycholegal Education: Training for Forum and Function." Pp. 567–576 in Dorothy K. Kagehiro and William S. Laufer (eds.), *Handbook of Psychology and Law.* New York: Springer-Verlag.

FRIEDMAN, LAWRENCE M., and STEWART MACAULAY. 1977. *Law and the Behavioral Sciences.* 2nd ed. Indianapolis: Bobbs-Merrill.

FRIEDMAN, LAWRENCE M., and ROBERT V. PERCIVAL. 1978. "A Tale of Two Courts: Litigation in Alameda and San Benito Counties." Pp. 69–79 in Sheldon Goldman and Austin Sarat (eds.), *American Court Systems: Readings in Judicial Process and Behavior.* San Francisco: W. H. Freeman & Company Publishers.

HALL, JEROME. 1952. *Theft, Law and Society.* 2nd ed. Indianapolis: Bobbs-Merrill.

HANS, VALERIE P. 1992. "Jury Decision Making." Pp. 56–76 in Dorothy J. Kagehiro and William S. Laufer (eds.), *Handbook of Psychology and Law.* New York: Springer-Verlag.

INCIARDI, JAMES A., ALAN A. BLOCK, and LYLE A. HALLOWELL. 1977. *Historical Approaches to Crime: Research Strategies and Issues.* Beverly Hills, CA: Sage Publications.

KATZ, JAMES EVERETT. 1978. *Presidential Politics and Science Policy.* New York: Praeger.

KERSHAW, DAVID N. 1969. *The Negative Income Tax Experiment in New Jersey.* Princeton, NJ: Mathematica.

KESSLER, JOAN B. 1975. "The Social Psychology of Jury Deliberations." Pp. 69–93 in Rita James Simon (ed.), *The Jury System in America: A Critical Overview.* Beverly Hills, CA: Sage Publications.

KOEHLER, JONATHAN J. 1992. "Probabilities in the Courtroom: An Evaluation of the Objections and Policies." Pp. 167–184 in Dorothy J. Kagehiro and William S. Laufer (eds.), *Handbook of Psychology and Law.* New York: Springer-Verlag.

KRAMER, GEOFFREY P., and NORBERT L. KERR. 1989. "Laboratory Simulation and Bias in the Study of Juror Behavior: A Methodological Note," *Law and Human Behavior* 13 (1): 89–99.

KUTCHINSKY, BERL. 1973. "The Effects of Easy Availability of Pornography on the Incidence of Sex Crimes: The Danish Experience," *Journal of Social Issues* 29 (3): 163–181.

LAVALETTE, MICHAEL and ALAN PRATT (EDS.) 1997. *Social Policy: A Conceptual and Theoretical Introduction.* Thousand Oaks, CA: Sage Publications, Inc.

LEMPERT, RICHARD. 1989. "Humility Is a Virtue: On the Publicization of Policy-Relevant Research," *Law & Society Review* 23 (1): 145–161.

LOH, WALLACE D. 1984. *Social Research in the Judicial Process: Cases, Readings, and Text.* New York: Russell Sage Foundation.

MACAULY, STEWART. 1979. "Lawyers and Consumer Protection Laws," *Law & Society Review* 14 (1): 115–171.

MANGIONE, THOMAS W. 1995. *Mail Surveys.* Thousand Oaks, CA: Sage Publications, Inc.

McCALL, GEORGE J. 1978. *Observing the Law: Field Methods in the Study of Crime and the Criminal Justice System.* New York: Free Press.

McGARRELL, EDMUND F. 1988. *Juvenile Correction Reform: Two Decades of Policy and Procedural Change.* Albany: State University of New York Press.

MILLER, FRANK W. 1969. *Prosecution: The Decision to Charge a Suspect with a Crime.* Boston: Little, Brown.

MINTZ, MORTON, and JERRY S. COHEN. 1976. "Human Guinea Pigs," *Progressive* 40 (12) (December): 32–36.

MONAHAN, JOHN, and LAURENS WALKER. 1991. "Judicial Use of Social Science Research," *Law and Human Behavior* 15 (6) (December): 571–584. 1998. *Social Science in Law: Cases and Materials.* 4th ed. Westbury, NY: The Foundation Press, Inc.

MOREHOUSE, THOMAS. 1972. "Program Evaluation: Social Research versus Public Policy," *Public Administration Review* 32 (6) (November–December): 868–874.

MORRIS, ROBERT. 1979. *Social Policy of the American Welfare State: An Introduction to Policy Analysis.* New York: Harper & Row, Pub.

MORSE, JANICE M., and PEGGY ANNE FIELD. 1995. *Qualitative Research Methods.* 2nd ed. Thousand Oaks, CA: Sage Publications, Inc.

MOYNIHAN, DANIEL P. 1969. *Maximum Feasible Misunderstanding.* New York: Free Press. 1989. "Toward a Post-Industrial Social Policy," *Public Interest* 96 (Summer): 16–27.

MULLARD, MAURICE and PAUL SPICKER. 1998. *Social Policy in a Changing Society.* New York: Routledge.

NADER, LAURA, and HARRY F. TODD, JR. 1978. "Introduction: The Disputing Process." Pp. 1–40 in Laura Nader and Harry F. Todd, Jr. (eds.), *The Disputing Process—Law in Ten Societies.* New York: Columbia University Press.

NAGEL, STUART S. 1969. *The Legal Process from a Behavioral Perspective*. Homewood, IL: Dorsey.

NAGEL, STUART S. 1993. *Legal Scholarship, Microcomputers, and Super-Optimizing Decision-Making*. Westport, CT: Quorum Books, 1993.

NAGEL, STUART S., and MARIAN NEEF. 1977. *The Legal Process: Modeling the System*. Beverly Hills, CA: Sage Publications.

NATHAN, RICHARD P. 1988. *Social Science in Government: Uses and Misuses*. New York: Basic Books.

NATIONAL COMMISSION ON THE CAUSES and PREVENTION OF VIOLENCE. 1969. *To Establish Justice, To Insure Domestic Tranquillity*. Final Report. Washington, DC: U.S. Government Printing Office.

NEWMAN, DONALD J. 1966. *Conviction: The Determination of Guilt or Innocence without Trial*. Boston: Little, Brown.

NEWSWEEK. 1986. "A Salvo in the Porn War"(July 21): 18.

NOCK, STEVEN, and PAUL W. KINGSTON. 1990. *The Sociology of Public Issues*. Belmont, CA: Wadsworth.

OHLIN, LLOYD E. 1975. "Report on the President's Commission on Law Enforcement and Administration of Justice." Pp. 93–115 in Mirra Komarovsky (ed.), *Sociology and Public Policy: The Case of Presidential Commissions*. New York: Elsevier.

ORR, LARRY L. 1998. *Social Experiments: Evaluating Public Programs with Experimental Methods*. Thousand Oaks, CA: Sage Publications, Inc.

PODGORECKI, ADAM. 1974. *Law and Society*. London: Routledge & Kegan Paul.

POSNER, RICHARD A. 2001. *Frontiers of Legal Theory*. Cambridge: Harvard University Press.

PUNCH, MAURICE. 1989. "Researching Police Deviance: A Personal Encounter with the Limitations and Liabilities of Field-Work," *British Journal of Sociology* 40 (2): 177–204.

REASON, PETER and HILARY BRADBURY (EDS.). 2001. *Handbook of Action Research, Participative Inquiry and Practice*. Thousand Oaks, CA: Sage Publications.

REED, B. J., and JOHN W. SWAIN. 1997. *Public Finance Administration*. 2nd ed. Thousand Oaks, CA: Sage Publications, Inc.

ROESCH, RONALD, STEPHEN L. GOLDING, VALERIE P. HANS, and N. DICKON REPPUCCI. 1991. "Social Science and the Courts: The Role of Amicus Curiae Briefs," *Law and Human Behavior* 15 (1) (February): 1–11.

ROGERS, JAMES M. 1988. *The Impact of Policy Analysis*. Pittsburgh: University of Pittsburgh Press.

ROSSI, RICHARD H., and KATHERINE LYALL. 1976. *Reforming Public Welfare: A Critique of the Negative Income Tax Experiment*. New York: Russell Sage Foundation.

SCOTT, ROBERT A., and ARNOLD R. SHORE. 1979. *Why Sociology Does Not Apply: A Study of the Use of Sociology in Public Policy*. New York: Elsevier.

SHORT, JAMES F., JR. 1975. "The National Commission on the Causes and Prevention of Violence: Reflections on the Contributions of Sociology and Sociologists." Pp. 61–91 in Mirra Komarovsky (ed.), *Sociology and Public Policy: The Case of Presidential Commissions*. New York: Elsevier.

SCHUTT, RUSSELL K. 2001. *Investigating the Social World, The Process and Practice of Research*. 3rd ed. Thousand Oaks, CA: Pine Forge Press.

SIMON, RITA JAMES (ED.). 1975. *The Jury System in America: A Critical Overview*. Beverly Hills, CA: Sage Publications.

SKOLNICK, JEROME H. 1994. *Justice without Trial: Law Enforcement in Democratic Society.* 3rd ed. New York: Macmillan.

SUCHMAN, EDWARD A. 1967. *Evaluative Research: Principles and Practice in Public Service and Social Action Programs.* New York: Russell Sage.

SUDNOW, DAVID. 1975. "Normal Crimes: Sociological Features of the Penal Code in a Public Defender Office," *Social Problems* 12 (3) (Winter): 255–276.

TOBY, JACKSON. 1980. "Crime in American Public Schools," *Public Interest*, no. 58 (Winter): 18–42.

TOMASIC, ROMAN. 1985. *The Sociology of Law.* London: Sage Publications.

U.S. DEPARTMENT OF JUSTICE. 1995a. Annual Report of NIJJDP, Fiscal Year 1994. National Institute for Juvenile Justice and Delinquency Prevention. Office of Juvenile Justice and Delinquency Prevention. Law Enforcement Assistance Administration (March). Washington, DC: U.S. Government Printing Office. 1995b. Criminal Victimization in the United States, 1986. Attorney General's Commission on Pornography. Final Report. Vols. 1 and 2 (July). Washington, DC: U.S. Government Printing Office.

U.S. OFFICE OF ECONOMIC OPPORTUNITY. 1970. Preliminary Results of the New Jersey Graduated Work Incentive Experiment, February 18. Washington, DC: U.S. Government Printing Office.

VAGO, STEVEN. 1999. *Social Change.* 4th ed. Upper Saddle River, NJ: Prentice Hall.

WADE, LARRY L. 1972. *The Elements of Public Policy.* Columbus, OH: Merrill Company.

WALKER, NIGEL, and MIKE HOUGH (EDS.). 1988. *Public Attitudes to Sentencing: Surveys from Five Countries.* Aldershot, England: Gower.

WEISS, CAROL. 1998. *Evaluation Research: Methods for Studying Programs and Policies.* 2nd ed. Upper Saddle River, NJ: Prentice Hall.

WESTOFF, CHARLES F. 1975. "The Commission on Population Growth and the American Future: Its Origins, Operations, and Aftermath." Pp. 43–49 in Mirra Komarovsky (ed.), *Sociology and Public Policy: The Case of Presidential Commissions.* New York: Elsevier.

WILLIAMSON, JOHN B., DAVID A. KARP, and JOHN R. DALPHIN. 1977. *The Research Craft: An Introduction to Social Science Methods.* Boston: Little, Brown.

ZEISEL, HANS. 1967. "The Law." Pp. 81–99 in Paul F. Lazarsfeld, William H. Sewell, and Harold Wilensky (eds.), *The Uses of Sociology.* New York: Basic Books.

ZHANG, SHELDON. 1998. "In Search of Hopeful Glimpses: A Critique of Research Strategies in Current Boot Camp Evaluation," *Crime & Delinquency* 44 (2) (April): 314–334.

ZIMRING, FRANKLIN E. 1989. "Methods for Measuring General Deterrence: A Plea for the Field Experiment." Pp. 99–108 in Martin Lawrence Friedland (ed.), *Sanctions and Rewards in the Legal System: A Multidisciplinary Approach.* Toronto: University of Toronto Press.

Index

Mazzarella, Mark, 99, 145
McAdam, Doug, 178, 188
McCall, George J., 409, 432
McCann, Michael W., 164, 186, 189
McCarthy, Joseph, 113, 386
McChesney, Fred S., 374, 401
McConville, Sean, 17–18, 33
McCubbin, Michael, 208, 240
McElrath, Karen, 211, 237, 242
McGarrell, Edmund F., 422, 432
McGillis, Daniel, 254, 298
McGuire, Gail M., 178, 189
McGuire, Kevin T., 166, 189
McIntyre, Lisa J., 3, 8, 30, 33, 52, 79, 371, 401
McKay, Robert B., 378, 401
McLaren, Roy C., 132, 151
McLaughlin, Andrew M., 179, 188
McLeod, Maureen, 194, 241
McMichael, Philip, 303, 335, 338
Mead, Margaret, 331, 338
Mechanical solidarity, 51–52
Med-arb, 258
Mediation, 249, 252–253, 258, 268, 276, 292
Medicaid, 264, 280
Medicalization, 207–208, 214
Medicare, 306, 327
Meier, Andrew, 16, 33
Meier, Robert F., 191, 195, 215, 238–239, 243
Melling, Tom, 113, 148
Mellon, Andrew, 154
Mellor, Philip A., 192, 244
Meltsner, Michael, 384, 396, 402
Mermin, Samuel, 18, 33
Merton, Robert K., 61–62, 79
Meschievitz, Catherine S., 249, 294, 299
Meyer, Thomas J., 212, 243
Miceli, Thomas J., 247, 299
Michaels, Priscilla, 59, 79
Miethe, Terance D., 201, 243
Milgram, Stanley, 316–317, 338
Milken, Michael R., 109
Milkis, Sidney M., 122, 146, 185
Mill, John Stuart, 318
Miller, Arthur Selwyn, 306, 338
Miller, Frank W., 409, 432
Miller, James C., 39, 80
Miller, Roger Leroy, 211, 239
Miller, Susan L., 67, 75, 79
Mills, C. Wright, 320, 338
Mills, Miriam K., 294
Milor, Vedat, 14, 33
Minitrials, 258
Minow, Martha L., 67, 74, 78
Mintz, Morton, 411, 432
Miranda v. Arizona, 161
Missouri Compromise, 311
Missouri Plan, 360
Missouri Public Interest Research Group, 180
Mitchell, Michael, 103, 143
Mnookin, Robert H., 253, 295
Mock trials, 101, 183, 409
Model Code of Professional Responsibility, 389
Model Rules of Professional Conduct and Code of Judicial Conduct, 389, 401
Modernization, 37–38, 42–43, 58, 72, 308–309

"Modernization of Law, The" (Galanter), 42–43
Modern legal systems, 38–39, 42–43, 50–52, 72, 317
Mohammed, 315
Mokrzycki, Edmund, 14, 31
Moment in the Sun (R. and L. T. Reinow), 176
Monahan, John, 30, 152, 186, 189, 416, 430, 432
Mondale Bill, 175
Montesquieu, Baron de, 44–45, 79
Monthly Review, 183
Moog, Robert, 267, 299
Moore, Charles A., 201, 243
Moore, Mark Harrison, 135, 148
Moral Compass of the American Lawyer, The (Zitrin and Langford), 352
Moral development
  stages of, 330
More, Harry W., 129, 131, 142, 147
More, Thomas, 351
Morehouse, Thomas, 423, 432
More Guns, Less Crime (Lott), 206
"More Scorn and Less Money Dim Law's Lure" (Johnson), 378
Mores, 192, 195, 235, 304, 322–325, 327, 330, 334, 352
Morgan, Richard E., 264, 299
Morgenthau, Hans, 21, 34
Morgenthau, Robert M., 205, 243
Morin, Paul, 208, 240
Morris, Norval, 142
Morris, Robert, 416, 432
Morse, Janice M., 404–405, 432
Moses, 50, 315
Moses, Jonathan, 363, 401
Moynihan, Daniel Patrick, 173, 189, 230, 243, 416, 422, 432
Mulcahy, Aogan, 108–109, 148
Mullard, Maurice, 417, 430, 432
Munk, Nina, 131, 148
Muris, Timothy J., 374, 401
Muto, Hiromi, 124, 147
Myers, Ken, 380, 386, 401
My Lai massacre, 314
Mystery of Capital, The (De Soto), 2

Nader, Laura, 18, 34, 248, 276, 299, 407, 432
Nader, Ralph, 176, 180, 189, 234, 243, 289, 311, 384, 401
Naffine, Ngaire, 67–68, 71, 79
Nagel, Stuart S., 225, 234, 243, 304–305, 338, 412, 416, 421, 430, 433
Nagpaul, Hans, 370, 401
Narby, Douglas J., 107, 148
Nasheri, Hedie, 107, 148
Nathan, Richard P., 422, 433
Nation, Carrie, 177
Nation, The, 183
National Association for the Advancement of Colored People, 166
National Association of Broadcasters, 181
National Association for Public Interest Law, 289–290
National Center for State Courts, 270
National Commission on the Causes and Prevention of Violence, 413, 417, 433

National Environmental Policy Act, 290
National Fertility Studies, 419
National Highway Traffic Safety
    Administration, 120
National Institute of Drug Abuse, 212
National Labor Relations Board, 121
National Law Journal, 390
National Maritime Union, 179
National Organization for Women, 264
National Rifle Association, 119, 327
National Security Agency, 230
National Service Legal Corps, 373
National Weather Service, 120
Nation Under Lawyers, A (Glendon), 27
Natural Gas Pipeline Safety Act, 176
Natural law, 44–45, 60, 73
Natural Resources Defense Council, 290
Naysnerski, Wendy, 290, 299
Neacsu, E. Dana, 65, 79
Neef, Marian, 412, 433
Negley, Glenn, 316, 338
Negotiation, 249, 252–253, 258, 276, 288, 292
Nelson, Robert L., 356, 401
Nettler, Ronald L., 17, 29, 31
Neusner, Jacob, 17, 34
New Jersey Guaranteed Income Experiments,
    411
New Leader, 183
Newman, Donald J., 110, 143, 409, 433
New Republic, 183
Newsweek, 170, 179, 189, 228, 243, 263, 299, 352,
    401, 418, 433
New York Times, 103, 105, 148, 170, 183, 196,
    204–206, 226, 243, 255, 277, 299, 349, 365,
    370, 373, 377–378, 383, 401
Nimkoff, Meyer F., 328, 338
Nisbet, Robert A., 61, 79, 307, 338
Nixon, Richard, 178, 228–229, 231
Nock, Steven, 404, 433
Nolo Press, 388
Nonet, Philippe, 38, 57, 63, 79
Norms, 3, 9–10, 19, 21–23, 28, 37–38, 43, 46, 50,
    58–60, 68–69, 84, 98, 110, 113–115, 132, 140,
    153–155, 157, 174, 191–195, 197, 235,
    252–253, 256, 263–265, 278, 304, 310–311,
    313–315, 317, 330–331, 334, 355, 390–392,
    405
Nossel, Suzanne, 349, 396, 401
Novak, William J., 127, 148
Novick, Sheldon M., 54, 79
Nuremberg war crimes trials, 314

O'Barr, William M., 5, 29, 31
Oberschall, Anthony, 227–228, 243
O'Brien, Timothy L., 217, 221, 243
Observational methods, 405, 408–411, 413, 428
Occupational Health and Safety Act, 177
Occupational Safety and Health
    Administration, 121, 289
O'Connell, John P., Jr., 110, 148
Office of Economic Opportunity, 373, 411–412,
    434
Official Guide to U.S. Law Schools 2000, 362, 367,
    375, 379–380, 401
Ogloff, James R. P., 3, 30, 34, 104, 151

Ohlin, Lloyd E., 417, 433
O'Leary, Dennis, 131, 148
Olson, Walter K., 269, 294, 299, 365, 367–369, 401
Ombudsman, 254
Omnibus Crime Control and Safe Streets Act,
    218
Operation Chaos, 228
Operation Greylord, 392
Operation Rescue, 264
Operation Shamrock, 230
Oppenheim, Jerrold, 172, 186
O'Reilly, Robert C., 281, 299
Organic analogy, 61
Organic solidarity, 51–52
Organized crime, 15–16, 109, 200, 213, 218–220,
    264
Organized Crime Control Act, 218
Orleans, Sonya, 318, 338
Ornstein, Norman J., 115–116, 148, 158, 189
Orr, Larry L., 422, 433
Osakwe, Christopher, 360, 398
Osborn, Fairfield, 176, 189
Osborne, Randal, 108, 148
Ostrom, Brian J., 108, 146
Outward Bound, 421
Oxford University, 344

Packer, Herbert L., 219, 238, 243, 383, 401
Page, Clarence, 278, 299
Palay, Thomas, 395
Palermo, George B., 107–108, 148, 353, 401
Palmer, Michael, 83, 149, 247, 252, 294, 299
Palmer, Stacy E., 284, 299
Paringaux, Roland-Pierre, 16, 34
Parker, Patricia, 356, 399
Parks, Rosa, 177
Paragon Cable, 286
Parole, 111, 196, 204, 206, 263
Parsons, Talcott, 24, 34, 50, 62, 79, 228
Participant observation, 405, 408–409
Passell, Peter, 387, 401
Pastore, Ann L., 128, 148, 206, 243
"Path of the Law, The" (Holmes), 54
Patterson, Samuel C., 113, 118, 147
Payne, John, 365, 399
Peak, Kenneth J., 135, 149
Pear, Robert, 373, 402
Pearce, Frank, 223, 243
Peay, Jill, 208–209, 243
Peel, Robert, 127
Penn, Stanley, 222, 239
Pepinsky, Harold E., 57, 79, 137, 149
Penrod, Steven D., 105, 149
Percival, Robert V., 266–267, 296, 407, 431
Peremptory challenge, 99, 102
Perlez, Jane, 15, 34
Peterson, Ruth D., 199, 204, 239
Pettigrew, Thomas F., 172, 189
Philips, Susan U., 91, 149
Piaget, Jean, 38, 79
Pierce, Glenn L., 201, 244
Pierce, Richard J., Jr., 158, 189
Pinkele, Carl F., 91, 149
Pipkin, Ronald M., 353, 381–383, 397
Pitulla, Joanne, 391, 402

Sherman, Lawrence W., 59, 80
Sherman Anti-Trust Act, 223, 225
Sherry, Suzanna, 27, 32, 352, 398
Shibutani, Tamotsu, 192, 244
Shilling, Chris, 192, 244
Shore, Arnold R., 416, 418–421, 423, 430, 433
Short, James F., 417–418, 433
Shover, Neal, 221, 238, 245
Shulins, Nancy, 352, 402
Shuman, Daniel W., 361, 402
Sierra Club, 117, 179–180, 289
Silent Spring (Carson), 176
Silverglate, Harvey A., 281, 298
Simenhoff, Mark, 396
Simmel, Georg, 25
Simon, David R., 224, 238, 245
Simon, Leonore, 232, 245
Simon, Rita James, 100, 150, 171, 190, 412, 430, 433
Simonsen, Clifford E., 131, 142, 150
Simpson, A. W. B., 30, 344, 402
Simulated juries, 101, 105, 409
Sinclair, Upton, 176
Situ, Yingyi, 288, 300
Skapska, Grazyna, 14, 31
Skerry, Peter, 262, 300
Skolnick, Jerome H., 133, 137–138, 150, 405, 409, 434
Slonim, Scott, 116, 150
Smigel, Erwin O., 357, 379, 402
Smith, Adam, 53
Smith, Anne Kates, 171, 190
Smith, Bruce, 129, 150
Smith, Clay J., Jr., 349, 396, 402
Smith, Craig S., 14, 35, 201, 245
Smith, Dwayne M., 203, 238, 245
Smolowe, Jill, 205, 245
Snipes, Jeffrey B., 191, 239
Snow, David A., 178, 188
Social change, 20–21, 24, 28, 42, 44, 48, 52, 161, 177, 302–339, 384, 406, 419, 423
    advantages of law in creating, 313–319
    as cause of legal changes, 305–307, 333–334
    as effect of legal changes, 307–325, 333–334, 384
    efficacy of law as an instrument of, 311–313
    limitations of law in creating, 319–325
    reciprocity between law and, 303–305
    resistance to, 325–333
Social conflict, 2–4, 10, 20, 22–24, 28, 38, 41–42, 55–56, 59, 62–65, 73, 113, 153, 155, 157, 165, 194, 247–248, 250–253, 256, 258, 264–265, 267, 271, 274–276, 283–284, 288–289, 292, 303, 319–321, 328, 334
Social control, 2–4, 10, 19–22, 25, 28, 37–38, 46, 49, 55–58, 60, 64, 84, 120, 191–246, 305, 340, 407, 417–418
    formal, 192–210, 235, 305
    informal, 192–195, 235, 305
Social disorganization, 22, 221
Social engineering, 3, 20, 304, 325
Socialization, 191–192, 235, 309, 317, 329–330, 340, 394
    into legal profession, 381–385, 394

Social mobility, 58, 132, 227, 307, 309, 342, 344–345, 351, 358, 393
Social movements, 165, 178–180, 185, 311, 313, 327
Socialist law, 12–17, 28
    objectives, 13–14
Social Policy, 183
Social Security, 327, 333, 373, 388, 426
Social Security Administration, 252, 270, 412
Social Structure and Law (Evan), 57
Social Structure of Right and Wrong, The (Black), 57
Society, 366, 402
Society
    paradigms of, 22–26, 28, 60, 65, 73
    researching law in, 404–434
Society of Gentlemen Practicers in the Courts of Law and Equity, 345
Sociological jurisprudence, 4, 37
Sociological Justice (Black), 22, 57
Sociologists
    roles of, 26–29
Sociology
    contributions to enacted policy of, 420–422, 429
    contributions to policy recommendations of, 417–420, 429
    impact on social policy of, 415–422, 429
Socratic method (see *case method*)
Sonn, Tamara, 17, 34
Souryal, Sam S., 18, 35, 131, 150
Southern University, 284
Spangler, Eve, 351, 396, 402
Special Services Staff, 229
Spector, Malcolm, 177, 190, 358, 402
Spence, Gerry, 27, 35
Spencer, Herbert, 45–46, 54, 62, 80
Spicker, Paul, 417, 430, 432
Spirit of Laws, The (Montesquieu), 45
Spite of Innocence, In (Radelet, Bedau, and Putnam), 205
Spitzer, Robert J., 119, 150, 206, 245
Sportsman's Paradise Homeowners Association, 179
Stalin, Josef, 15
Standing, 271–272, 293
Stare decisis doctrine, 159, 162, 407
Starr, June, 30
Status, 22, 41–43, 46–48, 50, 115, 139–140, 154–155, 167, 181, 207, 211, 221, 249, 253, 268, 273, 313–314, 326, 329, 342, 345, 355–356, 378–379, 390–391, 405, 407, 421
Statutory law, 12–13, 21, 28, 37, 40–42, 52, 57, 110, 122, 125, 153, 156, 158, 162–165, 184, 198, 201, 207, 210, 216, 264, 268, 280, 288, 290, 305, 308, 310, 318, 322, 370, 409, 424
    interpretation of, 163
Stead, Deborah, 15, 35, 98, 150
Stearns, Linda Brewster, 178, 186, 291, 295
Stefancic, Jean, 71, 74, 77
Stein, Laura, 68, 80
Stenning, Philip C., 131, 150
Stern, Eric, 221, 246
Stevens, Amy, 362, 378, 391, 403
Stevens, Dennis J., 206, 245

449